CLASSIC JAZZ

SCOTT YANOW

Backbeat
Books

San Francisco

Published by Backbeat Books
600 Harrison Street, San Francisco, CA 94107
An imprint of the Music Player Network
United Entertainment Media

Distributed to the book trade in the U.S and Canada by
Publishers Group West, 1700 Fourth Street, Berkeley, CA 94710

Distributed to the music trade in the U.S. and Canada by
Hal Leonard Publishing, P.O. Box 13819, Milwaukee, WI 53213

Cover Design by Richard Leeds
Text Composition by Impressions Books and Journals Services
Front Cover Photo of Louis Armstrong by Michael Ochs Archives.com
Back Cover Photo of Fats Waller by Ray Avery

Printed in the United States of America

Library of Congress Cataloging-in-Publication Data

Yanow, Scott.
  Classic jazz / by Scott Yanow.
    p. cm. — (Third ear)
  Includes bibliographical references, discographies, and index.
  ISBN 0-87930-659-9
    1. Jazz—History and criticism. 2. Jazz—Discography. 3. Jazz musicians—United States.
  I. Title. II. Series.

ML3508 .Y38 2001
781.65′3—dc21   2001043707

02 03 04 05 06 5 4 3 2 1

CONTENTS

INTRODUCTION

This book begins in an unusual way, with an apology. I had planned for over a year to call my study of 1920s music *Classic Jazz*, not knowing that veteran jazz writer Floyd Levin had a book coming out with the same title. While Floyd's book (which I can easily recommend) deals with his experiences with New Orleans and trad musicians from the 1940s to the present, Third Ear's *Classic Jazz* is primarily about jazz from 1917 to 1932, an unnamed period that represents jazz's first 15 years on records.

Rather than producing one homogeneous type of music, the 1920s were full of overlapping genres, music that cannot simply be placed under the categories of "Dixieland" or "New Orleans jazz." *Classic jazz* is the most logical term to use for the freewheeling combos, jazz-inspired dance bands, early classic blues singers, stride pianists, and big bands of the pre-swing era.

According to the stereotypical, not totally accurate, story of the beginnings of jazz, jazz came from ragtime and the blues, was born in New Orleans, and quickly became Dixieland. With the closing of New Orleans' red-light Storyville district in 1917, so the myth continues, most of the top New Orleans musicians went up the Mississippi to Chicago and eventually east to New York, spreading the joy of Dixieland worldwide throughout the roaring '20s. The music is then supposed to have served as the perfect soundtrack for wearing raccoon coats, dancing the Charleston, sitting on flagpoles, and drinking bootleg gin in speakeasies. The balloon burst in 1929 with the Wall Street crash. The final blow to early Dixieland was the end of Prohibition, leading to the rise in the mid-1930s of more sophisticated swing big bands, or so the story goes.

But the real story of the origins of jazz is quite a bit different and more complex. Jazz, ragtime, and the blues were all actually born about the same time (Buddy Bolden became prominent before Scott Joplin), New Orleans was not necessarily jazz's only birthplace, few musicians who were not pianists worked regularly in Storyville bordellos, and the Mississippi River does not go all the way north to Chicago! Most importantly, Dixieland was only one aspect of the 1920s jazz scene, and mid-1930s swing was not necessarily more sophisticated than the music of the previous decade.

One of the joys of listening to jazz of the 1920s is hearing musical stories, songs, and ideas told for the first time, before they were adopted and altered by later generations. For example, "'Tain't Nobody's Business If I Do" was a hit for Jimmy Witherspoon in the late 1940s and a trademark song for Billie Holiday. But how many realize that Bessie Smith recorded the same song in 1923? Or that "In the Mood" (one of the biggest hits for Glenn Miller) actually debuted in 1930 as Wingy Manone's "Tar Paper Stomp"? Or that Dizzy Gillespie's "Groovin' High" from 1945 was based on the chords of "Whispering," a million-seller for Paul Whiteman from 1920?

Jazz evolved at a dizzying pace during the 1920s. Music that sounded advanced in 1922 was considered quite dated by 1927, new ideas that debuted one year became major parts of the musical language six months later and were sometimes discarded a year later, and the technical quality of records improved rapidly. Listeners who are into the music can easily guess (within a year) when a particular recording was made, usually whether the band was black or white, and quite often where the musicians were based.

The 1920s were an era of great contradictions. After winning World War I, the United States seemed to be (on the surface) a more liberated country than previously, finally shaking off the restrictions of the

Victorian era. Dresses became shorter, many more women entered the workforce than had been there earlier, dancing became more exciting and sensuous, some movies actually hinted strongly at sex, the economy was prosperous, and jazz seemed to be everywhere as the country experienced something like a decade-long party.

But a closer look reveals that Republicans ruled the White House, liquor was illegal (even if gangsters and bootleggers made it widely available), the Ku Klux Klan was at the height of its popularity (with lynchings of blacks being commonplace), racism was institutionalized even in the North, big business had few restrictions, poverty was actually widespread (particularly in rural areas), and there was no safety net. It was a great period to be rich and white, but the poor and the blacks were barely tolerated by the average middle-class citizens. However, despite that, blacks were often the main innovators of jazz and had a direct effect on all of popular music.

Each book in the Third Ear series has the potential difficulty of drawing boundary lines in deciding who to include and emphasize and who to leave out. Because *Classic Jazz* essentially cuts off after 1932 (except in discussing the later years of the early jazz greats), this was less of a problem. Every musician and band who recorded before 1933 was eligible for inclusion, along with a few undocumented legends. The main question was, if a particular person had retired from performing in January 1933, would that individual be considered significant in jazz history?

I started listening to music from the classic jazz era very early on, shortly after I "discovered" 1950s Dixieland while in high school. There is a charm to the period that is very difficult to recreate. Part of the music's ambiance is due to its restrictions. All records available to the public before the late 1940s were released on '78's, and that format could accommodate only around three minutes of music per song; four minutes on special releases. Solo space was necessarily brief, which was an incentive for musicians to make ideal use of every second. Prior to 1927, drummers were not able to use their full set on record dates, for fear that the bass drum in particular would cause a major technical distortion in the music. Drummers had to function more as percussionists, often putting the emphasis on cymbals, woodblocks, and sometimes a washboard, making every sound count. Virtually all of the music of the 1920s was played at danceable tempos (no real slow ballads or radical tempo changes) since nearly all nonclassical music (other than novelty acts and rural blues performers) was considered dance music first and foremost, particularly by record company executives.

While the primitive recording quality in the 1920s may initially put some listeners off, in most cases the music is quite listenable once you get used to the prestereo sounds, adding to the feeling that things just sounded different in the 1920s, a magical musical era.

During the past decade, a large percentage of the most important 1920s jazz recordings have been reissued on CD, often in comprehensive form in addition to intelligent samplers. Unlike with most other genres of music, the great majority of reissues of 1920s recordings tend to be produced by real fans of the music, not major label executives who smell a quick buck (as they do with the music of the swing era) and endlessly repackage the same old recordings in commercial "best of" or ludicrous "theme" samplers.

I used a rating system for the CD reviews. Since most 1920s reissues are quite good (particularly in their packaging), very few of the CDs received evaluations lower than 5. Here are what the ratings mean:

★ Limited edition box set—Most highly recommended for completists and veteran collectors, but make sure to get it while you can!

10 A gem that belongs in every serious jazz collection

9 Highly recommended

8 A very good release

7 An excellent acquisition

6 Good music but not quite essential

5 Decent but not one of the era's more important works

4 So-so

3 A disappointing effort with just a few worthwhile moments

2 A weak release

1 Stinks!

Although, as the author of this book I am solely responsible for any errors that might have crept in, there are several people whom I would like to thank: Dorothy Cox, Matt Kelsey and the staff at Backbeat Books, for trusting me and believing in this important project; Brian Ashley, who got me started in the jazz writing business back in 1976 when he formed *Record Review*; the much-maligned but invaluable jazz publicists (including Ann Braithwaite, Lynda Bramble, Lori Hehr, and Terri Hinte) who make life much easier for jazz journalists; Vanessa Ellis, who was quite helpful behind the scenes; the late Benson Curtis, whose daily KRHM-FM radio show *Strictly from Dixie* introduced me to jazz; the many dedicated record collectors who are wise enough to greatly value this timeless music and, in some cases, reissue it for the rest of us to enjoy; those musicians, such as the members of the Fly By Night Jazz Band, who have sought to keep this music alive through live performances; and the Buddy Boldens of the world, the many pioneers who made forgotten and undocumented but very significant contributions to classic jazz, helping it develop into the remarkable music that it became.

I am dedicating this book to the late, great singer Susannah McCorkle, who would have enjoyed it. I also wish to give a special thanks to my wife, Kathy, and my daughter, Melody, for their love and support.

THE BEGINNINGS OF JAZZ

Among the most common questions that newcomers have about jazz are: "What is it?" "When did it start?" and "Where did it come from?" As luck would have it, none of those questions can be answered to everyone's satisfaction!

Scholars, musicians, and fans have tried for decades to define what jazz is and isn't. The problem is that jazz continues to evolve and a definition that fits today will seem overly restrictive ten years from now. The closest I have been able to come in defining this very vital music, which ranges from classic jazz and bebop to the avant-garde and fusion, is to say that jazz is a type of music that emphasizes improvisation and always has the feeling of the blues. The "feeling of the blues" refers to bending notes and putting one's soul into the music rather than actually playing a 12-bar blues. If anything, my definition is too open, since there are other idioms that would fit (such as improvised rock and the blues itself) that, despite being relatives of jazz, are not actual jazz styles. But all of jazz does have at least some improvising and the all-important blues feeling, at least in an abstract fashion.

Because jazz was born over 20 years before it was ever recorded, there is not one obvious moment in history that we can point to as the birth of jazz. Symbolically, when Buddy Bolden (jazz's first star) formed his first band in 1895, jazz could be said to have solidified and been born, but it probably existed in rudimentary form a little earlier.

Throughout its history, one of the strengths of jazz is that it has borrowed and taken from other styles of music. The same is true of its beginnings. Jazz in the late 1800s drew from the many types of music that were around. African rhythms from up to two centuries before had been passed down from generation to generation and were combined in irresistible fashion with the rhythms of marches to create syncopations that made parades in New Orleans sound particularly infectious. From black spirituals that were performed in church and work songs (sung in the fields by workers doing physical labor) came the blues and some traditional melodies, along with the idea of passionately bending notes. There were no bent notes in classical music! From classical music came intonation, technique, and discipline. Popular melodies of the day (ranging from Stephen Foster tunes to sentimental ballads) helped form part of jazz's early repertoire. Minstrel shows gave some musicians an opportunity to tour and play before new audiences (even if the settings were often dreadful and the performers were in blackface). Improvising pianists (often heard in bar settings) gradually developed both ragtime and stride piano. And concert orchestras (the most notable of which were led by John Phillip Sousa and Arthur Pryor) brought a rich variety of melodies and styles to small towns.

New Orleans, being a major port, boasted many overlapping musical cultures, including those brought by French and Spanish immigrants, former black slaves and their descendants, and former residents of Cuba and Latin America. Music was a major part of day-to-day life, and by the mid-1890s brass bands were everywhere. There were countless excuses to have a parade or a celebration, including holidays, funerals, parties, and social functions. New Orleans developed a brass band tradition, with mobile groups providing constant work for both black and white musicians.

Out of this fertile musical environment came jazz. Brass band musicians, who would often play lengthy versions of songs while marching, began to improvise a bit, infusing their music with bluish notes, melodic variations, and new ideas. Thus was jazz born!

JAZZ: 1895–1916

The first jazz recordings were not made until 1917, so the music's first two decades went completely undocumented. Until around 1910, jazz was mostly confined to the southern United States, with New Orleans as its center.

The main popular music of the 1895–1916 period (particularly 1899–1914) was ragtime. Although sometimes mistakenly called a style of jazz, ragtime is actually an independent type of music, differing from jazz in that it is generally not improvised and does not have a blues feeling. While jazz has sometimes been called America's classical music (latter-day proponents hoped to "uplift" it to an art form rather than having it considered merely as entertainment), in reality ragtime has more in common with classical music than jazz.

Classic ragtime's song structure usually has four themes performed in the format of A-A-B-B-A-C-C-D-D. Its highly appealing syncopated rhythms are a logical bridge between marches and early jazz.

The earliest known rag to be composed was Tom Turpin's "Harlem Rag," from 1892, although it was not published until 1897. Scott Joplin published his first two songs in 1895, but it was the publication of his "Maple Leaf Rag" in 1899 that really launched the ragtime era. Ragtime was largely thought of as a solo piano music, and it coincided with the peak in popularity of the piano itself, an era when a large percentage of families used the piano for its main entertainment. In those days, when the recording industry was in its infancy and no blacks (other than a few spiritual groups) were recorded, the success of new songs was judged by their sheet music sales. "Maple Leaf Rag" sold over 75,000 copies of sheet music during its first year, an enormous number for the period.

Joplin, who was born November 24, 1868 in Bowie City, Texas, was ragtime's most talented and influential composer. Joplin lived in St. Louis during 1885–93, playing piano in local clubs and bars and developing his songwriting abilities. In 1894 he appeared with a band at the Chicago's World's Fair and he formed the Texas Medley Quartet, with whom he performed in vaudeville. In 1895 he moved to Sedalia, Missouri, where his works began to be published by his supporter John Stark.

After "Maple Leaf Rag" caught on, other composers (most significantly James Scott and Joseph Lamb) had their rags published. Ragtime became so popular that pieces that had nothing to do with the style (such as Irving Berlin's "Alexander's Ragtime Band") were quickly written to take advantage of the craze. John Philip Sousa included orchestrated versions of ragtime in his repertoire, and James Reese Europe arranged ragtime pieces that were danced to by the famous team of Vernon and Irene Castle.

Strangely enough, there were very few solo piano ragtime records made during the 1900–20 period (Joplin and Scott never recorded, and Lamb's only record was in 1959), but there were a fair number of ragtime banjo records (most notably by Vess Ossman and Fred Van Eps) and orchestrated ragtime performances. Few of these early recordings have been reissued yet on CD, so fans should search for the LP *Kings of the Ragtime Banjo* (Yazoo 1044), which has seven numbers apiece featuring Ossman (from 1900–10) and Van Eps (1911–23) and the two-LP set *Ragtime* (RCA Jazz Tribune 45687). The latter twofer has quite a few remarkable performances from 1900–25 (with one number from 1930), including ragtime numbers from Sousa, Arthur Pryor's band, James Reese Europe, the Victor Military Band, Ossman, Van Eps, pianist Felix Arndt ("Desecration Rag"), Conway's Band ("Hungarian Rag"), and others, with the tunes including "Trombone Sneeze," Tom Turpin's "St. Louis Rag," "At a Georgia Camp Meeting," "Maple Leaf Rag" (performed by the United States Marine Band in 1909), "The Ragtime Drummer" (a drum feature by James I. Lent from 1912), and "The Memphis Blues" from 1914.

Ragtime was near its creative height in 1904, when the St. Louis World's Fair held a ragtime contest. However, the music was running out of steam by 1910. Scott Joplin wanted to take ragtime far beyond its roots and establish it as American's main music. He staged a ballet (*The Ragtime Dance*) and wrote two ragtime operas (*The Guest of Honor* and *Treemonisha*) but was unable to gain financial backing for the latter, the major frustration of his life. A backlash against ragtime by those who considered the music primitive compared to European classical, spurred on by the fact that it was dominated by black composers (other than Joseph Lamb), meant that ragtime could grow only so much. Joplin, who began to show the effects of syphilis in 1910, wrote his last two rags in 1914 and died in 1917, at the age of 48.

The ragtime era died along with Scott Joplin, for 1917 was coincidentally the year that jazz debuted on records. Although "Maple Leaf Rag" would become a jazz standard and novelty ragtime (a series of complicated workouts for virtuoso pianists) was in vogue for a time in the 1920s (particularly the pieces of Zez Confrey), ragtime went underground. There was a mini-ragtime revival in the mid-1940s, thanks to pianist Wally Rose's occasional rag features with Lu Watters' Yerba Buena Jazz Band, and the 1950 publication of *They All Played Ragtime*, by Rudi Blesh and Harriet Janis, increased interest in the style. But the commercialized and often-corny "honky tonk" music of the 1950s pushed ragtime back underground. In the mid-1970s, with its inclusion in the soundtrack of the film *The Sting* (which made Joplin's "The Entertainer" into a surprise pop hit), ragtime had a major renaissance. Even though the fad lasted only a couple of years, the music has had a larger visibility since that time, with such composers as David Thomas Roberts and Reginald Robinson adding new pieces to the classic ragtime repertoire.

Musicians in New Orleans and throughout the South were well aware of ragtime, and the structures of the music (with its multiple themes) were an influence. However, jazz developed on a parallel path. At the time that cornetist Buddy Bolden formed his initial group in 1895, music was a major part of daily life in New Orleans and other nearby cities. Born September 6, 1877, in New Orleans, Bolden was considered so powerful a player that he was a significant name in New Orleans by 1900. He performed at dances, parades, and parties and was the musician cited the most by survivors of the era. Although he allegedly recorded a cylinder in 1898, no recording of Bolden has ever been found. Tragically, he was also jazz's first martyr. In 1906 he began to suffer from mental illness, and the following year, after a few incidents, Bolden was committed to Jackson Mental Institution, where he spent his final 24 years before passing away on November 4, 1931.

During Buddy Bolden's period of prominence, New Orleans jazz began to form. The emphasis was on ensembles, melodic improvising, and fairly basic chord changes. The best players of the era infused the music with the blues. Generally the cornetist (or trumpeter) was in charge of the melody, the trombonist played harmonies, and the clarinetist roamed fairly free, creating countermelodies and fills. Rhythm sections consisted of banjo (or guitar), tuba (or string bass), and drums, occasionally with a violin added. The best bands were able to play parades (where additional horns were employed) and dances alike. In the early days, pianists were mostly featured as soloists (since marching band pianos did not exist!).

Some pianists were employed in the bordellos of Storyville (New Orleans' red-light district), while others played dances, where they emulated a full orchestra.

While the repertoire grew and the names changed, New Orleans jazz music did not evolve much during 1900–15. Since there were no recordings, jazz remained a local folk music. Some musicians left town, with Bill Johnson in 1909 being one of the earliest; his Creole Orchestra was among the very first groups to play jazz in New York City (1915). But jazz itself did not have its name until 1916, when Johnny Stein's Jass Band in Chicago began to gain attention. That particular outfit lasted only a few months before the New Orleans sidemen (Nick LaRocca, Eddie Edwards, Alcide "Yellow" Nunez, and Henry Ragas) broke away after a dispute to form the Original Dixieland Jazz Band. The attention that they were getting by the end of the year set the stage for jazz's breakthrough in 1917.

IMPORTANT EVENTS: 1895–1916

1895   Buddy Bolden forms his first band.

1898   Ma Rainey at the age of 12 appears in the show "A Bunch of Blackberries" in Columbus, Georgia.

1899   Scott Joplin's "Maple Leaf Rag" launches the Ragtime era. Duke Ellington is born.

1900   Twenty-eight-year-old Bill Johnson starts playing bass.

1901   Manuel Perez begins leading the Imperial Orchestra. Louis Armstrong is born.

1902   This was the year that Jelly Roll Morton (then 16) would later claim to have invented jazz. Scott Joplin writes "The Entertainer," "The Ragtime Dance," and "Elite Syncopations."

1906   Freddie Keppard forms the Olympia Orchestra.

1907   Fate Marable first begins playing on riverboats. King Oliver starts his rise to fame. Buddy Bolden is committed.

1908   Nick LaRocca leads his first band. Eight-year-old Sidney Bechet sits in with Freddie Keppard's group. Richard M. Jones begins a nine-year stint playing piano at Lulu White's Mahogany Hall.

1909   Bill Johnson leaves New Orleans, introducing jazz to California.

1910   Oscar Celestin starts leading the Tuxedo Band. Ida Cox tours with White and Clark's Minstrels.

1911   Scott Joplin completes *Treemonisha*.

1912   Kid Ory moves to New Orleans and forms one of the city's top groups. Tony Parenti as a 12-year-old plays with Papa Jack Laine's Reliance Band. Ma Rainey stars with the Moses Stock Company, a show that includes Bessie Smith. Louis Armstrong is arrested and confined to a waif's home. Baby Dodds takes up the drums. W. C. Handy writes the "Memphis Blues." Tony Jackson moves to Chicago. James P. Johnson starts playing professionally in New York.

1913   Jimmie Noone joins Freddie Keppard's band, and Lorenzo Tio works with Oscar Celestin. Mamie Smith moves to New York and begins working in vaudeville. James Reese Europe makes his first recordings.

1914   Jelly Roll Morton and Ed Garland both visit Chicago. Sidney Bechet leaves New Orleans and begins traveling throughout the South. W. C. Handy writes "St. Louis Blues." Bill Johnson sends for Freddie Keppard to join his Original Creole Orchestra in Los Angeles.

1915   Bill Johnson's Original Creole Orchestra brings jazz to New York City. Chris Kelly moves from his home town of Plaquemine Parish to New Orleans, where he quickly becomes one of the city's top cornetists. Sam Morgan puts together his jazz band. Jelly Roll Morton plays jazz in San Francisco. Manuel Perez visits Chicago with the Arthur Sims band. Sidney Bechet and Buddy Petit form the Young Olympia Orchestra in New Orleans. Noble Sissle and Eubie Blake meet in Baltimore.

1916   Johnny Stein's band makes a strong impression in Chicago for a few months. A dispute leads Nick LaRocca, Eddie Edwards, Yellow Nunez, and Henry Ragas to depart Stein's band to form the Original Dixieland Jazz Band. Phil Napoleon makes his recording debut, as a classical cornetist. Paul Mares and Leon Roppolo are members of Tom Brown's band.

JAZZ: 1917–1932

In 1917, ragtime (which had been dropping in popularity since 1912) officially ended its golden age when Scott Joplin died. Woodrow Wilson began his second term as President, the United States entered World War I, Russia had its Communist revolution, and the music world had its own revolution!

Prior to 1917, few listeners outside of the South and isolated sections of the United States had ever heard jazz music. That all started to change in 1917. On January 30, the Original Dixieland Jazz Band became the first jazz group to record. When its two selections ("Darktown Strutters Ball" and "Indiana") were rejected by the Columbia label (which felt the music was too uninhibited, barbaric, and spontaneous), the ODJB went to the Victor label and on February 26 cut "Livery Stable Blues" and the "Original Dixieland One-Step." Victor wisely rushed out this release, and "Livery Stable Blues" (which featured the three horn players emulating animals during the many two-bar breaks) became the hit that launched the Jazz Age.

Early jazz as played by the ODJB was indeed somewhat barbaric, especially compared to what had been heard on records previously. Early jazz sounded nothing like classical music, genteel dance bands, ragtime, or Sousa's marching bands. Jazz offered spontaneity, freedom, and opportunities for group and individual expression that were much different than merely reading notes from a piece of paper. The records of the ODJB brought jazz to many listeners who had never heard the music before, and its influence during 1917–22 was huge. In fact, as can be heard on other jazz records from that five-year period, most of the more uninhibited jazz combos sound like close relatives of the pioneering group. And after the end of World War I, the ODJB repeated their success by visiting England and introducing jazz to Europe, with the result that other ODJB imitators could be heard on the European continent during the first half of the 1920s.

In reality, jazz began to spread around the globe from the day the first jazz records were released. This was consistent with the migration of jazz from the South that had begun gradually around 1910. Although some jazz-history books claim that jazz left New Orleans in 1917 with the government's closing of Storyville, the city's red-light district, and even though that event actually did lead more musicians to venture up North, this out-migration was occurring anyway as the city's musicians sought to escape the racism of the South in search of better work opportunities. Some went to California (including, at various times, Jelly Roll Morton, King Oliver, and Kid Ory), while others did indeed go up the Mississippi (generally to St. Louis), playing on riverboats. Some toured throughout the South and Midwest in vaudeville, while others took a chance and went directly to New York. In addition, some New Orleans jazz musicians chose to stay home.

Because only white jazz bands recorded during 1917–19 (other than a few rare exceptions, such as James Reese Europe's orchestra), it is still difficult to know exactly what most jazz sounded like during that era. We can only speculate how Freddie Keppard and King Oliver sounded in 1919, how far back Jelly Roll Morton played music that would be considered jazz, and what the scene in New Orleans was really like during the period.

While 1917–19 could be considered the ODJB era, in 1920 the blues craze began. Mamie Smith, filling in for Sophie Tucker, had the opportunity to make the first blues record, "Crazy Blues." After "Crazy Blues" became a surprise hit, many female singers (both black and white) were documented by record labels, in hopes of duplicating Smith's success. While quite a few of the vocalists were taken from vaudeville and were not really blues singers, the best (such as Ethel Waters and Alberta Hunter) were flexible enough to do justice to both blues and pop songs. And in 1923, with the first recordings of Bessie Smith and Ma Rainey, the blues became an integral part of the record industry, evolving parallel to jazz.

By the early 1920s, jazz was being played in many cities, but the most important events were taking place in Chicago (the center of jazz during 1920–27) and New York. While the Original Memphis Five was among the first groups in New York to swing and James P. Johnson was developing into the king of stride pianists, many of the other musicians in the Big Apple who attempted to play jazz were technically skilled but rhythmically inflexible, with the horn players often using vaudeville novelty effects (such as slap-tonguing, obvious tonal distortions, and corny humor). In contrast, Chicago was the home for many of the top transplanted New Orleans musicians. The New Orleans Rhythm Kings during 1922–23 took the first large step ahead of the ODJB, featuring a fine clarinet soloist in Leon Rappolo, a fresh repertoire, clean and swinging ensembles, and a more advanced rhythm section.

The year 1923 was the breakthrough year for jazz, and the first time that black jazz musicians were extensively recorded. Kid Ory's band (as Spikes' Seven Pods of Pepper Orchestra) had recorded two songs in Los Angeles the previous year, but 1923 brought the recording debuts of Jelly Roll Morton, Sidney Bechet, King Oliver, Johnny Dodds, and Louis Armstrong, among many others. Oliver's Creole Jazz Band (which had actually been playing in Chicago before the NORK) proved to be the premiere group in jazz, a classic New Orleans jazz band that emphasized ensembles while having occasional short solos. Louis Armstrong's spot on "Chimes Blues" was a hint of things to come.

By 1923–24, the Original Dixieland Jazz Band was considered ancient history. Much more popular were the large dance bands (such as Paul Whiteman's orchestra), which were touched but not dominated by jazz. Nightlife was flourishing in the United States as never before, with nightclubs and speakeasies (most of which were run by gangsters) featuring jazz bands that were uninhibited yet also providing background music for dancers.

From nearly the beginning, jazz had been the most integrated of all art forms. To musicians, it did not matter if a player was black or white; what mattered was whether or not the musician could play. But even in New York and Chicago in the 1920s, jazz was largely segregated. Whites could usually go to black clubs but not the other way around. Occasionally a white musician would sit in with a black band, but the opposite was almost never true in public. There was some mixing at private jam sessions (where musical ideas were exchanged) but not on bandstands before paying customers. Record dates were mixed much more often than club performances, since it was obviously much easier to disguise the race of the players that way.

During this era, blacks and whites to an extent had a different approach, although they developed in similar ways. The stereotype, which was sometimes true, is that whites were better technically trained and had superior instruments and more "legitimate" sounds. Blacks, in contrast, were more adventurous improvisers, were much more conversant with the blues, and swung more than the typical white player. However, there were many exceptions, and, after the world became much more integrated in later decades, those two approaches permanently merged.

Two major events occurred during 1924–26 that greatly changed jazz. Louis Armstrong, after leaving King Oliver's band in 1924, moved to New York to join Fletcher Henderson's orchestra. His swinging style, ability to infuse any song with the blues, use of space to dramatic effort, beautiful tone, and brilliant ideas moved jazz several years forward. Armstrong's ideas were studied closely by Don Redman, whose arrangements for Fletcher Henderson made that ensemble jazz's top big band. Group improvisation as heard in King Oliver's band in 1923 was replaced by an emphasis on individual solos and arranged ensembles. Armstrong's *Hot Five* and *Hot Seven* recordings of 1925–28 showed his fellow jazz musicians that the potential for individual self-expression was unlimited.

The other major event was the transformation of recording techniques from acoustic to electric. Acoustical sound recording (which began in 1877 and was dominant until 1925) gave listeners only an approximate idea what instruments really sounded like, often having a rather tinny sound. The development of electrical recording (which was adopted during 1925–27) resulted in much more lifelike reproductions and made it possible to hear all of the instruments in a larger band. A complete drum set could at last be recorded (starting in 1927), along with quieter and more subtle vocalists. Recording engineers could worry less about making sure that all of the instruments were being heard and concentrate more on what the musicians were playing! To cite one example, had Duke Ellington's more atmospheric pieces been recorded acoustically, they surely would have had half the impact on the music world that they did.

During 1925–29, many new jazz musicians appeared on the scene, inspired and influenced by Louis Armstrong's swinging approach. The best ones, such as cornetist Bix Beiderbecke (who debuted on records in 1924), learned from Satch's innovations while developing fresh styles of their own. During these prime years of the classic jazz era, nearly all of the dance orchestras became more jazz-oriented, both soloists and singers loosened up their approach, and jazz first became noticed and taken seriously overseas, although in the United States it was widely regarded as just entertaining dance music. An exodus of Chicago-based musicians to New York took place during 1927–28 (including King Oliver, Jelly Roll Morton, and the Austin High Gang), making the Big Apple the main center of the jazz world, with Harlem becoming the home for many black bands.

By 1929, jazz seemed to be everywhere, whether it was Paul Whiteman's dance band, the jungle music of Duke Ellington, the nightly jam sessions in Kansas City, rent party marathons featuring pianists James P. Johnson and Fats Waller, or Louis Armstrong starring in the show *Hot Chocolates*. However, things soon changed drastically. The stock market crash in the fall of '29 resulted in the end of the classic jazz era during 1930–32. With the rapid rise of unemployment, consumers had less money to spend on records. The recording industry collapsed while radio (which offered free entertainment) boomed. The public started to prefer soothing vocalists and upbeat dance music over the wilder jazz sounds of the late 1920s, looking to forget the recklessness of the previous decade. Freewheeling jazz went underground.

The best white musicians went into the studios, working on radio and on records with commercial orchestras, making a lucrative living but not getting to play jazz very often. Those who were strong jazz players but not so technically skilled scuffled but managed to survive. Black musicians did not have the option of working in the segregated studios. Those that were most fortunate became members of one of the big bands in Harlem (such as the orchestras of Duke Ellington, Cab Calloway, Chick Webb, Luis Russell, and Fletcher Henderson) and were able to flourish. However, there were only a limited number of slots available, and many of the former jazz stars dropped out of the spotlight and, in many cases, out of music altogether, no longer recording or even being thought of much. While Louis Armstrong, Duke Ellington, and Cab Calloway became national figures, King Oliver, Jelly Roll Morton, and Johnny Dodds were completely forgotten. By 1933, the classic jazz era was over and the times were changing.

EVOLUTION OF THE INSTRUMENTS IN JAZZ

Jazz sounded much different in 1932 than it did in 1917. Part of that is due to the greatly improved recording quality, but much of it had to do with the development of new styles and approaches. The functions of some of the instruments used in jazz changed quite a bit during this 15-year period.

In 1917 the cornet was almost always the lead voice in jazz ensembles. This tradition went back to Buddy Bolden and continued in New Orleans with such "kings" as Freddie Keppard, King Oliver, and Louis Armstrong. More often than not, as jazz began to emerge on records, the cornetists were the leaders (including Nick LaRocca of the Original Dixieland Jazz Band, Phil Napoleon with the Original Memphis Five, and Paul Mares with the New Orleans Rhythm Kings) and were in charge of stating the melody. As jazz evolved from an ensemble-oriented music to an idiom that emphasized solos, the cornet was mostly replaced by the trumpet, due to the latter's more forceful sound. While LaRocca, Napoleon, and Frank Guarente of the Georgians had fairly smooth sounds, many trumpeters/cornetists of the 1917–22 period (particularly on records and those based in New York) used staccato phrasing, thought that "getting hot" meant playing the same phrase at double the speed and volume, and did little other than play the melody. Johnny Dunn, who was often guilty of those deficiencies, was among the first to utilize the plunger mute on records to distort his sound. King Oliver in 1923 modernized that approach, which found its creative height later in the decade with Bubber Miley.

But it was Oliver's sideman, Louis Armstrong, who really revolutionized the trumpet in jazz. By 1925 Armstrong, who never lost sight of the melody while displaying very strong improvising skills and legato phrasing, became extremely influential. Ensembles became secondary to solos, and Satch reinforced the trumpet as the leading instrument in jazz. He remained the dominant force on his instrument until the rise of bebop in the mid-1940s. While such exciting players as Henry "Red" Allen, Jabbo Smith, and Reuben "River" Reeves tried their best to challenge Satch by the late 1920s, a large part of their ideas actually originated with Armstrong. Some of the other trumpeters and cornetists of the 1920s had a cooler approach to swinging, most notably Bix Beiderbecke (whose golden tone and choice of notes were quite original), Joe Smith, and Arthur Whetsol. But by 1932 (particularly after the death of Beiderbecke), nearly every trumpeter in jazz sounded like a relative of Louis Armstrong!

The trombone emerged from New Orleans primarily as a harmony instrument that was played percussively. Kid Ory best exemplified this approach. When jazz began to be documented, some musicians treated the trombone as a novelty instrument, one whose slides and roars were used (and abused) in humorous settings; this was a carryover from vaudeville and marching band music. Although George Brunies of the NORK was sometimes guilty of that, he was one of the first worthwhile trombone soloists to emerge on records. Other important pre-1927 pioneers included Charlie Green (a superior blues player), Charlie Irvis (an unacknowledged pioneer in using the plunger mute), and the remarkable Tricky Sam Nanton (a star with Duke Ellington for nearly 20 years). During 1926–27, Miff Mole emerged as one of the first trombonists to truly liberate his horn from its percussive function, treating it as a solo instrument that could be played nearly with the facility of a trumpet. While Mole's unusual style (with its wide interval jumps and eccentric choice of notes) was well utilized with Red Nichols' groups, it was soon overshadowed by the legato playing of Jimmy Harrison and particularly Jack Teagarden, whose arrival in New York in 1928 was a major event. Teagarden gradually became the main influence on his instrument, although there was always room for other voices to develop, including J. C. Higginbotham, Lawrence Brown, Dickie Wells, and Tommy Dorsey (who had the prettiest tone).

The clarinet's function in New Orleans jazz was to create countermelodies behind the trumpet and serve as a secondary solo instrument. While Sidney Bechet and Johnny Dodds were major New Orleans soloists with distinctive sounds, the clarinet often appeared on records (starting with Larry Shields on the Original Dixieland Jazz Band's "Livery Stable Blues") as a device to create silly sounds and odd tonal distortions. This "gaspipe" style was heard in the 1920s in the playing of Ted Lewis, Wilton Crawley, Boyd Senter, Fess Williams, and others, and for a time this style retarded the development of both the clarinet and jazz.

But while Bechet and Dodds were singular voices who generally did not influence many of their contemporaries, the rise of Jimmie Noone (who had a smoother and more generic sound) was particularly significant. He made a strong impression on Benny Goodman (the future King of Swing), and his playing uplifted the clarinet. Also quite important were Don Redman's use of clarinet trios in his arrangements for Fletcher Henderson and the playing of such musicians as Buster Bailey, Pee Wee Russell, Frank Teschemacher, and Jimmy Dorsey. By 1930 swinging clarinetists had won the battle over their gaspipe counterparts.

Prior to the 1920s, saxophones were fairly insignificant in jazz, being used as a poor substitute for a trombone or for novelty effects. But by the end of the decade, the sax would be considered one of jazz's most important instruments. The tenor saxophone's first hero was Coleman Hawkins. He began recording with Fletcher Henderson's orchestra in 1923. Although his early dates found him playing percussively and using dated effects (such as slap-tonguing), Hawkins learned quickly from Louis Armstrong's example and developed his own exciting style. After he recorded "The Stampede" with Henderson in 1926, Hawkins was the acknowledged leader on his instrument and an influential force. The only important alternative to Hawkins' thick tone and advanced solos (which revealed his complete mastery of harmonies and chord structures) during this time was Bud Freeman, who had a lighter tone and would be an influence years later on Lester Young.

The alto saxophone was actually utilized more extensively in jazz before Coleman Hawkins' rise to prominence, primarily as a "sweetener" on jazz dates, such as the addition of Benny Krueger on the ODJB records of 1920–21. It was considered a substitute melody instrument with dance bands early in the decade and did not emerge as an important solo voice until Jimmy Dorsey began to record in 1926. By the end of the 1920s, Johnny Hodges (with Duke Ellington) and Benny Carter had joined Dorsey as the most important altoists.

Other types of saxophones had their champions in the 1920s. The baritone sax had its first great soloist when Harry Carney joined Duke Ellington in 1927. The soon-to-be-extinct C-melody sax (which is voiced between the tenor and the alto) was brilliantly played by Frankie Trumbauer. And the bass sax (which would be replaced by both the baritone sax and the string bass) was never played with more power and creativity than by Adrian Rollini. But most big bands of the early 1930s used only tenors and altos, with baritone as a double for one of the saxophonists. Despite a few solos by Alberto Socarras and (in the early 1930s) Wayman Carver, the flute was still 20 years away from its first acceptance in jazz. And the violin, which had sometimes been used in very early New Orleans jazz bands, was (like the alto sax in the early '20s) seen as a sweetener, with the exception of the great jazz soloists Joe Venuti and Eddie South.

As the ragtime era ended and jazz took over, the stride piano style of James P. Johnson and his contemporaries became a major attraction. Johnson "strided" with his left hand, keeping the time by alternating between bass notes and chords that were an octave or two higher while his right hand played melodic variations. The basic style did not change much during the 1920s, making the piano a miniature orchestra and essentially a one-man band. Johnson, his pal Willie "the Lion" Smith, and his protégé Fats Waller were the pacesetters. While blues and boogie-woogie pianists had an alternate and simpler style, the first pianist to really break away from stride was Earl "Fatha" Hines. Hines loved to suspend time, breaking up the rhythms with his left hand while his right played startling breaks, somehow never missing a beat.

The piano was such an all-encompassing rhythm machine that other rhythm instruments (particularly the bass and tuba) were not necessary in small groups. In fact, having a bass on a record that had James P. Johnson or Fats Waller was somewhat of a frivolity.

Most larger groups had either a banjo or a guitar playing rhythm. Because the banjo was much louder, it overshadowed the guitar prior to 1926–27, although few (other than the remarkable Harry Reser) soloed much. By 1927, with the rise of electrical recording, volume was no longer as essential as flexibility, and the clanging of the banjo was soon considered a liability. Guitarist Eddie Lang's ability to play complex chords and single-note solos, and his gift of uplifting every session no matter what the style made him greatly in demand for record dates, as it did Carl Kress and Dick McDonough. The guitar has always been an important instrument in blues, with Lonnie Johnson being the first blues guitarist to "cross over" and add his solo strength to jazz dates. But with the exception of these players and a few others, guitarists during this period were largely restricted to the background, where they solidified the rhythm section. They would not start being electrified until 1938–39 and in most cases they were more felt than heard.

Many jazz combo dates of the 1920s had piano, banjo, and drums as their rhythm section and sounded complete. Larger bands, however, usually used a tuba or a string bass to fill in the ensembles. The tuba was louder and added force to the music, but the bass could play four notes to the bar without the musician having to gasp for air! Steve Brown with Jean Goldkette's orchestra in 1926–27 showed just how flexible the bass could be, frequently swinging the big band during a song's final chorus. Wellman Braud (with Duke Ellington) and Pops Foster (with Luis Russell) were also important pacesetters, and the changeover from acoustic to electric recording made using a string bass more feasible. But it was not until the rise of the many big bands of the early 1930s and the gradual lightening of most pianists' left hand before the tuba became largely extinct outside of Dixieland and the bass was considered an essential instrument.

When bands from later decades try to recreate the sound of a 1920s group, the most frustrating aspect is usually the drum part. Prior to Gene Krupa in 1927, drummers on early records could utilize only part of their drum set and not their bass drum. Although in person they undoubtedly had a heavier sound, on records drummers functioned as percussionists, emphasizing woodblocks, cowbells, cymbals, and other simple sounds so as not to overpower the music. Among the early drummers who overcame that limitation to develop their own identities were the ODJB's Tony Spargo, Ben Pollack, Baby Dodds, and Zutty Singleton. Other individuals who developed their own approaches after they were finally able to use their full drum sets on records were Krupa (whose bass drum work tried to compensate for the absence of a string bass), Chick Webb, and Dave Tough. Drum solos were extremely rare during this period, and, other than an occasional cymbal crash, the drums were seen very much as a background instrument.

Jazz singing had to largely wait for both the rise of Louis Armstrong and the development of electrical recording before it became anything but an annoyance! In the early days, and to an extent until the beginning of the swing era, vocalists were prized as much for their volume and ability to make words understandable as they were for their choice of notes, tone, and ability to swing. Many records in the 1920s had insipid vocalists wasting a chorus before the musicians had an opportunity to solo. The singing of such warblers as Irving Kaufman, Jack Kaufman, Scrappy Lambert, Smith Ballew, and Wesley Vaughan has not grown in value through the years!

Prior to 1925, nearly the only male vocalist worth listening to was the unjustly overlooked Cliff Edwards ("Ukulele Ike"), while the females fared much better with the best classic blues singers, including Bessie Smith, Ethel Waters, and Alberta Hunter. The majority of the most rewarding male vocals from 1926–32 are by musicians who occasionally sang. Louis Armstrong's phrasing, ability to scat, and sense of swing were a major influence, as was Jack Teagarden's similar approach; both affected Bing Crosby, who brought a jazz sensibility and a blues feeling into pop music. Although Cab Calloway and the Mills Brothers did not play any instruments, they sounded very much like jazz musicians in their vocals. But as a rule, nonmusician male vocalists from this time period (such as Rudy Vallee, Russ Colombo, and Chick Bullock) were outside of jazz (even when on jazz records) and are to be tolerated or (at worst) avoided!

In general, females adapted better to singing jazz than males during the second half of the 1920s. In addition to Bessie Smith and Ethel Waters, such new voices as Annette Hanshaw, Ruth Etting (the Bing Crosby of female singers), Mildred Bailey, and the Boswell Sisters recorded frequently, and their recordings are well worth hearing today. But unlike in the years since, all but the most famous vocalists of the classic jazz era were considered a small part of the music, rather than being the stars. Many of the singers were not even credited on the records which sometimes merely stated "With Vocal Refrain." It is a pity that more of the inferior singers did not follow the unintentional advice and refrain from vocalizing!

BIOGRAPHIES

Although it is tempting to sum up the classic jazz era of 1917–32 with a few major names (Louis Armstrong, King Oliver, Jelly Roll Morton, James P. Johnson, Paul Whiteman, Earl Hines, Duke Ellington, etc.), there were many other important contributors to the music of that period. In addition to the bandleaders and the top classic blues singers, I have made an effort to include entries on virtually all of the key sidemen of the period, many of whom never led their own record dates.

Discussed are the survivors of the pre-1917 era who were still active in the 1920s (such as Freddie Keppard), the musicians whose prime period was in that decade, and quite a few performers who made their major impact in the swing era but already showed great promise on records by 1932. Since 1932 is the cutoff point, some musicians who were just beginning to become significant (such as Art Tatum and Bunny Berigan) are left out, while others (Claude Hopkins and Cab Calloway) just made the cut.

The division between jazz and blues often overlapped. Listeners who enjoy classic jazz will also want to check out the blues-oriented recordings of Blind Lemon Jefferson, Blind Blake, Blind Willie McTell, Big Bill Broonzy, Georgia Tom Dorsey, and Tampa Red, in addition to the classic female blues singers who are included in this book (often because of the jazz accompaniment). The division between jazz and pop music was also often arbitrary during the era, with most important dance bands having at least a sampling of their recordings being jazz-oriented. I included a cross section of those orchestras.

The CD and LP reviews naturally focus on the pre-1933 recordings led by the artists in question. In some cases (particularly when an artist's career ended just a little bit past the 1932 cutoff), a few of the later recordings are also included. And throughout the book, I have endeavored to mention every single significant jazz recording of the period. I hope that in time, all of the best music from the 1920s will be made available on CD. Thanks to such labels as Jazz Oracle, Frog, Timeless, and Classics (among others), the situation has greatly improved during the past five years.

SYLVESTER AHOLA

b. May 24, 1902, Gloucester, MA, d. 1995, Gloucester, MA

Sylvester Ahola was a relatively minor name in his native United States, but for a time he was the most significant American musician in England. Nicknamed "Hooley" (Finnish for "embouchure"), Ahola was a technically skilled cornetist and an expert sight-reader who could play melodic solos. He started on drums at six, two years before he switched to cornet. Ahola played locally in the New England area during 1921–25, moved to New York, and was with Paul Specht during 1925–26, including a two-month visit to England. He worked briefly with the California Ramblers, Bert Lown, Peter Van Steeden, and Adrian Rollini's orchestra (August–September 1927), playing next to Bix Beiderbecke with Rollini's band.

After the Rollini group folded, Ahola (whose biggest influence was Red Nichols) moved to England to join the Savoy Orpheans. He quickly became so in demand for record dates that it seemed as if he lived in the studios during the next four years, appearing on more than 3,000 titles during 1927–31! In addition to his work with the Savoy Orpheans and Bert Ambrose's orchestra (joining the latter in October 1928), Ahola recorded with a remarkable number of dance bands and vocalists, over 190 dates in 1929 alone.

Eventually other British musicians, who felt that Ahola was getting most of the best jobs, rebelled. A group of English trumpeters drew up a petition in protest in March 1930, and the result was that Ahola, a foreigner, was banned from recording with any group other than that of his main employer, Ambrose. The number of his appearances on records dropped dramatically.

Ahola moved back to New York in August 1931 and settled in as a studio player, performing in commercial settings with dance bands during the remainder of the decade, including with Ray Noble, Peter Van Steeden, and the NBC staff orchestra. In 1940 Sylvester Ahola (who ironically never led any record dates of his own except for a few titles in 1926 that were never released) returned to his home town, Gloucester, and worked mostly outside of music during the remainder of his life, other than playing locally with the Cape Ann Civic Symphony into the 1980's. He can be heard in prime form on a couple of LPs put out by the British Retrieval label in the early 1980s (*Phillip Lewis Rhythm Maniacs* Vols. 1 and 2), and his unique life is documented in great detail (along with all of the recording sessions) in Dick Hill's book *Sylvester Ahola — The Gloucester Gabriel* (Scarecrow Press, 1993).

ED ALLEN

b. Dec. 15, 1897, Nashville, TN, d. Jan. 28, 1974, New York, NY

Ed Allen was a decent cornetist who recorded an awful lot due to his friendship with Clarence Williams. He grew up in St. Louis and started playing with groups when he was 16. Allen worked in Seattle for a period, played with Charlie Creath on riverboats for two years, led a band in New Orleans (1923), was with Earl Hines the following year in Chicago, and moved to New York by mid-1925, working with Joe Jordan's Sharps and Flats in *Ed Daily's Black and White Show* for a year. He also worked regularly with Allie Ross' band (which be-

came the Leroy Tibbs Orchestra in 1930) and Earle Howard (1932–33).

Starting in 1927 and continuing for a decade, Allen recorded regularly with Clarence Williams, including 160 titles on dates led by the pianist. In addition, with Williams' sponsorship, the cornetist appeared on sessions backing singers Anna Bell, Laura Bryant, Mary Dixon, Katherine Henderson, Bertha Idaho, Sara Martin, Clara Smith, Eva Taylor, and Bessie Smith (most notably on "Nobody Knows You When You're Down and Out") plus combo dates with the Alabama Jug Band, the Barrelhouse Five, the Blue Grass Foot Warmers, the Birmingham Serenaders, Dixie Washboard, the Gallon Jug Band, Joe Jordan, Willie "the Lion" Smith, Leroy Tibbs, and TeRoy Williams. Not a virtuoso by any means, Allen was expert with mutes and offered a subtle and bluesy lead voice.

After Clarence Williams became semiretired in 1938, Allen (who was 40) stopped recording altogether. He played primarily with second-level dance hall bands and was with Benton Heath's little-known ensemble during 1945–63. Ed Allen appeared on four numbers on a record with Cliff Jackson in 1961, but otherwise he was totally forgotten after Clarence Williams retired, despite living until 1974.

HENRY "RED" ALLEN

b. Jan. 7, 1908, Algiers, LA, d. Apr. 17, 1967, New York, NY

Henry "Red" Allen was the most advanced trumpeter to emerge from New Orleans during the second half of the 1920s. He never became a major name with the general public on the level of a Louis Armstrong, but Allen was a significant player for nearly 40 years. He seemed to rise to prominence in 1929 from out of nowhere and generally sounded more modern than the settings in which he found himself, playing solos that were quite conversational with unpredictable phrasing. He was also an expressive vocalist and a consistently colorful performer.

His father, Henry Allen Sr. (1877–1952), was the leader of one of New Orleans' top brass bands, although the elder Allen unfortunately never recorded. Red played drums, ukulele, violin, and alto horn early on before switching to trumpet. He was always proud to play and march with his father's band. Allen, who co-led a kid's group with clarinetist John Casimir, picked up important experience in the early 1920s (when he was a young teenager) playing on riverboats with Fate Marable. In 1927 he first moved up North to work with King Oliver. Allen made his recording debut during this period with Clarence Williams but became homesick after a few months and returned to New Orleans. After working locally and with Fate Marable again, the 21-year-old was ready to hit the big time.

In 1929 Allen was offered his choice between two major jobs in New York. Although he could have joined Duke Ellington (as Bubber Miley's replacement, a position that Cootie Williams would take), he decided to become a member of Luis Russell's band because he knew more of the musicians. Allen immediately became the band's main star, overshadowing fellow trumpeter Bill Coleman, who would soon depart due to his lack of solo space. Some of Allen's finest recorded solos with Russell were on "Jersey Lightning," "Saratoga Shout," and "Louisiana Swing."

The great success of Louis Armstrong's records for Okeh inspired other labels to try to get trumpet stars of their own. Jabbo Smith signed with Brunswick, Reuben "River" Reeves was snatched up by Vocalion, and Red Allen began recording as a leader for Victor on July 16, 1929. Unlike Smith and Reeves (both of whom would never surpass their output of 1929), Allen's recordings helped launch a major solo career. His first session resulted in outstanding solos on "It Should Be You" and "Biff'ly Blues," and he led five recording dates during 1929–30, mostly using musicians from Russell's or-

chestra. He also recorded during the period with Victoria Spivey, Don Redman, Jelly Roll Morton, and Spike Hughes plus an outstanding meeting with Pee Wee Russell as part of Billy Banks' Rhythmakers in 1932.

Red Allen's career was just getting started. He left Luis Russell's band in 1932, spent a few months with Charlie Johnson, and then became a well-featured soloist with Fletcher Henderson's orchestra (1933–34) and the Mills Blue Rhythm Band (1934–37). Although he headed many record dates during 1933–37, Allen did not become a major name during the swing era, spending 1937–40 playing anonymously with the Russell big band when it functioned as the backup group for Louis Armstrong. However, from 1940 until his death in 1967, Henry "Red" Allen led heated combos, which ranged from Dixieland to jump music and early R&B, always performing exciting music and keeping the legacy and fire of the best New Orleans jazz alive and modern.

9 1929–1933/July 16, 1929–Nov. 9, 1933/Classics 540
7 The Henry Allen Collection Vol. 2/July 16, 1929–Dec. 17, 1930/JSP 333
8 1933–1935/Nov. 9, 1933–July 19, 1935/Classics 551

These three CDs contain all of Henry "Red" Allen's recordings during his first six years as a leader on records. *1929–1933* begins with one of Allen's great performances ("It Should Be You") and includes such gems as "Biff'ly Blues," "Swing Out," "Pleasin' Paul," "Sugar Hill Function," "Roamin'," and "I Wish I Could Shimmy Like My Sister Kate." The 16 selections from 1929–30 (including two vocal numbers for Victoria Spivey) have Allen using the nucleus of the Luis Russell Orchestra, while the seven performances from 1933 (two of which were previously unreleased) costar Coleman Hawkins and draw much of their personnel from the Fletcher Henderson Orchestra.

While Vol. 1 of the British JSP label's Red Allen series mostly duplicates *1929–1933* (cutting off in 1930 and also including Allen's date with Victoria

Spivey's sister, *Sweet Pease Spivey*), Vol. 2 is quite valuable for it has 17 alternate takes from Allen's 1929–30 dates (including numbers by both Spivey sisters), highlighted by two exciting (and very different) versions of "It Should Be You." The CD concludes with the four somewhat obscure Luis Russell recordings of October-December 1930, which usually elude being reissued.

All of Allen's work as a leader in the 1930s and early '40s has been reissued by Classics. *1933–1935*, which brings the trumpeter into the beginning of the swing era, has plenty of memorable performances (such as "You're Gonna Lose Your Gal," "Pardon My Southern Accent," "Rug Cutter Swing," "Believe It Beloved," "Rosetta," and "Truckin'"). The supporting cast includes Coleman Hawkins, Horace Henderson, Dicky Wells, Buster Bailey, Cecil Scott, J.C. Higginbotham, and Albert Nicholas. Although not every selection is a classic, the leader's cheerful vocals and explorative trumpet keep the proceedings stimulating and often unpredictable.

AMBROSE

b. Sept. 15, 1896, London, England, d. June 12, 1971, Leeds, England

Bert Ambrose (simply known professionally as Ambrose) led one of the top British dance bands of the 1920s and '30s. Ambrose, who was born in London, moved to the United States to live with his aunt when he was 15. He played violin with Emil Coleman (1916), freelanced with several orchestras, and directed the band at New York's Club de Vingt (1917–20). He visited England in 1920–21 (performing with local groups) before permanently moving back to his native country in 1922.

Ambrose headed a seven-piece band at the Embassy Club in late 1922; within a few years it had expanded to ten pieces and was growing in popularity. Ambrose became quite famous nationally during the period when he led his big band at the Mayfair Hotel in London (March 1927–July 1933),

broadcasting regularly on the BBC starting in 1928. Ambrose's orchestra was primarily a dance band, but it was flavored with jazz and for a time he featured the two Americans Sylvester Ahola and clarinetist Danny Polo.

Ambrose led an orchestra at the Embassy during 1933–36 and headed a series of smaller groups until 1956, becoming exclusively involved in management during his final 15 years.

LPS TO SEARCH FOR

The best currently available Ambrose set is the two-CD *Swing Is in the Air* (Avid 690), but those recordings are primarily from 1935–39. Three British LPs have highlights from the 1930–32 period: *The Golden Age of Ambrose* (EMI 41 2525), *Faithfully Yours* (Saville 159), and *Hits of 1931* (EMI/World 419). The music alternates between jazz-flavored pieces ("'Leven Thirty Saturday Night" on *The Golden Age* is considered a classic), novelty numbers, and ballad vocal features for Sam Browne and occasionally Elsie Carlisle. A CD reissuing Ambrose's best jazz recordings of the 1920s is long overdue.

JIMMY ARCHEY

b. Oct. 12, 1902, Norfolk, VA, d. Nov. 16, 1967, Amityville, NY

A top-notch trombonist, Jimmy Archey was flexible enough throughout his long career to span from classic jazz and swing to Dixieland. He began playing trombone when he was 12 and was working locally within a year. Archey studied music at the Hampton Institute during 1915–19, played with Quentin Redd in Atlantic City for a year, and moved to New York in 1923. In the 1920s Archey performed in many different situations, working with Lionel Howard, the house band at Ed Small's, the Lucky Sambo Revue (1925–26), Tan Town Topics, Edgar Hayes (1926–27), John C. Smith, Joe Steele, Bill Benford, and Charlie Skeets. Archey, who recorded with Fats Waller (1927), James P.

Johnson (1929), Joe Steele (1929), Clarence Williams (1930), Red Allen (1930), and Mamie Smith (1931), gained some recognition for his work with King Oliver (1929–31) and Luis Russell's orchestra (1930 and 1931–37), including two years in which Russell's group mostly backed Louis Armstrong.

Later years found Archey working with the big bands of Willie Bryant (1938–39), Benny Carter (1939–40), Ella Fitzgerald, Coleman Hawkins, and Claude Hopkins, freelancing in New York, and playing Dixieland from 1947 on, including with Mezz Mezzrow, Bob Wilber, his own band (1950–52), and Earl Hines (1955–62) in San Francisco. Although he was not from New Orleans and did not play trad jazz much in his earlier days, Jimmy Archey ended up his career working regularly with New Orleans revival groups up until shortly before his death in 1967.

LIL HARDIN ARMSTRONG
b. Feb. 3, 1898, Memphis, TN, d. Aug. 27, 1971, Chicago, IL

Louis Armstrong was always the love of Lil Hardin Armstrong's life, and, although a fine pianist, singer, and bandleader, she would remain in Satch's shadow even after they were divorced in 1938.

Lil Hardin studied music for three years at Fisk University, moved to Chicago in 1917, and at first worked as a song demonstrator in Jones' Music Store. Within a short time she was playing piano professionally, including with Sugar Johnny's Creole Orchestra and Freddie Keppard. Hardin led a band at the Dreamland in 1920 and became a member of King Oliver's Creole Jazz Band in 1921. Her solid playing (which generally found her pounding out the beat four-to-the-bar) and her technical skills were major assets, although she was never a major soloist. In 1922 Oliver sent to New Orleans for his young protégé, Louis Armstrong, to join him on second cornet. Although at first Lil considered Louis to be overly rural and unsophisticated, in a

short while she realized that he was both charming and a superior player to Oliver.

In 1923 King Oliver, Louis Armstrong, and Lil Harden made their recording debuts with Oliver's band, and the result was classic New Orleans jazz from the finest jazz group to be on record up to that time. On February 5, 1924, Lil and Louis were married. A money dispute had led the Dodds brothers to leave Oliver, but the loyal Louis stayed on for a time, as did his wife. However, Lil knew that her husband should not be playing second cornet to anyone and that as long as he stayed with his hero's band and played a supporting role, Armstrong would never be the star that he could become. In mid-1924 she successfully persuaded Louis to accept an offer to join Fletcher Henderson's big band in New York, a decision that changed jazz history and started Louis Armstrong on his way to being the most famous and influential of all jazz musicians.

While Louis was in New York, Lil Armstrong led a band in Chicago. When he returned to Chicago in late 1925, at first Louis was a featured soloist with her group, although constant ribbing by other musicians that he was just a sideman in his wife's band soon led Louis to depart so as to join the orchestras of Carroll Dickerson and Erskine Tate. However, when he led his famous *Hot Five* recording sessions, Louis used Lil on piano, and her rhythmic playing was a major plus in a group that had only Johnny St. Cyr's banjo joining her in the rhythm section. In addition, she occasionally contributed a humorous vocal (as on "That's When I'll Come Back to You") and wrote a few of the songs, including one that became a standard ("Struttin' with Some Barbecue").

Lil Harden was on all of her husband's *Hot Five* and *Hot Seven* recordings of 1925–27; she also recorded with the New Orleans Wanderers and the New Orleans Bootblacks. However, Lil's career soon separated from Louis'. He used Earl Hines on his *Savoy Ballroom Five* classics of 1928, and the only time that Louis and Lil recorded together again was on a single title ("Blue Yodel No. 9") with country singer Jimmy Rodgers in 1930. As Louis' star rose, Lil was left behind. They separated in 1931 and ended their 14-year marriage in 1938. Lil, who never remarried or stopped loving Louis, worked with Freddie Keppard (1928) and Johnny Dodds (with whom she recorded during 1928–29). She earned a teacher's diploma at the Chicago College of Music in 1928 and a postgraduate diploma from the New York College of Music the following year. Ms. Armstrong freelanced in the 1930s (often leading bands), led a series of fine swing-oriented recordings, and was a house pianist for the Decca label in the late 1930s.

Moving back to Chicago in 1940, Lil Harden Armstrong worked steadily at clubs through the decades (including with Red Allen and Zutty Singleton) but slipped into obscurity, other than appearing in the 1961 *Chicago and All That Jazz* television special, the same year she recorded her final album. She died in 1971 while playing "St. Louis Blues" at a Louis Armstrong memorial concert, less than two months after her former husband's death.

LOUIS ARMSTRONG

b. Aug. 4, 1901, New Orleans, LA, d. July 6, 1971, New York, NY

Although jazz certainly existed before Louis Armstrong (Buddy Bolden debuted with his first band 27 years before Satch first appeared in Chicago with King Oliver), and there were important giants that preceded him (including Jelly Roll Morton, James P. Johnson, Freddie Keppard, Sidney Bechet, and Oliver), Armstrong had the biggest impact of any jazz musician of the 1920s. Whether it was emphasizing legato phrasing rather than staccato, transforming jazz from an ensemble-oriented music into one showcasing solos by virtuosos, popularizing both scat singing and hornlike vocalizing, showing how to infuse pop songs with the blues, making dramatic statements through the inventive use of silence and dynamics, and (via his sunny personality) making jazz quite accessible to millions who had never heard it before, Armstrong's contributions are so vast as to very difficult to measure. Certainly jazz would have been a lot different if he had not existed.

Although it was believed during his lifetime that he was born on July 4, 1900, a posthumous search for his birth certificate revealed that Louis Armstrong was actually born August 4, 1901. He grew up in a very poor environment in the slums of New Orleans, abandoned by his father and raised by his mother. Armstrong sang in a vocal group on the streets for pennies as a youth, enjoyed hearing the city's many brass bands, and first started fooling around on the cornet when he was ten. On New Year's Eve of 1912, he shot off a pistol in the air in celebration and was promptly arrested. Since Armstrong's mother was not able to supervise him very closely, he was sent to live in a waif's home. This would prove to be the biggest break of his life.

While in the waif's home, Armstrong learned self-discipline and began seriously playing the cornet, performing with the school's band. Released after two years, he emerged as a promising young musician. Armstrong worked at odd jobs as a teenager during the day, and at night had chances to play with local bands. His idol was King Oliver (who gave him a few informal tips on cornet playing). When Oliver left New Orleans in 1919, he recommended Armstrong for his spot with Kid Ory's band. "Little Louis" also played on riverboats with Fate Marable's group and developed very quickly.

In 1922 King Oliver, who was based at Chicago's Lincoln Gardens, decided to expand his Creole Jazz Band and sent to New Orleans for his protégé. Armstrong was thrilled to get the offer and, although initially nervous, fit right in with the group from the start, happily playing second trumpet with his idol and spontaneously harmonizing two-bar breaks with Oliver. Although already a stronger player than Oliver, Armstrong went out of his way not to outshine his hero. He debuted on records with the Creole Jazz Band in 1923, taking his first solo on "Chimes Blues." While Oliver's nickname was "Dippermouth," Armstrong's was originally "Satchelmouth," later garbled by an English journalist into "Satchmo."

While with Oliver, Armstrong married the band's pianist, Lil Hardin (his second of four wives). In 1924 Lil, knowing that her husband would never be a star if he played second cornet forever, persuaded a reluctant Louis to leave Oliver and accept an offer by Fletcher Henderson to join his orchestra in New York. At the time the New York jazz players were mostly musically behind their Chicago counterparts (who were just beginning to record), particularly rhythmically, although they did not initially realize it! At the start of his first rehearsal with Henderson, Armstrong was looked down upon by the other musicians due to his primitive clothes and rural manners. But that changed as soon as he started playing. He immediately became the band's top soloist and an influential force. Don Redman loosened up his arrangements, Coleman Hawkins learned how to phrase, and the New York jazz world began to swing, thanks in large part to the impact of Louis Armstrong.

The cornetist was with Henderson's big band from October 1924 until November 1925. In addition to his work with the orchestra, he recorded on blues dates behind Alberta Hunter, Margaret Johnson, Maggie Jones, Virginia Liston, Ma Rainey, Clara Smith, Bessie Smith (including "St. Louis Blues"), Trixie Smith, Eva Taylor, Sippie Wallace, and the team of Grant & Wilson. He also teamed up with Sidney Bechet in Clarence Williams' Blue Five, battling the soprano saxophonist successfully and taking an astounding solo on "Cake Walking Babies from Home."

When he left Henderson's orchestra and returned to Chicago, Armstrong at first worked with his wife's band and then with Erskine Tate's Vendome

Orchestra and the Carroll Dickerson Orchestra. Although he performed in big bands at night, taking dramatic solos and becoming a very popular local attraction, Satch (who also recorded blues dates in Chicago during 1925–26 with Blanche Calloway, Chippie Hill, Baby Mack, Hociel Thomas, Sippie Wallace, and Nolan Welsh) made his biggest impact with his series of Hot Five and Hot Seven recordings. The early Hot Fives (with Johnny Dodds, Kid Ory, Lil Armstrong, and Johnny St. Cyr) found Satch breaking out of the New Orleans ensemble style with exciting statements. It was obvious that a soloist of his caliber should not be confined to just a few short breaks or a chorus; "Cornet Chop Suey" is just one of several masterpieces, while "Heebie Jeebies" (during which Armstrong allegedly dropped the sheet music and improvised nonsense syllables) was a major factor in making scat singing popular. In 1927 Armstrong switched permanently to trumpet, and his Hot Sevens from that year (with Pete Briggs and Baby Dodds being added and John Thomas filling in for Ory on trombone) contain particularly brilliant playing on "Wild Man Blues" and "Potato Head Blues." The last Hot Five dates of '27 have Armstrong constructing a perfect solo on "Struttin' with Some Barbecue" and trading off joyfully with guest Lonnie Johnson on "Hotter Than That." Ironically enough, the Hot Five appeared in public only once (at a special concert held by the Okeh label), but it certainly sounded like an organized group and it was the most influential band of the era.

If anything, Armstrong was a better soloist in 1928 than he was the year before. Leading the Savoy Ballroom Five (also known informally as the Hot Five although actually a sextet/septet), Armstrong matched wits with the brilliant Earl Hines, propelled by Zutty Singleton's inventive percussion. While the rest of the band (Fred Robinson, Jimmy Strong, Mancy Cara, and sometimes Don Redman) played a supportive role, Armstrong and

Hines constantly challenged each other, most obviously on their duet recording of "Weatherbird." "West End Blues," always Armstrong's favorite recording of his own playing, features a remarkable opening cadenza, some impressive wordless vocalizing, and a dramatic closing statement. As a whole, it is one of the finest jazz recordings of all time and by itself would have made Armstrong immortal.

As 1929 began, Louis Armstrong's fame was primarily in jazz and in the Chicago music world. That would soon change. Given an offer to play in New York, he relocated, taking the Carroll Dickerson Orchestra with him (to the surprise of his bookers). He appeared in a featured role in *Hot Chocolates* at Broadway's Hudson Theatre, introducing Fats Waller's "Ain't Misbehavin'." Armstrong's recordings started using various big bands, with Satch in the spotlight throughout, usually on both vocals and trumpet. Rather than playing jazz originals, he started focusing on pop songs, turning them into jazz. Having already introduced "Muskrat Ramble," "Big Butter and Egg Man," "Basin Street Blues," and "St. James Infirmary," he helped such tunes as "Ain't Misbehavin'," the antiracism protest song "Black and Blue," "When You're Smiling," "Rockin' Chair," "I'm Confessin' That I Love You," "Body and Soul," "Lazy River," "Star Dust," and "Sleepy Time Down South" (his permanent theme song) become standards. His recordings of 1929–31, although not as innovative as his earlier Hot Fives, are generally of very high quality and helped to make Armstrong into a national star.

Satch used Luis Russell's big band as his backup group for six months in 1930, and he led the Les Hite Orchestra in California during 1930–31. Armstrong and Vic Berton were busted for marijuana possession in 1931. But he was soon bailed out, and the incident did nothing to hurt his rapidly growing popularity. Now known internationally, Satch first visited Europe in July 1932 and was an immediate hit overseas. His 1932–33 recordings were not at the same high level as his earlier sessions (the big band was underrehearsed), but they sold well, particularly considering that it was the early Depression years.

In 1933 Armstrong returned to Europe. Since he was having management troubles (which would be solved when Joe Glaser took over his affairs in 1935) and his trumpet chops were overworked, Armstrong mostly took it easy, staying 29 months, having only one recording session, doing some touring, and appearing in his first performance film (playing classic versions of "I Cover the Waterfront" and "Dinah"). After he returned to the United States in 1935, he would lead a big band for 12 years, act in movies, and, in 1947, disband his orchestra in favor of forming his All-Stars. Louis Armstrong stayed quite busy during his final 24 years, consolidating his earlier innovations and retaining his positions as both America's goodwill ambassador and the most famous jazz musician in the world.

⭐ Portrait of the Artist As a Young Man/Apr. 6, 1923–Oct. 1934/Columbia 57176

🔢 Louis Armstrong/King Oliver/Apr. 6, 1923–Dec. 22, 1924/Milestone 47017

⭐ Louis Armstrong and the Blues Singers/Oct. 16, 1924–July 16, 1930/Affinity 1018

The four-CD set *Portrait of the Artist As a Young Man* does a fine job of summing up Louis Armstrong's first 11 years on records, with three selections from his period as a sideman with King Oliver, five tunes with the bands of Clarence Williams and Fletcher Henderson, 13 backing various blues singers, one apiece with the Erskine Tate and Carroll Dickerson orchestras, 24 Hot Five and Hot Seven numbers, and 28 selections with Armstrong's big band of 1929–34. However, this box has been superceded by the Complete Hot Five and Hot Seven Recordings reissue and other, more complete reissue series. *Louis Armstrong/King Oliver*, which has 18 of the Creole Jazz Band's recordings plus seven numbers that feature Satch with Clarence Williams'

Red Onion Babies, has also been topped by more comprehensive sets (the King Oliver Retrieval double CD and Williams' Classics series which are reviewed under Oliver's and Williams' names).

But the six-CD *Louis Armstrong and the Blues Singers* cannot be beaten for what it covers: all 120 selections in which Armstrong accompanies other singers. Although not all of the music is essential, there are quite a few timeless gems here, including Ma Rainey's "See See Rider Blues," Virginia Liston's "Early in the Morning," Maggie Jones' "Anybody Here Want to Try My Cabbage," Alberta Hunter and Sidney Bechet on "Nobody Knows the Way I Feel Dis Morning," Armstrong and Bechet romping with Eva Taylor on "Cake Walking Babies from Home," Bessie Smith's "St. Louis Blues" and "Careless Love," Perry Bradford's "I Ain't Gonna Play No Second Fiddle If I Can Play the Lead," Chippie Hill's "Trouble in Mind," Lillie Delk Christian's "Too Busy" (which has Satch singing an exuberant vocal that easily overshadows the rather weak singer), Victoria Spivey's "How Do You Do It That Way," and country singer Jimmie Rodgers' "Blue Yodel No. 9."

⭐ **The Complete Hot Five and Hot Seven Recordings/Nov. 11, 1925–Mar. 5, 1929/Columbia/Legacy 63527**

🔟 **Hot Fives, Vol. 1/Nov. 12, 1925–June 23, 1926/Columbia/Legacy 44049**

🔟 **Hot Fives and Sevens, Vol. 2/June 28, 1926–May 13, 1927/Columbia/Legacy 42253**

🔟 **Hot Fives and Sevens, Vol. 3/May 13, 1927–June 28, 1928/Columbia/Legacy 44422**

🔟 **Louis Armstrong and Earl Hines, Vol. 4/May 9, 1927–Dec. 12, 1928/Columbia/Legacy 45142**

Louis Armstrong's Hot Five and Seven records are among the most essential performances for any jazz record library. In all there were 33 songs by the 1925–27 Hot Five, 11 from the Hot Seven, and 19 by the 1928 Savoy Ballroom Five. In addition, three big band selections (one by Armstrong's Stompers in 1927 and two from Carroll Dickerson in 1928) are usually included in these collections. Strange as

it seems, it was not until French Columbia reissued all of the music in the 1970s that the complete Armstrong Hot Fives and Sevens were available in a coherent fashion. Typically, Columbia in the United States waited until 1988 before it came out with the same music on its domestic label, 60 years after the music was originally recorded!

In 2000, a four-CD set was reissued containing all 66 selections plus a variety of other performances that either were by the same personnel or were mistakenly issued in 1929 under the Hot Five name. Producer Phil Schaap (who can be a bit fanatical at times) included the great 66 plus the two numbers (and the rare alternate take of "Drop That Sack") from Lil's Hot Shots (the Hot Five under a different name), sessions featuring Butterbeans and Susie ("He Likes It Slow"), Hociel Thomas, Johnny Dodds (his 1927 date with Armstrong, Roy Palmer, Barney Bigard, and Earl Hines), and Lillie Delk Christian (fortunately just the session that resulted in "Too Busy"), the 1929 jam session "Knockin' a Jug," and a couple of big band numbers from 1929. Logic would have said eliminate all of these "extras," other than Lil's Hot Shots and Butterbeans and Susie (which did use the Hot Five personnel) and have it be a three-CD set, but that is a minor reservation. Get this box!

For listeners who just want a smaller sampling of Armstrong's 1925–28 recordings, the four single-CD Columbia/Legacy reissues puts out the 66 numbers in a logical fashion. *Vol. 1* has the first 16 Hot Fives, including "Gut Bucket Blues" (during which Armstrong introduces the members of the band), "Come Back Sweet Papa," "Heebie Jeebies," "Cornet Chop Suey," and "Muskrat Ramble." *Vol. 2* is split evenly between Hot Fives (including "Jazz Lips," "Big Butter and Egg Man," and the strangely atmospheric "Skid-Dat-De-Dat") and Hot Sevens ("Willie the Weeper," "Wild Man Blues," and "Potato Head Blues"). *Vol. 3* finishes off both the Hot Sevens and the Hot Fives ("Struttin' with Some

Barbecue," "Got No Blues," and "Hotter Than That") and begins the Savoy Ballroom Five series ("Fireworks" and "A Monday Date"). *Vol. 4* has the three big band numbers plus all of the rest of Armstrong's 1928 sessions ("West End Blues," "Basin Street Blues," "Weather Bird," and "St. James Infirmary"). But the four-CD box (which has all of this music plus more) is the best buy.

9 Louis in New York, Vol. 5/Mar. 5, 1929–Nov. 26, 1929/Columbia/Legacy 46148

10 St. Louis Blues, Vol. 6/Dec. 10, 1929–Oct. 9, 1930/Columbia/Legacy 46996

9 You're Driving Me Crazy, Vol. 7/Oct. 16, 1930–Nov. 3, 1931/Columbia/Legacy 48828

In 1929, Louis Armstrong relocated to New York. After recording a lone jam session number ("Knockin' a Jug"), he was heard principally with big bands during the next 18 years, with occasional exceptions. Somewhat overshadowed by his Hot Fives and Sevens, Armstrong actually recorded many gems with big bands during 1929–31. *Vol. 5* has "Knockin' a Jug" (Armstrong's first time on records with Jack Teagarden), his early "pop" sides ("I Can't Give You Anything but Love," "Mahogany Hall Stomp," and "Ain't Misbehavin' "), dates backing singers Seger Ellis (a horrible vocalist!) and Victoria Spivey, and two never-before-released alternate takes of "After You've Gone." *Vol. 6* has four more previously unissued alternates (including two "new" versions of "St. Louis Blues") plus such gems as "Song of the Islands," "Blue, Turning Grey over You," "Dear Old Southland" (a duet with pianist Buck Washington), "I'm Confessin'," "Body and Soul," and the remarkable "I'm a Ding Daddy from Dumas," which has some brilliant scat singing by Satch that is topped by an absolutely perfect solo. *Vol. 7* brings the Louis Armstrong story up to November 1931 with "Shine," "I'll Be Glad When You're Dead, You Rascal You" (the best version ever of that song), and beautiful renditions of "Memories of You" and "Sweethearts on Parade."

8 1931–1932/Nov. 3, 1931–Dec. 21, 1932/Classics 536

6 Laughin' Louis/Dec. 8, 1932–Apr. 26, 1933/Bluebird 9759

7 1932–1933/Dec. 21, 1932–Apr. 26, 1933/Classics 529

★ Complete RCA Victor Recordings/July 16, 1930–Aug. 1, 1956/RCA 68682

8 1934–1936/Oct. 1934–Feb. 4, 1936/Classics 509

There should have been a Vol. 8 in Columbia's Armstrong reissue series since there were 16 performances made during November 4, 1931–March 11, 1932, but the label never got around to it. Filling the gap (but unfortunately skipping the alternates of "Wrap Your Troubles in Dreams" and "Star Dust") is Classics' *1931–1932*, highlighted by "Home," "The New Tiger Rag," and "Lawd, You Made the Night Too Long." That CD also has the first Victor session (and part of the second) from December 1932.

While the domestic *Laughin' Louis* takes a "best of" approach toward Armstrong's erratic but intriguing 1932–33 recordings, there are two better alternatives. *1932–1933* has the master takes of all of Armstrong's Victor sessions (other than the ones included in *1931–1932*), with the highlights being a "Medley of Armstrong Hits," "I've Got the World on a String," the classic "Hustlin' and Bustlin' for Baby," "Basin Street Blues," and "St. Louis Blues." However, the four-CD *Complete RCA Victor Recordings* has not only all of that music but eight alternate takes, Armstrong's one number ("Blue Yodel No. 9") backing country singer Jimmie Rodgers, and two CDs of material from 1946–47 (plus two numbers from 1956), much of which is classic (particularly "Jack-Armstrong Blues").

Reaching into the swing era is *1934–1936*, which has Armstrong's first Decca recordings with the Luis Russell Orchestra (1935–36) and his lone 1934 session in Europe, during which he performs exciting versions of "St. Louis Blues," "Tiger Rag," "St. Louis Blues," and the eccentric "Song of the Vipers."

In reality, no jazz collection is complete without a healthy supply of Louis Armstrong records.

LOVIE AUSTIN

> b. Sept. 19, 1887, Chattanooga, TN, d. July 10, 1972, Chicago, IL

Lovie Austin (who was born Cora Calhoun) was a talented pianist-arranger who inspired Mary Lou Williams. She studied music at Roger Williams University (in Nashville) and Knoxville College. Her second marriage was to a variety artist with whom she toured in theaters for a time as Austin and Delaney. Austin also toured with Irving Mills' Blue Babies and played in New York with the Club Alabam Show.

Lovie Austin is remembered today chiefly for her many recordings of the 1924–26 period, particularly those with her Blues Serenaders that had such sidemen as Tommy Ladnier, Bob Shoffner, Natty Dominique, Kid Ory, Albert Wynn, Jimmy O'Bryant, and Johnny Dodds. Fortunately all of those recordings have been reissued on a single CD by the Classics label. Although Austin's own playing is often inaudible, her ability as an organizer, arranger, and bandleader are very much in evidence. During this period, Austin was also a house pianist for Paramount Records, playing and recording with many classic blues singers, including Ma Rainey, Ida Cox, Alberta Hunter, and Ethel Waters.

All of this activity came to an end after 1926. Lovie Austin worked for 20 years in Chicago as the musical director for the Monogram Theatre, and in the late 1940s became the pianist at Jimmy Payne's Dancing School. Because she made extremely few records after 1926 (other than a recording in 1961 with Alberta Hunter), Lovie Austin is destined always to be underrated, but few female instrumentalists of the 1920s were as significant.

9 1924–1926/Sept. 1924–Aug. 1926/Classics 756
This perfectly done Classics CD has all 16 selections recorded by Lovie Austin's Blues Serenaders, including ten cuts with Jimmy O'Bryant and Tommy Ladnier or Bob Shoffner in the frontline ("Steppin' on the Blues," "Charleston, South Carolina," and "Rampart Street Blues" stand out) and six with the Natty Dominique-Kid Ory-Johnny Dodds lineup. In addition, Austin and variations of her group are heard on selections backing singers Edmonia Henderson, Ford and Ford, and Viola Bartlette. This is certainly the one Lovie Austin CD to get.

BUSTER BAILEY

> b. July 19, 1902, Memphis, TN, d. Apr. 12, 1967, Brooklyn, NY

One of the most technically skilled clarinetists of the 1920s, Buster Bailey had a long career. He started on clarinet when he was 13, taking lessons along the way from Franz Schoepp, of the Chicago Symphony, who also taught Benny Goodman. Two years later, when he was 15, Bailey was a member of W.C. Handy's orchestra, touring with the composer during 1917–19. After leaving Handy, Bailey moved to Chicago, where he worked with Erskine Tate's orchestra (1919–23) and was Johnny Dodds' replacement with King Oliver (late 1923 to October 1924). He gained quite a bit of recognition when he joined Fletcher Henderson's orchestra in the fall, right about the same time as Louis Armstrong. Bailey recorded frequently with Henderson during this period (October 1924–July 1927) and ranked with the top clarinetists of the era. He gave the impression of being able to play anything effortlessly, and his style was light-years ahead of the "gaspipe" clarinetists who had formerly been in vogue.

Bailey played briefly with Oscar "Bernie" Young's band in Milwaukee, was back with Henderson for a year (late 1927 to late 1928), visited Europe with Noble Sissle (May 1929), and had stints with Edgar Hayes and Dave Nelson. A second period with Noble Sissle (1931–33) was followed by his third stint with Henderson (January–September 1934). During the swing era, Bailey worked with the Mills Blue Rhythm Band (October 1934–November 1935), Fletcher Henderson a fourth and final time (1936–37), Louis Armstrong, and Stuff Smith. However, his most important association was as a member of the John Kirby Sextet (May 1937 to summer of 1944 and occasionally during 1945–46), where his cool tone, virtuosity, and versatility made him an invaluable asset. Buster Bailey's later jobs were generally in Dixieland (which he often sounded overqualified to play), including working with trombonist Wilbur DeParis (1947–49), Red Allen (1950–51 and the second half of the 1950s), trombonist Big Chief Russell Moore (1952–53), cornetist Wild Bill Davison (1961–63), the Saints and Sinners (1963–64), and finally the Louis Armstrong All-Stars, from 1965 until Buster Bailey's death in 1967. His only date as a leader before 1934, a pair of trio numbers ("Papa De Da Da" and "Squeeze Me"), is available on his CD *1925–1940* (Classics 904), which mostly covers his dates during the swing era.

MILDRED BAILEY

b. Feb. 27, 1907, Tekoa, WA, d. Dec. 12, 1951, Poughkeepsie, NY

Mildred Bailey's career took place mostly after the classic jazz era, but she made a couple of important contributions to early jazz. Inspired by Ethel Waters and Bessie Smith, she would in turn be an influence on Lee Wiley. Bailey went to school in Spokane, worked as a song demonstrator, and sang on the radio in Los Angeles. When her brother singer Al Rinker and his friend Bing Crosby came down to Los Angeles in 1927 in hopes of finding work, Bai-

The first female singer to be a regular part of a big band, Mildred Bailey began her career in the classic jazz era.

ley was a major help in getting them jobs with Paul Whiteman's orchestra, launching their careers. Two years later, Bailey herself began a four-year period as a member of Whiteman's orchestra. She was the first female vocalist to be a regular part of a big band, beginning a trend that would result in most swing-era orchestras having a "girl singer."

During her period with Whiteman, Bailey became closely identified with the two Hoagy Carmichael songs "Georgia on My Mind" (which she first recorded in 1931) and "Rockin' Chair" (from 1932). In fact, for a time she was billed as "The Rockin' Chair Lady." Bailey, who recorded a single title apiece with Eddie Lang's orchestra (her recording debut in 1929) and Frankie Trumbauer, began leading her own sessions in 1931. In 1933 she married xylophonist Red Norvo. They left Whiteman and within a few years were known as "Mr. and Mrs. Swing," recording many gems during the swing era, both with their big band and on the singer's own sessions.

7 Volume One/Oct. 5, 1929–Mar. 2, 1932/the Old Masters 103
8 Volume Two/Dec. 1, 1931–Feb. 2, 1934/the Old Masters 104
All of Mildred Bailey's recordings up to February 1934 are contained on these two CDs. *Volume One* has Bailey's early dates with Eddie Lang (1929's "What Kind of Man Is You"), Frankie Trumbauer ("I Like to Do Things with You" from 1930), and Jimmie Noone (two songs from early 1931). In addition, the singer is backed on various tracks by the Casa Loma Orchestra, Paul Whiteman, and Matty Malneck. Among the better numbers are "You Call It Madness," "Wrap Your Troubles in Dreams," "Home," and her earliest recording of "Georgia on My Mind." *Volume Two*, which starts with a couple of leftover tracks from 1931, has more numbers in which Bailey is accompanied by commercial orchestras (including "I'll Never Be the Same" and "Rockin' Chair"), but in 1933 her backup becomes much more jazz-oriented. The Dorsey Brothers Orchestra (with trumpeter Bunny Berigan) help Bailey

swing hard on "Is That Religion," "Harlem Lullaby," and "Doin' the Uptown Lowdown"; she is also quite touching on "There's a Cabin in the Pines." *Volume Two* concludes with five performances (the instrumental "Emaline," "Ol' Pappy," and two takes of "Junk Man") with an all-star group that includes Benny Goodman and Coleman Hawkins. The latter date launched Mildred Bailey's prime years as one of the top swing singers and closed the book on her early period.

PAUL BARBARIN

b. May 5, 1899, New Orleans, LA, d. Feb. 17, 1969, New Orleans, LA

One of the most important New Orleans drummers, Paul Barbarin is included in this book because he was part of Luis Russell's pacesetting rhythm section during 1928–32. His father, Isadore, played trumpet and alto horn in brass bands, three of his brothers were musicians, and Barbarin was guitarist Danny Barker's uncle. He started on clarinet at 15 before switching to drums the following year, working with the Silver Leaf Orchestra and the Young Olympia Band. Barbarin developed a flexible style and was equally adept at both parades and dances, swinging with subtlety. Barbarin left New Orleans for Chicago around 1917, playing locally while having a day job for a few years at the stockyards. By 1920 he was playing music full time, including with Art Simms, the Tennessee Ten, Freddie Keppard, Jimmie Noone, and his own band. After spending 1923–24 in New Orleans, Barbarin was back in Chicago as a member of King Oliver's Dixie Syncopators (1924–27), with whom he recorded. Another short period in New Orleans, playing with Armand Piron, preceded the drummer's move to New York, where he joined Luis Russell. As part of arguably the finest rhythm section in jazz at the time (along with Russell, Pops Foster, and guitarist Will Johnson), Barbarin gave power, momentum, and swing to the all-star band. He also had an opportunity to record with Jelly Roll Morton in 1929.

Paul Barbarin remained an important force in trad jazz during his last 35 years, playing again with the Luis Russell Orchestra during 1935–39, when it was Louis Armstrong's backup band, Joe Robichaux's New Orleans Rhythm Boys, Red Allen (1942–43), and Sidney Bechet (1944). He eventually moved back to New Orleans, where he was a significant force in the revival movement, composing "Bourbon Street Parade" and "The Second Line" and leading a variety of bands, including the Onward Brass Band in the 1960s.

ROY BARGY

b. July 31, 1894, Newaygo, MI, d. Jan. 16, 1974, Vista, CA

A fine novelty ragtime pianist, Roy Bargy was able to span from classic jazz to classical music in his career. Bargy started 12 years of piano lessons when he was five, growing up in Toledo, Ohio. Although he had planned to become a classical pianist, Bargy decided to work in popular music instead, at first playing piano and organ for silent movies and organizing his own school orchestra. In 1919 he began cutting piano rolls and in 1920 was hired as pianist, arranger, and musical director for the Benson Orchestra of Chicago. In addition to the piano rolls, in 1922 and 1924 Bargy recorded six novelty ragtime piano solos, including his most famous composition, "Pianoflage."

Bargy worked in the mid-1920s with Isham Jones and had a long stint (1928–40) with Paul Whiteman, which gave him a chance to play both concert music (such as "Rhapsody in Blue") and jazz. Roy Bargy ended up his career as Jimmy Durante's musical director (1943–63).

LPS TO SEARCH FOR

Piano Syncopations (Folkways 35) has all six of Bargy's solo piano records plus the 11 piano rolls he cut of his own compositions. In addition to "Pianoflage," Bargy's pieces include "Knice and Knifty," "Sunshine Capers," "Ruffenreddy," "Sli-

pova," and "Justin-Tyme." He was definitely a talented and versatile player.

SIDNEY BECHET

b. May 14, 1897, New Orleans, LA, d. May 14, 1959, Paris, France

Sidney Bechet was among the very first major jazz soloists (other than pianists) to appear on records. Although Louis Armstrong (a lifelong rival) recorded before him (with King Oliver), Bechet (who made his recording debut with Clarence Williams' Blue Five on July 30, 1923) emerged as a dominant force first. A brilliant soprano saxophonist and clarinetist whose wide vibrato made him both much loved and much despised by jazz listeners, the fiery Bechet loved to lead ensembles, rarely playing second fiddle to any trumpeter.

Bechet played clarinet as a child, sitting in with Freddie Keppard's band when he was only eight. He was largely self-taught at first, taking a few lessons later on from Lorenzo Tio, Big Eye Louis Nelson, and George Baquet, all of whom he soon surpassed. Bechet played in New Orleans with the Silver Bells Band, Buddie Petit's Young Olympians (1909), John Robichaux, the Olympia Band, and the Eagle Band (1911–12). He also doubled on cornet during the period (though never on record) and was such a strong player that he gave clarinet lessons to Jimmie Noone, who was actually two years older! In 1914 Bechet began traveling throughout the South, often with traveling shows and carnivals. By 1917 he was in Chicago, playing with Lawrence Duhe, King Oliver, and Freddie Keppard. Bechet became a member of Will Marion Cook's Southern Syncopated Orchestra, traveling with the huge band to New York and, in June 1919, Europe. Bechet caused a sensation overseas (where the only jazz group that had been heard previously was the Original Dixieland Jazz Band), was written about in a famous and insightful review by Swiss conductor Ernest Ansermet, and bought his first soprano sax in London. The soprano became Bechet's main in-

The fiery Sidney Bechet was the first major jazz horn soloist on records, taking outstanding soprano-sax solos in 1923.

strument (he featured it early on in "Song of Songs"), although he continued doubling on clarinet into the 1940s.

After leaving Will Marion Cook, Bechet played in London with a small band led by drummer Benny Payton. He worked in different situations in France and England during 1920–21 until being deported from Great Britain over an assault charge. By the fall of 1921, he was in New York, playing with shows. Bechet was often utilized by Clarence Williams for record dates during 1923–25, most notably with Williams' Blue Five, including showcases on "Wild Cat Blues" and "Kansas City Man Blues" plus a few collaborations with Louis Armstrong. Of the latter, Bechet and Armstrong are quite outstanding on "Cake Walking Babies from Home," and Bechet is remarkable on bass sarru-

sophone on "Mandy, Make Up Your Mind," his only recording on that extinct instrument. Bechet also recorded with Rosetta Crawford, Maureen Englin, Alberta Hunter (including "Nobody Knows the Way I Feel Dis Mornin' "), Margaret Johnson, Virginia Liston, Sara Martin, Mamie Smith, Eva Taylor, Sippie Wallace, the Red Onion Jazz Babies, and the Get Happy Band (two titles in 1925). Bechet worked for a few months with Duke Ellington's Washingtonians in 1924 (he and Ellington were longtime mutual admirers), played with James P. Johnson, and had a club in Harlem (Club Basha), utilizing the young Johnny Hodges in his band.

In September 1925, Bechet was ready to roam again. Because he spent so much of the next six years overseas, his influence on American jazz musicians was much less than would be expected of someone with his stature. Bechet went to Paris with the *Revue Negre*, which featured Josephine Baker (who became a huge hit) and Claude Hopkins' orchestra. After leaving the show in February 1926, Bechet toured Russia for three months, spent time in Berlin leading a band, and played all over the continent. He first joined Noble Sissle's orchestra in the summer of 1928. After working with Benny Payton in France, Bechet (whose hot temper and unpredictable personality became legendary) was jailed in Paris for 11 months due to a shooting incident with banjoist Mike McKendrick. After his release, he played in Berlin and Amsterdam before returning to New York. Bechet rejoined Sissle in early 1931 (recording with the orchestra) and in 1932 co-led the New Orleans Feetwarmers with Tommy Ladnier. That explosive band (which Bechet hoped would help bring back New Orleans jazz) recorded six numbers on September 15, 1932, but folded by early 1933. For a few months Bechet operated the Southern Tailor Shop with Ladnier in New York. But because they spent more time playing at jam sessions in the backroom than they did attending to business, that venture also failed.

Bechet rejoined Noble Sissle's orchestra (1934–38), a steady job during the Depression but one that kept him out of the spotlight. Things began to look up in 1939, when Bechet had a hit recording of "Summertime" for the new Blue Note label. He worked fairly often during the 1940s (helped out by the New Orleans revival movement) and recorded steadily. And then, in an unexpected final chapter, Sidney Bechet moved to France in 1949 and during his final decade was treated as a national hero overseas.

★ The Victor Sessions-Master Takes 1932–43/Sept. 15, 1932–Dec. 8, 1943/Bluebird 2402

The definitive Sidney Bechet release, this three-CD set has all of the selections (but not the alternate takes) from Bechet's small-group dates of 1932–43. The Noble Sissle recordings are absent, but all of Bechet's sessions as a leader (including his overdubbed "one man band" recordings of "The Sheik of Araby" and "Blues of Bechet" from 1941) are included plus his 1938 "Really the Blues" date with Tommy Ladnier and Mezz Mezzrow and his 1939 session with Jelly Roll Morton. Of greatest relevance to the classic jazz era are the six 1932 numbers with the New Orleans Feetwarmers. It would be difficult to find hotter performances than these versions of "I've Found a New Baby," "Maple Leaf Rag," and "Shag."

BIX BEIDERBECKE

b. Mar. 10, 1903, Davenport, IA, d. Aug. 6, 1931, Queens, NY

In many ways, Bix Beiderbecke symbolized the 1920s. He rose to prominence with the rise of the Jazz Age, drank far too much bootleg liquor, and perished shortly after the Depression hit. He played intuitively (particularly in the early days) and was drawn to a wild new music that his parents disapproved of. And he was one of the first (some would say the very first) white musicians to carve out his own original voice in a music dominated by blacks. One part of the legend that is often told is untrue: that he was frustrated playing the often-commercial music of Paul Whiteman and that that situation somehow led to his death. But the rest of the story reads, to a large extent, like a Hollywood movie.

Leon Beiderbecke was born and grew up in Davenport, Iowa, to a conservative family. "Bix" was a family nickname that had also been applied to his father and grandfather. From an early age, Beiderbecke's musical talents were obvious. When he was four he picked out songs on his family's piano. He was given classical piano lessons but used to make his teachers mad by "improving" the written music. Hearing one of his older brother's records in 1918 ("Tiger Rag" by the Original Dixieland Jazz Band), Bix informed his parents that he wanted to play cornet, and a short time later he purchased his first horn. He also was a pianist in a local band, playing

Cornetist Bix Beiderbecke's up-and-down life perfectly typified the 1920s and the early Depression years.

purely by ear because he had not bothered to really learn how to read music.

After his graduation from high school, Bix was sent by his parents to Lake Forest Military Academy in 1921, in the vain hope that he would learn self-discipline and forget about this jazz music. As it turned out, the school was only 35 miles north of Chicago, the center of jazz at the time! Beiderbecke was soon violating his school's curfew by going to local nightclubs in search of jazz. He enjoyed the music of the New Orleans Rhythm Kings, having a few opportunities to sit in with the band. Needless to say, Bix was eventually caught and was expelled from the academy near the end of his first year.

During 1922–23, Beiderbecke worked on his cornet playing and freelanced. He was impressed and influenced by the playing of Emmett Hardy, and he befriended Louis Armstrong, whom he first heard performing on a riverboat. In October 1923, Beiderbecke joined a new band, the Wolverines, that started out with the New Orleans Rhythm Kings as their role model before developing their own sound. Between February and October 1924, the Wolverines recorded 16 songs, Bix's recording debut. Already at that early point, Beiderbecke had a beautiful and haunting tone, and a style that was cool on the outside but full of inner fire. The Wolverines' records were quickly noticed, and Red Nichols even copied Bix's first solo ("Jazz Me Blues") note for note on George Olsen's recording of "You'll Never Get to Heaven with Those Eyes." Although the band (a septet/octet with the fine tenor player George Johnson) was excellent and George Brunies of the NORK sat in on one date, Beiderbecke quickly emerged as the solo star. Among the more notable recordings were "Riverboat Shuffle" (the first time a Hoagy Carmichael song was waxed), "Royal Garden Blues," and "Big Boy" (on which Bix took a rare piano solo).

In September 1924, the Wolverines traveled to New York, where they made a strong impression, particularly their cornetist. Beiderbecke was soon offered a job with Jean Goldkette's orchestra. After training Jimmy McPartland to replace him, Bix joined Goldkette, but only for a brief time. It soon became apparent that his sight-reading was rather weak, and Goldkette reluctantly let Beiderbecke go, promising to hire him again when he could cut the charts. The Wolverines (after one recording date with McPartland) struggled along for a couple of years without Bix before breaking up.

In 1925 Beiderbecke was with Charlie Straight's band for four months before being fired for still not being able to read music well. He made just one record date that year (with the Rhythm Jugglers, introducing his "Davenport Blues"), attended the University of Iowa for two weeks (before being expelled for being in a drunken brawl), and worked in St. Louis with an orchestra led by Frankie Trumbauer. While with Trumbauer, Bix finally improved his sight-reading. Jean Goldkette happily rehired Beiderbecke in March 1926. With the addition of Trumbauer, Goldkette soon had his strongest orchestra, an ensemble that won a "battle of the bands" contest over Fletcher Henderson while visiting New York in October 1926. Unfortunately difficulties with the record producer at the Victor label resulted in most of the Goldkette recordings being merely commercial dance band performances, often featuring vocalists who had nothing to do with the music the band usually played. There was precious little solo space for Beiderbecke, whose only classic chorus with the band was on its final recording, "Clementine."

The greatest musical year in Bix Beiderbecke's life was 1927, when he was at the peak of his powers. He began recording regularly with groups assembled by Trumbauer. "Singin' the Blues" has Bix's most famous improvisation, and he is also in brilliant form on "I'm Comin' Virginia" (which has his longest cornet solo), "Way Down Yonder in New Orleans," and "Ostrich Walk." Beiderbecke started leading his own series of Dixieland-oriented dates under the name of Bix and His Gang; "Jazz Me Blues," "Royal Garden Blues," and "At the Jazz Band Ball" are three of the high points. In addition, he composed four impressionistic piano pieces, recording "In a Mist" as a piano solo although he never got around to waxing "Candlelights," "Flashes," and "In the Dark." The Goldkette Orchestra broke up in the summer, Bix and Tram played for two months with the sadly unrecorded Adrian Rollini Orchestra, and, after the latter band's collapse, the pair joined Paul Whiteman. Playing with the "King of Jazz" was considered very prestigious by Beiderbecke, a sign that he had "made it" and could perform the most complex charts.

Bix became a member of the Paul Whiteman Orchestra at the busiest time in the bandleader's career. Not only was Whiteman constantly on the radio and performing at concerts, but in mid-1928 he switched from the Victor label to Columbia. He made dozens of recording dates to finish off his Victor contract, and followed that with a large number for his new label. Beiderbecke was featured in short solos on many records, including "There Ain't No Sweet Man That's Worth the Salt of My Tears," "San," "Dardanella," and "You Took Advantage of Me" (which has a famous tradeoff between Bix and Tram), although he was most proud of his ability to play the trumpet part in George Gershwin's Concerto in F. In addition, Beiderbecke continued recording with Trumbauer and on his own Bix and His Gang dates.

Late in 1928, the cornetist's excessive drinking and the very heavy schedule began to catch up with him. He spent time in the hospital with pneumonia, came back for a short time, but in January 1929 suffered a nervous breakdown. Because Bix's position had by then become very important in the orchestra's sound (taking key solos on many Bill Challis arrangements), Whiteman hired soundalike Andy Secrest to fill in for him. When Beiderbecke returned sooner than expected, Whiteman kept both cornetists. Bix continued to decline throughout 1929, his playing became erratic (he really fumbles on "Futuristic Rhythm" with Trumbauer on March 8), and he eventually suggested that Secrest take his place on Trumbauer's future recordings. A cross-country trip did not help his health, and on September 13, after taking a short solo with Whiteman on "Waiting at the End of the Road," he collapsed.

Paul Whiteman, who was quite fond of the cornetist, kept Bix on his payroll and sent him home to Davenport in the hope that he would recover. Beiderbecke checked into a hospital for a time, took occasional gigs, and tried to stop drinking, but he was not strong enough to beat his addiction. In 1930 he recorded a few times (including a session of his own, with Irving Mills' Hotsy Totsy Gang, and with his pal Hoagy Carmichael), but his tone had clearly deteriorated. Bix turned down an offer to rejoin Whiteman and disappointed the members of the Casa Loma Orchestra by sounding quite weak during a tryout.

On August 6, 1931, at the age of 28, Bix Beiderbecke died from pneumonia. Perhaps if there had been an Alcoholics Anonymous in the 1920s or if the quality of the liquor had been better, Bix might have recovered from his alcoholism and become a major voice during the swing era instead of merely being one of jazz's most famous martyrs.

10 Bix Restored, Vol. 1/Feb. 18, 1924–Jan. 18, 1939/Sunbeam BXCD 1–3

10 Bix Restored, Vol. 2/Sept. 28, 1927–Feb. 28, 1928/Sunbeam BXCD 4–6

9 Bix Restored, Vol. 3/Feb. 28, 1928–June 18, 1928/Sunbeam BXCD 7–9

Collectors of 1920s music are generally well aware that every recording by Bix Beiderbecke is valuable. Not only did Bix play beautifully prior to 1929 (and occasionally afterwards), but his career (both his rise and fall) can easily be traced through his recordings, going from the optimism of his early days to the world-weariness of the later dates.

There had previously been a few attempts to reissue all of Beiderbecke's recordings (including a notable 14-LP box by the Joker label), but the current Sunbeam series is the most complete. These three-CD sets include not only all of the recordings on which Bix solos, but also selections with Jean Goldkette and especially Paul Whiteman in which Beiderbecke is known to be present even if he cannot be heard! Thus far there have been three volumes (a fourth set in the future will wrap up his career), and this is the most logical way to acquire his recordings. *Vol. 1* has all of the Wolverine sessions plus Bix's dates with the Sioux City Six (his first meeting on records with Frankie Trumbauer), Jean Goldkette (a lone solo from 1924 and the intriguing if frustratingly compromised sessions of 1926–27), the Rhythm Jugglers ("Toddlin' Blues" and "Davenport Blues"), and the first Trumbauer dates (highlighted by "Singing the Blues," "Clarinet Marmalade," "Ostrich Walk," and "I'm Comin' Virginia"). Also on this three-fer is Bix's recording of "In a Mist" and (to show his full legacy) Jess Stacy's piano solos from 1935 and 1939 of Beiderbecke's other piano pieces.

Vol. 2 has more dates with Trumbauer, the beginning of the Bix and His Gang series, sessions with the Broadway Bellhops and Willard Robison, and the start of Beiderbecke's association with Paul Whiteman, including "Changes," "Ol' Man River," "San," "Mississippi Mud," "There Ain't No Sweet Man," "From Monday On," and other pieces in which Bix is inaudible (including the two-part "Grand Fantasia from Wagneriana"). *Vol. 3* has 69 selections from a 111-day period; two dates led by Trumbauer, one from Bix and His Gang, and the bulk (including "Borneo," "Louisiana," "You Took Advantage of Me," and "'Tain't So, Honey, 'Tain't So") by Paul Whiteman's orchestra. Beiderbecke was still in strong form at the end of *Vol. 3*, but he must have already begun to feel exhausted from all of the activity!

9 And the Chicago Cornets/Feb. 18, 1924–Jan. 26, 1925/Milestone 47019

9 Vol. 1: Singin' the Blues/Feb. 4, 1927–Sept. 30, 1927/Columbia 45450

8 Vol. 2: At the Jazz Band Ball/Oct. 1927–Apr. 3, 1928/Columbia 46175

For collectors who are not acquiring the Sunbeam sets, these three CDs might suffice. The Milestone set has the Beiderbecke Wolverine recordings, his dates with the Sioux City Six and the Rhythm Jugglers, plus the two Wolverine selections with Jimmy McPartland in Bix's place ("When My Sugar Walks Down the Street" and "Prince of Wails") and the unrelated seven selections from the Bucktown Five, a 1924 quintet with Muggsy Spanier and Volly DeFaut.

Columbia's *Vol. 1* sticks to 1927 and has the classic Frankie Trumbauer recordings with Bix, "In a Mist," two trio numbers with Tram, Eddie Lang, and Bix on piano, and the Broadway Bellhops date. This CD acts as a perfect introduction to the musical magic of Beiderbecke. *Vol. 2* is almost on the same level, featuring more Trumbauer sides, the full Chicago Loopers date, the early Bix and His Gang titles, and numbers cut with the orchestras of Russell Gray and Lou Raderman.

TOMMY BENFORD

b. Apr. 19, 1905, Charleston, WV, d. Mar. 24, 1994, Mt. Vernon, NY

Tommy Benford is best known for recording with Jelly Roll Morton in 1928 (including "Shreveport Stomp") and 1930. The younger brother of tuba player Bill Benford (who also recorded with Morton), the drummer studied music at the legendary Jenkins Orphanage in South Carolina and toured with the school band, visiting England as early as 1914, when he was nine. He began working professionally in 1920 with the Green River Minstrel Show. After playing with the Marie Lucas Orchestra in Washington, D.C., Benford moved to New York, where he worked with many groups, including Charlie Skeete, Elmer Snowden, Edgar Hayes, and Fats Waller in addition to Morton.

Benford spent most of the 1930s (starting in 1932) in Europe, working along the way with Eddie South, Freddy Taylor, Garland Wilson, and Willie Lewis. Back in the U.S., he played in Dixieland settings for years, including with bands led by Snub Mosley (1946–48), Bob Wilber (1948–49), Jimmy Archey (1950–52), Rex Stewart, and Muggsy Spanier, toured with the Saints and Sinners (1963–68), was part of Bob Greene's World of Jelly Roll Morton (1973–74), and was a longtime member of Clyde Bernhardt's Harlem Blues and Jazz Band (1973–81). Tommy Benford was active into the late 1980s as one of the last surviving members of Jelly Roll Morton's bands.

BEN BERNIE

b. May 30, 1891, New York, NY, d. Oct. 20, 1943, Beverly Hills, CA

A popular bandleader in the 1920s and early '30s who often featured jazz-oriented performances, Ben Bernie was also an ok singer and an occasional songwriter. Bernie studied at the New York College of Music and played violin in vaudeville. He formed his first dance band (the Hotel Roosevelt Orchestra) in 1922 and during the next 11 years became quite popular, recording hundreds of titles and appearing regularly on the radio. In 1925 Bernie and his band appeared on what is probably the first sound short film ever to feature a jazz group, playing "Sweet Georgia Brown" (a Maceo Pinkard song that lists Bernie as cowriter). The historic clip, which features a fine Jack Pettis tenor solo, is available as part of the video *At the Jazz Band Ball*.

Among the other musicians to spend time in Bernie's orchestra were pianist-arranger Al Goerning, Bill Moore, classical pianist-comedian-actor Oscar Levant, and altoist Dick Stabile. After the early 1930s, Ben Bernie became better known as a radio personality than as a bandleader, dubbing himself "The Old Maestro" and acting in the films *Wake Up and Live* (1937) and *Love and Hisses* (1938).

LPS TO SEARCH FOR

Ben Bernie CDs are not exactly common, so look for *Ben Bernie and His Hotel Roosevelt Orchestra* (Sunbeam 11), a strong sampling of his more jazz-oriented sides. The music dates from 1924–30 and has a very memorable version of "Crazy Rhythm" (featuring Bernie's vocal), an early rendition of "Sweet Georgia Brown," a few vocals by Scrappy Lambert, and hot recordings of "Miss Annabelle Lee" and "Cannon Ball Rag."

VIC BERTON

> b. *May 7, 1896, Chicago, IL, d. Dec. 26, 1951, Hollywood, CA*

A very busy drummer during the second half of the 1920s, the consistently creative Vic Berton was also jazz's first tympanist. The son of a violinist, Berton (who was born Victor Cohen) started on violin and piano, but by the time he was seven he was playing drums in the pit orchestra at the Alhambra Theatre in Milwaukee. He studied tympani extensively, at 16 was appearing with the Milwaukee and Chicago Symphony orchestras, and played with Sousa's band during World War I. In the early 1920s, Berton moved to Chicago, where he worked with the bands of Art Kahn, Paul Beise, and Arnold Johnson. He managed the Wolverines during 1924–25, once in a while playing with them although Vic Moore was the band's regular drummer.

By 1926, Berton was living in New York and being noticed by other musicians. He made many re-

cordings with Red Nichols' Five Pennies and Nichols' other recording groups, showing how the tympani could be used colorfully in classic jazz and making every sound count in his drumming. Berton also freelanced quite extensively, working with Roger Wolfe Kahn (1926), Don Voorhees, and Paul Whiteman (part of 1927), among many others, appearing on quite a few recordings. However, with the onset of the Depression and the change in the musical atmosphere, Berton moved to Los Angeles, where he played with Abe Lyman and became a studio musician, working for years at Paramount Studios and Twentieth Century Fox; he also worked occasionally as percussionist with the L.A. Philharmonic. In 1935 Vic Berton was back in New York, leading three record dates (resulting in 13 titles) that displayed both his drumming and tympani playing in a swing setting. However, that was his only real return to jazz, and he soon went back to the prosperous anonymity of the Hollywood studios.

JIMMY BERTRAND

> b. *Feb. 24, 1900, Biloxi, MS, d. Aug. 1960, Chicago, IL*

Jimmy Bertrand was not only a significant drummer and washboard player in Chicago during the 1920s (appearing on many records), but he could be considered jazz's first xylophonist, predating Red Norvo and inspiring Lionel Hampton (one of his students, along with drummer Big Sid Catlett). He moved to Chicago with his family in 1913 and was a long-term member of Erskine Tate's Vendome Orchestra (1918–28). In addition to titles with Erskine Tate in 1923 and 1926, Bertrand appeared on records during 1926–29 with his Washboard Wizards (four sessions with such sidemen as Johnny Dodds, Jimmy Blythe, Natty Dominique, Punch Miller, Darnell Howard, and, on one date, Louis Armstrong), Tiny Parham, Ma Rainey, Blind Blake, the Kansas City Stompers, and the Midnight Rounders. In addition, he played xylophone with

Elzadie Robinson on one session in 1928 and took a xylophone solo on "Transatlantic Stomp" that year with E.C. Cobb and his Corn Eaters.

It is surprising that the colorful Jimmy Bertrand did not become a notable name in jazz. Perhaps he would have if he had lived in New York instead of choosing to stay in Chicago. After leaving Erskine Tate, Bertrand worked with Dave Peyton (1928), Eddie South (1931–33), Reuben "River" Reeves, and Walter Barnes (1938) in addition to leading bands of his own. Jimmy Bertrand recorded with the Memphis Nighthawks (1932), Eddie South (1932), and the Chicago Rhythm Kings (1936) but dropped out of music permanently in 1945 to work in a meat packing plant.

BARNEY BIGARD

b. Mar. 3, 1906, New Orleans, LA, d. June 27, 1980, Culver City, CA

Barney Bigard is famous for being a longtime clarinetist with both Duke Ellington's orchestra and the Louis Armstrong All-Stars, but he actually started out his career as one of the top tenor saxophonists of the mid-1920s. He came from a very musical family: His uncle Emile Bigard (a violinist) taught young Barney music, his brother Alex was a drummer, and among his cousins were Natty Dominique and Armand J. Piron. Bigard started on the E-flat clarinet when he was seven, taking lessons from Lorenzo Tio Jr., although many of his early jobs found him playing tenor as much as clarinet. He began his career freelancing in New Orleans, including with Albert Nicholas (1922) and Luis Russell. In late 1924, Bigard moved to Chicago to join King Oliver's Dixie Syncopators on tenor. He stayed with Oliver off and on until mid-1927 and recorded with Jelly Roll Morton on two occasions (in 1926 and a trio date in 1929). On November 17, 1926, Bigard had his finest recording session on tenor, recording four titles with Luis Russell's sextet and showing that at the time he was really second on that instrument to Coleman Hawkins.

In January 1928, Bigard joined Duke Ellington's orchestra (replacing Rudy Jackson), working almost exclusively as a clarinetist, a post in which his New Orleans sound and distinctive style were considered major assets. Bigard proved to be an invaluable soloist during the next 14½ years, staying until June 1942, contributing the main melody to "Mood Indigo," and consistently being one of Ellington's most reliable sidemen. Although he finally left Duke's band to get off the road, Barney Bigard would not exactly be staying home all that much in future years, working with Freddie Slack (1942–43), Kid Ory (1946), the Louis Armstrong All-Stars (1947–52, 1953–55, 1960–61), Ben Pollack, Cozy Cole (1958–59), Johnny St. Cyr's Young Men of New Orleans, Art Hodes, Eddie Condon, and his own groups.

EUBIE BLAKE

b. Feb. 7, 1883, Baltimore, MD, d. Feb. 12, 1983, New York, NY

An important early ragtime pianist and composer, Eubie Blake was also a significant composer for Broadway shows. After decades in obscurity, he emerged as the last survivor of the ragtime era, joyfully performing his songs while in his 90s. Born James Hubert Blake, he started played organ when he was six, soon switched to piano and was playing in public in the late 1890s, composing "Charleston Rag" in 1899. Blake worked mostly in the Baltimore area during the ragtime years, both in sporting houses and with medicine shows. During 1907–15 he played solo piano at the Goldfield Hotel in Baltimore and composed such songs as "Chevy Chase" and "Fizz Water Rag."

Starting in 1915, Blake teamed up with singer Noble Sissle in vaudeville. They spent a period working with James Reese Europe and in the 1920s were known as the Dixie Duo. The Sissle and Blake team co-led an orchestra in the early 1920s, appeared in some pioneering sound film shorts and they both produced and wrote the music for *Shuffle*

Along (1921), the first all-black musical on Broadway; usually Blake wrote the music while Sissle was the lyricist. Other shows that they collaborated on in the 1920s included *Revue Negre, Plantation Review, Rhapsody in Black,* and *Bamville Review.* In 1927 the team split up, but they worked together on an occasional basis in later years.

Blake recorded as a bandleader in 1931 and freelanced for decades. Of his songs, three ("I'm Just Wild About Harry," "You're Lucky to Me," and "Memories of You") became standards. The pianist played music on only a part-time basis during 1946–68, but he was rediscovered, recorded the double LP *The Eighty-Six Years of Eubie Blake* in 1969, and made a major comeback. Late in life Blake proved to be a very entertaining performer, playing and singing his music for amazed audiences during the next dozen years. At age 95 Blake took a bow at the opening of the Broadway revue *Eubie.* Eubie Blake performed regularly in public until he was 98, living five days past his 100th birthday.

LPS TO SEARCH FOR

Although Eubie Blake recorded 13 numbers without Noble Sissle during 1917–22, all are pretty scarce these days. In 1931 he cut 14 selections with a 12-piece dance band. Seven are on *Eubie Blake/ Frank Tanner* (Harrison G), mostly featuring vocals by Dick Robertson. The orchestra does not include any major soloists and Blake is not heard from much, but the music swings well. Also on this collector's album are seven numbers from 1936 by the San Antonio-based Frank Tanner and his Rhythm Kings, a decent if unidentified octet.

RUBE BLOOM

b. Apr. 24, 1902, New York, NY, d. Mar. 30, 1976, New York, NY

Rube Bloom, a skilled songwriter who is best known for "Give Me the Simple Life," appeared on many jazz records as a pianist in the 1920s. Self-taught, he developed quickly as a teenager and started working as an accompanist in vaudeville shows in 1919. Bloom recorded with the Sioux City Six in 1924 and during the next seven years recorded frequently with Red Nichols, Miff Mole, Frankie Trumbauer (the groups with Bix Beiderbecke), Eddie Lang, Joe Venuti, and the Dorsey Brothers among others. He recorded six tunes (including his "The Man from the South") with the Bayou Boys in 1930, using Adrian Rollini, Benny Goodman, and Tommy Dorsey as sidemen. Bloom also wrote original piano compositions that he recorded as a novelty ragtime soloist (23 piano solos during 1926–28 and four in 1934), most notably the haunting "Soliloquy." Eight of his solos are included on *Novelty Ragtime Piano Kings* (Folkways 41), an LP that he shares with Arthur Schutt.

Rube Bloom did not record in a jazz setting again after 1934, but he made a strong impact on jazz as a songwriter, composing (in addition to "Give Me the Simple Life") such standards as "Don't Worry 'Bout Me," "Truckin'," "Fools Rush In," "Day In, Day Out," "Stay on the Right Side, Sister," and "Penthouse Serenade."

JIMMY BLYTHE

b. May 20, 1901, Keene, KY, d. June 14, 1931, Chicago, IL

Although pianist Jimmy Blythe's life is almost a complete mystery, he was quite active in the 1920s, being equally skilled in freewheeling jazz and blues settings. Blythe, who grew up in Kentucky, moved to Chicago in 1918, recorded dozens of piano rolls in the early 1920s, and started appearing on records in 1924. His "Chicago Stomp," from 1924, is considered by some to be the first full-length boogie-woogie recording. During 1924–31 Blythe was on many recordings, including some piano solos, accompanying singers Viola Bartlette and Alexander Robinson, jamming with Johnny Dodds in several settings, leading Blythe's Sinful Five, the State Street Ramblers, and the Washboard Wizards, and also recording with the Midnight Rounders, J.C. Cobb and his Grains of Corn, Jimmy Bertrand, Lonnie Johnson, the Dixieland Thumpers, and the Chicago Footwarmers, in addition to piano duets with Buddy Burton and Charlie Clark (his cousin).

Jimmy Blythe died at the age of 30 from meningitis, only three months after his final recording.

9 **Jimmy Blythe/Apr. 1924–Mar. 20, 1931/RST 1510**

With the exception of his work with the State Street Ramblers, Lonnie Johnson, Johnny Dodds, and Buddy Burton (which are available elsewhere), this CD from the Austrian RST label gives listeners the complete Jimmy Blythe. He is featured on eight piano solos (including the historic "Chicago Stomp"), accompanying Viola Bartlette and Alexander Robinson, playing two duets with Charles Clark, and jamming good-time music with his Sinful Five, Birmingham Bluetette, the Midnight Rounders, and the Washboard Wizards. Among the sidemen are W.E. Burton, Jimmy Bertrand, Punch Miller, Darnell Howard, and singer Half Pint Jaxon. Blythe is particular strong on the more blues-oriented material.

PETER BOCAGE

b. July 31, 1887, Algiers, LA, d. Dec. 3, 1967, New Orleans, LA

The main soloist with Piron's orchestra, cornetist Peter Bocage had a fairly simple melodic style and a gentle sound. He began playing professionally as a violinist, working with Tom Albert, the Eagle Band, the Superior Orchestra, and the Peerless Orchestra during 1906–10. A friend of Bunk Johnson, Bocage taught Bunk how to read music in exchange for some cornet lessons. He developed quickly on his new instrument and freelanced in New Orleans, playing with the Onward Brass Band, the Tuxedo Brass Band, the Excelsior Brass Band, Oscar Celestin, and Fate Marable (1918). Bocage was a fixture with Armand J. Piron's New Orleans Orchestra during 1919–28, recording 17 selections with Piron

during two visits to New York. Bocage, whose mellow tone and subtle improvising consistently uplifted the music, cowrote "Mama's Gone Goodbye" with Piron.

After Piron's orchestra broke up in 1928, Bocage performed with the Creole Serenaders for a decade (unfortunately that band never recorded), worked outside of music as an insurance salesman, had a brief but unsuccessful stint with Sidney Bechet in 1945, and became more active in the 1950s and '60s. Although past his prime, Peter Bocage organized a new version of the Creole Serenaders, worked with the Eureka Brass Band, and led three albums (doubling on trumpet and violin) late in his life.

STERLING BOSE

b. Feb. 23, 1906, Florence, AL, d. June 1958, St. Petersburg, FL

Sterling Bose never really caught on, but in the 1920s he was a talented trumpeter who could be relied upon for brief and fiery solos. Bose started working professionally in the early '20s and was based in St. Louis for several years starting in 1923. He played with the Crescent City Jazzers and recorded eight titles with the Arcadian Serenaders (a hot band influenced by the New Orleans Rhythm Kings) in 1925. Bose appeared with a variety of groups in the Midwest and was with the Jean Goldkette Orchestra during 1928–29, making some records with the big band and sounding pretty close at times to Bix Beiderbecke.

Bose worked with the Ben Pollack Orchestra during 1930–33 and then spent the next decade alternating between studio work and stints with swing orchestras, including Joe Haymes (1934–35), Tommy Dorsey (1935), Ray Noble (1936), Benny Goodman (1936), Glenn Miller (1937), Bob Crosby (1938–39), Bobby Hackett (1939), Bob Zurke (1939–40), Jack Teagarden (1940), Bud Freeman (1942), and Bobby Sherwood (1943). He played Dixieland at Nick's (1943–44), worked in

Chicago (1945–47), and permanently relocated to Florida, having a regular gig at the Soreno Lounge in St. Petersburg during 1950–57. Seriously ill for a long period, Sterling Bose committed suicide in 1958.

BOSWELL SISTERS

There were many sister vocal groups in the 1920s, including the Keller Sisters (who recorded with Jean Goldkette), the Brox Sisters, and the Hannah Sisters. Most, at best, featured appealing voices and little else, but the Boswell Sisters were on a completely different level altogether. Not only were they the finest of all the sister groups of the past century, but the Boswell Sisters were arguably the most rewarding jazz vocal ensemble prior to Lambert, Hendricks, and Ross in the late 1950s.

Connie (1907–76), Martha (1908–58), and Helvetia (1909–88) were born and raised in New Orleans. Connie contracted polio during infancy and was never able to walk; she always appeared in public in a well-hidden wheelchair. Each of the sisters played instruments early on, with Connie learning cello, piano, alto sax, and trombone, Vet playing violin, and Martha (the only one to record on her instrument) becoming a fine pianist. The Boswells were encouraged in their singing by Emmett Hardy (an early associate), performed locally, and as teenagers in 1925 made their recording debut with "Nights When I'm Lonely" and a solo feature for Connie on "I'm Gonna Cry."

After creating a stir in the late 1920s in Los Angeles, where they appeared on radio five nights a week, the Boswells began recording regularly in 1930. From the start they offered something much different than most vocal groups of the time. Their adventurous arrangements (organized mostly by Connie and Martha) had surprise tempo and key changes, mixed together lyrics and hot scatting, built up to unpredictable conclusions, and swung hard. Connie was always the solo voice, but the harmonies of Vet and Martha were just as important.

Although some radio listeners called in to ask where the melody was and many initially assumed that the white siblings were black, the Boswell Sisters became a hit in 1931, when they appeared regularly at New York's Paramount Hotel.

The Boswell Sisters had spots in several films (best is their version of "Crazy People" in 1932's *The Big Broadcast*), they visited Europe in 1933 and 1935, and, other than the Mills Brothers, they had no competition among jazz vocal groups. Many of their records featured top jazz soloists, including Bunny Berigan, the Dorsey Brothers, and Joe Venuti, and they still sound fresh and exciting today.

The group came to a premature end in 1936 when all three sisters got married and both Vet and Martha decided to retire. Connie Boswell (whom Ella Fitzgerald always cited as her main influence) continued with a solo career that included memorable recordings with Bob Crosby's orchestra, short appearances in a variety of movies, and a role in the late 1950s television series *Pete Kelly's Blues*, although she individually never reached the creative heights of the Boswell Sisters.

10 The Boswell Sisters Collection, Vol. 1/Mar. 19, 1931–Apr. 9, 1932/Nostalgia Arts 3007

8 The Boswell Sisters Collection, Vol. 2/Mar. 25, 1925–Apr. 19, 1932/Nostalgia Arts 3008

9 The Boswell Sisters Collection, Vol. 3/Feb. 19, 1932–Apr. 11, 1933/Nostalgia Arts 3009

7 The Boswell Sisters Collection, Vol. 4/Mar. 25, 1932–Dec. 13, 1934/Nostalgia Arts 3022

7 The Boswell Sisters Collection, Vol. 5/Apr. 19, 1932–Feb. 12, 1936/Nostalgia Arts 3023

All of the Boswell Sisters' regular studio recordings are being reissued on five CDs from the Danish Nostalgia Arts label (which is available through Storyville); *Vol. 4* and *Vol. 5* were scheduled but not yet released as of this writing. *Vol. 1* temporarily bypasses the sisters' first recordings but chronologically reissues all of their recordings from a 13-month period, including two obscure numbers cut with Victor Young's orchestra. The backup bands

The Boswell Sisters showed that vocal groups could
swing, improvise, and take chances.

(which include the Dorsey Brothers, Jack Purvis, Joe Venuti, Eddie Lang, Bunny Berigan, and a host of others) are top-notch, clearly inspiring the Boswells. No collection is complete without these versions of "When I Take My Sugar to Tea," "Roll On, Mississippi, Roll On," "Shout, Sister, Shout," "Heebie Jeebies," "River, Stay 'Way from My Door," "Was That the Human Thing to Do," "Put That Sun Back in the Sky," "Everybody Loves My Baby," "There'll Be Some Changes Made," and "If It Ain't Love." Classic jazz at its best.

Vol. 2 is a gap filler. It has the 1925 selection ("Nights When I Am Lonely"), the Boswell's six recordings from 1930, some rare alternate takes, guest appearances originally issued under other orchestra's names, including those of Jackie Taylor,

the Brunswick Concert Orchestra, Victor Young, Red Nichols, and Don Redman, plus a few multi-artist medleys in which the Sisters make an appearance. Although not as essential or as consistent as *Vol. 1* or *Vol. 3*, this disc has its moments, including different versions of "Heebie Jeebies," "Put That Sun Back in the Sky," and "Was That the Human Thing to Do."

After a few additional alternate takes, *Vol. 3* continues the Boswell Sisters' chronology from June 17, 1932, through April 11, 1933, including exciting versions of "Old Yazoo," "We Just Couldn't Say 'Goodbye,' " "Down Among the Sheltering Palms," "Sentimental Gentleman from Georgia," "Crazy People," and "Forty-Second Street." *Vol. 4* starts off with seven alternate takes and then covers the second half of 1933 and 1934. Bunny Berigan gets off a few hot solos, and, even though the backup groups are a little more tightly arranged than usual on some selections, there are plenty of noteworthy selections, including "Coffee in the Morning," "Rock and Roll," "If I Had a Million Dollars," and "The Object of My Affection." *Vol. 5* has two alternates, wraps up 1934, and has the Sisters' eight numbers from 1935 and four from early 1936. The later selections are a little more conservative than the earlier ones due to the wishes of record company executives, but there was certainly no decline in the Boswell Sisters' voices. It is a pity that they chose to end their singing careers just as the swing era was catching on, leaving a gap that would be filled by the less adventurous Andrews Sisters.

7 The Boswell Sisters 1930–1935/1930–July 19, 1935/Retrieval 79009

7 Syncopating Harmonists from New Orleans/1930–1935/Take Two 406

5 That's How Rhythm Was Born/Mar. 21, 1932–May 28, 1935/Legacy/Columbia 66977

5 Okay, America!/May 25, 1931–July 19, 1935/Jass 622

The Retrieval CD has some interesting material not previously available. There are six studio records, three of which (an alternate of "Sleep, Come on and Take Me" and two songs from September 18, 1934) were not released before. In addition, the Boswell Sisters (accompanied just by Martha Boswell's piano) are heard performing on three radio broadcasts in 1930 and one (with an orchestra) in 1931, mostly singing tunes that they otherwise never recorded. An extra bonus is that the liner notes have an interview with Vet Boswell.

Syncopating Harmonists from New Orleans also includes some historic material. There are nine regular studio records but also nine numbers from 1930 radio shows plus two cuts from the 1935 *Dodge Show*; none of the radio material had been released before.

The other two discs have been superceded by the Nostalgia Arts series. *That's How Rhythm Was Born* has 20 recordings by the Boswells (mostly from 1932–34), programmed in random order. It is a good introduction but is no longer all that important. *Okay, America* was a significant CD when it was released in 1992 (although largely an expanded version of an earlier LP) since it includes lots of alternate takes, medleys, and obscure guest appearances. But all of the music (other than Connie Boswell's solo vocal on an alternate of "Washboard Blues" with the Casa Loma Orchestra) is in the Nostalgia Arts series, especially on *Vol. 2*.

Note that, due to the release of Nostalgia Arts' *Vol. 2* and *Vol. 3*, which duplicate much of their content in superior fashion, the ratings of *That's How Rhythm Was Born* and *Okay America* are lower than they were in my previous book *Swing*.

LPS TO SEARCH FOR

On the Air 1931–1936 (Totem 1042) has additional Boswell Sisters radio appearances, dating from 1930–31 and 1935–36, that add to their legacy. Connie Boswell, one of the best jazz singers of the 1930s (although she did not achieve major commercial success) is heard on some of her most rewarding solo performances from 1931–35 on *The Early Solos* (Take Two 209) and *Under a Blanket of Blue* (Take Two 216). *Send in My Shoes* (MCA 16989) features the final six recordings by the Boswell Sisters (from 1936) followed by 24 of Connie Boswell's most jazz-oriented recordings of 1937–41, including two duets with Bing Crosby, "Mama Don't Allow It," "Martha," "That Old Feeling," and a remarkable version of "Home on the Range."

PERRY BRADFORD

b. Feb. 14, 1893, Montgomery, AL, d. Apr. 20, 1970, New York, NY

An important figure behind the scenes in 1920s jazz and blues and an occasional singer, Perry Bradford hurt his cause a bit with his bragging, but his contributions were significant. He grew up in Atlanta and worked in minstrel shows as early as 1906, as a teenager. During the next dozen years, Bradford performed as a solo pianist, primarily at theaters (spending 1909–11 in Chicago before moving to New York in 1912) and composing songs. He became Mamie Smith's musical director, managing the singer and helping her in 1920 to become the first blues singer to record; "Crazy Blues" was Bradford's song.

During 1923–27 Perry Bradford's Jazz Phools were featured on seven recording dates (14 selections in all) with Bradford's sidemen including Louis Armstrong, Buster Bailey, Charlie Green, Bubber Miley, and James P. Johnson. However, by the late 1920s, the singer (who never recorded on piano) was fading out of the music scene. Although he ran a publishing company and helped get black performers on the radio, by the swing era Bradford was quite obscure. In 1965 Perry Bradford wrote his autobiography, *Born with the Blues*, exaggerating his own significance to early jazz a bit, probably to counteract the fact that no one knew who he was anymore.

WELLMAN BRAUD

b. Jan. 25, 1891, St. James Parish, LA, d. Oct. 29, 1966, Los Angeles, CA

In the late 1920s, after Steve Brown was no longer prominent, the top bassists in jazz were Wellman Braud and Pops Foster. Braud started playing violin when he was seven and later played trombone, guitar, and drums before switching to bass. He picked up early experience playing in string trios in New Orleans. After moving to Chicago in 1917, Braud worked with John Wickliffe, the Original Creole Orchestra, Charlie Elgar (1920–22), Will Vodery's Plantation Revue (1923) in London, and Wilbur Sweatman, also performing with several shows. In mid-1927 Braud joined Duke Ellington's orchestra and during the next eight years was quite prominent

with Ellington, making sure that his bass could always be heard on Duke's records. Ellington learned from Braud, and, consistently through the years, his bassists were better recorded than were those with other bands.

After leaving Duke in 1935, Braud worked with Jimmy Noone, Kaiser Marshall, the Spirits of Rhythm, Hot Lips Page (1938), Edgar Hayes, Jelly Roll Morton, Sidney Bechet (1940–41), Al Sears, and Garvin Bushell (1944). He largely retired from music in the mid-1940s to manage a pool hall and later on a meat-marketing business. Braud came back briefly to play with Bunk Johnson in 1947 and then returned in 1956 to work with Kid Ory, spending his last years freelancing in the Los Angeles area, including with clarinetist Joe Darensbourg and singer Barbara Dane. Wellman Braud died of a heart attack in 1966 at age 75.

PETE BRIGGS

b. 1904, Charleston, SC, d. 1970s?

Pete Briggs is primarily known for being the tuba player with Louis Armstrong's Hot Seven in 1927. He began his career touring with the Jim Jam Jazzers in the early 1920s and also worked with the Lucky Boy Minstrels (1923). Settling in Chicago, Briggs was a member of the Carroll Dickerson Orchestra in 1926 and continued with the band the following year, when it was renamed the Louis Armstrong Stompers. On the Hot Seven dates, Briggs' steady rhythm and occasional breaks helped make the ensembles quite solid and added to their color. He worked briefly with Jimmie Noone, was back with Dickerson in 1928, and traveled to New York with the orchestra when it accompanied Louis Armstrong in 1929. Briggs, who switched to string bass around this time, played in New York with the Edgar Hayes Orchestra (1929–30) and Vernon Andrade, freelanced out of the spotlight, worked with trumpeter Herman Autrey (1943–44) in Philadelphia, and then permanently retired from music to run his own farm.

LAWRENCE BROWN

b. Aug. 3, 1907, Lawrence, KS, d. Sept. 5, 1988, New York, NY

Lawrence Brown really fits much more securely in the *Swing* book than in this book due to his many years with Duke Ellington, but he was also one of the best trombonists of the late 1920s. The son of a minister, Brown was an oddity in the jazz world, because he never smoked, drank, or gambled. He studied piano, violin, and tuba before switching to trombone. Brown took classes in medicine at Pasadena Junior College but also played in the school orchestra and was inspired to become a full-time musician. He was an important part of the early Los Angeles jazz scene, working with Leon Herriford, Curtis Mosby's Blue Blowers, and Paul Howard's Quality Serenaders and recording with Howard in 1929–30, taking many short solos. Brown was part of the house band at Sebastian's Cotton Club in Culver City, led by Les Hite, an ensemble that recorded with Louis Armstrong in 1930.

In the spring of 1932, the trombonist joined Duke Ellington, where he remained until March 1951, becoming one of Duke's most reliable and fluent soloists, offering a major contrast to the more primitive sounds of Tricky Sam Nanton. Later on, Lawrence Brown was with Johnny Hodges' combo (1951–55), freelanced a bit, and was back with Duke Ellington for another ten-year run (1960–70) before retiring from music.

STEVE BROWN

b. Jan. 13, 1890, New Orleans, LA, d. Sept. 15, 1965, Detroit, MI

Steve Brown was one of the first important string bassists on records. He originally played tuba in a band led by his brother, trombonist Tom Brown. After switching to bass, he went to Chicago with his brother's band in May 1915. Brown freelanced locally for many years, was a member of the New Orleans Rhythm Kings in 1922, and also worked with Murphy Steinberg, the Original Memphis Mel-ody Boys, and the Midway Dance Orchestra. During 1924–27 Brown was a major part of the Jean Goldkette Orchestra. Frequently during the last chorus of their recordings, Brown put down his bow and really swung the rhythm section. In fact, he was one of the main reasons that jazz bands eventually switched from having a tuba to employing a swinging bassist.

But ironically, by the time the switch was taking place, Brown had already become obscure. He went with the other key Goldkette alumni to Paul Whiteman's orchestra in late 1927 but chose to stay only four months. After a short second stint with Goldkette, Steve Brown settled in Detroit, where he played on just a part-time basis for decades, including making a rare recording with Frank Gillis' Dixie Five in 1950.

ABBIE BRUNIES

b. Jan. 19, 1900, New Orleans, LA, d. Oct. 2, 1978, Biloxi, MS

The Brunies family was one of the most important in early New Orleans jazz. Henry Brunies was a violinist and his wife Elizabeth played piano. Their daughter Ada was a guitarist and their six sons all played music: bassist Rudy, cornetist Richie, George and Henry on trombones, Merritt Brunies (cornet and valve trombone), and cornetist Abbie Brunies, not to mention Albert "Little Abbie" Brunies, a nephew who played drums. While Ada, Rudy, and Richie were not professionals, George, Henry, Merritt, and Abbie all had significant careers.

Abbie, the fifth of the six sons, started playing professionally in 1910, freelancing in New Orleans as a teenager. In 1919 he led a band that played at a roadhouse just outside of New Orleans called the Halfway House. The Halfway House Orchestra (ranging from five to seven pieces) stayed together for nine years, recording 22 selections during 1925–28, some of the best music to be documented in New Orleans during the decade. Brunies' mellow and generally low-register cornet was a strong asset to the band's ensembles.

After the Halfway House Orchestra broke up, Abbie Brunies freelanced in New Orleans, spent periods outside of music, ran a café in Biloxi, Mississippi (where he moved in 1946), and made one final record in 1957 with his brother Merritt Brunies, *The Brunies Brothers Dixieland Band* (American Music AMCD 077).

9 **Halfway House Orchestra/Jan. 22, 1925 – Dec. 17, 1928/Jazz Oracle 8001**

This single CD has all 22 recordings by the Halfway House Orchestra, including four selections not released until the 1970s. The first session (resulting in "Pussy Cat Rag" and "Barataria") includes the ill-fated clarinetist Leon Rappolo (doubling on alto). Otherwise, the band, which is sometimes reminiscent of the New Orleans Kings, features the leader on cornet, Charlie Cordella or Sidney Arodin on clarinet, altoist Joe Loyacano, and a four-piece rhythm section that is driven by Chink Martin on tuba or bass. Their versions of "Maple Leaf Rag" and "Let Me Call You Sweetheart" are quite memorable, while many of the group's originals deserve to be revived by current-day trad bands.

GEORGE BRUNIES

b. Feb. 6, 1902, New Orleans, LA, d. Nov. 19, 1974, Chicago, IL

The most famous of the Brunies brothers, George Brunies was an important trombonist in the Dixieland world for decades. By the time he was eight, he was already playing alto horn in Papa Jack Laine's band. Brunies (who was self taught and never learned to read music) switched to trombone, playing in a variety of bands throughout New Orleans as a teenager. In 1920 he moved to Chicago, playing with drummer Joe "Ragababy" Stevens and Elmer Schoebel, and in a riverboat band on the S.S. *Capitol*. In 1921, Brunies joined the Friar's Society Orchestra, which soon became the New Orleans

Rhythm Kings, playing in the frontline opposite his two childhood friends Paul Mares and Leon Rapollo. Brunies recorded with the NORK during 1922–23, taking a famous recorded solo on "Tin Roof Blues." After the NORK broke up, he played briefly with Eddie Tancil, recorded with the Wolverines, and became a regular member of Ted Lewis' Orchestra (1924–35). Brunies' playing added a strong jazz content to the music of the corny Lewis.

Unlike the careers of his siblings and his frontline partners with the NORK, George Brunies' career was just starting. In later years the trombonist (who on the advice of a numerologist dropped two of the E's from his name and became known as Georg Brunis!) worked with Louis Prima, Sharkey Bonano, Bobby Hackett, Muggsy Spanier's Ragtimers (1939), Art Hodes, Eddie Condon, Wild Bill Davison, and his own bands, staying active into the early 1970s.

MERRITT BRUNIES

b. Dec. 25, 1895, New Orleans, LA, d. Feb. 5, 1973, Biloxi, MS

The fourth of the six musical Brunies brothers, Merritt Brunies was a fine cornetist. He first played with the Brunies family band and freelanced around New Orleans. Brunies led the Original New Orleans Jazz Band (1916–18), which at various times also included brothers George, Henry, and Albert. The group visited Chicago briefly, and Merritt played in Los Angeles with Angelo Schiro and in San Francisco with Chris Mann. He returned to Chicago after those gigs. When the New Orleans Rhythm Kings left the Friars Inn in 1923, Merritt put together his own Friars Inn Orchestra and took its place. Merritt Brunies' Friars Inn Orchestra (which also included Henry Brunies on trombone) was based at that venue for two years and lasted until 1926, recording 17 selections. One of the songs that the band played was the standard "Angry," cowritten by Merritt and Henry.

Merritt Brunies played in Chicago until the late 1920s, when he moved permanently to Biloxi, Mississippi, becoming a policeman and playing music only on a part-time basis during the remainder of his life. He returned to records one time, playing valve trombone with a band he co-led with cornetist Abbie Brunies in 1957.

LPS TO SEARCH FOR

Up Jumped the Devil (Retrieval 124) has not only all 15 recordings by Merritt Brunies' Friars Inn Orchestra but two previously unreleased test pressings. The band features Merritt and Henry Brunies, clarinetist Volly DeFaut, and up to three saxophones, along with a three-piece rhythm section and an occasional violin. Its repertoire includes some future jazz standards (such as "Clarinet Marmalade" and "Sugar Foot Stomp"), a few originals, current pop tunes, and the novelty "Masculine Women! Feminine Men!"

TEDDY BUNN

b. 1909, Freeport, NY, d. July 20, 1978, Lancaster, CA

Teddy Bunn, a fine single-note soloist, was one of the top guitarists of the early 1930s, ranking with Eddie Lang, Carl Kress, Lonnie Johnson, and Dick McDonough. Bunn was largely self-taught and first worked accompanying a calypso singer. In 1929 he began to emerge, recording as a guest with Duke Ellington on September 16 and beginning a two-year association with the Washboard Serenaders (1929–31). Bunn worked and recorded with the Spirits of Rhythm (1932–1937), being the main soloist with the unusual group, which also included three singers who played tiples and a drummer-vocalist. Bunn had a second stint with the Spirits of Rhythm during 1939–41 and recorded along the way with Jimmie Noone, Johnny Dodds, Trixie Smith, J.C. Higginbotham, Sidney Bechet, Lionel Hampton, and Mezz Mezzrow. But after he re-

corded four unaccompanied guitar solos for Blue Note in 1940, Bunn surprisingly became obscure.

In later years Teddy Bunn switched to electric guitar and played mostly with R&B groups. He remained active into the early 1970s but rarely appeared again on records and was almost completely forgotten by the jazz world.

9 Teddy Bunn/Sept. 16, 1929–Mar. 28, 1940/RST 1509

A large portion of Teddy Bunn's recordings are on this recommended single CD. He is heard with Red Allen backing pianist-singer Walter Pichon in 1929, having eight vocal duets with Spencer Williams in 1930 (Clarence Profit or James P. Johnson help out on piano), and accompanying singers Buck Franklin (1931) and Fat Hayden (1939) plus on six alternate takes from 1938 record dates with Mezz Mezzrow. Best are Bunn's four selections (plus an alternate take) from 1940, unaccompanied guitar solos, including a version of "King Porter Stomp."

BUDDY BURTON

b. Feb. 1890, Louisville, KY, d. July 6, 1977, Louisville, KY

It seems strange to think that pianist W.E. "Buddy" Burton was alive until 1977 because virtually nothing was heard from him after 1936. A multi-instrumentalist, Burton played not just piano but organ, drums, percussion, and kazoo, in addition to taking vocals. He worked at a variety of jobs in his native Louisville before moving to Chicago in 1923. Burton recorded on drums (1923) and kazoo (1925) with Jelly Roll Morton but did most of his recordings in 1928, when he was heard as a soloist (singing and playing piano), dueting with Jimmy Blythe, backing blues singers Tillie Johnson and Mae Mathews, and playing with the Dixie Four and the Harlem Trio.

Otherwise, Burton recorded two numbers in 1929, some duets with pianist Bob Hudson in 1932 and accompanied singer Irene Sanders in 1936. Nothing much else is known about his life. Buddy

Burton lived in Chicago until returning to Louisville in 1965.

9 W.E. "Buddy" Burton and Ed "Fats" Hudson/Feb. 1928–Apr. 2, 1936/RST 1511

All of Buddy Burton's recordings (other than his dates with Jelly Roll Morton) are on this obviously definitive CD, including a previously unreleased (and very charming) piano-trombone duet with Roy Palmer, "The Trombone Slide." Highlights include the two-part "Ham-Fatchet Blues," "Dustin' the Keys," "Five O'Clock Stomp," and three versions of "Block and Tackle." Rounding out the CD is a pair of vocals by the very obscure banjoist Ed "Fats" Hudson, accompanied by Jimmy Blythe on the pianist's final recording.

GARVIN BUSHELL

b. Sept. 25, 1902, Springfield, OH, d. Oct. 31, 1991, Las Vegas, NV

A technically skilled reed player rather than a major jazz improviser, Garvin Bushell was on records nearly from the beginning of recorded jazz. He started on piano at six, switching to clarinet when he was 13. Bushell studied at Wilberforce University and moved to New York in 1919. Although in other time periods, Bushell (who played clarinet, tenor sax, alto sax, soprano sax, oboe, and bassoon) could have been active as a classical musician, only the jazz and blues worlds were open to him in the early 1920s. He worked with Mamie Smith's Jazz Hounds (with whom he recorded in 1921), Ethel Waters' Black Swan Jazz Masters (1921–22), and the house band at Leroy's. Bushell toured Europe and South America during 1925–27 with Sam Wooding. Back in the United States, he performed with the *Keep Shufflin'* revue, making records with a quartet from the show (James P. Johnson, Fats Waller on organ, and Jabbo Smith) as the Louisiana Sugar Babes. Those relaxed and intriguing recordings find Bushell tripling on clarinet, alto, and bassoon, being one of the first recorded jazz bassoon soloists.

Garvin Bushell's other associations included Otto Hardwicke (1931), Fess Williams (1933), Fletcher Henderson (late 1935), Cab Calloway (1936–37), Chick Webb (1937–39), and the Ella Fitzgerald Orchestra (1939–41). More of a section player than a soloist, Bushell also led low-profile groups in the 1940s, worked with Bunk Johnson (1947), played bassoon with the Chicago Civic Orchestra (1950), was with the Fletcher Henderson reunion band (1958), and succeeded Omer Simeon as a member of Wilbur DeParis' New New Orleans Jazz Band (1959–64). Garvin Bushell, whose oboe and bassoon playing was utilized in the backgrounds of records by Gil Evans and John Coltrane, lived in Puerto Rico for a time before settling in Las Vegas, spending his last couple of decades primarily as a music teacher.

HENRY BUSSE

b. May 19, 1894, Magdeburg, Germany, d. Apr. 23, 1955, Memphis, TN

Henry Busse may not rank high as a jazz cornetist, but he was one of the most famous soloists in jazz during the 1920s, primarily because of his association with the Paul Whiteman Orchestra. He freelanced during the World War I years and first joined Paul Whiteman's dance band in 1918, originally being co-leader before ceding the ensemble to the more charismatic Whiteman. As Whiteman became famous as "The King of Jazz," Busse gained recognition as his best soloist of the first half of the 1920s, taking well-known solos on "Wang Wang Blues," "Hot Lips" (written by Henry Lange and Lou Davis in 1922 for Busse), and "When Day Is Done." Busse's solo choruses, though rarely ever changing, had their charm.

However, by 1928 Busse (who was making $350 a week) was frequently being passed over for solos in favor of Bix Beiderbecke. Some tunes (such as "Mary" and "Love Nest") had short solos by both Busse and Bix (the older cornetist sounds dated), while other charts had almost nothing for Busse to do. In April 1928, after an argument with Whiteman, Busse left the band (he was replaced by the soundalike Harry Goldfield) and soon started his own big band.

Henry Busse led an orchestra for the next 27 years, never altering his sound (with its exaggerated vibrato), his solos, or his repertoire (which always included "Hot Lips" and "When Day Is Done"). He met an unusual end, dying from a heart attack while playing at the National Undertakers Convention in Memphis, Tennessee!

HAPPY CALDWELL

b. July 25, 1903, Chicago, IL, d. Dec. 29, 1978, New York, NY

Although Albert "Happy" Caldwell had a long career, he is best known for his work in the late 1920s. Caldwell studied pharmacy in high school, but, after beginning on clarinet in 1919, he switched to music, studying with his cousin Buster Bailey. Caldwell played with Bernie Young during 1922–23 (with whom he made his recording debut in 1923) and soon was doubling on tenor, which became his main instrument. Caldwell freelanced in the New York area, including with Mamie Smith's Jazz Hounds, Elmer Snowden (1925), Thomas Morris, Willie Gant's Ramblers, Cliff Jackson, the *Keep Shufflin'* revue (1927), and Arthur Gibbs (1927–28). Caldwell recorded with Eddie Condon in 1928 and was on Louis Armstrong's famous jam session recording of "Knockin' a Jug" the following year.

Although a contemporary of Coleman Hawkins', Caldwell lacked Hawkins' musical curiosity and harmonic knowledge, never really advancing through the years. He worked along the way with Charlie Johnson, Fletcher Henderson, Vernon Andrade (1929–33), Tiny Bradshaw (1934), Louis Metcalf (1935), Fats Waller, and his own bands (which were sometimes called the Happy Pals). Happy Caldwell recorded with Jelly Roll Morton in 1939, freelanced for decades at low-level musical jobs, and much later in life (the early 1970s) played with Clyde Bernhardt's Harlem Blues and Jazz Band.

CALIFORNIA RAMBLERS

Although often overlooked when 1920s big bands are discussed, the California Ramblers were one of the first jazz orchestras and certainly the most prolific jazz band of the era, recording an estimated 628 titles during 1921–31 (not counting alternate takes or sessions by other groups using the name during 1935–37)! Nor does this include the Ramblers' recordings under the pseudonyms of the Vagabonds and Ted Wallace's orchestra or the many small group sides by the Little Ramblers, the Goofus Five, the Five Birmingham Babies, and the Varsity Eight which drew its personnel from the larger band.

The California Ramblers never played in California and actually comprised a group of top New York-based players. They were formed in Ohio by banjoist Ray Kitchenman, relocating to New York by November 1921, when they made their recording debut. Starting out without any famous names, along the way the Ramblers' sidemen included Adrian Rollini (a prominent force on many records), Red Nichols, Chelsea Quealey, Bill Moore, Miff Mole, altoist Bobby Davis, Tommy Dorsey, Jimmy Dorsey, Stan King, and many other top white players of the era. Although they spent much of their life in the recording studios, the California Ramblers did sometimes play in public, being based at the Ramblers Inn near New York during part of the 1920s. Managed and led in later years by Ed Kirkeby (Fats Waller's future manager), who sometimes took vocals, the California Ramblers were at their musical prime during 1924–27, evolving into a first-class but rather routine dance band by 1928 but still recording quite steadily through 1931. During their best recordings, the California Ramblers were a perfect representative of solid mainstream jazz of the mid-1920s, the type of music that made the youth of the era want to dance.

9 1925–1928/May 14, 1925–Feb. 10, 1928/Timeless 053
6 Edison Laterals 2/Nov. 5, 1928–Oct. 9, 1929/Diamond Cut 301D

The Timeless CD has some of the California Ramblers' strongest jazz recordings from a three-year period. The 25 selections are only a drop in the bucket (not even 4 percent of the band's total output). It is a pity that all of the group's dates have not been reissued. But for a single CD of the Ramblers, this is as good as it gets. Among the key players are Chelsea Quealey, trombonist Abe Lincoln, Bobby Davis, and especially Adrian Rollini; Red Nichols and the Dorsey Brothers also make appearances. The tunes include "Everything Is Hotsy Totsy Now," "The Girl Friend," "She Knows Her Onions," "Stockholm Stomp," "Vo-Do-Do-De-O Blues," "Nothin' Does-Does Like It Used to Do-Do-Do," and "Make My Cot Where the Cot-Cot-Cotton Grows."

Edison Laterals 2 features the California Ramblers during a later period, when they were strictly a dance band and their jazz content had greatly decreased. Although Phil Napoleon and Miff Mole are on "Button Up Your Overcoat," Adrian Rollini is on three songs, and drummer Stan King was still aboard, the group was mostly inhabited by no-names, fine musicians but no one who stands out individually. The repertoire on this set of rarities (originally recorded for the Edison label during the label's waning days) includes "You're the Cream in My Coffee," "My Sin," "Tiptoe Through the Tulips," and other period pieces, expertly played.

LPS TO SEARCH FOR

Miss Annabelle Lee (Biograph 12020) and *Hallelujah* (Biography 12021) reissue 12 songs apiece from the California Ramblers' huge discography. The former set (from 1925–27) includes "Charleston," "Collegiate," "Manhattan," and "Sweet Man" among others, while *Hallelujah* (which dates from 1925–29) has such titles as "Oh! Mabel," "When Erastus Plays His Old Kazoo," "Blue River," and "Clementine." In both cases, the music is drawn from the catalog of Edison (though not duplicating the cuts on *Edison Laterals 2*), and some of the selections are more extended than usual, clocking in at over four minutes apiece.

Two albums from the Old Masters label, *Volume One* (The Old Masters 20) and *Volume Two* (The Old Masters 25), unfortunately do not contain liner notes, recording dates, or personnel. *Volume One* (which like the second volume has 16 selections) is completely different than the Timeless and Edison sets, featuring such numbers as "Is She My Girl Friend," "Cheatin' on Me," "Crazy Words—Crazy Tune," and "Ain't She Sweet." In contrast, *Volume Two* is of lesser interest, since it has only four numbers (two of which are by the Little Ramblers) that are not duplicates from Timeless' *1925–1928*.

BLANCHE CALLOWAY

b. 1902, Baltimore, MD, d. Dec. 16, 1978, Baltimore, MD

The older sister of Cab Calloway, Blanche Calloway was a successful singer before Cab hit it big. She sang locally in Baltimore in the early '20s and was at New York's Ciro Club in the mid-1920s before relocating to Chicago. Blanche recorded a pair of blues in 1925 (accompanied by Louis Armstrong and Richard M. Jones) and appeared with shows and revues. In 1931 she worked with Andy Kirk's orchestra in Philadelphia, recording three numbers, including "I Need Lovin' " (one of her trademark songs). She tried her best to take over Kirk's orchestra but, other than tempting away a couple of the trumpeters, was unsuccessful.

However, Calloway soon formed a fine big band (including Ben Webster on tenor, pianist Clyde Hart, and drummer Cozy Cole) and had four record dates in 1931 plus one apiece in 1934 and 1935; highlights include "Just a Crazy Song," "Make Me Know It," "You Ain't Livin' Right'," and a remake of "I Need Lovin'." Her flamboyance and extroverted nature were obvious influences on her younger brother, but there was room for only one Calloway in the top echelons of the music business. After struggling for years, in 1938 she declared bankruptcy and broke up her orchestra. Blanche Calloway continued singing now and then, ran a cosmetic company, and in the 1960s was the director of a Florida radio station.

LPS TO SEARCH FOR

In her career, Blanche Calloway recorded two blues in 1925, five sessions (resulting in 18 songs) in 1931, and eight additional numbers in 1934–35. *Blanche Calloway* (Harlequin 2057) has four of the five dates from 1931, leaving out the three titles that she recorded while using the Andy Kirk Orchestra. On such numbers as "Just a Crazy Song," "Sugar Blues," "Without That Gal," and "Make Me Know It," Blanche Calloway sings with plenty of spirit and sass, showing that she was in the same league with her better-known brother.

CAB CALLOWAY

b. Dec. 25, 1907, Rochester, NY, d. Nov. 18, 1994, Hockessin, DE

Cabell "Cab" Calloway's main impact was during the swing era, but he started leading his big band a few years before that period and was a major name by 1931. The younger brother of Blanche Calloway, he grew up in Baltimore and Chicago, studying at Crane College. Calloway appeared in the *Plantation Days* show (1927), freelanced in several capacities, and was the relief drummer and master of ceremonies at the Sunset Café in 1928. He led the Alabamians (a group from Chicago!) at the Savoy for a time in 1929, but the band was not strong enough to compete in New York when Calloway relocated. Cab gained his initial recognition when he was featured in the *Hot Chocolates* show, a revue that featured Fats Waller's music and Louis Armstrong.

In 1930 Calloway took over the Missourians, a strong jazz group that was struggling for work and on the verge of breaking up. The unit was soon renamed the Cab Calloway Orchestra. After making a few recordings, in February 1931 Calloway's band became the house orchestra at the Cotton Club. The charismatic singer/performer was a sensation, his recording of "Minnie the Moocher" was a major hit, and his radio broadcasts made him a national star. Calloway was a talented jazz singer and an inventive if sometimes silly scatter whose gyrations and showmanship on stage often overshadowed the music, although he always had top-notch bands. Cab Calloway appeared in many movies during the swing era and kept his underrated big band together up to 1948, remaining a show business legend to the end of his life.

10 Cab Calloway and the Missourians/ June 3, 1929–Dec. 23, 1930/JSP 328

This CD contains all 14 recordings by the Missourians along with the group's first ten selections as the Cab Calloway Orchestra; the latter are also included on the Classics label's *1930–1931*. The Missourians numbers are often quite heated and offer plenty of proof that the group was one of the top bands of 1929–30, even though it never prospered. Its lineup includes R.Q. Dickerson and Lammar Wright on trumpets, both of whom get to solo. The 14 songs are all group originals, including such spirited pieces as "Market Street Stomp," "400 Hop," "Swingin' Dem Cats," and "Stoppin' the Traffic." The numbers with Cab Calloway (which directly preceded "Minnie the Moocher") show that the singer was pretty exciting from the start. Highlights include a spectacular version of "St. Louis Blues," "Happy Feet," "Some of These Days," "Nobody's Sweetheart," and a classic rendition of "St. James Infirmary."

10 1930–1931/July 24, 1930–June 17, 1931/Classics 516
10 1931–1932/July 9, 1931–June 7, 1932/Classics 526

One of the most colorful of all performers, Cab Calloway
was not only a showman but a highly original jazz singer.

9 1932/June 7, 1932 – Dec. 7, 1932/Classics 537
8 1932 – 1934/Dec. 7, 1932 – Sept. 4, 1934/Classics 544

Twelve CDs from the Classics label trace the history of Cab Calloway on record (sans alternate takes) from 1930 until his big band's last dates in 1947; the first four discs fit into the classic jazz era. *1930 – 1931* documents Calloway during an 11-month period in which he went from complete unknown to major star. "Minnie the Moocher" (from March 3, 1931) made him immortal, but there are many gems to be heard on this set, including "St. Louis Blues," "St. James Infirmary," "Blues in My Heart," and "Six or Seven Times." *1931 – 1932* is on the same high level, with many memorable selections, including "Bugle Call Rag" (which has a famous arrange-

ment), "Trickeration," "Kickin' the Gong Around," "Corinne Corinna," "Cabin in the Cotton," "Minnie the Moocher's Wedding Day," and "Dinah."

If any proof were needed that swing existed before Benny Goodman hit it big in 1935, Cab Calloway's early recordings serve as perfect evidence. *1932* is highlighted by "Old Yazoo," "Reefer Man," "Old Man of the Mountain," "I've Got the World on a String," the weird "Dixie Doorway," and "Beale Street Mama." *1932 – 1934* finds Calloway increasing his fame, signing up with the Victor label, and remaking "Minnie the Moocher" and "Kickin' the Gong Around." Other highlights on that CD include "Doin' the New Low-Down" (with Don Redman's orchestra and the Mills Brothers),

"The Lady with the Fan," the swinging "Harlem Camp Meeting," "'Long About Midnight," and "Margie." The big band was used very much in support of the singer, and one by one over time the cast of the Missourians left; there were just five of them still with the Cab Calloway band by the end of 1932.

MANCY CARA

b. 1900, Charleston, WV, d. 1950s?

Mancy Cara (whose last name was possibly Carr) recorded on banjo and guitar with Louis Armstrong's Savoy Ballroom Five in 1928, appearing on such records as "West End Blues" and "Basin Street Blues." After moving to Chicago, Cara worked with Carroll Dickerson in 1924, played with Lottie Hightower's Night Hawks the following year, and then returned to Dickerson (with whom he recorded four numbers). Cara had a background role on the Armstrong recordings, keeping the rhythm steady behind Satch and Earl Hines on the classic Savoy Ballroom Five sessions. He also recorded with Armstrong behind singers Lillie Delk Christian and Victoria Spivey.

Mancy Cara went to New York with Dickerson's orchestra and Armstrong in 1929 (recording a few further sessions with the trumpeter) but did not stay long, returning to Chicago in 1930 and eventually settling back in his native West Virginia, dropping out of music after the early 1930s.

MUTT CAREY

b. 1891, Hahnville, LA, d. Sept. 3, 1948, Elsinore, CA

Thomas "Mutt" Carey was a New Orleans trumpeter who appeared on just a few recordings in 1922, though he lived long enough to have a comeback in the mid-1940s. The youngest of 17 children, Carey originally played drums, guitar, and alto horn, not starting on the trumpet until he was already 22, in 1913. He worked in New Orleans with his brother Jack Carey's Crescent Brass Band, Fran-

kie Dusen, King Oliver (a major influence on his early style), Jimmy Brown, and Bebe Ridgeley. Carey first became a member of Kid Ory's band in 1914. Due to his ability to play very softly, he was billed as the "Blues King of New Orleans."

The trumpeter left New Orleans in 1917, when he toured in vaudeville with Mack's Merrymakers, a quartet that included Johnny Dodds. After playing in Chicago with Lawrence Duhe, he found that he hated the winter weather and returned home. In 1919 Kid Ory sent for Carey to join his band in California, and that climate appealed to him much more. The Ory band helped to introduce jazz to Los Angeles, and, when King Oliver passed through the area in 1921, audiences who had never heard him thought that he was a Mutt Carey imitator! In 1922, with Ory's band (billed on record as Spikes' Seven Pods of Pepper Orchestra), Carey recorded two instrumentals that are considered the first recordings by a black New Orleans band, plus four numbers backing singers Roberta Dudley and Ruth Lee. Otherwise he went unrecorded until 1944. In 1925 Ory left Los Angeles to join King Oliver in Chicago. Carey took over his group, which he expanded and renamed the Liberty Syncopators and later the Jeffersonians. Carey's orchestra often worked in the silent film studios during the next few years (providing atmospheric music for Hollywood film sets) until the rise of sound pictures and the onset of the Depression forced him out of music. He spent years working as a Pullman porter and as a mailman.

Fortunately Carey was able to make a comeback. In February 1944 he worked with Kid Ory's band on the Orson Welles' radio series. The group became quite popular and made some records, and Carey (whose playing was erratic at times) worked steadily with Ory until the summer of 1947, leading a record date of his own. Mutt Carey put together a new band at that point and was hopeful about the future but died of a heart attack at the age of 57 while on vacation in 1948.

BILL CARLSEN

b. July 1904, Clay Center, KS, d. Dec. 1979, FL

Bill Carlsen was a decent saxophonist (playing tenor and alto in addition to clarinet) who led an important territory band based in Milwaukee. He grew up in Kansas, attended the University of Kansas as a chemistry major for two years, and also went to the University of Wisconsin. Carlsen dropped out of school before he graduated so he could play music. He worked with Fred Dexter's orchestra in Milwaukee (1925–26), a band that played regularly at the Wisconsin Roof Theatre. In 1926 Dexter gave up the group, and Carlsen became the new leader of the Wisconsin Roof Orchestra, playing at the Wisconsin Roof (and broadcasting on the radio) for a five-year period. His big band was based at Milwaukee's Modernistic Ballroom and the Futuristic Ballroom during 1932–36, working in Chicago until 1941 and recording during 1926–31 and 1940. Bill Carlsen broke up the band when the United States entered World War II. He worked as a flight instructor and ended up his career as a meteorologist on local television.

7 1926–1931/Oct. 1926–Mar. 1931/Jazz Oracle 8014

The best jazz recordings of Bill Carlsen's band are on this CD, rare titles that were originally listed as being by Devine's Wisconsin Roof Orchestra, Bill Carlsen's orchestra, or simply the Wisconsin Roof Orchestra. All of the music was formerly quite rare. None of the sidemen in the ten-piece band were destined for fame and the soloists are generally just adequate, but the ensembles are appealing and the music frequently swings well for the time. Among the 23 titles are "Shanghai Honeymoon," "Black Maria," "New St. Louis Blues," "Farewell Blues," "Clarinet Marmalade," "Milenberg Joys," and two versions of "Tiger Rag."

HOAGY CARMICHAEL

b. Nov. 22, 1899, Bloomington, IN, d. Dec. 27, 1981, Rancho Mirage, CA

One of America's finest songwriters, Hoagy Carmichael was responsible for such songs as "Stardust" (originally an uptempo stomp!), "Georgia on My Mind," "The Nearness of You," "Skylark," "Up the Lazy River," and "Rockin' Chair." He was also a personable singer, a decent pianist, and an occasional movie actor.

Howard Hoagland "Hoagy" Carmichael was part of the 1920s jazz scene and always retained a strong love for that era's music. Carmichael played piano in Indianapolis at dances and in jazz bands, even while taking law classes. He was a good friend of Bix Beiderbecke, and "Riverboat Shuffle" (a future Dixieland standard) was his first song to be recorded, by the Wolverines in 1924. After a bit of turmoil, Carmichael abandoned his parents' plans for him to become a lawyer, instead choosing to play jazz piano, singing, and trying to play trumpet. Carmichael recorded with Hitch's Happy Harmonists (1925), worked a little with Jean Goldkette (1927), and recorded "Washboard Blues" with Paul Whiteman but mostly freelanced. He led some record dates of his own during 1927–30, using such sidemen as Andy Secrest, Tommy Dorsey, Jimmy Dorsey, Jack Teagarden, and Joe Venuti plus local players from the Midwest. One session from 1930 (which also included Benny Goodman and Bud Freeman) teamed Bix Beiderbecke and Bubber Miley.

With the onset of the Depression, Carmichael found himself in much more demand for his songwriting abilities than for his jazz playing, although he did catch on as a personality, appearing in 14 films during 1937–54. Hoagy Carmichael's early days are recounted in his two autobiographies: *The Stardust Road* (1946) and *Sometimes I Wonder* (1965).

10 Stardust, and Much More/Nov. 18, 1927–Mar. 1, 1960/Bluebird 8333

Many of Hoagy Carmichael's key recordings of 1927–34 are on this disc, which has 19 vintage

Even as a world-famous songwriter, Hoagy Carmichael talked about his love of 1920s jazz.

numbers plus versions (both from 1960) of "Stardust" that begin and end the collection. Starting with "Washboard Blues" (recorded with Paul Whiteman), Carmichael is heard with Jean Goldkette's orchestra ("So Tired") and Sunny Clapp's Band O' Sunshine, as a solo pianist-vocalist (including playing "Lazybones" and a different version of "Stardust") and heading all-star bands. The last is highlighted by the original version of "Rockin' Chair," "March of the Hoodlums," "Rockin' Chair" (with Bix Beiderbecke and Bubber Miley), "Georgia on My Mind," and "Up the Lazy River." Jimmy Dorsey, Tommy Dorsey, Joe Venuti, Red Norvo, Bud Freeman, Benny Goodman, and Jack Teagarden are among those making notable appearances.

LPS TO SEARCH FOR

Curtis Hitch and Hoagy Carmichael (Fountain 109) has nine recordings by the Happy Harmonists, a septet led by pianist Hitch during 1923–25. Its final two recordings ("Boneyard Shuffle" and "Washboard Blues") have Carmichael in Hitch's place. Also on this generous 19-selection LP are the first three numbers ever released under Carmichael's name (including an uptempo instrumental version of "Stardust"), five unrelated selections by pianist Eric Seidel's band in 1927, and two cuts from Carmichael's Collegians: "March of the Hoodlums" and a version of "Walkin' the Dog" that has Hoagy taking a very rare cornet solo. *Star Dust* (Historical 37) duplicates six of the selections on the Fountain LP and the Bluebird CD but also contains six other cuts from 1929–30, including rare versions of "Rockin' Chair" and "March of the Hoodlums."

HARRY CARNEY

b. Apr. 1, 1910, Boston, MA, d. Oct. 8, 1974, New York, NY

The most loyal of all sidemen, Harry Carney was a fixture in Duke Ellington's orchestra during nearly its entire existence. Carney was the definitive baritone saxophonist of the prebop era. Not only did his huge sound set the standard for baritonists, but he practically introduced the baritone sax to jazz as a significant solo instrument. Carney started on piano and played clarinet before switching early on to alto sax. He worked in Boston with local groups (taking lessons from Benny Waters) and in 1927 moved to New York, where he gigged with Fess Williams and a couple local groups. Carney (who considered his main influences to be Coleman Hawkins and Adrian Rollini) joined Ellington in June 1927, playing alto at first but soon switching his focus to baritone while also occasionally doubling on bass clarinet and clarinet. Forty-seven years later Harry Carney was still with the Duke Ellington Orchestra. He passed away in 1974, a few months after Duke.

BENNY CARTER

b. Aug. 8, 1907, New York, NY

Benny Carter has had one of the most productive careers in music history, being a major musician from 1927 up to the present time. Although his reputation as a brilliant altoist, arranger, composer, bandleader, and occasional trumpeter grew during the swing era, he was also one of the top altoists and arrangers of the 1920s. Carter began on piano as a youth, taking lessons from his mother. Inspired by his cousin Cuban Bennett, Carter saved up for a trumpet in 1921. But after buying one, he became frustrated and traded it in for a C-melody sax because he could not master the trumpet in a couple of hours!

Carter started working professionally in 1923, and in August 1924 he joined June Clark's band on alto. Carter worked with Billy Paige's Broadway Syncopators, Lois Deppe's Serenaders, Earl Hines (playing baritone sax in late 1924), Horace Henderson's Collegians (1925–26), and briefly with Fletcher Henderson. The altoist was a member of Charlie Johnson's Paradise Ten (1927–28), with whom he made his recording debut. After a short time with Horace Henderson, Carter gained some fame working with Fletcher Henderson (on and off during 1928–31). Since Don Redman had departed, Carter also had the opportunity to contribute a lot of arrangements to Henderson's book; "Blues in My Heart" was his first original to become a standard. After leaving Henderson, Carter led McKinney's Cotton Pickers (1931–32), but the band was quickly declining during this period. However, he began seriously doubling on trumpet and soon organized a big band of his own that lasted three years (1932–35). In addition, Carter contributed arrangements to other bands and organized a series of fascinating all-star recording sessions for Spike Hughes.

As the swing era began, Benny Carter was playing trumpet with Willie Bryant's orchestra, would soon begin a busy three-year period in Europe, and still had over 60 years of accomplishments ahead of him!

9 1929–1933/Sept. 18, 1929–May 19, 1933/Classics 522
9 1933–1936/May 19, 1933–Apr. 1936/Classics 530

The *1929–1933* CD, although released under Benny Carter's name, has just five selections that he actually led (during 1932–33), including "Six Bells Stampede" and three numbers on which he sings (showing that even Carter is human!). However, he is a major part on the other all-star dates: two songs with the Little Chocolate Dandies, five cuts with the Chocolate Dandies, and the first 11 numbers that bassist Spike Hughes led while in the United States in 1933. The "Dandies" sides include such notables as Rex Stewart, Bobby Stark, J.C. Higginbotham, Jimmy Harrison, Coleman Hawkins, and

Fats Waller, highlighted by "Six or Seven Times," "Bugle Call Rag," and "Dee Blues." The Hughes recordings feature many of the who's who of 1933 jazz (including Red Allen, Dicky Wells, Hawkins, tenor saxophonist Chu Berry, and flutist Wayman Carver) on fairly advanced arrangements ("Nocturne," "Pastorale," "Air In D-flat," and "Donegal Cradle Song" were far from conventional!) plus jam session versions of "Bugle Call Rag" and "Sweet Sue, Just You."

1933–1936 starts off with the last three numbers from the Hughes project (including a Red Allen feature on "How Come You Do Me Like You Do") and the third Chocolate Dandies session (the first one was actually by McKinney's Cotton Pickers in 1929), which teams Carter (on alto and trumpet) in an octet with trumpeter Max Kaminsky, Chu Berry, and pianist Teddy Wilson. Carter's two 1933–34 big band sessions (including "Blue Lou," "Symphony in Riffs," and "Synthetic Love") are also on this CD, along with eight numbers cut in London in 1936 (including "Just a Mood") that have the multitalented Carter not only on alto and trumpet but on clarinet, tenor, and piano!

CASA LOMA ORCHESTRA

The Casa Loma Orchestra ranks with the big bands of Fletcher Henderson and Duke Ellington as the most important and influential of the early jazz orchestras on the bands of the swing era. Originally one of Jean Goldkette's many big bands, the ensemble was initially known as the Orange Blossom Band and based in Detroit when it was scheduled to play at the Casa Loma Hotel in Toronto, Canada. Although the gig fell through when that venue never opened, the band took its name from the hotel, became independent of Goldkette, and was reformed as a co-op that was owned by all of the founding musicians. One of its saxophonists, Glen Gray (b. June 7, 1900, Metamore, IL, d. August 23, 1963, Plymouth, MA), was elected the band's president; he would be its official leader by the late 1930s.

The Casa Loma Orchestra made their recording debut in 1929, and they predated the swing era with swinging charts, although some later critics would call the often-crowded Gene Gifford arrangements mechanical sounding. The band's best soloists from the early days included clarinetist Clarence Hutchenrider and trombonist/singer Pee Wee Hunt; Kenny Sargent offered ballad vocals. On such songs as "China Girl," "San Sue Strut," "Casa Loma Stomp," "White Jazz," "Black Jazz," and the haunting "Smoke Rings" (their theme song), the Casa Loma Orchestra proved to be among the top swing bands before the word "swing" was actually applied to their music. Although overshadowed by its successors (such as Benny Goodman, whose original orchestra was inspired by the Casa Lomans), the band would make it through the swing era and into the 1940s.

7 Best of the Big Bands/Dec. 18, 1931–Dec. 24, 1934/Columbia 45345

Some of the early recordings by the Casa Loma Orchestra have been made available on CD by the Scottish Hep label, but unfortunately those discs were unavailable to be reviewed. Best of the Big Bands seems to have been tossed together so quickly that it was decided not to bother listing such information as recording dates and personnel! The music (not reissued in chronological order) dates from a three-year period and includes several gems, such as the original version of "Smoke Rings," "Black Jazz," "Maniac's Ball," "Casa Loma Stomp," and "Limehouse Blues." In addition to Pee Wee Hunt and Clarence Hutchenrider, trumpeter Sonny Dunham is heard on some of the later tracks. Excellent music that deserves much more comprehensive and logical treatment; quick, someone call the Classics label!

LPS TO SEARCH FOR

Casa Loma Stomp (Hep 1010) contains some of the group's finest recordings of 1929–30, including "China Girl," "San Sue Strut," and "Casa Loma

Stomp." Four of the songs are duplicated on *Casa Loma Orchestra 1929/1932* (Harrison N), but the latter collector's LP also contains the original version of "Smoke Rings," a heated "Clarinet Marmalade," and a rare publicity record version of "Casa Loma Stomp." *Casa Loma Orchestra—Vol. 2 1930–1937* (Harrison T) has a couple of additional selections from 1930 but dates mostly from 1933–35 (along with the 1937 version of "Smoke Rings"), including such "killer-dillers" as "Ol' Man River," "Jungle Fever," "Panama," and "Avalon."

FLOYD CASEY

b. 1900, Poplar Bluff, MI, d. Dec. 7, 1967, New York, NY

A drummer who doubled on washboard, Floyd Casey was closely associated with Clarence Williams' bands for a decade. Casey started out working on riverboats in the early 1920s in the Midwest, also playing with Ed Allen's Whispering Gold Band (1922), Dewey Jackson, and Jimmy Powell's Jazz Monarchs (1925–26), making his recording debut with Powell while in St. Louis in 1926. In 1927 Casey moved to New York, where he appeared on the majority of Williams' records during 1927–37, not only dates under the pianist's name but sessions with the Dixie Washboard Band, the Barrel House Five Orchestra, Bessie Smith (1931), the Alabama Jug Band, and the Birmingham Serenaders (1935). After 1937, Casey worked in dance halls and in obscure bands in New York for many years, including Benton Heath's ensemble in the 1950s. Floyd Casey recorded with Elmer Snowden in 1961 and was active in trad jazz settings until a few years before his death.

OSCAR CELESTIN

b. Jan. 1, 1884, Napoleonville, LA, d. Dec. 15, 1954, New Orleans, LA

Oscar "Papa" Celestin was a major New Orleans bandleader in the 1920s who survived long enough to make a comeback during his last few years. Celestin briefly played guitar and mandolin before settling on trumpet. After moving to New Orleans in 1906, he worked with the Indiana Brass Band, Henry Allen Sr.'s Excelsior Brass Band, the Algiers Brass Band, and the Olympia Band. Celestin led the Tuxedo Band (1910–13), co-led the Original Tuxedo Orchestra with trombonist William Ridgley during 1917–25, and renamed the latter the Tuxedo Jazz Orchestra after Ridgley dropped out. Although not a major trumpeter, Celestin always led excellent bands and could take effective short solos. He recorded five sessions in New Orleans during 1925–28, 15 numbers that are highlighted by "Original Tuxedo Rag," "Station Calls," and "It's Jam Up."

After the Depression hit, Celestin broke up his band, retired from music except for occasional gigs, and worked in a shipyard. In 1946, when he was 62, Oscar Celestin noticed that conditions had greatly improved and he made a comeback with a new version of the Tuxedo Jazz Orchestra (featuring veteran clarinetist Alphonse Picou), becoming a major tourist attraction in New Orleans during the eight years that preceded his death in 1954.

9 **Celestin's Original Tuxedo Jazz Orchestra/Sam Morgan's Jazz Band/Jan. 23, 1925–Dec. 13, 1928/Jazz Oracle 8002**

This CD has all 17 recordings by Oscar Celestin's Original Tuxedo Jazz Orchestra in the 1920s, including a previously unreleased alternate take of "Station Calls." The five sessions, all recorded in New Orleans (during location trips by Okeh and Columbia), do an excellent job of giving today's listeners a good idea of what Celestin's ensemble sounded like; pity that all of the key New Orleans bands were not as well documented. The supporting cast includes trumpeter Kid Shots Madison, altoist Paul Barnes, cornetist Ricard Alexis (who is excellent), pianist Jeannette Kimball, and (in 1928) banjoist Narvin Kimball. In addition, this CD has all eight selections (recorded in 1927) by Sam Morgan's spirited band, including "Sing On," "Down by the Riverside," and "Bogalusa Strut." Best known among Morgan's sidemen is trombonist Jim Robinson. The joyful ensembles are most impressive.

BILL CHALLIS

b. July 8, 1904, Wilkes-Barre, PA, d. Oct. 4, 1994, Wilkes-Barre, PA

Bill Challis was one of the top arrangers of the 1920s, and much of his work for Paul Whiteman is considered classic. Challis was self-taught on piano and played C-melody sax in high school. He studied economics and philosophy at Bucknell University but also led the student band and eventually chose music for his career. After graduating in June 1925, Challis worked with Dave Harmon's group as a saxophonist and arranger. The following year he became Jean Goldkette's staff arranger, and among his charts from 1926–27 are "Sunday," "My Pretty Girl," and "Clementine." When Goldkette broke up the band and many of his top sidemen (including Bix Beiderbecke and Frankie Trumbauer) joined Paul Whiteman's orchestra, Challis followed and worked regularly for Whiteman during 1927–30. He was responsible for many of the band's most jazz-oriented arrangements, including "San," "Ol' Man River," "Changes," "Dardanella," "Louisiana," "'Tain't So, Honey, 'Tain't So," "Because My Baby Don't Mean Maybe Now," and "Oh Miss Hannah." Challis also wrote for Frankie Trumbauer's small-group dates with Bix Beiderbecke, and he helped Bix document his four piano pieces (including "In a Mist"), hurriedly writing down the music as Beiderbecke improvised.

In the 1930s, Challis led a radio orchestra and contributed arrangements to many bands, including those of Fletcher Henderson, Frankie Trumbauer, the Dorsey Brothers, Glen Gray, and Artie Shaw, also writing for pop sessions. Among his more notable later projects were writing for Bobby Hackett, Bucky Pizzarelli (orchestrating Beiderbecke's piano

pieces for a guitar quintet), the Manhattan Transfer, and Vince Giordano's Nighthawks. The Nighthawks' recording from 1986 gave Bill Challis one last opportunity to revise his original Jean Goldkette arrangements, which still sounded exciting nearly 60 years after their debut.

CHARLESTON CHASERS

The name of "The Charleston Chasers" was used for a series of recording groups during the 1925–31 period by studio bands that did not play in public. The first Charleston Chasers session was in 1925 and featured trumpeter Leon McConville, Miff Mole, and Arthur Schutt. Fifteen songs were recorded by a version of the Chasers in 1927–28 that was similar to Red Nichols' Five Pennies, with Nichols, Miff Mole, Jimmy Dorsey, or Pee Wee Russell and usually Arthur Schutt, Dick McDonough, Joe Tarto, and Vic Berton. In 1929 the Chasers were reborn as a Phil Napoleon-led band with Mole or Tommy Dorsey, Benny Goodman, Fud Livingston, or Jimmy Dorsey, a rhythm section, and singers Eva Taylor (who is in particularly strong form during her six numbers) and Roy Evans. The fourth and final version of the Charleston Chasers, on February 9, 1931, used an 11-piece group with trumpeter Charlie Teagarden, Jack Teagarden, Glenn Miller, Benny Goodman, and Gene Krupa. Two songs had pop vocals by Paul Small, but it is the classic renditions of "Basin Street Blues" and "Beale Street Blues" (with Jack Teagarden's singing) that are the high points (and final acts) of this group's existence.

9 **The Charleston Chasers Vol. 1/Aug. 28, 1925–Feb. 20, 1930/ Timeless 1–040**

All of the Charleston Chasers sessions are on this CD except for four of the numbers from 1930 and the classic 1931 date. It does make one wonder what will also be included on Vol. 2! Among the more memorable selections are "After You've Gone," two surprisingly effective numbers with

Kate Smith, "Davenport Blues," "Delirium" (which has Vic Berton playing a metallophone!), "Imagination," "Moanin' Low," "Lovable and Sweet," and "What Wouldn't I Do for That Man."

JUNIE COBB

b. 1896, Hot Springs, AK, d. ca. 1970

The brother of trumpeter Jimmy Cobb, Junius "Junie" Cobb was a highly versatile player who was expert on piano, banjo, clarinet, and saxophones. He started playing music when he was nine, getting piano lessons from his mother. Cobb played with Johnny Dunn as a teenager. After moving to New Orleans to study house building, Cobb bought a clarinet, which he quickly learned. He attended college for a short time, moved to Chicago, and at first worked as a pianist. Cobb led a band, played clarinet with Everett Robbins' Jazz Screamers (1921) and Mae Brady's orchestra, and was King Oliver's banjoist during 1924–25 and 1926–27 (although he never recorded with Oliver). Cobb recorded on alto and clarinet with the Pickett-Parham Apollo Syncopators (1926) and played banjo with Jimmie Noone's Apex Club Orchestra during 1928–29. He led freewheeling record dates during 1926–29, nine hot numbers (including his popular "Once or Twice") that featured him on clarinet, tenor, and alto.

Cobb, who headed a group in Paris during part of 1930, chose to stay in Chicago and largely faded away during the swing era. He freelanced (including with singer Annabelle Calhoun) and mostly worked as a solo pianist during 1946–55 before becoming a part-time player. In 1961 Cobb made his final record (for Riverside), playing piano with a local septet that included Ikey Robinson. Junie Cobb, who worked with Jasper Taylor's Creole Jazz Band in 1962, continued being a solo pianist in the 1960s, although he also played banjo with Walbridge's Hot Four in 1967, three years before his death.

9 The Junie Cobb Collection 1926–29/June 1926–Oct. 24, 1929/Collector's Classics 14

Virtually all of Junie Cobb's recordings from the 1920s (everything but his two numbers with the Pickett-Parham Apollo Syncopators and his work on banjo with Jimmie Noone) are on this single CD. There are no liner notes, but all of the relevant recording information is here and the music (mostly from 1928–29) is programmed in chronological order. Cobb's nine numbers as a leader have been expanded to 13 with the inclusion of an alternate take of "Endurance Stomp" and three selections from a previously unissued session (including a "new" version of "Once or Twice"). Cobb is heard on a couple of quartet numbers playing clarinet next to Johnny Dodds and with his Grains of Corn (which sometimes include brother Jimmy Cobb on trumpet, Alex Hill, and Bill Johnson), the State Street Stompers (a quartet with Hill, guitarist Tampa Red, and Jimmy Bertrand), and the Windy Rhythm Kings. In addition, there are four numbers (by the Kansas City Tin Roof Stompers and the Kansas City Stompers) that are similar in style but do not include Cobb, and two classic cuts ("Transatlantic Stomp" and "Barrelhouse Stomp") with E.C. Cobb and his Corn-Eaters; Bertrand takes an early xylophone solo on "Transatlantic Stomp." Highly recommended to fans of small-group 1920s Chicago jazz.

ZINKY COHN

b. Aug. 18, 1908, Oakland, CA, d. Apr. 26, 1952, Chicago, IL

Zinky Cohn was a remarkable Earl Hines sound-alike, a talent that both helped and hindered his career. Cohn grew up in Chicago, studying at the Chicago Music College. He played with Roy Palmer in 1928 and was with Jimmie Noone's Apex Club Orchestra (as Hines' replacement) from June 1929 into 1931, recording with the clarinetist during that period and also 1933–35. He also recorded two cuts apiece with Harry Dial and Frankie Franko's Louisianians in 1930.

Cohn's brilliant playing should have made him famous, but the pianist spent little if any time in New York, failed to record any dates as a leader, and never developed a musical personality of his own. He worked in Europe accompanying Arlene and Norman Selby, played in Chicago with Walter Barnes (1931), Erskine Tate, Alex Calamese's Virginia Ramblers, Eddie South (off and on during 1933–37), and Carroll Dickerson (1934–35), made his last recordings in 1936 with singer Bob Howard, and occasionally rejoined Noone. Starting in 1937, Zinky Cohn worked mostly as a piano teacher and also as the business manager of the local musicians union, virtually retiring from full-time playing at the age of 29.

LEE COLLINS

b. Oct. 17, 1901, New Orleans, LA, d. July 3, 1960, Chicago, IL

Lee Collins had the potential to be a major trumpet star, but his decision to stay in New Orleans and Chicago after both of their golden ages had ended resulted in fewer recordings and much less acclaim than he deserved. Collins started playing trumpet when he was 12 and was a professional three years later. He organized the Young Eagles with Pops Foster and worked with the Columbia Band, the Young Tuxedo Orchestra, Oscar Celestin, and many other groups in New Orleans. After a brief period in Florida, in 1924 Collins moved to Chicago to play with King Oliver as Louis Armstrong's replacement. His recording debut was four primitively recorded numbers with Jelly Roll Morton, including his "Fish Tail Blues," which Morton later claimed as his own and retitled "Sidewalk Blues." After six months, Collins returned to New Orleans, where (partly by default) he was one of the best trumpeters in town. Fortunately he made one significant recording session while home, four exciting titles with the Jones-Collins Astoria Hot Eight, re-

issued on *Sizzling the Blues* (Frog 5), which show just how powerful a player he was in his prime.

In 1930, Collins played briefly with Luis Russell in New York (subbing for the vacationing Red Allen) and then moved to Chicago, five years after the Windy City's musical prime. Although Collins was quite active in the 1930s, playing with Dave Peyton, W. McDonald's Chicago Ramblers, Johnny Dodds, and Zutty Singleton and recording with many blues-oriented groups (including Richard M. Jones, Lil Johnson, and Victoria Spivey), no one outside of the city really noticed. Collins, who led bands in Chicago into the 1950s and recorded with Chippie Hill (1946) and Little Brother Montgomery (1947), mostly missed the New Orleans revival movement. Both of his European tours with Mezz Mezzrow (1951 and 1954) found him becoming quite ill, and he retired altogether after his second trip. Lee Collins did, however, write a fascinating autobiography (*Oh Didn't He Ramble*) in which he discussed many of the early New Orleans trumpeters who never recorded.

EDDIE CONDON

b. Nov. 16, 1905, Goodland, IN, d. Aug. 4, 1973, New York, NY

Eddie Condon, a very significant propagandist for trad jazz in the 1940s and '50s and leader of a series of all-star bands, was also an important part of the Chicago scene of the 1920s. Condon started on ukulele before switching to banjo and, by the mid-1920s, rhythm guitar. He played with Bill Engleman's band in Cedar Rapids (September 1921) and Hollis Peavey's Jazz Bandits (1922). Condon met Bix Beiderbecke early on and in 1924 was a member of the Austin High Gang (which included Gene Krupa, Frank Teschemacher, Bud Freeman, Jimmy McPartland, and Joe Sullivan). Never really a soloist, Condon was a fine rhythm player who worked with many bands in the Chicago area during 1924–28, including those of Bob Pacelli, Charlie Pearce,

A fine rhythm guitarist, Eddie Condon was most significant for his ability to put together freewheeling all-star bands.

Charles "Murphy" Podolsky, Irving Rothschild, Roy Peach, Louis Panico, and Jack Gardner.

On December 6 and 8, 1927, Condon led the McKenzie-Condon Chicagoans, recording "Sugar," "China Boy," "Nobody's Sweetheart," and "Liza." These important sessions were the recording debuts of Condon, Teschemacher, Freeman, Sullivan, Krupa, and bassist Jim Lannigan (with McPartland heard on cornet) and are considered the epitome of classic Chicago jazz. In 1928 Condon moved to New York, where he led three record dates during 1928–29 (including features for Teschemacher and Jack Teagarden) and appeared as a sideman on sessions with Louis Armstrong ("Mahogany Hall Stomp"), Fats Waller, and Billy Banks (1932). Condon, who led two further sessions in 1933 (high-

lighted by two versions of Bud Freeman's "The Eel"), toured with Red Nichols (1929) and worked with Red McKenzie's Mound City Blue Blowers (1930–31 and 1933) but largely struggled during the early years of the Depression, when freewheeling jazz was out of vogue. However, after playing with the comedy band of Mike Reilly and Eddie Farley (1935) and co-leading a group with clarinetist Joe Marsala in 1936, in 1937 he began working regularly at Nick's. The following year, when he led some classic titles for the new Commodore label, Eddie Condon was well on his way to becoming one of the leaders of Dixieland.

ZEZ CONFREY
b. Apr. 3, 1895, Peru, IL, d. 1971, Lakewood, NJ

Edward Elzear "Zez" Confrey was not a jazz pianist, but in the 1920s his virtuosic novelty ragtime playing and inventive compositions made him one of the best-known pianists of the era. Confrey studied piano at the Chicago College of Music and originally planned to become a concert pianist. However, he soon discovered that there was much more money to be made in popular music. Confrey worked in vaudeville, made piano rolls, and composed difficult but catchy piano pieces that he recorded, also selling many copies of the sheet music. The year 1921's "Kitten on the Keys" was a huge hit that quickly made him a national celebrity, and his other compositions included "Stumbling," "Dizzy Fingers," and "Nickel in the Slot" (an imitation of a nickelodeon). On February 12, 1924, Confrey had a major spot at Paul Whiteman's Aeolian Hall Concert (the same event that featured the debut of George Gershwin's *Rhapsody in Blue*), introducing his "Three Little Oddities" and getting a big ovation for "Kitten on the Keys."

By the late 1920s (when radio had replaced the parlor piano as the center of entertainment), there was less demand for piano pieces and the spotlight moved off of Zez Confrey (who continued writing music into the 1950s).

DOC COOK

b. Sept. 3, 1881, Louisville, KY, d. Dec. 25, 1958, Wurtsboro, NY

Charles "Doc" Cook, a pianist and arranger, was most significant as a major bandleader in 1920s Chicago. Cook worked in Detroit as early as 1909 as a composer and arranger. In Chicago he led bands at Harmon's Dreamland Ballroom during 1922–28. Among his sidemen along the way were Freddie Keppard, Jimmie Noone, Joe Poston, George Mitchell, and Johnny St. Cyr. The big band recorded in 1923 and 1926–27 (21 titles in all, none of which actually have Cook playing) under the names of Cook's Dreamland Orchestra, Cookie's Gingersnaps (a sextet), and Doc Cook's

14 Doctors of Syncopation. After the Dreamland association ended, Cook worked at other Chicago clubs during 1928–30, moved to New York, and was staff arranger at R.K.O. and Radio City Music Hall into the early 1940s before leaving full-time music.

COON-SANDERS NIGHTHAWKS

The first group to make it big on the radio, the Coon-Sanders Nighthawks, although lacking any significant soloists, was a superior ensemble band whose optimistic spirit symbolized the 1920s. Pianist Joe Sanders (born October 15, 1894, in Thayer, Kansas) sang with church choirs and studied music, but for a time it looked like he might have a career in baseball as a pitcher, where he earned the nickname of "The Old Left-Hander." However, Sanders chose music as his career. While serving as a sergeant at Camp Bowie, Texas, during World War I, he led a combo called the Camp Bowie Jazz Hounds. Drummer Carleton A. Coon (born February 5, 1894, in Rochester, Minnesota) also sang, led a band while a teenager, and was a captain during the war. In December 1918, Sanders was on leave. He stopped in a Kansas City music store, picked out a few songs to play, and started singing one of the tunes. Coon happened to be in the store at the same time and spontaneously harmonized with Sanders; they soon became good friends.

After getting out of the military and briefly running a booking agency for bands, Coon and Sanders decided to form a group of their own, the Coon-Sanders Novelty Orchestra. Featuring Sanders' arrangements and plenty of good-natured vocal interplay from the co-leaders, the group played in the Midwest. They recorded four numbers in 1921 (only one was released) and on December 5, 1922, made their first radio broadcast on WOAF in Kansas City. Because their radio show was on late, from midnight until 2 a.m., the band was renamed the Coon-Sanders Nighthawks. Within a short time, the

The Coon-Sanders Nighthawks (here seen in its early days) was the first jazz-oriented band to be a hit on the radio.

band gained fame far beyond Kansas City. In 1924 the orchestra relocated to Chicago (they were based at the Blackhawk Restaurant during 1926–30) and began recording on a regular basis for Victor. Counting their first record (which was made for Columbia), there were 82 selections in all, including such gems as "Brainstorm," "Roodles," "Slue Foot," "Ready for the River," and "Here Comes My Ball and Chain."

Disputes with the Victor label resulted in the Coon-Sanders Nighthawks' not making any recordings during 1930–31, although they would have two record dates in March 1932 during the end of a six-month stay in New York. Back in Chicago, the band was settling into a residency at the Hotel Sherman when Carleton Coon had surgery for an abscessed tooth that he had neglected. He contracted blood poisoning from the operation. After a few

weeks, on May 4, at the age of 38, he died. The band struggled on for a year, but audiences missed the interplay between Coon and Sanders. The magic was gone, and the Nighthawks disbanded in April 1933. Joe Sanders led another big band for a decade but without gaining the earlier group's popularity. In later years he worked in the studios and in the 1950s was a regular member of the Kansas City Opera Company. He passed away on May 15, 1965, in Kansas City, Missouri.

8 Coon-Sanders Nighthawks, Vol. 1/Mar. 24, 1921–Dec. 21, 1925/the Old Masters 111
10 Coon-Sanders Nighthawks, Vol. 2/Mar. 9, 1926–June 9, 1928/the Old Masters 112
8 Coon-Sanders Nighthawks, Vol. 3/Aug. 13, 1928–Feb. 12, 1929/the Old Masters 113
8 Coon-Sanders Nighthawks, Vol. 4/Feb. 12, 1929–Mar. 24, 1932/the Old Masters 114

7 The Best of Coon-Sanders/Apr. 5, 1924–Mar. 24, 1932/Retrieval 79019

Every recording by the Coon-Sanders Nighthawks is included on the four CDs from The Old Masters label. *Vol. 1* has the band's lone 1921 recording ("Some Little Bird") and its first 22 selections for Victor, including such numbers as "Night Hawk Blues," "Red Hot Mama," "Some of These Days," "Who Wouldn't Love You," and "Flamin' Mamie." By mid-1924, the Coon-Sanders sound was quite recognizable, and its personnel became quite stable within a year, with no personnel changes at all from late 1925 until at least early 1930. *Vol. 2* features the group at its peak, particularly on such classics as "My Baby Knows How," "Brainstorm," "I Ain't Got Nobody" (a famous arrangement), "Roodles, "Slue Foot," and "Hallucinations." So tight are the ensembles and the joyous vocals that it is easy to miss the fact that there are actually very few solos.

Vol. 3 has a few departures. There are four titles from a session that the Coon-Sanders Orchestra recorded under the pseudonym of the Louisiana Rhythm Kings (for the rival Vocalion label); two of those songs are instrumentals, while two others have vocals by Harry Maxfield instead of Coon and Sanders. In addition, this CD has a 27½-minute radio show (called *The Maytag Frolic*) from January 17, 1929, featuring the band playing quite a few songs, including several that they never recorded otherwise. Of the conventional recordings, "What a Girl! What a Night," "Little Orphan Annie," and particularly "Here Comes My Ball and Chain" are highlights. *Vol. 4* wraps up the recorded history of the band with 13 selections from 1929 (including "Kansas City Kitty" and "After You've Gone") and the nine numbers that the Nighthawks cut in 1932 (including the ironically titled "What a Life! (Trying to Live Without You)," which Joe Sanders sang). Also on the CD is one of two piano solos ("Improvisation") that Sanders made on March 9, 1932; pity that its companion, "Intangibility," was not in-

cluded too. But that minor quibble aside, this is a perfectly done series.

Collectors just desiring a sampling of the Coon-Sanders recordings might want to pick up the Retrieval disc, which has 24 of their very best selections although unfortunately not "My Baby Knows How" or "I Ain't Got Nobody."

THE COTTON PICKERS

The name of this group (no relation to McKinney's Cotton Pickers) was used by the musicians in the Original Memphis Five for their Brunswick recordings of 1922–26. The 36 titles usually had Phil Napoleon, trombonist Charlie Panelli, Jimmy Lytell, and Frank Signorelli in the personnel, although there were substitutes (Miff Mole is on the first four titles, Frankie Trumbauer is on eight songs, and Phil Napoleon's spot on the last 12 tunes was taken by Roy Johnson, Red Nichols, or Mickey Bloom). In 1929 the Cotton Pickers name was revived for four sessions, with such players as Tommy Dorsey (trumpet on two dates and trombone on one other), Glenn Miller, Jimmy Dorsey, and a returning Phil Napoleon heard from. While the earlier group stuck mostly to instrumentals, in 1929 Hoagy Carmichael and torch singer Libby Holman (heard on "Moanin' Low") had two vocals apiece.

8 The Cotton Pickers/July 1922–Apr. 19, 1925/Timeless 1–029

Twenty-four of the Cotton Picker's first 30 recordings are on this CD. Phil Napoleon or Roy Johnson is on trumpet, Miff Mole or Charles Panelli is on trombone, and the clarinet slot is filled by Bennie Kruger, Jimmy Lytell, or Larry Abbott. Other notables passing through include Frankie Trumbauer, Frank Signorelli, and Rube Bloom. The music is excellent for the period (particularly the 1922–23 sides) and is essentially melodic and danceable early jazz that includes future standards and such superior obscurities as "Got to Cool My Doggies Now," "Snakes Hips," and "Walk Jenny, Walk." Hopefully the missing six selections will show up on another CD eventually.

IDA COX

b. Feb. 25, 1896, Cedartown, GA, d. Nov. 10, 1967, Knoxville, TN

One of the great classic blues singers, Ida Cox differed from many of her contemporaries who recorded in the 1920s by being primarily a blues rather than vaudevillian singer. Cox sang in choirs as a child, ran away from home at age 14 to tour with White and Clark's Minstrels in 1910, and gradually became a major attraction. She had a long-time marriage to pianist Jesse "Tiny" Crump, who often accompanied her. Cox moved to Chicago in 1922, and in 1923 she made her recording debut, recording 86 songs (not counting alternate takes) during the next six years, including "I've Got the Blues for Rampart Street," "Graveyard Dream Blues," "Wild Woman Don't Have the Blues," and "Death Letter Blues." During this period, Cox ranked second to Bessie Smith among blues singers (with Ethel Waters close behind), touring with her *Raisin' Cain"* show and heading the *Darktown Scandals* company.

Although the recordings stopped after two titles in 1929, Cox managed to keep working on a lower level during the 1930s, mostly in the South. Later in the decade she made a comeback, appearing at the Spirituals to Swing concert in December 1938, recording seven songs in 1939 (plus four more in 1940), and performing at Café Society. She worked regularly until suffering a heart attack in 1945. In 1961 Ida Cox came out of retirement to make a final record, an underrated gem for Riverside that has Coleman Hawkins and Roy Eldridge as sidemen.

9 Vol. 1 (1923)/June 1923 – Dec. 1923/Document 5322
9 Vol. 2 (1924 – 1925)/Mar. 1924 – Apr. 1925/Document 5323
8 Vol. 3 (1925 – 1927)/Apr. 1925 – July 1927/Document 5324
8 Vol. 4 (1927 – 1938)/July 1927 – Dec. 24, 1938/Document 5325
6 The Uncrowned Queen of the Blues/June 1923 – Aug. 1924/ Black Swan 7

All of Ida Cox's recordings from the 1920s (other than some alternate takes) are on the four Document CDs. The blues singer's 1923 sessions comprise *Vol. 1*, including "Any Woman's Blues," "Graveyard Dream Blues," "Ida Cox's Lawdy, Lawdy Blues," "I've Got the Blues for Rampart Street," and "Bear Mash Blues." Other than the last title, Cox's backing is provided by Lovie Austin, with and without her Blues Serenaders (Tommy Ladnier and Jimmy O'Bryant). An expanded version of the Blues Serenaders, sidemen from Fletcher Henderson's orchestra, and (on two songs) a banjo-guitar duo (the Pruitt Twins) help Cox on *Vol. 2*, which is highlighted by "Chicago Monkey Man Blues," "Blues Ain't Nothing Else But," "Wild Women Don't Have the Blues," and "Death Letter Blues." Some of the lines on "Chicago Monkey Man Blues" would show up years later in "Goin' to Chicago." In fact, Ida Cox was a greatly underrated (and often plagiarized) lyricist who wrote many phrases that were used by other blues and jazz singers for many decades. *Vol. 3* is mostly from April 1925 – July 1926 and, in addition to the Blues Serenaders, Cox is joined on various tracks by Dave Nelson, Jesse Crump, and banjoist Papa Charlie Jackson (who shares the vocals on the two-part "Mister Man"). Among the better-known selections are "Southern Woman's Blues," "Coffin Blues," and "'Fore Day Creep."

Except for the final two selections (taken from the 1938 Spirituals to Swing concert) and two numbers from 1929 in a trio with Roy Palmer and Tiny Parham, *Vol. 4* is from 1927 – 28. Cox is accompanied for three of the five sessions just by Jesse Crump's piano, excelling quite well in the intimate setting. But no hits resulted and her recording career stopped after 1929.

The singer's 11 selections from 1939 – 40 (plus eight alternate takes) with top swing players are on *Vol. 5* (Document 5651), while her 1961 album *Blues for Rampart Street* has been made available in the Original Jazz Classics series (OJC-1758). *The Uncrowned Queen of the Blues* has 20 of Ida Cox's first recordings, bypassing seven numbers plus the alternate takes. Although the choices are excellent, this CD will not satisfy either completists or those wanting a definitive CD by the blues singer, since it does not go past 1924.

WILTON CRAWLEY

b. July 18, 1900, Smithfield, VA, d. Nov. 1967, Anne Arundel, MD

The most outlandish and flamboyant of all the gaspipe clarinetists of the 1920s (making the other ones sound dull and colorless in comparison), Wilton Crawley was a master at slap tonguing, odd tonal distortions, and laughing through his horn. Crawley, who grew up in Philadelphia, was taught clarinet by his father when he was ten. He developed a variety act that featured his wild clarinet playing, good-humored singing, juggling, and skills as a contortionist! In fact, it was said that he apparently found it difficult to separate his two talents (music and contortionism), so it was somewhat tricky to record him in the studio! Despite that difficulty, Crawley recorded 14 titles with small groups during 1927–28 (often including Eddie Lang and pianist Eddie Heywood Sr.) but is best known for his three combo dates of 1929–30, two of which include Jelly Roll Morton. Best are "You Oughta See My Gal," "I'm Her Papa, She's My Mama," and "Big Time Woman."

Crawley spent most of 1928 with Lew Leslie's *Blackbirds* show and toured Europe during 1930–32. Wilton Crawley's career faded away after 1932. Based on his recordings, he could have been a strong jazz clarinetist, but comedy and novelty effects interested him more. At the latter, he had few competitors.

8 Wilton Crawley/May 31, 1927 – June 3, 1930/Jazz Oracle 8020
All of the clarinetist's recordings are on this CD except for his final two selections from his 1930 date; those are scheduled to be included in *George McClennon and Wilton Crawley* (Jazz Oracle 8025). This 26-selection CD (which runs over 79 minutes) is full of Crawley's wide array of sounds and effects along with some solid playing on occasional choruses. The first 17 numbers (three of which were previously unreleased) have Crawley showcased in trios and quartets with such sidemen as Eddie Lang, Lonnie Johnson, and Eddie Heywood Sr. In truth, a little goes a long way! Crawley is also heard on his last three dates with musicians taken from Luis Russell's band (including Red Allen, Charlie Holmes, and Russell himself) plus Teddy Bunn and (on several memorable numbers) Jelly Roll Morton. Some of the performances are filled with hilarity— the other musicians sound quite surprised by Wilton Crawley's colorful and bizarre playing. Unique music from the greatest of the gaspipe clarinetists!

CHARLIE CREATH

b. Dec. 30, 1890, Ironton, MO, d. Oct. 23, 1951, Chicago, IL

Charlie Creath was one of the top bandleaders in 1920s St. Louis. Among his sidemen were Ed Allen, Leonard Davis, Dewey Jackson, Lonnie Johnson, Pops Foster, and Creath's brother-in-law Zutty Singleton. Starting on alto, Creath switched to trumpet as a teenager. He played early on with circus bands and in theater shows. After leading a band in Seattle, Creath moved to St. Louis in 1918. In 1921 he put together his Jazz-O-Maniacs, a hot outfit that on 12 selections recorded during 1924–27 proved to be a particularly strong group. All of that music is available on *Jazz in Saint Louis* (Timeless 1–036).

Not a major player himself, Creath was wise to feature Leonard Davis or Dewey Jackson on several of his selections. But after illness knocked him out of action during much of 1928–30, Creath's earlier fame was gone. Mostly playing alto and accordion in later years, he worked with Harvey Lankford's Synco High Hatters (1933), co-led a band with Fate Marable in the mid-1930s, ran a nightclub in Chicago, and ended up working outside of music.

The Rhythm Boys (Al Rinker, Bing Crosby, and Harry Barris) was a good-humored trio that launched Crosby's solo career.

BING CROSBY

b. May 3, 1903, Tacoma, WA, d. Oct. 14, 1977, Madrid, Spain

The most famous and (not counting Louis Armstrong) most influential singer in popular music of the 1930–45 period, Harry Lillis "Bing" Crosby did not always sing jazz, but he kept a warm spot in his heart for Dixieland and 1920s music. The older brother of bandleader-vocalist Bob Crosby, Bing took the vocal innovations of Louis Armstrong and Jack Teagarden, and brought them into pop music.

Crosby sang in his local high school band and ordered a drum set through the mail, which he taught himself to play. While studying law at Gonzaga University in Spokane, Washington, he met vocalist Al Rinker and was soon playing drums and singing with Rinker's Musicaleaders. After graduating in 1925, Crosby decided to discard his potential law career and instead formed a duo with Rinker, appearing in vaudeville in Los Angeles and staying with Rinker's sister, Mildred Bailey. Through Bailey, Crosby and Rinker met Paul Whiteman, who hired and teamed them with the colorful singer-pianist-songwriter Harry Barris as the Rhythm Boys. The good-humored vocal group (whose carousing sometimes caused the bandleader headaches) recorded both with Whiteman and as a trio, appearing in *The King of Jazz* in 1930 (singing "Mississippi Mud") and gaining a national reputation. In addition, Crosby had some solo vocals with Whiteman, including "Muddy Water," "Mary,"

"Ol' Man River," "Make Believe," and "'Tain't So, Honey, 'Tain't So."

In 1931 the Rhythm Boys left Whiteman and joined Gus Arnheim's orchestra in Los Angeles. However, it was only a short time before Crosby's great success as a soloist led the unit to break up. One of the first singers to really master the use of the microphone, Crosby saved listeners from all of the boy tenors and pompous semioperatic singers that had been dominating pop music. His relaxed and friendly delivery had a much more natural feel than that of most of the singers who had recorded before him, and it revolutionized pop music. Bing had tremendous success with his series of 15-minute radio programs on CBS, and his recordings resulted in such hits as "Just One More Chance," "I Found a Million-Dollar Baby," "Please," "Brother Can You Spare a Dime," and "June in January." Crosby appeared in the 1932 movie *The Big Broadcast* (with Eddie Lang as his accompanist), but within a few years his association with jazz would only be occasional as he enjoyed great success on radio and records and in movies and live appearances. However, on such early records as "Dinah," "Shine," "Some of These Days," "St. Louis Blues" (with Duke Ellington), and "My Honey's Loving Arms," Bing Crosby showed that he could be a top jazz singer whenever he wanted. His love for early jazz and Dixieland (shown in the films *Pennies from Heaven, The Birth of the Blues,* and *High Society*) would be quite consistent throughout his long career.

9 1926–1932/Dec. 22, 1926–Feb. 11, 1932/Timeless 1–004
★ Bing—His Legendary Years: 1931 to 1957/Nov. 23, 1931–Dec. 27, 1957/MCA 4–10887

1926–1932 is a superior summation of Bing Crosby's early years, particularly his recordings from 1927–29. Crosby's best solo sides with Paul Whiteman (including "Muddy Water," "Mary," "Ol' Man River," and "Make Believe") are included, along with specialties with the Rhythm Boys and other Whiteman vocalists (highlighted by "Changes," "From Monday On," "Louisiana," "You Took Advantage of Me," and "Happy Feet"). In addition, Crosby is heard with Sam Lanin, the Dorsey Brothers Orchestra, and, during 1930–32, Gus Arnheim ("One More Time"), the Mills Brothers ("Dinah"), and Duke Ellington (1930's "Three Little Words" with the Rhythm Boys and solo on 1932's "St. Louis Blues"). It is not a "complete" reissue series (which is long overdue) but a very good sampler of early Bing.

The four-CD box *Bing—His Legendary Years* has many of the highlights from a 26-year period in the singer's career. Classic jazz collectors will be most interested in the first disc, which includes his early ballad hits, such as "Out of Nowhere," "Just One More Chance," "I'm Through with Love," "I Found a Million-Dollar Baby," and "June in January."

LPS TO SEARCH FOR

A variety of LPs have early Crosby material not included on *1926–1932*. The two-LP set *Volume I: The Early Jazz Years* (Columbia 201) consists of 32 selections from the same time period while duplicating only five songs; its gems include "Wa-Da-Da," "I'll Get By," "Louise," and "Sweet Georgia Brown." *Wrap Your Troubles in Dreams* (RCA 584) has four Paul Whiteman selections already on *1926–1932* but also such 1930–31 recordings as "It Must Be True," the adventurous arrangement of "I Surrender Dear," "I'm Through with Love," and "Just One More Chance." *Bing Crosby in Hollywood 1930–1934* (Columbia 43) has Crosby's studio recordings of the music from the films *The King of Jazz* (not all of those songs feature Bing), *The Big Broadcast, College Humor, Too Much Harmony, Going Hollywood, We're Not Dressing,* and *She Loves Me Not,* including "Happy Feet," "Please," "Learn to Croon," "The Day You Came Along," and "Temptation." And true Bing Crosby fans will want to search for *A Bing Crosby Collection Volumes I, II, and III* (Columbia 35093, 35094, and 35748) since they contain rarities from the 1929–34 period, including "Anyone Can See with Half an Eye I'm Crazy Over You!"

BERNIE CUMMINS

b. Mar. 14, 1900, Akron, OH, d. Sept. 22, 1986, Palm Beach, FL

Although far from a major name, Bernie Cummins led a series of fine bands in the 1920s and early '30s. He originally planned to be a dancer, but a leg injury incurred while playing football convinced him to be a drummer instead. He began working locally as a teenager. In 1923 Cummins moved to Cincinnati, where he led a six-piece band and the following year began recording for the Gennett label, making some excellent jazz-oriented dance band records during 1924–25 as the group gradually grew to eight pieces. By 1927, Bernie Cummins' Orchestra was 12 pieces, he was no longer playing drums (instead fronting the band and taking occasional vocals), and his ensemble was based in New York, playing major hotels. The band became more commercial as time progressed, but Bernie Cummins kept leading very musical orchestras until he retired in 1959.

8 1924–1930/ Jan. 28, 1924–Nov. 4, 1930/Timeless 1–058
This CD features Bernie Cummins' bands on 15 selections from 1924–25, two from 1927, and nine from 1930. There were never any major soloists in Cummins' groups but the musicianship is high, the vocals are easy to take, and the ensembles swing. Such tunes as "Ida," "Dancin' Dan," "When," "Words," "Make My Cot Where the Cot-Cot-Cotton Grows," and "Hand Me Down My Walking Cane" show why the band was popular during the era. This is fine 1920s mainstream hot dance music. Hopefully Cummins' equally rewarding early 1930s dance band recordings will eventually be reissued too.

LEONARD DAVIS

b. July 4, 1905, St. Louis, MO, d. 1957, New York, NY

Leonard Davis was a solid trumpeter with a beautiful tone and a wide range. Those assets ironically worked against him because they resulted in his becoming a lead trumpeter rather than a soloist. However, he did have one day of greatness.

Leonard "Ham" Davis grew up in St. Louis, where he played locally. He made his recording debut with Charlie Creath (1924–25), moved to New York, and worked with Charlie Skeets, Edgar Hayes (1927), Arthur Gibbs, and Charlie Johnson (1928–29). During a date with Eddie Condon's Hot Shots on February 8, 1929, Davis took beautiful solos on "I'm Gonna Stomp, Mr. Henry Lee" and particularly the blues "That's a Serious Thing"; they have been reissued (happily with two takes apiece) on *The Indispensable Jack Teagarden* (RCA Jazz Tribune 66606). Oddly enough, there would never be any real encore. Davis worked with many other groups, including those of Elmer Snowden (1930–31), Don Redman, Russell Wooding, Benny Carter (1933), Luis Russell (1934–37), and Edgar Hayes (1938), Sidney Bechet's nonet (1940), George James (1943) and Alberto Socarras. But in each situation, Leonard Davis' tone was used as an anonymous part of the ensemble, and his solo talents remained undiscovered.

VOLLY DEFAUT

b. Mar. 14, 1904, Little Rock, AK, d. May 29, 1973, So. Chicago Heights, IL

One of the first significant clarinet soloists to pop up on records, Voltaire "Volly" DeFaut never fulfilled his early potential. He grew up in Chicago, started on violin when he was six, and switched to saxophone and clarinet when he was 14. DeFaut worked with Sig Meyers (1922), the New Orleans Rhythm Kings (briefly in 1923), Mel Stitzel, the Midway Gardens Orchestra, and Art Kassel. On recordings with the Stomp Six and the Bucktown Five (both Muggsy Spanier groups) in 1924, Jelly Roll Morton (1925's "My Gal"), and Merritt Brunies' Friars Inn Orchestra (1924–26), DeFaut showed that he was near the top of his field at that moment in time. However, his later associations with Ray Miller, Isham Jones, and Jean Goldkette (1928–29) were less eventful. DeFaut was a studio musician for radio station WGN for a decade, had a dog-breeding business, served in the Army during World War II (luckily getting to play music), and worked mostly in the Chicago area into the late 1960s. Volly DeFaut recorded with pianist Art Hodes in 1953 and 1968 but remained quite obscure despite his talent.

SIDNEY DEPARIS

b. May 30, 1905, Crawfordsville, IN, d. Sep. 13, 1967, New York, NY

Sidney DeParis was one of the better trumpeters of the late 1920s. The younger brother of trombonist Wilbur DeParis (1900–1973), Sidney studied music with his father, who led a carnival band that played in vaudeville. After touring with his Dad's group in the South, DeParis worked with Sam Taylor in Washington, D.C. (1924), and relocated to New York. He played with Andrew Preer's Cotton Club Orchestra (making his recording debut) and was one of the key players with Charlie Johnson's Paradise Ten during 1926–31 (other than a year spent with Wilbur DeParis' group in Philadelphia). DeParis was featured on several records with Johnson (including "Walk That Thing" and "The Boy with the Boat"). He also recorded seven titles with McKinney's Cotton Pickers in November 1929.

The 1920s were just the first of three main periods for DeParis. During the 1930s he worked primarily with big bands, including Fletcher Henderson (1931), Don Redman (1932–36), Willie Bryant, and Benny Carter (1940–41). He also recorded with Jelly Roll Morton (1939), Sidney Bechet, and Willie "the Lion" Smith. After a period

of freelancing, Sidney DeParis spent his last playing years (1943–62) performing colorful Dixieland with Wilbur DeParis' New New Orleans Jazz Band.

HARRY DIAL

b. Feb. 17, 1907, Birmingham, AL, d. Jan. 25, 1987, New York, NY

A minor figure as a drummer and a good-time singer, Harry Dial had a fairly long career. He grew up in St. Louis, playing drums locally as a youth. Dial became a professional in August 1921, leading his first band in 1922 (when he was 15). He worked with Dewey Jackson, Fate Marable (1923–26 on riverboats) and Jimmy Powell's Jazz Monarchs. After moving to Chicago in 1928, Dial played with violinist Wilson Robinson, Clifford King's Big Band (1928–29), Jerome Pasquall, and many little-known groups. He led three record dates in 1930, resulting in six titles, including two that feature Omer Simeon and Zinky Cohn; all six songs have been reissued in *That's My Stuff* (Frog 7).

Dial was with Louis Armstrong for a couple of months in 1933, worked with Ira Coffey's Walkathons, and moved to New York in 1934. He freelanced with many groups, including those of Sam Wooding, Fats Waller (1935), and Ed Allen (1937–40). Harry Dial recorded with his own band (which included Reuben Reeves) during 1946–47, was based at Small's Paradise during 1947–55 and cut LPs in 1961 and 1965, staying active into the late 1960s.

CARROLL DICKERSON

b. 1895, d. Oct. 1957, Chicago, IL

Carroll Dickerson led one of the top big bands in Chicago during the 1920s. Dickerson, who played violin but rarely soloed, was based at the Entertainers' Café (1921) and the Sunset Café (1922–24). After going out on tour for 48 weeks in 1925, he returned to the Sunset Café (1926). When his star sideman, Louis Armstrong, took over the band,

Dickerson moved to the Savoy Dance Hall (1927–29), where, after a period, Armstrong rejoined him.

Dickerson led only two recording dates in his career (both in 1928), which resulted in four songs. Five of the members of Louis Armstrong's Savoy Ballroom Five, trumpeter Willie Hightower, and pianist Gene Anderson were among the 11 musicians who recorded "Missouri Squabble" and "Black Maria"; those two numbers are included on *Hot Stuff* (Frog 28). The second session resulted in "Symphonic Raps" and "Savoyagers' Stomps," featuring Satch and Earl Hines. Other sidemen who performed with Dickerson along the way included Johnny Dunn, Tommy Ladnier, and Buster Bailey.

In the spring of 1929, the Dickerson Orchestra went with Louis Armstrong to New York, a move that did not please the bookers, who had sent for only the trumpeter. The ensemble played under Satch's leadership for a short time and was based at Connie's Inn during 1929–30 before disbanding. Carroll Dickerson worked with the Mills Blue Rhythm Band and King Oliver on violin, returning to Chicago in the early 1930s. He continued leading bands (though they went completely undocumented) into the 1940s.

R.Q. DICKERSON

b. 1898, Paducah, KY, d. Jan. 21, 1951, Glen Falls, NY

R.Q. (Roger Quincey) Dickerson was an underrated soloist who worked with several bands that were associated with the Cotton Club. Dickerson grew up in St. Louis, playing professionally in local theaters starting in 1918. In 1923 he toured with Wilson Robinson's Bostonians, a group that, after violinist Andrew Preer emerged as its leader, became the house band of the Cotton Club. As the Cotton Club Orchestra, they recorded six songs in 1925, and Dickerson also appeared on two songs recorded by Harry's Happy Four. The Cotton Club band cut only one additional title under Preer's name ("I've Found a New Baby" in 1927) before

its leader's unexpected death. After being renamed the Missourians, the band recorded 14 exciting selections during three sessions in 1929–30. Dickerson (who had a lyrical style) shared the trumpet solos with Lammar Wright. After the Depression hit, the Missourians were on the verge of breaking up when they were taken over by the up-and-coming Cab Calloway. Renamed the Cab Calloway Orchestra, the ensemble soon flourished (although in a subsidiary role), especially after Cab recorded "Minnie the Moocher" on March 3, 1931. R.Q. Dickerson stayed with the orchestra into 1931 before choosing to leave music altogether. He was only 33 and spent most of his remaining 20 years as a cab driver.

BABY DODDS

b. Dec. 24, 1898, New Orleans, LA, d. Feb. 14, 1959, Chicago, IL

The younger brother of Johnny Dodds, Warren "Baby" Dodds was one of the most innovative drummers of the 1920s. The youngest of six children (thus his lifelong nickname), Dodds started playing drums in 1912, when he was 13. Early on he worked at parades with Bunk Johnson, Willie Hightower, Frankie Dusen's Eagle Band, and Oscar Celestin and also performed throughout New Orleans. Dodds played on the *S.S. Sydney* with one of Fate Marable's most legendary bands (1918–21). Along with his brother, he was sent for by King Oliver to join the Creole Jazz Band. Dodds joined Oliver in San Francisco (1921), relocating to Chicago the following year. He worked with Oliver's Creole Jazz Band (making his recording debut in 1923) until a money dispute caused the Dodds Brothers to leave in early 1924.

A fixture in Chicago, Baby Dodds worked with (among others) Honore Dutrey, Freddie Keppard, Willie Hightower, Lil Armstrong, Charlie Elgar, Hugh Swift, and Johnny Dodds (at Kelly's Stables). His most notable recordings were with his brother, Louis Armstrong's Hot Seven, and Jelly Roll Morton. His 1927 trio performance of "Wolverine Blues" with Morton and Johnny Dodds is a great example of his talents. On that selection Baby Dodds (a master of dynamics) can be heard playing a variety of different patterns that he constantly changed. Gene Krupa and Dave Tough were among the many drummers who listened closely to Dodds and were influenced by his alert and stimulating style.

Dodds was off records during much of the Depression, but he continued playing in Chicago while helping Bill Dodds (one of his other brothers) run a taxi service. He was the house drummer at the Three Deuces during 1936–39 and recorded with Johnny Dodds in 1940, just before his older brother's sudden death. In the 1940s Baby Dodds worked with Jimmie Noone (1940–41), Bunk Johnson (1944–45), Art Hodes (1946–48), and Miff Mole (1948–49), appearing on occasional records (including with Sidney Bechet) and performing with Mezz Mezzrow in France at the Nice Jazz Festival in 1948.

During 1945–46, Baby Dodds became the first musician to record unaccompanied drum solos, valuable documents (recorded for Circle and Folkways) that show today's listeners just how advanced and colorful his style really was. He also led some combo dates during the period. Dodds had a stroke in the spring of 1949, mostly recovered, played on a part-time basis, and survived a second stroke in 1950. After working with Natty Dominique (1951–52), his health really started declining, but he played on an occasional basis until 1957. Fortunately, before his death in 1959, Baby Dodds completed his fascinating memoirs (*The Baby Dodds Story*, Louisiana State Univ. Press), which were released posthumously.

JOHNNY DODDS

b. Apr. 12, 1892, New Orleans, LA, d. Aug. 8, 1940, Chicago, IL

One of the greatest jazz clarinet players of all time and arguably the definitive clarinetist of the 1920s, Johnny Dodds had a very distinctive and appealing tone in both his upper and lower registers, and he was able to cut easily through any ensemble. Although renowned for his emotional sound and ability to play blues, Dodds was also a strong improviser who could essay the chord changes of the era without any difficulty. The older brother of Baby Dodds, he did not begin on clarinet until he was already 13, in 1905. Self-taught except for some lessons with Lorenzo Tio Jr., Dodds played strictly by ear. In 1912 he began working with Kid Ory (who led the city's top jazz group), freelancing around the city for the next few years. Dodds played with Fate Marable on the *S.S. Capitol* in 1917, toured with Billy and Mary Mack's Merrymakers (1918), and in 1921 (along with Baby Dodds) joined King Oliver's Creole Jazz Band.

Dodds played with Oliver through early 1924, appearing on his first records with the cornetist in 1923 and making major contributions to the classic band's ensembles. A fight over money led the Dodds brothers to depart. The clarinetist played with Honore Dutrey and Freddie Keppard (spring 1924) before putting together a band that played at Bert Kelly's Stables on and off into 1930. Dodds appeared on many records in the 1920s, including backing singers Viola Bartlette, Butterbeans and Susie, Ford and Ford, Edmonia Henderson, Teddy Peters, Elzadie Robinson, Hociel Thomas, and Sippie Wallace. Dodds can be heard jamming with such hot (and sometimes overlapping combos) as Lovie Austin's Blues Serenaders, King Oliver (a guest shot in 1926 on "Someday Sweetheart), Junie Cobb, Freddie Keppard, the Dixieland Jug Blowers, Jimmy Bertrand's Washboard Wizards, the Chicago Footwarmers (including "Oriental Man" and "Brush Stomp"), Jasper Taylor, the State Street Ramblers, Blind Blake, the Paramount Pickers, and the Beale St. Washboard Band.

Dodds managed to mostly hold his own with a

One of the most distinctive of all clarinetists, Johnny Dodds had a style that perfectly fit black Chicago jazz of the 1920s.

rapidly emerging Louis Armstrong on the remarkable series of Hot Five and Hot Seven recordings (1925–27), including "Muskrat Ramble," "Willie the Weeper," "Wild Man Blues," "Potato Head Blues," "Weary Blues," and "Struttin' with Some Barbecue." He also appeared with the same combo for another label as Lil's Hot Shots and in similar recording groups (with George Mitchell in Armstrong's spot) called the New Orleans Bootblacks and the New Orleans Wanderers (resulting in a classic "Perdido Street Blues"). Dodds made some dates with Jelly Roll Morton in 1927 (including trio versions of "Wolverine Blues" and "Mr. Jelly Roll" with Morton and brother Baby). In addition, Dodds (who frequently teamed up with cornetist Natty Dominique) led sessions of his own during 1927–29; "Come on and Stomp, Stomp, Stomp" was one of the high points.

The recordings came to an end in 1929, and, although Dodds worked regularly in Chicago in the 1930s and had fortunately invested his money in property (including apartment houses), he struggled a bit. Things began to look up in 1938 when he made his only trip to New York for a record date (six titles) that also featured the young trumpeter Charlie Shavers. Unfortunately Dodds had a heart attack in May 1939 and was inactive until January 1940. He began to play again on a part-time basis and recorded two final selections on June 5 (Dominique's subpar playing largely sank that date) but died from a second heart attack two months later. Johnny Dodds' early death (he was 48) took place right before the New Orleans revival movement would have certainly revived his career.

9 Blue Clarinet Stomp/July 5, 1928–Feb. 7, 1929/Frog 3

There are a few different ways to acquire Johnny Dodds' recordings. The single CD from Frog has all of the music that the clarinetist recorded as a leader on his six sessions of 1928–29 but not his five dates of 1927. The main advantage to this release is that it includes all of the alternate takes, including previously unreleased versions of "Too Tight" and "My Little Isabel." Dodds is heard in trios on two sessions and in a sextet (with Natty Dominique, Honore Dutrey, Bill Johnson, Baby Dodds, and Charlie Alexander or Lil Armstrong on piano) for the remaining tunes. Among the highlights are "Blue Clarinet Stomp," "Bull Fiddle Blues," "Too Tight," and "Indigo Stomp." The CD concludes with Sippie Wallace's "I'm a Mighty Tight Woman," Dodds' last recording (other than his date with the Beale St. Washboard Band) until 1938.

8 1926/May 19, 1926–Dec. 26, 1926/Classics 589
9 1927/Jan. 19, 1927–Aug. 10, 1927/Classics 603
9 1927–1928/Oct. 5, 1927–July 5, 1928/Classics 617
7 1928–1940/July 6, 1928–June 5, 1940/Classics 635

The four Classics Johnny Dodds releases are unusual for the label, for rather than just reissuing the music from dates led by the clarinetist (which would fill two CDs), they also have his most important sideman combo sides (other than his sets with Morton and the Louis Armstrong Hot Five and Seven). As usual with Classics, no alternate takes are included. On *1926*, Dodds is heard as a sideman with Jimmy Blythe, the New Orleans Wanderers, the New Orleans Bootblacks, Freddie Keppard, Junie Cobb, and the Dixieland Jug Blowers. The music is mostly quite exciting (he certainly uplifts the jug band), particularly the New Orleans Wanderers and Bootblacks sessions, but most of the selections (particularly those of Blythe, Keppard, and Cobb) are easily available in more complete form elsewhere.

1927 has dates with Keppard, Blythe, and Jimmy Bertrand along with duets with Tiny Parham, trios with Lil Armstrong and Bud Scott, and a session by Dodds' Black Bottom Stompers that has Louis Armstrong, Roy Palmer, Barney Bigard (on tenor), Earl Hines (his only recording with Dodds), Bud Scott, and Baby Dodds; "Melancholy" is the classic of that date. *1927–1928* has the exciting Chicago Footwarmers recordings ("Brush Stomp" and the various versions of "Oriental Man" are classics), dates with Blythe, Jasper Taylor, and the State Street Ramblers, and two of Dodds' sessions as a leader, including the one that resulted in "Come on and Stomp, Stomp, Stomp." *1928–1940* is comprised of the music (but no alternates) from Dodds' last four dates as a leader in the 1920s, the Sippie Wallace selection, the titles with the Beale St. Washboard Band, and his sessions from 1938 and 1940.

In summary, the first three Johnny Dodds' Classics CDs can be acquired with only two titles from *1927–1928* duplicating music on Frog's *Blue Clarinet Stomp*. *1928–1940* has the later Dodds dates but not the alternates from the 1928–29 sessions. It is difficult at times to be a completist!

7 Blue Clarinet Stomp/Dec. 11, 1926–Feb. 7, 1929/Bluebird 2293
5 South Side Chicago Jazz/Apr. 21, 1927–July 24, 1929/MCA/Decca 42326

Making things even a more confusing, Bluebird's *Blue Clarinet Stomp* covers the same basic period of time as Frog's *Blue Clarinet Stomp*. Included on the Bluebird but not the Frog set are two of the trios that Dodds made with Jelly Roll Morton and three cuts with the Dixieland Jug Blowers. But the Frog CD (which duplicates 16 of the 21 selections) has versions of six numbers from January–February 1929 that are left out of the Bluebird CD plus Sippie Wallace's "I'm a Mighty Tight Woman." The edge goes to the Frog set and the Classics.

South Side Chicago Jazz is a sampler and is easy to pass by unless available for a budget price. There are titles of Dodds with Bertrand, Blythe, and the Beale Street Washboard Band plus eight numbers as a leader. But at 16 cuts and with only a couple of the sessions being complete, this is a lesser release.

LPS TO SEARCH FOR

All of Johnny Dodds' recordings as a leader and as a sideman are available on CD in one form or another. But two LP reissues are worth getting if the material is not already owned on CD. *Johnny Dodds and Kid Ory* (Columbia 16004) has the eight numbers by the New Orleans Bootblacks and the New Orleans Wanderers (exciting performances, including "Gate Mouth," "Papa Dip," and "Perdido Street Blues") plus four numbers by the Chicago Footwarmers (including "Oriental Man"). However, there are mistakes in the personnel listing (Joe Clark, not Stump Evans, is on alto), and none of the selections were actually led by Dodds or Ory.

The Complete Johnny Dodds (RCA 74110/111) has all of the clarinetist's sessions for labels now owned by RCA. This two-LP set, in addition to including the trios with Jelly Roll Morton, the Dixieland Jug Blowers date, and the inevitable number with Sippie Wallace, completely duplicates Frog's *Blue Clarinet Stomp* CD except for leaving out the rare alternate takes of "Too Tight" and "My Little Isabel." But this twofer will be difficult to find.

Confused yet?

NATTY DOMINIQUE

> *b. Aug. 2, 1896, New Orleans, LA, d. Aug. 30, 1982, Chicago, IL*

A rather limited cornetist, Anatie "Natty" Dominique had a lot of power; his colorfully erratic solos made him particularly memorable. The cousin of Barney Bigard and the uncle of trumpeter Don Albert, Dominique started out on drums before studying cornet with Manuel Perez. He played at many parades in New Orleans, including with Perez's Imperial Band. Dominique moved to Chicago in June 1913, working by day as a cigar maker and not playing music full time until the early 1920s. Among Dominique's most important associations in the '20s were Carroll Dickerson's orchestra (where at one point he played second trumpet behind Louis Armstrong), Al Simeon's Hot Six, Jimmie Noone, and Johnny Dodds (with whom he worked regularly starting in 1928). Dominique recorded with Jelly Roll Morton (a pair of lesser-known band sides in 1923), Jimmy Bertrand (1926), Lovie Austin, Jimmy Blythe, Sippie Wallace, and most importantly Dodds, including with the Chicago Footwarmers, the Dixieland Thumpers, and the State Street Ramblers. Dominique (who was capable of colorful outbursts) can be heard at his best on such numbers as "Brush Stomp," "Oriental Man," and "Lady Love," but at other times his technical limitations are more obvious.

Dominique worked with Johnny and Baby Dodds in Chicago on and off through the 1930s, but his playing gradually declined. He appeared on a session apiece with Dodds (the clarinetist's last recordings) and Noone in 1940, but he was out-of-tune and helped ruin both efforts. Heart trouble soon forced the cornetist to stop playing, and he worked at an airline for years. Natty Dominique was able to resume playing part time in the late 1940s and recorded a few so-so selections during 1953–54, gigging into the 1970s. One can only imagine how he sounded by then!

JIMMY DORSEY

> *b. Feb. 29, 1904, Shenandoah, PA, d. June 12, 1957, New York, NY*

Best known for his work as a swing-era big bandleader, Jimmy Dorsey was also one of the finest reed players (both on alto and clarinet) of the 1920s. The older brother of Tommy Dorsey and the son of a coal miner who became a music teacher and band director, JD started as a child on cornet, playing in his father's band from the time he was seven. At 11, in 1915, he switched to alto and was soon also playing clarinet, although he still picked up a trumpet every once in a while in the 1920s. With brother Tommy, he formed Dorsey's Novelty Six and later

Dorseys' Wild Canaries, playing regularly in Baltimore starting around 1919. Both brothers joined Billy Lustig's Scranton Sirens in 1921. By September 1924, Jimmy was in New York playing with the California Ramblers, and during the next six years he worked steadily in jazz, appearing in countless settings. Among his most significant associations were the orchestras of Jean Goldkette, Ray Miller, Vincent Lopez, Paul Whiteman, and Ted Lewis (with whom he visited Europe in 1930). Dorsey appeared on records with those ensembles plus Red Nichols' Five Pennies and Frankie Trumbauer's orchestra (next to Bix Beiderbecke, including on "Singin' the Blues"). His set chorus on tunes that utilized the chord changes of "Tiger Rag" was particularly impressive, as was his showpiece on "Beebe" (which he recorded in 1929 and 1932) and his quintet session (with Spike Hughes' Three Blind Mice) in 1930. Since he slightly predated Benny Carter and Johnny Hodges, JD can be thought of jazz's first significant alto saxophonist.

Starting in 1928, Jimmy co-led the Dorsey Brothers Orchestra, which was strictly a recording group for its first five years. Well trained as a musician, Dorsey worked steadily in the studios during the first half of the 1930s, being (along with Benny Goodman) one of the first-call clarinetists. Eventually tiring of the commercial work, Jimmy and Tommy Dorsey decided to form a real group in 1934, and for a year the Dorsey Brothers Orchestra was a successful big band before the battling Dorseys went their separate ways. Jimmy Dorsey would be ultimately successful (after a slow start) in the swing era, even though his own playing was often overshadowed or used as a prop on commercial vocal-oriented performances.

TOMMY DORSEY

b. Nov. 19, 1905, Shenandoah, PA, d. Nov. 26, 1956, Greenwich, CT

The "Sentimental Gentleman of Swing" led one of the most popular of all swing-era big bands (an orchestra whose diversity and skills as a dance band were comparable to Paul Whiteman's in the 1920s) and was famous for his very pretty tone on trombone. Prior to that success, Tommy Dorsey worked steadily in the 1920s. The younger brother of Jimmy Dorsey, TD was also taught music by their father, learning trumpet and trombone. He co-led Dorseys' Novelty Six and Dorsey's Wild Canaries with Jimmy and in 1921 joined Billy Lustig's Scranton Sirens. Starting in 1925, Dorsey was kept busy appearing in both jazz and dance band settings, including working with Jean Goldkette, Paul Whiteman, Vincent Lopez, Roger Wolfe Kahn, Fred Rich, and other orchestras. His ballad expertise on trombone contrasted with his "dirty" and primitive trumpet playing, which can be heard at its best on the four quartet/quintet titles that he led during 1928–29; he rarely played trumpet in later years.

Tommy Dorsey kept busy during the early Depression years working in the studios and co-leading the Dorsey Brothers Orchestra as a recording band starting in 1928. In 1932 the group (as an octet with trumpeter Bunny Berigan) recorded TD's future theme song, "I'm Getting Sentimental Over You." In 1934 Tommy and Jimmy Dorsey teamed up to form a working band, but it was only a matter of time before the siblings (who loved each other but could not stop fighting over trivial matters) broke up their musical relationship. Tommy Dorsey then took over the Joe Haymes Orchestra and had many successes during the next decade, getting back together with Jimmy in a new Dorsey Brothers Orchestra in the 1950s.

DORSEY BROTHERS ORCHESTRA

Tommy and Jimmy Dorsey, who first played music together as children, started co-leading record dates under the title of the Dorsey Brothers Orchestra in 1928. Their records of 1928–33 ranged from superior dance music and commercial ballads to hot jazz; sidemen included trumpeter Leo McConville, Glenn Miller, Bud Freeman, Adrian Rollini, Arthur

Schutt, Frank Signorelli, Eddie Lang, Joe Tarto, Chauncey Morehouse, Stan King, and most (by 1931) notably Bunny Berigan. The orchestra also backed up Bing Crosby, Mildred Bailey, and Ethel Waters on record dates.

In 1934 Tommy and Jimmy Dorsey decided to forgo their jobs in the studios and make the Dorsey Brothers Band a working unit. For a year they had increasing success, with Glenn Miller providing many arrangements and with vocals provided by Bob Crosby (succeeded in the spring of 1935 by Bob Eberle) and Kay Weber. How this particular ensemble would have fared with the competition of the swing era is not known, for in May 1935, while playing at the Glen Island Casino, the battling Dorseys had an argument over the tempo of "I'll Never Say 'Never Again' Again" and Tommy stormed off the bandstand. Both brothers would have major successes in the swing era, but that is another story!

7 The Dorsey Brothers Orchestra, Vol. 1—1928/Feb. 14, 1928–Nov. 21, 1928/Jazz Oracle 8004
8 The Dorsey Brothers Orchestra, Vol. 2—1929–1930/Jan. 26, 1929–Jan. 13, 1930/Jazz Oracle 8005
8 The Dorsey Brothers Orchestra, Vol. 3—1930–1933/Nov. 7, 1930–Apr. 8, 1933/Jazz Oracle 8006

All of the Dorsey Brothers Orchestra's recordings of 1928–31 (including alternate takes) are on these three perfectly realized CDs, plus the siblings' specialty numbers from 1932–33. From the start, the Dorseys' recordings were essentially hot dance music rather than freewheeling jazz. Most of their selections utilize a medium-size orchestra (some use additional personnel), arranged ensembles, a vocal (which is often mediocre), and short solos from the co-leaders. Best on *Vol. 1* are "Mary Ann," "My Melancholy Baby," and two numbers ("It's Right Here for You" and "Tiger Rag") that feature Tommy Dorsey jamming on trumpet with a rhythm section that includes Eddie Lang. The most ambitious selection is the two-part "Was It a Dream" by the Dorsey Concert Orchestra, but it gets interesting only near its conclusion. *Vol. 2* has Bing Crosby

guesting on three numbers for the January 26, 1929, session (including "Let's Do It" and "My Kinda Love"). Tommy Dorsey (who played almost as much trumpet as trombone during 1929 before largely giving the former instrument up) has two more features with a rhythm section ("Daddy, Change Your Mind" and "You Can't Cheat a Cheater") but is overshadowed by Jimmy Dorsey's two outstanding showcases ("Beebe" and "Praying the Blues"). In addition, there is another two-part recording ("Lover, Come Back to Me") that does not come across as well as "Was It a Dream," various dance band numbers, and a hot version of "Breakaway."

Vol. 3 has 15 more dance band numbers (some of which were issued under the band name of the Travelers) with mediocre vocals by Scrappy Lambert, Wes Vaughan (who is stuck singing "I Can Make Most Anything but I Can't Make a Man!"), Elmer Feldkamp, and Tony Sacco. Earlier sessions had also featured Smith Ballew, Irving Kaufman, Seger Ellis, and Bill Dutton; only Bing Crosby was listenable. "Sweet and Hot," "Parkin' in the Moonlight," and "Home" are among the best of the numbers on *Vol. 3*, and happily Bunny Berigan is heard (often taking short solos) on the dozen from 1931. His talent was obvious even at this early point. *Vol. 3* concludes with Jimmy Dorsey featured on two versions apiece of "Beebe" and "Oodles of Noodles" (the latter's middle section would later become his theme song, "Contrasts"), while Tommy Dorsey is showcased on three renditions of the rather intriguing "Three Moods" (which partly shows off his background in Arthur Pryor-type prejazz music) and two of the Gershwin ballad "Maybe."

8 Mood Hollywood/Sept. 24, 1932–Oct. 17, 1933/Hep 1005
7 Harlem Lullaby/ Feb. 1933–July 1933/Hep 1006
5 Best of the Big Bands/Sept. 14, 1932–Apr. 23, 1934/Columbia/Legacy 48908

The two Hep CDs pick up where the Jazz Oracle series ends off. Seven songs (plus four alternate takes) feature the Dorsey Brothers in an octet, with the great swing trumpeter Bunny Berigan often stealing the show (particularly on "Someone Stole Gabriel's Horn"). The original rendition of "I'm Getting Sentimental Over You" is also included (in two versions) with a vocal by Jean Bowes. *Mood Hollywood* concludes with an orchestra date arranged by Bill Challis that has vocals by Johnny Mercer, Mildred Bailey, and Jerry Cooper. On *Harlem Lullaby*, the Dorsey Brothers group (the same octet with Berigan) accompanies Bing Crosby on three numbers (including two takes of "Stay on the Right Side of the Road") and Mildred Bailey for eight songs (highlighted by "There's a Cabin in the Pines"). There are also four numbers in which the Dorsey Brothers Orchestra interacts with Ethel Waters (including the original version of "Stormy Weather"). Although the Dorseys are purely in a supportive role, they make their presence felt many times throughout these vintage vocal recordings.

During 1934–35, the Dorsey Brothers Orchestra recorded around 120 titles, but only a scattered few have been reissued coherently. The generically titled *Best of the Big Bands*, instead of concentrating on the working band's output, skips all over the place, with 11 of its 16 titles actually being from the 1932–33 studio groups and only five cuts (four of which have dull vocals) from the actual orchestra. To be fair, most of the Dorsey Brothers' big band's work was made for Decca (which has largely neglected those recordings), but the title to the Columbia CD is quite inaccurate. Get the Jazz Oracle and Hep releases instead.

LPS TO SEARCH FOR

The Decca Sessions (MCA 1505) is rather chintzy, with just ten selections (under a half-hour of music) and graphics so ugly that it is difficult to read the personnel listing. However, the selections (dating from August 1934 to February 1935) are among the more jazz-oriented recordings by the Dorsey Brothers Orchestra, including "Dippermouth Blues,"

"St. Louis Blues," "Milenberg Joys," and "Honeysuckle Rose."

JOHNNY DUNN

b. Feb. 19, 1897, Memphis, TN, d. Aug. 20, 1937, Paris, France

The evolution of jazz was so rapid in the 1920s that Johnny Dunn, who was considered one of the pacesetters among cornetists in 1921, was thought of as hopelessly out of date in 1926! Dunn went to Fisk University in Nashville and had a solo act in Memphis, where he was discovered by W.C. Handy. He became a member of Handy's band in 1917 and then came to New York. His feature on "Sergeant Dunn's Bugle Call Blues" (the basis for "Bugle Call Rag") gave him some fame. He was one of the pioneers at creating wa-wa effects with the plunger mute, and his double-time breaks, although rhythmically inflexible (and rather repetitive), created a sensation.

Dunn was a member of Mamie Smith's Jazz Hounds during 1920–21 (appearing on many of Smith's records) and accompanied Edith Wilson in the show *Put and Take*. During 1921–23 Dunn recorded 18 selections with Wilson and 14 instrumentals with his Original Jazz Hounds. He worked with Will Vodery's Plantation Orchestra in 1922 and first visited Europe in 1923 with the *Dover to Dixie* revue. However, Dunn failed to evolve with the times, and the Chicago musicians (many of whom were originally from New Orleans) were beginning to surpass the more overconfident New Yorkers. During a visit to Chicago, Dunn saw Louis Armstrong playing at the Dreamland and wanted to show him up. He went onstage, asked for Armstrong's horn, and tried to sit in. It was not until he played the first couple of notes that he realized that the song was in seven sharps!

In 1926, Dunn was back in Europe, playing with *The Blackbirds of 1926* show and recording in London with the Plantation Orchestra. In the United States in 1927, he led a short-lived big band. In

1928 Dunn made his last and finest recordings, four numbers with Jelly Roll Morton (including "You Need Some Lovin' " and "Sergeant Dunn's Bugle Call Blues") and two (including the rollicking "What's the Use of Being Alone") with the twin pianos of James P. Johnson and Fats Waller. Although his playing on both dates was quite effective and he was still just 31, Dunn's contributions to jazz history were over. He rejoined Lew Leslie's *Blackbirds* company and moved permanently back to Europe. Johnny Dunn spent the remainder of his life playing in Europe (including leading a group called the New Yorkers) in obscurity.

7 Johnny Dunn & Edith Wilson, Vol. 1/Sept. 13, 1921–Sept. 29, 1922/RST 1522

8 Johnny Dunn, Vol. 2/Dec. 1922–Mar. 26, 1928/RST 1523

9 Johnny Dunn/Sept. 13, 1921–Mar. 26, 1928/Frog 33

Every Johnny Dunn recording (except for his dates with Mamie Smith) are on the two RST CDs. *Vol. 1* has Dunn playing a supporting role behind singer Edith Wilson on 16 selections, mostly vaudevillian-type blues, including "He May Be Your Man but He Comes to See Me Sometimes." Wilson was a good singer for the time period but certainly not in Bessie Smith's (or even Mamie Smith's) league. The other eight numbers are of greater interest (particularly the original version of "Bugle Blues") since they are instrumentals featuring Johnny Dunn's Original Jazz Hounds. However, *Vol. 2* is a much more interesting set overall. There are only two Edith Wilson cuts, Dunn is heard leading his Jazz Hounds on eight selections (including "Jazzin' Babies Blues" and "I Promise Not to Holler, but Hey! Hey!"), and there are two numbers in which he is backed just by pianist Leroy Tibbs and banjoist Samuel Speed. In addition, Dunn's 1926 session with the Plantation Orchestra is here, along with his 1928 recordings with Jelly Roll Morton, James P. Johnson, and Fats Waller.

The Frog CD skips all of the Edith Wilson recordings and leaves out one of Dunn's early dates (which resulted in "Put and Take" and "Mournful Blues") but adds a second take of "Sergeant Dunn's Bugle Call Blues" from the Morton session and otherwise has everything that is on the RST releases. Since the Edith Wilson selections are not that significant, with the exception of the two left-out Dunn cuts, this CD gives listeners the "complete" Johnny Dunn and is the logical acquisition.

HONORE DUTREY

b. 1894, New Orleans, LA, d. July 21, 1935, Chicago, IL

Honore Dutrey, a fine ensemble player who had a distinctive tone of his own, played trombone alongside King Oliver, Louis Armstrong, and Johnny Dodds in Oliver's Creole Jazz Band in 1923. He had started out working in New Orleans, including with Oliver (as early as 1907), the Melrose Brass Band (1910), John Robichaux, and a group co-led by Buddy Petit and Jimmie Noone. After a long stint with the Silver Leaf Orchestra (1913–17), Dutrey served in the Navy during World War I. An accident in the powder room of a ship permanently damaged his lungs, and Dutrey was often short of breath during his remaining years. After his discharge, he moved to Chicago and resumed playing (using an inhaler), working with Oliver off and on during 1920–24. Dutrey led a band during the first half of 1924 and later worked with Carroll Dickerson, Johnny Dodds, and Louis Armstrong's Stompers (with whom he recorded "Chicago Breakdown" in 1927). Honore Dutrey (who recorded with Richard M. Jones, the Chicago Footwarmers, and Johnny Dodds during 1928–29) retired from music in 1930 and died at the age of 40 due to his weak lungs.

CLIFF EDWARDS

b. June 14, 1895, Montreal, Quebec, Canada, d. July 17, 1971, Hollywood, CA

Although it has rarely been acknowledged, Cliff Edwards (best known as "Ukulele Ike") was one of the very first jazz singers on record (no significant male jazz vocalist preceded him), and he was documented scatting a couple of years before Louis Armstrong recorded "Heebie Jeebies." Edwards, who sang and played ukulele and kazoo, left home as a teenager to work in show business. He started out working in St. Louis-area bars, struggled for quite a few years, became quite successful in vaudeville, and graduated to Broadway shows. In 1924, Edwards (who often sang in a falsetto voice) introduced "Fascinatin' Rhythm" in the Gershwin show *Lady Be Good*. He was one of the stars of the *Ziegfeld Follies of 1927*, introduced "I'll See You in My Dreams," and made "Singin' in the Rain" famous in the film *The Hollywood Revue of 1929*.

Edwards first recorded in 1922 on kazoo with Bailey's Lucky Seven and Ladd's Black Aces. During 1923–33 he recorded over 125 titles, often interacting with top jazz musicians, including Adrian Rollini, Red Nichols, Miff Mole, Jimmy Dorsey, and Eddie Lang. He was one of the few male singers on records during that era that are still listenable; most others sound like rejected opera singers, second-rate boy tenors, or tone-deaf drunks! But unfortunately in the 1930s, Edwards became a not-too-successful gambler and an alcoholic with large alimony payments. He worked as a B-movie actor (appearing in reportedly 105 films, usually as weak comedy relief), drank and gambled away all of his earnings, and largely threw away his career.

In 1939 Edwards had what should have been a major break, being cast as the voice of Jiminy Cricket in the film *Pinocchio* (singing "When You Wish Upon a Star"). But other than making some radio transcriptions in the mid-1940s, he slipped away after the film was completed. In the 1950s Ukulele Ike made another comeback, singing on a Dixieland-flavored album in 1956 for the Disney label, making some children records, and being employed for a time by Disney. But again he drank away his opportunities. Cliff Edwards spent most of his later years in complete obscurity, poverty, and an alcoholic haze.

LPS TO SEARCH FOR

Cliff Edwards is long overdue to have his more significant recordings reissued on CD. The only CDs that are readily available are *Singing in the Rain* (Audiophile 17), which contains some of his radio transcriptions of 1943, and *Ukulele Ike Sings Again* (Disney 60408), his surprisingly effective 1956 set, which finds him singing in a good-humored and largely unchanged style from the 1920s.

Of his LPs, *Cliff Edwards and His Hot Combination 1925–26* (Retrieval 203) features Ukulele Ike singing mostly obscurities in spirited fashion, assisted by Red Nichols, Miff Mole, Dick McDonough, Adrian Rollini, and Frankie Trumbauer; the only standards among the 18 songs are "Remember," "Dinah," "Clap Hands, Here Comes Charlie," and "Sunday," but several of the others deserved to be. *The Vintage Recordings of Cliff Edwards* (Totem 205) dates from 1928–34 (with two test pressings from 1944) and includes "I'll See You In My Dreams," "It's Only a Paper Moon," "I Can't Give You Anything but Love," and "Singin' in the Rain." *I'm a Bear in a Lady's Boudoir* (Yazoo 1047) has a couple of rare "party" records from the 1930s along with 11 songs from 1924–30, including "Hard-Hearted Hannah," the two-part "Stack O' Lee," "It Had to Be You," and a repeat of "I'll See You in My Dreams." Also worth checking out is *I Want a Girl* (Totem 1014), which is mostly radio performances from 1944.

But considering his popularity during his prime years, it is surprising that no collectors' jazz label has really dug into Cliff Edwards' recorded legacy and fully reissued his early groundbreaking recordings.

FRED ELIZALDE

b. Dec. 12, 1907, Manila, Philippines, d. Jan. 16, 1979, Manila, Philippines

Fred Elizalde was one of the first musicians based in England to make an impression in the jazz world, although his career in jazz was actually quite brief.

Born in the Philippines, he began playing piano as an infant and composed a minuet when he was four! Elizalde had extensive classical training in three countries: England, Spain, and the United States (attending Stanford in California), making his recording debut in Hollywood with eight selections in June 1926. While attending Cambridge University in England later in 1926, he became the leader of the Quinquaginta Ramblers, playing piano and arranging. After leaving in June 1927, Elizalde freelanced as an arranger.

Elizalde opened at London's Savoy Hotel in 1928 with a group comprising both English and American musicians (including such former members of the California Ramblers as Adrian Rollini, Bobby Davis, and Chelsea Quealey plus Fud Livingston and later on tenor-saxophonist Arthur Rollini). The band (which recorded frequently during 1928–29) grew gradually until it was 21 pieces at its height. But because jazz was far from accepted in England at the time, its contract at the Savoy was not renewed in September 1928. After a tour of England and Scotland, in late 1929 Elizalde broke up the orchestra.

Fred Elizalde studied classical music in Spain and under Maurice Ravel in France (1930–32), made a few final jazz recordings (mostly piano solos) in England during 1932–33, and then spent the rest of his life playing and composing classical music.

8 The Best of Fred Elizalde and His Anglo American Band/ Jan. 15, 1928–Dec. 4, 1929/Retrieval 79011

Fred Elizalde's big band recorded 39 selections in 1928 and four others in 1929. Twenty-two of its best recordings are on this single CD. Featured are such fine players as trumpeters Chelsea Quealey and Norman Payne, Bobby Davis on clarinet and alto, Adrian Rollini (on bass sax, goofus, and hot fountain pen), Fud Livingston, Arthur Rollini, and guitarist Al Bowlly (who would become famous in England in the 1930s) on three vocals. Elizalde takes some piano solos and provided the arrange-

ments, which are mostly quite jazz-oriented, making this the finest non-American jazz orchestra of the 1920s.

DUKE ELLINGTON

b. Apr. 29, 1899, Washington, DC, d. May 24, 1974, New York, NY

Edward Kennedy "Duke" Ellington's accomplishments during the 1926–32 period as composer, arranger, pianist, and bandleader are so large that, if he had passed away when he was in his mid-thirties, he would still be remembered today. Fortunately he lived several decades longer and never lost his creativity or his hunger to create new music.

Growing up in Washington, D.C., Ellington studied piano when he was seven. For a time it looked as if he would be an artist (he studied art in high school), and he was offered an art scholarship to Brooklyn's Pratt Institute. However, by then his main interest was music, so he turned the scholarship down. Intrigued by the ragtime and stride pianists that he heard around D.C., Ellington (who earned the lifelong name of "Duke" due to his suave and sophisticated nature) did his best to emulate the keyboardists. He also slowed down James P. Johnson piano rolls to half-speed so he could copy the fingering. In 1917 he wrote his first composition, "Soda Fountain Rag." Ellington, who during a period earned a living as a sign painter, was wise enough to put a very large ad in the Yellow Pages about his band, even before he had a regular group! By 1918 he was supplying several bands a night for parties and dances, making cameo appearances with each of the groups. At the same time, Duke hurriedly worked to improve his piano technique and repertoire. But where he gained his genius for composing and arranging from is not known and probably cannot be explained.

After several years of working around D.C., in 1923 Ellington first went to New York, traveling up North with Sonny Greer and Otto Hardwicke to join Wilbur Sweatman's band. But the gig did not

As composer, arranger, and bandleader, pianist Duke Ellington was leading the way by 1928.

last long and, after a period of struggling, the trio returned home. A few months later, Elmer Snowden formed the Washingtonians, a group consisting of his banjo, Hardwicke, Greer, Arthur Whetsol, and Fats Waller. However, by the time the musicians arrived in New York, Waller had unaccountably left town. Snowden immediately sent to Washington, D.C., for Ellington to fill the piano spot. The Washingtonians worked in New York for a few months. But in early 1924 a dispute over money resulted in Snowden's being ousted and Ellington's becoming the band's leader.

Within a short time, Duke Ellington and the Washingtonians were playing regularly at the Hollywood Club (which was soon renamed the Kentucky Club), an association that lasted for three years. When Whetsol decided to return to Washington,

D.C., to attend medical school, Bubber Miley took his place. The addition of Miley to the formerly sweet band (with Charles Irvis soon joining on trombone) gave the orchestra a unique "jungle" sound featuring unusual tone colors and sounds. For a few months in 1924, Sidney Bechet (Ellington's favorite musician) was also in the Washingtonians, although unfortunately that version of the band never recorded.

Ellington gained important experience writing the score for the *Chocolate Kiddies* revue, which ran for two years in Germany (1924–26). In November 1924 his sextet (with Fred Guy on banjo as Snowden's replacement) recorded two impressive numbers ("Choo Choo" and "Rainy Nights"), but this was a premature start. The band's next four sessions (1925–26) had shifting personnel, and the eight resulting songs were erratic and surprisingly primitive. But on November 29, 1926, with the recording of "East St. Louis Toodle-oo" (Ellington's theme song until 1941) and "Birmingham Breakdown," the Duke Ellington sound was born. The personnel of the band by then consisted of Miley, Louis Metcalf, Tricky Sam Nanton (who replaced Irvis and built upon his innovations), Hardwicke, Prince Robinson on tenor, Ellington, Guy, Bass Edwards on tuba, and Greer.

The year 1927 was the turning point for Ellington. Irving Mills became Duke's manager, helping the band achieve and maintain a busy recording schedule with quite a few labels. "Black and Tan Fantasy" and "Creole Love Call" (Adelaide Hall's singing on the latter is considered the first wordless vocal) debuted, and Harry Carney (the band's baritonist until 1974!), Rudy Jackson, and Wellman Braud all joined Ellington. Most importantly, the orchestra passed an audition at the Cotton Club and became the famous club's house band, starting on December 4, 1927, continuing regularly into 1931 and on an occasional basis throughout the 1930s. Working at the Cotton Club meant that Ellington's orchestra was broadcasting regularly (becoming well known in the process), and he had the opportunity to develop his talents as an arranger-composer, writing material for both his orchestra and a bit for the club's famous floor shows.

During 1928, Duke Ellington's band became quite famous, eventually being billed as his "Famous Orchestra." Barney Bigard took over on clarinet, Johnny Hodges became Duke's alto soloist, and among the Ellington songs receiving their first recordings were "Jubilee Stomp," "Black Beauty," and "The Mooche." In January 1929, Bubber Miley's alcoholism and unreliability resulted in his being one of the few musicians that Ellington ever fired; Cootie Williams took his place. That year, Ellington made his debut on films in the 1929 short *Black and Tan*. Louis Metcalf departed, Arthur Whetsol returned, and Freddie Jenkins joined on

third trumpet, with Juan Tizol becoming the band's valuable valve trombonist. The orchestra recorded constantly, with 1930 bringing "Old Man Blues" (which Ellington and his band performed in the Amos and Andy movie *Check and Double Check*), "Rocking in Rhythm," and a major hit in "Mood Indigo."

While the Depression slowed down or short-circuited the careers of many other top black jazz musicians, Duke Ellington continued to grow in stature. In 1929 he had recorded his first extended piece, a two-sided jam on "Tiger Rag." In 1931 his two-part "Creole Rhapsody" inspired a lot of discussion about jazz as an art form and "serious" music. The year 1932 found him writing "It Don't Mean a Thing If It Ain't Got That Swing" (which was the debut for his longtime singer Ivie Anderson), while his version of "The Sheik of Araby" featured Ellington's new trombonist, Lawrence Brown. In 1933 "Sophisticated Lady" and "Drop Me Off in Harlem" were introduced and the Duke Ellington Orchestra for the first time visited Europe, where the bandleader was rightfully considered a genius.

Although he had already made his place in jazz history with his famed "jungle band," Duke Ellington (who had 41 more years of accomplishments ahead of him) was just getting started!

7 The Birth of a Band, Vol. 1/Nov. 1924–Dec. 1926/EPM 5104

The Birth of a Band is well titled, for this French CD has every Duke Ellington record prior to 1927. Included is his lone piano roll ("Jig Walk"), the eight early numbers by the orchestra (including "Choo Choo" and "Rainy Nights"), and dates in which Duke backs Alberta Hunter, Jo Trent, Sonny Greer (who sings on "Oh, How I Love My Darling"), Florence Bristol, Irving Mills, and Alberta Jones. The CD concludes with the Ellington Orchestra finding its sound during November–December 1926 with "East St. Louis Toodle-oo," "Birmingham Breakdown," "Immigration Blues," and two takes of "The Creeper." Although some of the early band performances are rather weak, this disc does Ellington collectors a major service by making everything available.

⭐ **The Centennial Edition**/Jan. 10, 1927–Dec. 1, 1973/RCA 09026–63386
🎱 **Early Ellington**/Oct. 26, 1927–Jan. 10, 1934/Bluebird 6852
7️⃣ **Jungle Nights in Harlem**/Dec. 19, 1927–Jan. 9, 1932/Bluebird 2499
7️⃣ **Jubilee Stomp**/Mar. 26, 1928–May 9, 1934/Bluebird 66038

During 1927–32, Duke Ellington recorded around 280 performances, including alternate takes and multiple versions of the same song (often re-arranged) on different days. All of the priceless music is owned by either RCA/BMG, Universal/Decca, or Sony/Columbia. The remarkable 24-CD set called *The Centennial Edition* has every selection that Ellington recorded for RCA Victor over a 46-year period. The first seven discs cover the 1927–34 period and allegedly will someday be issued as a separate set. Since Ellington's best work overall from this period was for Victor, hopefully this music will become available in that fashion. But true Ellington collectors will want to get this limited-edition 24-CD box anyway while it is still around; it cannot be improved upon.

The only single CDs that have been released thus far that focus on Duke's early Victor recordings are all quite incomplete and overlap in chronology (often splitting up a particular session between a couple CDs), although no individual performance is duplicated. *Early Ellington*, which contains "Black and Tan Fantasy," "Creole Love Call," "Black Beauty," "Mood Indigo," and "Rockin' in Rhythm," is the best overall. *Jungle Nights in Harlem* has some offbeat material, including the two-part "A Night at the Cotton Club" (narrated by Irving Mills), and a pair of three-song medleys, while *Jubilee Stomp* includes a classic version of "Bugle Call Rag" and a variety of atmospheric mood pieces.

🔟 **Early Ellington**/Nov. 29, 1926–Jan. 20, 1931/GRP/Decca 640
9️⃣ **Okeh Ellington**/Mar. 22, 1927–Nov. 8, 1930/Columbia 46177

All of Duke Ellington's 67 performances for labels now owned by Universal are on the three-CD *Early Ellington*, starting with the initial version of "East St. Louis Toodle-oo" and including such tunes as "Black Beauty," "The Mooche," the two-part "Tiger Rag," "Wall Street Wail," "Cotton Club Stomp," "Mood Indigo," and "Creole Rhapsody." Since the RCA box is so expensive and its samplers fall short of definitive, this three-fer is the perfect place to begin collecting recordings from the first period of Duke Ellington.

On nearly the same par as *Early Ellington* is the two-CD *Okeh Ellington*, which has the master takes (but unfortunately not the alternates) from Duke's 50 recordings for the Okeh (now Sony) label during 1927–30. Containing some of the same titles as the Victors (but often with different frameworks), highlights include "Black and Tan Fantasy," "Sweet Mama," "Doin' the New Low-Down," "Saturday Night Function," "Double Check Stomp," "Old Man Blues," and "Mood Indigo."

But missing from all of these reissue sets, in addition to the alternates of the Okehs, are the Sony-owned sessions of 1931–33.

LPS TO SEARCH FOR

They will not be easy to find, but an extensive series of 15 two-LP sets from French CBS that were put out in the 1970s have all of Ellington's recordings (including alternate takes) for the Sony labels. Of greatest relevance to classic jazz is *Vol. 1 1925–1928* (CBS 67264), *Vol. 2 1928–1930* (CBS 68275), *Vol. 3 1930–1932* (CBS 88000), *Vol. 4 1932* (CBS 88035), and *Vol. 5 1932–1933* (CBS 88082). Until Sony gets its act together, these are the best Ellington reissues of the Okeh/Columbia material; each twofer is overflowing with exciting gems.

RUTH ETTING

b. Nov. 23, 1897, David City, NE, d. Sept. 24, 1978

Ruth Etting was a very likable jazz-influenced pop singer who in the late 1920s introduced many standards.

In some ways, Ruth Etting was the Bing Crosby of female singers, although her impact was not on Bing's level. Like Crosby, she was essentially a pop singer of the early 1930s who was influenced by jazz and helped bring jazz phrasing into the mainstream of popular music.

Ruth Etting moved to Chicago in 1915, when she was 17, attending the Chicago Academy of Fine Arts, where she studied costume design. But soon she gained a job as a chorus girl, working as a dancer and an occasional singer. After marrying Martin Snyder (the gangster "Moe the Gimp") in 1922, with his help she landed a job broadcasting with Abe Lyman's orchestra and began to become known. Etting started appearing on records in 1926 (she recorded 203 songs during the next 11 years).

She was billed as "The Recording Sweetheart," and moved to New York, where she appeared in the *Ziegfeld Follies of 1927*, having a hit with "Shakin' the Blues Away." In the Eddie Cantor show *Whoopee!*, she introduced "Love Me or Leave Me," and in 1930's *Simple Simon*, Etting caused a big stir with "Ten Cents a Dance." She also appeared in 35 film shorts and three full-length movies (*Roman Scandals* is the best known), in addition to being a regular fixture on radio. Etting, who occasionally used jazz musicians on her records (Rube Bloom and later Frank Signorelli were her pianists, with Joe Venuti, Eddie Lang, Tommy Dorsey, and Jimmy Dorsey sometimes making appearances), stayed busy until deciding in 1937, for a variety of reasons, to retire.

Ruth Etting made a minor comeback in 1947 when she began hosting a radio show and was still singing in the mid-1950s when a semifictional movie on her life (*Love Me or Leave Me*, starring Doris Day and James Cagney) was released. She permanently retired later in the decade.

8 Ten Cents a Dance/Apr. 14, 1926 – Sept. 29, 1930/Living Era 5008

Although she was not really a jazz singer (since she did not improvise), Ruth Etting had an appealing cry in her voice, could swing, and was a superior interpreter of lyrics. The 20 selections on this excellent sampler CD (which is not programmed in chronological order and unfortunately does not include a complete personnel listing) has many of the highlights of her first four years on records, including "Ten Cents a Dance," "Mean to Me," "Dancing with Tears in My Eyes," "Shakin' the Blues Away," "You're the Cream in My Coffee," and "Love Me or Leave Me."

LPS TO SEARCH FOR

Love Me or Leave Me (Columbia 5050) used to be the definitive Ruth Etting LP. But of its dozen songs, the six main ones are on Living Era's *Ten Cents a Dance. Ruth Etting* (Biograph 11) has nine (out of 14) songs not on the CD, including "Glad Rag Doll," "Ain't Misbehavin'," and "Deed I Do." *Reflections 1927 – 35* (Totem 203) is the best buy of the three LPs, for all 14 songs are "new," including "Varsity Drag," "All of Me," "Everything I Have Is Yours," and "What About Me."

Queen of the Torch Singers (Broadway Intermission 143) is filled with Ruth Etting rarities. The eight studio selections (other than "All of Me") are somewhat obscure, including "Don't Tell Her What Happened to Me" and "Home." In addition, there are six numbers that were cut during the singer's August – September 1936 visit to London (a year before her retirement), five songs taken from the soundtracks of film shorts, and a 1947 rendition of Etting's theme song, "Shine On, Harvest Moon."

JAMES REESE EUROPE

b. Feb. 22, 1881, Mobile, AL, d. May 10, 1919, Boston, MA

James Reese Europe was a pioneering black bandleader who directly preceded jazz. Europe grew up in Washington, D.C., studied piano and violin, and worked as the assistant director of the U.S. Marine Band. In 1904 he moved to New York, where he worked as pianist for and director of musical comedies and traveling shows. Europe formed the Clef Club Orchestra, and during the 1910s his Society Orchestra accompanied dancers Vernon and Irene Castle, including in the show *Watch Your Step* (1912).

Europe's Society Orchestra (which sometimes consisted of trumpet, clarinet, three violins, two pianos, drums, and a full five-piece banjo section) became the first black nongospel group to record in 1913. Although historical revisionists have claimed that his was the first jazz band to make it on records (over three years before the Original Dixieland Jazz Band), a listen to the eight selections that Europe recorded during 1913 – 14 (which include such tunes as "Too Much Mustard," "Down Home Rag," and "Castle Walk") reveal the influence of ragtime rhythms but no real jazz. Hopefully someday these intriguing eight titles (recorded for Victor) will be reissued on the same CD!

The ambitious Europe presented a Carnegie Hall concert featuring 125 musicians and singers nearly a decade before Paul Whiteman's famous Aeolian Concert of 1924. As a lieutenant in the U.S. Army during World War I, Europe directed the 369th Infantry Regiment band (dubbed the Hell-Fighters), which toured Europe. The band had a triumphant run in the United States during the first few months of 1919 and made four record dates (resulting in 24 titles, including "St. Louis Blues," "Darktown Strutters' Ball," "Memphis Blues," and "Clarinet Marmalade") that show the influence of jazz and ragtime although never really cutting loose; Noble Sissle was the orchestra's vocalist. But an argument in Boston came to a violent end when Europe was stabbed to death by his snare drummer, Herbert Wright. Whether James Reese Europe would have made an impact on the jazz world in the 1920s will never be known.

⑧ James Reese Europe's 369th U.S. Infantry "Hell Fighters" Band/Mar. 3, 1919–May 7, 1919/Memphis Archives 7020
⑧ Featuring Noble Sissle/Mar. 3, 1919–May 7, 1919/IAJRC 1012

Both of these CDs contain exactly the same music. The IAJRC set has the selections programmed in chronological order (the Memphis Archives disc has the order shuffled), and IAJRC does a better job of identifying the personnel, but the difference in the booklets (48 pages for Memphis Archives, 12 for IAJRC) means that the edge overall goes to Memphis Archives. As for the music, it includes vocals by Noble Sissle, march rhythms, novelties, rags, waltzes, and future jazz standards. Europe's band at the time comprised four trumpets, four trombones, seven clarinets (!), two saxophones, two baritone horns, tuba, and two drums. The style in general is prejazz dance music, with Europe's versions of such tunes as "St. Louis Blues," "Darktown Strutters' Ball," and "Clarinet Marmalade" hinting at early jazz, almost swinging in spots. Intriguing and historic performances.

STUMP EVANS

b. Oct. 18, 1904, Lawrence, KS, d, Aug. 29, 1928, Douglas, KS

A potentially great saxophonist, Paul "Stump" Evans had a tragically brief life. Nicknamed "Stump" due to his small height, he started out on alto horn, played trombone in his high school band, and changed to alto and baritone in the early 1920s before settling on C-melody sax. Evans worked in Chicago with Bernie Young, King Oliver (1923 and 1926), Jimmy Wade, and Erskine Tate. Along the way he recorded with Oliver, Wade, Young, Tate, Ollie Powers, and most notably Jelly Roll Morton in 1927 (including "Jungle Blues," "Beale Street Blues," and "The Pearls"). But Stump Evans contracted pulmonary tuberculosis and never recovered, dying when he was just 23.

GEECHIE FIELDS

b. 1903, GA, d. 1950s?

Trombonist Julius "Geechie" Fields is remembered primarily for his participation on three record dates by Jelly Roll Morton. Fields was raised in the famous Jenkins Orphanage in South Carolina, touring with the orphanage's band. He moved to New York in 1924 and freelanced with several bands, including those of Earle Howard, Charlie Skeete, and Bill Benford (1929–30). Fields recorded with Thomas Morris (1926) and Clarence Williams (1929) in addition to his Jelly Roll Morton sessions (1928 and 1930). The 1928 Morton date resulted in the trombonist's most famous solo, "Mournful Serenade." Geechie Fields left full-time music in the 1930s, working as a boxing coach and a trainer for an athletics club.

DUDLEY FOSDICK

b. 1902, Liberty, IN, d. June 27, 1957

The first great jazz mellophone soloist (Don Elliott would be the second, 30 years later), Dudley Fosdick was also a very valuable ensemble player. He attended Northwestern University and Columbia University, making his debut playing with his brother Gene Fosdick's Hoosiers, with whom he recorded in 1922. Fosdick, who worked with Ted Weems (1924–25), the Melody Artists, Don Voorhees, and Roger Wolfe (1928–29), is best known for his many recordings with Red Nichols' Five Pennies (and related groups, such as Miff Mole's Molers and the Louisiana Rhythm Kings) during 1928–29; among the highlights are "Avalon," "My Gal Sal," and "On the Alamo."

After the 1920s ended, Dudley Fosdick had a second stint with Ted Weems (1931–33), spent a decade with Guy Lombardo (1936–46), and worked in the studios into the mid-1950s, teaching late in life at the Roerich Academy of Arts. It is a pity that he did not continue as a jazz soloist in the 1930s; the mellophone has yet to catch on!

POPS FOSTER

b. May 18, 1892, McCall, LA, d. Oct. 30, 1969, San Francisco, CA

One of the top bassists of the late 1920s, George "Pops" Foster had a long career and kept the tradition of percussive slap bass solos alive into the late 1960s. Foster moved to New Orleans with his family when he was ten, in 1902. After playing cello for three years, he switched to bass. Foster worked in New Orleans with many groups, including Rosseals' Orchestra (1906), Jack Carey, the Magnolia Orchestra, Kid Ory, the Tuxedo Brass Band, the Eagle Brass Band, Armand Piron, and King Oliver, doubling on tuba so he could perform at parades. Foster played with Fate Marable on riverboats during 1917–21, worked in St. Louis with Charlie Creath and Dewey Jackson, and was part of the Kid Ory (later Mutt Carey) band in Los Angeles (1923–25). After a second period in St. Louis with Creath and Jackson (Foster managed to miss Chicago altogether), the bassist moved in 1928 to New York, where he was briefly with King Oliver.

Pops Foster really came into his own as a member of the Luis Russell Orchestra, being part of one of the great rhythm sections of the era and ranking at the top with Wellman Braud among jazz bassists. Foster's thumping sound was well recorded with Russell during 1929–31 and influenced other bandleaders to replace their tuba with string bass. He stayed with Russell's orchestra long after it was taken over by Louis Armstrong in 1935, lasting until 1940. After that, Pops Foster became an important member of the New Orleans revival jazz movement, playing with (among many others) Sidney Bechet, Art Hodes, Bob Wilber, and Earl Hines (at San Francisco's Hangover Club during 1956–61)

and writing his memoirs *The Autobiography of a New Orleans Jazzman* (published posthumously in 1971).

BUD FREEMAN

b. Apr. 13, 1906, Chicago, IL, d. Mar. 15, 1991, Chicago, IL

From the time Coleman Hawkins recorded his influential solo on "Stampede" with Fletcher Henderson in 1926 until the arrival of Lester Young in New York in late 1936, almost every tenor saxophonist in jazz sounded like a close relative of Hawkins. Lawrence "Bud" Freeman was one of the very few exceptions, a player with a softer tone and an angular style who helped make the tenor sax acceptable in Dixieland settings.

Freeman was a member of the Austin High School Gang that was inspired to start playing jazz after hearing the records of the New Orleans Rhythm Kings and the Original Dixieland Jazz Band. He started on C-melody sax in 1923, switching permanently to tenor in April 1925, but it took him a few years to develop. In his earliest days, Freeman's style was quite primitive and he would often just emphasize one note in his solo, swinging that note until his fellow musicians made fun of him. But by the time he made his recording debut with the McKenzie-Condon Chicagoans in 1927, Freeman nearly had his style together, and he already sounded unlike any other saxophonist.

Freeman worked in Chicago with the Blue Friars, Husk O'Hare's Wolverines, Charles Pearce, and Thelma Terry. Along with many of the other top Chicago players, Freeman moved to New York in late 1927, working with Ben Pollack. On a lark, he sailed to France with Dave Tough in mid-1928, staying a few months before returning home. Back in Chicago, Freeman led his first record date (which resulted in "Crazeology" and "Can't Help Lovin' Dat Man"). In New York the tenor saxophonist worked and recorded with Red Nichols and freelanced during 1929–33, including playing with the orchestras of Roger Wolfe Kahn and Gene Kardos.

Freeman moved back to Chicago in 1933, the year he began to emerge as a mature jazz player, recording his complex original "The Eel" with Eddie Condon. Ironically, although he was the last of the Austin High School Gang to develop into a top-notch musician, Freeman worked more than the other Eddie Condon-associated players during the swing era, being a soloist with the big bands of Joe Haymes (1934–35), Ray Noble (1935), Tommy Dorsey (1936–38), and Benny Goodman (1938). Most of the rest of Bud Freeman's career was spent playing small-group swing and Dixieland, and he was quite active into the late 1980s, living to be 84.

JAN GARBER

b. Nov. 5, 1897, Morristown, PA, d. Oct. 5, 1977

Jan Garber, who was billed as "The Idol of the Airwaves," led one of the top "sweet" bands of the 1930s and '40s, a close competitor to that of Guy Lombardo. However, during the 1924–30 period, Garber's orchestra generally played high-quality dance music along with some hot jazz. Garber attended the University of North Carolina and played violin in the Philadelphia Symphony Orchestra around 1915. He switched to popular music and in 1921 with pianist Milton Davis co-founded the Garber-Davis Orchestra; Chelsea Quealey and Harry Goldfield (later with Paul Whiteman) were the trumpeters. In 1924, Garber and Davis went their separate ways and the Jan Garber Orchestra was formed. During the next six years, Garber's band, although not having any major soloists (other than Jimmy McPartland on one session in 1930), worked and recorded pretty steadily, playing jazz-influenced dance music.

In 1930 Garber began to change his band, and by 1933 his orchestra sounded a great deal like Guy Lombardo's. Except for a flirtation with swing during 1942–43, Jan Garber's importance to jazz had ended.

7 **The Hot Years 1925–30/June 29, 1926–Jan. 24, 1930/The Old Masters 119**

Most of Jan Garber's music would never interest jazz collectors. However, this one CD from The Old Masters will have its appeal to 1920s music fans. The music is melodic, there are some decent solos, and the vocals are generally ok. Among the better songs are "Sister Kate," "Tiger Rag" (taken from a movie soundtrack), "Steppin' Around" (with guest banjoist Harry Reser), "'Round Evening," "She's a Great Great Girl," "When a Woman Loves a Man," and this particular Garber group's one hit, "Baby Face."

ED GARLAND

b. Jan. 9, 1885, New Orleans, LA, d. Jan. 22, 1980, Los Angeles, CA

Bassist Ed "Montudi" Garland lived long enough to be one of the grand old men of jazz. Garland started on drums in his native New Orleans and sometimes played snare or bass drum in parades. As a teenager he switched to tuba and mellophone, later on taking up the string bass while continuing to double on tuba. Garland worked with Buddy Bolden (1904), Freddie Keppard (1908), Kid Ory's Brownskin Babes (by 1910), the Imperial Orchestra, John Robichaux, and the Eagle, Security, Excelsior, and Superior bands. In 1914 Garland moved to Chicago, where he led a group and worked with Manuel Perez, Lawrence Duhe, Freddie Keppard, and Sugar Johnny's Creole Band.

Garland (who by then was strictly a string bassist) was part of the early King Oliver Creole Jazz Band in 1920, visiting the West Coast with Oliver in 1921, and deciding to settle in Los Angeles. He worked and recorded with Kid Ory (including making records accompanying singers Ruth Lee and Roberta Dudley). But because he stayed in Los Angeles rather than returning to Chicago with Ory in 1925, Ed Garland did not become famous and made no other recordings until 1944. Garland played with Mutt Carey (1925–27), led bands, and worked on and off during the 1930s and early '40s, including with Jelly Roll Morton's last, short-lived group in 1940. Ed Garland became part of the New Orleans revival movement as a member of Kid Ory's Creole Jazz Band (1944–55), later working with Earl Hines, Turk Murphy, the Legends of Jazz, and other New Orleans-based jazz musicians, staying active until shortly before his death at age 95. He was the last living link to Buddy Bolden.

THE GEORGIANS

The concept of featuring a small combo taken out of a big band was quite popular during the swing era, with such famous units emerging as the Benny Goodman Trio, Quartet, and Sextet, Artie Shaw's Gramercy Five, and Tommy Dorsey's Clambake Seven. The practice actually originated in the 1920s, first with the Virginians (which was drawn out of the Paul Whiteman Orchestra) and then with the Georgians, an advanced unit headed by trumpeter Frank Guarente.

Guarente (born October 5, 1893, in Montelmilleto, Italy) began playing trumpet while in his native Italy. He moved to the United States in 1910, played in Pennsylvania, and moved to New Orleans in 1914. While there, he traded lessons with King Oliver, teaching Oliver classical technique while King gave Guarente pointers on hot jazz playing. After serving in the Army during World War I, working in Texas, and playing with Charlie Kerr's band in Philadelphia, Guarente joined Paul Specht's orchestra in 1921. In addition to his work with the big band, Guarente (starting in the fall of 1922) directed the Georgians, a septet/octet from Specht's ensemble that had four horns and a three-piece rhythm section that included Arthur Schutt and Chauncey Morehouse. While Specht's orchestra, based at the Hotel Alamac, played at the main ballroom, after the regular job was over the Georgians performed for dancers at the Alamac's nightclub, the Congo Room. Performing arrangements by Guarente (one of the best trumpeters on record

during the era) and Schutt, the Georgians recorded 42 selections during 1922–24 that hold their own with the top jazz bands of the period. The music swings, and the arrangements avoid the wooden quality of most charts of the time.

The Georgians broke up in May 1924 when Guarente went to Europe. During his four years overseas, he led the New Georgians, a successful venture for a time. The trumpeter returned to the United States in 1928, rejoining Specht for two years, but by then his solo style was considered out of date. After leaving Specht, Guarente was used primarily as an anonymous studio player, working with Victor Young's orchestra (1930–36) on radio and as a section player until retiring in 1941. He passed away on July 21, 1942, in New York City.

The name of the Georgians was also used for a variety of studio bands during 1924–29, featuring Leo McConville, Red Nichols, Sylvester Ahola, and Charlie Spivak in Guarente's former spot but without the same artistic success of the original group.

9 **The Georgians 1922–23/Nov. 29, 1922–Nov. 17, 1923/Retrieval 79003**

The Georgians have long been one of the most overlooked bands in early jazz, with Frank Guarente being one of the top unknown trumpeters. This CD has the group's first 24 recordings. In addition to Guarente, the musicians include Ray Stilwell, Russ Morgan, or Archie Jones on trombone, Johnny O'Donnell and one of three other players on reeds, Arthur Schutt, banjoist Russell Deppe, and Chauncey Morehouse. The music (all instrumentals) is of the same high caliber as that of the Original Memphis Five of the period, with the melodic ensembles, concise solos, and strong musicianship showing that there was some excellent jazz to be heard before King Oliver's band recorded. Since there were 20 other selections recorded before Guarente's departure (and 25 additional selections during 1925–29 with other trumpeters), hopefully there will be other volumes released of the Georgians' music in the future.

GEORGE GERSHWIN

b. Sept. 26, 1898, New York, NY, d. July 11, 1937, Beverly Hills, CA

Throughout his relatively brief life, George Gershwin constantly crossed musical boundaries. He was one of America's top songwriters, and his "I Got Rhythm" and "Lady Be Good" became two of the most popular chord changes for jazz improvisers.

From the time he had the hit "Swanee" in the 1919 show *Sinbad* up until 1937, Gershwin was a fixture in American music, constantly invigorating popular music with superior songs written for shows, revues, and Hollywood films. Although not a major jazz improviser himself, Gershwin was quite impressed by the playing of James P. Johnson and Fats Waller and sought to put the feeling of jazz and blues even into his extended and more classical-oriented works. Gershwin worked now and then with Paul Whiteman in the 1920s, writing *Rhapsody in Blue* for Whiteman's 1924 Aeolian Hall concert (performing it himself during the debut and its initial recording) and also composing Concerto in F for Whiteman. One of Gershwin's later projects was the folk opera *Porgy and Bess*, a show that introduced quite a few jazz standards, including "Summertime."

Before his premature death from a brain tumor at the age of 38, many of George Gershwin's songs (quite a few uplifted by the words of his brother, lyricist Ira Gershwin) were on their way to becoming standards, including such gems as "Fascinating Rhythm," "Somebody Loves Me," "Our Love Is Here to Stay," "They Can't Take That Away from Me," "A Foggy Day," "'S Wonderful," "The Man I Love," "Embraceable You," "I've Got a Crush on You," "Nice Work If You Can Get It," and "But Not for Me."

8 The Piano Rolls/Sept. 1916–June 1933/Elektra Nonesuch 79287

7 The Piano Rolls, Vol. Two/Jan. 1916–Mar. 1921/Nonesuch 79370

5 Gershwin Performs Gershwin/June 26, 1931–Apr. 30, 1934/ Music Masters 5062

★ I Got Rhythm—The Music of George Gershwin/Nov. 5, 1923–Mar. 10, 1992/Smithsonian Collection 4–7247

During 1916–27, George Gershwin made around 130 piano rolls, music that has been little heard since the late 1920s. In the early to mid-1990s, two CDs were released by Nonesuch that contain 28 of these performances. *The Piano Rolls* has Gershwin exclusively playing his own pieces (including a two-piano version of *An American in Paris* from 1933). In addition to *Rhapsody in Blue* and some of his early hits ("Sweet and Lowdown," "Swanee," and "Kickin' the Clouds Away"), such obscurities as "Scandal Walk," "Idle Dreams," and "Novelette in Fourths" add to the Gershwin legacy. *Vol. Two* is a bit more unusual, because only two of the 16 selections ("Rialto Ripples" and "From Now On") are Gershwin songs. Overall, this CD puts the emphasis on Gershwin's pianistic skills on such numbers as "Havañola," "Singin' the Blues," "Jaz-o-Mine," "Kangaroo Hop," and "Pastime Rag No. 3."

Gershwin Performs Gershwin has some intriguing moments. He is heard as a pianist on two *Music by Gershwin* radio shows from 1934, including performing his full-length "Variations on 'I Got Rhythm'." Gershwin is also heard playing a couple of other "variations" (of "Fascinating Rhythm" and "Liza") on a 1932 *Rudy Vallee Show*, rehearsing an orchestra in 1931 on his *Second Rhapsody*, and rehearsing a few numbers with the cast of *Porgy and Bess* in 1935. From a jazz standpoint, the piano pieces are of greatest interest, although much of this historic CD (particularly the *Porgy and Bess* section) is really worth hearing only once.

The four-CD Smithsonian box is quite wide ranging, divided into Gershwin and the Popular Song, On Stage and Screen, In the Concert Hall, and Gershwin and Jazz. Although many of the 71 performances are from later decades (only two of the jazz performances fit into the classic jazz era), listeners do get Cliff Edwards' "Fascinating

Rhythm," Ethel Waters' "I Got Rhythm," and Gershwin playing the classic original version of *Rhapsody in Blue* with Paul Whiteman, his three Preludes (1926), and his Variations on "I Got Rhythm" (1934).

GENE GIFFORD

b. May 31, 1908, Americus, GA, d. Nov. 12, 1970, Memphis, TN

Guitarist Gene Gifford was one of the top arrangers of the preswing era, being quite notable for his contributions to the Casa Loma Orchestra. Gifford grew up in Memphis, played banjo in his high school band, and studied arranging. He worked on banjo with Bob Foster in Arkansas, toured with Lloyd Williams and Watson's Bell Hops, first appeared on record in 1927, and switched to guitar while playing with Blue Steele (1928–29). After working with Henry Cato's Vanities Orchestra (1928) and Jean Goldkette, Gifford joined the Orange Blossoms in 1929; the band soon changed its name to the Casa Loma Orchestra.

Gifford played guitar and banjo with the big band through 1933 but was most significant as the Casa Loma's main arranger during 1929–39. Gifford composed such numbers as "Black Jazz," "White Jazz," and the band's theme song, the haunting "Smoke Rings." Although his busy writing was sometimes criticized for sounding a bit mechanical and excitable at faster tempos, it helped set the stage for the swing era and became quite influential; his "Casa Loma Stomp" (from 1930) could have been written and recorded five years later.

Gifford also freelanced as an arranger, contributing charts to other orchestras (including that of Fletcher Henderson) and leading his only record date, in 1935. After leaving the Casa Lomans, Gene Gifford continued in music on just a part-time basis, working as an audio consultant and a radio engineer, ending his life as a music teacher in Memphis.

JEAN GOLDKETTE

b. Mar. 18, 1899, Valenciennes, France, d. Mar. 24, 1962, Santa Barbara, CA

A classical pianist, Jean Goldkette was a very important leader of big bands in the 1920s even though he very rarely played with his own orchestras. Goldkette lived in France, Greece, and Russia as a youth, moving with his family to the United States in 1911. Trained as a concert pianist, he chose to become involved in popular music instead. Goldkette became the musical director of the Benson Orchestra of Chicago, moving in 1921 to Detroit, where at first he ran a second Benson Orchestra. He acquired an unfinished Chinese restaurant, transformed it into the Graystone Ballroom, and used the establishment (which was soon recognized as Detroit's top nightclub) as a home base for his bands. Goldkette had a knack for organizing orchestras, and by the late 1920s his organization (the National Amusement Corp.) controlled over 20 bands. Two would break away and become independent: the Orange Blossoms (which became the Casa Loma Orchestra) and McKinney's Cotton Pickers.

The Jean Goldkette Orchestra first recorded in 1924, with Tommy Dorsey, Jimmy Dorsey, Bill Rank, and Joe Venuti in the personnel. Bix Beiderbecke was briefly in the band in the fall of 1924, but his poor reading skills forced Goldkette to let him go, with the promise that he would be rehired when he could read music much better. Two versions of the Goldkette Orchestra recorded in 1926, and by October Bix was with the stronger group, one whose lineup included Bill Rank, Don Murray, Frank Trumbauer, Venuti, Eddie Lang, Steve Brown, and Chauncey Morehouse plus arranger Bill Challis. That ensemble defeated Fletcher Henderson's orchestra at a "battle of the bands" contest. Unfortunately the Victor label did not allow Goldkette's band to cut loose in the studios, saddling it with guest vocalists who were not part of the band and demanding that the soloists mostly stick to the melody. Because of that policy, only on a few occasions (most notably "My Pretty Girl," "Clementine," and the final chorus of several other numbers when bassist Steve Brown swung the ensembles) did the Goldkette Orchestra hint on records at being the great jazz band that it apparently was in person.

In the fall of 1927, the Jean Goldkette Orchestra broke up, and several of his top players at first joined Adrian Rollini's orchestra before they were eventually signed up by Paul Whiteman. By December 1927, Goldkette was recording with a new orchestra, one that had cornetists Andy Secrest and Sterling Bose. The band lasted until 1929, and other sidemen along the way included trombonist Pee Wee Hunt, Volly DeFaut, and (briefly) Hoagy Carmichael.

Goldkette appeared as a piano soloist with the Detroit Symphony Orchestra in 1930 and then largely dropped out of music, other than occasionally forming bands in the mid-1940s. In later years he worked as an agent and a classical pianist. In 1959 Jean Goldkette (who was still just 60) brought back some of the old arrangements for a record date, *Dance Hits of the '20s in Stereo* (RCA/Camden 548), that utilized studio musicians and just one alumnus, Chauncey Morehouse.

LPS TO SEARCH FOR

The Jean Goldkette Orchestra's recordings with Bix Beiderbecke have been reissued under the cornetist's name. *1924–1929* (The Old Masters 47) has 14 other recordings, seven from before the Bix period (1924 and 1926) and seven from 1927–29, after Beiderbecke had departed. While the early titles (such as "I Want to See My Tennessee," "Where the Lazy Daisies Grow," and "Dinah") often have spots for Tommy Dorsey, Jimmy Dorsey, and Joe Venuti, the later songs include "Here Comes the Showboat" (with a tradeoff by cornetists Andy Secrest, Sterling Bose, and Nat Natoli) and a few numbers arranged by Don Redman. There are still many pre- and post-Bix Goldkette recordings that have yet to be reissued.

BENNY GOODMAN

b. May 30, 1909, Chicago, IL, d. June 13, 1986, New York, NY

Benny Goodman was one of the finest clarinetists of all time and is still a household name 15 years after his death. Although he did not become famous with the general public until 1935, the future "King of Swing" was a major clarinetist in the 1920s too.

Goodman began playing clarinet when he was ten and developed very quickly, taking lessons from Franz Schoepp (who also taught Buster Bailey and Jimmie Noone) for two years. In 1921, when he was 12, BG won a talent contest by imitating Ted Lewis. The following year he joined the Musicians Union and began playing in Chicago with other talented youngsters, including Jimmy McPartland, Bud Freeman, and Frank Teschemacher. Goodman worked with Murph Podolsky, Chuck Walker's Meteorgnoes, and Jules Herbevaux, and on steamboats, meeting Bix Beiderbecke in 1923 (who made a strong impression on him). After stints with Arnold Johnson and Art Kassel (1924–25), in August 1925 the 16-year-old joined Ben Pollack's orchestra.

Goodman traveled to California, back to Chicago, and eventually to New York with Pollack, making his recording debut in December 1926 and working with the drummer's band off and on until September 1929. At that early point, Goodman was a very skilled clarinetist and his sound was recognizable, if sometimes a bit "hotter" and "dirtier" than it would become. He was influenced by Jimmie Noone and Frank Teschemacher but was already showing strong originality. Goodman led four small-group record dates during 1928–29, including recording a humorous imitation of Ted Lewis on "Shirt-Tail Stomp" and heading his first trio session (with pianist Mel Stitzel and drummer Bob Conselman), seven years before the famous Benny

Goodman Trio with Teddy Wilson and Gene Krupa.

After leaving Pollack, Goodman worked with Red Nichols (October 1929–January 1930) and then became a very busy studio musician during the early years of the Depression. He appeared on the radio constantly, made countless recordings as a mostly anonymous sideman (including with Sam Lanin, Nat Shilkret, Meyer Davis, Ben Selvin, and Johnny Green), and played in the pit bands of Broadway shows (such as *Strike Up the Band* and *Girl Crazy*). Goodman, who often doubled on alto or baritone for these commercial sessions, also occasionally recorded in a jazz setting, including with Nichols, Ted Lewis (!), Eddie Lang/Joe Venuti, Adrian Rollini, and the Charleston Chasers, and as a leader. His six record sessions as a leader from 1930–31 were dominated by commercial dance music, but his dates of 1933–34 were much more jazz oriented, sometimes including such sidemen as Jack Teagarden, Billie Holiday (her recording debut), Mildred Bailey, Coleman Hawkins, and Gene Krupa.

Although Goodman made a lucrative living during the Depression years in the studios, he grew tired of playing dance music and had the itch to lead a big band. In 1934 he put together his first orchestra, a 12-piece band that played at Billy Rose's Music Hall, recorded for Columbia, and in November 1934 landed a spot on the NBC radio program *Let's Dance*, often using Fletcher Henderson arrangements. When the show ended in May 1935, Benny Goodman could not have foreseen the sensation his band would cause just three months later when they played at the Palomar Ballroom in Los Angeles, launching the swing era.

8 **B.G. and Big Tea in NYC/Aug. 29, 1929–Oct. 1934/GRP/Decca 609**

Some of Benny Goodman's most rewarding early sessions as a sideman are on this CD. The young clarinetist is heard on eight numbers with Red Nichols' Five Pennies (including "Indiana," "China Boy," and "The Sheik of Araby"), four tunes with Irving Mills' Hotsy Totsy Gang (a 1930 date that also has Bix Beiderbecke in the lineup), five decent selections with Adrian Rollini from 1934, and, best of all, the four exciting numbers with the Joe Venuti-Eddie Lang All-Star Orchestra: "Beale Street Blues," "After You've Gone," "Farewell Blues," and "Someday Sweetheart." Jack Teagarden (who is often the costar) is on all 21 selections, and other notables include Gene Krupa, Joe Sullivan, and Charlie Teagarden.

LPS TO SEARCH FOR

The two-LP set *A Jazz Holiday* (MCA/Decca 4018) duplicates part of *B.G. and Big Tea in NYC* but also contains ten selections with Goodman as a leader in the 1920s, including "Wolverine Blues," "Jungle Blues" (which has his only recording on trumpet), "Shirt-Tail Stomp" (a funny takeoff on Ted Lewis), and two cuts by the very first Benny Goodman Trio: "That's a-Plenty" and "Clarinetitis."

The Sunbeam label was formed in the 1970s, originally to reissue Benny Goodman's recordings. Particularly valuable are the many LPs taken from the clarinetist's early obscure sessions, although some have jazz as a contrast rather than a constant. *The Rare B.G.* (Sunbeam 112) repeats the trio numbers from *A Jazz Holiday* but also has Goodman's sideman appearances with the All-Star Orchestra, Johnny Marvin, Irene Beasley, the Ipana Troubadors, Mills Musical Clowns, Dot Dare (Annette Hanshaw), and the Dixie Daisies, all dating from 1928. *With the Whoopee Makers* (Sunbeam 114) features Goodman, Jimmy McPartland, and Jack Teagarden playing hot dance music, often saddled with so-so vocalists but creating some short solos on such songs as "Futuristic Rhythm," "It's Tight Like That," and "Four or Five Times," often heard in multiple versions. *Benny Goodman on the Side* (Sunbeam 107) dates from 1929–31 and has the clarinetist playing with Jack Pettis, Mills Merry Makers, Carl Fenton, Sammy Fain ("the crooning composer"), James Melton, Art Gillham ("the whispering pianist"), and Phil Hughes' High Hatters.

Although Benny Goodman is listed as the leader of the majority of the sessions on *In a Melotone Manner* (Sunbeam 106) and *Melotone Melodies* (Sunbeam 157), which date from 1930–31, the music is strictly early-Depression dance music, the musicians are taken from the studios, and vocals dominate. *Featuring Benny Goodman Vols. 1–3* (Sunbeam 108, 109, and 110) are in the same vein except that Ben Selvin is the leader (despite the many pseudonyms used). Goodman takes a short solo on each of the 48 numbers (which are mostly from 1931), but the pleasant music contains few moments of hot jazz.

Of greater interest to early-swing collectors are *The Early Years Vols. 1–3* (Sunbeam 138, 139, and 140), recordings that set the stage for Goodman's rise to prominence. *Vol. 1* starts out with dance music from 1931 but also contains dates from 1933 with Jack Teagarden, Gene Krupa, and (on two numbers) Billie Holiday. *Vol. 2* has Goodman's 1934 all-star session with Mildred Bailey and Coleman Hawkins, appearances by Teagarden and Teddy Wilson, and BG's first official big band recording (including two versions of "Bugle Call Rag"). And on *Vol. 3*, after four unusual numbers issued under the name of Harry Rosenthal and using much different instrumentation, Goodman's big band (which was almost recognizable) is heard on their last recordings for the Columbia label, made right before they found fame on the Victor label.

THE GOOFUS FIVE

The Goofus Five, like the Little Ramblers (which recorded for Columbia) and the Five Birmingham Babies (the Pathe label's version), was a quintet taken from the lineup of the California Ramblers. *Goofus* is the name given a miniature saxophone that sounds like a mouth organ and was occasionally played by Adrian Rollini. The band (which recorded for Okeh) originally consisted of Rollini, Bill

Moore, pianist Irving Brodsky, banjoist Tommy Felline, and Stan King. It soon grew beyond five pieces with the addition of Bobby Davis on reeds, tenor saxophonist Sam Ruby, and trombonist Abe Lincoln. In 1926, Chelsea Quealey took over on trumpet. That version of the band (with a few minor personnel changes) stayed intact into the fall of 1927. However, the later recordings by the Goofus Five (from 1928–29) are essentially the full California Ramblers under a different name.

9 **The Goofus Five/May 12, 1926–Aug. 10, 1927/Timeless 1–017**

The prime period of the Goofus Five is documented in full on this CD, which contains all 24 recordings made with the Quealey-Rollini lineup, after cutting 25 earlier selections during 1924–25. Although there are occasional vocals, the emphasis is on heated melodic jazz, featuring a strong frontline (Quealey, Lincoln or Al Philburn on trombone, Davis, Ruby, and Rollini), excellent songs (many of which became standards), and plenty of spirit. The music was not as adventurous as that of Louis Armstrong's Hot Five during the period, but it has its own charm and spirit.

CHARLIE GREEN
b. 1900, Omaha, NE, d. Feb. 1936, New York, NY

One of the finest trombonists of the mid-1920s, Charlie Green was a superior blues player who could also play more complex arrangements. He worked early on with brass bands, the Omaha Night Owls (1920), Red Perkins, carnival bands, and other groups in the Omaha area. In 1924 Green joined the Fletcher Henderson Orchestra. On their recording of "Charlie, My Boy," he proved to be the band's first swinging soloist on records, preceding Louis Armstrong by a few months. In fact, because he emerged before Jimmy Harrison and Jack Teagarden, Green ranks as one of the very first trombonists (along with Miff Mole) to "liberate" his instrument from its earlier percussive roots.

Green was a fixture with Fletcher Henderson (1924–27 and 1928–29), and he appeared on many notable recordings with Bessie Smith during 1924–30 (including "Trombone Cholly"). He also recorded with Perry Bradford (a 1925 session with Louis Armstrong), Ida Brown, Ida Cox, Maggie Jones, Ma Rainey, Clara Smith, Trixie Smith, George Williams, and Leona Wilson.

After leaving Henderson in 1929, Green played with many groups, including June Clark, the *Keep Shufflin' Revue*, Zutty Singleton, Benny Carter (1929–31), Elmer Snowden, Louis Armstrong (1932), Jimmie Noone, McKinney's Cotton Pickers, Sam Wooding, Don Redman, Chick Webb (1932–33 and 1934), Louis Metcalf, and Kaiser Marshall. His death was unexpected and quite avoidable. Unable to get into his home one cold snowy evening, Charlie Green spent the night sleeping in front of his home and froze to death!

SONNY GREER

b. Dec. 13, 1895, Long Branch, NJ, d. Mar. 23, 1982, New York, NY

Duke Ellington's longtime drummer, Sonny Greer was never a virtuoso, but he added an important range of colors and percussive effects to the band, helping to form its "jungle sound." Greer started playing drums while in high school and freelanced around New Jersey. He worked in Washington, D.C., with Marie Lucas in 1919 and met Duke Ellington (who was four years younger) at that time. Greer first played with Ellington in 1920, was part of the Washingtonians during their first unsuccessful visit to New York in 1923, and was with them again when they returned. He would remain associated with Duke Ellington's orchestra for 28 years.

While at the Cotton Club (1927–31), Greer looked very impressive, being placed high up on the stage and surrounded by an expensive setup that included a gong, tympani, skulls, vibes, and chimes in addition to his drums. He was a significant part of the Duke Ellington sound until his drinking and general unreliability resulted in his departing in 1951. Sonny Greer remained active on a part-time basis into the late 1970s, working with Johnny Hodges, Red Allen, Tyree Glenn, and Brooks Kerr although never duplicating his former prominence.

FERDE GROFÉ

b. Mar. 27, 1892, New York, NY, d. Apr. 3, 1972, Santa Monica, CA

Ferde Grofé's writing for Paul Whiteman in the 1920s played a major role in developing the distinctive orchestral sound of the "King of Jazz." Grofé grew up on the West Coast, where he studied piano and violin. At 14 he worked as a pianist in dance halls in the San Francisco area, and a few years later he became a member of the Los Angeles Symphony Orchestra, on viola. Around 1914, Grofé started working with drummer Art Hickman in a large group, helping to develop the concept of big band dance band music.

In 1919 Grofé joined Paul Whiteman's orchestra as arranger and pianist. Though he would soon give up the keyboard position, Grofé was Whiteman's chief writer until 1933, enjoying combining together the rhythms of jazz with elements of classical music. Among his more notable accomplishments were arranging the hit versions of "Japanese Sandman," "Whispering," and "Three O'Clock in the Morning," orchestrating George Gershwin's *Rhapsody in Blue*, and composing *The Grand Canyon Suite*. After leaving Paul Whiteman in 1933, Ferde Grofé wrote for the movie studios.

FRED GUY

b. May 23, 1899, Burkesville, GA, d. Nov. 22, 1971, Chicago, IL

Fred Guy's banjo helped keep the rhythm of the Duke Ellington Orchestra steady during its early days. Guy grew up in New York, worked with Joseph C. Smith's orchestra, and led a band. When

Elmer Snowden departed the Washingtonians in the spring of 1924 and Duke Ellington became its leader, Guy was hired on banjo. Guy (who began doubling on guitar a few years later) can be heard prominently on many of the Ellington records of the late 1920s, although he never soloed. After 1934 he played guitar exclusively, and Guy's importance (and audibility) dropped sharply after that. He was a member of the Duke Ellington Orchestra for 24 years, staying until January 1949. But when Guy departed, Duke never felt compelled to add a rhythm guitarist to his band again. Fred Guy retired to Chicago, where he managed a local ballroom for over 20 years, committing suicide in 1971 after many years in obscurity.

ADELAIDE HALL

b. Oct. 20, 1901, Brooklyn, NY, d. Nov. 7, 1993, London, England

Adelaide Hall, who had a very long career, is remembered primarily for recording "Creole Love Call" with Duke Ellington on October 26, 1927, considered the first wordless vocal in jazz (not counting scat vocals). Hall started working in theaters and shows in the early 1920s, was featured in the chorus line of *Shuffle Along* in 1921, went to Europe in May 1925 with the *Chocolate Kiddies* revue, and appeared in New York in *Desires of 1927*.

Never a member of the Ellington Orchestra, Hall was nevertheless in top form as a guest when she recorded "Creole Love Call" and "The Blues I Love to Sing." She was in *Blackbirds of 1928* on Broadway (helping to introduce "I Can't Give You Anything but Love"), recorded with Lew Leslie's Blackbird Orchestra (1928), visited England in 1931, and in 1932 brought pianist Art Tatum (who made his recording debut with Hall) to New York as her regular accompanist. The singer appeared regularly on stage in the 1930s (including in *Brown Bodies* and *The Cotton Club Revue*), recorded again with Ellington ("I Must Have That Man" and "Baby" in 1932), visited Europe in 1936 (recording with Willie Lewis in Paris), and settled in England, becoming a British citizen in 1938. Adelaide Hall worked steadily in England throughout the remainder of her long life, mostly as a cabaret and show singer.

8 **Hall of Memories/Oct. 26, 1927–June 23, 1939/Conifer 169** This is certainly the one Adelaide Hall CD to get, for it has virtually all of the jazz high points of her career (except for the 1932 reunion session with Duke Ellington). The singer is heard on her 1927 Ellington collaborations, with Lew Leslie's Blackbird Orchestra ("I Must Have That Man" and "Baby"), backed by two piano duo teams (including, on "You Gave Me Everything but Love," Art Tatum and Francis Carter), guesting with the Mills Blue Rhythm Band in 1933, singing two selections with Willie Lewis four years later, and interacting with Fats Waller (who plays organ) on 1938's "That Old Feeling."

FRED "SUGAR" HALL

b. 1898, New York, NY, d. Oct. 6, 1954, New York, NY

A pianist and songwriter, Fred "Sugar" Hall led an underrated series of hot dance band records during 1925–30. Born Fred Arthur Ahl, Hall worked early on with publishing houses as a song plugger and staff composer. During the second half of the 1920s he led over 150 sides, some of which were issued as the Hometowners, the Pennsylvania Melody Syncopators, Arthur Fields and His Assassinators, and the Tin Pan Paraders. During 1926–32, Hall often teamed up with singer Arthur Fields (who is on many of the records) to cowrite songs, the best known of which is "I Got a Code in By Dose." After the Depression made Sugar Hall's style of happy dance music out of vogue, he largely dropped out of music, making his final recordings in 1932.

The 24 selections included on this collectors' CD form a strong sampling of Sugar Hall's recording career. The personnel included Jack Mollick or Mike Mosiello on trumpet (Leo McConville guests on one date), trombonist Harry Blevins, Eddie Grosso on clarinet and alto, banjoist Albert Russo, Al Morse on tuba, Joseph May on drums, Hall on piano and occasional scat vocals, regular vocals by Arthur Fields, and a special treat in the excellent jazz harmonica of Phillip d'Arcy (who also plays violin and second piano). The music includes some notable novelty numbers (such as "What a Funny World This Would Be," "On the Night We Did the Boom-Boom by the Sea," "I'm Wild About Horns on Automobiles," and "She's the Sweetheart of Six Other Guys"). In terms of jazz, the high points are "'Tain't No Sin," "Harmonica Harry," and "Come On, Baby."

LIONEL HAMPTON

b. Apr. 12, 1908, Louisville, KY

The most famous vibraphonist in the world and a major attraction for over 60 years, Lionel Hampton actually began his career as a talented drummer in the 1920s. Hampton grew up in Birmingham, Kenosha (Wisconsin), and Chicago (where he moved with his family in 1916). Early on he played drums in Major N. Clark Smith's Chicago Defender Newsboys' Band. Hampton worked in Chicago as a teenager and took xylophone lessons from Jimmy Bertrand, his idol. In 1928 he moved to California, where he played with the Spikes Brothers and Curtis Mosby's Dixieland Blue-Blowers. As drummer with Paul Howard's Quality Serenaders, Hampton made his recording debut in 1929, and he proved to be one of the most impressive players in the top-notch band.

Next up was an association with Les Hite, who led the orchestra at Sebastian's Cotton Club in Culver City. When Louis Armstrong visited Los Angeles in 1930, he used Hite's big band as a backup group. At a recording session, Armstrong noticed a set of vibes in the studio, and he asked Hampton if he could play a few notes behind him. Luckily, Hamp had been practicing on vibes, and his playing with Armstrong on "Shine" and "Memories of You" rank as the first significant appearances of the vibraphone on a jazz record.

During the first half of the 1930s, Hampton appeared on many movie soundtracks with Hite, studied music at USC, and by 1934 was leading his own band. He can be seen as a masked drummer with Louis Armstrong during "Skeleton in the Closet" in the 1936 film *Pennies from Heaven.* Lionel Hampton was playing in obscurity at the Paradise Café in Hollywood in 1936 when he was seen by Benny Goodman. Fame would be just around the corner!

W.C. HANDY

b. Nov. 16, 1873, Florence, AL, d. Mar. 28, 1958, New York, NY

W.C. Handy was known as "The Father of the Blues." Although not that great a musician himself, he composed quite a few standards, many inspired by the songs and lyrics that he heard performed by street musicians during his travels. William Christopher Handy played cornet with the Bessemer Brass Band and led a vocal quartet at the Columbian Exposition of 1893 in Chicago. He toured as a cornet soloist with Mahara's Minstrels (1896–1903), becoming its musical director. Handy led an orchestra in the South for quite a few years, but it was as a composer that he made his mark. He wrote "Memphis Blues" in 1912; originally it was a campaign song named "Mr. Crump." "St. Louis Blues" (1914) was a huge hit, and it was followed by such future standards as "Yellow Dog Blues" (1914), "Beale Street Blues" (1916), "Ole Miss," "Hesitatin' Blues," and "Careless (or Loveless) Love" (1921).

In 1917 Handy took his Memphis Orchestra to New York, where he recorded during 1917, 1919, and 1922–23. Handy's cornet playing was very straight, even for the time period. And although his ensemble performed mostly his compositions, from the jazz standpoint it was weak. After his band broke up in 1923, other than a short stint with Jelly Roll Morton in 1926, Handy worked primarily as a music publisher for his Handy Brothers Music Company. He did occasional theater work during 1932–36 and in 1939 recorded four of his songs with an all-star septet, but those mostly showed that his playing had not advanced since 1917 and that he had no conception of jazz. An eye disease caused him to gradually go blind by the early 1940s. W.C. Handy (who published his autobiography, *Father of the Blues*, in 1941) was in failing health during his later years before passing away at the age of 84.

4 W.C. Handy's Memphis Blues Band/Sept. 21, 1917–May 1923/Memphis Archives 7006

Out of print for many decades and long a question mark to collectors, 16 of W.C. Handy's recordings (including his ten earliest) are reissued on this 1994 CD. Unfortunately the music does not live up to expectations. The songs (nearly all of them Handy compositions) are excellent, but the playing by the band (consisting of Handy's very stiff cornet, a trombone, four reeds, three violinists including Darnell Howard, piano, tuba, string bass, and drums) is quite awkward rhythmically, and the solos are nothing to brag about. It is interesting to hear such early versions of "St. Louis Blues," "Yellow Dog Blues," and "Muscle Shoals Blues," but the music overall is disappointing.

ANNETTE HANSHAW

b. Oct. 18, 1910, New York, NY, d. Mar. 13, 1985, New York, NY

One of the first great female jazz singers (although she is often left out of jazz history books), the teenaged Annette Hanshaw in the late 1920s ranked near the top of her field, along with Bessie Smith, Ethel Waters, the Boswell Sisters, and Mildred Bailey. She gave proper feeling to the lyrics, sometimes wrote additional verses to songs, improvised, and always swung. If she had had the desire to continue, Hanshaw would be much more famous today.

Annette Hanshaw began her recording career when she was just 15 (discovered by her future husband, Herman Rose, who was the A&R man for the Pathe label), sounding quite mature from the start. Billed as "The Personality Girl," her trademark became saying "That's all!" (which she had spontaneously ad-libbed on one of her first recording dates) at the end of her records. Hanshaw's recordings of 1926–34 are much more jazz oriented than those of Ruth Etting and feature such major sidemen as Red Nichols, Miff Mole, Jimmy Lytell, Adrian Rollini, Joe Venuti, Eddie Lang, Vic Berton, Benny Goodman, Manny Klein, Phil Napoleon, Jimmy Dorsey, Tommy Dorsey, Jack Teagarden, and Muggsy Spanier. Her recordings of "I'm Gonna Meet My Sweetie Now," "It All Depends on You," "Get Out and Get Under the Moon," "Daddy, Won't You Please Come Home," "Lovable and Sweet," and "My Future Just Passed" are particularly definitive.

In addition, Hanshaw (who on records sometimes expertly mimics Helen Kane, the boop-boop-a-doop girl) recorded under such pseudonyms as Gay Ellis, Patsy Young, and Dot Dare and appeared regularly on radio. But the singer hated to perform in public, and in 1936 (at the age of 25 and two years after her last recordings) she retired from singing. Annette Hanshaw worked outside of music during the remainder of her life (never thinking of making a comeback) and was always surprised when record collectors who tracked her down knew who she was.

7 Volume 5, 1928–29/June 12, 1928–Jan. 17, 1929/Sensation 769 748 022
10 Volume 6, 1929/Feb. 20, 1929–Sept. 20, 1929/Sensation 769 748 023

One of the great jazz singers of the era, Annette Hanshaw was remarkably young considering her accomplishments.

7 Lovable but Sweet/Sept. 12, 1926–Feb. 3, 1934/Living Era 5220

The Canadian Sensation label is scheduled to re-issue every Annette Hanshaw recording, on ten CDs. *Volume 5* and *Volume 6* are the only ones out as of this writing. The former set begins two years after the singer began recording. Unfortunately ten of its 25 selections find Hanshaw singing with Frank Ferera's Hawaiian Trio, a group consisting of steel guitar, conventional guitar, and ukulele. Although Hanshaw sounds fine, she is mostly in a supporting role and there is an awful lot heard from the steel guitar! The other 15 selections (which include "I Can't Give You Anything but Love," "That's Just My Way of Forgetting You," "My Blackbirds Are Bluebirds Now," and "You're the Cream in My Cof-fee") are mostly on a higher level, although the four cartoonish Helen Kane imitations (best is the hu-morous "Is There Anything Wrong in That") will not be to everyone's taste.

Volume 6 only has four Frank Ferera numbers, and those are easily offset by classic renditions of "A Precious Little Thing Called Love," "Mean to Me," "Lover Come Back to Me," "Big City Blues," "My Sin," "I Get the Blues When It Rains," "I've Got a Feeling I'm Falling," "Am I Blue," "Daddy, Won't You Please Come Home," "True Blue Lou," and "Lovable and Sweet." The backup groups on this strong CD include Jimmy Dorsey, Tommy Dor-sey (on trumpet), and Phil Napoleon.

Although Annette Hanshaw collectors are ad-vised to wait for the other eight Sensation CDs to be released, *Lovable and Sweet* is an excellent sampler that spans virtually the singer's entire recording career. The 25 selections are highlighted by "Black Bottom," "Big City Blues," "Lovable and Sweet," "Little White Lies," "Fit As a Fiddle," and "Let's Fall in Love," with appearances along the way by Red Nichols, Miff Mole, the Dorsey Brothers, Benny Goodman, Manny Klein, and Jack Teagarden.

LPS TO SEARCH FOR

Since the Sensation label is scheduled to reissue all of Annette Hanshaw's recordings, her LPs will be duplicated in time. But for now, they fill in important gaps. The British Retrieval label reissued her first 47 recordings (dating from September 1926 up until the end of 1927) on the *Early Years, Vols. 1– 3* (Retrieval 201, 202, and 205). The first set includes such numbers as "Black Bottom," "Don't Take That Black Bottom Away," "My Baby Knows How," and "One Sweet Letter from You," with Red Nichols, Miff Mole, and Jimmy Lytell making appearances; two numbers have the teenage singer accompanying herself on piano. *Vol. 2* mostly features Hanshaw accompanied by just one or two musicians, with the more memorable selections including "He's the Last Word," "I'm Gonna Meet My Sweetie Now," and "It All Depends on You." The last of the three Retrieval sets has notable contributions by Joe Venuti, Adrian Rollini, Eddie Lang, Vic Berton, and composer-pianist Willard Robison. Among the better cuts are "I'm Somebody's Somebody Now," "Miss Annabelle Lee," and "The Song Is Ended."

While all but one of the 20 selections on *Vol. 1 Lovable and Sweet* (World/EMI 246) is covered on the Sensation CD, *Vol. 2 She's Got It* (World/EMI 247) has 20 numbers from a slightly later period (December 1929–February 1931), including "Cooking Breakfast for the One I Love," "My Future Just Passed," "Little White Lies," and "Would You Like to Take a Walk." *The Personality Girl* (Sunbeam 511) consists of Hanshaw's last 16 commercially available recordings, dating from 1932– 34. Although tiring of the show-biz life, she still retained enthusiasm in her singing, as can be heard on "Say It Isn't So," "Fit As a Fiddle," "Moon Song," "I Cover the Waterfront" (one of the finest versions ever of that standard), "Don't Blame Me," and even "This Little Piggy Went to Market." *It Was So Beautiful* (Sunbeam 512) is a 16-song sampler spanning 1927–36 that includes nine numbers not covered by the other CDs and LPs, including "Lila," "'Cause I Feel Lowdown," "Moonlight Saving Time," and a medley from a private acetate recording in late 1936 that ranks as the singer's final recording. Taken as a whole, it is obvious that Annette Hanshaw could have been a major star during the swing era. It is a pity that she did not have the desire to continue, even turning down movie roles.

OTTO HARDWICKE

b. May 31, 1904, Washington, DC, d. Aug. 5, 1970, Washington, DC

Otto "Toby" Hardwicke was one of Duke Ellington's most important early sidemen, even though he was taken for granted in later years. Hardwicke started on bass when he was 14, working with Carroll's Columbia Orchestra in 1920. After switching to C-melody sax, he played with Duke Ellington (a childhood friend) in Washington, D.C. Hardwicke traveled to New York with Duke in 1923 for their first visit (playing with Wilbur Sweatman) and again later that year for their more successful attempt at breaking into the big time. Hardwicke played alto, C-melody, and occasionally soprano, baritone, and bass saxophones while with Elmer Snowden's Washingtonians, where his sweet sound helped define the tone of the original group. He remained with the band after Ellington took over, staying until 1928.

In 1928 Hardwicke sailed to Paris, where he worked with Noble Sissle and several local groups. Back in the United States, he played with Chick

Webb (1929), led an orchestra in 1930 that actually beat Ellington's in a battle of the bands, and once again played with Elmer Snowden. Hardwicke rejoined Ellington in 1932 and took a famous recorded solo on "Sophisticated Lady" (a song that he cowrote with Duke) but otherwise was greatly underutilized as a soloist, since Johnny Hodges was the band's main altoist. Otto Hardwicke stayed with Ellington (mostly playing section parts) off and on until leaving after they had an argument in 1946. He freelanced a little (including recording two songs as a leader in 1947) before permanently retiring from music to work in hotel management and run a farm in Maryland.

EMMETT HARDY

> b. June 12, 1903, New Orleans, LA, d. June 16, 1926, New Orleans, LA

Emmett Hardy is a lost legend, a cornetist who never recorded and is remembered primarily because Bix Beiderbecke (who was actually a few months older) considered him an important influence. Hardy started on piano and guitar before switching to cornet at 12. In 1917 he worked with Papa Laine's Band and a few years later played with Brownlee's orchestra. In January 1921 Hardy left New Orleans to tour with singer Bee Palmer's group (which also featured Leon Roppolo). The band played in the Midwest, including Davenport, Iowa (Bix's hometown), and Peoria, Illinois. After Palmer's ensemble broke up, Hardy and Roppolo returned to Davenport, where they worked with Carlisle Evans' group during February 13–May 30. Beiderbecke heard Hardy often during this period, even spending some time practicing with him. In June, Hardy returned to New Orleans, where he led a group and freelanced. In late 1923 or early 1924 he moved to Chicago when the New Orleans Rhythm Kings were planning to expand to two cornets and three reeds.

But a dispute with the local Musicians Union led to Hardy's returning to New Orleans. Soon after his return, Emmett Hardy contracted pulmonary tuberculosis. He later developed an infection from an appendectomy and died in 1926, having played cornet for the last time at a party on his 23rd birthday, four days before his death.

JIMMY HARRISON

> b. Oct. 17, 1900, Louisville, KY, d. July 23, 1931, New York, NY

Jimmy Harrison, along with Jack Teagarden (a good friend whom he slightly preceded), liberated the trombone from its early role as a percussive harmony instrument, showing that it could be played with the legato phrasing of a trumpet. Harrison grew up in Detroit, teaching himself the trombone when he was 15. After spending time in Toledo, Ohio, helping to run the family restaurant and playing semipro baseball, he played and sang in a touring minstrel show. In 1919 Harrison began working in Atlantic City with his own group, also having stints with Charlie Johnson and Sam Wooding. After freelancing in Detroit and Toledo, the trombonist went to New York in 1923 with Fess Williams. Among his many associations during the next few years was playing in the bands of June Clark, Billy Fowler, Duke Ellington (briefly), and Elmer Snowden.

One of the most fluent trombonists of the period, Harrison is best known for his work and recordings with Fletcher Henderson (1927–30), taking solos on many records, along with occasional vocals (in a conversational style reminiscent of Bert Williams). He also recorded with the Blue Rhythm Orchestra, the Chocolate Dandies, the Georgia Strutters, the Gulf Coast Seven, Charlie Johnson, Sara Martin, Charlie Skeete, Bessie Smith, Eva Taylor, Chick Webb, and Clarence Williams. But in the summer of 1930, Jimmy Harrison became ill while on tour with Henderson and had to retire. He rejoined Henderson for a little while in 1931 but soon died of stomach cancer, when he was just 30.

COLEMAN HAWKINS

b. Nov. 21, 1904, St. Joseph, MI, d. May 19, 1969, New York, NY

One of the true giants of jazz, Coleman Hawkins was jazz's first significant tenor saxophonist. Hawkins was always proud of how modern a soloist he was, whether in 1923 or 1963. He studied music in Kansas City, at Washburn College in Topeka, Kansas, and in Chicago. Hawkins originally played piano (at five) and cello (at seven), starting on tenor when he was nine. He played with school bands and became a professional musician when he was 16, performing in Kansas City. Hawkins had virtually no predecessors in jazz on tenor (the instrument had been used mostly for novelty effects or as a poor substitute for the trombone), so he invented his own style completely from scratch; it would take until 1926 before he had his approach fully together.

Hawkins performed in a Kansas City theater orchestra, where he was discovered by Mamie Smith, with whom he toured and recorded during 1921–23. At the time Hawkins had a strong tone and an impressive technique, but his style was quite dated, and he often used slap-tonguing in his solos and played staccato runs. After the association with Smith ended, the young tenor began recording with Fletcher Henderson in August 1923, officially joining the orchestra in January 1924 and staying a decade. In the fall of 1924, when Louis Armstrong joined Henderson, his dramatic solos, use of space, and swinging lines had a major impact on Hawkins, who gradually modernized his style. By 1926, when he starred on "Stampede" (the first great tenor sax solo on records) with Henderson, Hawkins was recognized for the first time as a giant.

Coleman Hawkins worked steadily with Henderson, also making some notable freelance recordings along the way, including with McKinney's Cotton Pickers, the Mound City Blue Blowers (on "One Hour" he recorded one of the first significant ballad solos), the Chocolate Dandies, and Red Allen plus (starting in 1933) dates of his own as a leader. Because he was one of Henderson's main stars, it was a major blow in 1934 when Hawk, frustrated that the band was not prospering, left Henderson, sailing to England to play with Jack Hylton. It would be the beginning of an important five-year period overseas, just another chapter in the long career of the great Coleman Hawkins, a major force on the modern jazz scene into the mid-1960s.

9 **1929 – 1934/Nov. 14, 1929 – Mar. 8, 1934/Classics 587**
Some of Coleman Hawkins' most important early sessions away from Fletcher Henderson are included on this CD. Hawk is heard on six numbers with the Mound City Blue Blowers (including the famous versions of "One Hour" and "Hello Lola"), which find the tenor playing alongside such musicians as Pee Wee Russell, Glenn Miller, Muggsy Spanier, and Jimmy Dorsey. In addition, Hawkins is featured on three selections with Jack Purvis (a septet with J.C. Higginbotham and Adrian Rollini), a set with Horace Henderson (which is really the Fletcher Henderson band) highlighted by his ballad feature "I've Got to Sing a Torch Song," and his first six songs as a leader. The last includes three tunes with an octet taken from Henderson's orchestra costarring Red Allen and J.C. Higginbotham and three intriguing duets with pianist Buck Washington. Essential music.

CLIFFORD HAYES

Clifford Hayes, a decent country-style violinist, led a series of recording sessions that straddled the boundaries between jazz and blues. Very little is known about his life, including when and where he was born and when he passed away. What is known is that Hayes recorded with Sara Martin (1924), he led the first jug band on records, and he was teamed with banjoist Cal Smith in such groups as the Old Southern Jug Band, Clifford's Louisville Jug Band, the Dixieland Jug Blowers (1926–27), and Hayes' Louisville Stompers (1927–29). Johnny Dodds was prominent on one of the dates by the Dixieland Jug Blowers, and the sophisticated Earl Hines was on some of the selections from the rather primitive Louisville Stompers. Clifford Hayes last recorded in 1931 (all of his sessions as a leader are on four RST CDs); nothing at all is known about his later activities.

8 Vol. 1/Sept. 16, 1924–Dec. 10, 1926/RST 1501
9 Vol. 2/Dec. 10, 1926–Apr. 30, 1927/RST 1502
8 Vol. 3/June 6, 1927–Feb. 6, 1929/RST 1503
7 Vol. 4/Feb. 6, 1929–June 17, 1931/RST 1504

Vol. 1 of the four RST CDs (which are titled Clifford Hayes and the Louisville Jug Bands) has some rather historic recordings. Clifford Hayes is heard leading a trio with banjoist Curtis Hayes and Earl McDonald on jug behind blues singer Sara Martin on ten numbers from September 1924; these are considered the earliest of all jug band recordings. In addition, Hayes is featured with the Old Southern Jug Band (the same group with cornetist Theo Boone and banjoist Cal Smith in Sara Martin's place) and Clifford's Louisville Jug Band (recorded six months later with the identical lineup) and on one number ("Boodle-Am-Shake") in late 1926 with the Dixieland Jug Blowers. As a bonus, there are four selections from Whistler and His Jug Band, a similar quartet without Hayes.

Vol. 2 has the other dozen numbers from the Dixieland Jug Blowers, including six in which Johnny Dodds is a rather notable guest; "House Rent Rag" has a humorous monologue. The group otherwise consists of Hayes on violin, altoist Lockwood Lewis, three banjos, and the enthusiastic Earl McDonald on jug. Also on this disc are eight selections from McDonald's Original Louisville Jug Band and four additional titles from Whistler's Jug Band. *Vol. 3* has the ten later songs by the Dixieland Jug Blowers (with the rather primitive trombonist Hense Grundy, two reeds, Hayes, pianist Johnny Gatewood, and Cal Smith on banjo and guitar, along with a few guest vocalists but no jug player) plus the same group (without the reeds) performing as Clifford Hayes' Louisville Stompers. Seven of the 14 Stompers numbers have Earl Hines taking Gatewood's place, somehow fitting into the rather basic good-time music.

Vol. 4 wraps up the overview of the jug band era with a lot of different sessions. There are three additional titles from Hayes' Louisville Stompers (two with Hines and "You Gonna Need My Help" with singer Sippie Wallace), two cuts by the Kentucky Jazz Babies (Hayes, Gatewood, Cal Smith, and trumpeter Jimmy Strange), eight from Phillips' Louisville Jug Band (an unusual band consisting of C-melody sax, what is called a walking-cane flute, guitar and "jazzhorn"), four cuts by singer-vocalist Kid Coley (backed by Hayes' violin), two final numbers by Whistler and his Jug Band, and features for singers Jimmie Rodgers, Ben Ferguson, and John Harris in which they are accompanied by groups, including Hayes and Earl McDonald on jug.

Fans of historic jug bands should consider these four CDs to be essential, although more general classic jazz collectors may want to just acquire *Vol. 2.*

LENNIE HAYTON

b. Feb. 13, 1908, New York, NY, d. Apr. 24, 1971, Palm Springs, CA

Lennie Hayton is best known as an arranger and musical director, often for his wife, Lena Horne. Less known is that Hayton appeared on numerous jazz dates during the second half of the 1920s. He started playing piano when he was six and studied music extensively. Hayton worked with Spencer Clark (1926), the Little Ramblers, Cass Hagan's orchestra (1927), and the Paul Whiteman Orchestra (September 1928–May 1930), playing second piano with the last. Along the way he recorded with Bix and His Gang ("Ol' Man River"), the Charleston Chasers, the Mason-Dixon Orchestra, Red Nichols' Five Pennies, Jack Pettis, Frank Trumbauer (1928–30), Joe Venuti, and Paul Whiteman, providing solid if not overly distinctive piano.

Lennie Hayton, who led a two-song record date in 1928, had his own band for a time in the 1930s, served as the musical director for Bing Crosby, led an orchestra during 1937–40 (eight songs were recorded), and then left jazz altogether. In later years he worked for MGM (1941–53) and with Lena Horne.

LUCILLE HEGAMIN

b. Nov. 29, 1894, Macon, GA, d. Mar. 1, 1970, New York, NY

One of the very first classic blues singers to appear on record (just three months after Mamie Smith), Lucille Hegamin worked steadily in the 1920s. Born Lucille Nelson, early on she sang in a church choir in Georgia, first touring when she was 15 with the *Leonard Harper Revue*. Married to pianist Bill Hegamin during 1914–23, she worked with Jelly Roll Morton and Tony Jackson (premiering his "Pretty Baby") and throughout the West Coast. In late 1919 Hegamin moved to New York, where she began recording on November 1920, starting with "The Jazz Me Blues" and "Everybody's Blues." Her "I'll Be Good but I'll Be Lonesome" and "Arkansas Blues" from February 1921 were hits. Hegamin toured with her Blue Flame Syncopators and later on the Dixie Daisies, being billed for a time as "The Chicago Cyclone—Blues Singer Supreme." Hegamin performed at clubs and in several Broadway shows in the 1920s, working with Doc Hyder's Southerners in the latter part of the decade. All in all, she recorded 94 selections during 1920–26 and two songs in 1932. After performing at Atlantic City during 1933–34, she left music, becoming a nurse in 1938.

In the 1960s, Lucille Hegamin made a brief comeback, recording four songs for a Bluesville LP and three selections for an album for the Spivey label in 1962 in addition to appearing at a few charity benefits before permanently retiring from music.

8 Vol. 1/Nov. 1920–Apr. 30, 1922/Document 5419

7 Vol. 2/July 16, 1922–Oct. 1923/Document 5420

8 Vol. 3/Oct. 1923–Mar. 4, 1932/Document 5421

6 Alternate Takes and Remaining Titles/Nov. 1920-Jan. 1926/ Document 1011

Lucille Hegamin was more of a vaudeville singer than a strict blues vocalist, but she was versatile and talented. *Vol. 1* has her first 24 recordings, including "The Jazz Me Blues," "Arkansas Blues," "Wang Wang Blues," "Wabash Blues," and two versions of a familiar blues song that she introduced: "He May Be Your Man but He Comes to See Me Sometimes." In addition, there are a pair of instrumentals ("Strut Miss Lizzie" and "Sweet Mama, Papa's Getting Mad") from her backup group (the Blue Flame Syncopators), a four-horn octet that includes her husband Bill Hegamin on piano and Kaiser Marshall. On *Vol. 2*, Hegamin is accompanied by such groups as the Blue Flame Syncopators, the Dixie Daisies, her Bang-Up Six from Georgia, and Sam Wooding's Society Entertainers (with the personnel of these bands mostly being either obscure or completely unknown) or pianists J. Russell Robinson or Cyril Fullerton. Considering how early these recordings are, the recording quality is not bad, and Hegamin's easy-to-understand interpretations are enjoyable. Highlights of the second disc include "I've Got What It Takes but It Breaks My Heart to Give It Away," "Beale St. Mama," "Aggravatin' Papa," "Down Hearted Blues," "Saint Louis Gal," and "Dina."

Vol. 3 mostly has the singer's recordings from 1923–26, with her backed by the Dixie Daisies, J. Russell Robinson, or (on a couple of 1926 selections), Clarence Williams' group. In addition, her two selections from 1932 (with backing by pianist Irving Williams) wrapped up her recording career for many years; she would not record again until 1960. *Vol. 3* includes such fine numbers as "Rampart St. Blues," "If You Don't Give Me What I Want I'm Gonna Get It Somewhere Else," "Hard-Hearted Hannah," "Alabamy Bound," "Dinah," and "Poor Papa." *Alternate Takes and Remaining*

Titles finishes the complete reissuance of Lucille Hegamin's 1920–32 recordings, with four songs formerly bypassed and 18 alternate takes.

FLETCHER HENDERSON

b. Dec. 18, 1898, Cuthbert, GA, d. Dec. 29, 1952, New York, NY

Fletcher Henderson was the leader of the finest big band of the 1920s before the rise of Duke Ellington in 1927–28 (Paul Whiteman was his only real competitor), a masterful talent scout, an adequate pianist, and a skilled arranger whose work began to blossom around 1930. The older brother of Horace Henderson, Fletcher (who gained the nickname of "Smack" for the way he smacked his lips) began playing piano when he was six. He attended Atlanta University College during 1916–20, earning degrees in chemistry and mathematics. Henderson came to New York in 1920 in hopes of doing postgraduate research and gaining work as a chemist, but he quickly found that there was no great demand for black chemists. So he shifted gears and acquired a job as a song demonstrator for the Pace-Handy Music Company. Distinguished and soft-spoken, Henderson moved up swiftly and was soon the recording manager for Harry Pace's short-lived Black Swan record label. Henderson led the band accompanying Ethel Waters (autumn 1921–summer 1922), with whom he toured.

After leaving Waters, Henderson became the house pianist for several labels (especially Paramount), backing many blues and vaudeville singers. Among the vocalists he accompanied on record dates during 1921–26 were Faye Barnes, Birleanna Blanks, Bessie Brown, Ida Brown, Gladys Bryant, Ida Cox, Katie Crippen, Maud De Forrest, Ethel Finnie, Emma Gover, Rosa Henderson, Edna Hicks, Mattie Hite, Alberta Hunter, Mary Jackson, Maggie Jones, Emma Lewis, Viola McCoy, Ozie McPherson, Hazel Meyers, Josie Miles, Julia Moody, Ma Rainey, Inez Richardson, Bessie Smith, Clara Smith, Trixie Smith, Mary Straine, Hannah Sylvester, Inez Wallace, Ethel Waters, Lulu Whidby, Esie Whitman, George Williams, Edith Wilson, Lena Wilson, and the team of Coot Grant and Leola Wilson.

Henderson, who worked a bit in 1922–23 with violinist Shrimp Jones' band, began leading record dates of his own in 1921 and quite often throughout 1923. In early 1924 he brought a band into the Club Alabam. By the summer, his orchestra was working regularly at the Roseland Ballroom, its home base for the next decade. The early band included Don Redman (clarinet, alto, and the main arranger), Coleman Hawkins, and trumpeters Elmer Chambers and Howard Scott. While Redman's arrangements sounded futuristic at times, rhythmically both the ensembles and the solos were generally quite stiff and awkward. The first time that the band swung on records was on the second half of "Charley, My Boy" on July 30, 1924.

In October 1924, Louis Armstrong joined the Fletcher Henderson Orchestra, and it was obvious from his first notes that he was on a different plane altogether. Armstrong's legato lines, use of space, and ability to tell a story while infusing pop tunes with the blues had a major effect. Redman's arrangements began to loosen up and swing, Hawkins modernized his style, and the other musicians developed quickly. By the time Satch left to return to Chicago in the fall of 1925, Henderson's orchestra was entering its peak period. The who's who of black jazz played with Henderson during 1925–34, including such up-and-coming stars as Joe Smith, Tommy Ladnier, Rex Stewart, Bobby Stark, Cootie Williams, Red Allen, Charlie Green, Benny Morton, Jimmy Harrison, Sandy Williams, J.C. Higginbotham, Dickie Wells, Buster Bailey, Coleman Hawkins, Ben Webster, Lester Young (although he never recorded with Henderson), Benny Carter, Russell Procope, Hilton Jefferson, John Kirby, Israel Crosby, Kaiser Marshall, Walter Johnson, and Sid Catlett. Fats Waller was a guest on some recordings, and, when Redman departed in

One of the great talent scouts, Fletcher Henderson led an all-star big band for over a decade.

1927 to join McKinney's Cotton Pickers, soon Benny Carter and Horace Henderson were contributing charts.

However, there were lost opportunities along the way. After being involved in a car accident in 1928, Henderson seemed less interested in business and the band failed to prosper, making relatively few recordings during 1928–30, when it was at its peak. Henderson did develop into a top arranger in the early 1930s. But the Depression did not help business, and in 1934, right before the swing era started, things began to fall apart. A frustrated Coleman Hawkins left the band after a decade to go to Europe. Although the personnel was still full of all-stars, Henderson's orchestra was overshadowed by Duke Ellington, Chick Webb, Jimmie Lunceford,

and others. To raise cash, Henderson began contributing many arrangements to the library of the new Benny Goodman orchestra, helping to define the sound of the swing era. But in early 1935 he broke up his big band altogether.

In 1936 Henderson put together a new orchestra and had a hit in "Christopher Columbus" (featuring trumpeter Roy Eldridge and tenor saxophonist Chu Berry), but within three years he had to disband due to the heavy competition. Henderson played with the Benny Goodman Sextet a bit in 1939 and then worked primarily as an arranger. He had other big bands in 1941, 1943, 1945, and 1946–47, but none were particularly successful. After working as Ethel Waters' accompanist (summer 1948–December 1949), he led a sextet at Café Society in New

York in December 1950. However, Fletcher Henderson suffered a major stroke that month and never played again, passing away two years later at the age of 54.

10 **A Study in Frustration/Aug. 9, 1923 – May 28, 1938/Columbia/Legacy 57596**

This magnificent three-CD box set (which was formerly four LPs) contains the absolute cream of Fletcher Henderson's recordings. The 64 selections (all but eight from 1923 – 33) dispenses fast with the early pre-Louis Armstrong period (with just two selections) and then emphasizes the glory years. Among the many high points are "Shanghai Shuffle," two versions of "Sugar Foot Stomp," three of "King Porter Stomp," "The Stampede" (Coleman Hawkins' famous feature), "Henderson Stomp," "St. Louis Shuffle," "Oh Baby," "Clarinet Marmalade," and "Honeysuckle Rose." Filled with essential music, this set is highly recommended to listeners not exploring Henderson's many Classics releases.

5 **1921 – 1923/June 1921 – June 11, 1923/Classics 794**
5 **1923/June 25, 1923 – Apr. 24, 1924/Classics 697**
6 **1923 – 1924/Nov. 30, 1923 – Jan. 29, 1924/Classics 683**
6 **1924/Feb. 1924 – May 6, 1924/Classics 683**
6 **1924, Vol. 2/May 21, 1924 – Aug. 29, 1924/Classics 657**

It is ironic that the most prolific period of Henderson's recording career was in the years before Louis Armstrong transformed his orchestra into a swinging outfit. *1921 – 1923* has some real rarities along with the leader's only three unaccompanied piano solos. The selections from 1921 are quite primitive, while the ones from 1923 find the Henderson Orchestra slowly forming its identity. *1923* has the first recordings of Coleman Hawkins with the band, but the group (a nonet by the end of the year) did not seem to realize yet that it was not swinging! *1923 – 1924, 1924,* and *1924, Vol. 2* mostly feature syncopated dance music, tricky arrangements, and solos that rely as much on effects as on ideas. Charlie Green joined Henderson in June 1924 (he was the

group's first strong soloist), and "Charley, My Boy" from July 30 hints at the future. But before Armstrong arrived, Henderson's big band was suffering from the same rhythmic problems as Paul Whiteman's orchestra.

10 **Louis with Fletcher Henderson 1924 – 1925/Oct. 7, 1924 – Oct. 21, 1925/Forte 38001/2/3**
3 **Fletcher Henderson and Louis Armstrong/Oct. 10, 1924 – Oct. 21, 1925/Timeless 1 – 003**
7 **1924, Vol. 3/Sept. 8, 1924 – Nov. 24, 1924/Classics 647**
7 **1924 – 1925/Dec. 1924 – Nov. 16, 1925/Classics 633**

Louis Armstrong's year with Fletcher Henderson did a great deal to change jazz forever. His recordings with Henderson (particularly the early ones) find him sounding a decade ahead of the previously overconfident band. The Forte three-CD set has all 65 performances (including 22 alternate takes) that Armstrong made with Henderson, including "Shanghai Shuffle, "Copenhagen," "Everybody Loves My Baby," and "Sugar Foot Stomp." In contrast, the Timeless release is a mess. This single CD has just ten complete performances from Armstrong's period with Henderson, along with 14 excerpts, some of which splice in his solos from other takes. That would be fine, except that the music is not programmed in chronological order (so Satch's development cannot be traced), and not all of his solos are included! Nice try though.

1924, Vol. 3 begins with the session before Armstrong arrived, while *1924 – 1925* concludes with the first one after he left. In between, these two CDs have the master takes of the cornetist's stay with Henderson, but the Forte set is much preferred.

8 **1925 – 1926/Nov. 23, 1925 – Apr. 14, 1926/Classics 610**
9 **1926 – 1927/Apr. 14, 1926 – Jan. 22, 1927/Classics 597**
9 **1927/Mar. 11, 1927 – Oct. 24, 1927/Classics 580**
9 **1927 – 1931/Nov. 4, 1927 – Feb. 5, 1931/Classics 572**

The Fletcher Henderson Orchestra was at its peak during the time covered by these four CDs, although it took over five years to record as much material as it had during June 1923 – August 1924! Right after Armstrong left the band, the key soloists were Joe Smith, Charlie Green, Buster Bailey, and Coleman Hawkins. Tommy Ladnier and guest Fats Waller are among the stars on *1926–1927* (which includes "Stampede," "Henderson Stomp," and "The Chant"), while Jimmy Harrison joins Ladnier, Bailey, and Hawkins on *1927*. The arrangements by Redman were really swinging by this time, and the orchestra featured some of the most significant soloists in jazz. Unfortunately Henderson recorded only 17 numbers during 1928–30, so a lot of gems were undoubtedly not documented. But *1927–1931* still contains many exciting moments. Rex Stewart, Bobby Stark, Benny Carter, Bailey, and Hawkins star, and the high points include "King Porter Stomp," "Oh Baby," and "Raisin' the Roof."

8 1931/Feb. 5, 1931–July 31, 1931/Classics 555
7 1931–1932/July 31, 1931–Mar. 11, 1932/Classics 546
9 1932–1934/Dec. 9, 1932–Sept. 12, 1934/Classics 535
7 The Indispensable Fletcher Henderson/Mar. 11, 1927–Aug. 4, 1936/RCA 66676
6 Hocus Pocus/Apr. 27, 1927–Aug. 4, 1936/Bluebird 9904
7 Tidal Wave/Apr. 1, 1931–Sept. 25, 1934/GRP/Decca 643

Some of the arrangements on *1931* are a bit generic, but Stark, Stewart, Hawkins, and Benny Morton uplift the material. *1931–1932* finds the band recording commercial material (such as "Strangers") along with two songs in which they back the vocals of child star Baby Rose Marie and a few tunes in which they sound like the Casa Loma Orchestra. But the strength of the solos keeps the music quite listenable and swinging. *1932–1934* features the orchestra regaining its stride, with the high points including "New King Porter Stomp" (which has Bobby Stark's greatest solo), "Honeysuckle Rose," "Yeah Man," "Queer Notions," Hawkins' feature on "It's the Talk of the Town," "Limehouse Blues," "Big John's Special," and "Down South Camp Meeting." Even with Hawkins gone, the Henderson Orchestra still featured Red Allen, Bobby Stark, Ben Webster, and Hilton Jefferson, among many others, during its closing period.

The Indispensable Fletcher Henderson and *Hocus Pocus* are both samplers of Henderson's periods on the Victor label (1927, 1931–32, 1934, and 1936). All of the music on the 21-song *Hocus Pocus* is duplicated on the two-CD 36-song *Indispensable* set (except for an alternate take of "Mary Had a Little Lamb" from 1936). In turn, all of that music (except two alternate takes) is on the individual Classics CDs. *Tidal Wave* is better, since it reissues five complete sessions, two from 1931 (including "Sugar Foot Stomp," "Radio Rhythm," and a tribute to Bix Beiderbecke on "Singin' the Blues") and three from 1934 (highlighted by "Limehouse Blues," "Big John's Special," and "Down South Camp Meeting"). The only number not also in the Classics series is an alternate take of "Memphis Blues."

Listeners wanting to hear the rest of the Fletcher Henderson Orchestra story are advised to also acquire *1934–1937* (Classics 527) and *1937–1938* (Classics 519).

HORACE HENDERSON

b. Nov. 22, 1904, Cuthbert, GA, d. Aug. 29, 1988, Denver, CO

The younger brother of Fletcher Henderson, Horace Henderson was actually a better pianist and a talented arranger who emerged as a top writer before Fletcher developed his skills. Nevertheless, Horace stayed in Fletcher's shadow throughout his career.

He started playing piano at 14, attending Atlanta University for a year and Wilberforce College for three. While at the latter, Henderson formed the Wilberforce Collegians, a band that worked during summer vacations starting in 1924. The group eventually broke away from the college and toured as the Horace Henderson Orchestra (1926–27) and the Dixie Stompers (in 1928). Henderson broke up the band in late 1928, worked with Sammy Stewart, and then led a new orchestra during 1929–31. In 1931, Don Redman took over the big band, with

Henderson remaining as its pianist until early 1933. During this era he also contributed arrangements to other bands and guested now and then with his brother's orchestra, playing piano on Fletcher's 1931 recordings of "Hot and Anxious" and "Comin' and Goin.' " During 1933–34, Horace worked often with Fletcher's big band, splitting the piano duties and contributing some swinging arrangements, including "Yeah Man," "Queer Notions," and "Big John's Special."

In 1933 Henderson used the nucleus of Fletcher's band for his debut recording as a leader, which has been reissued on Coleman Hawkins' *1929–34* (Classics 587). During the swing era, he wrote arrangements for such ensembles as the Casa Loma Orchestra, Benny Goodman ("Japanese Sandman" and "Dear Old Southland"), Charlie Barnet, Tommy Dorsey, Jimmie Lunceford, Earl Hines, and his brother (who used 30 of his charts, including his 1936 hit "Christopher Columbus"). Henderson led a big band of his own during 1937–40 (recording five fine sessions in 1940), but it never caught on. Horace Henderson worked in music into the early '80s, including leading a series of mostly unrecorded bands in Los Angeles, Chicago, Minneapolis, Las Vegas, and Denver, but never realized his potential.

ROSA HENDERSON

b. 1896, Henderson, KY, d. Apr. 6, 1968, New York, NY

A classic blues singer, Rosa Henderson was no relation to Fletcher or Horace Henderson. Born Rosa Deschamps, she first started singing professionally as a teenager in 1913 with her uncle's carnival troupe. She worked in vaudeville, married Douglas "Slim" Henderson, and by 1923 was becoming a fairly big name. Henderson spent the 1920s performing in musical comedies and visited London in 1928 to perform in *Showboat*. She recorded over 89 titles (counting alternate takes) during 1923–27, some under the pseudonyms of Flora Dale, Rosa

Green, Mae Harris, Mamie Harris, Rose Henderson, Sara Johnson, Sally Ritz (her sister's name!), Josephine Thomas, Gladys White, and Bessie Williams.

After her husband died in 1928, Henderson lost interest in show business, recording two final titles in 1931 and retiring the following year. Rosa Henderson worked outside of music (including in a New York department store) for decades, appearing as a singer at a few charity benefits in the 1960s.

7 Vol. 1/Apr. 1923–Dec. 1923/Document 5401
7 Vol. 2/Feb. 13, 1924–Sept. 1924/Document 5402
8 Vol. 3/Sept. 1924–May 14, 1926/Document 5403
7 Vol. 4/May 14, 1926–Aug. 19, 1931/Document 5404

Rosa Henderson recorded quite a bit, particularly during 1923–26. All of her recordings are available on her four Document CDs. *Vol. 1* has her mostly backed by pianist Fletcher Henderson, with one number apiece using sidemen from Henderson's early band and the Virginians; Coleman Hawkins pops up on "It Won't Be Long Now," while Thomas Morris and pianist Louis Hooper help out on two numbers. None of these songs became a hit, but quite a few are memorable, including "I Ain't No Man's Slave," "So Long to You and the Blues," and such colorful titles as "He May Be Your Dog but He's Wearing My Collar" and "Got the World in a Jug, the Stopper's in My Hand." *Vol. 2* continues in the same vein, with the singer backed mostly by Henderson and his sidemen. Best are "I'm a Good Gal but I'm a Thousan' Miles from Home," "West Indies Blues," "My Papa Doesn't Two-Time No Time," "Strut Yo' Puddy," and "Somebody's Doing What You Wouldn't Do."

Vol. 3 is the strongest of the four Document CDs. The backup groups (usually the Choo Choo Jazzers or the Kansas City Five) include Rex Stewart, Louis Metcalf, Bubber Miley, and Cliff Jackson, while the songs include such gems as "Hard-Hearted Hannah," "Don't Advertise Your Man," "Nobody Knows the Way I Feel Dis Mornin'," "Get It Fixed," and "What's the Matter Now" (one of two songs with Fats Waller on piano). *Vol. 4* is most notable for the six numbers in which Rosa Henderson is accompanied by James P. Johnson, including her two selections from 1931. Despite the lack of hit records, Rosa Henderson deserves to be ranked as one of the better classic blues singers of the 1920s.

J.C. HIGGINBOTHAM

b. May 11, 1906, Social Circle, GA, d. May 26, 1973, New York, NY

Jack "J.C." Higginbotham was one of the top jazz trombonists of the early 1930s, a boisterous and exciting soloist. Higgy, who grew up in Cincinnati, first played bugle before switching to trombone. He worked with J. Neal Montgomery (1921) and pianist Harvey Quiggs but spent a few years learning tailoring at a training school and working as a mechanic for General Motors. In 1924 Higginbotham decided to become a full-time musician, working during the next few years with Wesley Helvey, pianist Eugene Landrum, Wingie Carpenter, drummer Eugene Primus, and pianist Jimmy Harrison (no relation to the trombonist). In September 1928, while visiting New York, Higginbotham sat in with Chick Webb's band at the Savoy Ballroom. Luis Russell was in the audience and immediately signed him up. The enthusiastic trombonist became a key soloist with Russell (1928–31), starring next to Red Allen, Charlie Holmes, and Albert Nicholas. He recorded two numbers as a leader ("Give Me Your Telephone Number" and "Higginbotham Blues") in 1930 with a septet taken from Russell's band.

Higginbotham had productive stints with Fletcher Henderson (1931–33 and 1937), Benny Carter (1933), the Mills Blue Rhythm Band (1934–36), and the Luis Russell Orchestra when it was functioning as Louis Armstrong's backup band (1937–40). J.C. Higginbotham played primarily small-group Dixieland during the rest of his episodic career (often with Red Allen) while undergoing a long decline due to his alcoholism.

ANDREW HILAIRE

b. 1900, New Orleans, LA, d. 1936, Chicago, IL

Drummer Andrew Hilaire is best remembered for his playing on three Jelly Roll Morton recording sessions from 1926, dates that resulted in such titles as "Black Bottom Stomp," "The Chant," and "Doctor Jazz." He was based during his entire career in Chicago. Hilaire was with Lil Harden's group (1921) and played regularly with Doc Cook's Dreamland Orchestra during 1924–27, recording with Cook and taking two vocals. He also worked in theaters and had stints with Jerome Pasquall (1930) and Eddie South (1931). Andrew Hilaire, who led bands during his last couple of years, suffered from asthma, which led to his early death.

ALEX HILL

b. Apr. 19, 1906, North Little Rock, AK, d. Feb. 1, 1937, North Little Rock, AK

Alex Hill was a very talented arranger-composer and pianist who unfortunately died quite young. Hill started off taking piano lessons from his mother. As a teenager he became a professional musician, working with Alphonso Trent and leading a band in 1924. He was the musical director of a traveling revue until he decided to stay in Los Angeles in 1927. Hill did studio work in Hollywood and played locally, including with Mutt Carey's Jeffersonians. The following year he moved to Chicago, where he worked with Jimmy Wade, Carroll Dickerson, Jerome Pasquall, and Jimmie Noone (1928–29), both playing piano and contributing arrangements. His "Beau-Koo Jack" was recorded by Louis Armstrong's Savoy Ballroom Five.

Moving to New York in 1929, Hill worked with Sammy Stewart (1929–30) and became a staff arranger for Irving Mills. Hill contributed charts for Duke Ellington, Benny Carter, Claude Hopkins, Andy Kirk, Paul Whiteman, Eddie Condon, Mezz Mezzrow, Willie Bryant, Mills Blue Rhythm Band, Fats Waller's big band, and others. He led five record dates during 1929–30 and 1934, just singing and doing the writing for the last sessions. Alex Hill led a big band in November 1935, playing at the Savoy and appearing to be in a very good position at the beginning of the swing era. But his health unexpectedly declined quickly in 1936, and Alex Hill died of tuberculosis in 1937 at the age of 30.

9 **1928–1934/Oct. 9, 1928–Oct. 19, 1934/Timeless 1–050**

The majority of Alex Hill's most important recordings are on this well-conceived release. The pianist-arranger is featured with Albert Wynn's Gut Bucket Five, Jimmy Wade's Dixielanders, Jimmie Noone, Junie Cobb's Grains of Corn, Eddie Condon (1933), and the Hokum Trio. In addition, Hill's five sessions as a leader are reissued in full, including such gems as "Dyin' with the Blues," "Ain't It Nice," and "Functionizin'." His potential (particularly as a writer) is well displayed in the four titles from 1934, and it seems clear that Alex Hill would have been an important contributor to the swing era had he been fortunate enough to live to a decent age.

BERTHA "CHIPPIE" HILL

b. Mar. 15, 1905, Charleston, SC, d. May 7, 1950, New York, NY

One of the best blues singers of the 1920s, Bertha "Chippie" Hill grew up as one of 16 children. She worked as a dancer at LeRoy's in Harlem when she was 16 and toured as a singer and dancer with Ma Rainey's troupe. After appearing in a variety of theaters, Hill settled in Chicago in 1925, working briefly with King Oliver. During 1925–29, she recorded 24 selections (Louis Armstrong is in the backup group on ten numbers), including two versions of "Trouble in Mind," a standard that she introduced. Hill worked regularly in Chicago until 1930, at which time she left full-time music to raise her seven children.

The singer, who retired altogether by 1940, was discovered by writer Rudi Blesh in 1946, working

in a bakery. He persuaded her to appear on his *This Is Jazz* radio series the following year. She made a full comeback, appearing at New York clubs, making a few recordings, playing at Carnegie Hall with Kid Ory, appearing at the Paris Jazz Festival in 1948, and working with Art Hodes in Chicago. But it all came to a tragic end when 45-year-old Chippie Hill was hit by a car in Harlem in 1950.

8 **Complete Recorded Works/Nov. 9, 1925–Mar. 18, 1929/Document 5330**

All of Chippie Hill's 1920s recordings fit snugly on this single CD, a difficult disc to improve upon. With backing from Louis Armstrong, Richard M. Jones (with and without his Wizards), Georgia Tom Dorsey, and Tampa Red, Hill is quite consistent. One of the last classic blues singers to be discovered, she already sounded quite mature by 1925 (when she was 20). Among the better tunes are "Lonesome, All Alone and Blue," "Pleadin' for the Blues," "Some Cold Rainy Day," "Christmas Man Blues," and of course "Trouble in Mind."

EARL HINES

b. Dec. 28, 1903, Duquesne, PA, d. Apr. 22, 1983, Oakland, CA

Earl Hines was considered the first "modern" jazz pianist because, rather than keeping the beat with a steady stride, he broke up the rhythm with his left hand, suspending time during wild breaks, but always coming back without missing a beat. In addition, his right hand often played octaves so as to ring clearly over ensembles; this was dubbed "trumpet style." Although he had a long career full of highlights, some of Hines' greatest work was done in the 1920s, particularly during 1928.

The son of a father who played trumpet and a mother who was an organist and the brother of a pianist, Earl "Fatha" Hines (who grew up in Pittsburgh) started out on cornet, switching to piano when he was nine. Singer Lois Deppe discovered the teenager in the early 1920s, got him a job with

Earl Hines, possessor of the trickiest left hand in jazz, had quite a remarkable year in 1928.

Arthur Rideout's orchestra, and used Hines in his Pittsburgh Serenaders, with whom he made his recording debut, in 1923, taking a solo on "Congaine."

After performing with Harry Collins' orchestra in Pittsburgh, Hines moved to Chicago, where he was immediately in great demand. The pianist worked with Sammy Stewart's Ten Knights of Syncopation, Erskine Tate's Vendome Orchestra, and Carroll Dickerson (1925–26). When Louis Armstrong took over Dickerson's group at the Sunset Café in 1927, Hines became the band's musical director. Hines and Armstrong recorded first on a Johnny Dodds session (April 22, 1927) and again on May 9 with the trumpeter's big band ("Chicago Breakdown").

Together with Zutty Singleton, they ran a short-lived club for a few months.

For Hines, 1928 was a truly remarkable year. Nightly he played at the Apex Club with Jimmie Noone's quintet/sextet. He made his first recordings of the year with Noone on May 16 and June 14 (including "Four or Five Times" and "Every Evening"). On June 26 he made the most of a record date with the untalented singer Lillie Delk Christian; Louis Armstrong, Noone, and Mancy Cara were also aboard, and Satch really uplifted "Too Busy." Things became serious during June 27–29 as the pianist helped Armstrong make history with the first Savoy Ballroom Five recordings, debuting his own "A Monday Date," "Sugar Foot Strut,"

"Fireworks," and the astounding "West End Blues" among the eight songs. On July 2, Hines, Noone, and Bud Scott backed blues singer Stovepipe Johnson on "I Ain't Got Nobody." Three days later, Hines and Armstrong recorded "Knee Drops" with the small group and two exciting numbers with Carroll Dickerson's Savoyagers. On August 23 and 25, Hines performed five additional songs with Noone's band, including "A Monday Date," "Apex Blues," and "Oh Sister, Ain't That Hot?"

By December, Hines was busy organizing his first big band, but he had a few more recordings to make first. Back with Armstrong, December 4 yielded "No, Papa, No" and the original version of "Basin Street Blues." The following day the Savoy Ballroom Five recorded three numbers (including "Save It Pretty Mama") and Hines performed the remarkable duet with Armstrong, "Weather Bird," in which the two most advanced musicians of the time battled and challenged each other. December 7 found the Savoy Ballroom Five playing "Muggles." On December 8–9, Hines recorded his first ten piano solos, remarkable showcases that included two versions apiece of "A Monday Date" and "Blues in Thirds" (one of the latter was named "Caution Blues"). On December 11 and 12, Lillie Delk Christian returned to the studios (with Hines, Armstrong, Noone, and Cara) for two songs apiece. December 12 also had the final date by the Savoy Ballroom Five (including the earliest recording of "St. James Infirmary") and two more piano solos by Hines (highlighted by "57 Varieties"). And then, to top off the year, on his 25th birthday Earl Hines had his first gig at Chicago's Grand Terrace Ballroom with his new big band!

Although Hines recorded in 1929 with Clifford Hayes' Louisville Stompers (somehow fitting in with the primitive band) and two titles with Omer Simeon, and in 1931 he had a reunion recording date with Noone, his main work for the next 20 years would be with his orchestra. They recorded nine numbers in 1929 and, after 2½ years off re-cords, the big band recorded fairly steadily during 1932–35 and 1937–42, working mostly at Chicago's Grand Terrace Ballroom until 1940. Omer Simeon and Darnell Howard were among the musicians spending years with Hines (trumpeter Walter Fuller and trombonist Trummy Young were two of his other stars), and the pianist easily made the transition to swing. In fact, he was a strong influence on Jess Stacy, Joe Sullivan, and Nat King Cole and a lesser one on Teddy Wilson and Art Tatum. Singers Billy Eckstine and Sarah Vaughan got their start with Hines, and in 1943 he (almost unwittingly) led the first (but, sadly, unrecorded) bebop big band, with Charlie Parker (on tenor) and trumpeter Dizzy Gillespie among his sidemen. Whether heading his orchestra (which lasted until 1948), touring with the Louis Armstrong All-Stars (1948–51), playing Dixieland in San Francisco during the 1950s, or touring the world as a legendary and still chance-taking pianist (starting after his rediscovery in 1964), Earl Hines was simply one of the greatest jazz pianists of all time.

10 1928–1932/Dec. 8, 1928–June 28, 1932/Classics 545
9 1932–1934/July 14, 1932–Mar. 27, 1934/Classics 514

1928–1932 contains essential music for all jazz collections. It starts off with Earl Hines' dozen piano solos of 1928, including "Blues in Thirds," "Chicago High Life," two versions of "A Monday Date," "Chimes in Blues," "Caution Blues," and "57 Varieties." If this were all that Hines recorded in his career, he would be still be remembered, for these performances are full of miraculous moments. Also on this CD are the ten Hines big band recordings of 1929 (including "Everybody Loves My Baby," "Beau-Koo Jack," and "Grand Piano Blues"), the original 1932 version of the big band's theme, "Deep Forest," and a Hines piano solo on "Glad Rag Doll."

1932–1934 has all of Hines' other big band recordings of the period prior to his signing with the Decca label, plus piano solo versions of "Love Me Tonight" and "Down Among the Sheltering

Palms." The early swing band featured the key voices of trumpeter-vocalist Walter Fuller, Darnell Howard (clarinet, alto, and violin), Omer Simeon (on clarinet, alto, and baritone), and trombonist Trummy Young, plus two early vocals from Herb Jeffries. Among the better numbers are "Blue Drag," the original rendition of Hines' "Rosetta," "Cavernism," "Bubbling Over," and "Madhouse," although, in truth, the two piano solos take honors.

LPS TO SEARCH FOR

Earl Hines 1929 (Raretone 24003) is for completists, for not only does it have the ten Hines big band numbers from 1929 (plus his piano solo version of "Glad Rag Doll") but six rare alternate takes that are equally as exciting.

JOHNNY HODGES

b. July 25, 1906, Cambridge, MA, d. May 11, 1970, New York, NY

Johnny Hodges had the most beautiful tone of any saxophonist in jazz. A major altoist and a fine soprano saxophonist (although he gave up the latter instrument in 1940), Hodges was an integral part of the Duke Ellington Orchestra for decades, quite skilled on stomps and blues, but particularly renowned for his work on ballads.

Hodges started on drums and piano, switching to saxophone when he was 14. He had lessons on soprano sax from Sidney Bechet, played a bit in Boston, and in 1924 succeeded Bechet in Willie "the Lion" Smith's group at the Rhythm Club in New York. Hodges gigged with Bechet a bit at Club Basha in 1925 and freelanced, including with Chick Webb and Luckey Roberts. On May 18, 1928, Hodges joined the Duke Ellington Orchestra (replacing the departed Otto Hardwicke). Until he left to lead his own group in March 1951, Hodges was considered Ellington's top soloist. His playing uplifted the Ellington Jungle Band of 1928, and his style was so timeless that it still sounds fresh decades later.

Johnny Hodges led a jump band that sounded like an Ellington small group during 1951–55 before returning to Duke's orchestra for the remainder of his life (1955–70).

CHARLIE HOLMES

b. Jan. 27, 1910, Boston, MA, d. Sept. 12, 1985, Boston, MA

An underrated altoist influenced by Johnny Hodges, Charlie Holmes was a childhood friend of Hodges and Harry Carney in Boston. A skilled musician who played oboe with the Boston Civic Symphony Orchestra in 1926, Holmes was always more interested in jazz. He moved to New York with Carney in 1927 and worked with Chick Webb, Henri Saparo, Joe Steele, and George Howe. Holmes was briefly with Luis Russell in 1928 and the following year became a key soloist with Russell's orchestra, soloing on quite a few records and holding his own with Red Allen, J.C. Higginbotham, and Albert Nicholas.

Holmes' later years were anticlimactic. He was with the Mills Blue Rhythm Band (1932) but soon returned to Russell, staying with the big band during the five years (1935–40) when it functioned primarily as Louis Armstrong's backup group. The altoist's later associations included the Cootie Williams big band (1942–45), John Kirby (1947), Billy Kyle, and, after a long period of semiretirement, the Harlem Blues and Jazz Band (in the 1970s). Charlie Holmes never really fulfilled his potential, although he sounds quite good on his early records with Red Allen, J.C. Higginbotham, King Oliver, and particularly Luis Russell.

CLAUDE HOPKINS

b. Aug. 24, 1903, Alexandria, VA, d. Feb. 19, 1984, New York, NY

Although fitting more into the swing era, Claude Hopkins' big band started just early enough to belong in this book. A very talented stride pianist,

Hopkins grew up in Washington, D.C. He began playing piano when he was seven, and, despite studying to be a doctor, he chose music as his career, after studying at Howard University and Washington Conservatory. Hopkins first led a band in Atlantic City in the summer of 1924. He worked with Wilbur Sweatman (1925) and sailed to Europe so his orchestra could accompany Josephine Baker.

Back in New York, Hopkins led a few groups during 1926–29 that unfortunately never recorded. In 1930 his new orchestra was based at the Savoy Ballroom, switching to Roseland (1931–34), where it replaced Fletcher Henderson. The band had its recording debut on May 24, 1932, a date that included its theme song ("I Would Do Anything for You," which Hopkins cowrote) and a very colorful arrangement by Jimmy Mundy on "Mush Mouth." Other sessions during 1932–33 yielded a Hopkins feature on "Three Little Words" (actually from a radio transcription session), "Canadian Capers," and "California, Here I Come" among the highlights.

Despite its head start, the Claude Hopkins Orchestra (which was based at the Cotton Club during 1935–36) did not catch on commercially and actually declined as the decade progressed. There were no recordings at all in 1936, and, after much turnover (Jabbo Smith was with the orchestra in 1937), it broke up in 1940. Claude Hopkins (who led a few other short-term big bands) mostly freelanced in small groups during the remainder of his life, recording a pair of outstanding solo piano sets as late as 1972.

9 **1932–1934/May 24, 1932–Jan. 1, 1934/Classics 699**
All of Claude Hopkins' big band recordings are available on three CDs. *1934–1935* (Classics 716) and *1937–1940* (Classics 733) have their moments. However, *1932–1934* is easily the best of the trio. It includes four studio sessions plus two radio transcription dates. With such key players as trumpeter-singer Ovie Alston, trombonist Fernando Arbello,

clarinetist Edmond Hall, tenor saxophonist Bobby Sands, and ballad singer Orlando Roberson, this was a potentially great orchestra. Unfortunately it peaked too early, but that does not lessen the appeal of this swinging CD, which shows that the Claude Hopkins Orchestra ranked high among Harlem big bands of the early 1930s.

DARNELL HOWARD
b. July 25, 1895, Chicago, IL, d. Sept. 2, 1966, San Francisco, CA

An exciting clarinetist who had a 50-year career, Darnell Howard had the unusual double of clarinet and violin. The son of musicians, Howard started on violin when he was seven before taking up the clarinet. He began playing professionally in 1912, freelancing in the Midwest. In September 1917, Howard joined W.C. Handy's orchestra on violin, going to New York with the band and making his recording debut. Howard soon returned to his native Chicago, where he resumed freelancing, including playing with Charlie Elgar in 1921. Now mostly on clarinet, Howard visited London with the Plantation Days band (led by James P. Johnson) in 1923 and again the following year with the Singing Syncopators. In Chicago, he played with Carroll Dickerson, Dave Peyton, and King Oliver's Dixie Syncopators (the last on clarinet, alto, and soprano). Howard visited Shanghai, the Philippines, and Japan with the Singing Syncopators during 1925–26. Back in Chicago he worked again with Oliver, played simultaneously with the orchestras of Erskine Tate and Carroll Dickerson (1926–27) and worked with Jimmy Wade's Dixielanders (1928), Dave Peyton (1929–30), and groups of his own. Along the way he recorded in 1926 with Elgar's Creole Orchestra, Luis Russell, Jelly Roll Morton, and King Oliver and in 1929 with Jimmy Bertrand's Washboard Wizards, Junie Cobb (on violin), Alex Hill, and Reuben Reeves. There would be further appearances on freewheeling sessions by the State

Street Ramblers (1931) and the Memphis Nighthawks (1932).

Darnell Howard was an important member of the Earl Hines big band during 1931–37. In later years he worked with the Coleman Hawkins Orchestra (1941), Kid Ory (1945), Muggsy Spanier (1948–53), Bob Scobey, Jimmy Archey, and Earl Hines' Dixieland band (1955–62), also recording with pianist Don Ewell. The clarinetist remained quite active up until his death in 1966.

PAUL HOWARD

b. Sept. 20, 1895, Steubenville, OH, d. Feb. 18, 1980, Los Angeles, CA

A decent tenor saxophonist, Paul Howard led one of Los Angeles' finest bands of the late 1920s, the Quality Serenaders. Howard began on cornet and learned alto, clarinet, oboe, bassoon, flute, and piano before settling on tenor. After moving to Los Angeles in 1913, Howard started playing professionally with Wood Wilson's Syncopators in 1916. He worked with Satchel McVea's Howdy Band, Harry Southard's Black and Tan Band and both King Oliver and Jelly Roll Morton when they visited Los Angeles. Howard was with Harvey Brooks' Quality Four in 1923 (making his recording debut in February 1924) and formed his Quality Serenaders in 1924.

Based at Sebastian's Cotton Club (1927–29) and the Kentucky Club, the Quality Serenaders (heard in the backgrounds of a few movies) were featured on four exciting recording sessions (resulting in a dozen titles) during 1929–30, all of which have been reissued on *Hot Stuff* (Frog 28). The octet (which grew to ten pieces by 1930) featured two future swing all-stars (trombonist Lawrence Brown and Lionel Hampton on drums) and was a hard-driving unit. After the group broke up in the early 1930s, Howard worked with Ed Garland's 111 Band, Freddie Washington, Lionel Hampton (1935), and Eddie Barefield's orchestra (1936–37). Paul Howard led a group that played regularly at

Virginia's, near Los Angeles, during 1939–53 (but never recorded), before he retired from music.

SPIKE HUGHES

b. Oct. 18, 1908, London, England, d. Feb. 2, 1987, London, England

A fine bassist and an adventurous arranger-composer in the late 1920s, Patrick "Spike" Hughes unfortunately did not remain a jazz musician for long. Hughes played bass with the band at Cambridge University, and on his record dates of 1930–32 (with his Decca-Dents) he used some of the top British jazz musicians plus Americans Sylvester Ahola and Bobby Davis. His Three Blind Mice (a rhythm section from the larger band) accompanied Jimmy Dorsey on one memorable session. Hughes, who toured with Jack Hylton (1931–32), in 1933 went to New York City, where he led all-star black groups (using Benny Carter's big band as a nucleus) on four superb record dates, playing mostly his own compositions; his sidemen included Henry "Red" Allen, Dicky Wells, flutist Wayman Carver, Coleman Hawkins, Chu Berry, and Carter, among others.

Perhaps Hughes realized at that point that his career was not going to get any better. Right after the height of his 1933 sessions, he retired from playing bass, despite only being 24. Instead Spike Hughes, who was a critic for *Melody Maker* in England during 1931–44, became a full-time music journalist and was involved in composing classical music, largely turning his back on jazz.

9 Volumes 1 & 2/Mar. 12, 1930–Nov. 5, 1930/Kings Cross 001/002

8 Volumes 3 & 4/Nov. 19, 1930–Nov. 20, 1932/Kings Cross 003/004

10 1933/Apr. 18, 1933–Oct. 16, 1933/Retrieval 79005

These three CD releases have every recording led by Spike Hughes. The two Kings Cross reissues are both double-CD sets. *Volumes 1 & 2* feature such interesting soloists as trumpeters Sylvester Ahola,

Max Goldberg, and Norman Payne, altoist Philip Buchel, clarinetist Danny Polo, and Buddy Featherstonhaugh on tenor. In addition, Muggsy Spanier guests on one cut, and Jimmy Dorsey sounds quite remarkable (particularly on "I'm Just Wild About Harry") during his session with Hughes' Three Blind Mice. Not all of the music is classic (some of the vocals are just adequate), but there is an awful lot of rewarding music to be heard, much of it little known. The same can be said for *Volumes 3 & 4,* which almost comes up to the same level, features Hughes' leading larger bands, and has Norman Payne and Buddy Featherstonhaugh often taking solo honors. Overall, this pair of two-CD sets contain some of the finest British jazz of the era.

1933 has the 14 selections that Hughes led while in the United States, plus two record dates (with eight numbers plus a previously unissued alternate take of "Devil's Holiday") by the 1933 Benny Carter big band. On the Hughes sessions, the bassist contributed nine adventurous works, adapted one traditional theme, and let the band jam (to an extent) on four standards. The 14- to 15-piece bands are filled with some of the top black musicians of the era, with Allen, Wells, Carter, Carver, Hawkins, and Berry all having solo space. Spike Hughes' writing at times was influenced by Duke Ellington and classical music but comes across as quite original overall. It is a pity that he let this be his final act in jazz.

ALBERTA HUNTER

b. Apr. 1, 1895, Memphis, TN, d. Oct. 18, 1984, New York, NY

A major singer with a long and episodic career, Alberta Hunter's reappearance in the 1970s found her exceeding her earlier popularity. Hunter ran away from home when she was 11 and was soon working as a singer, performing in Chicago-area clubs throughout her teenage years. After moving to New York, she recorded regularly starting in 1921, being one of the first classic blues singers on record, although she always had a much wider repertoire than just blues. Hunter's "Downhearted Blues" in 1923 became a big hit for Bessie Smith. Her own recordings from the decade (sometimes using Josephine Beatty, her half-sister's name, as a pseudonym) generally featured the top players of the era as sidemen, including Louis Armstrong, Sidney Bechet, Fats Waller, King Oliver, Fletcher Henderson, the Original Memphis Five (an early integrated session from February 1923), Duke Ellington, and Eubie Blake.

Hunter always reached beyond blues in her career, costarring with Paul Robeson in the London production of *Showboat* (1928–29), working in Paris, and singing straight ballads and cabaret music with John Jackson's orchestra in England. She spent most of the 1930s in Europe, returning to New York in 1939, singing swing tunes quite credibly. Hunter did extensive touring for the U.S.O. during World War II and stayed active until 1956, when she retired from music and became a nurse, at the age of 61. She did come back briefly for a couple of recordings in 1961 but otherwise worked as a nurse for 20 years. When she was 82 in 1977, it was decided that she should be retired from the nursing field, since she was believed to be 65! So Alberta Hunter returned to music, having a very successful run at the Cookery in New York, recording three albums for Columbia, and delighting audiences with her double entendre lyrics. Before her death at age 89, she was one of the last living links to the early 1920s.

7 1921–1923/May 1921–Feb. 1923/Document 5422
8 1923–1924/Feb. 1923–Nov. 6, 1924/Document 5423
8 1924–1927/Nov. 6, 1924–Feb. 26, 1927/Document 5424
9 1927–1946/May 20, 1927–1946/Document 5425
6 Alternate Takes/May 1921–Feb. 1924/Document 1006

All of Alberta Hunter's early recordings are on these five CDs, other than her eight selections from 1950. *1921–1923* has her first 22 recordings. The technical quality of these often-scratchy transfers is a bit erratic and not every song is classic, but there are excellent versions of "Someday Sweetheart,"

"Downhearted Blues" (a year before Bessie Smith had a hit with Hunter's song), "I'm Going Away Just to Wear You Off My Mind," and possibly the earliest recording of "'Tain't Nobody's Biz-ness." Eubie Blake is on piano for two numbers, Fletcher Henderson and his pickup groups of the time also help out, and three selections find Hunter accompanied by the Original Memphis Five.

1923–1924 has some very interesting backup musicians, with Joe Smith on two numbers, Fats Waller jamming on "Stingaree Blues" and "You Can't Do What My Last Man Did," Lovie Austin's Blues Serenaders making a few appearances, and two tunes ("It's Gonna Be a Cold Cold Winter" and "Parlor Social De Luxe") being among the very first recordings of Duke Ellington. Hunter's better performances include "Aggravatin' Papa," "Loveless Love," and "Old-Fashioned Love." *1924–1927* has the Red Onion Babies (with Louis Armstrong on five numbers and Sidney Bechet on three) uplifting such tunes as "Nobody Knows the Way I Feel Dis Mornin'" and "Everybody Loves My Baby." Other selections feature Perry Bradford's Mean Four, pianists Clarence Williams and Mike Jackson, plus some unidentified musicians. Hunter is heard throughout in her early prime, including on "Your Jelly Roll Is Good," "I'm Hard to Satisfy," "Everybody Mess Around," and "Heebie Jeebies."

1927–1946 has Hunter accompanied by Fats Waller (on piano or organ) on "Sugar," "Beale Street Blues," and "I'm Going to See My Ma." There are also a couple numbers from 1929, excellent sessions from 1939 (with Buster Bailey, Lil Armstrong, Wellman Braud, and trumpeter Charlie Shavers) and 1940 (backing by pianist Eddie Heywood Jr.), along with two numbers from 1945. Alberta Hunter really did improve with age, and her style was quite timeless, fitting into each decade even while her basic approach was unchanged from the early days.

Alternate Takes, which has 22 alternates from the 1921–24 period (including two more versions of "Downhearted Blues"), is strictly for completists due to the sometimes-noisy sound quality and the lack of much difference between these recordings and the originally issued takes. Still, kudos to the Document label for making all of this music available.

JACK HYLTON

b. July 2, 1892, Great Lever, Lancashire, England, d. Jan. 29, 1965, London, England

Jack Hylton was the leader of one of the most popular British dance bands of the late 1920s and 1930s. Early on he was billed as "The Singing Millboy," dancing and singing in shows from the age of seven. Hylton played organ in a London theater in 1913 and occasionally performed piano but would be most notable as a bandleader. After serving in the Army during World War I and freelancing as a pianist, he began leading his orchestra in 1921. By the end of the decade, he was one of England's biggest names, the country's Paul Whiteman, mixing dance music with jazz. The Jack Hylton Orchestra appeared in vaudeville, on stage, constantly on the radio (starting in 1926), on tours of the European continent, and on many records, some of which were jazz oriented. Hylton, who visited the United States with a nucleus of musicians in 1935–36, helped coordinate Duke Ellington's visit to England in 1933 and used Coleman Hawkins as a guest in 1934.

Jack Hylton kept his big band together into 1940. In later years he worked as a theatrical producer.

LPS TO SEARCH FOR

Jack Hylton and His Orchestra (GNP/Crescendo 9017), which dates from 1931–33, has a remarkable "Ellingtonia Medley" that finds the band sounding very close to Duke Ellington's on "Black and Tan Fantasy," "Mood Indigo," "It Don't Mean a Thing," and "Bugle Call Rag." Other highlights include "St. Louis Blues," "Black and Blue Rhythm," "Some of These Days," a "42nd Street

Medley," and a version of "Dinah" where the group imitates Guy Lombardo, Tommy Dorsey, Louis Armstrong, Bing Crosby, and Joe Venuti, among others. *Jack's Back* (GNP/Crescendo 9018), which has 14 numbers from 1932–33, is a bit more conventional as the orchestra alternates between early swing and sweet dance music.

CHARLIE IRVIS

b. 1899, New York, NY, d. 1939, New York, NY

One of the pioneers in using the plunger mute on the trombone to create unusual tonal distortions, Charlie Irvis was a predecessor to Tricky Sam Nanton. Irvis started his career working with Lucille Hegamin's Blue Flame Syncopators (1920–21). He gigged with Willie "the Lion" Smith and was an early member of the Washingtonians (1924–26), initially led by Elmer Snowden but soon taken over by Duke Ellington. Irvis helped Bubber Miley create the original "jungle" sound, although he departed before Ellington made it big working at the Cotton Club. Instead, Irvis worked with Charlie Johnson (1927–28), Jelly Roll Morton (1929–30), and the short-lived Bubber Miley Orchestra (1931). In addition to appearing on some very early Ellington recordings and with Johnson and Morton, Irvis recorded with Alberta Hunter, Thomas Morris (1923 and 1926), Fats Waller (1927 and 1929), and most notably Clarence Williams (1924–27), including the Blue Five sessions with Louis Armstrong and Sidney Bechet.

With the rise of the Depression, Charlie Irvis faded out of the spotlight. He worked again with Elmer Snowden and Charlie Johnson but was largely forgotten years before his death at age 40.

CLIFF JACKSON

b. July 19, 1902, Culpeper, VA, d. May 24, 1970, New York, NY

Cliff Jackson was a major stride pianist. His two recording sessions with his Crazy Kats resulted in three of the hottest performances of the classic jazz era: "Horse Feathers," "Torrid Rhythm," and "The Terror." Jackson worked in Washington, D.C., and Atlantic City early on, moved to New York in 1923, and played with Happy Rhone's Club Orchestra (1925), Lionel Howard's Musical Aces (1926), and Elmer Snowden. He recorded with Bob Fuller and Elmer Snowden in 1927, and that same year he formed the Crazy Kats. In 1930, the Crazy Kats recorded two numbers under Jackson's name and nine songs (highlighted by "The Terror") as Marvin Smolev's Syncopators; Smolev was the musical director of the Grey Gull label. Best known among the sidemen were trumpeter Henry Goodwin and Rudy Powell on clarinet and alto.

After the band broke up in the early 1930s, Jackson worked mostly as a soloist, occasionally backing singers. He played with Sidney Bechet in 1940–41, led a trio, and during 1943–51 was the house pianist at Café Society Downtown, taking time off to tour with Eddie Condon in 1946. Jackson worked steadily if without much acclaim during the 1950s and played with Garvin Bushell (1959), J.C. Higginbotham (1960), trumpeter Joe Thomas (1962), and Tony Parenti at Ryan's (1963–67). Cliff Jackson married singer Maxine Sullivan and recorded some solo recordings in 1969, working in a club the night before he died at age 67.

LPS TO SEARCH FOR

Cliff Jackson and His Crazy Kats (Retrieval 119) has all 11 titles by Jackson's band from 1930 plus an alternate version of "The Terror." Although some of the tunes are commercial, even the least interesting arrangements have some hot solo breaks, and few more blazing performances have been recorded than "Horse Feathers." This must have been a very exciting band to see live!

DEWEY JACKSON

b. June 21, 1900, St. Louis, MO, d. 1994, St. Louis, MO

Dewey Jackson was considered St. Louis' top jazz trumpeter throughout the 1920s and '30s even though he barely recorded. Jackson began his career playing with Tommy Evans (1916–17) and George Reynolds' Keystone Band. He worked on a riverboat with Charlie Creath (starting in 1919) and led the Golden Melody Band during 1920–23. After playing on the *S.S. Capitol* with Fate Marable in 1924, Jackson led the St. Louis Peacock Charleston Orchestra.

During the next 15 years, the trumpeter alternated between having groups and playing on the river with Marable or Creath. Other than a four-month period performing at the Cotton Club with Andrew Preer's orchestra in 1926, Jackson spent virtually his entire career working in the St. Louis area or on riverboats, staying active (in later years with Dixieland bands) into the 1960s. His only recordings, other than possibly accompanying singers Missouri Anderson, Luella Miller, and Bert Hatton during 1926–27, were four songs cut as a leader on June 21, 1926 (including "She's Crying for Me" and "Going to Town"), that have been reissued on *Jazz in Saint Louis* (Timeless 1–036), two hot numbers ("Butter-Finger Blues" and "Crazy Quilt") with Charlie Creath's Jazz-O-Maniacs on May 2, 1927, and a pair of Dixieland standards ("Washington and Lee Swing" and "Tailgate Ramble") in a sextet led by tuba player Singleton Palmer (September 30, 1950) that were put out by the obscure Disco label on a '78'. Although there is so little recorded evidence, Dewey Jackson shows on his own date and the session with Creath that he was one of the more exciting trumpeters of the mid-1920s, one who almost missed being documented altogether.

PRESTON JACKSON

b. Jan. 3, 1904, New Orleans, LA, d. Nov. 12, 1983, Blytheville, AR

Preston Jackson was a talented trombonist with a distinctive tone. Born James Preston McDonald, he moved to Chicago in 1917. In 1920 (when he was 16) his mother bought him his first trombone. Within nine months, Jackson was playing locally with a variety of lesser-known groups while taking lessons from Honore Dutrey and Roy Palmer. Jackson worked with Teddy Weatherford, Art Simms (1925), and especially Oscar "Bernie" Young (1923, including his debut recordings, and 1925–30) in Milwaukee. Along the way he recorded as a leader, in 1926 (included on *Alexander, Where's That Band*—Frog 13) and with Richard M. Jones.

In the 1930s, Jackson played in Chicago with Dave Peyton (1930), Erskine Tate, Louis Armstrong (1931–32), Frankie "Half Pint" Jaxon (1933), Carroll Dickerson, Jimmie Noone, Zilner Randolph's W.P.A. Band, and Roy Eldridge, among others. In the 1940s he played just part-time (though he did record as a leader in 1946). But Preston Jackson stayed active into the 1970s, ending his career playing with veteran musicians in New Orleans and touring Europe.

RUDY JACKSON

b. 1901, Fort Wayne, IN, d. 1968, Chicago, IL

Rudy Jackson was one of the first of the ex-Ellingtonians. He grew up in Chicago, playing clarinet locally starting in 1918. Jackson was in Carroll Dickerson's group in the early 1920s and worked with King Oliver (late 1923 to mid-1924), Billy Butler, Vaughn's Lucky Sambo Orchestra, and others, having a second stint with Oliver in 1927. Jackson was with Duke Ellington's orchestra during June–December 1927, taking clarinet solos on five record dates with Ellington. Unfortunately Jackson made Duke a bit mad when he passed off Oliver's "Jazzin' Babies' Blues" as his new composition, which Ellington named "Creole Love Call," and that deception partly led to Jackson's being replaced by Barney Bigard.

Rudy Jackson's later experiences included touring Europe with Noble Sissle (1929–33), playing with Teddy Weatherford in India and Ceylon, and being based in the Far East until after World War II, when he returned to Chicago and retired from music.

TONY JACKSON

b. June 5, 1876, New Orleans, LA, d. Apr. 20, 1921, Chicago, IL

An early inspiration for Jelly Roll Morton, who called him the greatest piano player and singer in New Orleans, Tony Jackson (who unfortunately never recorded) was reportedly a major ragtime pianist who helped pave the way for jazz. Jackson played piano in New Orleans brothels as early as the 1890s, being a regular in Storyville. He traveled throughout the South until 1912, when he permanently left New Orleans to settle in Chicago. Jackson played duos with Glover Compton and accompanied the Whitman Sisters but worked mostly solo until dying from syphilis when he was 44. Tony Jackson composed "Pretty Baby" (which became a standard), "The Naked Dance," and "Michigan Water Blues," all of which Jelly Roll Morton recorded.

FREDDIE JENKINS

b. Oct. 10, 1906, NY, d. July 12, 1978, Tarrant County, TX

Freddie Jenkins (nicknamed "Posey") was a colorful player whose heated Louis Armstrong-inspired solos were a contrast in Duke Ellington's orchestra to the plunger work of Bubber Miley and Cootie Williams, and the lyricism of Arthur Whetsol. Jenkins worked early on with the 369th Regiment Cadet Band, attended Wilberforce University, gigged with Edgar Hayes' Blue Grass Buddies, and performed regularly with Horace Henderson's Collegians during 1924–28. He made his recording debut on a Clara Smith session in 1928.

Jenkins worked steadily with Duke Ellington from October 1928 until April 1934, appearing on many records, including "Tiger Rag" and "When You're Smiling." He can be seen quite prominently during the Ellington Orchestra's performance of "Old Man Blues" in the 1930 Amos and Andy film *Check and Double Check*. Jenkins' only record outside of the sphere of Ellington during this period was a two-song session with the Musical Stevedores in 1929.

A serious lung ailment forced Jenkins to retire in 1934, when he was just 27. Jenkins started a comeback in 1935, recording six titles during his only date as a leader. He was with Luis Russell for a few months in 1936, spent part of 1937–38 back with Ellington, recorded with Rex Stewart in 1937, and co-led a band with bassist Hayes Alvis. But later in 1938, his lung ailment returned and he was urged to permanently give up playing trumpet. His doctor's advice must have been good, for Freddie Jenkins (who later on worked as a songwriter, press agent, disc jockey, real estate broker, and as an insurance salesman) lived 40 more years!

BILL JOHNSON

b. Aug. 10, 1872, New Orleans, LA, d. Dec. 3, 1972, New Orleans, LA

Bassist Bill Johnson was a major New Orleans jazz pioneer. He has been cited by some as being the first bassist to regularly pluck his instrument as opposed to bowing it, reportedly because a drunk had broken his bow one night!

One of the oldest jazz musicians to be active on the scene in the 1920s, Johnson played guitar when he was 15 and did not start on bass until 1900, when he was already 28. He worked regularly in New Orleans, including with the Peerless Orchestra and Frankie Dusen's Eagle Band, doubling on tuba in order to play parades. Johnson was one of the first jazz musicians to leave New Orleans, moving to California in 1909. In 1914 he sent for Freddie Keppard and some other top musicians, forming the Original Creole Orchestra, which played on the Orpheum Circuit, helping to introduce the as-yet-unnamed new jazz music to Los Angeles, Chicago, and New York. The Original Creole Orchestra lasted until 1917. Johnson formed a similar group the following year and supposedly recorded one title ("Tack It Down"), but unfortunately that performance was never released.

Johnson joined King Oliver's Creole Jazz Band in 1921 on guitar and banjo, playing with Oliver into 1923. He appeared on the first recording by Oliver's famed band, taking the famous vocal break ("Oh, play that thing!") on the original version of "Dippermouth Blues." Johnson led a band in Chicago for many years and also worked on bass with Johnny Dodds and Freddie Keppard. During 1928–29 he recorded with the Chicago Footwarmers, the Dixie Four, singer Marie Grinter, Ikey Robinson, the State Street Ramblers, Tampa Red, and Sippie Wallace, in addition to several sessions with Johnny Dodds and having one two-song date as a leader.

Despite being an important early bassist, Johnson never gained the fame he deserved; had the 1918 selection been released at the time, he would have been the first jazz string bassist on records. In the 1930s he worked with the Smitzer Trio, Johnson performed with Bunk Johnson in 1947, and he played regularly in Chicago into the 1950s. Bill Johnson retired in the early 1960s and lived to be several months older than 100 before passing away in his native New Orleans.

CHARLIE JOHNSON

b. Nov. 21, 1891, Philadelphia, PA, d. Dec. 13, 1959, New York, NY

Charlie Johnson led one of the finest bands of the 1920s. Johnson started out playing trombone, freelancing in the New York area from 1914. However, after he moved to Atlantic City, he switched to piano. Never really a soloist, Johnson was more of an accompanist who had a knack for putting together bands full of young all-stars. He led a series of groups starting in 1918 and recorded four titles with classic blues singer Mary Stafford in 1921. His

Paradise Ten was based at Small's Paradise during 1925–35. Johnson's band recorded five notable sessions during 1925–29, featuring such sidemen as Thomas Morris, Jabbo Smith, Leonard Davis, Sidney DeParis, Charlie Irvis, Jimmy Harrison, Benny Carter, and Benny Waters plus guest vocalist Monette Moore. At different times, Carter (who made his recording debut with Johnson) and Waters contributed arrangements. After the band closed at Small's in 1935, Charlie Johnson faded from the scene, playing on only an occasional basis into the early 1950s and never recording again.

9 **The Compete Charlie Johnson Sessions/Oct. 1925–May 8, 1929/Hot 'n' Sweet 5110**

All of Charlie Johnson's recordings as a leader are on this CD: 14 titles plus ten alternate takes, so this would be a difficult disc to improve upon. Among the highlights are "Don't You Leave Me Here," "You Ain't the One," "Charleston Is the Best Dance After All," and three takes of the exciting "Walk That Thing." Jabbo Smith steals the show on a couple of occasions, but a large percentage of Johnson's sidemen were major players, and both the ensemble work and the solos are on a consistently high level.

JAMES P. JOHNSON

b. Feb. 1, 1891, New Brunswick, NJ, d. Nov. 17, 1955, New York, NY

The king of stride pianists, James P. Johnson was one of the greatest jazz pianists of all time and arguably the most influential of the 1920s, particularly before the rise of Fats Waller, Earl Hines, and Art Tatum. Johnson had piano lessons from his mother as a youth and was playing at rent parties as a young teenager. A professional by 1912, Johnson played solo piano in clubs, toured in vaudeville, cut piano rolls (starting in 1917), and also did theater work. Moving the music beyond ragtime, Johnson "strided" with his left hand (moving back and forth between bass notes and chords that were played an

James P. Johnson was the definitive stride pianist and a major songwriter.

octave or two higher) while his right improvised an endless series of melodic variations. Although Johnson did not invent stride piano, he solidified the ideas of his predecessors from the previous two decades into an exciting new style that perfectly fit the music of the 1920s.

Johnson first recorded in 1921, and during the next decade he recorded such classic piano works as "Carolina Shout" (a test piece for young pianists), "Keep Off the Grass," "Snowy Morning Blues," "You've Got to Be Modernistic," and "Jingles." He also led some combo dates, recorded as an accompanist to a variety of classic blues singers (including memorable encounters with Bessie Smith and Ethel Waters), and was the star of countless rent parties and jam sessions, often with his

friends Willie "the Lion" Smith and Fats Waller (his protégé). But that was not all. Johnson wrote such standards as "If I Could Be with You One Hour Tonight," "Old-Fashioned Love," and the theme song of the 1920s, "The Charleston." He worked as musical director for the *Dudley Black Sensations/Smart Set* revues, led the Harmony Seven (1922), and visited England with the *Plantation Days* show. In 1923 he scored the Broadway musical *Runnin' Wild* (which included "The Charleston" and "Old-Fashioned Love"), and in July 1928 he debuted his extended work *Yamecraw* at Carnegie Hall. Johnson also worked in *Keep Shufflin'* with Fats Waller in 1928 and directed the band in 1929 for the Bessie Smith short film *St. Louis Blues*.

After a very busy decade, Johnson spent most of

the 1930s out of the limelight, concentrating on composing large-scale orchestral works, including *Harlem Symphony, Jassamine, Symphony in Brown,* and a blues opera called *De Organizer.* Unfortunately much of his "serious" work from this era was rarely performed and some of it has since been lost. After appearing at John Hammond's Spirituals to Swing concert in December 1938, Johnson began performing more regularly again. The revival of interest in classic jazz found Johnson working steadily in the 1940s, including appearing at some of Eddie Condon's Town Hall concerts. He survived a stroke in October 1946 and remained active until a more severe stroke in 1951 ended his playing days, four years before his death. James P. Johnson was a major influence on many pianists, including Fats Waller, Duke Ellington (who used to slow down James P.'s piano rolls so he could learn the fingerings), Art Tatum, and Thelonious Monk.

6 Carolina Shout/May 1917–June 1925/Musical Heritage Society 512358
6 Parlor Piano Solos/May 1917–June 1921/Biograph 150
5 Runnin' Wild/1921–1926/Tradition 1048

The music on each of these CDs is made up of James P. Johnson piano rolls. Although somewhat metronomic (as piano rolls tend to be), these "performances" are of particular interest because the great pianist did not get around to recording all of these songs, some of which were his own compositions. *Carolina Shout,* in addition to the title cut (a song that is on all three discs in different versions), is most notable for "The Charleston" (which Johnson did not record until the 1940s and never as a piano solo), "Steeplechase Rag," "Harlem Strut," and "Farewell Blues." *Parlor Piano Solos* has such obscurities as "When It's Cherry Time in Tokio," "Roumania," "Don't Tell Your Monkey Man," "It Takes Love to Cure the Heart's Desire," "Fascination," and "Stop It"; the latter three songs were written by Johnson. Nowhere on the outside of *Runnin' Wild* does it say that the music is piano

rolls rather than piano solos, a fact mentioned only near the end of the liner notes. The exact dates are also not given, and the playing time is rather brief. Still, a four-song "Runnin' Wild Medley," "Harlem Choc'late Babies on Parade," and "What a Fool I've Been" are rarities, and none of the music is repeated from the other two CDs.

10 Harlem Stride Piano/Aug. 1921–Nov. 18, 1929/Hot 'n' Sweet 151032
9 1921–1928/Aug. 1921–June 18, 1928/Classics 658

These two CDs cover largely the same ground, with a slight edge given to the Hot 'n' Sweet disc. In both cases there are James P. Johnson's 11 piano solos from 1921–27 (including "The Harlem Strut," "Keep Off the Grass," "Carolina Shout," and "Snowy Morning Blues"), a band version of "Carolina Shout" from 1921, and six combo selections; two are duets with Louis Metcalf that have vocals by Perry Bradford. The Hot 'n Sweet disc also has Johnson's piano roll version of "Charleston" and six selections from 1929 (including two more piano solos and four band tracks). The Classics disc, which has three fewer selections, has Johnson's two numbers with Johnny Dunn and Fats Waller ("What's the Use of Being Alone" and "Original Bugle Blues") plus an additional number with Perry Bradford ("Lucy Long"), but those three cuts are also available elsewhere.

9 1928–1938/Oct. 19, 1928–Aug. 31, 1938/Classics 671
9 Snowy Morning Blues/Jan. 21, 1930–Sept. 22, 1944/GRP/Decca 604

If you purchase Classics' *1921–1928,* it would also make sense to acquire *1928–1938,* since it logically continues the James P. Johnson story. The pianist is heard with the Gulf Coast Seven (a Perry Bradford-led sextet in 1928 that is filled with Duke Ellington sidemen), in 1938 with a freewheeling Pee Wee Russell group, and on his own solos and band sides of 1929–31. Highlights include unaccompanied renditions of "What Is This Thing Called Love," "You've Got to Be Modernistic," and "Jingles," and a couple of duets with Clarence Williams (including the humorous "How Could I Be Blue"). For listeners who prefer just to hear Johnson's piano, *Snowy Morning Blues* has his four piano solos of 1930 plus 16 duets with drummer Eddie Dougherty from 1944, including eight songs associated with Fats Waller and eight of Johnson's best compositions (such as "A Porter's Love Song to a Chambermaid" and "Old-Fashioned Love").

Other recommended James P. Johnson CDs from the post-classic jazz era include *1938–1942* (Classics 711), *1943–1944* (Classics 824), *1944* (Classics 835), *1944 Vol. 2* (Classics 856), *1944–1945* (Classics 1027), *1945–1947* (Classics 1059), and *The Original James P. Johnson 1942–1945* (Smithsonian/Folkways 40812).

LONNIE JOHNSON

> *b. Feb. 8, 1899, New Orleans, LA, d. June 16, 1970, Toronto, Canada*

A major blues guitarist and singer for 45 years, Lonnie Johnson also appeared on a variety of jazz recordings during the second half of the 1920s, showing that he was as advanced as any guitarist of the era other than Eddie Lang. Johnson started out playing guitar and violin in his native New Orleans. He worked in London during 1917–19. But arriving back home, he discovered that most of his family had died in the flu epidemic. After working on riverboats with Fate Marable and freelancing, in 1922 Johnson moved to St. Louis, where for two years he worked in a steel foundry during the day while gigging at night on guitar, violin, and piano. A turning point in his career occurred in 1925 when he won a talent contest sponsored by the Okeh label, leading to the launch of his very productive and prolific recording career, starting by taking a vocal and playing violin on Charlie Creath's "Won't Don't Blues."

Although most of his recordings feature Johnson as a solo performer, usually singing and playing

blues and occasional ballads, his jazz associations were quite notable. Johnson recorded with Louis Armstrong's Hot Five ("I'm Not Rough," "Savoy Blues," and most notably "Hotter Than That"), Duke Ellington ("Hot and Bothered" and "The Mooche"), McKinney's Cotton Pickers, the Chocolate Dandies, Victoria Spivey, Clara Smith, Clarence Williams, Blind Willie Dunn's Gin Bottle Four (a group also including Eddie Lang, King Oliver, and Hoagy Carmichael) and ten exciting guitar duets with Lang.

Lonnie Johnson was active as a blues performer into the late 1960s. His later jazz associations included playing a couple of years with singer Putney Dandridge's band in the 1930s, recording and working with Johnny Dodds and Jimmie Noone in Chicago, duet recordings with Elmer Snowden, and some Dixieland dates in the 1960s.

7 Vol. 1/Nov. 4, 1925–Aug. 13, 1926/Document 5063
8 Vol. 2/Aug. 13, 1926–Aug. 12, 1927/Document 5064
9 Vol. 3/Oct. 3, 1927–Feb. 21, 1928/Document 5065
9 Vol. 4/Mar. 9, 1928–May 8, 1929/Document 5066
9 Vol. 5/May 15, 1929–Jan. 23, 1930/Document 5067
7 Vol. 6/Jan. 23, 1930–Feb. 11, 1931/Document 5068
7 Vol. 7/Feb. 11, 1931–Aug. 12, 1932/Document 5069
6 Steppin' on the Blues/Nov. 4, 1925–Aug. 12, 1932/Columbia/Legacy 46221

Lonnie Johnson's most significant jazz sessions of the 1920s were made as a sideman. All of his recordings as a leader during 1925–32 are on the seven Document CDs, and although many are strictly solo blues performances, there are also quite a few jazz-oriented selections, particularly the rare instrumentals. On *Vol. 1*, Johnson plays not only guitar but at various times violin, banjo, and harmonium; three selections (including "Johnson's Trio Stomp") are instrumentals. *Vol. 2* puts the emphasis on Johnson's guitar on "To Do This, You Got to Know How," "I Done Tol' You," "Steppin' on the Blues," "Four Hands Are Better Than Two," and "Woke Up with the Blues in My Fingers." *Vol. 3* has nine instrumentals among the 25 selections (including "6/88 Glide" and "Playing with the Strings"), and Jimmy Blythe pops up on three songs. *Vol. 4* is most notable for Johnson's vocal duets with Victoria Spivey on "New Black Snake Blues," "Toothache Blues," and "Furniture Man Blues" (each of which is a two-part performance), five guitar duets with Eddie Lang (including "A Handful of Riffs" and "Have to Change Keys to Play These Blues"), Johnson's date with Blind Willie Dunn's Gin Bottle Four, and some vocal duets with Spencer Williams.

Vol. 5 has the other five duets with Lang (including "Bull Frog Moan" and the accurately titled "Hot Fingers"), more vocal duets with Spencer Williams and Victoria Spivey ("You Done Lost Your Good Thing Now"), "Wipe It Off" (which teams Johnson with Clarence Williams and James P. Johnson), and such titles as "From Now on Make Your Whoopee at Home," "She's Making Whoopee in Hell Tonight," and "Another Woman Booked Out and Bound to Go." *Vol. 6* sticks mostly to blues, with appearances by Spencer Williams and Clara Smith, while *Vol. 7* (other than two songs that add pianist Fred Longshaw) is strictly solo blues and good-time vocal numbers.

Although the sampler *Steppin' on the Blues* claims that four performances are previously unissued (which might have been true when this 1990 CD was released), they are all included in the Document series. The 19 selections include seven solo instrumentals (two are duets with Lang) and two numbers on which Johnson accompanies singer Texas Alexander. But compared to the Document series, this release is a frivolity.

The Documents are filled with gems and particularly recommended to collectors of early blues. Lonnie Johnson's recordings of 1937–47 have also been made fully available through this remarkable European label. However, an overview that has just Johnson's main jazz performances and instrumentals is long overdue to be compiled.

WALTER JOHNSON
b. Feb. 18, 1904, New York, NY, d. Apr. 26, 1977, New York, NY

A solid drummer, Walter Johnson was an important transitional figure between early jazz and swing. He started his career playing with Freddie Johnson's Red Devils (1924), Bobby Brown, Elmer Snowden (1925 and 1927–28), and Billy Fowler. Johnson gained his greatest recognition for his work with Fletcher Henderson's orchestra (1929–34), where he was quite influential on the upcoming big band drummers, even though he has since been underrated. Johnson's later work included the big bands of Sam Wooding, LeRoy Smith, Fletcher Henderson again (1936–37), Lucky Millinder (1938–39), Claude Hopkins, Edgar Hayes, Coleman Hawkins (1940), Claude Hopkins, and Henderson for a third time (1941–42). Walter Johnson had a longtime association with altoist Tab Smith (1944–54) but spent his later years working as a bank guard.

CLAUDE JONES
b. Feb. 11, 1901, Boley, OK, d. Jan. 17, 1962, Atlantic Ocean, NJ

A fine trombonist who was a reliable sideman, Claude Jones had many notable musical associations, although he never became famous himself. Jones started playing music early on, originally trumpet and drums before taking up the trombone when he was 13. He attended Wilberforce College but dropped out of his law classes to work with the Synco Jazz Band (1922). Jones stayed with the group, which became McKinney's Cotton Pickers, until the spring of 1929. Primarily a big band trombonist who could take very capable and concise solos, Jones also worked with Fletcher Henderson (1929–31), Don Redman (1931–33), back with Henderson (1933–34), Chick Webb, Cab Calloway (1934–40), Coleman Hawkins (1940), and Henderson a third time (1941) in addition to the combos of Zutty Singleton and Joe Sullivan. He recorded with Jelly Roll Morton and Sidney Bechet in the late 1930s. Jones' later career included stints with the big bands of Benny Carter (1942), Don Redman, Cab Calloway, Duke Ellington (1944–49), and Machito, and brief returns to Henderson (1950) and Ellington (1951). Claude Jones retired from music altogether in the early 1950s to become an officers' mess steward on the liner *S.S. United States*.

ISHAM JONES

b. Jan. 31, 1894, Coalton, OH, d. Oct. 19, 1956, Hollywood, FL

One of America's great songwriters, Isham Jones wrote such songs as "It Had to Be You," "I'll See You in My Dreams" "The One I Love Belongs to Somebody Else," "There Is No Greater Love," and "On the Alamo." Jones was also an important bandleader in the 1920s and '30s. He played tenor sax and in the early days string bass, first leading a band in 1912, when he was 18. In 1915 Jones moved to Chicago, where he had a trio that gradually grew to 11 pieces by 1921. During 1922–24, his orchestra featured trumpeter Louis Panico, performing first-class jazz-influenced dance music. Jones' orchestra visited London in 1924 and upon its return to Chicago became less jazz oriented, evolving into a high-quality dance band. Jones weathered the Depression but gradually lost interest in his ensemble, which by 1936 was featuring the young clarinetist-altoist-singer Woody Herman. When Jones decided to break up his big band that year, Herman took over the nucleus of the orchestra and started his own successful group. Isham Jones led another orchestra during 1937–38 and recorded as late as 1947 but was happy in his later years to run a general store in Colorado, moving to Florida in 1955, a year before his death.

9 1922–1926/Mar. 1922–May 6, 1926/Timeless 067
7 Swinging Down the Lane/Apr. 24, 1924–Dec. 15, 1930/Memphis Archives 7014
7 Vol. 1/Oct. 8, 1929–Mar. 31, 1931/Parklane 101

8 The Isham Jones Centennial Album/Apr. 29, 1935 + Nov. 2, 1937/Viper's Nest 156

There are only three duplicates between the 23-cut Timeless CD and the 18 numbers on the Memphis Archives release. The former set has 17 of the better performances that Louis Panico recorded with Jones during 1922–24 (skipping over their cornball hit of "Wabash Blues"), including "Those Longing for You Blues," "Aunt Hagar's Children Blues," "Somebody's Wrong," and "Never Again." Listeners can appreciate why Panico was held in such high regard during this early period. The CD also has six numbers from 1925–26, including "Riverboat Shuffle" and "Charleston," before Jones' music became much more commercial. *Swinging Down the Lane*, in addition to six Panico appearances, has two selections by the Ray Miller Orchestra (with Jones conducting), eight numbers from 1925–26, and two somewhat out-of-place selections from 1930.

With the exception of "Stardust" and alternate versions of two songs, all 24 numbers on the Parklane CD have vocals by either Frank Sylvano or Eddie Stone. The music is purposely quite danceable and soothing, the type of commercial big band performances that were popular in the early 1930s, although there are occasional jazz moments, particularly from trumpeter Whitey Moeller. The better tunes include "What's the Use," "Miss Hannah" and "My Baby Just Cares for Me." *The Isham Jones Centennial Album* has some particularly intriguing music. The first 17 selections feature a surprisingly jazz-oriented version of the Isham Jones Orchestra, dating from 1935. The ensemble, a big band with three violins and the young Woody Herman prominently featured, has both string bass and tuba, which contributes to a very powerful sound. The music (which includes "Blue Room," "King Porter Stomp," "Sugar Foot Stomp," and a medley of Jones' hits) is reminiscent of Benny Goodman's orchestra, except that Goodman was still a couple of months away from making it big! The CD concludes with five selections from Jones' completely unknown orchestra of 1937, tunes that swing surprisingly hard, considering the leader's reputation for sweet music.

MAGGIE JONES

b. 1900, Hillsboro, TX, d. 1940s?

Maggie Jones is best known for leading two sessions in 1924 that include Louis Armstrong among her sidemen. She was born Faye Barnes, moved to New York City in the early 1920s, and worked regularly in theaters during the 1920s, billed as "The Texas Nightingale." During 1923–26 she recorded 40 selections (counting alternate takes), proving to be an excellent second-level blues singer. Jones worked with the Clarence Muse Vaudeville Company in 1927 and co-owned a dress shop. During 1928–29 she had a small part in Lew Leslie's *Blackbirds of 1928*. Maggie Jones returned to Texas in the early 1930s and was performing at least as late as 1934, although her whereabouts and activities after that engagement are unknown.

8 Maggie Jones, Vol. 1/Aug. 1923–April 16, 1925/Document 5348

7 Maggie Jones, Vol. 2/Gladys Bentley/May 1925–Mar. 1929/ Document 5349

The first Document CD contains Maggie Jones' first 24 recordings. Her six titles with Louis Armstrong and Fletcher Henderson include "Anybody Here Want to Try My Cabbage," "Screamin' the Blues," and "Good-Time Flat Blues" (which reappeared as "Farewell to Storyville" in the 1946 Louis Armstrong movie *New Orleans*). Charlie Green and Henderson help out on four other numbers, while most of the other accompaniment is more obscure. Among the better non-Armstrong tunes are "You Can't Do What My Last Man Did," "Early Every Morn," and "Undertaker's Blues."

The second disc starts out with Jones' final 16 recordings. While Bob Fuller's clarinet on a few numbers is unfortunate, Jones is assisted by Henderson's Hot Six (with Joe Smith) on two cuts and by Louis Metcalf on four others. Among the highlights are "Cheatin' on Me," "You Ain't Gonna Feed in My Pasture Now," and "Mama Stayed Out the Whole Night Long." It seems strange that Maggie Jones' recording career would end in 1926, for she was still improving with age.

The remainder of the second CD has the only eight numbers that singer-pianist Gladys Bentley recorded (other than one appearance with the Washboard Serenaders). Bentley sometimes worked as a male impersonator (due to her low voice and her large features), and her recordings (solos and four duets with Eddie Lang) are a bit primitive and obvious in their humor, but still quite musical and not without interest.

RICHARD M. JONES

b. June 13, 1892, Donaldsville, LA, d. Dec. 8, 1945, Chicago, IL

Richard Myknee Jones was an adequate pianist who was more significant as a bandleader and songwriter. He began his career when he was 12, playing tuba with the Claiborne Williams Band. Jones, who performed with the Eureka Brass Band on alto horn and cornet, eventually specialized on piano. He played regularly at Lulu White's Mahogany Hall (a famous bordello) during 1908–17 and often led bands in New Orleans. Jones, who also played with John Robichaux and Armand J. Piron, wrote a song in 1915 ("Lonesome Nobody Cares") that was featured by Sophie Tucker.

After performing with Oscar Celestin in 1918, Jones moved to Chicago and worked in Clarence Williams' publishing company, learning the music business. Jones played with Bernie Young and Willie Hightower but more importantly became a powerful manager of the "race" department of the Okeh label in the mid-1920s, organizing many record dates. As a leader he recorded a pair of piano solos in 1923 and led his Jazz Wizards (sidemen included

Albert Nicholas, Johnny St. Cyr, cornetist Shirley Clay, Preston Jackson, Ikey Robinson, Roy Palmer, and Omer Simeon) on a total of 22 numbers during 1925–29. In addition, Jones recorded as a sideman with many singers, including Chippie Hill and Blanche Calloway. As a songwriter he had his greatest success with "Trouble in Mind," "Jazzin' Babies' Blues," "Riverside Blues," and, in the 1930s, "Red Wagon."

Jones spent 1931–32 back in New Orleans and then resettled in Chicago and worked as a talent scout for record labels (especially Decca), playing on an occasional basis and leading a few sessions during 1935–36. Richard M. Jones spent his last years doing defense work during World War II, leading a final record date in 1944 and acting as a talent scout for the Mercury label.

7 1923–1927/June 1, 1923–July 20, 1927/Classics 826
7 1927–1944/Nov. 7, 1927–Mar. 23, 1944/Classics 853

All of Richard M. Jones' recordings as a leader are on these two CDs. Not all of the music is classic, and some of the group sides (which are not very well recorded technically) are a little disappointing, but both discs have their moments of interest. *1923–1927* features Jones as a solo pianist (two numbers from 1923), with several versions of his Jazz Wizards (Albert Nicholas gets solo honors on the early trios, while the later quintet/sextets are a bit more erratic), and on two songs apiece with singer Lillie Delk Christian, Don Nelson's Paramount Serenaders, and cornetist Willie Hightower's Night Hawks. *1927–1944* has plenty of variety. The 1927–28 band sides are erratic, but Jones' 1929 band is greatly uplifted by Omer Simeon and Roy Palmer, his six 1935 big band titles are rare and swinging, and he is featured as a singer in 1936's "Trouble in Mind" and "Black Rider" (Lee Collins is strong in support). The CD concludes with four worthwhile numbers from 1944 with a veteran sextet, also including Bob Shoffner, Preston Jackson, Darnell Howard, John Lindsay, and Baby Dodds.

JIMMY JOY

b. 1902, Mount Vernon, TX, d. Mar. 1962, Dallas, TX

Born James Maloney, Jimmy Joy led a fine band in Texas. He began playing clarinet while he was young and attended Texas A&M and the University of Texas, Austin, majoring in business administration. To raise money, he organized a band called the Soul Killers as early as 1920. Joy led college groups during summer vacation and off hours. In 1922 his group was renamed Jimmy's Joys (and billed as "exterminators of gloom"). After being repeatedly called Jimmy Joy, the clarinetist adopted the name legally in 1927. The Joys performed on an extensive vaudeville tour in 1923, began making recordings, became full-time musicians, and worked fairly steadily throughout Texas, Louisville, and occasionally the West Coast into the 1940s. Although Wilbur Sweatman had a reputation for playing three clarinets at once, he never recorded that trick. Jimmy Joy, however, did occasionally play two clarinets simultaneously on records.

Jimmy's Joys recorded during 1923–29, and the Jimmy Joy Orchestra made one final date in 1940, a few years before the band broke up. The clarinetist continued playing in the Dallas area until his death in 1962.

LPS TO SEARCH FOR

Jimmy's Joys (Arcadia 2017D) is a two-LP set that has all of Joy's 1923–29 recordings except alternate takes. Originally a sextet influenced by the NORK and to a lesser extent the ODJB, the band grew to 11 pieces by 1928 but never lost its youthful spirit, as can be heard on such numbers as "Wolverine Blues," "Riverboat Shuffle," "Everybody Stomp," "From Monday On," and "Harmonica Harry."

ROGER WOLFE KAHN

b. Oct. 19, 1907, Morristown, NJ, d. July 12, 1962, New York, NY

The son of multimillionaire Otto Kahn, Roger Wolfe Kahn led high-quality jazz-influenced dance orchestras during the second half of the 1920s. Kahn played violin when he was seven and learned piano, woodwinds, and brass but did not solo on records, actually appearing (on alto and tenor) on only the first session under his name. Only 16 when he started leading his big band (purchasing Arthur Lange's orchestra), Kahn was based at the Hotel Biltmore throughout his main musical years. During the period he also owned a booking office and a nightclub, and wrote such songs as "Crazy Rhythm" and "Imagination."

Though primarily a dance band, the Roger Wolfe Kahn Orchestra did feature jazz soloists, and along the way its recordings featured such notables as Miff Mole, Joe Venuti, Eddie Lang, Jack Teagarden (who sat in on the classic "It's a Great Great Girl"), Dudley Fosdick, Arthur Schutt, Vic Berton, Jimmy Dorsey, and (in 1932) Artie Shaw.

Roger Wolfe Kahn left music in 1934 to work in aviation as a test pilot.

8 1925–1932/Mar. 10, 1925–Nov. 9, 1932/Jazz Oracle 8013
This generous 25-selection CD (which has nearly 79 minutes of music) contains nearly all of the musical high points of Roger Wolfe Kahn's recording career. The only important omission is the master take of "It's a Great Great Girl" (the alternate take is here), possibly left out because it has been reissued on other sets. Kahn's orchestra recorded mostly syncopated dance music, with scattered jazz solos from Miff Mole, Joe Venuti (often with backing by Eddie Lang), and lesser-known players. Most of these numbers are quite listenable (except perhaps for the purposely corny "Fit As a Fiddle"), and the better performances include "Hot-Hot-Hottentot," "Jersey Walk," "Where the Wild, Wild Flowers Grow," "Crazy Rhythm," and "It Don't Mean a Thing." The famous torch singer Libby Holman is on two songs from 1930. A pretty definitive reissue.

PECK KELLEY
b. Oct. 22, 1898, Houston, TX, d. Dec. 26, 1980, Houston, TX

The legendary pianist John "Peck" Kelley is most famous for his desire not to be famous! Kelley led Peck's Bad Boys in Texas starting in the early 1920s, and among his sidemen were Leon Roppolo, Jack Teagarden, and Pee Wee Russell. Kelley preferred to stay in his native Texas, and he constantly refused offers to go North and record, turning down Paul Whiteman, Bob Crosby, Jimmy Dorsey, Tommy Dorsey, and Bing Crosby. The farthest that he traveled were brief visits to St. Louis (1925), Shreveport (1927), and New Orleans (1934). Kelley, whose piano style was considered very advanced in the 1920s, was saluted (if anonymously) in the 1930s Will Bradley big band hit "Beat Me Daddy, Eight to the Bar."

Peck Kelley modernized his style through the decades and by the 1950s was showing the influence of George Shearing and Lennie Tristano. After having gone a lifetime without making a single recording, in 1957 he relented and recorded for Commodore; the sessions were not released until 1983, three years after his death. Other private dates from the early 1950s were released by the collector's Arkadia label, but there is no hint as to how the successfully elusive Peck Kelley really sounded in the 1920s.

CHRIS KELLY
b. Oct. 18, 1885 or 1890, Plaquemine Parish, LA, d. Aug. 19, 1929, New Orleans, LA

Chris Kelly is a lost early jazz legend, a popular cornetist who never recorded, was never even photographed, and died young. He studied cornet with Jim Humphrey, moved to New Orleans in 1915, and worked in Humphrey's society band at first. Within a couple of years, Kelly was considered one of the city's top cornetists. He took over clarinetist Johnny Brown's band in 1919 and during the next decade played regularly at dance halls, cabarets, and dances throughout New Orleans. Kelly was most famous for his highly expressive version of "Careless Love" and for his work with the plunger mute. But he never seemed to have the desire to leave New Orleans, and his fame was only regional.

Chris Kelly, an alcoholic who apparently drank a huge amount of liquor, died from a heart attack in 1929, when he was either 38 or 43.

HOWARD KENIN

b. 1901, Portland, OR, d. July 21, 1970

Violinist Howard Kenin led an excellent orchestra in Portland, Oregon, that sometimes sounded a bit like Jean Goldkette's. Kenin earned a law degree in the early 1920s but was more interested at the time in performing music. He played with George Olsen's orchestra when it was based in Portland but, rather than go East with the group, he elected to stay home and put together his own big band. Kenin's orchestra played regularly at the Multnomah Hotel for a few years, and during 1929–30 his band was based at the Coconut Grove in Los Angeles. Howard Kenin dropped out of music in the early 1930s, working as a lawyer and eventually becoming an important official in the American Federation of Musicians, serving as its president during 1958–70.

7 Herman Kenin and the Garden Dancing Orchestra/May 29, 1927–Apr. 26, 1929/The Old Masters 124

The first 17 selections on this CD (dating from 1927–29) are the most rewarding recordings made by Herman Kenin's Multnomah Hotel Orchestra. The Portland band (which had ten pieces along with occasional spots on violin for the leader) often utilized arrangements that made them swing like Goldkette's big band, even though they lacked any major soloists; the personnel is completely obscure. The vocals by Van Fleming, Gene Dahlgren, Ted O'Hara, and Ken Allen are mostly easy to take. Also on this CD are six selections from the Garden Danc-

ing Palace Orchestra, a group based in Spokane, Washington, that was led by violinist Lillian Frederic. Its brand of dance music is complementary to Kenin's, making this an enjoyable CD full of real obscurities.

FREDDIE KEPPARD

b. Feb. 27, 1890, New Orleans, LA, d. July 15, 1933, Chicago, IL

Buddy Bolden never recorded, but Freddie Keppard, his successor as king cornetist of New Orleans, fortunately did, giving today's listeners a glimpse at what jazz might have sounded like in 1910. Keppard began on mandolin, violin, and accordion (his older brother, Louis Keppard, played guitar) before settling on cornet. At 12 he started played with John Brown's band, and four years later he founded the Olympia Orchestra, also working with Frankie Dusen's Eagle Band during the period. With Bolden's mental illness putting him permanently out of action by 1906, Keppard was considered New Orleans' top cornetist while he was still a teenager.

In 1914 Keppard left New Orleans to join Bill Johnson's Original Creole Orchestra in Los Angeles. Keppard traveled with Johnson, including appearing in Chicago (1914) and New York City (1915), helping to introduce jazz (which did not yet have a name) to those cities. The cornetist was often worried about other brassmen stealing his stuff, so he sometimes covered his right hand with a handkerchief when he played so that other musicians could not see his fingering. In addition, in 1916 the Victor label supposedly offered Keppard an opportunity to make records (a year before the Original Dixieland Jazz Band), but he turned them down for the same reason, a bad decision in the long run!

In 1918 Keppard settled in Chicago, where during the next ten years he often worked as a sideman, including with Doc Cook's Gingersnaps, Erskine Tate, Ollie Powers, and Jimmie Noone. Keppard finally did record for the first time in 1923 (two

Of all the major musicians to record in the 1920s, Freddie Keppard reaches the furthest back, to New Orleans of 1906.

songs with Tate), and he made a few other titles with Cook in 1924. Those technically primitive dates give only a glimpse of the cornetist, but he can be heard under better circumstances on six sessions cut between June 1926 and January 1927 on dates led by Cook, Jimmy Blythe, Jasper Taylor, and (on one occasion) Keppard himself. The cornetist (still just 36) sounds pretty strong on these selections, especially "Stock Yards Strut" (his greatest recording), "Salty Dog," "Here Comes the Hot Tamale Man," and "Messin' Around." It is fascinating to hear his playing because his training was in brass bands, he had a powerful sound, and the influences of marches and ragtime are apparent. He also emphasized colorful and percussive outbursts.

Keppard should have had a long career, but as an alcoholic he drank between a half-gallon and three quarts of liquor a day. By 1928, when Keppard worked with Charlie Elgar at Chicago's Savoy Ballroom, he was erratic and definitely on the decline. After suffering from tuberculosis for a few years, Freddie Keppard died in 1933 at the age of 43.

9 **The Complete Freddie Keppard 1923/27/June 23, 1923 – Jan. 1927/King Jazz 111**

Freddie Keppard appeared on 25 recordings during his career, all of which fit on this single CD from the Italian King Jazz label. The earliest selections (two numbers with Erskine Tate's Vendome Orchestra in 1923 and six cuts with Cook's Dreamland Orchestra the following year) are difficult to listen to, although there are brief moments of interest on the latter. The real Freddie Keppard emerges on nine numbers from 1926 with Doc Cook (including "Messin' Around," "Spanish Mama," and two versions of "Here Comes the Hot Tamale Man"), three cuts with Jimmy Blythe's Ragamuffins (which also include Roy Palmer, Johnny Dodds, Jasper Taylor, and Trixie Smith), two songs with Jasper Taylor, and two numbers (plus an alternate take) with his own Jazz Cardinals. Papa Charlie Jackson sings the two versions of "Salty Dog" quite effectively, and Freddie Keppard hints strongly on "Stock Yards Strut" at why he was rated so high in the early days of jazz.

STAN KING

b. 1900, Hartford, CT, d. Nov. 19, 1949, New York, NY

One of the top drummers of the 1920s, Stan King ranked near the top, with Vic Berton and Chauncey Morehouse, among the white jazz and studio players. King first played locally in Connecticut, becoming a full-time musician when he joined Barney Rapps' group. He was a member of the much-recorded California Ramblers (1922–26) and worked with Roger Wolfe Kahn, Jean Goldkette, Paul Whiteman, Jack Albin's orchestra, and Bert Lown's Hotel Biltmore Orchestra (1929–31). King performed with the Dorsey Brothers Orchestra for the show *Everybody Welcome* and then became a studio musician, working on radio and recordings. Among Stan King's later jazz associations were playing with the early Benny Goodman Orchestra (1934), Joe Haymes (1935), the Three T's (1936), and Bob Zurke's big band (1939–40).

ANDY KIRK

b. May 28, 1898, Newport, KY, d. Dec. 11, 1992, New York, NY

Andy Kirk, who played bass sax and tuba but never soloed or wrote any music, led a successful big band during the swing era that made its initial impression in the late 1920s. Kirk grew up in Denver and spent short periods playing piano and alto sax before learning tuba and bass sax. He worked in George Morrison's band (starting in 1918) alongside another future bandleader, Jimmie Lunceford. In 1925 Kirk moved to Dallas, where he joined Terrence Holder's Dark Clouds of Joy. A money dispute led Holder to depart in January 1929, and Kirk was elected the leader of the new Twelve Clouds of Joy.

During 1929–30, Kirk's orchestra (which became a major part of the Kansas City nightlife scene) recorded 19 selections. Most notable among the sidemen were pianist Mary Lou Williams (who was not a regular member of the group until 1931 but was already providing many of their most swinging arrangements) and violinist Claude Williams (one of the extremely few 1920s veterans still active in 2001). One of the top territory bands of the era, Andy Kirk's Twelve Clouds of Joy survived a take-over attempt by Blanche Calloway in 1931 and worked steadily in Kansas City despite not making any records during 1932–35. However, in 1936 the band was signed to Decca and had a hit record with Pha Terrell's vocal on "Until the Real Thing Comes Along." The group gained a certain amount of fame during the next decade, even if Andy Kirk by then was merely a baton-waving frontman.

10 1929–1931/Nov. 7, 1929–Mar. 2, 1931/Classics 655
This CD has all 25 recordings by Andy Kirk's early orchestra, including two numbers originally issued as being by John Williams' Memphis Stompers and three selections in which the band accompanied Blanche Calloway. One of the hottest bands in Kansas City at the time, Kirk's Twelve Clouds of Joy featured Mary Lou Williams, Claude Williams, John Williams on baritone, clarinetist John Harrington, and trumpeters Gene Prince and Edgar "Pudding-head" Battle. Highlights include "Blue Clarinet Stomp," "Cloudy," "Lotta Sax Appeal," "Mary's Idea," and "Once or Twice." All that is missing are Andy Kirk's five alternate takes (four from the Calloway date).

ED KIRKEBY

b. Oct. 10, 1891, Brooklyn, NY, d. June 12, 1978, Mineola, NY

Ed Kirkeby, who took occasional vocals on records in the 1920s, was not a musician but a manager who mostly worked behind the scenes. Born Wallace Theodore Kirkeby, he started working for Columbia Records in 1916 as a salesman and within a year had been promoted to assistant recording manager. He helped Columbia organize and sign Earl Fuller's Jazz Band (which featured Ted Lewis) as an early competitor to the Original Dixieland Jazz Band. In 1920, Kirkeby was hired by the California Ramblers, which he soon reorganized. He gained the formerly Ohio-based band a foothold in New York and helped set up an extremely busy recording schedule for the group. In 1926 Kirkeby first recorded as a vocalist with the band, and he took occasional vocals in their later sessions. In 1927 Kirkeby started leading dates of his own, using the pseudonym of Ted Wallace. In addition to recordings by Ted Wallace and his Campus Boys, Kirkeby recorded as Eddie Lloyd's Singing Boys (or sometimes as Eddie Lloyd) and Ed Kirkeby Wallace.

Kirkeby managed the Pickens Sisters (1932–34) In 1935 he switched to the Victor label as an A&R man and continued producing records. In 1938 Kirkeby became Fats Waller's manager, a job he held until Waller's death in 1943. In 1966 he wrote of the experiences in the book *Ain't Misbehavin'*. In later years Ed Kirkeby managed other musicians and singers, including the Deep River Boys, staying active until 1977.

7 Volume One/June 27, 1927–Feb. 4, 1930/The Old Masters 110

Ed Kirkeby takes vocals on only four of the 24 performances included on this CD (including the last three cuts); Smith Ballew is heard from often, with appearances by Russell Douglas and Scrappy Lambert. The titles from 1927 feature musicians from the California Ramblers (including Chelsea

Quealey, trombonist Abe Lincoln, altoist Bobby Davis, and Adrian Rollini), although within a year the style by Ted Wallace's Campus Boys evolved into dance music played by top studio musicians. But virtually all of these formerly rare selections are well worth hearing for fans of superior dance band music, and there are also some jazz solos to hold listeners' interest. Among the titles are "Who-oo? You-oo, That's Who," "Zulu Wail," "There's Something Spanish in Your Eyes," "I May Be Wrong, but I Think You're Wonderful," and "Love Ain't Nothing but the Blues."

CARL KRESS

b. Oct. 20, 1907, Newark, NJ, d. June 10, 1965, Reno, NV

A major guitarist who succeeded Eddie Lang as New York's top jazz guitarist before becoming buried in the studios, Carl Kress had a very sophisticated chordal style. He started on piano, switching to banjo and eventually doubling on guitar. Kress joined Paul Whiteman's orchestra in 1926, when he was 18, and then worked regularly during the second half of the 1920s, appearing on many recordings and in the studios. Kress was with Bix Beiderbecke and Frankie Trumbauer on the Chicago Loopers' date and played on scores of records with Red Nichols, Miff Mole, and the Dorsey Brothers (among many others). Kress was so advanced at voicing chords that when he recorded a pair of classic guitar duets with Eddie Lang in 1932 ("Pickin' My Way" and "Feeling My Way"), Lang played the single-note lines over Kress' chords. He also teamed up with Dick McDonough in 1934 and recorded some intriguing solo guitar pieces, unique showcases that have been reissued on Eddie Lang/Carl Kress/Dick McDonough (Retrieval 79015). But Kress mostly stayed in the studios for decades, not recording much jazz after the late 1930s. During his last few years, Carl Kress became a little more prominent, collaborating and recording with guitarist George Barnes in duets in the early 1960s.

GENE KRUPA

b. Jan. 15, 1909, Chicago, IL, d. Oct. 16, 1973, Yonkers, NY

One of the most famous names of the swing era and the first drummer to be considered a superstar, Gene Krupa got his start in the 1920s. He studied percussion, played drums during summer vacation while in high school starting in 1925, and worked around Chicago with Al Gale, Joe Kayser, Leo Shukin, Thelma Terry, Mezz Mezzrow, the Benson Orchestra (1927–28), and other bands. He made his recording debut on the Condon-McKenzie Chicagoans dates of 1927, becoming the first drummer to be captured on record using a full drum set, including bass drum. In fact, Krupa's heavy reliance on the bass drum during the era led many other drummers to utilize a heavier approach (as if compensating for the lack of a string bass) until the rise of Jo Jones in late 1936.

In 1929 Krupa moved to New York, where he worked with Red Nichols (both on jazz dates and in theater bands) and recorded with Bix Beiderbecke. The early Depression years were spent playing commercial music with Irving Aaronson's Commanders, Russ Colombo, Mal Hallett, Buddy Rogers and in the studios. It was a comfortable but dull existence, so Krupa was delighted to join Benny Goodman's orchestra in November 1934, just in time for the famed *Let's Dance* radio series. From then on it would only be a matter of time before Gene Krupa became the first internationally famous drummer.

TOMMY LADNIER

b. May 28, 1900, Florenceville, LA, d. June 4, 1939, New York, NY

One of the more exciting trumpeters of the mid- to late 1920s, Tommy Ladnier unfortunately did not survive long enough to take advantage of the New Orleans revival of the 1940s. Ladnier grew up near New Orleans and early on took trumpet lessons

with Bunk Johnson. In 1917 he moved to Chicago, where he worked with drummer John H. Wickliffe. Ladnier played in St. Louis with Charlie Creath, violinist Milton Vassar, and Ollie Powers. Making his recording debut in 1923, Ladnier backed classic blues singers Ida Cox, Julia Davis, Edna Hicks, Alberta Hunter, Edmonia Henderson, Monette Moore, Ma Rainey, Ethel Waters, and the team of Ford and Ford. In addition, Ladnier was on no less than five takes of "Play That Thing" with Ollie Powers, may have appeared on two early numbers with Jelly Roll Morton, and definitely cut seven titles with Lovie Austin's Blues Serenaders (1924–25), playing next to Jimmy O'Bryant.

After working briefly with Fate Marable and King Oliver, Ladnier went to Europe with Sam Wooding's *Chocolate Kiddies* in June 1925. He spent a year with Wooding (with whom he recorded in Berlin) and worked in Poland with Louis Douglas' revue before returning home. He gained his greatest recognition when he was Fletcher Henderson's main trumpet soloist (1926–28), being featured on such records as "The Chant," "Clarinet Marmalade," "Snag It," "Tozo," "I'm Comin' Virginia," "St. Louis Blues" and several versions of "St. Louis Shuffle." During this era, Ladnier's style was mature, falling somewhere between King Oliver's and Louis Armstrong's. He also appeared as a sideman on record dates by Clarence Williams, Eva Taylor, Bessie Smith, and Clara Herring.

After leaving Henderson, Ladnier worked with Sam Wooding's orchestra again for a year in Europe and stayed overseas for stints with Benny Peyton, Harry Flemming's Blue Birds, Louis Douglas, and his own band in France, returning to the United States with Noble Sissle's Sizzling Syncopators in 1931. He teamed up with Sidney Bechet in the New Orleans Feetwarmers. Although hot jazz was out of favor, the Feetwarmers did work a bit at Harlem's Saratoga Club and at the Savoy, recording an explosive session in 1932. Ladnier and Bechet also co-ran the Southern Tailor Shop during this era,

The most sophisticated guitarist of the 1920s, Eddie Lang had the ability to make any musician and singer sound better than they actually were.

but their backroom jam sessions took more of their time than their day job and the store folded. When Bechet rejoined Sissle's band, Ladnier disappeared from the jazz scene and was not heard from in New York City for five years.

In 1938, French jazz critic Hugues Panassie, who was in the United States to record some New Orleans-style bands, conducted a long search for Ladnier, finding him in upstate New York, where the trumpeter played locally and drank constantly. Ladnier was recorded a few times by Panassie, including an erratic date with Mezz Mezzrow and Sidney DeParis, and a more successful outing with Bechet and Mezzrow that resulted in the classic "Really the Blues." He also appeared with Bechet in a revived New Orleans Feetwarmers at John

Hammond's first Spirituals to Swing concert at Carnegie Hall. But his comeback quickly ended when Tommy Ladnier died from a sudden heart attack a week after his 39th birthday.

EDDIE LANG

b. Oct. 25, 1902, Philadelphia, PA, d. Mar. 26, 1933, New York, NY

Eddie Lang was the top jazz guitarist of 1925–33 and the first jazz virtuoso on the instrument. Born Salvatore Massaro, he started on violin when he was seven and was a childhood friend of Joe Venuti. Although Lang played violin in public in 1917 after 11 years of lessons, he soon switched to banjo and started doubling on guitar, quickly becoming a very sophisticated player whose chord voicings were quite advanced for the era. Lang worked with Chuck Granese's Trio (1918), Charlie Kerr (1920–23), Bert Estlow, Vic D'Ipplito, and Billy Lustig's Scranton Sirens (which included the Dorsey Brothers). He was a member of Red McKenzie's Mound City Blue Blowers (1924–25) and was soon discovered, becoming a very busy freelance guitarist who worked constantly on radio and recordings. His success and popularity (along with the development of better recording equipment) resulted in the guitar's replacing the banjo in most bands by the late 1920s.

Throughout his career, Lang often teamed up with violinist Joe Venuti, including with Roger Wolfe Kahn (1926–27), Jean Goldkette, Adrian Rollini's big band (1927), and Paul Whiteman (1929–30). Among his most notable recordings were duets with Venuti ("Stringin' the Blues"), dates with Venuti's Blue Four, guest spots with Frankie Trumbauer's orchestra (including "Singin' the Blues" with Bix Beiderbecke), duets with Lonnie Johnson (during which Lang used the pseudonym of "Blind Willie Dunn" so as to hide the fact that those were integrated dates), and a pair of memorable duets with Carl Kress ("Pickin' My Way" and "Feelin' My Way"). Lang, whose solos tended to be single-note lines (although his chord voicings were a major reason why so many commercial bands and singers hired him for their recordings), also recorded 20 selections as a leader during 1927–29, mostly showcases for his guitar, although two sessions found him at the head of combos that sometimes included the Dorsey Brothers, Hoagy Carmichael (on piano), and Mildred Bailey (making her recording debut on "What Kind o' Man Is You").

Eddie Lang appeared in a wonderful 90-second performance with Venuti in the 1930 Paul Whiteman film *The King of Jazz*. He stayed busy in the studios during the early 1930s, spent part of 1932 with Roger Wolfe Kahn's orchestra, and then became Bing Crosby's accompanist; he can be seen playing "Dinah" with Crosby in the 1932 movie *The Big Broadcast*. But tragically his life was cut short in 1933 due to complications resulting from a tonsillectomy, a major loss to jazz. Eddie Lang was just 30.

10 **Eddie Lang/Carl Kress/Dick McDonough/Apr. 1, 1927– Aug. 8, 1939/Retrieval 79015**

Collectors of early acoustic guitar records will have to get this release. Included are all of Eddie Lang's dates as a leader, except for his six titles leading bands. There are a dozen numbers featuring the guitarist either unaccompanied or joined by Arthur Schutt, Frank Signorelli, or Rube Bloom on piano, with the emphasis being very much on his guitar. Highlights include "Eddie's Twister," "Perfect," "Add a Little Wiggle," and "There'll Be Some Changes Made." Lang's two classic guitar duets with Carl Kress are also here; they are so perfect that they deserve to be orchestrated for a full band. In addition, the four Carl Kress-Dick McDonough duets from 1934 and 1937 (including "Chicken-à-la-Swing") and Kress' six solo recordings of 1938–39 (highlighted by "Peg Leg Shuffle," "Sutton Mutton," and the three movements of "Afterthoughts") round out this definitive set. This is how jazz guitar sounded in the United States before Charlie Christian. Only Django Reinhardt was on the level of these three masters.

JIM LANNIGAN

b. Jan. 30, 1902, Chicago, IL, d. Apr. 9, 1983, Elburn, IL

Bassist Jim Lannigan was one of the lesser-known members of the famed Austin High School Gang. He studied violin and piano as a youth and sometimes played piano and drums with the Austin High School Blue Friars before switching to bass and tuba. Lannigan was quite active in the Chicago jazz scene of the 1920s, working with Husk O'Hare, the Mound City Blue Blowers, and Art Kassel (for two years) plus other local bands. He recorded on the

McKenzie-Condon Chicagoans dates in 1927 (on both bass and tuba) and also appeared on records in 1928 with the Chicago Rhythm Kings, the Jungle Kings, the Louisiana Rhythm Kings, and Frankie Teschemacher. Unlike many of his associates, Lannigan did not emigrate to New York. He worked locally in Chicago, spent four years with Ted Fio Rito's orchestra, became a staff musician at NBC in 1937, and was with the Chicago Symphony Orchestra during 1953–68.

Although working mostly outside of jazz, Jim Lannigan did have occasional reunions with the Chicagoans, recording in later years with Jimmy McPartland (1939), Bud Jacobson's Jungle Kings (1945), Bud Freeman (1946), and drummer Danny Alvin (1950).

GEORGE E. LEE

b. Apr. 28, 1896, Kansas City, MO, d. Oct. 1958, San Diego, CA

George E. Lee led one of the more popular bands in Kansas City during the 1920s and '30s. Lee played baritone sax and piano in a U.S. Army Band in 1917. After his discharge, he returned to his native Kansas City, where he headed George E. Lee's Singing Orchestra during 1920–40. His band recorded two numbers in 1927 (Lee was on tenor on that occasion) but had grown much more sophisticated by 1929, when it recorded six songs, including three backing the vocals of Lee's sister Julia Lee (who would become much more famous in the 1940s). By then Lee, who was doing his best to compete with Bennie Moten, was using the arrangements of Jesse Stone. Other than Julia Lee, the best-known sideman was tenor saxophonist Budd Johnson.

Unfortunately there were no further recordings, and Lee retired from music in 1940, moving to Detroit, where he ran a nightclub, and permanently settling in San Diego after World War II. All of George E. Lee's recordings are included in *What Kind of Rhythm Is That* (Frog 31).

MIN LEIBROOK

b. 1903, Hamilton, OH, d. June 8, 1943, Los Angeles, CA

A versatile musician who played bass sax, tuba, and string bass (three instruments with similar functions but requiring very different technical skills), Wilford "Min" Leibrook (whose nickname, Min, was borrowed from a cartoon character) was on many records in the 1920s, sometimes as a substitute for Adrian Rollini. Leibrook started on cornet before switching to bass sax and tuba. He played with the Ten Foot Band in Chicago and the Wolverines (playing tuba on all of their recordings) and recorded with the Sioux City Six. By 1927, Leibrook was playing primarily bass sax. He was a member of the Paul Whiteman Orchestra during 1927–31, also appearing on quite a few famous recordings with Frankie Trumbauer (1928–30), Bix Beiderbecke, and Hoagy Carmichael. After the Whiteman years ended, Min Leibrook worked as a bassist with Eddie Duchin (1935), Lennie Hayton's orchestra, and the Three T's (December 1936), eventually settling in Los Angeles, where he worked in the studios during his final years before his premature death at age 40.

ED LEWIS

b. June 22, 1909, Eagle City, OK, d. Sep. 18, 1985, Blooming Grove, NY

Ed Lewis, who worked for many years as the lead trumpeter with Count Basie's big band, in the 1920s was a major soloist with Bennie Moten's orchestra. Lewis grew up in Kansas City, Missouri. He originally played baritone horn with a few local groups. In 1925 Lewis switched to trumpet, playing briefly with Paul Bank and Laura Rucker before spending six years with Bennie Moten (1926–32). Lewis, one of the first black trumpeters to be clearly influenced by white players (particularly Red Nichols and Bix Beiderbecke), split the solo space during his Moten years with Lammar Wright (and later Booker Washington).

After leaving Moten in February 1932, Lewis' sight-reading abilities and strong technical skills led to his being a first trumpeter rather than a soloist. He played with Thamon Hayes' Kansas City Skyrockets, Pete Johnson, Jay McShann, Harlan Leonard, and Count Basie (1937–48). Ed Lewis worked outside of music after leaving Basie (including as a cab driver) but continued playing part time, including touring Europe with the Countsmen in 1984, a year before his death.

TED LEWIS

b. June 6, 1892, Circleville, OH, d. Aug. 25, 1971, New York, NY

A popular entertainment figure who was in reality a cornball singer and a musician (clarinet and alto) with somewhat questionable taste, Ted Lewis helped in his own way to popularize jazz. Born Theodore Leopold Friedman, Lewis started out playing music in a local boy's band in Ohio. He first became a bandleader in 1910 and in 1915 moved to New York, where he joined an ensemble led by pianist Earl Fuller. Lewis recorded with Earl Fuller's Famous Jazz Band during 1917–18, playing clarinet in a gaspipe style that, though fine for the time, would be out of date within a few years; he never bothered to update his approach. In 1919 he and the other sidemen left Fuller, with Lewis becoming the leader of the quintet. Very popular in vaudeville, Lewis made "Me and My Shadow" and his theme, "When My Baby Smiles at Me" (which he first recorded in 1920), famous, he helped to introduce "Blues My Naughty Sweetie Gives to Me," and his trademark phrase was "Is everybody happy?" His band (which in its early days sometimes featured laughing trombone from Harry Raderman) recorded frequently during the 1920s and gradually grew to ten pieces by 1924. George Brunies (straight from the New Orleans Rhythm Kings) joined Lewis that year for a lengthy stay, Sophie Tucker and Ruth Etting both recorded with Lewis,

and such players as Don Murray (1928–29), Frankie Teschemacher (1929), and Muggsy Spanier (who started a long stint in 1929) gave Lewis' music some credibility from a jazz standpoint. In addition, Fats Waller, Jack Teagarden, Benny Goodman (who had debuted as a youth imitating Lewis), and Jimmy Dorsey made guest appearances on recordings.

But, although he epitomized jazz to some listeners, the jazz world tended to laugh at Lewis' playing and singing. Ted Lewis, the "top-hatted tragedian of jazz," was active into the late 1960s, never changing his act, although he largely gave up playing clarinet (to the relief of many!) after the 1930s.

7 **Jazzworthy 1929–1933/Aug. 31, 1929–July 28, 1933/Challenge 79014**

Many of Ted Lewis' best jazz sides are on this CD. The music is sometimes a battle between "good" (swinging jazz) and "evil" (Lewis' hilariously dated clarinet, alto, and vocalizing), sometimes alternating between the two, such as on "Farewell Blues" and "Wabash Blues," with Frank Teschemacher sitting in on clarinet. George Brunies (who sometimes joined the "bad" side) and Muggsy Spanier contribute jazz solos along the way, Jimmy Dorsey and Benny Goodman are on some numbers, and Fats Waller guests (and takes vocals) on "I'm Crazy 'Bout My Baby," "Dallas Blues," and "Royal Garden Blues." Some of the music is rather corny (check out Lewis' vocal on "Dip Your Brush in the Sunshine!"), but this CD certainly never loses interest. A retrospective of Lewis' early recordings (he started leading dates in 1919) has yet to be compiled.

JOHN LINDSAY

b. Aug. 23, 1894, Algiers, LA, d. July 3, 1950, Chicago, IL

A fine musician, John Lindsay had the unusual double of string bass and trombone. He started out playing bass in his family band as a teenager. Lindsay served in the Army during World War I, moved to New Orleans, and played trombone with local bands, including those of John Robichaux and Armand Piron. He went to New York with Piron (with whom he recorded in 1923), toured with King Oliver (1924), worked in St. Louis with Dewey Jackson (1925), and finally settled in Chicago. Lindsay played with Willie Hightower (on trombone), Carroll Dickerson, and Lil Hardin, gradually shifting his emphasis to bass. He is best known for recording on bass with Jelly Roll Morton (three classic sessions in 1926). Lindsay toured with Louis Armstrong during 1931–32 and worked in Chicago in the 1930s with Jimmie Noone, Johnny Dodds, Richard M. Jones, and the Harlem Hamfats, appearing on many blues-oriented dates. John Lindsay was active locally up until his death in 1950.

JACK LINX

b. Dec. 3, 1899, Birmingham, AL, d. Nov. 1967, New York, NY

Very little is known about Jack Linx (who played clarinet, soprano, and alto). He led a fine dance band in Birmingham during the 1920s, which luckily was well documented during the Okeh label's annual field trips to Atlanta (1924–27). Jack Linx (who made no further recordings after 1927) retired from active playing (most likely in the 1940s) and ran a musical instrument store in New York during the 1950s and '60s.

7 Jack Linx and Maurice Sigler/Aug. 28, 1924–Mar. 16, 1927/ Jazz Oracle 8018

All of Jack Linx's recordings (23 titles, including one alternate take and two songs that were originally not released) are on this CD. The octet (known as Linx's Birmingham Society Serenaders) did not include any notable musicians (only banjoist Maurice Sigler had a later musical career) but improved year by year, sounding a bit nervous in 1924 but quite swinging by 1927. The results are decent mainstream jazz/dance music of the era, which surprisingly only has one vocal. Also on this generous CD

are the four titles that Sigler's Birmingham Merrymakers (a pickup group led by Maurice Sigler) made in 1924, music that is quite complementary to the Linx output.

VIRGINIA LISTON

b. 1890, d. June 1932, St. Louis, MO

An obscure but talented classic blues singer, Virginia Liston was on records for only a three-year period. She began performing blues in Philadelphia around 1912. Liston married pianist Sam Gray, and they toured vaudeville as Liston and Liston during 1920–23. Based in New York, Liston recorded 36 selections during 1923–26, touring with the *Eliza Scandals* revue in 1925. In 1926 Virginia Liston dropped out of music, moved to St. Louis, remarried, and spent her last years working with the church.

7 Vol. 1/Sept. 18, 1923–Oct. 25, 1924/Document 5446
7 Vol. 2/Lavinia Turner/Mar. 1921–May 29, 1926/Document 5447

Although Virginia Liston did not have any hits, quite a few of her recordings are memorable. *Vol. 1* has her first 23 recordings, including "You Thought I Was Blind but Now I See," "You Can Have It (I Don't Want It)," "Early in the Morning," and "You've Got the Right Key but the Wrong Keyhole." The latter two recordings find her backed by Clarence Williams' Blue Five at a time when the group included Louis Armstrong, Sidney Bechet, and Charles Irvis. All of the other recordings have Williams on piano, except for "Jail House Blues," which has a guitarist who might possibly be Bechet (in his only recording on the instrument). *Vol. 2* has Liston's last 13 recordings and, although the backup is not that exciting, there are excellent versions of "Papa De Da Da," "Make Me a Pallet," "Titanic Blues," and "You Can Dip Your Bread in My Gravy, but You Can't Have None of My Chops!" Also on the CD are the ten recordings of Lavinia Turner, a very good vaudevillian singer who recorded only during 1921–22. Although backed by bands on the majority of the tunes, this talented (if very obscure) singer is heard at her best on two selections from November 1921, on which she is accompanied by James P. Johnson's piano.

THE LITTLE RAMBLERS

In the 1920s, the key members of the California Ramblers also recorded for various labels as the Five Birmingham Babies, the Goofus Five, the University Six, the Vagabonds, and the Little Ramblers. The last group recorded 26 titles during 1924–27, featuring Bill Moore, Red Nichols, Roy Johnston, or Chelsea Quealey on trumpet, Tommy Dorsey or Herb Winfield on trombone, Bobby Davis, occasional tenor players, Adrian Rollini on bass sax and goofus, pianist Irving Brodsky, banjoist Tommy Felline, and Stan King or Herb Weil on drums. Their output (made for the Columbia label) was melodic but spirited jazz, mostly instrumentals, although there were guest vocals by Arthur Hall, Arthur Fields, Ed Kirkeby, and Billy Jones. When Rollini, Davis, and Quealey sailed to Europe in 1927, the group ceased to exist. In 1935–36 the Little Ramblers name was revived for five unrelated sessions by different groups; Rollini is on the first one (playing piano!).

7 The Little Ramblers/Sept. 18, 1924–July 8, 1927/Timeless 1–037

All of the Little Ramblers recordings from the 1920s, with the exception of the first four titles (which have Adrian Rollini just on goofus), are on this CD, plus an alternate take of "In Your Green Hat." The ensembles are well played, Rollini often takes solo honors, and Red Nichols is an asset on four numbers. Nothing too innovative occurs, but the music is pleasing and swinging in its own fashion.

FUD LIVINGSTON

b. Apr. 10, 1906, Charleston, SC, d. Mar. 25, 1957, New York, NY

Joseph "Fud" Livingston was a decent journeyman clarinetist and tenor saxophonist whose greatest skill was as an adventurous (almost avant-garde) arranger. Livingston played accordion and piano as a child before taking up the saxophone. He worked with Talmadge Henry in South Carolina (the summer of 1923), Ben Pollack (1924–25), the California Ramblers, and Jean Goldkette (1925), contributing inventive arrangements in addition to taking occasional solos. Livingston returned to Pollack for a year (1926–27) and moved to New York, where he worked with Nat Shilkret, Don Voorhees, and Jan Garber. Most important were his many freelance recording dates, including with Red Nichols, Miff Mole, Joe Venuti, Frankie Trumbauer, the All Star Orchestra, the Broadway Bellhops, Benny Goodman, Mendello and his Five Gee-Gees, the Midnight Airedales, the Mississippi Maulers, and Boyd Senter's Senterpedes.

Livingston spent March–June 1929 in England playing with Fred Elizalde. After performing with Paul Whiteman (June–September 1930), he worked mostly as an arranger, although he did play in the sax section of Jimmy Dorsey's big band during 1935–37. Fud Livingston, who contributed charts to many bands during the swing era, spent the 1940s working in Hollywood, ending his life as a pianist in New York bars in the 1950s.

BERT LOWN

b. 1903, d. Nov. 20, 1962, Portland, OR

Bert Lown, who was one of the composers of "Bye Bye Blues," led a fine jazz-oriented dance band in the late 1920s and early '30s. A violinist, Lown worked with cornetist Fred Hamm in 1925, one of the four cowriters of "Bye Bye Blues." Lown, who began leading his orchestra in early 1929 (no longer playing violin), made his first recordings on February 11 and cut 86 selections during the next four years. Miff Mole was on Lown's first two sessions, and Adrian Rollini and Stan King appeared on many of the dates during 1929–30; most of the other sidemen were pretty obscure. Lown's orchestra was based at the Biltmore Hotel in New York during 1929–31 and broadcast regularly. The Depression eventually did his band in, they broke up in 1933, and Bert Lown became active as a manager. He was outside of music by the 1940s and eventually worked for CBS-TV behind the scenes.

7 **Bert Lown and His Biltmore Hotel Orchestra/Apr. 25, 1929– May 18, 1933/The Old Masters 105**

Twenty-three of Bert Lown's best recordings (more than one-fourth of his total output) are on this single CD. Adrian Rollini, his successor Spencer Clark, Miff Mole, trumpeter Frank Cush, and trombonist Al Philburn are among the players having their spots, with vocals by Smith Ballew, the Biltmore Rhythm Boys, Elmer Feldkamp, and Ted Holt. The performances are typical of an early-Depression dance band, with only the first number ("Jazz Me Blues") finding the musicians cutting loose. Other titles include "Bye Bye Blues," "Lovin' You the Way I Do," "Heartaches," and "When I Take My Sugar to Tea."

JIMMIE LUNCEFORD

b. June 6, 1902, Fulton, MO, d. July 13, 1947, Seaside, OR

Leader of one of the top big bands of the swing era, Jimmie Lunceford began his career and his orchestra a few years earlier. Lunceford grew up in Denver, where he took music lessons from Paul Whiteman's father (Wilberforce Whiteman), had training on many instruments, and played alto with George Morrison's orchestra (1922). He earned a music degree from Fisk University (1926), playing in New York (including with Wilbur Sweatman and Elmer Snowden) during summer vacations. That same year, Lunceford started teaching music at Manassas High School in Memphis, gradually forming a band with his students that he called the Chickasaw Syncopators. They recorded two sides in 1927, reissued on *What Kind of Rhythm Is That* (Frog 31);

most notable among the players was Moses Allen (a bassist then on tuba who "preaches" on "Chickasaw Stomp") and drummer Jimmy Crawford. In 1929 the group (which had recently added altoist Willie Smith and pianist-arranger Edwin Wilcox) became professional. The ensemble recorded two titles in 1930 (including a reprise of Allen's preaching on "In Dat Mornin' ") and, finally leaving Memphis, spent time working in Cleveland and Buffalo. The Lunceford big band recorded two songs on May 15, 1933, that were not released until decades later (highlighted by "Flaming Reeds and Screaming Brass"). By then the nucleus of the Lunceford big band was in place. In September 1933, Lunceford and his musicians moved to New York. After they began playing regularly at the Cotton Club in January 1934 and signed with the Decca label, the Jimmie Lunceford Orchestra was on its way to stardom.

JIMMY LYTELL

b. Dec. 1, 1904, New York, NY, d. Nov. 28, 1972, Kings Point, NY

A fluent clarinetist, Jimmy Lytell was considered a valuable sideman in the 1920s, even though he was little known to the general public. Born James Sarrapede, he adopted the name of Lytell because he liked its sound when applied to movie actor Bert Lytell. The clarinetist became a professional musician in 1916, when he was 11. He was with the Original Indiana Five (1921), the Original Dixieland Jazz Band when he was still a teenager (as Larry Shields' replacement during 1922–24), and most significantly the Original Memphis Five (1922–25), with whom he recorded an enormous number of selections. One reason that Lytell never became famous is that he began to emphasize classical music by 1925, joining the Capitol Theatre Orchestra. He did record 16 numbers as a leader during 1926–28 (mostly in trios), but these are quite obscure and have yet to be reissued.

Jimmy Lytell spent the 1930s and '40s as a staff

musician at NBC. He was part of the reformed Original Memphis Five in 1949 and occasionally played in Dixieland settings in the 1950s but mostly worked as a studio player during his last four decades.

MATTY MALNECK

b. Dec. 9, 1903, Newark, NJ, d. Feb. 25, 1981, Hollywood, CA

A skilled composer who wrote "I'm Through with Love," "I'll Never Be the Same," and "Goody, Goody," Matty Malneck was one of the main violinists with Paul Whiteman's orchestra during its prime years. He played violin from an early age and was performing in dance bands from 1921. Malneck was with Whiteman during 1926–37 (he can be heard prominently on "San") and appeared on many records with other groups during the era, including with Frankie Trumbauer, Frank Signorelli, Jack Pettis, Annette Hanshaw, and Mildred Bailey. Not a major improviser, he was more notable for his arrangements, songwriting abilities, and tone. After leaving Whiteman, Matty Malneck led a small combo (usually featuring an accordion player) in the late 1930s and '40s before retiring from active playing.

WINGY MANONE

b. Feb. 13, 1904, New Orleans, LA, d. July 9, 1982, Las Vegas, NV

Joseph "Wingy" Manone was a melodic Dixieland trumpeter and a jivey good-humored singer, most influenced by Louis Armstrong in his phrasing and ideas. Manone "earned" the lifelong name of "Wingy" after losing his right arm in a streetcar accident when he was ten. Shortly after, Manone started playing trumpet, and he became a professional when he was 17. Wingy played on riverboats, was a member of the Crescent City Jazzers in Mobile in 1924, and recorded with the same group in St. Louis when they were called the Arcadian Serenaders. Manone was constantly on the road during the next few years, performing with a variety of territory bands, including Peck's Bad Boys (led by Peck Kelley) in Texas.

Manone first recorded as a leader in November 1925, but that session was never released. He had more success with four titles in 1927, four others in 1928, and six tunes (issued as by Barbecue Joe and His Hot Dogs!) in 1930. Of the last, his "Tar Paper Stomp" utilized a riff that would later be used by Joe Garland as the basis of his song "In the Mood," a huge hit for Glenn Miller nine years later. In addition, Manone recorded "Baltimore" with the Red Heads in 1927 and one date apiece with Benny Goodman (1929), Red Nichols (1930), and the Cellar Boys (1930). He had associations with the bands of Ray Miller, Charlie Straight, and Speed Webb but largely struggled until 1934.

At that point in time, unlike some of his contemporaries who had to wait for the New Orleans revival of the early 1940s before they could flourish, Manone began recording quite prolifically and became a hit on 52nd Street. Wingy Manone's popular freewheeling performances and recordings during the next decade would be the most rewarding of his career, and he helped keep New Orleans jazz alive during an era dominated by swing big bands.

10 The Wingy Manone Collection Vol. 1/Apr. 11, 1927– Sept. 19, 1930/Collector's Classics 3

10 The Wingy Manone Collection, Vol. 2/May 2, 1934–Sept. 26, 1934/Collector's Classics 4

Wingy Manone had his commercial breakthrough in 1935 with his happy recording of "The Isle of Capri." Fortunately he did record before that era, and his first 43 selections (not counting numbers with the Arcadian Serenaders, the Red Heads, and Red Nichols) are on the two Collector's Classics CDs. The quality is consistently high, and there are many exciting solos throughout the discs. *Vol. 1* has Manone's dates as a leader during 1927–28 (recorded in New Orleans with obscure personnel and in Chicago with Bud Freeman, Gene Krupa, and

Frank Teschemacher), his sessions as a sideman with Benny Goodman (1929) and the Cellar Boys (a quintet with Teschemacher and Freeman), and the Barbecue Joe and his Hot Dogs sides of 1930. Highlights include two versions of "Up the Country Blues," "After a While," the three takes of "Barrel House Stomp," "Tar Paper Stomp" (the future "In the Mood"), and "Big Butter and Egg Man."

Vol. 2 jumps to 1934 and has more very interesting material. Manone is heard with a band billed as "The New Orleans Rhythm Kings," a sextet/septet that plays songs associated with both the NORK and the ODJB while actually including only one of the former's alumni (George Brunies). Manone is also heard jamming "Shine" with a pickup quartet called the Four Bales of Cotton and leading two dates of his own. The first of the latter (with a sextet of musicians from Ben Pollack's orchestra) sounds typical of Manone's late 1930s recordings (although recorded five years earlier), but the date from August 15, 1934 (four songs and three alternate takes) has rather unusual personnel: Manone, Dicky Wells, clarinetist Artie Shaw (four years before he became famous), Bud Freeman, guitarist Frank Victor, bassist John Kirby, Kaiser Marshall, and either Teddy Wilson or Jelly Roll Morton on piano! Morton is on "Never Had No Lovin' " and "I'm Alone Without You," his only appearances on records during 1931–37.

FATE MARABLE

b. Feb. 12, 1890, Paducah, KY, d. Jan. 16, 1947, St. Louis, MO

Fate Marable was a legendary bandleader who led groups on steamships for the Streckfus riverboat line for many years. Marable, who played piano and calliope, first worked in public when he was nine. In 1907, when he was 17, Marable performed on the Steamboat J.S. in duos with violinist Emil Flindt. From then on, Marable spent virtually his entire career working on riverboats up and down the Mississippi. In 1917 he formed the Kentucky Jazz Band, and his sidemen along the way included Louis Armstrong, Johnny Dodds, Baby Dodds, Pops Foster, Zutty Singleton, Red Allen, altoist Earl Bostic, bassist Jimmy Blanton, and clarinetist Gene Sedric among many others, all young jazz musicians who picked up important experience playing with Marable.

Unfortunately Fate Marable's only recording session, "Frankie and Johnny" and "Pianoflage" in 1924 (reissued on *New Orleans In the '20s*—Timeless 1–014), is quite disappointing, poorly recorded, and erratically played, giving today's listeners no real idea as to the impact of his bands. Fate Marable, who sometimes co-led groups with Charlie Creath in the mid-1930s, stopped playing steamships in 1940 and worked in St. Louis clubs during his last years, before dying from pneumonia.

KAISER MARSHALL

b. June 11, 1899, Savannah, GA, d. Jan. 3, 1948, New York, NY

A reliable drummer during the 1920s, Kaiser Marshall was an unacknowledged influence on big band drummers. He grew up in Boston, first worked locally, and moved to New York in the early 1920s. Marshall was a member of the Fletcher Henderson Orchestra during 1923–30 and is best known for his many recordings with the pacesetting big band.

In 1931 he led the Czars of Harmony. The drummer freelanced (including subbing with Duke Ellington's orchestra for a month and with Cab Calloway for two) and had a stint with McKinney's Cotton Pickers. Marshall led bands during 1935–36, was in Europe with Bobby Martin's group in 1937, played with Edgar Hayes' big band in New York (1939), and was heard in Dixieland settings in the 1940s, including with Wild Bill Davison, Art Hodes, Sidney Bechet, and Bunk Johnson. Kaiser Marshall last recorded with Bechet and Mezz Mezzrow in mid-December 1947, just a couple of weeks before dying from food poisoning. One of the jams was posthumously titled "Kaiser's Last Break."

SARA MARTIN

b. June 18, 1884, Louisville, KY, d. May 25, 1955, Louisville, KY

Part of the older generation of classic blues singers who recorded in the 1920s, Sara Martin was often closely associated with Clarence Williams. Born Sarah Dunn, she sang in her church choir, was married and widowed quite early (married at 16 to a husband who died the following year), and sang in theaters as a teenager. She spent quite a few years outside of music working odd jobs. She married William Martin in 1908 and kept his name throughout her career. After his death in 1916, Martin returned to music, moving to Chicago, where she worked with shows and gained a third husband. There would be five spouses in all, with the last three marriages ending in divorce. Encouraged by Mamie Smith, Martin moved to New York in 1922, was introduced to Clarence Williams, and began recording. Her first record, "Sugar Blues," was a hit.

In 1923, Martin toured with W.C. Handy's orchestra and appeared on 20 record sessions. During the next couple of years she was at the height of her popularity, performing and recording constantly. But by 1928 her brand of old-time blues had gone out of style and, although she diversified and was singing more pop tunes in addition to acting, her recording career came to an end. Martin appeared in the obscure films *Hello Bill* (1927 with Bill "Bojangles" Robinson) and *Dark-Town Scandals Revue* (1930). After temporarily losing her voice in the early 1930s before a stage appearance, Sara Martin became very religious and performed from then on as a gospel singer, later operating a nursing home and working for her church back in Louisville.

8 Vol. 1/Oct. 17, 1922–July 12, 1923/Document 5395

7 Vol. 2/July 12, 1923–Mar. 19, 1924/Document 5396
7 Vol. 3/Mar. 19, 1924–Nov. 23, 1925/Document 5397
8 Vol. 4/Nov. 23, 1925–Dec. 1928/Document 5398

These four Document CDs have all of Sara Martin's recordings, except for six titles with Fats Waller, several with guitarist Sylvester Weaver, three with Robert Cooksey, ten with her jug band, and six that have not been found. All but those last six are available on other sets put out by Document.

Vol. 1 finds Martin mostly being accompanied by Clarence Williams' piano, with three songs having Eva Taylor joining for vocal duets. There are also two numbers with pianist-composer Shelton Brooks and three tunes with W.C. Handy's orchestra. Most memorable are "Sugar Blues," "I Got What It Takes," and "Nobody in Town Can Bake a Sweet Jelly Roll Like Mine." Other than four numbers with Williams' Blue Five (a band with Thomas Morris and Sidney Bechet), all of the music on *Vol. 2* has Martin accompanied by either Clarence Williams, pianist Porter Grainger, or guitarist Sylvester Weaver. The tunes include "New Orleans Hop Scop Blues," "Mistreated Mama Blues," and "Slow Down Sweet Papa, Mama's Catching Up with You."

Vol. 3 features accompaniment by Weaver, Williams, and pianist Lemuel Fowler along with a few band numbers. The repertoire by then was starting to include more jazz tunes. Highlights include "He's Never Gonna Throw Me Down," "Old-Fashioned Sara Blues," "Eagle Rock Me, Papa," "Daddy Ease This Pain of Mine," "I'm Gonna Hoodoo You," and "I'd Rather Be Blue Than Green." *Vol. 4* has Martin's last recordings. Her backup bands include Williams, Charles Irvis, Louis Metcalf, Eddie Heywood Sr., Bubber Miley, Richard M. Jones' Jazz Wizards, and King Oliver. There is plenty of variety in the songs, including "Yes Sir, That's My Baby," "That Dance Called Messin' Around," "What's the Matter Now," "How Could I Be Blue," "Cushion Foot Stomp," and (on her final session) three particularly powerful blues.

For listeners only wanting one Sara Martin CD, *Vol. 4* is the one to get.

DICK MCDONOUGH

b. July 30, 1904, New York, NY, d. May 25, 1938, New York, NY

Eddie Lang's death in 1933 left a huge hole in the recording industry, one partly filled by Carl Kress and Dick McDonough before the latter's own premature demise. McDonough started out on banjo, doubling on guitar by 1926, when he became one of the top session musicians in New York. During the following decade, McDonough appeared on countless recordings, including with the Dorsey Brothers, Cliff Edwards, Benny Goodman, Miff Mole, Red Nichols, Red Norvo, Jack Pettis, Jack Teagarden, Frankie Trumbauer, and the Boswell Sisters, plus many others.

Although he was initially considered a perfect fill-in for Lang, McDonough (whose chordal style was an influence decades later on Marty Grosz) quickly developed a strong reputation of his own. He occasionally teamed up with fellow guitarist Carl Kress (they recorded four duets in 1934) and was on an all-star record date with Fats Waller, trumpeter Bunny Berigan, Tommy Dorsey, and drummer George Wettling in 1937. During 1936–37, McDonough led his own radio dance band, which recorded 46 selections but surprisingly did not feature many solos from the leader. Unfortunately Dick McDonough was a rather extreme alcoholic, and he collapsed while working in the NBC studios on May 25, 1938, passing away at the age of 33.

RED MCKENZIE

b. Oct. 14, 1899, St. Louis, MO, d. Feb. 7, 1948, New York, NY

The master of the comb (which he wrapped with tissue paper and played like a kazoo), Red McKenzie was also a sentimental ballad singer and an important organizer of recording dates. McKenzie

grew up in Washington, D.C., and St. Louis. Early on he worked as a jockey (before breaking both arms in a fall), and he also had a job as a bellhop. McKenzie loved jazz and in 1923, for the fun of it, formed the Mound City Blue Blowers, a trio consisting of his comb, Dick Slevin on a conventional kazoo, and banjoist Jack Bland. On February 23, 1924, they made their first recording and "Arkansas Blues" became a big hit, selling over a million copies. The novelty group recorded a dozen numbers in all for Brunswick during 1924–25. Frankie Trumbauer guested on C-melody sax for two songs and by December 1924, Eddie Lang had joined to make the band a quartet. The identical band, as Red McKenzie's Candy Kids, made eight additional recordings for the Vocalion label during the same period.

With personnel changes, McKenzie kept the Mound City Blue Blowers together into 1932, gradually de-emphasizing his comb playing in favor of his singing. He recorded both as a leader (eight songs during 1927–30, some with Lang, Joe Venuti, Benny Goodman, Bud Freeman, Coleman Hawkins, and Fats Waller) and with later versions of the Mound City Blue Blowers (a dozen songs, including "Hello Lola" and "One Hour," which featured Hawkins, Pee Wee Russell, and Glenn Miller). In addition, as an important force behind the scenes, McKenzie helped gain record dates for the New Orleans Rhythm Kings, Bix Beiderbecke, the Spirits of Rhythm, and Eddie Condon. Although he did not play or sing on the two sessions, McKenzie also lent his name to the famous 1927 dates by the McKenzie-Condon Chicagoans.

As a singer, McKenzie appeared regularly with the Paul Whiteman Orchestra during 1932–33 and occasionally revived the Mound City Blue Blowers name for record dates during 1935–36 (including some performances featuring the heated trumpet of Bunny Berigan). Along the way he also recorded with the Midnight Airedales (1929), Red Nichols (1929–31), Adrian Rollini (1933), and the Spirits of Rhythm, leading further sessions during 1931–37. After 1937, McKenzie worked outside of music, as a beer salesman for a brewery in St. Louis, an ironic job for an alcoholic! In 1944 the forgotten singer was persuaded by his old friend Eddie Condon to appear at a few of his Town Hall concerts. Red McKenzie made a comeback during his last few years, doing a little bit of recording and leading a band at Ryan's before his death from cirrhosis of the liver at age 48.

LPS TO SEARCH FOR

Although Red McKenzie's recordings of 1935–37 are available on the two CDs *Red McKenzie* (Timeless 1-019) and *Mound City Blue Blowers 1935–1936* (Classics 895), his early work with the Mound City Blue Blowers and as a leader is both scattered and scarce. *Just Friends* (Emanon 2) puts the emphasis on McKenzie's singing on eight ballads from 1931–32 (plus an alternate take) with commercial studio orchestras. In addition, McKenzie is heard singing "Swanee Shuffles" with the Midnight Airedales (a Red Nichols group) in 1929 and on a few numbers from a 1936 broadcast with Jerry Sears' orchestra. But his most significant early work has not yet been gathered together coherently.

MCKINNEY'S COTTON PICKERS

During 1928–31, McKinney's Cotton Pickers was one of the finest groups in jazz, a big band that not only predated the swing era but defined the very best music of the classic jazz years. William McKinney (b. Sept. 17, 1895, Cynthiana, KY, d. Oct. 14, 1969, Cynthiana, KY) worked originally as a drummer in circuses. While in Springfield, Ohio, in the early 1920s, he took over the leadership of the Synco Septet. McKinney gave up being the group's drummer in 1923 in order to work as the band's business manager. After the ensemble played in the Midwest, Jean Goldkette signed them up as the house band for his Greystone Ballroom in Detroit; they were renamed McKinney's Cotton Pickers in

1926. In June 1927 Don Redman was lured away from Fletcher Henderson's orchestra in order to become the Cotton Pickers' musical director, arranger, clarinet, altoist, singer, and front man.

McKinney's Cotton Pickers recorded regularly for Victor during 1928–31. Among its key musicians (in addition to Redman) were trumpeters/cornetists John Nesbitt, Langston Curl, Joe Smith, and Rex Stewart, trombonists Claude Jones and Ed Cuffee, and saxophonists Milton Senior, George Thomas, Prince Robinson, and Benny Carter (who joined in 1930). The band introduced such numbers as "Gee Baby, Ain't I Good to You," "Baby Won't You Please Come Home," "I Want a Little Girl," and "Cherry." In addition, in November 1929 Redman led an all-star group (which had the band's nucleus plus such guests as Coleman Hawkins and Fats Waller) on recordings under the Cotton Pickers name.

In the summer of 1931, Don Redman departed to lead his own big band. Benny Carter took over the Cotton Pickers for a year, but its glory years were over and it recorded only two additional selections, in September. Carter left in 1932, the band broke up in 1934, and, although William McKinney organized similar groups into the early 1940s (no further recordings resulted), none made an impression or caught on.

10 Put It There, Vol. 1/July 11, 1928–Nov. 7, 1929/Frog 25

9 Cotton Picker's Scat, Vol. 2/Jan. 31, 1930–Dec. 18, 1930/Frog 26

7 Shag Nasty, Vol. 3/July 11, 1928–Sept. 8, 1931/Frog 27

9 1928–1929/July 11, 1928–Apr. 9, 1929/Classics 609

7 1929–1930/Nov. 5, 1929–Nov. 4, 1930/Classics 625

7 1930–1931/1939–1940/Nov. 4, 1930–Jan. 17, 1940/Classics 649

6 The Band That Don Redman Built/July 11, 1928–Nov. 3, 1930/Bluebird 2275

There are three logical ways to acquire the recordings of McKinney's Cotton Pickers. The three Frog releases contain the band's complete output. *Put It There*, which is highlighted by such gems as "Milenberg Joys," "Cherry," "There's a Rainbow 'Round My Shoulder," "I've Found a New Baby," and "Miss Hannah," has the master takes of the band's records from 1928–29. *Cotton Picker's Scat*, which fully covers 1930, is nearly at the same level, with "Honeysuckle Rose," "Baby, Won't You Please Come Home," and "I Want a Little Girl" all getting memorable treatment. *Shag Nasty* has the four titles from 1931, the band's 17 alternate takes, and their 1928 session as the Chocolate Dandies.

Classics reissues the same music but with no alternate takes. The Chocolate Dandies sessions are included on *1928–1929*, while *1930–1931/1939–1940* also has most of the 1939–40 sessions from the Don Redman big band and the four songs recorded by Redman's ensemble in 1932 under the name of vocalist Harlan Lattimore.

Quite typically, Bluebird (RCA's main domestic jazz label) has put out only a single sampler of recordings by McKinney's Cotton Pickers, 22 of their better titles (including "Four or Five Times," "Cherry," "I've Found a New Baby," and "Gee Baby, Ain't I Good to You"). This set is fine for general listeners but irrelevant to serious 1920s collectors, who will want every recording by one of the great bands of the period.

JIMMY MCPARTLAND

b. Mar. 15, 1907, Chicago, IL, d. Mar. 13, 1991, Port Washington, NY

Jimmy McPartland, whose original inspiration was Bix Beiderbecke, developed his own sound early on and was a fixture on the Dixieland scene for many decades. McPartland started on violin when he was five, switching to cornet ten years later. As a member of the Austin High Gang, McPartland (along with such friends as Bud Freeman, Frankie Teschemacher, Eddie Condon, Dave Tough, and older brother guitarist Dick McPartland) was initially inspired by the records of the Original Dixieland Jazz Band and by seeing the New Orleans Rhythm Kings and King Oliver play in Chicago.

McPartland's early associations included Al Haid (1923), Frisco Haase, Charles "Murph" Podolsky, and the Maroon Five. In late 1924 he became Bix Beiderbecke's replacement with the Wolverines, making his recording debut on the group's final session ("When My Sugar Walks Down the Street" and "Prince of Wails"). After a year with the Wolverines, McPartland worked with Art Kassel (1926) and appeared on the classic McKenzie-Condon Chicagoans sessions that helped to define Chicago jazz in 1927. He moved to New York later in 1927 and became a key soloist with Ben Pollack's orchestra (1927–29), playing next to Benny Goodman, Glenn Miller, and Jack Teagarden. In addition, the cornetist recorded with the Original Wolverines (1927), Eddie Condon, the All-Star Orchestra, Benny Goodman, Irving Mills' Hotsy-Totsy Gang, the Whoopee Makers, and Jimmy McHugh's Bostonians (1928–29).

McPartland weathered the Depression years by working in Broadway pit bands and playing commercial music with Russ Columbo, Horace Heidt, Smith Ballew, and Harry Reser (1933–35). After moving back to Chicago in 1936, Jimmy McPartland happily returned to jazz, playing freewheeling Dixieland during his final 55 years.

FRANK MELROSE

b. Dec. 26, 1907, Sumner, IL, d. Sept. 1941 Hammond, IN

A fine Jelly Roll Morton-influenced pianist whose difficulties with the crime world resulted in his early death, Frank Melrose was the brother of the important music publishers Walter and Lester Melrose. He started on violin before switching his focus to piano. Melrose worked in Chicago of the late 1920s, sometimes recording as Kansas City Frank (so as to hide the integrated nature of the sessions), making dates in 1929 with the Beale Street Washboard Band (which included Johnny Dodds), the Windy Rhythm Kings, and the Kansas City Tin Roof Stompers and in 1930 with the Cellar Boys.

Melrose also recorded 11 titles as a leader during 1929–30, all but two selections either as a piano soloist or in a duet.

In the 1930s Melrose worked in New York and the Midwest. He had a job as a machinist in a pressed-steel factory but continued playing music part time, including with trumpeter Pete Daily in Chicago in 1940. Although some standard discographies state that he died on January 9, 1941, Frank Melrose is apparently on records with Bud Jacobson's Jungle Kings on January 13 and March 9, 1941! He was murdered under mysterious circumstances, probably sometime in September 1941.

PAUL MERTZ

b. Sept. 1, 1904, Reading, PA

Although not a major jazz name himself, Paul Mertz performed with some rather significant groups in the 1920s. He started playing professionally in 1918 (when he was just 14) with local dance bands and theater orchestras. In 1922 Mertz toured with the Dorsey Brothers' Wild Canaries and studied briefly at the University of Detroit. He worked with a couple of versions of Jean Goldkette's orchestras during 1923–27, for whom he also contributed arrangements and recorded. Mertz, who also wrote for Red Nichols and recorded with Bix Beiderbecke's Rhythm Jugglers in 1925, left Goldkette in January 1927 to work with Fred Waring's Pennsylvanians, staying until 1929. After returning briefly to Goldkette in 1929, Mertz moved to Hollywood, where he arranged for Paramount Pictures, writing for the movies. He was in New York for a short period in the early 1930s (working with Nichols, Irving Aaronson's Commanders, and Horace Heidt), but otherwise he spent the rest of his career composing and arranging music for films, including for MGM and Columbia. In 1941 his "I'm Glad There Is You" became a standard. Since no confirmation has come through of his passing, Paul Mertz is apparently one of the very few survivors left of the 1920s jazz scene.

LOUIS METCALF

b. Feb. 28, 1905, Webster Groves, MO, d. Oct. 27, 1981, New York, NY

Louis Metcalf is remembered today chiefly for his short stint with Duke Ellington, although he actually had a pretty long musical career. His first instrument was drums, but he soon switched permanently to cornet. Metcalf worked with Charlie Creath's band in St. Louis as a teenager. By 1923 he was in New York playing with Jimmie Cooper's *Black and White Revue*. A fine soloist for the era, Metcalf worked during 1924–26 with Willie "the Lion" Smith, Andrew Preer's Cotton Club Syncopators, Elmer Snowden, Sam Wooding, and Charlie Johnson. He appeared on many records during 1924–29, including dates backing singers Butterbeans and Susie, Martha Copeland, Mary Dixon, Helen Gross, Rosa Henderson, Maggie Jones, Sara Martin, Viola McCoy, Hazel Meyers, Josie Miles, Lizzie Miles, and Mamie Smith, plus sessions with the Cotton Club Orchestra, Clarence Williams, James P. Johnson, the Musical Stevedores, the Jungle Town Stompers, Jasper Davis' orchestra, the Gulf Coast Seven, Harry's Happy Four, the Kansas City Five, the Original Jazz Hounds, the Wabash Trio, and King Oliver (filling in for Oliver on five numbers).

In late 1926, Metcalf was hired by Duke Ellington for his up-and-coming orchestra. He stayed with Duke until June 1928 but never really found his niche with the band. Metcalf's work with the plunger mute was never as warm or witty as that of Bubber Miley, and he was not as lyrical a soloist in general as Arthur Whetsol. He did have a fair amount of solo space (sounding best on "Harlem River Quiver" and "Bugle Call Rag"), but his role as a "hot soloist" was not as comfortable a fit as it would be for Freddie Jenkins later in 1928.

After leaving Ellington, Metcalf joined Jelly Roll Morton for a period. The first half of 1929 was spent with Luis Russell until a falling-out resulted in his being replaced by Henry "Red" Allen. Metcalf largely stopped recording after the Depression began but found work in various places, including with the Connie's Inn Revue and Vernon Andrade's orchestra, three years freelancing in Montreal, a brief stint with Fletcher Henderson (1935), on St. Louis-area riverboats, leading a big band, spending 1944–51 heading the International Band in Montreal, and freelancing in New York. In 1966 Louis Metcalf recorded a now-rare album for Victoria Spivey's Spivey label that featured him playing advanced swing and still sounding in his prime. But nothing came of it. When he died in 1981, Louis Metcalf was still known primarily for his work with Duke Ellington, which had ended 53 years earlier.

MEZZ MEZZROW

b. Nov. 9, 1899, Chicago, IL, d. Aug. 5, 1972, Paris, France

Mezz Mezzrow (born Milton Mesirow) made his greatest impact as a propagandist for New Orleans jazz and integration, a reefer salesman, an author (his colorful memoirs, *Really the Blues*), and the head of a record label (King Jazz) in the 1940s. An erratic but enthusiastic musician, Mezzrow began playing saxophone in 1917 while spending a brief time in jail. He always had a strong enthusiasm for ensemble-oriented jazz and by 1923 was associated with the slightly younger Austin High Gang. Mezzrow worked with Husk O'Hare's Wolverines (1926), recorded with the Jungle Kings, Frank Teschemacher, and the Chicago Rhythm Kings, and led the Purple Grackle Orchestra in 1928. A limited player who was at his best on blues chord changes, Mezzrow distrusted more modern developments in jazz. He reluctantly moved to New York in 1928 (following the other Chicago musicians who had already departed), worked a month with Ben Pollack, recorded with Eddie Condon (1928–29), visited Europe in 1929, and toured with Red Nichols.

Mezzrow led two interracial recording dates during 1933–34 (resulting in such numbers as "Free Love," "Dissonance," and "Sendin' the Vipers")

and a session apiece during 1936–37 but mostly scuffled during the Depression years until Hugues Panassie (an important French jazz writer who was a lifelong Mezz fan) used him in 1938 on the famous Panassie Sessions. Those dates teamed Mezzrow with the rediscovered Tommy Ladnier and on one occasion Sidney Bechet, including a classic version of "Really the Blues." After spending much of 1940–42 in jail for selling marijuana, Mezzrow ran the King Jazz label during 1945–48, recording frequently with Bechet and trumpeter Hot Lips Page in ensemble-oriented dates that emphasized blues. Mezz Mezzrow, who played at the Nice Jazz Festival in 1948, moved permanently to France in 1951.

9 1928–1936/Apr. 6, 1928–Mar. 12, 1936/Classics 713

An interesting variety of sessions is on this Classics CD, which actually has Mezz Mezzrow as the leader on only half of the selections. He is heard as a sideman on six exciting numbers with the Chicago Rhythm Kings, the Jungle Kings, Frank Teschemacher, and the Louisiana Rhythm Kings in 1928; the other musicians include Muggsy Spanier, Joe Sullivan, Eddie Condon, and Gene Krupa. Mezzrow's sessions of 1933–34 are also included, and the 10- to 11-piece groups fall between swing and classic jazz, with arrangements provided by Mezz, Benny Carter, Alex Hill, and trombonist Floyd O'Brien; sidemen include Max Kaminsky, Benny Carter, Bud Freeman, Teddy Wilson, and Willie "the Lion" Smith. In addition, there is a rare date led by tenor saxophonist Art Karle (all four numbers unfortunately feature singer Chick Bullock) and the first two titles from Mezzrow's 1936 session with trumpeter Frankie Newton.

LIZZIE MILES

b. Mar. 31, 1895, New Orleans, LA, d. Mar. 17, 1963, New Orleans, LA

Lizzie Miles was a rarity, a classic blues singer of the 1920s who made a comeback in the 1950s and exceeded her earlier fame. She was born Elizabeth

Mary Pajaund, leaving New Orleans in 1909 when she was 14 to perform as a novelty act with the Jones Brothers' Circus. Miles sang with circuses and minstrel shows during the next eight years. She spent 1918–20 in Chicago, performing with King Oliver, Freddie Keppard, and Charlie Elgar. In 1921 Miles (who considered Sophie Tucker and her half-sister, Edna Hicks, to be her main influences) moved to New York, where she made her recording debut the following year. During 1922–30 she recorded 57 songs, mostly with lesser-known musicians, other than for two songs in a trio with King Oliver, flutist Albert Socarras, and Clarence Williams, two duets with Jelly Roll Morton, and a pair of titles with Jasper Davis' group (which includes Louis Metcalf, Charlie Holmes, and Cliff Jackson). Miles, who spent much of 1924–26 in Europe, was knocked out of action during 1931–35 by a serious illness. She made a comeback and recorded eight songs in 1939. But since her good-time blues style was out of vogue, she was out of music altogether during 1942–50.

In the early 1950s, Miles made an unexpected comeback, working at the Hangover Club in San Francisco (1952), performing regularly with trumpeter Bob Scobey (1955–57), and recording with Scobey, trumpeter Sharkey Bonano, and clarinetist George Lewis. Lizzie Miles, who returned to her native New Orleans, was active musically until after the 1959 Monterey Jazz Festival, when she retired to devote herself to religion.

8 Vol. 1/Feb. 24, 1922–Apr. 25, 1923/Document 5458
7 Vol. 2/Apr. 25, 1923–Feb. 29, 1928/Document 5459
8 Vol. 3/May 2, 1928–Oct. 7, 1939/Document 5460
All of Lizzie Miles' recordings from the first part of her career are reissued on these three Document CDs. Although rarely accompanied by famous musicians, Miles' recordings mostly sound pretty good today, for her delivery was straightforward, sincere, and musical. *Vol. 1* has such numbers as "He May Be Your Man but He Comes to See Me Sometimes," "Hot Lips," "The Yellow Dog Blues," and

"You've Gotta Come and See Mama Every Night." *Vol. 2* has eight selections from 1923 and 14 from 1927–28, after she had returned from Europe. Among the better tunes are "When You Get Tired of Your New Sweetie," "Lonesome Ghost Blues," and two takes of "A Good Man Is Hard to Find." *Vol. 3* has some of Lizzie Miles' most jazz-oriented recordings. There are two selections with the trio of King Oliver, Albert Socarras, and Clarence Williams ("You're Such a Cruel Papa to Me" and "My Dif'rent Kind of Man"), a pair of tunes with a pickup group supposedly led by Jasper Davis ("Georgia Gigolo" and "It Feels So Good"), and a date in which she is accompanied by Jelly Roll Morton ("I Hate a Man Like You" and "Don't Tell Me Nothin' 'Bout My Man"). The CD concludes with eight selections from 1939, in which Miles (still sounding in prime form) is joined by the Melrose Stompers for a variety of good-time tunes.

BUBBER MILEY

b. Jan. 19, 1903, Aiken, SC, d. May 24, 1932, New York, NY

One of the great trumpeters of 1926–29, Bubber Miley deserves a large amount of the credit for the development of Duke Ellington's "jungle sound." A true master of the plunger mute (often played in conjunction with a straight mute), Miley was able to achieve a wide variety of haunting and memorable speechlike sounds. He lived in New York from the age of six, the brother of three sisters who sang professionally as the South Carolina Trio. Miley played trombone for a time before switching to cornet and finally trumpet. After serving in the Navy (1918–19), Miley worked with the Carolina Five, Willie Gant's Band, and Mamie Smith's Jazz Hounds (with whom he made his recording debut during 1921–22). After hearing King Oliver play at the Dreamland in Chicago, Miley began using the plunger mute. He was also inspired by Johnny Dunn, although in time he surpassed both Dunn and Oliver.

Miley played in many situations during 1922–25, including with Thomas Morris' Past Jazz Masters in 1923 and record dates with Perry Bradford, the Kansas City Five, the Six Black Diamonds, Helen Gross, Margaret Johnson, Louella Jones, Hazel Meyers, Julia Moody, and Monette Moore plus unusual duets with the reed organ of Arthur Ray. He first worked with the Washingtonians in September 1923, when the group was led by Elmer Snowden. Even at that early stage, Miley greatly impressed the band's pianist, Duke Ellington. In 1924, when Ellington took over the group, Miley was officially hired, and the band's identity immediately changed from a pretty-sounding sweet group to a gutbucket ensemble filled with the blues and unusual tonal distortions. Miley starred on Ellington's first two recordings ("Choo Choo" and "Rainy Nights," from November 1924). During the next 19 months, Miley was in and out of Duke's band a few times, making significant freelance recordings with Perry Bradford's Georgia Strutters, Sara Martin, Alberta Hunter, Martha Copeland, and Clarence Williams (four exciting titles, including "I've Found a New Baby" and "Jackass Blues").

Starting in June 1926, Miley and Tricky Sam Nanton (his musical equivalent on trombone) starred on dozens of Duke Ellington recordings, helping to make Duke a major success at the Cotton Club from late 1927. Miley cowrote some of the band's most atmospheric pieces, including "Black and Tan Fantasy," "Creole Love Call," "Doin' the Voom Voom," and Ellington's original theme song, the haunting "East St. Louis Toodle-oo." He can also be heard in memorable form on such numbers as "Jubilee Stomp," "The Mooche," "Hot and Bothered," "Bandanna Babies," "Diga Diga Do," and "Tiger Rag." Unfortunately by January 1929, Miley was an alcoholic and becoming unreliable. Because he had made his trumpet chair so indispensable to the band's sound, whenever Miley was absent, it was noticeable. After a few warnings, Miley was fired by Ellington; his place was filled by Cootie Williams for the next 11 years.

Although Miley only had three years left in his life, his post-Ellington period was busy. He visited France with Noble Sissle's orchestra in May 1929, played in New York with Zutty Singleton and Allie Ross, and in 1930 worked with Leo Reisman's white orchestra, usually appearing with the band during those segregated times hidden behind a screen. His haunting solo on Reisman's recording of "What Is This Thing Called Love" is quite memorable (despite the wretched vocal that follows), and he can also be heard on "Without Your Love." Other recordings of 1930 include four songs with Jelly Roll Morton ("Fussy Mabel" is a classic), "St. James Infirmary" with King Oliver, a Hoagy Carmichael session that includes Bix Beiderbecke (highlighted by "Rockin' Chair"), and six numbers as a leader (included on *Thumpin' and Bumpin'*—Frog 11, with the alternate takes being on *Don't You Leave Me Here*—Frog 12); "I Lost My Gal from Memphis" and "Black Maria" are particularly rewarding. In 1931 Miley accompanied dancer Roger Pryor Dodge in the *Sweet and Low* revue for several months and led a band backed by Irving Mills.

But tuberculosis, aggravated by his alcoholism, struck Bubber Miley down, and he died in 1932, when he was only 29.

GLENN MILLER

b. Mar. 1, 1904, Clarinda, IA, d. Dec. 16, 1944, English Channel

The leader of the most popular big band of 1939–42 (an orchestra's whose many hits served as the soundtrack of the era) and the remarkable Army Air Force Band of 1943–44, Alton Glenn Miller got his start in the 1920s. Miller grew up in Nebraska, Missouri, and Colorado, originally playing cornet and mandolin before switching to trombone by 1916. After graduating from high school, he had a stint with Boyd Senter (1921–22). Miller attended the University of Colorado and gigged in his spare time.

In 1926 he joined the Ben Pollack Orchestra, where he was at first the main trombone soloist in addition to contributing arrangements. However, in 1928 Jack Teagarden also became a member of Pollack's band, and Miller's solo opportunities were cut drastically. He realized at that early stage that his future was in writing music rather than being a trombonist, although he would continue to do both for some time.

Miller played with Paul Ash (1928) and Red Nichols (1929–30), appearing on some record dates (his finest solo was on "Hello Lola" with the Mound City Blue Blowers), working as a freelance arranger, and performing in theater orchestras for Broadway shows. Glenn Miller's most notable associations prior to forming his first big band in 1937 were with the Smith Ballew orchestra (1932), the Dorsey Brothers big band (1934–35), and Ray Noble (1935), contributing charts (often for ballads) and playing in the trombone section. He would hit it very big in 1939, but that's another story!

PUNCH MILLER

b. June 14, 1894, Raceland, LA, d. Dec. 2, 1971, New Orleans, LA

Ernest "Punch" Miller (who gained his nickname because his twin sister, Ernestine, had the middle name of Judy!) was a fine New Orleans trumpeter who never quite lived up to his potential. Miller had short periods playing bass drum, baritone horn, and trombone in parade bands before switching to cornet. After serving in the Army during World War I, Miller became an important part of the New Orleans jazz scene, playing with Kid Ory, Jack Carey, Fate Marable, and his own band. Miller left town to work in Dallas with Mack's Merrymakers (with whom he made his recording debut in January 1925) and settled in Chicago in 1926.

During the next few years, Miller worked with Kid Ory, Albert Wynn, Freddie Keppard, Chippie Hill, Tiny Parham, Omer Simeon, Jimmy Bertrand,

Jelly Roll Morton, Erskine Tate, Frankie Franko's Louisianians (on and off during 1929–35), Zilner Randolph's W.P.A. Band, and Walter Barnes, plus his own groups at local clubs. He appeared on recordings with the Levee Serenaders (a 1928 group with Jelly Roll Morton), Jimmy Wade, Albert Wynn, Tiny Parham (1928–29), Bertrand (1929), King Mutt's Tennessee Thumpers, Frankie "Half Pint" Jaxon, and Frankie Franko (1930), contributing a heated lead and concise solos.

Miller's decision to stay in Chicago in the 1930s rather than emigrate to New York resulted in his working mostly in low-level bands during the swing era. The comeback of Dixieland in the 1940s did not affect his life much, and the trumpeter continued playing in near-anonymity. In 1956 Punch Miller moved back to New Orleans, where he stayed active during his final 15 years, ironically finally having many opportunities to record once he was way past his prime.

8 Punch Miller 1925–1930/Jan. 22, 1925–Nov. 12, 1930/RST 1517

The great majority of Punch Miller's appearances on records during the classic jazz era are on this CD. In fact, it contains practically every one of his early sessions except those with the Levee Serenaders and Tiny Parham. Miller is heard in a supporting role behind Billy and Mary Mack, jamming at his early best with Albert Wynn (including versions of "She's Crying for Me" and "Parkway Stomp"), on two selections with Jimmy Wade's Dixielanders, sounding so-so on a good-time set with clarinetist King Mutt, in fine form with Jimmy Bertrand's Washboard Wizards (a quartet with Darnell Howard and Jimmy Blythe), backing the jivey singer Frankie "Half Pint" Jaxon, and in 1930 with Frankie Franko's Louisianians (excellent versions of "Somebody Stole My Gal" and "Golden Lily Blues"). This is the one Punch Miller CD to get, and far superior to his later work of the 1960s.

RAY MILLER

A busy bandleader in the 1920s, Ray Miller is nevertheless an obscure figure in jazz history. He worked as a singing waiter at the Casino Gardens in Chicago in 1916, the same time that the Original Dixieland Jazz Band was performing at that establishment nightly. Inspired by the ODJB, Miller (who played drums) put together a sextet that, with Tom Brown on trombone and trumpeter Earl Oliver, started making recordings in 1920. The group gradually expanded, was nine pieces in 1923, and went up to 13 by 1924. By then Miller was no longer playing drums, sticking to directing the band. Among the musicians who spent time with his orchestra in the 1920s were Miff Mole, Frankie Trumbauer, Rube Bloom, Volly DeFaut, and Muggsy Spanier (1928–29).

The Ray Miller Orchestra (which recorded both excellent jazz and dance music) spent periods playing in New York, Cincinnati, and Chicago. But nothing is known of Ray Miller's whereabouts after 1930.

8 1924–1929/Mar. 28, 1924–Dec. 21, 1929/Timeless 1–066
Twenty-four of the best recordings by Ray Miller's orchestra are on this CD. Most of the numbers are quite jazz oriented. Frankie Trumbauer, Miff Mole, and Muggsy Spanier ("That's a-Plenty" and "Angry") are heard from, and there is speculation (although unproven) that Bix Beiderbecke might be one of the two cornet soloists on the two takes of "Cradle of Love." Other highlights include "Lots o' Mama," "Mama's Gone, Goodbye," "Red Hot Henry Brown," "Spanish Shawl," "Weary Blues," and "My Honey's Lovin' Arms." Additional titles by Ray Miller are included in *The Obscure and Neglected Chicagoans* (IAJRC 1007).

MILLS BLUE RHYTHM BAND

The Mills Blue Rhythm Band straddled the boundary between early classic jazz and swing. The ensemble was originally known as the Blue Rhythm Band and was led by drummer Willie Lynch. After it became the Coconut Grove Orchestra, the group accompanied Louis Armstrong on a few recordings in 1930 (including "Dinah" and "Tiger Rag"). Producer Irving Mills took over the ensemble in early 1931, renaming it after himself and having it work at the Cotton Club as the relief band for Cab Calloway and Duke Ellington. Because it was a fill-in group, the Mills Blue Rhythm Band never really developed its own musical personality. However, it did make some fine recordings during 1931–37, with Edgar Hayes as the musical director (and main arranger) and such frontmen as Baron Lee, Billy Banks, and (starting in 1933) Lucky Millinder. Among its key members were Charlie Holmes (1931), Red Allen, J.C. Higginbotham, and Buster Bailey (1934–36) and, in its last year, altoist Tab Smith, pianist Billy Kyle, and trumpeters Harry "Sweets" Edison and Charlie Shavers. The Mills Blue Rhythm Band permanently broke up in 1938.

7 1931/Jan. 21, 1931-July 30, 1931/Classics 660
7 1931–1932/July 30, 1931–Sept. 23, 1932/Classics 676
8 1933–1934/Mar. 1, 1933–Dec. 11, 1934/Classics 686
9 1934–1936/Dec. 19, 1934–May 20, 1936/Classics 710
8 1936–1937/May 20, 1936–July 1, 1937/Classics 731

All of the recordings by the Mills Blue Rhythm Band are on these five Classics CDs (other than a few alternate takes). *1931* has lots of vocals (by Dick Robertson, Charlie Lawman, George Morton, and Chick Bullock), arrangements by Harry White and Edgar Hayes, and some hot numbers, including "Blue Rhythm," "Red Devil," and "Futuristic Jungleism." *1931–1932* finds Billy Banks taking over as the vocalist (he is a big improvement over the others). The highlights include "Savage Rhythm," "Snake Hips," "Heat Waves," "The Growl," and "Jazz Cocktail," but the arrangements are generally more exciting than the soloists.

By the time that the music on *1933–1934* was recorded, the Mills Blue Rhythm Band was improving, thanks to the addition of major stars (by 1934) in Red Allen, J.C. Higginbotham, Buster Bailey, and tenor saxophonist Joe Garland. "Ridin' In

Pictured here in a later period, the Mills Brothers were at their best in the 1930s when they sang uncanny imitations of instruments.

Rhythm," "Harlem After Midnight," and "The Stuff Is Here (and It's Mellow)" are some of the more exciting selections. Much of the best music by the Mills Blue Rhythm Band actually took place in the early part of the swing era and appears on *1934–1936*, including such swinging numbers as "Back Beats," "Ride Red Ride," Garland's "There's Rhythm in Harlem" (which is reminiscent of the yet-to-be-composed "In the Mood") and "Truckin'." *1936–1937* has the same group (with altoist Tab Smith and pianist Billy Kyle making the band even stronger) on a variety of hot tunes, including "St. Louis Wiggle Rhythm," "Merry-Go-Round," "Big John's Special," and "Algiers Stomp." As can be heard on the group's last recordings, during December 1936–February 1937,

the band had an almost complete turnover and emerged as a young and swinging ensemble (featuring Charlie Shavers and Harry "Sweets" Edison) that was not quite on the same level as the Red Allen version. Still, swing and vintage-jazz collectors will want all five of the Mills Blue Rhythm Band's discs.

MILLS BROTHERS

It is ironic that the Mills Brothers gained their most lasting fame after their importance to jazz had greatly diminished. The Mills Brothers originally consisted of Herbert Mills (1912–89), Harry Mills (1913–82), Donald Mills (1915–99), and John Mills (1910–36). The siblings (all born in Piqua, Ohio) started off singing in vaudeville shows in local theaters during the late 1920s. Their brilliance at imitating instruments found the group billed as "four boys and a guitar" yet often sounding as if they also had a trumpet, trombone, and bass too.

In 1931 the Mills Brothers went to New York and quickly became well known, recording regularly and appearing in the films *The Big Broadcast* (1932), *Twenty Million Sweethearts* (1934), and *Broadway Gondolier* (1935), among many other movies, usually for one or two songs. The Mills Brothers worked steadily throughout the 1930s, visited Europe, and had some collaborations, including recordings with the Duke Ellington Orchestra and (later in the decade) some delightful sessions with Louis Armstrong. After John Mills' unexpected death in 1936, the Mills Brothers' father, Herbert Mills (1882–1967), took his place. Since John had been the group's guitarist (the only instrument that they used), an outside guitarist had to be employed from then on.

The Mills Brothers continued in the same successful fashion until they had a major hit in 1942 with "Paper Doll." Shortly afterwards, they stopped imitating instruments and became a much more conventional vocal group, staying active (even after John Sr.'s retirement in 1957) into the 1970s. Donald Mills performed (with his son) as the last surviving Mills Brother as late as 1998.

10 Chronological, Vol. 1/Oct. 12, 1931–Apr. 14, 1932/JSP 301
10 Chronological, Vol. 2/May 1932–Feb. 24, 1934/JSP 302
9 Chronological, Vol. 3/May 29, 1934–Feb. 20, 1935/JSP 303
9 Chronological, Vol. 4/Oct. 28, 1935–June 29, 1937/JSP 304
9 Chronological, Vol. 5/Feb. 2, 1933–Aug. 23, 1938/JSP 320
9 Chronological, Vol. 6/May 30, 1935–Aug. 23, 1939/JSP 345

All of the Mills Brothers' recordings from their first eight years on records are on these six CDs by the British JSP label. The same music is currently being reissued in similar fashion by Nostalgia Arts. In addition to their studio recordings, the CDs also include some radio appearances, film soundtracks, and other rare items. *Vol. 1* finds the Mills Brothers introducing their unique sound to the world, and

they are particularly exciting on three renditions of "Tiger Rag," "Nobody's Sweetheart," "Sweet Sue," and a few numbers (including "Dinah" and "Shine") with Bing Crosby. *Vol. 2*, in addition to "The Old Man of the Mountain," "Coney Island Washboard," "Smoke Rings," "Swing It Sister," and "I've Found a New Baby," has the vocal group meeting up with Duke Ellington, Cab Calloway, Don Redman, Alice Faye, and Bing Crosby (a classic version of "My Honey's Lovin' Arms"). *Vol. 3* continues with such gems as "Put On Your Old Grey Bonnet," "Nagasaki," "Limehouse Blues," and two songs with film star Dick Powell.

Vol. 4 starts off with John Jr.'s last four recordings with the Mills Brothers before his death. The group came back together in mid-1936 and continued at the same high level, making its first joint recordings with Louis Armstrong (including "Carry Me Back to Old Virginny" and "In the Shade of the Old Apple Tree"), recording a couple of numbers with Ella Fitzgerald, and swinging on "Shoe Shine Boy," "Pennies from Heaven," and "The Love Bug Will Bite You." Also included on this CD are two Harry Mills solo records. *Vol. 5*, which has three earlier alternate takes, continues the Mills Brothers' evolution through 1938, including "Organ Grinder's Swing," a particularly memorable version of "Caravan," and more meetings with Louis Armstrong. *Vol. 6* wraps up the series (which could have continued at a high level into 1942) with two earlier alternate takes, a pair of numbers featuring Harry Mills with Andy Kirk's orchestra, and such tunes as "You Tell Me Your Dream," "Jeepers Creepers," and "Basin Street Blues." Although other singers have imitated instruments through the years, very few were ever at the remarkable level of creativity that the Mills Brothers in the 1930s attained every time they performed.

IRVING MILLS

b. Jan. 16, 1894, New York, NY, d. Apr. 21, 1985, Palm Springs, CA

Irving Mills is usually mentioned in jazz-history books as Duke Ellington's manager, but there was much more to him than that. Mills worked initially as a song demonstrator and a singer. In 1919 he founded the publishing company Mills Music with his brother, Jack Mills. Irving Mills worked in many capacities during the next 20 years: as a talent scout, record producer, band manager, singer, and underrated lyricist. As Duke Ellington's manager during 1926–39, he worked tirelessly, getting Duke booked at the Cotton Club, arranging radio hookups, and having Ellington record for many labels under pseudonyms. Although Mills did get his name as one of the composers on a lot of Ellington's originals during the period (many of which he had little if anything to do with), he did write the lyrics to "It Don't Mean a Thing" and "Mood Indigo."

In addition, Mills organized record dates for the Whoopee Makers and his Hotsy Totsy Gang, led and ran the Mills Blue Rhythm Band, founded the Master and Variety record labels in 1936, and along the way worked with Cab Calloway, Benny Carter, Fletcher Henderson, Jimmie Lunceford, and Don Redman. In 1939, financial disputes ended his partnership with Ellington. Staying active in management and music publishing for decades, Irving Mills (who assembled the cast for the 1943 black musical *Stormy Weather*) played mostly a behind-the-scenes role after 1939.

9 **Vol. 1/July 27, 1928-July 31, 1929/Sensation 24**
9 **Vol. 2/Sept. 20, 1929–May 3, 1931/Sensation 25**
A large chunk of Irving Mills' musical legacy is on these two CDs from the Canadian Sensation label. Included are all of the recordings (including alternate takes) by Mills' Hotsy-Totsy Gang (except two numbers on which they backed the tap dancing of Bill "Bojangles" Robinson), the selections by Mills' Merry Makers, and the one title ("At the Prom") cut by Mills' Modernists. Mills himself has only a few forgettable vocals, but his groups include plenty of all-stars. Heard on *Vol. 1* are such notables as Jimmy McPartland, Dudley Fosdick, Fud Living-

ston, Jack Pettis, Eddie Lang, Jack Teagarden, Benny Goodman, Tommy Dorsey, Jimmy Dorsey, and Miff Mole. Although the ensembles tend to be arranged, there are plenty of freewheeling solos. *Vol. 2* also has many of the same musicians in top form, plus the additional bonus of hearing Hoagy Carmichael on several numbers (including "Stardust") and a declining but still intriguing Bix Beiderbecke on the June 6, 1930, session. Irving Mills may have had very little direct involvement in this music (other than his two vocals), but it is fair to say that, were it not for his connections with record labels, the Hotsy-Totsy Gang would have never existed and a lot of fine music would have never been documented.

THE MISSOURIANS

Wilson Robinson's Syncopators was formed in the early 1920s and based in New York. In 1925 it became the Cotton Club Orchestra, serving as the house band at the Cotton Club during 1925–27 and recording seven titles in 1925. In 1927 it recorded an additional selection ("I've Found a New Baby") under the name of its leader, Andrew Preer. Preer unexpectedly died later that year and, after the ensemble toured with Ethel Waters, it was renamed the Missourians. Led by altoist-clarinetist George Scott, the Missourians played regularly at the Savoy Ballroom during 1928–29. The band is remembered today chiefly because it recorded a dozen exciting numbers at three recording sessions during 1929–30, including "Market Street Stomp," "Vine Street Drag," and "Prohibition Blues." The recordings have been reissued as *Cab Calloway and the Missourians* (JSP 328) and are reviewed in this book under Calloway's name.

But despite how spirited the ten-piece group sounded at its February 17, 1930, session, it was in financial doldrums and on the verge of breaking up. Cab Calloway, who was dissatisfied with his backup band (the Alabamians), took over the superior Missourians and renamed them the Cab Calloway Orchestra. Although the band would play a subsidiary role from then on, it would no longer have to worry about steady work!

GEORGE MITCHELL

b. Mar. 8, 1899, Louisville, KY, d. May 22, 1972, Chicago, IL

George Mitchell's lyrical sound, all-round musicianship, and ability to adapt to Jelly Roll Morton's music during five recording sessions (1926–27) are his greatest claims to fame, even though his period with Morton was actually quite brief. Mitchell began playing trumpet when he was 12. He worked in the South with the Louisville Musical Club Brass Band, the Rabbit's Foot Minstrel Show, A.G. Allen's Minstrels, and the L.M.C. Band. After moving to Chicago in late 1919, Mitchell played with Irving Miller's Brown Skin Models, Arthur Sims, Tony Jackson (1920), Clarence Miller, Doc Holly's Band, John Wickliffe, Carroll Dickerson (1923–24), and Doc Cook (1924–25). In 1926 he cut two songs with Luis Russell, accompanied Ada Brown on one recording date, and worked with Lil Armstrong's band. Mitchell recorded four titles apiece with the New Orleans Wanderers and the New Orleans Bootblacks, identical combos that were essentially the Louis Armstrong Hot Five with Mitchell in Satch's place and altoist Joe Clark added.

Most importantly, Mitchell recorded 17 selections with Jelly Roll Morton during 1926–27, and these include a large number of classic performances, highlighted by "Black Bottom Stomp," "The Chant," "Sidewalk Blues," "Dead Man Blues," "Someday Sweetheart," "Original Jelly Roll Blues," "Doctor Jazz," "Beale Street Blues," and "The Pearls." The cornetist is such an integral part of the music that it is difficult to know where he is reading Morton's charts and where he is improvising.

Mitchell also recorded with Johnny Dodds in 1927 (including "Come On and Stomp, Stomp, Stomp"), Doc Cook, Jimmie Noone (1928–29), and the Dixie Rhythm Kings, working at night with Dave Peyton's orchestra. Mitchell's last significant job was as a member of the original Earl Hines Orchestra (1929–31). But at that point, he apparently lost interest in music. Mitchell gigged briefly with banjoist Jack Ellis in the summer of 1931, appeared on a Frankie "Half Pint" Jaxon recording in 1933, and sometimes played with Elgar's Federal Concert Orchestra later in the 1930s. Otherwise, George Mitchell spent his last 41 years outside of music, working for many years as a bank messenger.

MIFF MOLE

b. Mar. 11, 1898, Roosevelt, Long Island, NY, d. Apr. 21, 1961, New York, NY

A highly original trombonist, Irving Milfred "Miff" Mole was a perfect match for Red Nichols in the mid- to late 1920s. Mole had violin lessons for three years starting when he was 11 and also played piano, but by the time he was 15 he had switched to trombone. Mole played with Gus Sharp's orchestra for two years, was in a band led by Jimmy Durante (who at the time was a jazz pianist), and in 1922 was a founding member of the Original Memphis Five. Other early associations included playing with Abe Lyman in California and working in New York with Sam Lanin, Ray Miller (1924–25), Russ Gorman, and Roger Wolfe Kahn (1926–27).

Mole first met Red Nichols while playing with Gorman. They recorded together quite frequently during 1925–29 as sidemen with each other's groups (Red Nichols' Five Pennies and Miff Mole's Molers) plus in such overlapping bands as the Arkansas Travelers, the Redheads, and Red and Miff's Stompers. The music that Nichols and Mole created, which was a bit avant-garde for the period, often featured whole-tone scales, unusual interval jumps, tricky arrangements, and hot solos. Mole's staccato runs and intervals were part of his early style, and he showed that the trombone could be played with as much adventure and unpredictability as the trumpet/cornet, freeing his instrument from its percussive role.

However, his style did not become influential, because in 1928 Jack Teagarden (with his more legato and blues-oriented approach) arrived in New York and was quickly considered both a sensation and a role model for other trombonists. Mole's association with Red Nichols ended in early 1929, and his string of recordings at the head of his Molers concluded on February 6, 1930. Mole, who was a staff musician on radio station WOR as early as 1927, had a longtime association with NBC (1929–38). By the time he emerged from the studios to become a member of the Paul Whiteman Orchestra (1938–40), Mole showed the strong influence of Teagarden himself and was a much more conventional trombonist than he had been earlier. He had a stint with Benny Goodman's big band (1942–43) and led Dixieland groups during 1943–47, having a minor hit with his version of "Peg o' My Heart." Miff Mole worked mostly in Chicago during 1947–54 (including with Muggsy Spanier) and, due to bad health, was only a part-time player in his last years.

9 Slippin' Around/Jan. 26, 1927–Feb. 6, 1930/Frog 19
8 Slippin' Around—Again/Feb. 11, 1927–Feb. 17, 1937/Frog 20

Other than two big band selections from 1937, these two CDs have all of Miff Mole's recordings as a leader prior to 1944. *Vol. 1* includes 14 numbers by Miff Mole's Molers of 1927–28, a recording band that was basically Red Nichols' Five Pennies (with Nichols, Mole, Arthur Schutt, Dick McDonough, and Vic Berton), along with Jimmy Dorsey, Joe Tarto, drummer Ray Bauduc, Fud Livingston, Adrian Rollini, and Eddie Lang. Mole's four numbers backing stage singer Sophie Tucker (who sounds pretty strong in 1927), four cuts with Red and Miff's Stompers, two by Nichols' orchestra, and a pair of test pressings from a Mole session in 1930 (with Phil Napoleon) wrap up this intriguing set. Highlights include adventurous versions of "Hurricane," "Delirium," "Davenport Blues," "Imagination," and "Feelin' No Pain."

Slippin' Around—Again starts off with six alternate takes (all formerly test pressings) and has the last dates by Mole's Molers, with Phil Napoleon taking over for Nichols and the members of the supporting cast, including Fosdick, Livingston, Schutt, Carl Kress, and Jimmy Dorsey. Also on this CD are two numbers from a radio broadcast in 1936 that feature Mole, and a pair of selections (plus an alternate take) from Mole's only session as a leader during the swing era, transitional performances that show the trombonist having lost much of his individuality in favor of sounding like Teagarden.

BILL MOORE

b. 1901, Brooklyn, NY, d. June 17, 1964, New York, NY

Trumpeter Bill Moore is a unique figure in music history because he was a light-skinned black who spent most of his life "passing" and appearing on recordings with otherwise completely white bands. Moore was the product of a mixed marriage, but he did not let that slow down his career, and few of his contemporaries realized that he was continually breaking down racial boundaries. Moore appeared on countless records in the 1920s, including with the California Ramblers (and their smaller groups the Five Birmingham Babies, the Goofus Five, and the Lumberjacks), Ben Bernie, Don Voorhees, Bert Lown, Jack Pettis, Irving Mills' Hotsy Totsy Gang, the Whoopee Makers, the Mississippi Maulers, the New Orleans Blackbirds, the Vagabonds, the Varsity Eight, Bailey's Dixie Dudes, the Broadway Broadcasters, Al Goering's Collegians, the Kentucky Blowers, the Little Ramblers, Fred Rich, and the Dorsey Brothers (1930–31), all of which were white bands. The trumpeter took short and hot solos on many of the sessions, and he proved to be a flexible and top-notch musician, adding a bit of jazz to many dance band dates. Whenever there was any doubt about Moore's ancestry, he billed himself as "The Hot Hawaiian," even though he had never been to Hawaii!

After 1930, Bill Moore left jazz altogether to work

full-time as a busy studio musician, being virtually the only black to appear on countless sessions, even if very few people ever realized it.

FREDDIE MOORE

b. Aug. 20, 1900, Washington, NC, d. Nov. 3, 1992, Bronx, NY

A primitive but entertaining drummer and washboard player, Freddie Moore was a throwback to the early 1920s stylistically, even when performing in the 1980s. He began playing drums at 12 and gained early experience working with traveling minstrel shows. After touring with William Benbow's *Get Happy* revue in 1926, Moore worked with Charlie Creath in St. Louis (1927), led a band in Detroit, and played regularly with Wilbur Sweatman (1928–31) in New York. He made his only recordings in the early period with King Oliver in 1930, touring with Oliver during 1931–32.

Moore worked in a variety of settings during his long career, including as a leader and with pianist Art Hodes, Sidney Bechet, trumpeter Bunk Johnson, clarinetist Bob Wilbur, Wilbur De Paris (1952–54), Mezz Mezzrow, Tony Parenti (1968–70), and trumpeter Roy Eldridge (1971). Freddie Moore specialized on washboard in his later years, playing with Bo Cantwell's Saturday Night Stompers at the Red Blazer in New York on a weekly basis until he was 92.

MONETTE MOORE

b. 1902, Gainesville, TX, d. 1962, Los Angeles, CA

An excellent classic blues singer, Monette Moore could also sing jazz quite effectively and had a wide-ranging career. She grew up in Texas, sang locally, and moved to New York in the early 1920s. Moore accompanied silent films on piano, began recording in 1923, and ironically had recorded all but a few of her early sessions by late 1925, when her career in vaudeville started to take off. She worked in musical comedies, on stage (including on Broadway), and ran her nightclub (Monette's Club) for a few

years in the early to mid-1930s. Moore, who recorded two titles in 1936, moved to Los Angeles in 1942 and during 1945–47 recorded six final songs. Among the highlights of Monette Moore's later years were appearing in the 1951 film *Yes Sir Mr. Bones*, having an occasional role on the *Amos 'n' Andy* television show, playing a small part in the 1954 version of the film *A Star Is Born,* and working at Disneyland during 1961–62, appearing with Louis Armstrong in the TV special *Disneyland After Dark* shortly before her death.

7 Vol. 1/Jan. 7, 1923-Nov. 1924/Document 5338
7 Vol. 2/Nov. 1924–Sept. 28, 1932/Document 5339

Other than one lost title and her appearances on a few numbers with Charlie Johnson's orchestra, these two CDs contain all of Monette Moore's recordings of 1923–32. *Vol. 1* has mostly obscure backing, other than for two cuts with Tommy Ladnier and Jimmy O'Bryant, one with Jimmy Blythe, and a few later contributions by Rex Stewart and Bubber Miley. Moore's voice is fine, and she sounds flexible on such numbers as "Sugar Blues," "Gulf Coast Blues," "Muddy Water Blues," and "I Wanna Jazz Some More." *Vol. 2* has further appearances by Miley and Stewart, along with spots for clarinetist Bob Fuller. None of these performances (which include "The Bye Bye Blues," "Put Me in the Alley Blues," "Undertaker's Blues," and "If You Don't Like Potatoes") were hits. Monette Moore was never on the level of a Bessie Smith, but her music contain solid mainstream singing for the period. *Vol. 2* is all from 1924–25, except for two numbers from 1926, three from 1927, and what may be Monette Moore's finest recording, a medley of "Shine on Your Shoes" and "Louisiana Hayride" from 1932 in which she is accompanied by Fats Waller. Ironically the Waller medley was not released for decades.

CHAUNCEY MOREHOUSE

b. Mar. 11, 1902, Niagara Falls, NY, d. Nov. 3, 1980, Philadelphia, PA

Chauncey Morehouse played drums on many sessions during the 1920s. He grew up in Chambersburg, Pennsylvania, and as a youth performed for silent movies in duos with his father, who played piano. In 1919, while still in high school, Morehouse formed the Versatile Five. He soon dropped out of school to become a professional musician. Morehouse was with Paul Specht's Society Serenaders during 1922–24 and recorded frequently with the Georgians. He performed with Howard Lanin, Ted Weems, and Jean Goldkette (1925–27), including recording with Goldkette's band during the period that Bix Beiderbecke and Frankie Trumbauer were members. Morehouse was with the short-lived Adrian Rollini Orchestra (September 1927) and worked with Don Voorhees before becoming a studio musician in 1929. Along the way Morehouse recorded with Trumbauer, Bix and his Gang, Joe Venuti, Hoagy Carmichael, Red Nichols, Miff Mole, the Dorsey Brothers, Wingy Manone, and many others.

After 1929, Morehouse worked primarily in the studios, in theaters, and anonymously on radio and (later on) television. In 1938 he had a short-lived big band that featured him playing chromatically tuned percussion he had designed himself, with Stan King playing more conventional drums. However, that orchestra (which recorded four numbers) did not last long, and Morehouse returned to the studios, in later years running an advertising agency, writing, and recording jingles. Chauncey Morehouse was active into the 1970s, occasionally appearing at Jean Goldkette reunions and Bix Beiderbecke tributes.

SAM MORGAN

b. Dec. 18, 1887, Bertrandville, LA, d. Feb. 25, 1936, New Orleans, LA

Sam Morgan, a New Orleans trumpeter, was most important as a bandleader who led two significant record sessions. Morgan led bands in New Orleans during 1915–25. He suffered a minor stroke in

1925 (at the age of 37) but within a year was back leading a new ensemble. In 1927 the Columbia label made a couple of field trips to New Orleans and on both occasions documented Sam Morgan's Jazz Band, for a total of eight songs. The only notable sideman was trombonist Jim Robinson (who would play with Bunk Johnson and George Lewis in future decades). But Morgan's group proved to be a spirited ensemble, and its recordings give listeners an excellent idea what the music sounded like in New Orleans a decade after the great exodus. The selections are available on *Celestin's Original Tuxedo Jazz Orchestra/Sam Morgan's Jazz Band* (Jazz Oracle 8002) and are reviewed in this book under Oscar Celestin's name.

Sam Morgan, who also ran a treasure-hunting service on the side, kept his jazz band together until 1932, when a second stroke forced him to retire.

THOMAS MORRIS

b. 1898, New York, d. 1940s

Thomas Morris was a primitive but expressive cornetist whose playing fit the mainstream of 1923 but would prove to be behind the times a few years later. Morris is a somewhat mysterious figure, and very little is known about his life outside of his playing career. He appeared on many records during 1923–27, including with Clarence Williams' Blue Five (sharing the frontline on a few occasions with Sidney Bechet), Fannie Mae Goosby, Helen Gross, Rosa Henderson, Jane Howard, Mike Jackson, Margaret Johnson, Mandy Lee, Sara Martin, Evelyn Preer, Mabel Richardson, Elizabeth Smith, Laura Smith, Mamie Smith, Eva Taylor, Sippie Wallace, Edna Winston, Buddy Christian's Jazz Rippers, the Dixie Jazzers Washboard Band, the Five Musical Blackbirds, the Get-Happy Band, George McClennon's Jazz Devils, the Nashville Jazzers, the New Orleans Blue Five, and several groups organized by Clarence Williams.

As a leader, Morris and his Past Jazz Masters recorded eight songs in 1923, while his Seven Hot Babies cut ten selections in 1926. The later dates (which feature Morris at his best) have such sidemen as Rex Stewart, Geechie Fields, Charlie Irvis, and Tricky Sam Nanton. But by 1927, Morris' unchanged if charming style sounded quite old-fashioned, particularly on three numbers with Charlie Johnson, where he is overshadowed by Jabbo Smith. Sometime after making his final recordings (on December 1, 1927, with Fats Waller), Morris left music, becoming a red cap at New York's Grand Central Station. During Thomas Morris' last few years, he joined Father Divine's religious cult and changed his name to Brother Pierre.

8 1923–1927/Feb. 1923–1927/Classics 823
9 When a 'Gator Hollers/July 13, 1926–Nov. 24, 1926/Frog 1
These two CDs unfortunately overlap. *1923–1927* has the master takes of all of Morris' sessions as a leader, plus dates with the New Orleans Blue Five, singer Margaret Johnson, and the Nashville Jazzers ("St. Louis Blues" from 1927). All of the music except for the eight 1923 selections and "St. Louis Blues is on the Frog CD, which benefits from the inclusion of 11 alternate takes. Since Morris was heard at his best throughout 1926, *When a 'Gator Hollers* gets the edge. Among the better selections are "Jackass Blues" (featuring Tricky Sam Nanton), "Georgia Grind," "The King of the Zulus," and "The Mess." The music is a bit primitive but always quite fun.

LEE MORSE

b. 1899, TN, d. Dec. 16, 1954, Rochester, NY

A fine cabaret singer from the 1920s who often used backing by top jazz players, Lee Morse gained a certain amount of popularity during her prime, although she is largely forgotten today. She was born Lena Taylor and grew up in Portland and Kooskia, Idaho. Her four older brothers had a popular vocal quartet, while her younger brother, Glen Taylor, became a U.S. Senator from Idaho.

After marrying as a teenager, Lee Morse began to sing professionally on the West Coast, usually backing herself on guitar. She played regularly in vaudeville during 1920–22, performed in a couple of plays on Broadway, and in 1924 debuted on record, recording prolifically for the rest of the decade. She was often joined by her Blue Grass Boys, which at various times included Benny Goodman, Tommy Dorsey, trumpeter Manny Klein, Rube Bloom, Harry Reser, and Eddie Lang, among others. She performed regularly on the radio during the late 1920s, although her excessive drinking and emotional personality caused her to miss some opportunities, including the chance to debut "Ten Cents a Dance" in a major show; Ruth Etting instead had the hit.

Lee Morse's career slowed down drastically in the early 1930s. She did have a record date in 1938 but, after marrying a third time, she settled in upstate New York, where she was content just to sing locally (recording as late as 1951) and host a radio show.

LPS TO SEARCH FOR

Two fine collections of Lee Morse's recordings of 1927–31 were put out on albums: *Lee Morse and Her Blue Grass Boys* (Take Two 201) and *Lee Morse Revisited* (Take Two 213). Morse's wide range, light Southern accent, and occasional (and usually unexpected) yodeling are constant surprises. She deserves to be better known.

BENNY MORTON

b. Jan. 31, 1907, New York, NY, d. Dec. 28, 1985, New York, NY

Benny Morton's career fit into both the classic jazz and swing eras. Morton played early on with the Jenkins' Orphanage Band. He gained experience working with the orchestras of Clarence Holiday (1923) and Billy Fowler (off and on during 1923–26). Morton made a strong impression during his periods with Fletcher Henderson (1926–28, 1931–

Jelly Roll Morton at the peak of his creative powers, leading the Red Hot Peppers in 1926.

32), which sandwiched a stint with Chick Webb (1930–31). A solid soloist and an excellent all-round musician, Morton spent much of the big band era with Don Redman (1932–37) and Count Basie (1937–40). His later associations included Joe Sullivan, the Teddy Wilson Sextet (1940–43), Edmond Hall (1943–44), Red Allen, Wild Bill Davison, and his own combos, performing with both Broadway show pit bands and Dixieland groups.

JELLY ROLL MORTON

b. Sept. 20, 1885, Gulfport, LA, d. July 10, 1941, Los Angeles, CA

A towering figure in jazz history, Jelly Roll Morton may have been inaccurate when in later years he claimed that he had invented jazz back in 1902, but he was one of the music's first major innovators. As

a distinctive pianist, Morton (along with James P. Johnson) helped smooth the transition between ragtime and classic jazz. As a composer, he contributed such songs to the jazz repertoire as "King Porter Stomp," "Milenberg Joys," "Wolverine Blues," "The Pearls," "Grandpa's Spells," "Mr. Jelly Roll," "Shreveport Stomp," "Black Bottom Stomp," "Winin' Boy Blues," "Don't You Leave Me Here," "Sweet Substitute," and "Wild Man Blues," among others. As an arranger, Morton made perfect use of the three-minute limitations of '78' records with a mixture of arranged passages, jammed ensembles, and concise solos. His recording of "Black Bottom Stomp" has so many ideas going on as to be miraculous. He was also a fine singer, though he took only one vocal on record in the 1920s ("Doctor Jazz"). As a bandleader, Morton could be a taskmaster, but he knew what he was talking about. Unfortunately his fame as a braggart hurt his reputation for years, and he had few friends when he needed them most, during his darkest days.

Born Ferdinand Joseph La Menthe, he started off playing guitar and trombone before settling on piano when he was ten. Morton, whose formative years are shrouded in legend, played in Storyville in his early days. During 1900–16 he worked at a variety of jobs, including as a pool hustler, a boxing promoter, a tailor, a gambling house manager, a hotel manager, a pimp, a comedian in traveling shows, and (whenever possible) a pianist. He played music in the South, was in Chicago as early as 1914, and played in San Francisco in 1915. Morton (who named himself "Jelly Roll") was based mostly in Los Angeles during 1917–22 but also appeared in Alaska, Wyoming, Denver, Tijuana, and throughout the West Coast.

In 1923 Morton moved to Chicago and began his recording career with a brilliant series of piano solos (introducing "King Porter Stomp," "Grandpa's Spells," "Wolverine Blues," and "The Pearls"), a few surprisingly primitive band sides, and a session with the New Orleans Rhythm Kings that was one of the first integrated jazz dates. Morton toured with bands in the Midwest (not actually working in Chicago that often) and recorded two duets with King Oliver in 1924. He made his finest band recordings during 1926–30, when he was signed to the Victor label, particularly his sessions of 1926–27 in Chicago and his first New York date in 1928. His use of dynamics, transitions, and arranged passages in what was essentially a New Orleans jazz band still sounds timeless, unpredictable, and highly appealing today.

Morton moved to New York in February 1928 and continued recording, although some of his sessions were less disciplined, sometimes using overly large bands of musicians not always familiar with his methods. Although thought of as fading in importance (particularly in comparison to the music of his arch-rival, Duke Ellington), Morton continued recording occasional classics until the contract with Victor ended, in 1930.

As with many other black musicians who were not associated with big bands in Harlem, Morton found his music out of favor by 1931. He was off records altogether (other than a guest spot with Wingy Manone in 1934) until 1938. Making matters worse, he had burned a lot of bridges along the way with his bragging and arrogance (much of which was actually a front), was ripped off by his publishers (several of his songs had become standards but he received almost no royalties), and found work very difficult to find. Morton struggled along, sometimes performing anonymously in pit bands for musical revues. During 1936–38, even as swing bands continually played hit versions of his "King Porter Stomp" on the radio, Morton performed at the Jungle Club in Washington, D.C., a dive in which the forgotten "founder of jazz" performed for mostly indifferent audiences.

Things began to look up a little in 1938. From May to July, Jelly Roll was interviewed extensively by Alan Lomax for the Library of Congress about the early days in New Orleans. But typically Morton was never paid at all for this work (which included many piano demonstrations and vocals), and the valuable performances and reminiscences were not made available to the public until after Jelly Roll's death. In late 1938 Morton returned to New York, secured some record dates, and made some wonderful solo sessions (some of which featured his charming singing) along with band sides that used Sidney Bechet and Red Allen. Unfortunately these performances did not enjoy any real commercial success. Overlooked by the jazz world, Morton had every right to be a bit bitter. When a *Ripley's Believe It or Not* radio program identified W.C. Handy as the originator of jazz and blues, Morton was so angry that he wrote a letter to *Downbeat*, claiming to have created jazz in 1902. Because of his reputation for bragging, his statements were laughed at and ridiculed, but, although sometimes exaggerated, many turned out to be quite true.

In late 1940, a frustrated Morton moved with all of his belongings to California with hopes of starting a new band, but his health quickly declined; he had asthma and a heart condition. Jelly Roll Morton was 55 when he died in the summer of 1941. If he had lived a few years longer, he would have been a major beneficiary of the New Orleans jazz revival movement, since trad and Dixieland bands have been performing his songs on a nightly basis ever since.

9 Jelly Roll Morton/June 9, 1923-Feb. 2, 1926/Milestone 47018
10 Ferd "Jelly Roll" Morton/July 17, 1923 – Apr. 20, 1926/Retrieval 79002
7 Piano Rolls/Sept. 1924 – 1926/Nonesuch 79363

The Milestone and Retrieval sets are almost identical. Both of the single CDs contain all 20 of Jelly Roll Morton's piano solos of 1923–24, some of the very best jazz on record during that era. Where they differ is that the Milestone disc has four of Morton's very early band sides (there were 16 in all during June 1923–February 1926) and the pianist's two duets with King Oliver (which are available elsewhere under Oliver's name), while the Retrieval Morton set also has his four exciting piano solos from 1926 (including excellent remakes of "The Pearls" and "King Porter Stomp").

Jelly Roll recorded possibly 16 piano rolls in his life, mostly from 1924, with "Dead Man Blues" cut two years later. Four are lost, but the other dozen are available on the Nonesuch CD ("Sweet Man" may or may not actually be by Morton), which does the best possible job of bringing the potentially metronomic performances back to life, adding a bit to Morton's huge legacy.

★ Jelly Roll Morton Centennial: His Complete Victor Recordings/ Sept. 15, 1926-Sept. 28, 1939/Bluebird 2361
6 1926 – 1934/Sept. 15, 1926 – Aug. 15, 1934/ABC 836 – 199

The five-CD set *His Complete Victor Recordings,* has every Morton performance for the Victor label, including all of the alternate takes. Taken as a whole, these 111 performances rank with the greatest work of any jazz musician from any era. Among the classics (and this is only a partial list) from 1926–30 are "Black Bottom Stomp," "The Chant," "Dead Man Blues," "Grandpa's Spells," "Doctor Jazz," "The Pearls," "Wolverine Blues," "Mr. Jelly Lord," "Kansas City Stomps," "Shreveport Stomp," "Seattle Hunch," "Tank Town Bump," "Fussy Mabel," "Low Gravy," and "Strokin' Away." The personnel includes George Mitchell, Kid Ory, Omer Simeon, Johnny St. Cyr, John Lindsay, Andrew Hilaire, Johnny Dodds, Stump Evans, Baby Dodds, Ward Pinkett, Geechie Fields, Tommy Benford, Red Allen, J.C. Higginbotham, Albert Nicholas, Barney Bigard, Zutty Singleton, Bubber Miley, and Morton himself. The final dozen performances are Morton's two band dates of September 1939, which have contributions by Sidney DeParis, Sidney Bechet, and Albert Nicholas. Although Morton's Victor recordings have also been made available in piecemeal fashion through the years, this is the ideal way to acquire the essential music.

Speaking of piecemeal, producer Robert Parker's "stereo" transformations of 16 Morton performances on *1926–1934* are not without interest, but they are a bit frivolous when compared to the Bluebird set. All of these performances (including two numbers with Johnny Dunn and one with Wingy Manone) are easily available elsewhere.

6 Kansas City Stomp/May 23, 1938-June 7, 1938/Rounder 1091
6 Animule Dance/May 23, 1938 – June 7, 1938/Rounder 1092
6 The Pearls/May 23, 1938 – June 7, 1938/Rounder 1093
6 Winin' Boy Blues/June 7, 1938 – Dec. 14, 1938/Rounder 1094
8 Last Sessions — Complete General Recordings/Dec. 14, 1939 – Jan. 30, 1940/GRP/Commodore 403

Jelly Roll Morton's Library of Congress recordings had formerly been released complete on eight LPs. The four Rounder CDs have just the music, cutting out most of Morton's colorful storytelling. The music has been pitch-corrected, and it is good to hear such fascinating sections as Jelly Roll showing the difference (by playing two versions of "Maple Leaf

Rag") between ragtime and jazz, and Jelly Roll demonstrating "Tiger Rag" in several styles; both of those illustrations are on the *Kansas City Stomp* CD. But Morton's talking deserves to be reissued too, so hopefully some label will eventually come out with everything, rather than just these intriguing excerpts.

Last Sessions has all of the pianist's final recordings. In fact, all that was left after these performances for Commodore were two songs from a slightly later radio broadcast. The CD has 13 solo performances, five of which (highlighted by "Winin' Boy Blues," "Buddy Bolden's Blues," and "Don't You Leave Me Here") have Morton's vocals. The dozen band sides of 1940 (with sextet and septets that include Red Allen and Albert Nicholas) are of lesser interest, other than "Sweet Substitute" and "Panama." Most of these songs were futile attempts at having a "hit," although the musicians play quite well. But get *Last Sessions* for the solo numbers, which show that Jelly Roll Morton still had so much left to give the uncaring world during the twilight of his life.

LPS TO SEARCH FOR

Rarities, Vol. 2 (Rhapsody 6030) contains a variety of unusual and sometimes scarce Morton items. He is heard on two of his 1923 band titles, "Soap Suds" in 1926 with the St. Louis Levee Band, four numbers with Johnny Dunn (1928), two songs apiece with Wingy Manone (1934), the Levee Serenaders (1928), and Edmonia Henderson (1926), and his four piano solos from 1926. The budget release *Jelly Roll Morton* (Alamac 2424) contains so-so live bootleg numbers from 1938 with a mediocre group but also has the pianist's final radio broadcast ("Winin' Boy Blues" and "King Porter Stomp"), from May 1940. And for those who want to acquire Jelly Roll Morton's complete Library of Congress recordings, both the Australian Swaggie label (S1311-S1318) and the Swedish Classic Jazz Masters label (CJM 2-CJM9) released all of the talking, singing, and playing on eight LPs.

CURTIS MOSBY

b. 1895, Kansas City, MO, d. 1960, CA

Curtis Mosby led one of the top jazz bands in Los Angeles during the second half of the 1920s. Born in Kansas City, Mosby learned drums and in 1918 had a band in Chicago. By 1921 he had moved to Oakland, California, where he ran a music shop in addition to heading a group. His band accompanied Mamie Smith on the road for two years; when Mosby ended this association in 1924, he settled in Los Angeles. Mosby's Dixieland Blue Blowers, in addition to making a two-song test pressing during 1924-25 that was not released until 75 years later, had three recording dates during 1927-29 that show how exciting a band it was despite its lack of major names. Tenor saxophonist Bumps Myers is the only band member to gain a little recognition years later. Mosby's Dixieland Blue Blowers appears prominently for a few minutes in the 1929 film *Hallelujah*, probably the first regularly working black orchestra to be heard and seen in a motion picture.

Mosby kept bands together into the early 1930s, touring with the show *Change Your Luck* during 1933-34. He ran the Club Alabam during 1940-47, with the house band being known as Mosby's Blue Blowers, although the leader was no longer playing drums by then. Curtis Mosby (who did not record again after 1929) also ran the Oasis Club for a few years starting in 1949.

8 **Curtis Mosby and Henry Starr/1924-1935/Jazz Oracle 8003**
The bulk of this CD is the complete output (other than the soundtrack from *Hallelujah*) by Curtis Mosby's Dixieland Blue Blowers, including the first-time release of the 1924-25 test pressing. While the value of the latter (which is scratchy) is more historic than musical, Mosby's eight selections (and four alternates) from 1927-29 are full of spirit and strong musicianship. Among the hotter numbers are "Weary Stomp," "Whoop 'Em Up Blues," "Hardee Stomp," and three versions of "Tiger Stomp."

The pianist during the 1927 session, Henry Starr (who sings on "In My Dreams") is featured on the second half of this disc. He is heard playing piano on four solo numbers from 1928–29, including two that have his vocals. Also, Starr is teamed with singer Ivan Harold Browning and a rhythm section in London in 1935, performing vocal duets on seven infectious and rather rare performances, including "Let's Go Ballyhoo," "Lulu's Back in Town," and "Truckin'."

BENNIE MOTEN

b. Nov. 13, 1894, Kansas City, MO, d. Apr. 2, 1935, Kansas City, MO

Pianist Bennie Moten was the leader of the top big band in Kansas City during the 1920s, an orchestra that dwarfed (and often swallowed up) its competitors. Moten played baritone horn when he was 12 but soon switched to piano, studying with two of Scott Joplin's pupils. He worked locally and led a ragtime trio (called BB & D) during 1918–21. In 1922 Moten expanded to a sextet that gradually grew to become a big band. The Bennie Moten Orchestra began recording in 1923, cutting 14 songs for the Okeh label during 1923–25, including a hit version of "South."

Moten and his orchestra were documented regularly by Victor during 1926–30. Although they visited New York in the fall of 1928, the big band remained based in Kansas City, where it gradually lured away most of the members of its top competitor, Walter Page's Blue Devils. By October 1929, Count Basie was the band's regular pianist on all of its recordings; Moten played only a few numbers a night in clubs. Other key sidemen included trumpeter Ed Lewis, Eddie Durham on trombone and guitar, future bandleader Harlan Leonard on reeds, baritonist Jack Washington, and (by 1930) trumpeter Hot Lips Page, singer Jimmy Rushing, and Bennie's brother Buster Moten on occasional accordion. The Depression brought hard times to the band, which cut only two titles in 1931 and a mar-

athon date on December 13, 1932. The latter session, which resulted in ten numbers, found the Bennie Moten Orchestra (with Ben Webster on tenor and bassist Walter Page) looking forward musically to both the future Count Basie Orchestra and the swing era in general on such numbers as "Moten Swing," "Blue Room," and "Lafayette."

Despite some personnel changes, the Bennie Moten Orchestra would probably have been a major force during the swing era. But tragically its leader died in 1935 at the age of 40 from complications following a tonsillectomy.

9 Vol. 1—Justrite/Dec. 13, 1926-Sept. 6, 1928/Frog 29

9 Vol. 2—Kansas City Breakdown/Sept. 6, 1928–July 18, 1929/Frog 30

8 1923–1927/Sept. 1923–June 11, 1927/Classics 549

8 1927–1929/June 11, 1927–June 17, 1929/Classics 558

7 1929–1930/July 17, 1929–Oct. 28, 1930/Classics 578

8 1930–1932/Oct. 28, 1930–Dec. 13, 1932/Classics 591

6 South/Dec. 13, 1926–July 17, 1929/Bluebird 3139

6 Basie Beginnings/Oct. 23, 1929–Dec. 13, 1932/Bluebird 9768

There are three different ways to collect Bennie Moten's recordings. The two Frog CDs have all of his performances during a nearly three-year period, including quite a few rare and in some cases never-before-released alternate takes. When this series is completed, particularly if it eventually covers Moten's earlier Okeh recordings too, this will be the band's definitive reissue program. Moten's orchestra was at the peak of its powers during the 1926–29 period, with highlights including "Kansas City Shuffle," "Sugar," "The New Tulsa Blues," "Moten Stomp," "Kansas City Breakdown," "Get Low Down Blues," "South," "Terrific Stomp," and "That Certain Motion."

Listeners satisfied with just the master takes of Bennie Moten's music will certainly enjoy the four Classics CDs. Although they bypass the 1923 recordings, which found the band backing singers Ada Brown and Mary Bradford, everything else is here (other than the alternate takes). The dozen Okeh recordings (including the original version of

"South") are on *1923–1927, 1927–1929* is duplicated in the Frog releases, and *1929–1930* (which has Count Basie taking over on piano) includes "New Goofy Dust Rag," "Band Box Shuffle," "Boot It," and "New Vine Street Blues." *1930–1932* (which has "The Count," "New Moten Stomp," and "Somebody Stole My Gal") is highlighted by the remarkable session of December 13, 1932.

Typically, the domestic Bluebird reissue series gives American listeners only a taste of Bennie Moten's music. *South* has 22 of the better selections from Moten's 1926–29 period, while *Basie Beginnings* has seven of the ten numbers from 1932 and some of the more rewarding performances of 1930–31. But why acquire those two discs when you can get the full picture from Frog or Classics?

DON MURRAY

> b. June 7, 1904, Joliet, IL, d. June 2, 1929, Los Angeles, CA

A promising clarinetist and saxophonist, Don Murray met an early and unnecessary demise. After studying at Northwestern University, Murray played tenor with the New Orleans Rhythm Kings in 1923. He was a member of Jean Goldkette's orchestra (doubling on clarinet and baritone sax) during 1924–27, including the period when Bix Beiderbecke and Frankie Trumbauer were key members. After working briefly with Adrian Rollini's big band (September–October 1927), Murray performed with Broadway theater orchestras and became a member of Ted Lewis' band in 1928. Along the way, he recorded with Bix Beiderbecke's Rhythm Jugglers in 1925 and in 1927–28 with Bix and his Gang, the Broadway Bellhops, the Chicago Loopers, Frankie Trumbauer, Cass Hagan's Park Central Hotel Orchestra, the All Star Orchestra, Joe Venuti, Jack Pettis, and Ted Lewis.

Murray was in Hollywood filming *Is Everybody Happy* with Lewis in 1929. A heavy drinker, he apparently fell on his head against a parked car and was rushed to a hospital. While making a recovery, Don Murray resumed drinking, against doctor's orders, and soon died, five days short of his 25th birthday.

TRICKY SAM NANTON

> b. Feb. 1, 1904, New York, NY, d. July 20, 1946, San Francisco, CA

A remarkable trombonist whose mastery with mutes (particularly the rubber plunger) resulted in the creation of all kinds of original and otherworldly sounds, Joe "Tricky Sam" Nanton (along with Bubber Miley) was a major factor in making Duke Ellington's "jungle band" a major success in its early days. Nanton picked up early experience playing with Earl Frazier's Harmony Five (1923–25), Cliff Jackson, and Elmer Snowden, and recording with Thomas Morris. Tricky Sam (Otto Hardwicke gave him his lifelong nickname) joined Ellington in mid-1926, replacing Charlie Irvis. During the next 19 years he was a major part of Duke's band, having short atmospheric solos on scores of records, whether they be moody ballads or stomps. Nanton worked quite well with Miley and, when the trumpeter was succeeded by Cootie Williams in 1929, Tricky Sam helped the younger trumpeter learn the intricacies of working with mutes and distorting the tone in a highly individual way. He also worked alongside Williams' successor, Ray Nance, in the 1940s.

Nanton played constantly with Ellington's orchestra until he suffered a stroke in late 1945. He came back in May 1946 but died suddenly in his hotel room two months later. Until the end, Tricky Sam Nanton was a vital link to Duke's jungle band of two decades before.

PHIL NAPOLEON

> b. Sept. 2, 1901, Brooklyn, NY, d. Sept. 30, 1990, Miami, FL

Phil Napoleon was the top trumpeter on records during 1921–22, but his early recordings would be overshadowed by the rise of Louis Armstrong. Born Filippo Napoli, Napoleon played trumpet in public for the first time when he was five. His four brothers (saxophonists George and Joe, guitarist Matthew, and drummer Ted) were all musicians, and two of his nephews, Teddy and Marty Napoleon, became swing pianists in the 1940s. At 12, Phil Napoleon ran away from home in Brooklyn and made it all the way down to New Orleans before he was caught. He recorded when he was 15, in 1916 (one year before the Original Dixieland Jazz Band), as a classical cornetist, but he was most interested in jazz. In late 1917 the teenager formed the first version of his Original Memphis Five, naming the group after W.C. Handy's "Memphis Blues."

After a period of freelancing, in 1921 Napoleon began to record in jazz settings. He waxed "Memphis Blues" and "The St. Louis Blues" in July 1921 with Lanin's Southern Serenaders, and the following month recorded hit versions of "Shake It and Break It" and "Aunt Hagar's Children's Blues." As the Original Memphis Five, Phil Napoleon, Miff Mole (later replaced by Charles Panelli), Jimmy Lytell, Frank Signorelli, and drummer Jack Roth (with occasional changes in personnel) recorded 111 titles during 1922–23 alone, not including their many recordings under the names of the Ambassadors, Bailey's Lucky Seven, the Broadway Syncopators, the Cotton Pickers, Jazzbo's Carolina Serenaders, Ladd's Black Aces, Sam Lanin, the Savannah Six, the Southland Six, and the Tennessee Ten. While most trumpeters in New York were indulging in novelty effects (sometimes laughing or crying through their horn) or "getting hot" by playing repetitive double-time runs, Napoleon already knew how to swing a song in tasteful fashion, uplifting melodies, adding a touch of blues to his solos, and expertly leading ensembles.

Napoleon's activities did not slow much during the 1920s. The Original Memphis Five recorded 43 songs in 1924, 22 in 1925. and 13 more in 1926. Although the Original Memphis Five name faded away, being used for only a dozen numbers during 1927–31, the trumpeter was on records accompanying singers Irene Beasley, Lew Bray, Seger Ellis, Annette Hanshaw, Alberta Hunter, Irving Kaufman, Lee Morse, Carson Robison, Leona Williams, and Leon Wilson. He was also on jazz dates with the California Ramblers, the Charleston Chasers, the Dorsey Brothers, the Emperors, the Hot Air Men, the Hotsy Totsy Gang, Miff Mole's Molers, the New Orleans Black Birds, Boyd Senter, and Milt Shaw. And, in addition, Napoleon recorded 29 selections during 1926–27 and 1929 under his own name.

Despite all of these recordings and performances, Napoleon never became that well known to the general public. In the 1930s he played mostly in the background with radio orchestras, his big band of 1938 went nowhere, and during part of the early 1940s he worked in the musical instrument business. In 1946 Napoleon returned to jazz, putting together a Dixieland band that by 1949 was known as the Memphis Five, performing regularly at Nick's in New York for seven years. In 1956 Phil Napoleon (who made his final recordings in 1960) settled in Florida, where he led a band into the mid-1980s. But by then, few of his listeners and fans probably knew of his importance to early jazz.

LPS TO SEARCH FOR

Two albums include some of the selections that Phil Napoleon recorded under his own name in the 1920s. *Featuring the Original Memphis Five* (IAJRC 26) has six Napoleon titles from 1926–27 with his 10- to 11-piece band (including "Tiger Rag" and "Clarinet Marmalade") plus eight selections from the Original Memphis Five of 1927–29. *1929–1931* (The Old Masters 13) has the last Original Memphis Five session (from 1931, with the Dorsey Brothers) along with Napoleon's dates with the Hot Air Men, one title ("You Made Me Love You") with Miff Mole's Molers, and the five-song session by Napoleon's Emperors from May 14,

1929 (also with the Dorsey Brothers plus Venuti and Lang).

DAVE NELSON

b. 1905, Donaldsonville, LA, d. Apr. 7, 1946, New York, NY

Dave Nelson was both the nephew and the protégé of King Oliver. He played violin and piano before settling on the trumpet, studying arranging with Richard M. Jones. Nelson moved to Chicago in the mid-'20s, working with Marie Lucas' Orchestra, Ma Rainey (with whom he recorded in 1926), Jelly Roll Morton, Edgar Hayes' Eight Black Pirates (1927), Jimmie Noone, Leroy Pickett, and Luis Russell (1929), also occasionally leading a band. Nelson, who recorded two songs with James P. Johnson in a group that also included King Oliver, joined his uncle's orchestra in the autumn of 1929. He played as part of the trumpet section, wrote many of the arrangements for Oliver's 1929–31 recording sessions, and took quite a few solos, due to Oliver's declining playing ability. Because he played in a similar style as his uncle (although his work with mutes was not on Oliver's level), it created confusion years later when collectors tried to figure out who was soloing on a particular selection.

After using King Oliver's band for two record dates under the titles of either the King's Men or Dave's Harlem Highlights (playing trumpet and singing on all seven numbers, which are available on *Thumpin' and Bumpin'*—Frog 11), Nelson left Oliver in 1931. Only 26 at the time, Nelson would seem to have had a bright future, but for unknown reasons he never really made it. Doubling on piano, he led obscure bands in New York and New Jersey, appeared on only one further record date (with Willie "the Lion" Smith in 1937), and spent his last four years as a staff arranger for the Lewis Publishing Co. Dave Nelson died from a heart attack when he was 41.

JOHN NESBITT

b. 1900, Norfolk, VA, d. 1935, Boston, MA

John Nesbitt was a key arranger and trumpet soloist with McKinney's Cotton Pickers. He began his career playing with Lillian Jones' Jazz Hounds and Amanda Randolph. Nesbitt joined William McKinney's Synco Septette in 1925 and stayed with the group after it became known as McKinney's Cotton Pickers. He was on the band's records of 1928–30 (often taking short solos influenced by both Louis Armstrong and Bix Beiderbecke) and wrote such arrangements as "Plain Dirt," "Travelin' All Alone," "Crying and Sighing," "Will You, Won't You Be My Babe," and "Zonky." Nesbitt also contributed a reworking of "Chinatown, My Chinatown" that Fletcher Henderson's orchestra recorded in 1930.

After leaving the Cotton Pickers in the summer of 1930, Nesbitt wrote for Luis Russell and played with Zach Whyte's Chocolate Beau Brummels, Speed Webb, and Earle Warren. But a serious stomach ailment resulted in John Nesbitt's early death right before the swing era began.

NEW ORLEANS OWLS

The New Orleans Owls were one of the finest bands active in New Orleans during the 1920s. The group's direct descendant was the Invincibles String Band (active during 1912–21), a band consisting of violin, mandolin, guitar, banjo, ukulele, piano, bass, and drums. Most of those musicians were involved in founding the New Orleans Owls in 1922, changing instruments so as to play jazz. The Owls recorded a total of 18 numbers during their five recording sessions of 1925–27; five of the Invincibles were still in the band, which then consisted of cornet, two reeds, piano, banjo, tuba, and drums. With the addition of a trombonist and a third reed in 1926, the Owls were a nonet, becoming a tentet when a second cornetist was added in 1927. None of the sidemen on the records (other than banjoist Nappy Lamare, who later played guitar with Bob Crosby) became famous, although near the end cornetist Johnny Wiggs, tenor saxophonist

Eddie Miller, and pianist Armand Hug spent time with the group before it broke up in 1929. The New Orleans Owls were a very effective bridge between the New Orleans Rhythm Kings (a major influence) and the hot dance bands of the late 1920s.

9 **The Owls' Hoot/Mar. 26, 1925-Oct. 26, 1927/Frog 2**

All 18 of the New Orleans Owls' recordings are on this CD, including such exciting numbers as "Stomp Off, Let's Go," "The Owl's Hoot," "Dynamite," "White Ghost Shivers," "The Nightmare," "Brotherly Love," and "That's a-Plenty." In addition, this generous disc has two numbers and two alternate takes from John Hyman's Bayou Stompers (a septet with cornetist Hyman, who would change his name to Johnny Wiggs, and the fluent harmonica of Alvin Gautreaux) and the final session of the New Orleans Rhythm Kings. The latter finds the NORK in New Orleans as a septet with Paul Mares, trombonist Santo Pecora, and clarinetist Charles Cordilla as the frontline, playing two versions apiece of "She's Cryin' for Me" and "Everybody Loves Somebody Blues."

NEW ORLEANS RHYTHM KINGS

In 1922, the New Orleans Rhythm Kings were the finest jazz group on record. Building from the innovations of the ensemble-oriented Original Dixieland Jazz Band, the NORK featured three fine soloists: cornetist Paul Mares (b. June 15, 1900, New Orleans, LA, d. Aug. 18, 1949, Chicago, IL), trombonist George Brunies, and the brilliant but ill-fated clarinetist Leon Roppolo (b. Mar. 16, 1902, Lutcher, LA, d. Oct. 14, 1943, LA).

Mares, Brunies, and Roppolo were childhood friends, growing up in New Orleans. As early as 1916, Mares and Roppolo played together in Tom Brown's band on the riverboat *Capitol*. In 1919 Mares left New Orleans to join drummer Gababy Stevens' group in Chicago. Brunies joined the same band the following year. In August 1921, Mares was hired to organize a group to back singer Bee Palmer

at Chicago's Friar's Inn. He sent for Roppolo and also used Brunies in the frontline. Within a few weeks, Palmer left and Mares was appointed leader of the Friar's Society Orchestra. After a short time, Mares renamed the band the New Orleans Rhythm Kings.

During August 29–30, 1922, the NORK had their first two of eight recording sessions, appearing as an octet, with the three main horns joined by Jack Pettis on C-melody sax, pianist Elmer Schoebel (who was the arranger, since he was the only member of the band able to read music at that point!), banjoist Lou Black, bassist Steve Brown, and drummer Frank Snyder. Mares' mellow and legato phrases were years ahead of Nick LaRocca's style, and his use of mutes was inspired by the as-yet-unrecorded King Oliver. Roppolo (who took one of the first notable horn solos on records during "Tiger Rag" from August 30) had purged the clarinet of any gaspipe and novelty effects, while Brunies proved to be an expert ensemble player.

There were also two sessions during March 12–13, 1923, that featured the NORK as a quintet (with pianist Mel Stitzel and drummer Ben Pollack) and that was highlighted by a famous solo from Brunies on "Tin Roof Blues," and two sessions from July 17–18, 1923, that had the NORK expanding to ten pieces. Pettis, Glenn Scoville, and Don Murray were added on saxophones, banjoist Bob Gillette and tuba player Chink Martin joined Pollack in the rhythm section, and either Jelly Roll Morton or Kyle Pierce were on piano.

The use of Morton made the NORK one of the first integrated bands on record, and his influence is certainly felt on such numbers as "Mr. Jelly Lord" and "Milenberg Joys." Other future Dixieland standards that the NORK introduced include "Farewell Blues," "Bugle Call Blues" (later renamed "Bugle Call Rag"), "Panama," "That's a-Plenty," and "Weary Blues." Bix Beiderbecke and the members of the Austin High Gang were among those who were greatly impressed by the NORK.

After the New Orleans Rhythm Kings period at the Friar's Inn ended, in the spring of 1923, they soon disbanded, an unfortunate move. Mares and Roppolo joined Al Siegal's band in New York, while Brunies played with Eddie Tancil. They returned to the Midwest for the reunion sessions with Morton, but then Roppolo (who played briefly with Peck Kelley in Texas) and Mares returned to New Orleans, while Brunies joined Ted Lewis' Orchestra for 11 years. In late 1924, Mares was offered a job with the Wolverines, where he would have succeeded Beiderbecke, but he chose to stay home.

In January 1925 Mares organized a new version of the NORK, with Roppolo, trombonist Santo Pecora, Charlie Cordilla on tenor, and a local rhythm section. They sound in top form on four titles (including "Golden Leaf Strut" and "She's Crying for Me Blues"). But Roppolo (who also recorded with the Halfway House Orchestra during this period) was suffering from very shaky mental health, and he soon suffered a mental breakdown, resulting in his being confined to a mental institution for his final 27 years. Unlike Buddy Bolden, Roppolo was coherent at times and even played in public in the early 1940s for a couple of nights with Santo Pecora and Abbie Brunies, but his life was tragic.

On March 26, 1925, the New Orleans Rhythm Kings had their final record date, with Roppolo absent and Charlie Cordilla switching to clarinet. Although Mares was just 25, he retired from full-time music and worked at his family's fur business. In 1934, Mares returned to Chicago and opened a barbecue restaurant. He began to play music again and on January 26, 1935, recorded four songs with his Friar's Society Orchestra in a largely unchanged and still relevant style. But unfortunately he did not have the old desire to play and again chose to drop out of music. Near the end of his life Paul Mares was planning a new group, but he passed away in 1949 before any project was started.

10 New Orleans Rhythm Kings and Jelly Roll Morton/Aug. 29, 1922-July 18, 1923/Milestone 47020

This essential CD has all of the master takes from the NORK's 1922–23 sessions, including versions of "Farewell Blues," "Panama," "Tiger Rag," "That's a-Plenty," and "Tin Roof Blues." In addition, the selections with Jelly Roll Morton are here too. The only thing missing are the poorly recorded alternate takes (which were previously put out on a double LP by Milestone), although the three alternates with Morton are included. The NORK was one of the most important jazz groups of the 1920s, and this CD is the best way to acquire their music. Their later sessions have also been reissued on CD, with the first New Orleans date (with Rappolo) coming out in the collection *New Orleans in the '20s* (Timeless 1–014), while the final NORK date is included in the New Orleans Owls' CD *The Owls' Hoot* (Frog 2).

ALBERT NICHOLAS

b. May 27, 1900, New Orleans, LA, d. Sept. 3, 1973, Basel, Switzerland

A fluent clarinetist with an appealing sound, Albert Nicholas emerged during the 1920s. Nicholas began playing clarinet when he was ten, taking lessons a few years later from Lorenzo Tio Jr. He performed with Buddy Petit, King Oliver, and Manuel Perez, served in the Merchant Marine (1916–19), and, after his discharge, worked in many New Orleans bands, including with the Maple Leaf Band, Arnold Dupas' Orchestra, and a group of his own. In May 1924 Nicholas went to Chicago, touring with King Oliver for seven weeks. After a long visit home, he rejoined Oliver, being a member of his Dixie Syncopators from December 1924 until August 1926. During this period Nicholas recorded with Oliver, Richard M. Jones, the Chicago Hottentots, and singers Wilmer Davis and Irene Scruggs. Nicholas spent a year in Shanghai, China with drummer Jack Carter's group, and also played in Egypt with Guido Curti, in Alexandria with Benedetti's Six Crackerjacks, and in Paris.

After returning to the United States in November 1928, Nicholas became a key member of Luis Russell's orchestra for five years, getting a lot of solo space and gaining recognition for his playing on Russell's records. He also recorded with Henry "Red" Allen, Fats Waller (1929), Jelly Roll Morton (1929–30 and 1939–40), Clarence Williams (1933), Alex Hill (1934), Freddie Jenkins (1935), and the Little Ramblers (1935).

Albert Nicholas, who always stuck to his original New Orleans style, had a long career that included work with Chick Webb, Sam Wooding, John Kirby, the Louis Armstrong big band (1937–40), Art Hodes, Bunk Johnson, Kid Ory, Ralph Sutton, and his own groups. In 1953 he moved permanently to Europe, where he worked steadily during the remainder of his life.

RED NICHOLS

b. May 8, 1905, Ogden, UT, d. June 28, 1965, Las Vegas, NV

Ernest Loring "Red" Nichols was one of the busiest cornetists of the 1920s. He started on cornet when he was five, studying with his father, a college music teacher. Nichols played with his father's brass band when he was 12, worked locally in Utah, and attended the Culver Military Academy in 1920. His career got going in 1922 when he recorded with the Syncopating Five. Nichols took over the group, renamed it the Royal Palms Orchestra, and led it during periods in Atlantic City and Indiana.

After hooking up with Sam Lanin in New York in late 1924, Nichols became one of the most recorded musicians in the world. Although his sound and style were influenced by Bix Beiderbecke, Nichols had an emotionally cooler sound, and some of his solos seemed worked out in advance. He had very impressive technical skills, was a superior arranger, and could read anything (unlike Bix). Because he had the ability to add a touch of jazz to any setting, Nichols was constantly in great demand, working with Harry Reser, Benny Krueger, Ross Gorman, Henry Halsted, Vincent Lopez, Don Voorhees, the California Ramblers, and many studio orchestras. He also spent a few months with Paul Whiteman's orchestra in 1927, and was always very proud that his replacement was Bix Beiderbecke.

It was as a bandleader that Nichols made his greatest mark. Starting in 1926, he recorded as a leader of his Five Pennies, having a surprise hit in 1927 with his version of "Ida, Sweet as Apple Cider." The original group included Miff Mole, Arthur Schutt, Eddie Lang, and Vic Berton (who doubled on tympani). Most of the Five Pennies recordings featured a band with more than five members; other key players included Dudley Fosdick (jazz's first mellophone soloist), Jimmy Dorsey, Pee Wee Russell, Benny Goodman, trumpeter Leo McConville, Gene Krupa, Jack Teagarden, and Glenn Miller. Nichols' collaborations with Mole (1926–28) often utilized whole-tone runs, unusual interval jumps, and lots of surprises—avant-garde 1920s jazz! During 1926–32, Nichols recorded an enormous number of recordings under such names as the Five Pennies, the Charleston Chasers, the Arkansas Travelers, the Red Heads, the Louisiana Rhythm Kings, the Wabash Orchestra, and Red and Miff's Stompers, among others. Nichols also led larger bands on some records, worked as a sideman (including with Miff Mole's Molers), and headed the orchestras for the shows *Strike Up the Band* and *Girl Crazy*.

Nichols was never that popular among his fellow musicians (he was a straight-laced disciplinarian), and he was in obscurity during the swing era, working in the studios and leading a low-level big band. After working in the shipyards for a time during World War II (1942–44), he made a comeback. At first playing with the Casa Loma Orchestra for a few months in 1944, Nichols formed a new version of the Five Pennies (a Dixieland sextet) that was based in Los Angeles. Leading one of the better trad

Red Nichols was the busiest cornetist of the 1920s.

bands of the 1950s (particularly when it featured Joe Rushton on bass sax), Nichols unexpectedly became quite famous when he was the subject of the 1959 movie *The Five Pennies*, a mostly fictional but very entertaining film that starred Danny Kaye, with Nichols playing his own cornet solos. Red Nichols' last five years found him in the spotlight, until he died of a heart attack in 1965, when he was 60.

8 Red Nichols and Miff Mole/Nov. 11, 1925-Sept. 14, 1927/ Retrieval 79010

6 Red Nichols on Edison 1924–27/Nov. 24, 1924–Feb. 28, 1927/Jazz Oracle 8007

5 Red Nichols and Miff Mole/Oct. 29, 1925–Dec. 10, 1930/ABC 836 185

7 Radio Transcriptions 1929–30/Aug. 29, 1927–Aug. 25, 1930/IAJRC 1011

It is surprising, considering how many 1920s CDs have been released in recent years, that only a small percentage of Red Nichols' recordings have been reissued during the past decade. These four CDs only hint at the wealth of material that exists.

The Retrieval CD has the most valuable music of the four discs. Nichols is heard on all of his dates with the Original Memphis Five, the Arkansas Travelers, and the Six Hottentots, plus four of his seven titles with the Hottentots. There is a lot of overlap of personnel on these selections, with Nichols and Miff Mole being constants and such players as Jimmy Lytell, Jimmy Dorsey, Rube Bloom, Frank Signorelli, Arthur Schutt, Joe Tarto, and Vic Berton making appearances. The music from the first date by the Arkansas Travelers ("Washboard Blues," "That's No Bargain," and "Boneyard Shuffle") is most significant, but the other tunes all have their surprising moments.

Red Nichols on Edison has 18 performances, eight of which are over four minutes long; the Edison label often put out 12-inch 78s that contained additional playing time. Because nine of the selections on the CD are alternate takes (four songs are heard in three versions apiece), this set will most be enjoyed by Nichols completists. The cornetist is heard on two numbers apiece with the Charleston Seven (an interesting pickup group from November 24, 1924, that includes Mole and Jack Pettis) and the 1925 version of the California Ramblers (that '78' was issued as by the Golden Gate Orchestra). There are also three versions of "Pardon the Glove" with Don Voorhees and four songs (plus seven alternates) with Red and Miff's Stompers. The latter group (which contributes this CD's most rewarding performances) consists of Nichols, Mole, Jimmy Dorsey, altoist Alfie Evans, Arthur Schutt, Joe Tarto, and Vic Berton playing "Alabama Stomp," "Stampede," "Hurricane," and "Black Bottom Stomp."

Engineer Robert Parker has the ability to make vintage recordings sound as if they are stereo recordings. His Jazz Classics series for the Australian Broadcasting Corporation includes a Red Nichols CD that has a few highlights from the 1925–30 period. Nichols is heard with Russ Gorman ("Rhythm of the Day"), on nine titles from Miff Mole's Molers that are available elsewhere, and on three songs with the Charleston Chasers. Surprisingly there are only three numbers by Nichols' Five Pennies ("Riverboat Shuffle," "Harlem Twist," and "Corrine Corrina") on this interesting but somewhat frivolous sampler.

Radio Transcriptions features Nichols in 1927, 1929, and 1930 performing music specifically for the radio, complete with announcements. The 1927 *Brunswick Brevity* series has versions of "Say It with Music" (used as a theme song) sandwiching such tunes as "I May Be Wrong," "They Didn't Believe Me," "On the Alamo," and "That's a-Plenty." There is also a *Brunswick Brevity* from

1929 and several episodes of *The Heat* series from 1930. Among Nichols' sidemen along the way are Glenn Miller (who provided some of the arrangements), Jack Teagarden, Jimmy Dorsey, Pee Wee Russell, Benny Goodman, Adrian Rollini, Joe Sullivan, and Gene Krupa.

LPS TO SEARCH FOR

Most of the treasures in Red Nichols' 1920s discography are long overdue to be reissued on CD. The best Nichols LP reissue series was put out by the Australian Swaggie label: *Red Nichols and His Five Pennies — Volumes One – Five* (Swaggie 836, 837, 838, 839, and 840). Included on these five albums are all of Nichols' recordings (with many intriguing alternate takes) with his Five Pennies from December 8, 1926, to February 8, 1929, plus his selections leading the Louisiana Rhythm Kings, the Captivators, and a larger orchestra, ending with a June 11, 1929, session. Just to name a few gems, *Vol. One* has the debut of the Five Pennies (including "That's No Bargain," "Boneyard Shuffle," and "Buddy's Habits"), showing how valuable a percussionist Vic Berton was. *Vol. Two* includes "Riverboat Shuffle," "Ida, Sweet As Apple Cider," "Feelin' No Pain," and "Avalon." *Vol. Three* contains some intriguing orchestra selections plus jams on "Panama," "Margie," and "Imagination." *Vol. Four* includes "Who's Sorry Now," "Alice Blue Gown," and "That's a-Plenty." And *Vol. Five* is highlighted by famous versions of "Indiana," "Dinah," and "On the Alamo." But the rise of CDs unfortunately put this very valuable series to a premature end before Nichols' music of the 1929–32 period could be fully explored.

Many other LPs (usually from collectors' labels) have released titles from Nichols' huge discography. *Real Rare Red* (Broadway 110) includes Nichols' very first session (private recordings from 1922 by his Syncopated Five) and rarities with Fred Rich, Billy Wynne, Jack Albin, Peggy English (a memorable version of "High, High, High Up in the

Hills"), Voorhees, and the cornetist's own bands. *Real Rare Red Volume II* (Broadway 120) featured Nichols with the Seven Missing Links, the Cotton Pickers, Sam Lanin, Arnold Brilhart, Frank Signorelli, Lee Morse, and others. *With Sam Lanin's Orchestra* (Broadway 105) has sideman sessions with a variety of bands led by recording director Sam Lanin (including the Melody Sheiks and the Okeh Melodians) from 1925–28. The 20-song *Red and Miff* (Saville 146) has some of Nichols' dates from 1927–31 along with eight numbers in which Nichols is a sideman with the Roger Wolfe Kahn Orchestra. *Red and Ben* (Broadway 103), in addition to six Ben Pollack performances from 1926–28 that are readily available on CD, has all ten of Nichols' selections leading the Wabash Dance Orchestra in 1928, a band that also includes trumpeter Manny Klein, Miff Mole, and Fud Livingston.

Mostly starting where the Swaggie series ended, *Starring Benny Goodman, 1929–31* (Sunbeam 137) and *1929–1932* (IAJRC 22) fill in more gaps, featuring Nichols' Five Pennies and orchestra. Filled with alternate takes but unfortunately not including liner notes or a very coherent personnel listing, the rather skimpy ten-song *Rarest Brunswick Masters* (MCA-1518) is a bit of a mess. Also without any notes but at least with complete sessions and 16 selections is *The Louisiana Rhythm Kings and Red and His Big Ten* (The Old Masters 35), featuring Nichols with expanded groups during 1930–31.

JIMMIE NOONE

b. Apr. 23, 1895, Cut-Off, LA, d. Apr. 19, 1944, Los Angeles, CA

Jimmie Noone, one of the big three of New Orleans clarinetists of the 1920s (along with Johnny Dodds and Sidney Bechet), had a smooth sound that at times made him sound like a predecessor of Benny Goodman. Born on a family farm ten miles outside of New Orleans, Noone started on guitar when he

was ten. He moved to New Orleans with his family in 1910, began on the clarinet, and took lessons from Lorenzo Tio Jr. and Sidney Bechet (who was only 13!). Noone's first professional job was subbing for Bechet with Freddie Keppard's band in 1913. He worked with Keppard for a year, formed the Young Olympia Band with Buddy Petit, and also played jobs with Kid Ory and Oscar Celestin.

The clarinetist spent part of 1917–18 in Chicago, working with Keppard in the Original Creole Band. He returned to New Orleans for a few months and then in the fall of 1918 went back to Chicago to join Bill Johnson's band. Noone worked on and off with Doc Cook's Gingersnaps during 1920–26, doubling on soprano sax for the only time in his career. He made his recording debut with Ollie Powers (1923) and can be heard soloing with Cook on records from 1924 and 1926–27.

Starting in the summer of 1926, Noone led a band at the Nest, which a few months later was renamed the Apex Club. Although that establishment closed in the spring of 1928, Noone would always call his group the Apex Club Orchestra. Most unusual about his band was that the ensemble featured an altoist (originally Joe Poston) who played the melody constantly while Noone (the only other horn) improvised on top. The 1928 version of the quintet/sextet was also quite notable for featuring Earl Hines on piano. Noone began recording as a leader that year, and among his more classic recordings are "Sweet Lorraine" (which he originally made famous, 12 years before Nat King Cole's hit version), "Four or Five Times," "Apex Blues," and "Oh Sister, Ain't That Hot?"

Noone, who also recorded in 1928 with Stovepipe Johnson and (in his only meetings with Louis Armstrong) Lillie Delk Christian, led combos in Chicago until 1943, even having a big band briefly in 1939. The Hines-soundalike pianist Zinky Cohn was in the piano slot during 1929–35, while Eddie Pollack took the ailing Poston's place during 1930–34.

In 1943 Noone moved to California, where he worked with Kid Ory's band on the Orson Welles radio series and recorded with the Capitol Jazzmen. Just when it seemed as if he would play a major part in the New Orleans revival movement, Jimmie Noone died from a heart attack, four days short of his 49th birthday. Decades later, his son Jimmie Noone Jr. emerged from nowhere to play reeds with the Cheathams, recording in the 1980s.

6 1923–1928/Sept. 1923-Mar. 30, 1928/Classics 604
10 The Jimmie Noone Collection, Vol. 1/May 16, 1928–Dec. 27, 1928/Collector's Classics 6
9 1928–1929/May 16, 1928–Apr. 27, 1929/Classics 611
9 1929–1930/June 21, 1929–Feb. 18, 1930/Classics 632
8 1930–1934/May 16, 1930–Nov. 23, 1934/Classics 641
7 1934–1940/Nov. 23, 1934–Dec. 11, 1940/Classics 651
7 Apex Blues/May 16, 1928–July 1, 1930/GRP/Decca 633

The Classics series as usual reissues the complete output of an artist sans alternate takes. *1923–1928* is quite unusual because none of the 23 selections were led by Jimmie Noone, despite the CD's coming out under his name. The clarinetist is heard on his two titles with Ollie Powers in 1923 and then on all 21 selections that he made with Doc Cook's groups, which happen to be Cook's entire recorded legacy. Since all of the latter numbers (except for the six songs from 1927–28) have also been reissued as part of *The Complete Freddie Keppard* by King Jazz, serious collectors who do not want a lot of duplicates will have to decide what is best.

Also a bit tough will be deciding whether to pick up *Vol. 1* in Collector's Classics' Noone series or *1928–1929* from Classics. The former has all of the clarinetist's dates as a leader in 1928, the year that Earl Hines was his pianist and Noone recorded such gems as "I Know That You Know," "Four or Five Times," "Apex Blues," "Sweet Lorraine," and "Oh, Sister, Ain't That Hot?" *Vol. 1* also has six alternate takes plus a version of "I Ain't Got Nobody" with Stovepipe Johnson. *1928–1929* has the same music but no alternate takes, instead including Noone's first five recordings of 1929 with his band.

Another tough choice, although if Collector's Classics continues its series, it will eventually make the Classics Noone CDs less significant.

For now, *1929–1930, 1930–1934,* and *1934–1940* are all recommended. Although there are occasional vocals along the way, the music is mostly pretty consistent. Eddie Pollack and Zinky Cohn prove to be fine replacements for Joe Poston and Earl Hines, cornetist George Mitchell and singers Mildred Bailey and Georgia White make worthy appearances, and by 1934–35 (when Jimmy Cobb was added on trumpet) Noone was showing that he fit in quite well with more swing-oriented music. *1934–1940* has a fine session in which Noone teams up (in 1937) with trumpeter Charlie Shavers and altoist Pete Brown, although his 1940 date with Natty Dominique is weak and his final studio session as a leader is weighed down by Ed Thompson's jivey vocals.

Apex Blues benefits from including liner notes but is less complete than the other CDs. The dozen master takes from the Noone/Hines band of 1928 are here, plus eight other numbers from 1928–30. It succeeds as "the best" of Jimmie Noone's Apex Club Orchestra. But since that band was so consistent, why not opt to put out everything instead?

RED NORVO
b. Mar. 31, 1908, Beardstown, IL, d. Apr. 6, 1999, Santa Monica, CA

The career of Red Norvo, jazz's first major (and practically only) xylophone soloist, and one of its most significant vibraphonists after he switched instruments in 1943, fits primarily in the swing era and later time periods. Born Kenneth Norville, Norvo started on piano, taking up the xylophone while in high school. In 1925, Norvo toured the Midwest with the Collegians, a marimba band. He worked in Chicago with Paul Ash and Ben Bernie, performed in vaudeville as a solo act (which included tap dancing), played on the radio, and studied mining on the side at the University of Missouri

(1926–27). After leading a band on Radio Station KSTP and working with Victor Young, Norvo became a member of the Paul Whiteman Orchestra (1931–32), although his role was somewhat undefined and he never recorded with that ensemble. However, Norvo's first recordings as a leader (eight numbers during 1933–34, including Bix Beiderbecke's "In a Mist" and "Dance of the Octopus") are classic and show off the great potential of his instrument. In late 1933, Red Norvo married Mildred Bailey (a few years later they would become known as "Mr. and Mrs. Swing") and his productive career (which would last into the mid-1980s) was fully under way.

10 Dance of the Octopus/Apr. 18, 1933-Mar. 16, 1936/Hep 1044
Red Norvo's first 26 recordings as a leader (recorded right before he formed his big band) are on this generous CD. In addition to numbers from his octet (an unusual group with the leader's xylophone and arranger Eddie Sauter's mellophone) in 1936 and his swing octets of 1934–35 (which include such future big bandleaders as clarinetist Artie Shaw, trombonist Jack Jenney, tenor saxophonist Charlie Barnet, pianist Teddy Wilson, and trumpeter Bunny Berigan) are four chamber jazz classics from 1933. Norvo's xylophone and marimba are showcased on "Knockin' on Wood" and "Hole in the Wall" in a quartet with Jimmy Dorsey, pianist Fulton McGrath, and bassist Artie Bernstein. Even better are two numbers with Benny Goodman (mostly on bass clarinet), Bernstein, and Dick McDonough: Bix Beiderbecke's "In a Mist" (one of its earliest recordings) and the playful "Dance of the Octopus."

ALCIDE "YELLOW" NUNEZ

b. Mar. 17, 1884, New Orleans, LA, d. Sept. 2, 1934, New Orleans, LA

An interesting if limited clarinetist, Yellow Nunez was a pioneer on records but missed his chance for immortality. He started out on guitar, working with violinist John Spriccio. Nunez switched to clarinet in 1902, when he was 18, performing with the Right at Em's Razz Band. He freelanced in New Orleans with many ensembles, including Papa Jack Laine's Reliance Band, Frank Christian, and Tom Brown. In March 1916, Nunez went to Chicago to join drummer Johnny Stein's group. A dispute resulted that ended up with four of the musicians (Nunez, Nick LaRocca, Eddie Edwards, and Henry Ragas) leaving to form the Original Dixieland Jazz Band; Tony Sbarbaro took over Stein's spot. However, Nunez had an argument with the fiery LaRocca on October 31, 1916, and he left the group; Larry Shields took his place.

While the Original Dixieland Jazz Band went on to fame the following year, Yellow Nunez led a band of his own and played with the obscure Bert Kelly. Nunez recorded 40 titles (not counting alternate takes) with Anton Lada's Louisiana Five during 1918–20. The lack of a trumpet in the group (which consisted of Nunez, trombonist Charles Panelli, pianist Joe Cawley, banjoist Karl Berger, and drummer Lada) made the band sound a bit empty since Nunez was not that strong a lead voice. Nunez also recorded with Harry Yerkes' Novelty Five and the Happy Six during 1919–20. After the Louisiana Five broke up, Yellow Nunez had a quartet, played in Oklahoma and Texas, and in 1927 returned to New Orleans, where he spent his last years playing in obscurity, slipping away into history.

JIMMY O'BRYANT

b. 1896, AK, d. June 24, 1928, Chicago, IL

Very little is known about Jimmy O'Bryant. An excellent clarinetist whose sound and style were influenced strongly by Johnny Dodds, O'Bryant worked with the Tennessee Ten (1920–21). He toured briefly in 1923 with a group co-led by Jelly Roll Morton and W.C. Handy and played with King Oliver (1924). He is best known for his recordings with Lovie Austin's Blues Serenaders (1924–25) and with his own Washboard Band (28 selections during 1924–26). In addition, O'Bryant appeared on sessions during 1923–26 backing blues singers Viola Bartlette, Ruth Coleman, Ida Cox, Julia Davis, Edmonia Henderson, Edna Hicks, Alberta Hunter, Ozie McPherson, Sodarisa Miller, Monette Moore, Ma Rainey, and Priscilla Stewart.

Jimmy O'Bryant worked with Paul Stuart's Wee Hours Serenaders in 1927 and then dropped out of the jazz scene, dying the following year of unknown causes at the age of 32.

7 Vol. 1/Nov. 1924-July 1925/RST 1518
7 Vol. 2 and Vance Dixon/Oct. 3, 1923–June 12, 1931/RST 1519

All of Jimmy O'Bryant's recordings as a leader are on these two CDs. *Vol. 1* starts off with two songs apiece in which O'Bryant, Tommy Ladnier, and Lovie Austin accompany singers Julia Davis and Sodarisa Miller. The remainder of the set is from the clarinetist's "Famous Original Washboard Band," a trio/quartet with Jimmy Blythe, Jasper Taylor on washboard, and (on six numbers) Bob Shoffner. The primitive recording quality of the Paramount pressings hurts the music a bit, although O'Bryant's many catchy originals (quite a few deserve to be revived) compensate. *Vol. 2* has the last nine numbers by O'Bryant; Shoffner is absent and Buddy Burton takes Taylor's place on the final seven cuts. Also on the CD is virtually the entire recording career of Vance Dixon, a decent if not major clarinetist. Dixon is heard with Lois Deppe's Serenaders on 1923's "Congaine" (which was also Earl Hines' first recording), on two numbers backing blues singer Hattie McDaniels in 1929 (who in the 1930s would become a well-known Hollywood character actress), and on all 11 of his selections as a leader. These include duets with pianist Kline Tyndall, selections with Dixon's Jazz Maniacs (a trio with Tyndall and banjoist Lawrence Dixon), and four cuts from 1931 with his Pencils. These two RST reissues, although not essential, are perfectly conceived.

KING OLIVER

b. May 11, 1885, Abend, LA, d. Apr. 8, 1938, Savannah, GA

Joe "King" Oliver was considered the top cornetist in jazz during 1915–23, although he is most famous today as Louis Armstrong's main inspiration. Oliver grew up in New Orleans, originally playing trombone before switching to cornet as a young teenager. Around 1907, while working days as a butler, he started playing with the major brass bands. Oliver was able to quit his day job a few years later when he became one of the busiest musicians in New Orleans, working with the Melrose Brass Band, the Olympia Band, the Onward Brass Band, the Magnolia Band, the Eagle Band, the Original Superior Band, Allen's Brass Band, Richard M. Jones' Four Hot Hounds, and Kid Ory, among many others. He earned the title of "King" after defeating both Freddie Keppard and Manuel Perez in cornet battles.

In March 1919, Oliver moved to Chicago, where he worked simultaneously with the bands of clarinetist Lawrence Duhe and Bill Johnson. The following year he received an offer to lead his own group at the Dreamland Café. Oliver formed the Creole Jazz Band, an ensemble that also included Honore Dutrey, Johnny Dodds, Lil Harden, and Baby Dodds. The group played in San Francisco for a few months in 1921 and also gigged a bit in Los Angeles. Returning to Chicago in 1922, Oliver's Creole Jazz Band was based at Lincoln Gardens. To make the ensembles even more exciting, Oliver sent to New Orleans for Louis Armstrong, whom he had informally tutored a few years earlier and who worshipped the older cornetist.

King Oliver was particularly expert at using plunger mutes to create a variety of wa-wa sounds (even imitating a baby), inspiring Bubber Miley, Paul Mares, Tommy Ladnier, and Muggsy Spanier, among others. When Armstrong joined the band,

An early version of King Oliver's Creole Jazz Band, when they were performing in California in 1921.

the two cornets often spontaneously harmonized their breaks (Satch knew Oliver's style very well) which amazed listeners, including the youngsters of the Austin High Gang, who were frequently in the audience. The Creole Jazz Band was the definitive classic New Orleans jazz group, an ensemble-oriented band filled with some of the most individual horn players of the period. In 1923 the band recorded for Gennett, Okeh, Columbia, and Paramount, performances that were closely studied by most of the other top jazz musicians. Oliver created a famous three-chorus solo on his own "Dippermouth Blues," and he joyfully led the exciting band through such tunes as "Snake Rag," "Froggie

Moore," "Jazzin' Babies' Blues," and "Buddy's Habits."

A dispute over money led the Dodds Brothers to depart in early 1924, and Louis Armstrong (urged on by his new wife, Lil Harden Armstrong) reluctantly departed a few months later, accepting an offer to join Fletcher Henderson's orchestra. Oliver kept the Creole Jazz Band going with substitutes (Bob Shoffner, Lee Collins, and Tommy Ladnier all spent time sitting in Armstrong's former spot) before the group broke up in the fall of 1924. Oliver, who recorded a couple of duets with pianist Jelly Roll Morton that year (including "King Porter Stomp") and backed the vaudeville team Butterbeans and Susie on one record, spent a few months as the featured soloist with Peyton's Symphonic Syncopators. In February 1925 he formed the Dixie Syncopators, performing regularly at Chicago's Plantation Café. The Dixie Syncopators' records from 1926–27 are excellent and show that Oliver was adapting well to the times. His group had grown in size, included such notable players as Kid Ory, Albert Nicholas, and Barney Bigard (on tenor), and utilized colorful arrangements. The cornetist's break on "Snag It" was often quoted by other brassmen, his version of "Sugar Foot Stomp" (a remake of "Dippermouth Blues") is considered classic, and Oliver introduced his new, original "Doctor Jazz," which Jelly Roll Morton made famous.

Oliver's Dixie Syncopators toured the Midwest in 1927 before settling in at New York's Savoy Ballroom. The cornetist made a major mistake when he turned down a long-term contract with the Cotton Club because he was not happy with the amount of money being offered; Duke Ellington would soon get the job! When the engagement at the Savoy ended, the Dixie Syncopators disbanded. Oliver chose to stick it out in New York, and, with the help of Clarence Williams, he appeared on many records during the second half of 1928, including with Texas Alexander, Katherine Henderson, Elizabeth Johnson, Sara Martin, Lizzie Miles, Hazel Smith, Victoria Spivey, and Eva Taylor, plus 21 selections with Williams' groups (highlighted by "Bozo" and "Bimbo").

Things should have been looking up for King Oliver in mid-1929. He started recording regularly as a leader for Victor, and he headed an excellent ten- or eleven-piece modern orchestra. Unfortunately, Oliver's neglect of his teeth (as a youth he had often consumed "sugar sandwiches") was making playing cornet quite painful. His solos on records became briefer, and some dates listed as by King Oliver's orchestra did not have a note by the leader. Occasionally he was able to come through (he sounds quite heroic on the exciting "Too Late"

in 1929), but Oliver's teeth continued to rot away. Guests Louis Metcalf, Punch Miller, Red Allen, Bubber Miley and (by 1930) Oliver's nephew Dave Nelson took many of the trumpet solos. The recordings ended altogether in April 1931.

Due to his musical flexibility and the name he had created for himself in the 1920s, Oliver should have been able to survive the Depression and perhaps even do well during the swing era. But instead it was a steep and steady decline. Oliver left New York with his band in 1931, touring the South and Midwest with less and less success. One misfortune followed another (many buses broke down along the way), the former king of cornetists was unable to play at all after a certain point, and he struggled in poverty. Oliver gamely led groups until 1937 and turned down possible financial assistance from old friends (including Louis Armstrong), out of pride, but things never improved. King Oliver ended up as a poolroom attendant in Savannah, Georgia, passing away at the age of 52. If he had lived five more years, he would have certainly been celebrated again, because a large faction of the 1940s Dixieland revival (led by Lu Watters' Yerba Buena Jazz Band) considered Oliver's Creole Jazz Band to be their main musical role model.

10 King Oliver's Creole Jazzband 1923–1924/Apr. 5, 1923–
Dec. 6, 1924/Retrieval 79007

All 37 performances by King Oliver's Creole Jazz Band are on this essential double CD. Since the recording quality is sometimes a bit primitive, in order to pick up the remarkable interplay by the four horns of Oliver, Armstrong, Dutrey, and Dodds, it is best to play the music loud and swim in it! Not only are the classics, such as "Canal Street Blues," "Chimes Blues" (which has Satch's first recorded solo), the two versions of "Dippermouth Blues," "Froggie Moore," "Snake Rag," "Sobbin' Blues," and "Buddy's Habits," worth listening to very closely, but so are even the lesser-known songs. This is vintage New Orleans jazz at its best. Rounding out the twofer is Oliver's 1924 date with Butter-beans and Susie and his two duets ("King Porter Stomp" and "Tom Cat") with Jelly Roll Morton.

8 Sugar Foot Stomp/Mar. 11, 1926–June 11, 1928/GRP/Decca 616

9 Vol. 1—Sugar Foot Stomp/Mar. 11, 1926–Apr. 27, 1927/ Frog 34

9 Vol. 2—Farewell Blues/Nov. 18, 1927–Apr. 15, 1931/Frog 35

The master takes of the first 22 selections recorded by King Oliver's Dixie Syncopators are on *Sugar Foot Stomp*, an excellent set highlighted by the first five performances: "Too Bad," "Snag It," "Deep Henderson," "Jackass Blues," and "Sugar Foot Stomp." For the complete story with all of the alternate takes ("Snag It" was actually performed four times) and Oliver's appearances on two songs with Irene Scruggs and one with Teddy Peters, listeners need to acquire the two Frog releases. *Vol. 2* also includes the last six titles by the Dixie Syncopators (from August–November 1928) and finishes off by skipping to 1931 for the final three sessions released under Oliver's name.

7 The New York Sessions/Oct. 8, 1929-Sept. 10, 1930/Bluebird 9903

9 King Oliver and His Orchestra/Jan. 16, 1929–Sept. 19, 1930/ RCA Tribune 66538

7 1928–1930/Aug. 13, 1928–Jan. 28, 1930/Classics 607

7 1930–1931/Mar. 18, 1930–Apr. 15, 1931/Classics 594

King Oliver's Victor sessions of 1929–30 resulted in 35 master takes in all, with the first seven actually featuring Louis Metcalf and Punch Miller rather than Oliver. Typically, the one domestic release (*The New York Sessions*) is a confusing 22-song sampler that includes one previously unreleased alternate take ("Olga") and two takes of "Nelson Stomp" while leaving out eight of Oliver's later numbers. The double CD from French RCA, simply called *King Oliver and His Orchestra*, has 32 performances, everything but "When You're Smiling" and second versions of "Everybody Does It in Hawaii" and "Frankie and Johnny." This is the best bet to acquire, despite the lack of alternates, and is highlighted by "Too Late," "I'm Lonesome, Sweetheart," "St. James Infirmary" (with Bubber Miley), "Edna," and "Struggle Buggy."

To confuse matters more (too many choices!), the two Classics CDs (*1928–1930* and *1930–1931*) have all of the master takes plus the 1931 sessions found in Frog 35 and the later Dixie Syncopators performances of 1928 included on Frog 34. For now the RCA Tribune set is best, although hopefully a more complete King Oliver Victor series (with the alternates) will emerge in time.

ORIGINAL DIXIELAND JAZZ BAND

The earliest jazz band ever to record, the Original Dixieland Jazz Band did not invent jazz, but they helped to popularize the new music and were the best band on records during 1917–21.

Nick LaRocca (b. Apr. 11, 1889, New Orleans, LA, d. Feb. 22, 1961, New Orleans, LA) played cornet as a child. He led his first group in 1908, worked steadily around New Orleans, and was a member of Papa Jack Laine's Reliance Band. In 1915 LaRocca started working with drummer Johnny Stein and on March 1, 1916, he left New Orleans with Stein to accept a job in Chicago. Stein's quintet also included clarinetist Alcide "Yellow" Nunez, trombonist Eddie Edwards (b. May 22, 1891, New Orleans, LA, d. Apr. 9, 1963, New York, NY), and pianist Henry Ragas (b. 1891, New Orleans, LA, d. Feb. 18, 1919, New York NY). Stein's Dixie Jass Band became a hit at Schiller's Café, attracting large crowds to listen and dance to their revolutionary music. After three months, LaRocca and the other sidemen wanted to break the contract so as to accept a higher-paying job elsewhere. Stein refused, and the band broke apart, with all of the sidemen joining LaRocca in his new Original Dixieland Jazz Band, playing at first at the Del 'Arbe for the additional money. Tony Sbarbaro (b. June 27, 1897, New Orleans, LA, d. Oct. 30, 1969, New York, NY), who would later change his

Jazz recordings began with the Original Dixieland Jazz Band in 1917.

name to Tony Spargo, replaced Stein on drums. At the end of October, Yellow Nunez lost an argument with LaRocca and was fired; Larry Shields (b. Sept. 13, 1893, New Orleans, LA, d. Nov. 21 1953, Los Angeles, CA) took over as clarinetist.

It was with the LaRocca-Edwards-Shields-Ragas-Sbarbaro lineup that the ODJB made history. They relocated to New York in early 1917 and became a sensation playing at Reisenweber's, helping to launch the jazz age. The band made its first recordings ("Darktown Strutters Ball" and "Indiana") on January 30, 1917, for Columbia, but the label got cold feet and refused to release the freewheeling music. So on February 26, the ODJB went to Columbia's main rival, Victor, and recorded the riotous "Livery Stable Blues" (which featured the horn

players imitating animals) and "Dixie Jazz Band One-Step." Victor immediately came out with the music, "Livery Stable Blues" became a giant hit, and the ODJB started a jazz craze. Even Columbia reversed itself and released their pioneering ODJB recordings.

The Original Dixieland Jazz Band stuck exclusively to ensembles, with no solos other than brief two-bar breaks. But the spirit in their playing, along with the spontaneity and the wide range of sounds, was something unheard of on recordings previously and in few places outside of New Orleans. It appeared quite barbaric to some and inspired a backlash a few years later by so-called reformers and moralists who considered the music overly titillating. But there would be no stopping jazz.

During 1917–18, the Original Dixieland Jazz Band introduced such tunes (and future standards) as "Darktown Strutters Ball," "Indiana," "Tiger Rag," "At the Jazz Band Ball," "Fidgety Feet," "Sensation," and "Clarinet Marmalade." The group recorded seven selections for the AV label (when Victor was having legal problems with patents) and ten additional sides for Victor. When Eddie Edwards was drafted in the fall of 1918, he was replaced by Emile Christian (b. Apr. 20, 1895, New Orleans, LA, d. Dec. 3, 1973, New Orleans, LA). The influenza epidemic of 1918–19 claimed Henry Ragas (who was just 27); J. Russell Robinson (b. July 8, 1892, Indianapolis, IN. d. Sept. 30, 1963, Palmdale, CA) took his place.

In 1919, the ODJB became the first jazz band to visit Europe, duplicating their American success and working regularly in England, where they recorded 17 titles, including some of their finest work. The ODJB's nine-month run at the Hammersmith Palais in London was considered major news.

Returning to the United States, the Original Dixieland Jazz Band faced serious competition from other derivative jazz bands based in New York, and they were being surpassed musically by other New Orleans musicians based in Chicago who had not recorded yet. Emile Christian departed upon Eddie Edwards' discharge from the Army; Christian mostly played in Europe in the 1920s and '30s before settling in New Orleans, working locally as both a trombonist and a bassist into the late 1960s. The ODJB, with altoist Bennie Krueger added to its recordings so as to conform to more "modern" trends, had a minor hit in J. Russell Robinson's "Margie" in late 1920. After six recordings with the band during December 1920–January 1921, Robinson went out on his own. He would have strong success as a songwriter in future years, including "Singin' the Blues," "Beale Street Mama," and "Portrait of Jenny."

With Frank Signorelli as its pianist, the ODJB waxed five songs in 1921, including "Jazz Me Blues," "Royal Garden Blues," and the humorous "Bow Wow Blues (My Mama Treats Me Like a Dog)," which included some syncopated barking! The ODJB continued playing through the end of 1924 but was considered rather prehistoric by that time since it never updated its sound or evolved. There were only four recordings after 1921, and by then Shields had left (moving to California), as had Signorelli, replaced by such obscure players as clarinetist Artie Seaberg, soprano saxophonist Don Parker, and pianist Henry Vanicelli. After LaRocca had a mental breakdown in January 1925 and was advised to give up music, the Original Dixieland Jazz Band broke up.

During the next 11 years, LaRocca ran a contracting business, Robinson was a successful songwriter, Sbarbaro continued playing (including leading four titles in 1935 under the name of the Original Dixieland Jazz Band that had nothing to do with the group's music), Shields was retired, and Edwards performed in society orchestras. In 1936 LaRocca was approached about getting the ODJB back together to appear in the movie *The Big Broadcast of 1937*. The cornetist turned down the offer since he did not think the band could regain its earlier form that quickly. However, he was convinced that the ODJB should return and reclaim its former glory. After a long period of practice, the ODJB appeared together on an Ed Wynn radio show, generating a lot of fan mail with their version of "Tiger Rag." An unlikely comeback was under way.

Although none of the musicians were all that old (LaRocca was the eldest at 47), their music had been considered out of date more than a decade earlier and swing was king by 1936. Partly to show that he was open to newer trends, LaRocca organized a 14-piece big band (which included Shields, Robinson, and Sbarbaro) that was just so-so, recording in September 1936. Much more successful were six remakes of vintage tunes by the Original Dixieland Jazz Band itself. But personality conflicts slowed down the band's momentum, and on February 1, 1938, the ODJB permanently broke up.

LaRocca, who had a prickly personality, retired from music and refused to participate in any of the future reunions. On February 18, 1938, there was a record date by the ODJB that included Shields, Sbarbaro, and Frank Signorelli, with Sharkey Bonano in LaRocca's place, but the six selections were mainly features for singer Lola Bard. During 1943–44 valve trombonist Brad Gowans, switching to clarinet and doing expert imitations of Shields (who by then had permanently retired), led a version of the ODJB with Edwards, Signorelli, Sbarbaro, and either Wild Bill Davison or Bobby Hackett on cornet. And during 1945–46 Eddie Edwards (who stayed active on a part-time basis into the 1960s) recorded with an ODJB that had Gowans, Sbarbaro, Wild Bill Davison, or Max Kaminsky, Gene Schroeder or Teddy Roy on piano, and (for the only time in its history) a bassist (either Bob Casey or Jack Lesberg). But it all came to nothing, for the Original Dixieland Jazz Band's main significance had been during 1917–19. Tony Sbarboro (doubling on kazoo) ended up being the only original member of the ODJB to remain a full-time musician, playing in later years with Phil Napoleon, Eddie Condon, and Tony Parenti.

10 The 75th Anniversary/Feb. 26, 1917-June 7, 1921/Bluebird 61098
10 The Complete Original Dixieland Jazz Band/Feb. 26, 1917–Sept. 25, 1936/RCA 66608
9 In England/Sept. 1917–Jan. 21, 1924/EMI Pathe 252716
8 1917/1923/Jan. 30, 1917–Apr. 20, 1923/Jazz Archives 158492

Happily, it is not that difficult to obtain all of the Original Dixieland Jazz Band recordings without too much duplication. The band recorded 53 titles during 1917–23, and all 23 of its RCA recordings are on the *The 75th Anniversary*, including the famous versions of "Livery Stable Blues," "Dixie Jass Band One-Step," "Tiger Rag," "Sensation Rag," "Margie," and even "Bow Wow Blues." *The Com-*

plete Original Dixieland Jazz Band is a two-CD set that not only has the 23 RCA numbers but all of the music from the ODJB's "comeback," the six quintet remakes, and the eight big band selections.

Despite the claim of being "complete," there are still 30 other vintage selections by the ODJB that were not made for Victor. Seventeen (all of the overseas records by the LaRocca-Christian-Shields-Robinson-Sbarbaro lineup) are on *In England*. Ranking with the group's finest work, some of these performances were originally on 12-inch 78s, and two are over four minutes in length. In addition to the many remakes, the highlights include "My Baby's Arms," "I've Got My Captain Working for Me Now," "I'm Forever Blowing Bubbles," "Mammy o' Mine," "I've Lost My Heart in Dixieland," and a charming version of "Alice Blue Gown." Also on this CD are five selections from four British bands of the 1917–24 period; interesting but not up to the level of the ODJB.

1917/1923 is a real gap-filler. It includes the two historic Columbia selections ("The Darktown Strutters Ball" and "Indiana," although it claims they are from May 31, 1917, rather than January 30), the seven cuts for the ASV label (including "At the Jass Band Ball" and "Oriental Jazz") and the band's four 1922–23 recordings, plus 11 Victor recordings that are duplicates. By acquiring the Bluebird, EMI Pathe, and Jazz Archives CDs, collectors will have every ODJB recording of 1917–23. Substitute the RCA twofer for the Bluebird and it truly will be the complete Original Dixieland Jazz Band.

ORIGINAL INDIANA FIVE

Despite its name, the members of the Original Indiana Five were not from Indiana but from New York City! The band was formed in 1922 and at the beginning consisted of leader-pianist Newman Fier, trumpeter Johnny Sylvester, trombonist Vincent Grande, clarinetist Johnny Costello, and drummer Tom Morton. The OIF began recording in 1923 and during the next six years cut 96 titles under the name of the Original Indiana Five plus some additional songs under different names, including six on dates led by Morton. Later in 1923, Nick Vitalo (on clarinet and alto) took over for Costello, Charles Panelli was on trombone, Harry Ford was the new pianist, banjoist Tony Colucci made the group a sextet, and Tom Morton became the band's leader. Other than the addition of Pete Pellezzi as the OIF's trombonist in the fall of 1925, the personnel stayed the same until late in 1926, when Tony Tortomas took over on trumpet.

The group, which played melodic and freewheeling jazz not all that much different from the Original Memphis Five's, stayed together until their breakup in 1929. Seventeen years later, there was a reunion band that gave the members an opportunity to perform Dixieland from 1947 to 1953.

8 Original Indiana Five, Vol. 1/1923-May 1, 1925/Jazz Oracle 8019
8 Everybody Stomp/Oct. 13, 1925–May 21, 1929/Frog 23

Until recently, recordings by the Original Indiana Five were very scarce, for the band was not even included in reissue series during the LP era. Fortunately that has changed. First the Frog label came out with *Everybody Stomp*, all 26 selections that the group made for the Harmony label (including three from 1929 that were issued under Tom Morton's name). The music is primarily from 1925–27, and the quintet/sextet plays their happy brand of music on such numbers as "Everybody's Doin' the Charleston Now," "So Is Your Old Lady," "I'd Leave Ten Men Like Yours to Love One Man Like Mine," and "Stockholm Stomp." After the Frog CD came out, the Jazz Oracle label initiated their own Original Indiana Five series, which fortunately will eventually release all of that band's recordings except for the ones already covered by Frog. *Vol. 1* starts at the very beginning with two sides by the Indiana Syncopators. In addition to the Original Indiana Five selections, it has one number in which vaudeville singer Benny Davis is backed by the group and six tunes by the same band when it re-corded under Johnny Sylvester's name. Listening to such titles as "Louisville Lou," "Staving Change," "I Wanna Jazz Some More," and "King Porter Stomp," it is obvious that the Original Indiana Five is one of the most underrated and overlooked groups of the 1920s, well worth discovering.

ORIGINAL MEMPHIS FIVE

The Original Memphis Five competed with the California Ramblers in the 1920s as the most prolific jazz group. Although the Ramblers won for quantity, the OMF always stuck to jazz and certainly built up a very impressive and huge discography of its own. Trumpeter Phil Napoleon initially formed the band in late 1917, but by the time it first recorded in April 1922 the ensemble performed strictly as a recording group, cutting 201 selections during 1922–31 (including 111 in 1922–23). The band originally consisted of Napoleon, Miff Mole, Jimmy Lytell, Frank Signorelli, and drummer Jack Roth. After 26 selections (made within a six-month period), Charles Panelli succeeded Mole. Other than occasionally using banjoist Ray Kitchenman, Mole sometimes returning to the trombone slot, and Red Nichols substituting on two titles in January 1926, the personnel stayed the same until December 1926. During this prime period, Phil Napoleon was one of the finest jazz trumpeters on record, and the OMF was the definitive mainstream jazz combo, emphasizing the melody while always swinging, balancing clean ensembles with concise solos. The same basic group (with augmented personnel) also recorded as Bailey's Lucky Seven, the Broadway Syncopators, the Cotton Pickers, Jazzbo's Carolina Serenaders, Ladd's Black Aces, the Savannah Six, the Southland Six, and the Tennessee Ten. In addition, the 1922–23 band backed the obscure but pleasing classic blues singer Leona Williams on all 16 of her recordings, before she disappeared into history.

Ray Bauduc succeeded Jack Roth on drums in December 1926. The Original Memphis Five name was used much less after 1926, with just six titles in 1927 (George Bohn was on clarinet and on four numbers Red Nichols was in Napoleon's place), three apiece in 1928 and 1929, and four in 1931. Napoleon was still present for the last ten titles, but for these last dates he was joined by Tommy Dorsey, Jimmy Dorsey, Frank Signorelli, and either Stan King or Ted Napoleon on drums. The Memphis Five name was revived by Phil Napoleon for his later Dixieland bands starting in the late 1940s.

8 The Original Memphis Five, Vol. 1/Apr. 22, 1922-Dec. 10, 1923/Collector's Classics 16

7 1922/1931/May 10, 1922–Nov. 24, 1931/Jazz Archives 159542

The Original Memphis Five's recordings have not yet been reissued in a coherent fashion. These two CDs are among the few that have brought back some of the music. The Collector's Classics set has all nine selections recorded in 1922 by Jazzbo's Carolina Serenaders (essentially the Memphis Five with an altoist added) and two from the Southland Six, plus a dozen cuts that were actually originally put out under the OMF name. The music (including "My Honey's Lovin' Arms," "Yankee Doodle Blues," "Chicago," "The Great White Way Blues," and even "That Barking Dog—Woof! Woof!") is excellent, and hopefully this will serve as a good start toward making all of this important band's music available. *1922/1931* duplicates only one selection (the aforementioned "Woof") and is a good overview, with a dozen numbers from 1922–23, eight from 1924–28, and two of the four numbers from the Original Memphis Five's final session, in 1931.

LPS TO SEARCH FOR

The Original Memphis Five (Folkways 26) has 16 selections from the band during 1922–24, including two songs put out by Ladd's Black Aces and one from the Tennessee Ten. Hopefully, comprehensive CD reissues will eventually make this fine LP obsolete in time.

KID ORY

b. Dec. 25, 1886, La Place, LA, d. Jan. 23, 1973, Honolulu, HI

Edward "Kid" Ory's "tailgate" style of trombone, using his horn to play rhythmic bass lines and harmonies in the front line behind the trumpet and clarinet, defined how the trombone was played before the late 1920s and how it was often utilized in later Dixieland bands. Ory started on banjo when he was ten, was soon doubling on valve trombone, and eventually switched permanently to slide trombone. He visited New Orleans often before moving there in 1912 (when he was already 25). During 1912–19 Ory led one of the city's top bands, an ensemble that featured King Oliver on cornet (followed by his successor, Louis Armstrong) and at various times Johnny Dodds, Sidney Bechet, and Jimmie Noone. In 1919 he moved to California, sending for several top New Orleans players and leading a band that spent periods in San Francisco, Los Angeles, and Oakland. Mutt Carey was the cornetist when Ory made his first records (as Spikes' Seven Pods of Pepper Orchestra) in 1922, the earliest recordings by a black New Orleans jazz band. In addition to those two instrumentals (which included "Ory's Creole Trombone"), the group backed singers Roberta Dudley and Ruth Lee on two songs apiece.

In late 1925, the trombonist gave the band (which was really known as Kid Ory's Brown Skinned Babies) to Carey and moved to Chicago so as to play nightly with King Oliver's Dixie Syncopators. Ory appeared on many important recordings during the next four years, including with Louis Armstrong's Hot Five and Hot Seven (where he introduced his "Muskrat Ramble"), King Oliver, Jelly Roll Morton, and Johnny Dodds. He also recorded with the Chicago Footwarmers, the New Orleans Bootblacks, the New Orleans Wanderers, Tiny Parham, Luis Russell, Lovie Austin, Viola Bartlette, Butterbeans and Susie, Ozie McPherson, Ma Rainey, Irene Scruggs, and Sippie Wallace. After leaving Oliver,

Ory worked with Dave Peyton (1927), Clarence Black, and Boyd Atkins' Chicago Vagabonds (1929).

As was true for many of the other New Orleans veterans, job opportunities dried up for Ory in 1930. He moved back to Los Angeles, freelanced with various local groups (including Mutt Carey's Jeffersonians), and in 1933 decided to leave music altogether to help his brother run a chicken farm, not playing trombone for a decade. However, with the rise of the New Orleans revival movement, Kid Ory returned to the scene in the mid-1940s and led one of the top New Orleans jazz bands of the 1944–61 period.

7 1922–1947/June 1922-Aug. 9, 1947/Document 1002

Included on this CD is a 1944 broadcast version of "Mutt's Blues" (with Mutt Carey and Jimmie Noone), two fairly rare Ory studio dates from 1945, and the trombonist's appearance on Rudi Blesh's *This Is Jazz* radio series in 1947. Of more relevance to classic jazz is the inclusion of all six performances from Spikes' Seven Pods of Pepper Orchestra in 1922: the four selections backing singers Roberta Dudley and Ruth Lee (which are ok) and most importantly the instrumentals "Ory's Creole Trombone" and "Society Blues," which, although primitively recorded, are well worth owning.

WALTER PAGE

b. Feb. 9, 1900, Gallatin, MI, d. Dec. 20, 1957, New York, NY

A top bassist during the swing era and famous for his association with Count Basie, Walter Page earlier in his career was the leader of one of the top territory bands of the 1920s, the Blue Devils. He started off playing tuba and bass drum in local brass bands. While in high school, Page learned string bass, and he became a professional soon after graduating, working in saxophonist Dave Lewis' band. Page was an early member of the Bennie Moten Orchestra in Kansas City (1918–23), often dou-

bling on baritone sax. During 1923–25 he worked with trombonist Emir Coleman's group, touring in Billy King's road show.

When the ensemble was stranded in Oklahoma City in 1925, Page became its leader, and during the next six years Walter Page's Blue Devils was the main competitor of Moten's orchestra. Among the Blue Devils' members at various times were the unrelated trumpeter Hot Lips Page, pianist Count Basie, tenor saxophonist Lester Young, and singer Jimmy Rushing. But one by one, Moten lured each of these artists and others into his better-paying orchestra.

Page's Blue Devils cut two selections at their lone recording date in 1929 (included on *What Kind of Rhythm Is That*—Frog 31). However, the Depression made work scarce for the band, and in 1931 Page finally threw in the towel. He gave the Blue Devils to trumpeter James Simpson and joined Moten himself. Walter Page played with Moten until 1934 and after Moten's death was an important part of Count Basie's influential rhythm section during 1936–42 and 1946–49. His four-to-the-bar walking behind soloists set the standard for bassists of the swing era.

ROY PALMER

b. Apr. 2, 1892, New Orleans, LA, d. Dec. 22, 1963, Chicago, IL

Roy Palmer had a colorful and percussive style on trombone that sounded at its best in freewheeling settings. Palmer played guitar in the Rozele Orchestra in 1906 and spent several years as a trumpeter before switching to trombone. He worked in New Orleans with Richard M. Jones (1911), Willie Hightower's American Stars (1914–15), and the Tuxedo and Onward Brass Bands. Palmer left his hometown in 1917 to play in Chicago with Sugar Johnny's Smith's band. During the next 15 years he worked with Tig Chambers, W.C. Handy, Johnny Dodds, Jelly Roll Morton, Freddie Keppard, and a variety of lesser-known groups. Along the way, Palmer recorded with Jelly Roll Morton (1924), Johnny Dodds' Black Bottom Stompers (a 1927 session that included Louis Armstrong), Ida Cox (1929), and Richard M. Jones (1929), but he can be heard at his most exuberant on good-time jazz dates with the State Street Ramblers (1931) and the Memphis Night Hawks (1932).

Roy Palmer, who last recorded with the Chicago Rhythm Kings in 1936, left full-time music in the 1930s to work for the Mazola Oil Company. In later years he operated a laundry business and was a music teacher.

TONY PARENTI

b. Aug. 6 1900, New Orleans, LA, d. Apr. 17, 1972, New York, NY

A brilliant clarinetist who was a fluent improviser, Tony Parenti first made his mark in the 1920s. He originally played violin before starting on clarinet. As a 12-year-old, Parenti was already playing with Papa Jack Laine in 1912. Other musical experiences for the teenager included associations with Nick LaRocca, Johnny Stein, and Johnny DeDroit. Parenti also played on riverboats and led a successful band starting in 1917. While still in New Orleans, Parenti recorded 20 selections during 1925–26 and 1928 with his Famous Melody Boys and his Liberty Syncopators and appeared on two cuts with trombonist Russ Papalia's orchestra.

In 1929 Parenti moved to New York, where he recorded the exciting "Old Man Rhythm" (quite a showcase) in a duet with pianist Vic Breidis. He worked in dance bands and as a CBS staff musician, substituted for Benny Goodman with Ben Pollack, and recorded with Red Nichols. After a long association with Ted Lewis (1936–42), Tony Parenti played Dixieland-oriented music during the remainder of his long career.

7 Strut Yo' Stuff/Jan. 22, 1925–June 28, 1929/Frog 4
All of Tony Parenti's dates as a leader in the 1920s

(with his Famous Melody Boys, Liberty Syncopators, and New Orleanians) are on this single CD. Most of the material was formerly quite rare. The first 19 performances (three of which are alternate takes) are from 1925–26, and Parenti (who is also heard on alto and baritone) sounds fine although not overly distinctive yet. His band (with Henry Knecht and either Albert Brunies or Leon Prima on cornets, trombonist Charles Hartman, tenor saxophonist Tony Papalia, pianist Vic Lubowski, banjoist Mike Holloway, Mario Finazzo on tuba, and drummer George Triay) sometimes seems a little wooden rhythmically, although there are some strong moments along the way. The material (which includes "Cabaret Echoes," "Dizzy Lizzie," "Strut Yo' Stuff," and "Up Jumped the Devil") is filled with songs well worth reviving. Musically, the four numbers from 1928 (with Johnny Hyman or Leon Prima on trumpet, Hartman, pianist Buzzy Williams, guitarist Jack Brian, and drummer Monk Hazel) show a great deal of improvement, while 1929's "Old Man Rhythm" was Parenti's best feature for the decade.

TINY PARHAM

b. Feb. 25, 1900, Kansas City, MO, d. Apr. 4, 1943, Milwaukee, WI

Tiny Parham's string of hot yet atmospheric recordings during the late 1920s still sound quite spirited and unique today. Hartzell Strathdene "Tiny" Parham grew up in Kansas City, where he started his professional career playing locally. After moving to Chicago, he co-led the Pickett-Parham Apollo Syncopators with violinist Leroy Pickett (1926–27), an outfit that recorded two songs in December 1926. Parham soon broke away to form his own unit, recording three numbers in 1927 and leading eight very productive record sessions during 1928–30 as Tiny Parham and His Musicians. Other than Punch Miller and Milt Hinton (heard on tuba in 1930), Parham's sidemen were mostly obscure, but they performed the leader's continually surprising arrangements quite well. In addition, Parham recorded in 1927 with Jasper Taylor (a group including Freddie Keppard), King Brady's Clarinet Band, Johnny Dodds (three duets), Ora Brown, and Hattie McDaniels, and in 1928 with singers Sharlie English and Priscilla Stewart.

The not-so-tiny pianist stopped recording after 1930 (other than three titles in 1940), leading his band until 1936. Tiny Parham spent his last years at low-level jobs, often playing organ in theaters, hotels, and movie houses.

10 1926–1929/Dec. 1926-July 22, 1929/Classics 661
10 1929–1940/Oct. 25, 1929–June 4, 1940/Classics 691
Tiny Parham's recordings as a leader are full of treasures. All of the master takes of his sessions are on his two Classics CDs. *1926–1929* has Parham on two numbers as co-leader of the Pickett-Parham Apollo Syncopators in 1926 and heading his "Forty" Five, a quintet that includes blues banjoist Papa Charlie Jackson (who sings "Jim Jackson's Kansas City Blues") and Kid Ory in 1927. Otherwise the music features Parham's Musicians, a sextet/septet from 1928–29 that consists of either Punch Miller or Ray Hobson on cornet, the haunting violin of Elliott Washington, trombonist Charles Lawson, Charlie Johnson on clarinet and alto, banjoist Mike McKendrick, Quinn Wilson on tuba, and Ernie Marrero on drums and washboard. The arrangements are unpredictable, clever, and certainly haunting, while the repertoire is full of obscure but high-quality originals. Among the more memorable selections are "The Head-Hunter's Dream," "Jogo Rhythm," "Stompin' on Down," "Blue Melody Blues," "Blue Island Blues," and "Washboard Wiggles."

1929–1940 has the same octet (with Punch Miller on cornet and Dalbert Bright taking Charlie Johnson's place) on nine sometimes-eerie selections from 1929, including "Sud Buster's Dream," "Dixieland Doin's," and "Black Cat Moan." Parham's 1930 group (Hobson, trombonist John

Thomas, Bright, Jimmy Hutchinson on clarinet and tenor, McKendrick, Milt Hinton making his recording debut on tuba, and drummer Jimmy McEndre) recorded 11 titles, including "Doin' the Jug Jug," "Back to the Jungle," and "Nervous Tension." The violin is missed, but the arrangements help make the music sound unique. *1929–1940* concludes with three numbers from 1940, played by a quartet with Parham doubling on organ and Darnell Howard on clarinet and alto, that serve as an anticlimactic close to Tiny Parham's career.

LPS TO SEARCH FOR

In 1985 the Australian Swaggie label came out with four LPs that contain the complete Tiny Parham (other than his 1940 session). All of the music on the first three volumes is on Parham's two Classics CDs but *Volume Four* (Swaggie 834) consists of 14 intriguing alternate takes from 1928–30 that were bypassed, including "new" versions of "The Head-Hunter's Dream," "Jogo Rhythm," "Blue Melody Blues," and "Nervous Tension."

MANUEL PEREZ

b. Dec. 28, 1871, New Orleans, LA, d. 1946 New Orleans, LA

Manuel (or Emanuel) Perez was an early cornetist who was actually six years older than Buddy Bolden. He played cornet in New Orleans bands starting in the 1890s, working with Robichaux's orchestra, the Imperial Orchestra (which he led during 1901–08), and the Onward Brass Band, being leader of the last during 1903–30. Perez's sidemen included King Oliver, Peter Bocage, Lorenzo Tio Jr., and Sidney Bechet. His attractive sound and technical skills were well respected, although he was overshadowed by the flashier Buddy Bolden, Freddie Keppard, and King Oliver.

Perez mostly stayed in New Orleans throughout his life, other than for visits to Chicago in 1915 (working with the Arthur Sims band), 1919, and the summer of 1927 (as a member of Charles Elgar's orchestra). Perez joined Elgar nearly a year after the band had its lone recording date; unfortunately the cornetist never recorded. After working in New Orleans during 1928–30, Perez (who was 58) retired from music, becoming a full-time cigar maker. He never had an opportunity to make a comeback because a series of strokes in the 1940s ruined his health. Lee Collins and Punch Miller considered Manuel Perez to be strong influences on their styles.

BUDDY PETIT

b. 1897, White Castle, LA, d. July 4, 1931, New Orleans, LA

Buddy Petit, along with Chris Kelly and Manuel Perez, never recorded and his music is therefore totally lost to history. Born Joseph Crawford, he adopted the last name of his stepfather, valve trombonist Joseph Petit, who ironically did get to record in 1945, at the age of 72! Following the older Petit (who founded the Olympia Brass Band), Buddy formed the Young Olympia Band with Sidney Bechet around 1915. The following year he co-led a group with Jimmie Noone, and in 1917 he went to Los Angeles to play with Jelly Roll Morton. Unfortunately Morton ridiculed Petit and the other New Orleans musicians for their out-of-date clothes and their habits of cooking in the dressing room and eating on the bandstand. When Petit quit the band, he threatened to kill Morton if he ever returned to New Orleans!

In 1918, when Bill Johnson sent for Petit to join his group in Chicago, the 21-year-old adamantly refused to leave the South; King Oliver went in his place and became famous. In contrast, Petit (who was praised years later by Punch Miller, Herb Morand, and Wingy Manone) stayed in New Orleans. And although he worked quite steadily in the 1920s, his fame never reached beyond the city limits. Other than visiting California briefly in 1922 with Frankie Dusen and occasionally played on riverboats, he chose to stay in New Orleans.

Buddy Petit, a heavy drinker, last played music on the day he died, collapsing from the combination of overeating and excessive drinking at a July 4th picnic. He was just 34.

JACK PETTIS

b. 1902, Danville, IL, d. 1960s?

Jack Pettis was a superior tenor and C-melody saxophonist who deserved to be better known but instead is a major mystery figure in jazz history. Pettis began playing the C-melody sax when he was 16 (reportedly buying his first horn on Armistice day in 1918), soon moving to Chicago and working locally. He first gained attention for his work with Elmer Schoebel and the New Orleans Rhythm Kings, recording with the latter group during four of its 1922–23 sessions. After leading a band that accompanied singer Ann Pennington in vaudeville, Pettis moved to New York, where he worked with Ben Bernie during 1924–30. He recorded frequently with Bernie and was caught with that orchestra in a pioneering sound film version of "Sweet Georgia Brown" (taking a strong solo) in 1925. In addition to his work with Bernie, Pettis recorded with the Ambassadors (1924), the New Orleans Black Birds (1928), Jimmy McHugh's Bostonians (1928), the Whoopee Makers (1929), and Irving Mills' Hotsy Totsy Gang (1928 and 1930). Best are his nine sessions as a leader during 1926–29, heading a variety of medium-size groups often known as Jack Pettis' Pets. Among his sidemen were Bill Moore, Tommy Dorsey, Jack Teagarden, Don Murray, Benny Goodman, Joe Venuti, Eddie Lang, and Dick McDonough, while the songs included three memorable Pettis' originals ("A Bag o' Blues," "Freshman Hop," and "Sweetest Melody"), all of which deserved to become standards.

Extremely little is known of Jack Pettis' life after he left Ben Bernie in 1930. At one point he had a group that accompanied singer Morton Downey, and in Los Angeles he led a session in 1937 that resulted in two titles ("Hawaiian Heat Wave" and "Swing Session in Siberia") that have yet to be reissued. After that, he disappeared from the music scene and has not been heard from since.

10 Jack Pettis/Nov. 1924–May 23, 1929/Kings Cross Music 005/006

This double CD is difficult to improve upon. There are 49 selections (2½ hours of music), many of the recordings were formerly rare, the repertoire is fresh, the musicianship is top-notch, and there are countless exciting moments. Jack Pettis' sessions as a leader are reissued in complete form (24 selections plus three alternate takes), along with his appearances with Al Goering's Collegians, the Ambassadors, the Whoopee Makers, Mills' Musical Clowns, and Irving Mills' Modernists plus one of Ben Bernie's most jazz-oriented dates. The only significant things that are missing are Pettis' work with the NORK and the Hotsy Totsy Gang (both of which are available elsewhere) and his elusive 1937 session. This twofer is filled with classic (if often overlooked) music.

WARD PINKETT

b. Apr. 29, 1906, Newport News, VA, d. Mar. 15, 1937, New York, NY

Ward Pinkett was a busy trumpeter during 1928–31 and showed a great deal of potential before alcohol did him in. Pinkett began playing cornet when he was ten, and he later attended the New Haven Conservatory of Music. The trumpeter played with the White Brothers Orchestra in Washington, D.C., worked with a traveling show, and eventually settled in New York. During 1926–34 Pinkett worked with Charlie Johnson, Willie Gant, Billy Fowler, Joe Steele, Charlie Skeete, Chick Webb (1929), Bingie Madison, Rex Stewart (1933), and Teddy Hill (1934), among others. Most importantly, Pinkett recorded 62 selections as a sideman. He started out taking fine solos on Jelly Roll Morton's 1928 recordings of "Georgia Swing," "Kansas City Stomps," and "Shoe Shiner's Drag." Pinkett also recorded with King Oliver (filling in for the ailing cornetist), Joe Steele's orchestra, Chick Webb's Jungle Band, Bubber Miley's Mileage Makers, Clarence Williams, Mamie Smith, and James P. Johnson. He can be heard at his best on Jelly Roll Morton's 1930 sessions, particularly "Strokin' Away" and "Low Gravy."

However, after 1931, the Depression and Pinkett's excessive intake of alcohol combined to drastically slow down his career. He had a last outburst of activity during 1935–36, when he worked with Albert Nicholas at Adrian Rollini's Tap Room and recorded with Freddy Jenkins' Harlem Seven and the Little Ramblers. But by 1936 Ward Pinkett was a hopeless alcoholic who refused to stop drinking and rarely ate. He died from pneumonia the following year, when he was just 30.

ARMAND J. PIRON

b. Aug. 16, 1888, New Orleans, LA, d. Feb. 17, 1943, New Orleans, LA

Armand J. Piron led an intriguing band that fell between society music and jazz. A violinist, Piron received lessons from his father, who was also an orchestra leader. He started playing professionally in 1904, led his first band in 1908, worked in the Peerless Orchestra in 1910, and led the Olympia Orchestra starting in 1912; Clarence Williams was the pianist with the last. Piron also worked with Williams in a publishing company, composing and gaining the publishing rights to many songs. However, his best-known original, "I Wish I Could Shimmy Like My Sister Kate," was probably purchased at a low fee from Louis Armstrong. The trumpeter, who felt cheated, always refused all requests to play that song.

Piron worked with Oscar Celestin (1916) and formed his most successful orchestra in 1918. He performed mostly in New Orleans during the next decade, other than for two brief visits to New York during 1923–24. During one of those trips, his nonet (which included trumpeter Peter Bocage, trombonist John Lindsay, and Lorenzo Tio Jr. on clarinet and tenor) recorded a dozen selections for the Victor label plus one song backing singer Ester Bigeou. Piron also accompanied singer Lela Bolden on two songs in New Orleans in 1924, and a field trip by the Victor label in March 1925 resulted in the final two recordings by Piron's New Orleans Orchestra, which was captured as a sextet.

Armand J. Piron led bands up until almost the time of his death, but he died in obscurity.

LPS TO SEARCH FOR

Piron's New Orleans Orchestra (Retrieval 128) contains all 18 recordings by Armand J. Piron, including his work with the two singers, his New York and New Orleans recordings with his ensemble, and an alternate take of "Red Man Blues." Among the more notable selections are "Bouncing Around," "Kiss Me Sweet," and "Mama's Gone Goodbye" (which Piron cowrote with Peter Bocage).

BEN POLLACK

b. June 22, 1903, Chicago, IL, d. June 7, 1971, Palm Springs, CA

One of the better drummers of the 1920s (Benny Goodman said that he was the first drummer he heard who evenly accented all four beats in a measure), an important bandleader, and a major talent scout, Ben Pollack never found the fame that he desired, but he did record some fine records along the way. Pollack began playing drums in school and first worked on a regular basis with Dick Schoenberg in 1921. After playing with pianist Izzy Wagner, he joined the New Orleans Rhythm Kings, with whom he made his recording debut in 1923. When the NORK broke up, Pollack played with Harry Bastin in Los Angeles for most of a year. After short periods in Chicago and New York, he returned to L.A. to take over the Bastin band, playing on the West Coast from October 1924 until the fall of 1925. By then, he was featuring a 16-year-old clarinetist named Benny Goodman.

Back in Chicago by the spring of 1926, Pollack (who was still just 22) built up his orchestra, which soon included Jimmy McPartland, Glenn Miller, and (by 1928) Jack Teagarden. The group, which began making records in December 1926 (the recording debuts of both Goodman and Miller), in 1928 relocated to New York, where it was the pit band for the Broadway show *Hello Daddy*. Although its recordings were often compromised (alternating between jazz choruses and commercial arrangements), Pollack's group (which for a time was called the Park Central Orchestra) recorded some good jazz and was one of the finest white bands of the era.

By playing commercial music and enduring plenty of personnel changes, Pollack's orchestra made it through the worst years of the Depression. But unfortunately it did not survive 1934. By then Pollack was mostly just conducting and often taking corny vocals. He was apparently more interested in promoting his girlfriend, Doris Robbins, as a singer and an actress than he was in the band. In fact, Pollack spent so much time trying to get Robbins a job in Hollywood that his sidemen voted to become an independent orchestra and dump the leader. A few months later the ensemble became the Bob Crosby Orchestra.

Quite discouraged, Pollack had another impressive band by 1936, featuring the young trumpeter Harry James (whom he had discovered in Texas). But after a few months (and three recording sessions), James was lured away to join a better-known orchestra led by a Pollack alumnus, Benny Goodman. Pollack continued leading bands until 1942 (with Muggsy Spanier, Andy Secrest, and Clyde Hurley all taking turns in the "hot trumpet" chair). But whenever his orchestra was on the verge of success, other bandleaders outbid him for his top sidemen. By 1942, he was just directing the touring band for Chico Marx, one that featured a young drummer-singer named Mel Torme. Pollack spent his later years running a booking agency, having a short-lived record label (Jewel), playing Dixieland with his Pick-a-Rib Boys in the 1950s, and owning a restaurant in Palm Springs. Quite despondent from the way his life ended up, Ben Pollack hung himself in 1971.

8 Volume 1 1926–1928/Dec. 9, 1926-Nov. 27, 1928/Jazz Oracle 8015

7 Volume 2 1928–1929/Dec. 3, 1928–Mar. 1, 1929/Jazz Oracle 8016

6 Volume 3 1929/Mar. 1, 1929–Nov. 27, 1929/Jazz Oracle 8017

The first three of a projected five-CD series documenting all of Ben Pollack's recordings as a leader through 1933 have been released by Jazz Oracle. The production values, as is typical for this collector's label from Canada, are perfect. However, listening to the music of Ben Pollack's orchestra can be a bit frustrating, similar to listening to Jean Goldkette's band with Bix Beiderbecke. While Goldkette's music was hurt by the interference of recording directors at Victor, Pollack's was compromised by the leader's desire to balance the jazz with commercially accessible music, although he himself was a fine jazz player.

Volume 1 of the Jazz Oracle series covers a nearly two-year period and is highlighted by "He's the Last Word," "Memphis Blues," "Buy Buy for Baby (Or Baby Will Bye Bye You)," and "The Whoopee Stomp" (one of three numbers released as by Jimmy McHugh's Bostonians). In addition to Goodman, McPartland, Miller, and Teagarden, the key players include Fud Livingston, Larry Binyon, or Bud Freeman on tenor and section saxophonist Gil Rodin. The 15 songs are joined by ten alternate takes (placed at the end of the CD), and in general even the least interesting song has a worthwhile jazz solo by one of the main voices. *Volume 2* finds the Pollack Orchestra (which, in addition to another date as McHugh's Bostonians, also recorded as the Louisville Rhythm Kings and a septet called Ben's Bad Boys) being quite busy during a three-month period. The vocals of Gene Austin, Dick Robertson, Irving Kaufman, Smith Ballew, Scrappy Lambert, and Pollack himself (who told him he could sing?) do not help, although Goodman, McPartland, and Teagarden (who should have been singing) have their spots. The better numbers include "Futuristic Rhythm," "Wang Wang Blues," "Yellow Dog Blues," a previously unreleased "Shirt Tail Stomp" (a satire of cornball bands), and "Louise." *Volume 3* completes the Goodman-McPartland period of Pollack's orchestra (Teagarden would stay until 1933), with such tunes as "Wait 'Til You See Ma Cherie," "My Kinda Love," and "True Blue Lou." By then Pollack was just directing the orchestra (Ray Bauduc was on drums), taking occasional insipid vocals (although Scrappy Lambert and Smith Ballew are also heard from) and ending some of the records by saying "For your pleasure, Ben Pollack."

LPS TO SEARCH FOR

The Jazz Oracle Ben Pollack series should make all of his previous LPs from the period obsolete. *1933–1934* (VJM 43) is slightly later and has all 16 selections from Pollack's band of 1934 (with four cuts from December 28, 1933). Trumpeter Yank Lawson, clarinetist Matty Matlock, Gil Rodin, tenor saxophonist Eddie Miller, guitarist Nappy Lamare, and drummer Ray Bauduc are in place, and the orchestra was beginning to look like Bob Crosby's. There are some good solos along the way, but once again Pollack's desire to make it big means that there are too many vocals and arranged ensembles. The bandleader's girlfriend, Doris Robbins (who has three vocals), fares better than expected.

JOE POSTON

b. 1895, Alexandria, LA, d. May 1942, Chicago, IL

Joe Poston was an alto saxophonist with an appealing tone. He played in Chicago with Doc Cook's Dreamland Orchestra (1922–24 and 1927), Fate Marable, and most notably Jimmie Noone's Apex Club Orchestra (1928–30). While with Noone, Poston had a unique role, playing melody statements constantly behind the leader's clarinet solos while rarely getting to solo himself. Unfortunately he was forced to retire prematurely due to bad health, and Joe Poston spent his last eight years in a sanatorium.

JACK PURVIS

b. Dec. 11, 1906, Kokomo, IN, d. Mar. 30, 1962, San Francisco, CA

Jack Purvis certainly had a bizarre life. Early on, he learned trumpet and trombone, playing in his high school orchestra and with dance bands in his native Kokomo as early as 1921, when he was 14. Purvis worked in Indiana for a period and in Lexington, Kentucky, with the Original Kentucky Night Hawks, taking some time off to learn how to pilot a plane. In 1926 he toured New England with Bud Rice. Purvis spent part of 1926–27 with Whitey Kaufman's Original Pennsylvanians, had a short stint on trombone with Hal Kemp, and in July 1928 visited France with George Carhart's band. He did not last long with Carhart, for he apparently bilked an American tourist out of his traveler's checks and was forced to flee the country! Purvis worked again with Hal Kemp's orchestra in 1929 (on trumpet) but had to leave the band when a tour of Florida was planned because a few years earlier he had run the short-lived School of Grecian Dancing in Miami, and he was still wanted in Florida on morals charges!

During 1929–30, Purvis appeared on records with Kemp, Smith Ballew, the California Ramblers, the Carolina Club Orchestra, Roy Wilson's Georgia Crackers, Ted Wallace, and Rube Bloom. As a leader, he cut two intriguing numbers on December 17, 1929, with Hal Kemp's rhythm section (a tribute to Louis Armstrong called "Copyin' Louis" and "Mental Strain at Dawn"). He also led a pair of interracial sessions in 1930 that included such players as J.C. Higginbotham, Coleman Hawkins, and Adrian Rollini. Purvis' playing is full of unexpected outbursts, unrealized potential, and some crazy chance-taking, just like his life.

After leaving Kemp, Purvis worked for a little while with the California Ramblers, recorded with the Dorsey Brothers, occasionally sat in as fourth trumpeter with Fletcher Henderson, and played with radio orchestras and Fred Waring (1931–32). He traveled through the South with Charlie Barnet in 1933, including talking his way into playing "The Carnival of Venice" with the New Orleans Symphony and working as a pilot in Texas, probably smuggling illegal goods out of Mexico. In Los Angeles, Purvis wrote for the George Stoll Orchestra and did some arranging for Warner Brothers (composing "Legends of Haiti" for a 110-piece orchestra) before working as a chef in San Francisco.

In 1935 Purvis returned to New York, made his final recordings with pianist Frank Froeba, played for a couple of weeks with Joe Haymes' orchestra, and then dropped out of sight. He probably worked as a ship's cook on a freighter for a period. While employed as a cook in Texas in June 1937, he was sent to prison for his involvement in a robbery in El Paso. In jail, Purvis directed and played piano with the prison band (the Rhythmic Swingsters), broadcasting on radio station WBAP regularly in 1938. Purvis was granted a conditional pardon in August 1940 but soon violated it and spent six more years in prison, until being released on September 30, 1946.

Jack Purvis spent the rest of his life outside of music, as a pilot (in Florida), a carpenter, and a radio repairman in San Francisco. He reportedly committed suicide in 1962. However, a man who looked like Jack Purvis showed up at a gig by cornetist Jim Goodwin, and they had long discussions about his life on two occasions. It was 1968!

CHELSEA QUEALEY

b. 1905, Hartford, CT, d. May 6, 1950, Las Vegas, NV

Chelsea Quealey was a versatile if underrated trumpeter who was a valuable part of many record dates and a fine melodic soloist. He first played saxophone but switched to trumpet before he became a professional. Quealey worked with Jan Garber (1925) and the California Ramblers (1926–27), recording with both groups plus six bands that were offshoots of the Ramblers: Five Birmingham Babies, the Vagabonds, the Varsity Eight, the University Six, the Goofus Five, and the Little Ramblers. In addition, Quealey recorded with the Arkansas Travelers, Arnold Brilhart, the Broadway Bellhops, Fred Rich, and Ted Wallace during 1926–27.

Quealey left the United States to sail to England in December 1927, working overseas for 18 months, including with Fred Elizalde's band. After he became ill in June 1929, Quealey returned home. He soon recovered and played with Don Voorhees and the California Ramblers again, having brief stints with Paul Whiteman and Ben Pollack. After the classic jazz era ended, Quealey worked with Mezz Mezzrow (1934), Isham Jones (1935–36), Joe Marsala, Frankie Trumbauer (1937), and Bob Zurke's big band (1939–40). Chelsea Quealey played Dixieland in New York (mostly at Nick's) in the 1940s and spent his last four years working in California and Las Vegas before passing away from heart trouble at the age of 45.

MA RAINEY
b. Apr. 26, 1886, Columbus, GA, d. Dec. 22, 1939, Rome, GA

One of the pioneer classic blues singers, Ma Rainey (who was born Gertrude Pridgett) can be somewhat inaccessible to today's listeners. Unlike her protégé, Bessie Smith, who was reasonably well recorded by Columbia, Rainey made all of her recordings for the primitive Paramount label; the surface noise and distant sound make the singer a bit difficult to enjoy at times, although she was one of the finest vocalists of the era.

Rainey (who would be known as "The Mother of the Blues") appeared in the show *A Bunch of Blackberries* in Columbus, Georgia, when she was 12, in 1898. She married William "Pa" Rainey in 1904, and they toured as "Rainey and Rainey—Assassinators of the Blues," performing with the Rabbit Foot Minstrels and Tolliver's Circus. By 1912, Rainey was a major name in the South. She starred with the Moses Stock Co., a revue that included the young Bessie Smith.

After the successes of Mamie Smith and Bessie Smith, Ma Rainey finally was given a chance to record, cutting 110 selections (counting alternate takes) during 1923–28, including "See See Rider" (which she helped make into a standard), "Ma Rainey's Black Bottom," "Dead Drunk Blues," "Blues the World Forgot," and "Titanic Man Blues." Her backup groups ranged from Lovie Austin's Blues Serenaders, all-stars from Fletcher Henderson's orchestra, and a band with Louis Armstrong to Rainey's Tub Jug Washboard Band, Blind Blake, and the duet of guitarist Tampa Red and pianist Georgia Tom Dorsey. Unlike Bessie Smith and Ethel Waters, Rainey stuck to the blues throughout her career, even after it went out of style. She headed her own tent show in the 1920s (featuring her Georgia Jazz Band) and was active until 1933, when, after the death of her sister and her mother, Ma Rainey retired.

7 Vol. 1, 1923–1924/Dec. 1923-Aug. 1924/Document 5581
8 Vol. 2, 1924–1925/Oct. 15, 1924–Aug. 1925/Document 5582
7 Vol. 3, 1925–1926/Jan. 1926–Aug. 1926/Document 5583
8 Vol. 4, 1926–1927/Dec. 1926–Dec. 1927/Document 5584
9 Vol. 5, 1928/June 1928–Dec. 1928/Document 5156

The European Document label has made available the complete Ma Rainey on five CDs (including all the alternate takes). The surface noise can sometimes make these performances rather forbidding. *Vol. 1* mostly features accompaniment from Lovie Austin's Blues Serenaders (with Tommy Ladnier and Jimmy O'Bryant), though there are also a couple of songs in which Rainey is backed just by the Pruitt Twins (siblings playing banjo and guitar). Although no major hits resulted (best known is "Ma Rainey's Mystery Record"), Paramount was inspired to keep on recording "The Mother of the

Blues." *Vol. 2* is quite notable, for it has Rainey's one session with Louis Armstrong, which resulted in "See See Rider Blues," "Jelly Bean Blues," and "Countin' the Blues." Other selections find Rainey joined by Fletcher Henderson sidemen, Austin's Blues Serenaders ("Cell Bound Blues"), various obscure players, or her regularly working group, the Georgia Band (with Lil Henderson on piano).

On *Vol. 3*, Ma Rainey performs such numbers as "Slave to the Blues," "Titanic Man Blues," "Stack O'Lee Blues," "Down in the Basement," and "Trust No Man." She is joined by three different bands, her working group plus ensembles with such notables as Joe Smith, Charlie Green, Buster Bailey, Coleman Hawkins, Albert Wynn, and Jimmy Blythe. *Vol. 4* sticks mostly to 1927 and has Rainey assisted by Blind Blake ("Morning Hour Blues"), Jimmy Blythe, Kid Ory, and Claude Hopkins, among others. Highlights include "Weepin' Woman Blues," "Don't Fish in My Sea," "Blues the World Forgot," "New Bo-Weevil Blues," and "Ma Rainey's Black Bottom."

Ma Rainey was heard at her best in her 1928 sessions, making it rather ironic that these were her final recordings. Most of the selections match her in a relatively intimate setting with pianist Georgia Tom Dorsey and guitarist Tampa Red, and listeners can really hear her artistry on "Hear Me Talking to You," "Victim of the Blues," "Blame It On the Blues," and "Tough Luck Blues." Her last two sessions feature her dueting with banjoist-singer Papa Charlie Jackson.

8 **Ma Rainey/Oct. 15, 1924-Sept. 1928/Milestone 47021**
For listeners who do not have to have everything Ma Rainey recorded, this excellent sampler should suffice. The 23 selections, programmed in chronological order, focus mostly on Rainey's later sessions (although her date with Louis Armstrong is of course included) and her best-known material. A fine introduction to the music of this poorly recorded but powerful blues pioneer.

BILL RANK

b. June 8, 1904, Lafayette, IN, d. May 20, 1979, Cincinnati, OH

A solid trombonist capable of playing excellent solos, Bill Rank is best remembered for his association with Bix Beiderbecke in several groups. Rank debuted in 1921 with Collins' Jazz Band. After playing in Indianapolis with Tade Dolan's Singing Orchestra, Rank was a member of Jean Goldkette's orchestra (1923–27) and the short-lived Adrian Rollini band. When Rollini's group broke up, Rank freelanced for a few months (including with Sam Lanin, Roger Wolfe Kahn, and Nat Shilkret) before joining Paul Whiteman's orchestra for a decade (December 1927–1938). The trombonist was on many important recordings in the 1920s, including all but one session led by Frank Trumbauer during 1927–31, the Bix and His Gang dates (1927), and record sessions with the Broadway Bellhops (1927), Joe Herlihy (1927), Eddie Lang, the Mason-Dixon Orchestra, and Joe Venuti, the last three in 1929.

After leaving Whiteman, Rank worked for four years in Hollywood studio orchestras (recording "Frenesi" with Artie Shaw), led a band in Cincinnati, and had a day job selling insurance. Bill Rank's last decade was more musically active, with him appearing at trad jazz festivals and Bix tribute concerts.

ANDY RAZAF

b. Dec. 16, 1895, Washington, DC, d. Feb. 3, 1973, Hollywood, CA

Born Andreamenentania Paul Razafinkeriefo (!), Andy Razaf (a descendant of the royal family of Madagascar) was one of the finest lyricists of the classic jazz era. He recorded as a singer now and then (including with Fats Waller, Fletcher Henderson, James P. Johnson, and Luis Russell) but was most significant for the music that he wrote for revues (including *Keep Shufflin'*, *Hot Chocolates*, and Lew Leslie's *Blackbirds of 1930*) and for his collaborations with Fats Waller, Don Redman, James P. Johnson, and Eubie Blake. Among Andy Razaf's lyrics are "Honeysuckle Rose," "Ain't Misbehavin'," "Keepin' Out of Mischief Now," "Black and Blue," "Stompin' at the Savoy," "Christopher Columbus," "The Joint Is Jumpin'," "Reefer Man," "That's What I Like About the South" (a hit for Phil Harris), and "Knock Me a Kiss."

DON REDMAN

b. July 29, 1900, Piedmont, WV, d. Nov. 30, 1964, New York, NY

One of jazz's first major arrangers (along with Jelly Roll Morton), Don Redman was largely responsible for the division of larger ensembles into separate trumpet, trombone, and reed sections. Redman was also a decent altoist and clarinetist, a friendly vocalist whose lyrics were often philosophical (he generally talked as much as he sang), and a significant bandleader. A musical prodigy, Redman began playing trumpet when he was three but soon shifted to reed instruments, learning clarinet, all of the saxophones, and oboe by the time he was 12. He studied music at Storer's College (graduating at 20) and the Chicago and Boston conservatories. Redman arrived in New York in 1922, working with Billy Paige's Broadway Syncopators.

Redman began recording with Fletcher Henderson (on alto, clarinet, and even oboe) in 1923, becoming an official member of Henderson's orchestra the following year. He was Henderson's top arranger during 1923–27, even if his charts have sometimes been mistakenly attributed to the leader. Redman's early arrangements, although advanced and futuristic, were often a bit awkward, especially rhythmically. However, after Louis Armstrong joined Henderson's big band in the fall of 1924, Redman learned from Satch's phrasing, and his arrangements began to swing ("Sugar Foot Stomp" and "The Stampede" are classics), setting the pace for jazz and inspiring the young Duke Ellington. In addition, Redman took one of the earliest scat vo-

cals on "My Papa Doesn't Two Time" (predating Armstrong) and contributed occasional clarinet and alto solos. He also appeared on sessions backing such blues singers as Bessie Smith, Ma Rainey, and Ethel Waters.

Redman was lured away from Henderson's orchestra in mid-1927 when he was offered the position of musical director of McKinney's Cotton Pickers. He led, arranged, played, and sang with the band during its best years. Redman also recorded with Louis Armstrong's Savoy Ballroom Five (1928) and the Chocolate Dandies, and composed "Cherry" and "Gee Baby, Ain't I Good to You." In mid-1931, Redman left the Cotton Pickers (which after his departure quickly went into a permanent decline) to lead his own big band. The Don Redman Orchestra, which ironically did not catch on with the general public during the swing era (even though its leader was one of the founders of swing), lasted until January 1940.

Redman worked as a freelance arranger after his big band broke up (arranging a hit version of "Deep Purple" for Jimmy Dorsey) and led the first American big band to visit Europe (1946–47) after World War II. Don Redman's later years were quite anticlimactic, working as the musical director for singer Pearl Bailey in the 1950s and making a few final recordings in 1958–59 on alto, soprano, and piano.

⑨ 1931–1933/Sept. 24, 1931-Feb. 2, 1933/Classics 543
The early Don Redman Orchestra recordings feature Sidney DeParis, trombonists Claude Jones and Benny Morton, clarinetist Edward Inge, tenor saxophonist Robert Carroll, and (on the first two sessions) Henry "Red" Allen. Highlights include "Shakin' the African," "Nagasaki," "How'm I Doin'," a two-part version of "Doin' the New Lowdown" (with guests Cab Calloway, the Mills Brothers, and tap dancer Bill "Bojangles" Robinson), and Redman's mysterioso theme, "Chant of the Weed." Considering how strong the music is throughout this enjoyable CD, the vocal-dominated perfor-

mances on its follow-up, *1933–1936* (Classics 553), are quite disappointing, making one wonder why Don Redman did not have a more logical career during the swing era.

REUBEN "RIVER" REEVES

b. Oct. 25, 1905, Evansville, IN, d. Sept. 1975, New York, NY

Reuben Reeves, like Jabbo Smith, had a single great year on records before sinking into obscurity. Reeves began on piano, switching to trumpet in high school. He moved to New York in February 1924 to study dentistry but soon decided to be a musician instead and relocated to Chicago. Reeves worked with Erskine Tate's orchestra (1925–28) and Dave Peyton, studied at the American Conservatory (earning a master's degree), taught music at a high school during the day, and formed a band that performed at the Regal Theatre.

Record producer Mayo Williams signed Reeves to the Vocalion label in the hope that he could duplicate the sales of Louis Armstrong's Hot Five and Hot Seven dates; for the same reason Brunswick signed up Jabbo Smith and Victor documented Red Allen. Other than two numbers made with Fess Williams' Joy Boys the previous year, Reeves' 15 selections for Vocalion in 1929 were his debut on record. The wild, exciting, and sometimes reckless performances (which also included Omer Simeon, Darnell Howard, Blanche Calloway, and Reuben's older brother, trombonist Gerald Reeves) were easily the trumpeter's finest moments on record.

Unfortunately Reeves' career went downhill from there. He worked with pianist Jerome Carrington, was a member of Cab Calloway's orchestra (1931–32), and in 1933 organized a 12-piece swing orchestra, the River Boys. Their only record date just barely hints at Reeves' fiery playing. The trumpeter freelanced in New York in the late 1930s, played trumpet with the 369th Infantry Band while in the National Guard, and served in the Pacific during World War II. Reuben "River" Reeves (who was

never rediscovered) worked with Harry Dial's Blusicians on a part-time basis during 1946–55 but ended up his life as a bank guard, having reached the peak of his career before his 24th birthday.

9 **Reuben Reeves and Omer Simeon/May 22, 1929–Dec. 14, 1933/RST 1516**

All 15 recordings by Reuben "River" Reeves' River Boys are reissued on this valuable CD, including "River Blues," "Papa 'Skag' Stomp," and "Bugle Call Blues"; the music is consistently exciting. Also on the disc are the four very musical but slightly disappointing selections from Reeves' 1933 big band, Omer Simeon's only dates as a leader during the era (two titles in a small group with Earl Hines), and the four selections from the Dixie Rhythm Kings, a 1929 septet with Simeon and both Shirley Clay and George Mitchell on cornets. Taken as a whole, this 25-song CD gives listeners a very healthy chunk of 1929 Chicago jazz.

HARRY RESER

b. Jan. 17, 1896, Piqua, OH, d. Sept. 27, 1965, New York, NY

The finest banjo player of the 1920s, Harry Reser was a virtuoso who played novelty ragtime features in addition to leading the Clicquot Club Eskimos. Reser began playing guitar when he was eight, had piano, violin, and cello lessons, and around 1916 settled on the banjo. After freelancing in Ohio and upstate New York, in December 1920 he arrived in New York City, where he worked for Nathan Glantz, Bennie Krueger, Sam Lanin, and Ben Selvin. Reser debuted on records with Milo Rega's Dance Orchestra in October 1921 and began to record regularly, both as a sideman and as a leader (starting in October 1922 as the head of the Okeh Syncopators). After visiting England with Paul Whiteman's orchestra in 1923, Reser (who recorded with Bessie Smith in 1924) began working on radio.

On December 3, 1925, the Clicquot Club Eskimos debuted on radio. During the next five years,

Reser recorded an enormous number of records as a bandleader. His group, usually consisting of either Earl Oliver or Tommy Gott on trumpet, trombonist Sammy Lewis, the reeds of Larry Abbott and Norman Yorke, pianist Bill Wirges, Jimmy Johnston on bass sax, and drummer Tom Stacks, was a major fixture on the radio, featuring the cheerfully odd vocals of Stacks along with lots of novelty effects and comedy. The Clicquot Club Eskimos was the main title of the ensemble (helping to sell the Clicquot Club soft drinks for a decade, with the band often dressed in Eskimo suits!), which also recorded under a bewildering assortment of names, including the Blue Kittens, the Bostonians, the Campus Boys, the Four Minstrels, the High Hatters, the Jazz Pilots, the Parlophone Syncopators, the Plantation Players, the Rounders, the Seven Little Polar Bears, the Seven Rag Pickers, the Seven Wildmen, the Six Hayseeds, the Six Jumping Jacks, and the Victorian Syncopators.

Of greater value are Reser's novelty ragtime showcases (most of which have not been reissued on CD). His playing is so remarkable on these complex works (starting with his 1922 version of Zez Confrey's "Kitten on the Keys" and, including a dozen of his own pieces) that he makes most banjoists (even today) sound quite primitive and limited in comparison.

After the early 1930s, Harry Reser worked primarily as a studio musician and in Broadway pit bands for the remainder of his life.

5 The Six Jumping Jacks, Vol. 1/Jan. 22, 1926-Nov. 10, 1926/ The Old Masters 120

6 The Six Jumping Jacks, Vol. 2/Dec. 24, 1926 – Feb. 28, 1928/ The Old Masters 128

A sampling of the music that Harry Reser and his band recorded as the Six Jumping Jacks is on these two CDs, programmed in chronological order. There is plenty of cornball humor throughout the performances, but some of the good-natured jokes and sound effects are so broad that listeners have to chuckle despite their dated nature. The musi-cianship is excellent and there are some hot solos in nearly every performance, but the emphasis is usually on Tom Stacks' vocals and the band's brand of humor. *Vol. 1* includes such numbers as "The Wind Blew Through His Whiskers," "She Was Just a Sailor's Sweetheart," "Masculine Women, Feminine Men," "I'm Just Wild About Animal Crackers," and "When You Dunk a Doughnut." *Vol. 2* has such oddities as "Cock-a-Doodle, I'm Off My Noodle," "The Coat and Pants Do All the Work," "You'll Never Get Nowhere Holding Hands" (which is quite funny), "I'm Gonna Dance Wit the Guy Wot Brung Me," and "Get 'Em in a Rumble Seat."

LPS TO SEARCH FOR

Banjo Crackerjack (Yazoo 1048) is a remarkable album, consisting of 14 showcases for Harry Reser's banjo, ten of which are his pieces. On such numbers as "Lollypops," "The Cat and the Dog," "Flapperrette," "Crackerjack," and "Kitten on the Keys," Reser shows why he was one of the finest banjo virtuosos of all time. This music certainly deserves to be on CD.

Duplicating a total of only one song from the two CDs from The Old Masters, *Banjo Virtuoso* (Broadway Intermission 122), *Banjo Virtuoso Vol. 2* (Broadway Intermission 152), and *Harry Reser's Novelty Groups* (Take Two 202) include numerous performances by the Clicquot Club Eskimos and a variety of Reser's other recording bands, with the emphasis as usual on humor and novelties. The Broadway Intermission LPs are particularly generous, having ten selections per side.

RHYTHM BOYS

Singers Bing Crosby and Al Rinker worked together early in their careers in Washington State as a duo (with Rinker on piano and Crosby on drums) and with a full band. While staying in Los Angeles at the home of Rinker's sister, Mildred Bailey, they were introduced to Paul Whiteman by Bailey and were hired. After the duo quickly flopped, White-man teamed them with singer-pianist Harry Barris, who was also a skilled songwriter. As the Rhythm Boys, the trio became a popular attraction with Whiteman's orchestra (1927–30), recording as a separate unit, while backed by Whiteman's big band and sometimes as part of a contingent of singers that also included Jack Fulton, Austin "Skin" Young, and Charles Gaylord. Among the Rhythm Boys' better recordings were "I'm Coming Virginia," "Mississippi Mud," "Out of Town Gal," "and "Happy Feet." Their cheerful interplay and humorous scatting, along with Barris' way of saying a drawn-out "pahh" at the end of their performances gave them their own musical identity. In addition, during this period Crosby had an occasional solo number.

The Rhythm Boys performed "Mississippi Mud" in the 1930 Whiteman film *The King of Jazz.* Shortly after the movie, the Rhythm Boys (who often caused Whiteman a lot of grief with their carousing) went out on their own, performing as an added attraction with Gus Arnheim's orchestra for about a year. But by then Bing Crosby was on his way to becoming America's most famous singer, and the Rhythm Boys broke up. Al Rinker ended up working behind the scenes, while Harry Barris (who should have become a major star himself) wrote songs (including "I Surrender Dear") and had tantalizingly brief (and usually unbilled) cameos in quite a few films.

FRED RICH
b. Jan. 31, 1898, Warsaw, Poland, d. Sept. 8, 1956

Fred Rich was a significant bandleader in the 1920s. Born in Poland, he settled with his family in New York City, taking up the piano. By 1915 he was accompanying silent pictures at a movie theater, and he later studied at the Damrosch Conservatory of Music. During 1922–28, Rich led his orchestra at the Astor Hotel in New York and appeared often on the radio, touring Europe a few times and re-

cording extensively starting in 1925. As musical director for the CBS network during 1928–38, Rich was a major force on radio and records. Although most of his records were more dance band-oriented than jazz, along the way Joe Venuti, Eddie Lang, Jimmy Dorsey, Tommy Dorsey, Bunny Berigan, and Benny Goodman took quite a few jazz solos.

In later years Fred Rich, who led bands until 1945, was the musical director for several radio stations and worked for United Artists (1942–52).

7 Volume One/Apr. 12, 1929-Nov. 19, 1930/The Old Masters 101

With the rise in popularity of danceable jazz-oriented orchestras and the beginning of the Depression, Fred Rich's brand of big band music appeared on hundreds of records. Some of his best recordings from 1929–30 are on this CD, which often has vocals by the Rollickers, Paul Small, or Smith Ballew. The Dorsey Brothers and Venuti and Lang (featured on "I Got Rhythm") are among the (mostly unidentified) musicians heard in the large ensembles. The performances are essentially jazz-flavored dance music, perfect for the audiences of the era and still quite listenable today.

JOSEPH ROBECHAUX
b. Mar. 8, 1900, New Orleans, LA, d. Jan. 17, 1965, New Orleans, LA

Pianist Joseph Robechaux was the nephew of John Robechaux, a notable New Orleans bandleader from the early years of the 20th century. The younger Robichaux began playing professionally in 1917, making his first trip up North to play with trumpeter Tig Chambers in Chicago during the summer of 1918. Back in New Orleans, the pianist worked with Oscar Celestin, William Ridgley, Davey Jones, Lee Collins, the Black Eagle Band, and Kid Rena during the 1920s, recording with the Jones-Collins Astoria Hot Eight and singer Christina Gray in 1929.

In 1931 Robechaux formed the New Orleans

Rhythm Boys, a septet that two years later traveled to New York. Union restrictions prevented the group from accepting regular work, but they did have five notable recording sessions during a four-day period in August 1933, 22 selections that fully show off the exciting high-powered band.

Joseph Robechaux continued leading the New Orleans Rhythm Boys throughout the 1930s, expanding to 14-pieces before disbanding in 1939. In later years he worked as part of the New Orleans revival, most notably with Lizzie Miles and George Lewis (1957–64).

LPS TO SEARCH FOR

Joe Robichaux and His New Orleans Boys (Folklyric 9032) has 16 of the band's best performances from 1933, including "Forty-Second Street," "King Kong Stomp," "I Would Do Anything for You," and "The Riff." The group may not have featured any major names, but it sure packed a great deal of power and momentum, sounding like a much larger band. More difficult to locate will be the two-LP *The Complete Joseph Robichaux* (Blu-Disc 1007/1008), which contains all 22 selections, two alternate takes, Robichaux's two numbers with singer Christina Gray from 1929, and five performances by boogie-woogie pianist Albert Ammons' Rhythm Kings from 1936.

ELZADIE ROBINSON

Virtually nothing is known of classic blues singer Elzadie Robinson's life other than her recordings, not even when or where she was born and died. During 1926–29, Robinson recorded 39 performances in all for Paramount (35 songs plus four alternate takes). Pianist Will Ezell was her accompanist on the majority of the selections, although there were also three songs (plus an alternate) cut with Johnny Dodds and Blind Blake. Elzadie Robinson (who was probably born in the South and based during her prime years in Chicago) had a strong voice and, although not on the level of the major singers, she made some fine recordings.

7 Vol. 1/Sept. 1926-May 1928/Document 5248
7 Vol. 2/Mar. 1924–May 1929/Document 5249

All of Elzadie Robinson's recordings are on these two CDs. *Vol. 1*, which has the first 22 selections, includes such numbers as "2:16 Blues," "Troubled with the Blues," "The Santa Claus Crave," and "Elzadie's Policy Blues." Sidemen include Ezell, Richard M. Jones, Johnny St. Cyr, Dodds, Blake, and Jimmy Bertrand (on xylophone). *Vol. 2*, which has Robinson accompanied by either Ezell or (on two songs) Tiny Parham, is at the same level with the highlights, including "Wicked Daddy," "Need My Lovin', Need My Daddy," and "Unsatisfied Blues." Wrapping up the CD are six alternate takes from the early blues singer Lottie Beaman that date from 1924 and are fine if a bit out of place.

FRED ROBINSON

b. Feb. 20, 1901, Memphis, TN, d. Apr. 11, 1984, New York, NY

Trombonist Fred Robinson is remembered for recording with Louis Armstrong's Savoy Ballroom Five in 1928. Early on he played in his native Memphis and attended Dana's Musical Institute in Warren, Ohio. In 1927 Robinson moved to Chicago, where he worked regularly with Carroll Dickerson's orchestra at the Savoy for two years. Although his role was relatively minor on the Armstrong records (particularly compared to Kid Ory's position during 1925–27), Robinson mostly fared well during his short solos and in support behind Satch and Earl Hines.

Robinson traveled to New York with Armstrong and Dickerson in May 1929, and he worked regularly during the next 25 years. His associations included Edgar Hayes (1929–30), Marion Hardy's Alabamians (1931), Don Redman (1931–33), Charlie Turner's Arcadians, Fats Waller (1937), Benny Carter, Fletcher Henderson (1938–39 and 1941), Andy Kirk (1939–40), George James (1943), Cab Calloway (1945), Sy Oliver (1946–50), and Noble Sissle (1950–51). Fred Robinson, who recorded with Jelly Roll Morton in 1939 but was considered pretty obscure after the 1920s, became a part-time player in 1954, having a day job in the New York subway system while still playing occasionally into the 1960s.

IKEY ROBINSON

b. July 28, 1904, Dublin, VA, d. Oct. 25, 1990, Chicago, IL

A talented banjoist-singer who also played guitar and occasionally clarinet and piano, Ikey Robinson (who fit comfortably into both the jazz and blues worlds) should have been a star. He started out working as a barber but always played music on the side, having a part-time band starting in 1918. In 1922 Robinson left the barbering behind, performing in his native Virginia with Harry Watkins' orchestra (1922–24) and Bud Jenkins' Virginia Ravens (1924–26). He moved to Chicago in 1926, working with the Alabamians, Jelly Roll Morton, and Clarence Moore. Robinson recorded with Sammy Stewart's Ten Knights of Syncopation (1928), Jabbo Smith (1929), and Clarence Williams during this period, leading sessions of his own in 1929, 1931, 1933, and 1935. While with Sammy Stewart in 1930, Robinson relocated to New York. He performed with Wilbur Sweatman and Noble Sissle (1931) and also as a leader.

Having failed to make a dent in the Big Apple, Robinson returned to Chicago in 1934, leading groups for decades but rarely recording after 1937. Ikey Robinson worked with Franz Jackson's Original Jazz All Stars in the 1960s, had opportunities to tour Europe, and reunited late in life with Jabbo Smith.

9 "Banjo" Ikey Robinson/Jan. 4, 1929-May 19, 1937/RST 1508
Every selection that Ikey Robinson ever led (except for two songs featuring Half Pint Jaxon's vocals) are on this single CD from the Austrian RST label. There is quite a bit of variety as Robinson is heard performing with a pair of good-time jazz/blues

groups (the Hokum Trio and the Pods of Pepper), heading a quintet that includes Jabbo Smith and Omer Simeon, singing the blues, accompanying vocalist Charlie Slocum, and leading the swing-oriented Windy City Five, playing clarinet on "Swing It." Enjoyable and mostly formerly rare music.

ADRIAN ROLLINI

b. June 28, 1904, New York, NY, d. May 15, 1956, Homestead, FL

A very talented and versatile musician, Adrian Rollini is still considered the king of the bass saxophone. The older brother of Arthur Rollini (who played tenor with Benny Goodman's orchestra in the mid-1930s), Rollini was a child prodigy on piano, playing a Chopin concert when he was four. That same year he led a band in New York, playing piano and xylophone. In 1922 (when he was 18) Rollini joined the California Ramblers, bought a bass sax, and mastered it within a week. He recorded frequently in the 1920s, not just on bass sax but on "hot fountain pen" (a miniature clarinet with a saxophone mouthpiece), the goofus (a tiny saxophone keyboard), vibes, and miscellaneous other instruments. Rollini starred on many records by the California Ramblers, the Little Ramblers, and the Goofus Five, also being prominent on sessions by Frankie Trumbauer, Red Nichols, and Joe Venuti. Harry Carney always cited him as one of his main influences.

Rollini led an unrecorded all-star band in 1927 for a couple of months that included the core of Jean Goldkette's recently disbanded orchestra (including Trumbauer and Bix Beiderbecke), but it did not last and Paul Whiteman ended up getting most of the musicians. Rollini spent December 1927–December 1929 in Europe (mostly London), where he worked with Fred Elizalde and other local bands. When he returned to the United States, he performed with Bert Lown's orchestra (1930–31) and become a studio musician for a few years. Surprisingly he did not lead any record dates in the 1920s, but he did have the opportunity to head 14 sessions of his own during 1933–35, ranging from so-so dance dates to more freewheeling jazz; very little has thus far been reissued on CD.

During that period (which also included his running of the club Adrian's Tap Room during 1934–36), Rollini gradually shifted his focus from playing bass sax to vibes, recording on the bass sax for the last time in early 1938. From then on, Adrian Rollini primarily led a vibes-guitar-bass trio, working in New York, Chicago, and finally (after the early 1950s) Florida.

LPS TO SEARCH FOR

Other than one of his dates that has been reissued under Benny Goodman's name, the sessions led by Adrian Rollini are pretty scarce. *1933–34* (Sunbeam 134) has three complete dates plus one song from another session; sidemen include Benny Goodman, Bunny Berigan, Arthur Rollini, and Dick McDonough, although the vocals of Herb Weil, Clay Bryson, Howard Phillips, Jane Vance, and Joey Nash dominate. *Original 1938–1940 Recordings* (Tax 8036) shows how Rollini ended up, as a melodic vibraphonist with a trio. Some of the selections have him playing vibes and xylophone in a quintet that also includes cornetist Bobby Hackett and drummer Buddy Rich. But the bass sax is missed.

LUIS RUSSELL

b. Aug. 6, 1902, Careening Cay, Panama, d. Dec. 11, 1963, New York, NY

Luis Russell led one of the finest big bands of 1929–31. Russell studied guitar, violin, organ, and piano in his native Panama, settling on piano. He first worked as a professional musician when he accompanied silent films in 1917. In 1919 Russell won $3,000 in a lottery, money he used to move with his mother and sister to New Orleans. For the next few years, Russell worked with a variety of bands in New Orleans, including one led by Albert Nicholas (1923). When the clarinetist left town the following year, Russell took over leadership of the group. Later in 1924, Russell moved to Chicago to play with Doc Cook. He soon joined King Oliver's band for two years, touring, recording and relocating to New York in 1927 with the cornetist. In 1926, while still in Chicago, Russell led two recording sessions, one apiece by his Hot Six and his Heebie Jeebie Stompers, with such sidemen as George Mitchell, Kid Ory, Albert Nicholas, Barney Bigard (during the second session Bigard took his finest tenor sax solos), Johnny St. Cyr, Bob Shoffner (heard at his early peak), Preston Jackson, and Darnell Howard.

In the summer of 1927, Russell joined George Howe's band, becoming its leader by October and playing at the Nest Club for a year before moving his group's home base to the Saratoga Club. After recording three numbers by his Burning Eight in early 1929 (with Louis Metcalf and the nucleus of his future group), Russell slightly changed his personnel and ended up with a classic jazz band. The Luis Russell Orchestra consisted of four major soloists (Henry "Red" Allen, J.C. Higginbotham, Albert Nicholas, and Charlie Holmes), a pair of underfeatured players (Bill Coleman and tenor saxophonist Teddy Hill), and one of the finest rhythm sections in jazz (with guitarist Will Johnson, Pops Foster, and Paul Barbarin). Russell was not a major soloist himself, but he was a talented arranger whose charts set off the soloists quite well. The band recorded 18 songs during 1929–30, including such gems as "Feelin' the Spirit" "Jersey Lightning," "Saratoga Shout," and "Louisiana Swing." In addition, the group accompanied Louis Armstrong for a few months (including appearing on some of Satch's records) and recorded as a smaller combo on dates headed by Red Allen, J.C. Higginbotham, Victoria Spivey, Sweet Pease Spivey, and (without Russell) Jelly Roll Morton.

After 1931, there would be only one further record date (in 1934 with Rex Stewart featured on cornet), and the group was in decline as more successful orchestras lured away its top members. In 1935, just as the swing era got going, the Luis Russell Orchestra became the backup band for Louis Armstrong, working steadily but anonymously behind the star. While it would be a good forum for J.C. Higginbotham, most of the other players (including Russell, who contributed some arrangements) were underutilized. In 1940 most of the group was let go, but Russell continued working with Satch until 1943. In the mid-1940s he led a new big band that was swing oriented, but it was unsuccessful and its recordings are not that impressive. Luis Russell permanently dropped out of jazz in 1948. He spent his later years running a candy and gift store, working as a chauffeur, and teaching music, giving a classical piano recital in 1959.

9 1926–1929/Mar. 10, 1926-Dec. 17, 1929/Classics 558
8 1930–1934/Jan. 24, 1930–Aug. 8, 1934/Classics 606
5 The Luis Russell Collection/Mar. 10, 1926–Aug. 8, 1934/Collector's Classics 7

The two Classics CDs have all of the recordings by the classic Luis Russell Orchestra except for five alternate takes. *1926–1929* begins with the early outings by Russell's Hot Six, his Heebie Jeebie Stompers, and his Burning Eight. Also included are two numbers in which Russell and a contingent from his early band accompany singer Ada Brown, two selections by the Jungle Town Stompers (featuring Louis Metcalf and Charlie Holmes), and Victoria Spivey's October 1, 1929, session with the Russell band. Best are the seven numbers (including "Feelin' the Spirit," "Jersey Lightning," and "Broadway Rhythm") from the 1929 Russell Orchestra. *1930–1934* finishes up this group's recorded legacy (including "Saratoga Shout," "Louisiana Swing," and "Panama") plus the two selections from J.C. Higginbotham's Six Hicks (the same basic group) and the six numbers from the 1934 edition of the band.

The Collector's Classics disc, which was formerly a gap filler, is unnecessary now that the Classics CDs are out, offering two alternate takes but otherwise just duplicating the sessions from 1926 and 1934 plus a 1929 date and a few of the weaker cuts from 1930–31.

PEE WEE RUSSELL
b. Mar. 27, 1906, St. Louis, MO, d. Feb. 15, 1969, Alexandria, VA

One of the most original and unpredictable of all clarinetists, Charles "Pee Wee" Russell had a long career, getting his start in the 1920s. Russell grew up in St. Louis and Muskogee, Oklahoma. He took lessons on violin, piano, and drums before switching to clarinet, inspired originally by Yellow Nunez. Russell worked in the Midwest, played on riverboats (as early as 1920), toured with tent shows, and worked with Peck Kelley's Bad Boys in Texas in 1924. He made his recording debut with Herbert Berger in St. Louis when he was 18 (November 1924) and in late 1925 was in Frank Trumbauer's band, becoming good friends and drinking buddies with Bix Beiderbecke. Russell also worked with Beiderbecke and Trumbauer with Jean Goldkette's orchestra in the summer of 1926, although he left before that ensemble recorded.

Pee Wee Russell first gained recognition after he went to New York in 1927 and recorded with Red Nichols (1927–29), including "Ida, Sweet as Apple Cider." Although sharing some similarities at the time with Frankie Teschemacher, Russell was already becoming an original player. Among his freelance recordings of 1927–29 were dates with the Charleston Chasers, Miff Mole, the Red Heads, Frankie Trumbauer (a session with Beiderbecke), Irving Brodsky, the Louisiana Rhythm Kings, the Hotsy-Totsy Gang, the Whoopee Makers, and the Mound City Blue Blowers. During 1931–33 there were sessions with Jack Teagarden, Jack Bland, Adrian Rollini, and Russell's first encounter with Eddie Condon.

On April 18,1932, Russell was a star with Henry "Red" Allen on one of the hottest of all recording sessions, a Billy Banks date that resulted in "Oh, Peter," "Bugle Call Rag," and "Margie." Russell was also featured on two other heated dates by vocalist Banks. The clarinetist primarily freelanced during the early years of the Depression and did studio work. Things began to look up when Russell became a member of Louis Prima's popular 52nd Street Band (1935–37), a job that he spoke fondly of years later. In 1938 he became closely associated with Eddie Condon, with whom he would play on and off for 30 years. Pee Wee Russell became a popular figure on the trad jazz circuit for decades despite being too eccentric and original a soloist to fit all that comfortably into conventional Dixieland settings.

CYRUS ST. CLAIR

b. 1890, Cambridge, MD, d. 1955, New York, NY

An enthusiastic tuba player, Cyrus St. Clair always made his presence felt. His father and uncle played tuba and, although he started on cornet, St. Clair eventually played the bass horn too. He moved to New York in 1925 (when he was already 35), working at first with Wilbur DeParis and Bobby Lee's Cotton Pickers. St. Clair was a member of Charlie Johnson's orchestra during its most significant years (1925–29). He recorded with Johnson and the Little Chocolate Dandies (1929), but most significant was his association with Clarence Williams (1926–37). In addition to appearing on scores of recordings released under the pianist's name, St. Clair was heard with Williams' bands on dates by Eva Taylor (1926–28), Le Roy Tibbs, King Oliver, Anna Bell, Katherine Henderson, Sara Martin, Bessie Smith (1929), the Lazy Levee Loungers (1930), and the Alabama Jug Band (1934).

St. Clair worked with Cozy Cole's Hot Cinders (1930) and freelanced in New York before retiring by the late 1930s; the tuba had long been out of favor. Cyrus St. Clair occasionally played music in

his later years (including recording with Tony Parenti and guesting on Rudi Blesh's *This Is Jazz* radio series in 1947) but mostly worked outside of music during his last 15 years, a victim of the tuba's decline in popularity.

JOHNNY ST. CYR

b. Apr. 17, 1890, New Orleans, LA, d. June 17, 1966, Los Angeles, CA

Johnny St. Cyr played banjo, guitar, and a six-string "guitar banjo" that he made himself by combining aspects of both instruments. A fine rhythm player, St. Cyr was also quite capable of taking fine single-string and chordal solos. Self-taught, he started playing guitar as a youth, working with Jules Baptiste and Manuel Gabriel in New Orleans as early as 1905. Although having a regular job as a plasterer, St. Cyr played with Freddie Keppard, the Olympia Band, Armand J. Piron, Oscar Celestin, Kid Ory (1914–16), and King Oliver. He became a full-time musician in order to work on the riverboats with Fate Marable (1917–19). St. Cyr also worked in New Orleans and St. Louis with Ed Allen's Whispering Gold Band, Charlie Creath, Amos White, and Manuel Perez.

In September 1923, St. Cyr moved to Chicago, where he played with King Oliver's Creole Jazz Band (making his recording debut on five sessions with Oliver). The banjoist-guitarist also worked now and then with Richard M. Jones, recording with Jones and the Chicago Hottentots. He was a member of Doc Cook's Dreamland Orchestra (1925–29), often doubling by working with Jimmie Noone at the Apex Club. The busy St. Cyr was on three Jelly Roll Morton record dates in 1926 (including such titles as "Black Bottom Stomp," "The Chant," and "Doctor Jazz") and made sessions backing singers Ada Brown, Lillie Delk Christian, Wilmer Davis, Chippie Hill, Hattie McDaniels, Elzadie Robinson, and Hociel Thomas. However, St. Cyr's greatest fame came about from his recording with Louis Armstrong's Hot Five and Hot Seven during 1925–27, often functioning as half of the rhythm section (along with pianist Lil Armstrong) behind Armstrong, Ory, and Johnny Dodds. He also appeared on the similar sessions of the New Orleans Bootblacks and New Orleans Wanderers plus Luis Russell's two dates from 1926.

After leaving Doc Cook in 1929, St. Cyr worked a bit in Indiana and eventually returned to New Orleans, going back to his day job as a plasterer while playing part time with local players. In the 1950s Johnny St. Cyr worked with Alphonse Picou and Paul Barbarin, moving in 1955 to Los Angeles, where he became a local fixture, performing regularly at Disneyland during 1961–66 with the ironically titled Young Men from New Orleans.

ELMER SCHOEBEL

b. Sept. 8, 1896, East St. Louis, IL, d. Dec. 14, 1970, St. Petersburg, FL

An important songwriter and bandleader, Elmer Schoebel wrote such standards as "Nobody's Sweetheart," "Farewell Blues," and "Bugle Call Rag." Schoebel started his career playing piano at silent movie houses in Illinois when he was 14. After touring with variety acts for a few years, he settled in Chicago. During 1922 Schoebel was a member of the New Orleans Rhythm Kings, with whom he recorded their first two sessions, playing piano and contributing arrangements.

In 1923 Schoebel led a band at the Midway Gardens that recorded a total of 13 selections as the Original Memphis Boys, the Chicago Blues Dance Orchestra, and the Midway Garden Orchestra. He spent 1925 playing in New York with Isham Jones but soon returned to Chicago, where he freelanced. In 1929, Schoebel led a record date that included Frank Teschemacher and drummer George Wetling, resulting in fine versions of two of his compositions: "Copenhagen" and "Prince of Wails." By the 1930s he was primarily an arranger and composer, becoming the musical arranger for Warner Brothers' New York publishing company. Elmer

Schoebel resumed playing in the 1940s (including with Conrad Janis and in 1958 with Blue Steele's Rhythm Rebels), although he did not record at all in his later years, settling in Florida and working up until his death at age 74.

ARTHUR SCHUTT

b. Nov. 21, 1902, Reading, PA, d. Jan. 28, 1965, San Francisco, CA

An intriguing pianist, Arthur Schutt frequently utilized ideas that sounded advanced in the 1920s but that by the '30s were out of vogue. He started working professionally at the age of 13, playing piano for silent movies. At 16, Schutt joined Paul Specht's orchestra, staying six years (1918–24) and recording with both the big band and the Georgians (for whom he wrote some of the arrangements). After leaving Specht, Schutt became in great demand for record dates, both as a pianist and as an arranger. He recorded with Red Nichols often during 1926–29 (including the early Five Pennies dates), and among his other more significant record dates were sessions with the Deauville Dozen (1925), Roger Wolfe Kahn (1925–29), the Red Heads, the Arkansas Travelers, the Charleston Chasers (1927–31), the Chicago Loopers (with Bix Beiderbecke), Joe Venuti, Miff Mole, Carl Fenton, the Six Hottentots, the Dorsey Brothers Orchestra (1928–31), the Wabash Dance Orchestra, Eddie Lang, the Cotton Pickers, the Louisiana Rhythm Kings, and Benny Goodman (1931 and 1934). As a leader, Schutt recorded nine novelty ragtime piano solos (during 1923, 1928–29, and 1934), all but one of which is included on the LP that he shares with Rube Bloom, *Novelty Ragtime Piano Kings* (Folkways 41). He also headed five scarce band sessions during 1929–30 that mostly feature vocals by Smith Ballew but have some spots for the Dorsey Brothers and trumpeter Leo McConville.

Although Arthur Schutt led a group briefly in the late 1930s, he worked primarily as a studio musician after 1930 and was rarely heard in jazz settings by the swing era.

BUD SCOTT

b. Jan. 11, 1890, New Orleans, LA, d. July 2, 1949, Los Angeles, CA

Bud Scott was one of the better rhythm guitarists and banjoists of the classic jazz era. Scott (who early on tripled on violin) began working in New Orleans as a young teenager, playing with John Robichaux's orchestra (1904), Buddy Bolden, and Freddie Keppard among many other groups. In January 1913 he left New Orleans as featured violinist with the Billy King Traveling Show. After moving to New York in 1915, he played in theater orchestras, usually on banjo. Scott was with Will Marion Cook's orchestra in 1921, moved back to New Orleans for a spell, and spent time in Chicago in 1923, including three months with King Oliver's Creole Jazz Band. It was Scott who contributed the famous "Oh Play That Thing" vocal to Oliver's second recording of "Dippermouth Blues."

Scott worked in California with Kid Ory and Curtis Mosby's Blue Blowers. Back in Chicago, he had a second stint with Oliver (recording with his Dixie Syncopators during 1926–27) and also played with Erskine Tate, Dave Peyton (1926–28 and 1929), Fess Williams, and Jimmie Noone's Apex Club Orchestra (1928), appearing on records with Noone, Jelly Roll Morton (1927), Johnny Dodds, and Willie Hightower. Scott spent the Depression years in the Los Angeles area, working with Leon Herriford, Mutt Carey's Jeffersonians, and his own trio. Late in life, Bud Scott (who appeared with Louis Armstrong in the 1946 film *New Orleans*) played regularly with Kid Ory's band (1944–48), until ill health forced his retirement.

CECIL SCOTT

b. Nov. 22, 1905, Springfield, OH, d. Jan. 5, 1964, New York, NY

A spirited clarinetist and tenor saxophonist who also occasionally played baritone, Cecil Scott was a fluent soloist who always sounded good-humored. Scott had a trio in high school in 1919, with his older brother, Lloyd Scott, on drums and pianist Don Frye. The group gradually expanded to become a septet by 1922 (Scott's Symphonic Syncopators), playing in the Midwest, making it to New York for the first of several times in 1924, and also working in Canada. Scott made his recording debut in 1924 with Clara Smith. In 1927 Scott's ensemble (which included Dicky Wells and pianist Don Frye) recorded three titles under Lloyd Scott's name (available on *Hot Notes*—Frog 8, with the alternate takes on *Don't You Leave Me Here*—Frog 12). In 1929, as Cecil Scott's Bright Boys (its new official name), the band cut four additional titles (included on *Thumpin' and Bumpin'*—Frog 11), including happily eccentric versions of "Lawd Lawd" and "In a Corner." The sidemen by the later date included trumpeters Bill Coleman and Frank Newton in addition to Wells, Frye, and the Scott brothers.

Cecil Scott led the Bright Boys until he was hurt in a car accident in the early 1930s. He recovered, recorded often with Clarence Williams (1930–37), and freelanced, including with Teddy Hill's NBC Orchestra (1936–37). In later years, Cecil Scott worked with Alberto Socarras' Latin band (1937–42), Hot Lips Page, Art Hodes, Henry "Chick" Morrison (1950–52), Jimmy McPartland, and Willie "the Lion" Smith, being an important part of the New York Dixieland scene.

ANDY SECREST

b. Aug. 2, 1907, Muncie, IN, d. 1977, Los Angeles, CA

Andy Secrest has a strange place in jazz history, being best known as the cornetist who was hired to fill in for an ill Bix Beiderbecke with Paul Whiteman's orchestra. Secrest started his career playing in Cincinnati with Freda Sanker's orchestra and in the Midwest with Ted Weems and Ray Miller. He joined the Jean Goldkette Orchestra in the fall of 1927, shortly after Bix Beiderbecke, Frank Trumbauer, and the other members of Goldkette's most famous big band had departed. Secrest made his recording debut with Hoagy Carmichael ("One Night in Havana") and also recorded with Goldkette.

In January 1929, Secrest was hired by Whiteman to take the place of Beiderbecke, who had suffered a mental breakdown after becoming an increasingly unreliable alcoholic. Quite a few of the orchestra's jazz-oriented arrangements had feature spots for Bix, so the 21-year-old (who had a similar sound, although without Beiderbecke's genius) took the cornetist's place, as Harry Goldfield had in 1928 taken over for Henry Busse. Even when Bix surprised everyone by returning a month later, Secrest remained with the band, just in case. Decades later, record collectors would constantly be arguing over which solos were by Beiderbecke and which by Secrest. Frankie Trumbauer's recording of "Baby, Won't You Please Come Home" really caused collectors to scratch their heads because Secrest takes a short break right before Bix has a solo chorus! Secrest's other key solos of the period were "What a Day" and "Alabamy Snow" with the Mason-Dixon Orchestra, "Nobody's Sweetheart," "Happy Feet," and "After You're Gone" with Whiteman, Eddie Lang's rendition of "March of the Hoodlums," and several numbers with Frankie Trumbauer, including "Nobody but You," "Shivery Stomp," and "Manhattan Rag."

Secrest played with Whiteman until 1932 (the year after Beiderbecke's death). He worked with Ted Weems (1933–34), moved to Hollywood, and became a studio musician, often performing as part of Victor Young's orchestra. In 1938 Secrest played for a few months with Ben Pollack's orchestra but soon returned to the anonymous world of the studios. For a short period starting in 1949 and continuing into the early '50s, he played at Dixieland festivals. But Andy Secrest never outgrew his image

as a Bix Beiderbecke imitator, and he ended up his life outside of music, selling real estate.

BEN SELVIN

b. 1898, NY, d. July 15, 1980, NY

The most recorded bandleader of the 1920s and possibly of all time, Ben Selvin was associated with a minimum of 9,000 recordings, under as many as 125 pseudonyms! A violinist, Selvin was performing as early as 1905. When he was 19, in 1917, he led the house band at the Moulin Rouge in Manhattan, an engagement that lasted seven years. He first recorded in 1919, and his version of "Dardanella" sold over a million copies, an enormous number for that time period. A freelancer throughout the next nine years, Selvin recorded over 300 titles by 1924 for nearly every label, and that pace accelerated during the 1920s, when he recorded an average of at least one session a week. He also continued leading orchestras in public.

In 1928 Selvin became a recording director for Columbia, and he oversaw most of the sessions for Columbia and its associated labels up until the mid-1930s. As a leader he recorded a remarkable number of dance band sessions during 1928–31, often using Benny Goodman, the Dorsey Brothers, Jack Teagarden, Adrian Rollini, Venuti and Lang, and Bunny Berigan to flavor the music with jazz. Things slowed down quite a bit during 1932–33, and in 1934 Selvin led his last session. Ben Selvin's later positions included being a vice president of the new Muzak company, being A&R director of Columbia during 1947–51, working for RCA during 1952–63, and cofounding Majestic Records.

7 Volume One/Feb. 3, 1930–Mar. 22, 1932/The Old Masters 102
7 Volume Two/Dec. 9, 1929–Feb. 27, 1931/The Old Masters 117

The 44 selections on these two CDs are just a drop in the bucket as far as Ben Selvin's activities go, but they are a fine sampling of the jazz-oriented dance music that he recorded during the early Depression years. Using many of the top white studio musicians, Selvin recorded both future standards and period pieces doomed for obscurity. *Volume One* includes "You're My Everything," "Makin' Faces at the Man in the Moon," a "Hot-Cha Medley," "Happy Days Are Here Again," and "When Yuba Plays the Rumba on the Tuba," among many others. *Volume Two* has two versions of "The Free and Easy," "Smile, Darn Ya Smile," "'Tain't No Sin," and "Cheerful Little Earful" among its highlights.

LPS TO SEARCH FOR

Although there are a few duplications, most of the 20 selections on *Cheerful Little Earful* (Saville 165), which dates from 1929–32, have not been reissued on CD yet and are representative of the first-class hot dance music that Ben Selvin was famous for.

BOYD SENTER

> b. Nov. 30, 1898, Lyons, NB, d. 1970s?

Boyd Senter was a technically skilled clarinetist and alto saxophonist who chose to play in a very dated "gaspipe" style. At nine, Senter began playing violin and drums, learning reed instruments as a teenager. He worked in local theaters in Nebraska starting when he was 17 and in 1920 joined the Marie Hart Saxophone Quartet. Senter led a band in Atlantic City (1921–22) and worked with Myers' Sax Band and the Chicago De Luxe Orchestra (1923), recording with Jelly Roll Morton (in 1924 on clarinet, kazoo, and banjo). His style was fully formed by then and Senter apparently saw no reason to update his playing. During 1924–30, Senter recorded 67 titles with his band (which was sometimes billed as Boyd Senter's Senterpedes). Most of the selections were showcases for Senter's often-silly playing, but during 1928–30 such musicians as Tommy Dorsey, Jimmy Dorsey, and Phil Napoleon appeared on some of his dates.

In the 1930s Senter settled in Detroit, where he led an orchestra. During World War II Boyd Senter ran an aircraft component company, returning to music after the war and playing in Michigan until the early 1960s, although not recording at all after 1930.

6 Jazzologist Supreme/Mar. 20, 1928 – June 19, 1930/Timeless 1–032

The last 24 recordings of Boyd Senter's recording career are on this single CD, including all of his larger band sides. It is strange, given Senter's excellent musicianship and the musicians that he utilized (top studio players, including Tommy Dorsey, Phil Napoleon, Jimmy Dorsey, Frank Signorelli, Carl Kress, and trumpeter Mickey Bloom) that he never was motivated to modernize his own playing. But there are some fine solos along the way, mostly from the sidemen, making this the Senter set to get by those who are curious about him.

BOB SHOFFNER

> b. Apr. 30, 1900, Bessie, TN, d. Mar. 5, 1983, Chicago, IL

Bob Shoffner mixed together aspects of the styles of King Oliver and Louis Armstrong to form his own individual voice. He grew up in St. Louis and at nine started playing drums and bugle. In 1911 Shoffner switched to trumpet and piano. He served in the Army during World War I and began playing professionally in 1919, working in St. Louis and on riverboats with Charlie Creath. Shoffner performed in the Midwest with territory bands (including Everett Robbins' Jazz Screamers), settling in Chicago in 1922. He played with Honore Dutrey at the Lincoln Gardens, was Louis Armstrong's first replacement with King Oliver's Creole Jazz Band in 1924, worked with Dave Peyton and Lottie Hightower's Nighthawks, and was back with Oliver during May 1925–February 1927. Shoffner recorded with Oliver (in a supporting role in 1926), Lovie Austin's Blues Serenaders, Ida Cox, Ozie McPherson, and Jimmy O'Bryant (ten songs).

The high point of Shoffner's recording career took place on November 17, 1926, with Luis Russell and the nucleus of King Oliver's band; he plays brilliantly on "Plantation Joys," "Please Don't Turn Me Down," "Sweet Mumtaz," and "Dolly Mine." But in 1927 lip troubles caused Shoffner to take much of the year off. Although he recovered, the momentum in his career dissipated. Shoffner, who should have moved to New York at that point, stayed in Chicago, working with Charles Elgar (1928), Erskine Tate, Jerome Carrington, and McKinney's Cotton Pickers (summer 1931), recording with Alex Hill (1929) and Half Pint Jaxon (1933). He freelanced in Chicago during the 1930s in low-profile jobs, finally moving in 1937 to New York, where he played with the Hot Lips Page Orchestra and led his own short-lived big band in 1940. But by the end of 1940, Shoffner took a day job with the government. He continued playing jazz on a part-time basis for a few years (recording with Richard M. Jones in 1944) before retiring from music altogether.

In 1957, tenor saxophonist Franz Jackson organized his Original Jass All-Stars, and he persuaded Shoffner to dust off his horn and resume playing. Bob Shoffner, who by then played in a swing style reminiscent of Rex Stewart, made a full comeback and appeared on five of Jackson's records before illness forced him to permanently retire in 1965.

FRANK SIGNORELLI

b. May 24, 1901, New York, NY, d. Dec. 9, 1975, New York, NY

Pianist Frank Signorelli was a valuable pianist in the 1920s who was at his best accompanying other soloists. Signorelli was a founding member of the Original Memphis Five in 1917, playing with that busy ensemble on and off up until September 1926 and occasionally until 1931. He was also J. Russell Robinson's replacement with the Original Dixieland Jazz Band in 1921 and during September–October 1927 was a member of Adrian Rollini's New Yorker Band, an all-star ensemble that included Bix Beiderbecke and Frankie Trumbauer.

Otherwise, Signorelli freelanced throughout the decade, appearing on many records, including with Bailey's Lucky Seven, Bix and his Gang (1927), the Charleston Chasers, the Cotton Pickers, the Dorsey Brothers Orchestra, Cliff Edwards, Annette Hanshaw, the Hotsy-Totsy Gang, Jazzbo's Carolina Serenaders, Ladd's Black Aces, Eddie Lang, Jimmy Lytell, Miff Mole, Phil Napoleon, Boyd Senter, the Tennessee Ten, Frankie Trumbauer (1927), Joe Venuti, and the Whoopee Makers plus on one session of his own (1926).

Frank Signorelli worked with Paul Whiteman in 1938 and during the 1940s and '50s often appeared in Dixieland settings (recording with Miff Mole as late as 1958), including with cornetist Bobby Hackett, Phil Napoleon, and a reformed version of the Original Memphis Five. However, he made his biggest impact as a composer, writing the standards "I'll Never Be the Same" and "Stairway to the Stars."

OMER SIMEON

b. July 21, 1902, New Orleans, LA, d. Sept. 17, 1959, New York, NY

Jelly Roll Morton's favorite clarinetist, Omer Simeon had a smooth style and a distinctive tone. He took lessons from Lorenzo Tio Jr. early on in New Orleans before moving to Chicago with his family in 1914. Simeon first worked professionally with his violinist brother in Al Simeon's Hot Six (1920) and spent 1923–27 with Charlie Elgar's Creole Band. Simeon recorded regularly with Jelly Roll Morton during 1926–28. Among the numbers that featured Simeon were "Black Bottom Stomp," "The Chant," "Doctor Jazz," "Shreveport Stomp," and (reluctantly on bass clarinet) "Someday Sweetheart."

Simeon played with King Oliver for part of 1927 (making a few records), spent part of 1928 in New York playing with Luis Russell, and then returned to Chicago. Unlike many of his contemporaries, Simeon was rarely unemployed for long. He was with Erskine Tate (October 1928–1930) and Jerome Carrington before becoming a longtime member of Earl Hines' orchestra (1931–41), doubling on alto sax. In addition, he recorded in 1929 with the Dixie Rhythm Kings, Richard M. Jones, Reuben Reeves, Ikey Robinson, Jabbo Smith, and Victoria Spivey, leading two songs on his own sessions.

Omer Simeon's later associations included the Coleman Hawkins Big Band (1941), Jimmie Lunceford's orchestra (1942–50), and Wilbur De Paris' New New Orleans Band (1951–59), which kept him working regularly until his death from throat cancer.

ZUTTY SINGLETON

b. May 14, 1898, Bunkie, LA, d. July 14, 1975, New York, NY

A top-notch New Orleans jazz drummer for decades, Arthur James "Zutty" Singleton's main accomplishment in the 1920s was recording on drums (mostly cymbals and woodblocks) with Louis Armstrong's Savoy Ballroom Five in 1928. Singleton, who was among the first drummers to use brushes, grew up in New Orleans. He played with Steve Lewis (1915) and John Robichaux, served in the Navy during World War I, and after his discharge worked in New Orleans with Oscar Celestin, "Big Eye" Louis Nelson, and Luis Russell (1921). Singleton left town to work on the riverboats with Fate Marable (1921–24, appearing on Marable's only recordings) and played in St. Louis with Charlie Creath for a year. Moving to Chicago, Singleton became a fixture around town, working with Doc Cook, Dave Peyton, Jimmie Noone, and other local musicians. In late 1927 he briefly ran a club with Louis Armstrong and Earl Hines, but the establishment did not last long. Singleton joined the Carroll Dickerson Orchestra in 1928 and recorded the classic Savoy Ballroom Five sides, making a strong impression playing with Armstrong and Hines. In the spring of 1929 he relocated to New York with Dickerson's band, recording with Jelly Roll Morton and

gigging along the way with Armstrong, Allie Ross, Vernon Andrade, Fats Waller (1931), Bubber Miley, Otto Hardwicke, and many lesser-known groups.

Zutty Singleton moved back to Chicago in 1933 with 37 more years of playing ahead of him. Among his most important later associations were Roy Eldridge (1936–37), Slim Gaillard in Los Angeles (1945), Wingy Manone, Eddie Condon, Art Hodes, Bobby Hackett, Mezz Mezzrow, Tony Parenti, and countless trad and Dixieland bands. He remained active until a stroke ended his career in 1970.

NOBLE SISSLE

b. July 10, 1889, Indianapolis, IN, d. Dec. 17, 1975, Tampa, FL

A singer, bandleader, and lyricist who was not a jazz performer himself, Noble Sissle employed many important jazz musicians as sidemen. Sissle led his first band in his native Indianapolis in 1914. The following year he moved to Baltimore, where he met pianist Eubie Blake. Sissle sang and played guitar with James Reese Europe's Society Orchestra (1915–16), was a lieutenant during World War I, and served in France as a drum major in Europe's 369th Division Band. After his discharge, he toured with Europe's orchestra (1918–19) until the leader's death. Sissle next formed a duo with Eubie Blake, both as a singer-piano team and as writers/producers for musical stage shows, including *Shuffle Along* (1921) and *Chocolate Dandies* (1924), historic Broadway revues that helped break down racial boundaries. Sissle and Blake made a series of records during 1920–27, appeared together in a couple of pioneering sound film shorts in the early 1920s, and performed in London in 1926.

In 1927 Sissle and Blake went their separate ways. After appearing again in London (this time as a solo act), Sissle formed the Sizzling Syncopators to play in Paris. He led orchestras during the next decade, visiting Europe for three different stays and recording in 1929–31, 1934, and 1936–38. Among his sidemen were Sidney Bechet, Tommy

Ladnier, Rudy Jackson, Buster Bailey, and (in 1936) the young singer Lena Horne. After leading a commercial band at Billy Rose's Diamond Horseshoe in New York during 1938–50 and touring with Eubie Blake for U.S.O. shows in World War II, Noble Sissle retired. In later years he managed a publishing company and had a few reunions with Blake.

LPS TO SEARCH FOR

Some of Noble Sissle's first recordings were last put out on *Early Rare Recordings, Vol. 1* (Stash 129) and *Vol. 2* (Eubie Blake Music 7). Most of *Vol. 1* (dating from 1920–24, with one cut from 1927) features the Sissle-Blake duo, including "Love Will Find a Way," "I'm Craving for That Kind of Love," and "Waitin' For the Evening Mail." The only exception is "Baltimore Buzz," which is played by the Shuffle Along Orchestra in 1921, conducted by Blake. *Vol. 2* puts the focus more on the pianist, who is heard solo ("Ma"), backing singers Irving Kaufman and Alberta Hunter, heading his 1931 dance band on "My Blue Days Blew Over," and performing two numbers with the Shuffle Along Orchestra. In addition, there are five more Sissle-Blake duets and three numbers in which Sissle is backed by an early orchestra.

All of the singer's big band recordings of 1931–36 are on *Noble Sissle and His Sizzling Syncopators* (Fat Cat Jazz 199), with the main soloist being the great Sidney Bechet. Among the highlights are two versions of "Loveless Love," "Roll On, Mississippi, Roll On," the instrumental "Polka Dot Rag," and "'Tain't a Fit Night Out for Man or Beast." Tommy Ladnier is heard on the 1931 dates, while Lena Horne in 1936 made her recording debut on "That's What Love Did to Me" and "I Take to You."

BESSIE SMITH

b. Apr. 15, 1894, Chattanooga, TN, d. Sept. 26, 1937, Clarksdale, MS

"The Empress of the Blues," Bessie Smith was one of the finest singers ever captured on record, a powerful force who as early as 1923 overcame the primitive technical quality of the era's recording equipment along with occasionally indifferent accompaniment to record performances that still sound fresh and exciting today. She sang locally in Tennessee at an early age, starting with the Moses Stock Co. (an ensemble that featured her early inspiration, Ma Rainey) and moving on in 1912 to Fats Chappelle's Rabbit Foot Minstrels. Smith toured with the Florida Cotton Pickers and became an increasingly popular performer whose renditions of blues were often so passionate as to be hypnotic. By 1919 she was leading her own *Liberty Belles* show, which was succeeded in 1922 by the *How Come* revue.

In New York in February 1923, Bessie Smith had her first recording session (other than a couple of slightly earlier titles that were never released). Her version of Alberta Hunter's "Downhearted Blues" was a big hit. During 1923–33, Smith recorded 160 titles and become the most famous of all blues singers. Among the songs that she helped make famous were "'Tain't Nobody's Biz-ness If I Do," "You've Been a Good Ole Wagon," "Careless Love," "I Ain't Goin' to Play No Second Fiddle," "Backwater Blues," "Muddy Water," "Trombone Cholly," "Send Me to the 'Lectric Chair," "Mean Old Bed Bug Blues," "Empty Bed Blues," "Nobody Knows You When You're Down and Out," and "Gimme a Pigfoot." She toured throughout the 1920s in revues (including her summer tent show *Harlem Frolics* during 1925–27 and *Mississippi Days* in 1928). And in 1929 (when she was still just 35), Smith appeared in her only film, a fascinating short called *St. Louis Blues* and featuring her rendition of the title cut.

The rise of the Depression and the change in the public's musical tastes brought hard times to most of the classic blues singers. Although she only had one record date after 1931, Smith still worked fairly

Bessie Smith, the Empress of the Blues and the most powerful singer of the 1920s.

regularly if with less prominence. In 1934 she toured in *Hot from Harlem*, a show that actually starred Ida Cox. In 1935 Smith played at the Apollo Theater a few times, to good reviews, and substituted for Billie Holiday in the show *Stars Over Broadway*. Things were on an upswing during 1936–37 as Smith worked at the Apollo Theatre with *The League of Rhythm* revue and toured with the *Broadway Rastus* show. She had largely reinvented herself as a bluish swing singer and was beginning to get noticed again.

But on September 26, 1937, Bessie Smith died in a car accident as a passenger; she was just 43. Had she lived, she would certainly have been involved in recording sessions set up by producer John Hammond and been a major part of Ham-

mond's famous From Spirituals to Swing concert at Carnegie Hall in 1938, which was posthumously dedicated to her.

9 The Complete Recordings, Vol. 1/Feb. 16, 1923–Apr. 8, 1924/Columbia/Legacy 47091

10 The Complete Recordings, Vol. 2/Apr. 8, 1924–Nov. 18, 1925/Columbia/Legacy 47471

10 The Complete Recordings, Vol. 3/Nov. 20, 1925–Feb. 16, 1928/Columbia/Legacy 47474

10 The Complete Recordings, Vol. 4/Feb. 21, 1928–June 11, 1931/Columbia/Legacy 52838

7 The Complete Recordings, Vol. 5/May 6, 1925–Nov. 24, 1933/Columbia/Legacy 57546

In the 1970s, with the publication of Chris Albertson's great biography *Bessie*, the Columbia label reissued all of Bessie Smith's 160 recordings on five double LPs. Twenty-five years later they duplicated the feat on five double CDs, put out in large boxes along with a booklet by Albertson filled with photos and stories. It is a pity that every top jazz artist does not receive such lavish treatment!

Although not every Bessie Smith recording is classic, the great majority are, and none of her performances are throwaways, so 1920s collectors will want each of these sets. *Vol. 1* has her first 38 recordings, including "Down Hearted Blues," "Baby, Won't You Please Come Home," "'Tain't Nobody's Biz-ness If I Do," "Far Away Blues" (one of three duets with Clara Smith), and "Ticket Agent, Ease Your Window Down." While the accompaniment (often just Clarence Williams or Fletcher Henderson on piano) is merely adequate on the earlier titles, by the time of *Vol. 2*, the Empress was often joined by Charlie Green, Joe Smith, and Buster Bailey. Nine of the numbers (including "St. Louis Blues," "Careless Love," and "I Ain't Goin' to Play No Second Fiddle") have the added benefit of Louis Armstrong sharing the stage with Bessie in exciting fashion. Other high points include an exuberant "Cake Walkin' Babies from Home," "The Yellow Dog Blues," and "At the Christmas Ball."

Vol. 3 continues at the same high level with "I Want Every Bit of It," "Back Water Blues" (from Smith's first session with her perfect accompanist, James P. Johnson), "After You've Gone," "Muddy Water," "There'll Be a Hot Time in the Old Town Tonight," "Trombone Cholly," "Send Me to the 'Lectric Chair," and "Mean Old Bed Bug Blues." *Vol. 4* traces Bessie Smith's career up to her final two record dates, including the two-part "Empty Bed Blues," the risqué "Kitchen Man," "Nobody Knows When You're Down and Out," and "Moan, You Moaners." The singer was still in prime voice during 1929–31, but the collapse of the recording industry resulted in her recording less and less.

Vol. 5 starts off with Smith's final recordings (including her 1933 date that resulted in "Gimme a Pigfoot"), the only five alternate takes from her ca-

reer, and the complete, nearly 15-minute soundtrack of her 1929 film *St. Louis Blues*. The second disc in *Vol. 5* is quite a bit different, 78 minutes of taped reminiscences of Ruby Smith (Bessie's niece) as she was interviewed in the 1960s by Chris Albertson. Perhaps it would have made better sense to have *Vol. 4* be a three-CD set that included the contents of the first half of *Vol. 5*, for the rather salty storytelling (which is more about Bessie Smith's personal life and preferences than about her music) are only intriguing to hear once.

CLARA SMITH

b. 1894, Spartanburg, SC, d. Feb. 2, 1935, Detroit, MI

One of the five unrelated Smith blues singers of the 1920s (along with Bessie, Laura, Mamie, and Trixie), Clara Smith had a sweet voice but was not on Bessie's level; if her accompaniment was weak, she could not save the record! Smith worked in theaters in the South starting in the early 1910s and was billed as "The World's Champion Moaner" and "Queen of the Moaners." She began recording in 1923 and during the next nine years was heard on 125 selections, including three duets with Bessie Smith (1923) and such numbers as "Every Woman's Blues," "I'm Gonna Tear Your Playhouse Down," "You Don't Know My Mind," "Don't Advertise Your Man," "Nobody Knows the Way I Feel Dis Mornin'" (with Louis Armstrong in the backup group), "Whip It to a Jelly," and "I'm Tired of Fattenin' Frogs for Snakes." Among the better musicians accompanying the blues-oriented singer were Armstrong, James P. Johnson, Coleman Hawkins, Charlie Green, Joe Smith, Freddy Jenkins, and Lonnie Johnson.

At the height of her career, Clara Smith appeared in many revues and theaters (usually in Harlem, although she visited the West Coast during 1924–25), running her own successful Theatrical Club. The Depression hurt business, but she continued working (particularly in New York, Detroit, and

Cleveland) until 1934, when heart trouble forced her to retire.

8 Vol. 1/June 1923–Jan. 29, 1924/Document 5364
8 Vol. 2/Jan. 31, 1924–Dec. 16, 1924/Document 5365
8 Vol. 3/Jan. 7, 1925–Nov. 10, 1925/Document 5366
8 Vol. 4/May 1, 1926–June 1, 1927/Document 5367
8 Vol. 5/July 30, 1927–Dec. 31, 1929/Document 5368
8 Vol. 6/July 21, 1930–Mar. 25, 1932/Document 5369

Clara Smith's complete recordings were first made available on seven Document LPs in the late 1980s, and the same music is now available on six CDs from the Austrian label. *Vol. 1* mostly has Smith joined by Fletcher Henderson's piano, although there are also three small-group sides and two duets ("Far Away Blues" and "I'm Going Back to My Used to Be") with Bessie Smith. Among the numbers are "I Got Everything a Woman Needs," "I Never Miss the Sunshine," and "I'm Gonna Tear Your Playhouse Down."

Vol. 2 covers 1924 and finds Smith assisted by Henderson and some of his sidemen (including Coleman Hawkins and Don Redman) on various tracks, although the numbers with Ernest Elliott (on alto and clarinet) are hurt by the gaspipe player. Among the better tunes are "Chicago Blues," "West Indies Blues," "Don't Advertise Your Man," "Back Woods Blues," and "Death Letter Blues." *Vol. 3* is highlighted by Smith's two dates with Louis Armstrong (best are "Nobody Knows the Way I Feel Dis Mornin'" and the two takes of "Court House Blues") plus "My Good-For-Nuthin' Man," "My Two Timing Papa," "When My Sugar Walks Down the Street" (a rare departure from the blues), and a collaboration with Bessie Smith on "My Man Blues."

By the time of *Vol. 4*, Clara Smith was accompanied by either so-so pianists or obscure players (other than two appearances by Joe Smith), unlike Bessie Smith, who was usually joined by the best musicians. On tunes such as "Rock, Church, Rock," "Whip It to a Jelly," "Ain't Nothin' Cookin' What You're Smellin'," "You Don't Know Who's

Shakin' Your Tree," and "That's Why the Undertakers Are Busy Today," the singer does her best to update her style with humor and creative lyrics.

Freddie Jenkins, Joe Smith, and Charlie Green appear on a session apiece with Clara Smith on *Vol. 5*, but it is James P. Johnson (heard on four songs, including "Oh! Mister Mitchell") who steals solo honors. The tunes include "Black Cat Moan," "Steamboat Man Blues," "Got My Mind on That Thing," and "Ain't Got Nobody to Grind My Coffee." As was often the case with the classic blues singers, Clara Smith did some of her finest work at the end of her recording career, when the recording quality had improved, as had the musicianship of her backing musicians. *Vol. 6* wraps up her legacy with four enjoyable vocal duets with Lonnie Johnson and such numbers as "Low Land Moan," "I Want a Two-Fisted Double-Jointed Man," "Unemployed Papa—Charity Working Mama," and "I'm Tired of Fattenin' Frogs for Snakes."

JABBO SMITH

b. Dec. 24, 1908, Pembroke, GA, d. Jan. 16, 1991, New York, NY

Jabbo Smith was one of the two or three best trumpeters of 1929, when he was just 20, yet within two years he was almost completely forgotten. Born Cladys Smith (a cousin's name was Gladys!), he gained the lifelong nickname of Jabbo by the time he was a teenager. Smith attended the Jenkins Orphanage in Charleston, South Carolina, from the time he was six, learning both trumpet and trombone. He played with the orphanage's band starting when he was ten but ran away from the home several times, successfully in 1925, when he was 16. After a short time in Philadelphia, he went to Atlantic City and was discovered by pianist Charlie Johnson. Smith was well featured with Charlie Johnson's Paradise Ten during 1925–28, recording exciting solos on "Charleston Is the Best Dance After All," "Paradise Wobble," and "You Ain't the One." He also recorded with Eva Taylor, Perry

Bradford's Georgia Strutters, and Duke Ellington (subbing for Bubber Miley on "Black and Tan Fantasy") but turned down a chance to join Ellington because he felt the job did not pay enough. It was a particularly bad decision on Smith's part because he was soon fired by Charlie Johnson's band due to his unreliability and excessive drinking.

Smith played in the pit orchestra of *Keep Shufflin'*, recording some of the show's songs in a quartet with James P. Johnson, Fats Waller (on organ), and Garvin Bushell's reeds (as the Louisiana Sugar Babes). The show closed in Chicago in November 1928, and Smith had short stints with many local bands, including those of Carroll Dickerson, Sammy Stewart, Earl Hines, Erskine Tate, Charles Elgar, and Tiny Parham. After Jabbo stole the show on a pair of records by Ikey Robinson's quintet in January 1929 ("Got Butter on It" and "Ready Hokum"), he was signed to Brunswick as the leader of the Rhythm Aces, a quintet with Omer Simeon or George James on reeds, Cassino Simpson, Alex Hill, Kenneth Anderson, or Earl Frazier on piano, Hayes Alvis or Lawson Buford on tuba, and Ikey Robinson. It was hoped that his record sales would rival Louis Armstrong's for the Okeh label. The 19 selections that Jabbo recorded in 1929 are advanced, sometimes reckless to the point of being death-defying and among the most exciting recordings of the period. Smith's playing is quite impressive (in range, speed, and ideas), he proved to be a fine singer, and, as a bonus, he takes an effective trombone solo on "Lina Blues." Smith's playing on "Till Times Get Better," "Jazz Battle," "Band Box Stomp," "Sweet and Low Blues," and "Decatur Street Tutti" is quite brilliant.

But 1929 would be the high point of Smith's career. After the records did not sell that well and the Depression hit, his solo career came to an end. Smith settled in Milwaukee and, although playing in the city, he went into complete obscurity. His few recordings later in the 1930s were disappointing in comparison to his earlier work, and his stint with Claude Hopkins' struggling big band (1936–38) was uneventful. After a period playing in Newark, he moved back to Milwaukee and worked at a day job. In 1961 he was persuaded by guitarist Marty Grosz to rehearse with his band (tapes were released decades later), but he soon retired again. In the early 1970s, Smith appeared at a traditional jazz festival in Holland on trombone, he began to play trumpet again (sounding quite feeble), and during 1979–82 he sang and played in the musical show *One Mo' Time*. But Jabbo Smith gave up playing trumpet in 1983 and made just a few later appearances singing. Sad to say, he was a has-been by the time he reached his 21st birthday!

10 1929–1938/Jan. 4, 1929-Aug. 22, 1929/Retrieval 79013
9 1929–1938/Jan. 29, 1929–Feb. 1, 1938/Classics 669
These two CDs are very similar. Both contain all 19 of Jabbo Smith's Rhythm Aces sides and a previously unreleased "Weird and Blue." The Retrieval disc also has the trumpeter's two numbers with Ikey Robinson, while the Classics CD skips those two cuts and instead has Smith's four selections from his 1938 session, his only date as a leader after 1929. Unfortunately those four numbers are quite routine (with three Jabbo vocals and very little of his trumpet), so the edge goes to the Retrieval release, despite its inaccurate title; it should just be called *1929*.

JOE SMITH

b. June 28, 1902, Ripley, OH, d. Dec. 2, 1937, New York, NY

Joe Smith was widely respected for his cool tone and lyricism, which was a major contrast to the "hot" trumpeters of his day. Smith's father led a brass band in Cincinnati, and all six of Joe's brothers played trumpet, including Russell Smith, who played lead with Fletcher Henderson for quite a few years. Joe was given trumpet lessons by his father and started his career locally in his native Ohio. After working in Pittsburgh, he went to Chicago in January 1922, joining the Black Swan Jazz Masters, a group backing Ethel Waters that included Fletcher Henderson. After six months, Smith toured with Mamie Smith (1922–23), played with Billy Paige's Broadway Syncopators, and became a very popular sideman for recordings, especially for classic blues singers. During the next decade (especially 1922–27), Smith recorded with such vocalists as Andrew Copeland, Ida Cox, Ethel Finnie, Rosa Henderson, Alberta Hunter, Maggie Jones, Ozie McPherson, Hazel Meyers, Josie Miles, Julia Moody, Ma Rainey (an eight-song session in 1926), Clara Smith, Mamie Smith, Trixie Smith, Mary Straine, Evelyn Thompson, and Ethel Waters (21 selections). As Bessie Smith's favorite cornetist (she liked him better than the competitive Louis Armstrong), Smith recorded 19 songs with the Empress of the Blues during 1924–27, including "Cake Walkin' Babies from Home," "The Yellow Dog Blues," "At the Christmas Ball," "Young Woman's Blues," "Muddy Water," and "Send Me to the 'Lectric Chair."

Joe Smith spent most of 1924 playing with the Noble Sissle/Eubie Blake show *The Chocolate Dandies*. Although he had first recorded with Fletcher Henderson as early as 1921 and was on most of the record dates of 1923 and early '24, Smith did not become a regular member of Henderson's orchestra until April 1925. His tone (even when using the plunger mute, he sounded laid back and a bit introverted) was much mellower than that of the other, more fiery trumpeters in Henderson's band. During his period with Henderson, Smith played alongside Louis Armstrong, Rex Stewart, Tommy Ladnier, and Bobby Stark and received his share of solo space.

Leaving Henderson in October 1928, Smith worked with violinist Allie Ross, McKinney's Cotton Pickers (summer 1929 until November 1930), Henderson again for a couple of months, Kaiser Marshall's group, and McKinney's Cotton Pickers for a second period (1931–32). In 1932 his health began to fail. After moving to Kansas City, Smith worked briefly with Bennie Moten and Clarence Love and in 1933 tried to play a job with Fletcher Henderson in Detroit but became seriously ill. Joe Smith spent his last few years in a sanatorium, dying in 1937 from paresis when he was just 35.

LAURA SMITH

b. Indianapolis, IN, d. Feb. 1932, Los Angeles, CA

The most obscure of the five Smith blues singers, Laura Smith until recently did not have any of her 30 recordings reissued. She started working in theaters around 1920 and made all of her recordings between 1924 and 1927. Unlike most of the other classic blues singers, Smith's best recordings were her earlier ones, for her voice sounded strained and a bit in decline by 1926–27, although she was making the transition from blues to jazz in her last sessions (including on "Don't You Leave Me Here"). Laura Smith worked in Chicago and Los Angeles during her final years, allegedly made a film (never discovered) in 1930, and died at an unknown age in 1932 from high blood pressure.

6 Vol. 1/Aug. 3, 1924–Mar. 1927/Document 5429

All of Laura Smith's recordings except for two lost numbers and her final four-song session are on this CD. She is heard at her best on the earlier titles (including "Texas Moaner Blues," "I'm Gonna Get Myself a Real Man," and "Humming Blues"), although the later dates include such potentially interesting tunes as "Jackass Blues," "When a Gator Hollers," and "Don't You Leave Me Here." In the backup groups are Clarence Williams, Thomas Morris, and Perry Bradford along with unidentified players. Laura Smith (whose final four songs from June 7, 1927, are included on *Edna Hicks/Hazel Meyers/Laura Smith*—Document 5431) was a minor singer who worked steadily without catching on or carving out a niche for herself.

MAMIE SMITH

b. May 26, 1883, Cincinnati, OH, d. Oct. 30, 1946, New York, NY

The first singer to record blues, Mamie Smith was not as blues oriented a vocalist as Bessie Smith, Ma Rainey, or Ida Cox, but she was a top-notch and versatile performer, capable of holding her own against nearly anyone. After touring in the Midwest, Smith moved to New York in 1913, performing with a white vaudeville group (The Four Mitchells) and singing in Harlem clubs. She worked in the show *The Smart Set,* sang at many New York clubs, and in 1920 appeared in *Maid of Harlem* at the Lincoln Theatre.

On February 14, 1920, Mamie Smith (who was sponsored by Perry Bradford) made her recording debut, singing "That Thing Called Love" and "You Can't Keep a Good Man Now." She was one of the first nongospel black performers captured on record; James Reese Europe's bands and comedian Bert Williams were two of her very few predecessors. The sales for her record were good, so on August 10 she recorded one of the songs from *Maid of Harlem,* "Crazy Blues," along with "It's Right Here for You." To everyone's surprise, this '78' (due to the success of "Crazy Blues") sold a million copies within six months and started a major blues craze. During the next four years, scores of singers (mostly black females working in vaudeville) were extensively recorded. Some (such as Alberta Hunter) were better than others, with the discovery of Bessie Smith in 1923 being a major event.

Mamie Smith recorded 91 selections, all but 18 during 1920–23. Although she recorded mostly in the acoustic era, Smith was always wise enough to use the very best musicians, and her records (which include such players as Johnny Dunn, Garvin Bushell, Buster Bailey, Coleman Hawkins, Bubber Miley, Joe Smith, Sidney Bechet, Thomas Morris, and Charlie Irvis) are still quite listenable today. It is a pity that she recorded relatively little during 1924–31, for her "Goin' Crazy with the Blues" (from 1926) is a classic, and her voice had, if anything, become stronger.

Smith toured with her Jazz Hounds during the 1920s, worked on and off throughout the 1930s (leading her Beale Street Boys) and appeared in several films, including *Jailhouse Blues* (1929), *Paradise in Harlem* (1939), *Mystery in Swing* (1940), *Sunday Sinners,* and *Murder on Lenox Avenue* (1941), some of the later ones with Lucky Millinder. Although she stopped recording after 1931 (it is surprising that she was not rediscovered during the swing era), Mamie Smith (who could be called the "First Lady of the Blues") was active up until 1944.

9 Vol. 1/Feb. 14, 1920-Aug. 18, 1921/Document 5357
8 Vol. 2/Aug. 18, 1921–May, 1922/Document 5358
8 Vol. 3/May, 1922–Aug. 15, 1923/Document 5359
9 Vol. 4/Aug. 16, 1923–1942/Document 5360

Succeeding five Document LPs released in the late 1980s, these four CDs reissue the complete Mamie Smith. *Vol. 1* has the historic "That Thing Called Love" and "Crazy Blues," plus "It's Right Here for You," "If You Don't Want Me Blues," "Royal Garden Blues" (one of four instrumentals by her Jazz Hounds), "I Want a Jazzy Kiss," and "Sax-o-Phoney Blues." From the start, Smith used many of the top musicians in New York, including Willie "the Lion" Smith, Johnny Dunn, Garvin Bushell, and Buster Bailey. *Vol. 2* has some of the best classic blues vocal performances on record in 1921, continuing into the middle of the following year. The titles include "Mama Whip, Mama Spank," "I'm Free, Single, Disengaged, Looking for Someone to Love," "Get Hot," and "Let's Agree to Disagree." Coleman Hawkins made his recording debut with Smith on some of these titles.

Vol. 3 has more backup by Johnny Dunn and Coleman Hawkins (who has a couple of solos), along with guest appearances by Joe Smith and Sidney Bechet ("Lady Luck Blues" and "Kansas City Man Blues"). *Vol. 4* hints at what Mamie Smith could have accomplished had she been recorded later in her career. There is one selection from 1923, six from September 1924 (including "Remorseful Blues" and "Good Time Ball"), and two sessions with Thomas Morris in 1926 that include "Goin' Crazy with the Blues" and "What Have You Done to Make Me Feel This Way." Also on this intriguing disc are three previously unreleased numbers from 1929 (including "My Sportin' Man"), the four songs from Smith's final recording date in 1931 (including "Don't You Advertise Your Man"), and three numbers from soundtracks in 1929, 1940, and 1942 that show that Mamie Smith still had "it" late in her career.

PINETOP SMITH

b. June 11, 1904, Troy, AL, d. Mar. 15, 1929, Chicago, IL

George Thomas, under the name of Clay Custer, recorded the first song using a boogie-woogie bass ("The Rocks") in 1923. Probably the most notable boogie-woogie piano solo record of the decade was Meade Lux Lewis' "Honky Tonk Train Blues," from December 1927. Clarence "Pinetop" Smith emerged in the late 1920s to follow Lewis as one of the first significant boogie-woogie pianists. Smith grew up in Birmingham, working in the Pittsburgh area early in his career. He had a wide range of musical jobs as a pianist, dancer, and comedian, spending some time accompanying Butterbeans and Susie, and Ma Rainey. Smith settled in Chicago in the late 1920s and was discovered by Cow Cow Davenport. On December 29, 1928, he recorded two numbers (including "Pine Top's Boogie Woogie"), and these were followed by two others on January 14, 1929, and four numbers the following day. There are 11 performances in all (counting three alternate takes), eight of which are on the LP *Piano in Style* (MCA-1332) along with four-song piano solo sessions from Jelly Roll Morton and James P. Johnson.

However, it would be a rather short career and life. Two months after his third recording date, Pinetop Smith was accidentally shot to death in a Chicago dance hall fight; he was only 24. Nine years later, the Tommy Dorsey Orchestra's adaptation of "Boogie Woogie" (based closely on "Pine Top's Boogie Woogie") helped launch the boogie-woogie revival of the late 1930s, immortalizing the ill-fated Pinetop Smith.

TRIXIE SMITH

b. 1895, Atlanta, GA, d. Sept. 21, 1943, New York, NY

There was no shortage of Smith singers in the 1920s. Even beyond Bessie, Clara, Laura, and Mamie, there were Clementine, Elizabeth, Hazel, Ivy, and even Kate Smith! Trixie Smith tends to be overlooked, but she ranks close to Bessie, Clara, and Mamie among the blues-oriented Smith vocalists. She attended Selma University, moved to New York in 1915, and sang in theaters and revues. With the great success of Mamie Smith's "Crazy Blues," the Black Swan label had a blues contest in 1921, and Trixie was the winner. Her award was a contract with the label. Trixie Smith recorded 16 titles for Black Swan during 1921–23 and 16 songs for Paramount during 1924–25. She introduced "He May Be Your Man but He Comes to See Me Sometimes" and probably "My Man Rocks Me with One Steady Roll." Her sidemen on records are such notables as James P. Johnson, Fletcher Henderson, Charlie Green, Louis Armstrong, Buster Bailey, and Joe Smith. She also recorded two songs with the Original Memphis Five in 1925.

Unlike the other key Smith singers, Trixie Smith did not record at all during the second half of the 1920s (although she continued working in shows and revues), but she did made a comeback, appearing at John Hammond's Spiritual to Swing concert in 1938 and recording seven titles during 1938–39, staying active until ill health forced her retirement in the early 1940s.

7 Vol. 1/Sept. 1921-Dec. 1924/Document 5332
8 Vol. 2/Jan. 1925–June 14, 1939/Document 5333
Trixie Smith recorded relatively little in her career

and all of her performances (48 in all) are on these two CDs. The first volume does not have any noteworthy accompaniment until the last five numbers (when Charlie Green helps out), but Smith sounds fine on "Trixie's Blues," "He May Be Your Man," "My Man Rocks Me," and "Freight Train Blues." *Vol. 2* has 13 performances (counting three alternate takes) from 1925, including Smith's numbers with the Original Memphis Five ("Everybody Loves My Baby" and "How Come You Do Me Like You Do"), her two sessions with Louis Armstrong (highlighted by "The World's Jazz Crazy and So Am I"), and four songs (including "Everybody's Doing That Charleston Now" and "Black Bottom Hop") with all-stars from Fletcher Henderson's orchestra. Smith's final recordings of the period are the two versions of "Messin' Around" from 1926 with a group consisting of Jimmy Blythe, Freddie Keppard, Roy Palmer, Johnny Dodds, and Jasper Taylor. Talk about finishing up on top! Also on *Vol. 2* are the seven numbers that Smith recorded in 1938 in a sextet with Sidney Bechet and trumpeter Charlie Shavers (including remakes of "My Daddy Rocks Me," "Trixie Blues," and "He May Be Your Man") and a lone title with Red Allen from 1939 that wrapped up her career.

WILLIE "THE LION" SMITH

b. Nov. 25, 1887 (or 1893), Goshen, NY, d. Apr. 18, 1973, New York, NY

Willie "the Lion" Smith recorded relatively little in the 1920s and did not really start emerging on records until 1935, but he was an important pioneer as a stride pianist and one of the stars at nightly rent parties, alongside his pals James P. Johnson and Fats Waller. Although he looked like a rough character, with his bowler hat, a cigar in his mouth, and his extroverted and bragging nature, Smith's piano playing was often quite sensitive and lyrical. Born William Henry Joseph Bonaparte Bertholoff, he began playing piano when he was six, appearing in

clubs in New York and Atlantic City starting in 1912. Smith was in the Army from November 1916 until late 1919, serving in France during World War I. He later claimed to be a war hero, earning the title of "The Lion" which he apparently gave himself! In 1920 he resumed playing regularly in New York clubs and recorded with Mamie Smith (six songs in 1920, including "Crazy Blues"), although his piano is largely inaudible.

Smith played at countless club dates and rent parties throughout the 1920s, developing a very original style and becoming an important early influence on Duke Ellington (who in the early 1940s would write "Portrait of the Lion" in tribute to Smith). Although a bit of a braggart at times, "The Lion" always seemed lovable, unlike the more abrasive Jelly Roll Morton, who was punished for the same sins. Smith played and acted in the Broadway play *The Four Walls* (1927–28) and was featured at Pod's and Jerry's in the late 1920s/early 1930s. His only recordings of the 1920s (other than the ones with Mamie Smith) were two songs with the Gulf Coast Seven (1925), three with the Blue Rhythm Orchestra (1925), two with the Georgia Strutters (1927), and possibly two with the Seven Gallon Jug Band (1929); a total of nine songs maximum.

Smith weathered the worst years of the Depression, accompanied Nina Mae McKinney, and played in 52nd Street clubs throughout the 1930s and much of the '40s. He recorded during 1933–34 with Clarence Williams, the Alabama Jug Band, and Mezz Mezzrow, leading his combo "The Lion and His Cubs" on records in 1935 and 1937. Smith's solo sessions of 1938–39 (which include such memorable and impressionistic originals as "Echoes of Spring," "Morning Air," "Passionette," and "Rippling Waters") made him immortal. Willie "the Lion" Smith remained active until the early 1970s, frequently playing in Dixieland settings or as a soloist and writing his memoirs (*Music on My Mind*) in 1965.

SNOOKS AND HIS MEMPHIS STOMPERS

Drummer Snooks Friedman (b. Feb. 10, 1906, Memphis, TN., d. Mar. 24, 1993, Memphis, TN) led a series of high-quality hot dance band records during 1931–32, 41 titles in all. Friedman began his career in the summer of 1923 playing with the Ole Miss Jesters. He worked with Meyer Davis during 1924–25 and took over Hip Bennett's band in Wisconsin for a period in 1925. In 1926 he formed the Memphis Stompers, recording eight titles with the band during 1928–29 in Memphis. The orchestra relocated to New York in 1929, playing at the Swanee Club, Roseland (for six months), and the Crazy Cat Club (1930). The height of its fame was reached in 1931, when it added a string quartet and performed at the Paramount Hotel. By then, Friedman was taking some of the vocals while hiring someone else to play drums so he could front the band.

Although there were no further recordings after a single date in 1932, Snooks Friedman kept his orchestra working in New York until the beginning of World War II. He served in the Navy during the war and spent much of the next 25 years leading Dixieland bands in the Memphis area before retiring in 1972.

8 Snooks and His Memphis Stompers/Feb. 4, 1928-Apr. 7, 1932/Parklane 100

With the exception of one number from Snooks Friedman's band in 1928 ("Memphis Stomp") and a very brief example of him reminiscing (for just 41 seconds in 1990), this CD consists of 22 of the best recordings of Snooks and His Memphis Stompers from 1931–32. There are no noteworthy names among the sidemen, but the ensembles are reasonably tight and the solos have plenty of spirit. Among the highlights are such happy numbers as "Hello Beautiful," "I'm Crazy 'Bout My Baby," "One More Time," "Roll On, Mississippi, Roll On," and "Nothing To Do but Love."

ELMER SNOWDEN

b. Oct. 9, 1900, Baltimore, MD, d. May 14, 1973, Philadelphia, PA

Elmer Snowden was a fine banjoist who recorded as a sideman and occasionally led hot combos in the 1920s. Snowden started playing banjo and guitar as a child. As a teenager in Baltimore, he worked with pianist Addie Booze (1914), Eubie Blake (1915), and Joe Rochester (1916–19). After Rochester's death in 1919, Snowden settled for a time in Washington, D.C., playing in a trio with Duke Ellington. He worked with Claude Hopkins (1921) and led a band that performed in Washington, D.C., and Atlantic City before moving to New York in September 1923. Snowden's band, called the Washingtonians, originally included Sonny Greer, Arthur Whetsol, Otto Hardwicke, and Fats Waller, but Waller skipped town before the ensemble arrived in New York. Snowden quickly sent for Duke Ellington to fill Fats' spot. Within a few months, Bubber Miley had taken Whetsol's place (completely changing the sound of the formerly sweet band) and Charles Irvis was added on trombone. However, a dispute over money resulted in Snowden's being ousted by the middle of the year, and Ellington became the group's new leader.

The banjoist worked with Ford Dabney's orchestra for a short time and then led several bands into the early 1930s. No recordings were made of his ensembles (one of which appeared in the 1933 short film *Smash Your Baggage*), which is a real pity because his sidemen at various times included Benny Carter, Otto Hardwicke, Jimmy Harrison, Dickie Wells, Rex Stewart, Roy Eldridge, Fats Waller, and drummers Chick Webb and Sid Catlett. Snowden did record during 1924–25 with Charles Booker, the Six Black Diamonds, the Kansas City Five, and Jake Frazier and made records with the trio of clarinetist Bob Fuller and pianist Lou Hooper in 1925–26 under several names (Bob

Fuller, the Pennsylvania Syncopators, the Rocky Mountain Trio, the Three Hot Eskimos, the Three Jolly Miners, and the Three Monkey Chasers!). Snowden also recorded in 1927 with Te Roy Williams and in 1929 with Jasper Davis, the Jungle Town Stompers, and the Musical Stevedores, accompanying such singers on records as Helen Gross, Rosa Henderson, Billy Higgins, Louella Jones, Maggie Jones, Viola McCoy, Josie Miles, Monette Moore, Bessie Smith, Clementine Smith, and Mamie Smith.

A dispute with the Musicians Union led Snowden to move in 1933 to Philadelphia, where he worked as a music teacher. In the early 1940s Elmer Snowden settled his union problems, returned to New York, and played music off and on into the late 1960s, including late-period duet recordings with Lonnie Johnson, a successful appearance at the 1963 Monterey Jazz Festival, and a 1967 tour of Europe.

LPS TO SEARCH FOR

Elmer Snowden did not lead any record dates of his own in the 1920s, but he recorded fairly frequently. *Elmer Snowden* (IAJRC 12) features Snowden as a sideman with Booker's Dixie Jazz Band, Te Roy Williams (excellent versions of "Oh Malinda" and "Lindbergh Hop"), the Musical Stevedores, the Jungle Town Stompers, Jasper Davis, and the Sepia Serenaders (1934) plus three trio numbers from 1963 with Darnell Howard and Pops Foster. In addition, the soundtrack of the short *Smash Your Baggage* (four songs) is included.

ALBERTO SOCARRAS

> *b. Sept. 18, 1908, Manzanillo, Oriente, Cuba, d. Aug. 26, 1987, New York, NY*

Although several critics (including Leonard Feather and Ira Gitler) have long stated that Wayman Carver (who was with Chick Webb's orchestra in the 1930s) was jazz's first flute soloist, Alberto Socarras actually preceded him. Taught flute by his mother,

Socarras played in a family band that accompanied silent movies in Cuba. With the upcoming rise of sound films, Socarras (who also played alto, soprano and clarinet) emigrated to New York in April 1927. After stints with trumpeter Vincent Sigler and Nilo Melendez, he gained a job working with Lew Leslie's Blackbirds Orchestra (1928–33). During this period, Socarras recorded with Leslie, Adelaide Hall, Clarence Williams (1927–30), Eva Taylor, Katherine Henderson, Margaret Webster, and Russell Wooding (1931). While those dates generally found Socarras on clarinet and alto, he played flute with Clarence Williams on "Shooting the Pistol" in July 1927 (probably the first jazz flute solo on records) and "Have You Ever Felt That Way," on "You're Such a Cruel Papa to Me" with Lizzie Miles (1928), and with Bennett's Swamplanders for a session in 1930.

Socarras worked as a studio musician and a freelance arranger in the 1930s (contributing charts to the bands of Vincent Lopez, Cab Calloway, and Tommy Dorsey). He led a rumba band in 1934, had short stints with the orchestras of Benny Carter, Sam Wooding, and Erskine Hawkins, and headed Latin bands on and off into the 1950s, making a rare jazz appearance on flute for a 1949 session with singer Babs Gonzalez. Alberto Socarras spent his later years playing classical music and teaching flute.

EDDIE SOUTH

> *b. Nov. 27, 1904, Louisiana, MO, d. Apr. 25, 1962, Chicago, IL*

One of the major jazz violinists to emerge during the 1920s (second only to Joe Venuti), Eddie South made his greatest impact later in the 1930s. South grew up in Chicago, where he was a child prodigy on violin. In more enlightened times, South would have had a career as a classical violinist, but there was no demand for black classical players in the 1920s. So, after having extensive classical training, he learned how to play jazz violin from Darnell

Howard. South, who studied at the Chicago College of Music, began to work professionally in Chicago in 1920. He played with Charles Elgar, Erskine Tate, Mae Brady's orchestra, and Jimmy Wade's Syncopators (where he was the musical director during 1923–27 and made his recording debut on three selections). A second stint with Tate and some work with Mike McKendrick's quartet preceded his first recordings as a leader (1927–28) and an extended stay (1928–31) in Europe, leading his group, the Alabamians. South studied in Paris and Budapest (gaining a lifetime love for gypsy melodies), recording overseas in 1929 and 1931.

After returning to the United States in 1931, South (who was billed as "The Dark Angel of the Violin") resumed working in Chicago. Although he never made it big on a commercial label, Eddie South (who recorded in France with Django Reinhardt and Stephane Grappelli in 1937) was an important violinist into the 1950s.

9 1923–1937/Dec. 1923–Nov. 23, 1937/Classics 707
Starting off with Eddie South's first recorded solo ("Someday Sweetheart" with Wade's Moulin Rouge Orchestra in 1923), this CD also contains his nine selections as a leader during 1927–31 (recorded in Chicago, New York, and Paris), six songs from 1933, and most of his Paris dates of 1937. South's sessions with his Alabamians are quite intriguing, for he often used gypsy melodies as the basis for his improvising, recording such offbeat material as "By the Waters of Minnetonka," "Two Guitars," "Marcheta," and "Hejre Kati." The 1933 selections (such as "Old Man Harlem" and "Nagasaki") with bassist Milt Hinton and Jimmy Bertrand are more conventional and harder swinging. Rounding out the CD are South's meetings on record with Stephane Grappelli and Django Reinhardt, including an improvisation on a Bach theme and a version of "Lady Be Good" that has the violins of South, Grappelli, and Michel Warlop jamming happily together. The remainder of Eddie South's early sessions as a leader can be heard on the rewarding *1937–1941* (Classics 737).

MUGGSY SPANIER
b. Nov. 9, 1906, Chicago, IL, d. Feb. 12, 1967, Sausalito, CA

Francis "Muggsy" Spanier was a top Dixieland player for four decades, always playing with enthusiasm, even if he could be rather predictable. Spanier started on drums before switching to cornet when he was 13. He developed quickly and was playing in public within two years. Spanier worked in Chicago with Elmer Schoebel (1921), Sig Meyers (1922–24), Charlie Straight, Charles Pierce, Floyd Town (1925–28), and Ray Miller. His main influence was King Oliver, mixed in with some Louis Armstrong. But from the start, Spanier had his own sound, as he showed on his impressive recordings with the Bucktown Five (1924), the Stomp Six, and in 1928 with Danny Altier, the Chicago Rhythm Kings, the Jungle Kings, the Louisiana Rhythm Kings, Charles Pierce, and Ray Miller.

Spanier found a secure job with the cornball performer Ted Lewis, giving some jazz credibility to Lewis' music during 1929–36, often playing next to George Brunies. In later years Spanier was with Ben Pollack's orchestra (1936–38), survived a serious illness, recorded "The Great 16" with an influential Dixieland octet in 1939, was a sideman with Bob Crosby (1940–41), and led his own big band (1941–43). From 1944 on, Muggsy Spanier was heard in freewheeling Dixieland combos (including for a period with Earl Hines), staying active until 1964.

THE SPIRITS OF RHYTHM
One of the most popular novelty or jive bands of the 1930s, the Spirits of Rhythm came together at the end of the classic jazz era. Comprising Leo Watson, Wilbur Daniels, and Douglas Daniels on vocals and tiples (small guitars), guitarist Teddy Bunn, bassist Wilson Myers, and drummer-vocalist Virgil

Scroggins, the Spirits of Rhythm first recorded in 1933 as The Five Cousins. The group recorded only nine songs (during 1933–34 and one cut from 1941) that were released at the time, but various unissued performances and collaborations have since come out. After the mid-1930s, the musicians had only occasional reunions, and the 1941 session (by Wilbur Daniels, Douglas Daniels, Teddy Bunn, Wellman Braud, and Leo Watson on drums) was their last on record. The Spirits of Rhythm's scatting was happily eccentric, and the good-time string band was a predecessor to the skiffle groups that would emerge in England in the late 1950s.

9 Spirits of Rhythm/Nov. 23, 1932-Sept. 4, 1941/Retrieval 79004

This CD is very much the complete Spirits of Rhythm. In addition to the original nine released selections, there are two earlier numbers by the Washboard Rhythm Kings with vocals by Leo Watson and Wilbur Daniels, four unissued performances by the Spirits, and their sessions with singers Red McKenzie (1934) and Ella Logan (1941). This very accessible and fun band is heard at its best on such tunes as "Nobody's Sweetheart," a few versions of "I Got Rhythm," "I'll Be Ready When the Great Day Comes," "Shoutin' in That Amen Corner," and "Exactly Like You," but all of the 24 numbers are quite enjoyable.

VICTORIA SPIVEY

b. Oct. 15, 1906, Houston, TX, d. Oct. 3, 1976, New York, NY

A top blues singer in the late 1920s who often accompanied herself on piano, Victoria Spivey (always a determined woman) was one of the few classic performers who survived and was able to make a comeback in the 1960s. Spivey played piano at the Lincoln Theatre in Dallas when she was 12, worked throughout the South (sometimes with Blind Lemon Jefferson), and first recorded in St. Louis in 1926, when she was 19, having a major

hit in "Black Snake Blues," which sold 150,000 copies. Spivey recorded 56 titles during 1926–31 (including seven two-sided songs) and was unusual in that she did not debut on records until the blues craze had already ended. Spivey had a more rural sound than many of her predecessors and considered her main influence to be Ida Cox. On her records, Spivey usually pushed for the best sidemen, and among her players were Lonnie Johnson (who on a few occasions sang vocal duets with her), King Oliver, Omer Simeon, Clarence Williams, Eddie Lang, the Luis Russell Orchestra, and Louis Armstrong ("Funny Feathers" and "How Do You Do It That Way").

Spivey had a major acting role in the 1929 black film *Hallelujah* (although Nina Mae McKinney got to play the "bad girl," a jazz singer). Spivey worked throughout the 1930s and '40s, directing Lloyd Hunter's Serenaders, singing with Jap Allen, making recordings in Chicago during 1936–37, and touring in shows. She left full-time music in 1952 to work as a church administrator but in 1961 had a recorded reunion with Lonnie Johnson and was inspired to form and run the Spivey label. Victoria Spivey was active into the early 1970s.

9 Vol. 1/May 11, 1926-Oct. 31, 1927/Document 5316
9 Vol. 2/Oct. 31, 1927–Sept. 24, 1929/Document 5317
8 Vol. 3/Oct. 1, 1929–July 7, 1936/Document 5318

One of the few classic blues singers to emerge on records as late as 1926, Victoria Spivey (only 19 at the time) sounded quite mature from the start. Her debut recording was her biggest hit ("Black Snake Blues"), one of 23 selections on *Vol. 1*. With John Erby or Porter Grainger usually on piano and some important appearances by Lonnie Johnson, Victoria Spivey sounds quite comfortable and passionate on such tunes as "Hoodoo Man Blues," "Got the Blues So Bad," "Steady Grind," "The Alligator Pond Went Dry," "T-B Blues," and "Dope Head Blues." *Vol. 2* has her two-sided double-entendre vocal duets with Lonnie Johnson ("New Black Snake Blues," "Furniture Man Blues," "Toothache

Blues," and "You Done Lost Your Good Thing Now"), three performances with Clarence Williams' Blue Five (featuring King Oliver and Eddie Lang), four numbers with Red Allen, an octet from Luis Russell's orchestra, and the two selections with Louis Armstrong.

Vol. 3 features Spivey on an additional four songs with Allen and Russell and matching wits on two-sided vocal duets with Porter Grainger and Howling Smith. In addition, she sings "Dreaming 'Bout My Man" with Hunter's Serenaders in 1931 and leads a swing sextet on four selections from 1936, trying her best to adjust to modern times with "Black Snake Swing."

BOBBY STARK

> b. Jan. 6, 1906, New York, NY, d. Dec. 29, 1945, New York, NY

Bobby Stark is one of the most consistently over-looked trumpeters of the 1920s, virtually unknown despite his exciting solos with Fletcher Henderson's orchestra. He played the alto horn at 15, studying piano and reeds before settling on trumpet. Starting in late 1925, Stark worked in New York with many bands, including those led by Edgar Dowell, Leon Abbey, Duncan Mayers, Bobbie Brown, Bobby Lee, Billy Butler, and Charlie Turner. He was also with an early version of McKinney's Cotton Pickers and Chick Webb's first group (1926–27). Most importantly, Stark was a featured soloist with Fletcher Henderson's orchestra from November 1927 to mid-1934 (other than a short period in 1932 that he spent with Elmer Snowden). Stark shared solo space along the way with Rex Stewart and Henry "Red" Allen, holding his own and taking classic solos on three versions of "King Porter Stomp" (from 1927, 1932, and 1933). He also recorded with the Chocolate Dandies (1930) and Horace Henderson (1933).

After leaving Henderson, Stark was with Chick Webb's orchestra (1934–40) but was hardly heard from, because Taft Jordan (who had a similar style) was given almost all of the solo space. It seems strange that Stark stayed with Webb's ensemble (even a year after the leader's death) instead of switching to another band that would feature him, for he ensured his own future anonymity. Bobby Stark spent 1942–43 in the Army, worked with Garvin Bushell and Benny Morton in 1944, and recorded with Helen Humes, dying prematurely when he was just 39.

STATE STREET RAMBLERS

The State Street Ramblers name was used for four different overlapping groups organized by Jimmy Blythe that recorded in 1927, 1928, and 1931. The first session had a quartet consisting of Blythe, Natty Dominique, Johnny Dodds, and Baby Dodds on washboard and was the most musical. Dominique and Blythe are joined by W.E. Burton on washboard and an unknown (and somewhat amateurish) altoist for a session in 1928. The second set from 1928 retained Blythe and Burton (who switched to kazoo), adding Baldy McDonald on alto, clarinetist Alvin Fernandez, Bill Johnson, and drummer Clifford Jones. When Blythe put together the 1931 sessions, he used James "Bat" Robinson on kazoo, Burton on washboard, banjoist Ed Hudson, Roy Palmer, and Darnell Howard, with the final three numbers featuring the Robinson-Hudson-Blythe-Burton quartet. The results in each case were spirited, rather primitive, and fun, with the 1931 performances being quite unusual for the early Depression era.

7 **State Street Ramblers, Vol. 1/Aug. 12, 1927-Mar. 19, 1931/ RST 1512**
9 **State Street Ramblers, Vol. 2/Mar. 19, 1931–Apr. 3, 1936/ RST 1513**

Vol. 1 has all of the music from the first three versions of the State Street Ramblers plus three selections from the fourth band. There are three songs (including "There'll Come a Day") from the Dodds-Dominique group, a variety of material from Ramblers #2 (including "Oriental Man," "My

Baby," and the very erratic "Tack It Down") and 11 songs from the rather wild Ramblers #3. The 23-song CD concludes with "Tiger Moan," "Barrel House Stomp," and "Georgia Grind" from the Roy Palmer-Darnell Howard Ramblers #4.

Roy Palmer is the main star of *Vol. 2*. First there are six numbers from Ramblers #4 (including "South African Blues" and "Sic 'Em Tige' ") and three jams from the quartet without Palmer and Howard. A similar group, the Memphis Nighthawks (also known as the Alabama Rascals) recorded exciting good-time music that was completely out of place in 1932. Its dozen selections team Palmer and Howard with cornetist Alfred Bell, either Bob Hudson or Buddy Burton on piano, Jimmy Bertrand, and an unidentified saxophonist and banjoist. The music is quite fun, with Palmer's percussive trombone leading the way on such tunes as "Georgia Grind," "Nancy Jane," and "Stomp That Thing." A highlight is a previously unissued Palmer-Hudson duet, the charming "The Trombone Slide." Concluding this generous 26-selection disc are the four numbers cut in 1936 by the Chicago Rhythm Kings, a similar sextet with Palmer, clarinetist Arnett Nelson, and Bertrand but not Jimmy Blythe, who, despite being listed, had actually passed away five years earlier!

REX STEWART

b. Feb. 22, 1907, Philadelphia, PA, d. Sept. 7, 1967, Los Angeles, CA

An exciting cornetist, Rex Stewart became famous for his half-valve technique (showcased on "Boy Meets Horn") while with Duke Ellington's orchestra in the 1930s and '40s, but he was already an impressive player in the 1920s. Growing up near Washington, D.C., Stewart played piano, violin, and alto horn before switching to cornet. He began working professionally when he was 14, picking up early experience performing on riverboats and touring with Ollie Blackwell's Jazz Clowns in 1921. Af-ter moving to New York in 1923, Stewart free-lanced, worked with Elmer Snowden (1925–26), and recorded with Helen Gross, Rosa Henderson, Lena Henry, Monette Moore, and Thomas Morris (1926).

Stewart first joined Fletcher Henderson's orchestra in 1926, when he was 19. But, although he sounds fine on such Henderson recordings as "Jackass Blues" and "Static Strut," he did not feel that he was up to playing in a position that a year earlier had been filled by Louis Armstrong. After eight months, he left Henderson, playing instead with lesser-known groups and with Horace Henderson's Collegians.

In 1928, when Stewart had much more confidence, he rejoined Fletcher Henderson, becoming one of the band's main soloists during 1928–30 and 1932–33. The time between these two Henderson periods was spent playing with Alex Jackson and McKinney's Cotton Pickers; he also recorded with the Little Chocolate Dandies (1929). Stewart left Henderson for the final time to lead a big band of his own (1933–34), and he worked with Luis Russell for a few months (starring on Russell's 1934 recording of "Old Man River").

In December 1934, the fiery cornetist joined Duke Ellington's orchestra, where during the next 11 years he became famous in the jazz world. Rex Stewart mostly led combos from 1946–66, playing swing and Dixieland, and during 1957–58 he organized and ran the Fletcher Henderson Reunion Orchestra.

MEL STITZEL

b. Jan. 9, 1902, Germany, d. Dec. 31, 1952, Chicago, IL

Mel Stitzel was a fixture in Chicago during the 1920s. Born in Germany, he grew up in Chicago and started playing piano at an early age. In 1923 Stitzel succeeded Elmer Schoebel with the New Orleans Rhythm Kings, for whom he composed "Tin

Roof Blues." The pianist, who also wrote "The Chant" (made famous by Jelly Roll Morton), played and arranged for several Chicago-area bands, including Floyd Town (1925), Louis Panico, and the Benson Orchestra of Chicago (1929). Stitzel recorded on only four occasions in the 1920s, but they were all classic dates: with the NORK (its March 12–13, 1923, sessions), the Bucktown Five (1924), and the Stomp Six (1925) and as a member of the first Benny Goodman Trio (1928).

Mel Stitzel freelanced in Chicago during the 1930s, led a Dixieland band in the 1940s, and played vintage tunes with drummer Danny Alvin in the early 1950s, shortly before his death.

JIMMY STRONG

b. Aug. 29, 1906, d. 1940s

Jimmy Strong was a solid if unremarkable clarinetist and tenor saxophonist who recorded with Louis Armstrong's Savoy Ballroom Five in 1928. Relatively little is known about his life. Strong began working in Chicago in the early 1920s, playing with Lottie Hightower's Night Hawks and the Helen Dewey Show (1925). He worked with the Spikes Brothers Orchestra in Los Angeles and back in Chicago was with Carroll Dickerson's orchestra (1927–29, including Dickerson's two recording dates) and Clifford "Klarinet" King's big band (1928). Strong's recordings with Armstrong included the classic Savoy Ballroom Five sessions (highlighted by "West End Blues," "Basin Street Blues," and "A Monday Date"), two songs backing Victoria Spivey, and some of Satch's big band dates of 1929 (including "Ain't Misbehavin' " and "Some of These Days").

Strong went to New York with Carroll Dickerson and Armstrong in 1929 but did not stay long, returning to Chicago. Among his more significant later jobs were associations with pianist Cassino Simpson (1931), Zinky Cohn (1937), Jimmie Noone's big band (1939), and his own groups into the early 1940s, but no recordings resulted after

1929. Jimmy Strong ended his career playing in Jersey City, New Jersey.

JOE SULLIVAN

b. Nov. 5, 1906, Chicago, IL, d. Oct. 13, 1971, San Francisco, CA

One of the first pianists to be influenced by Earl Hines, Joe Sullivan (who developed a similar style of his own) emerged during the 1920s. He studied piano at the Chicago Conservatory of Music, led a group in Indiana during the summer of 1923, and worked a bit on the vaudeville circuit. Sullivan was associated with the members of the Austin High School Gang in Chicago, made his recording debut with the McKenzie-Condon Chicagoans in 1927, and moved to New York in 1928. Among Sullivan's recordings of the 1928–33 period were sessions with Louis Armstrong ("Knockin' a Jug"), Billy Banks, the Chicago Rhythm Kings, Eddie Condon (1928–29, 1933), Benny Goodman (1929, 1933), the Jungle Kings, the Louisiana Rhythm Kings, Miff Mole, Red Nichols, Frank Teschemacher, and Joe Venuti (1933). The pianist worked with Red Nichols, Roger Wolfe Kahn, Red McKenzie's Mound City Blue Blowers (1931–32), and Ozzie Nelson, becoming Bing Crosby's regular accompanist in 1933. Sullivan recorded his first session as a leader (four piano solos, including "Gin Mill Blues" and an early, themeless version of his "Little Rock Getaway") in 1933. His earliest dates as a leader have been reissued on *1933–1941* (Classics 821).

Sullivan's later associations include the Bob Crosby Orchestra (1936 and 1939) and the Eddie Condon gang, but he worked primarily as a soloist or as the leader of a trio. Unfortunately alcoholism and his general disillusionment with the jazz scene resulted in Joe Sullivan's being only occasionally active during his last two decades.

THE SUNSHINE BOYS

During 1929–31, siblings Joe and Dan Mooney recorded 16 selections as the Sunshine Boys. Joe

Mooney (b. Mar. 14, 1911, Paterson, NJ, d. May 12, 1975, Fort Lauderdale, FL) had a long and episodic career, while Dan Mooney was known chiefly for his work with his brother. Joe Mooney went blind in the early 1920s, but that did not stop him from pursuing a musical career, originally as a pianist who sang. In 1926 Joe and Dan (who also sang) began collaborating on the radio. As the Sunshine Boys, they were regularly featured on a national radio show during 1929–36, recording 18 selections during 1929–31 with backup by such players as Joe Venuti, Dick McDonough, Tommy Dorsey, Carl Kress, Manny Klein, and, on one occasion, the Ben Selvin Orchestra.

After the brothers broke up the group in 1936, Dan Mooney dropped out of music while Joe Mooney became a pianist-arranger for Frank Dailey. He worked with Buddy Rogers (1938), contributed arrangements to a variety of bands (including Paul Whiteman and Les Brown plus vocal charts for the Modernaires), and in 1943 began a new career as an accordion player. The Joe Mooney Quartet (featuring accordion, clarinet, guitar, and bass, with the leader singing) was quite popular during 1946–49. In the 1950s Mooney moved to Florida, where he was mostly content to work locally as an organist, other than recording a hit vocal version of "Nina Never Knew" with the Sauter-Finegan Orchestra and making rare trips to New York for recordings, including albums during 1956 and 1963–65. Passing away in 1975, Joe Mooney is today considered something of a legendary cult figure, known only to a few appreciative listeners, many of whom probably are completely unfamiliar with his early work with the Sunshine Boys!

LPS TO SEARCH FOR

The Sunshine Boys (Retrieval 206) has all 16 of the selections recorded by the Sunshine Boys (including four titles that originally came out as by the Melotone Boys) plus their two numbers with Ben Selvin's orchestra. The charming vocal duo performs such tunes as "Huggable Kissable You," "Does My Baby Love Me," "When I Take My Sugar to Tea," and "Smile, Darn Ya, Smile."

JOE TARTO

b. Feb. 22, 1902, Newark, NJ, d. Aug. 24, 1986, Morristown, NJ

Born James Tortoriello, Joe Tarto would later in life be nicknamed "The Titan of the Tuba." He started on trombone when he was 12 before switching to tuba. Giving a false age, Tarto served in the Army during World War I when he was 15. After his discharge in 1919, he became a professional musician. Tarto worked with Cliff Edwards (1921–22), Paul Specht (1922–24), Sam Lanin, Vincent Lopez, and Roger Wolfe Kahn, in addition to being in the orchestras for several Broadway shows. Tarto stayed very busy in the 1920s, appearing on many record dates (most notably with Red Nichols, Miff Mole, the Dorsey Brothers, Eddie Lang, Phil Napoleon, Bix Beiderbecke, Ethel Waters, and the Boswell Sisters), sometimes doubling on bass. He was also an occasional arranger who contributed a few charts for Fletcher Henderson and Chick Webb.

In the early 1930s, Tarto became a studio musician, his main source of income for several decades. Joe Tarto, who occasionally performed with Paul Whiteman in the 1930s, frequently played Dixieland during his final 40 years and led the New Jersey Dixieland Brass Quintet into the 1980s.

LPS TO SEARCH FOR

Joe Tarto never led any record dates of his own, but a tribute album, *Titan of the Tuba* (Broadway Intermission 108), came out in 1980. Tarto is heard on sideman jobs with Cliff Edwards, various Sam Lanin groups, the Hottentots, Vincent Lopez, Harry Raderman, Nat Shilkret, Joe Venuti, the Carson Robison Orchestra, and the New Yorkers. In addition, there are three novelty numbers from a broadcast in the 1950s plus Tarto's arrangement of "Black Horse Stomp" for Fletcher Henderson's band of 1926.

ERSKINE TATE

b. Dec. 19, 1895, Memphis, TN, d. Dec. 17, 1978, Chicago, IL

Erskine Tate was a notable bandleader in the 1920s. He grew up in Chicago, studied violin at the American Conservatory of Music, and began playing professionally in 1912. Tate led the orchestra at the Vendome Theatre during 1919–28, using such sidemen as Louis Armstrong, Earl Hines, Freddie Keppard, Buster Bailey, Stump Evans, Omer Simeon, Jabbo Smith, Eddie South, Jimmy Bertrand, and bassist Milt Hinton, among others. Surprisingly he only led a pair of two-song recording dates; a couple of primitive numbers from 1923 with Freddie Keppard and classic versions of "Static Strut" and "Stomp Off, Let's Go" in 1926 with Louis Armstrong; the latter are frequently reissued in collections under Satch's name.

Tate led bands at other theaters in Chicago during the 1930s, including the Savoy Ballroom and the Cotton Club. By the 1940s (and continuing into the 1960s), Erskine Tate worked primarily as a highly respected music teacher of violin, saxophone, trumpet, guitar, and drums.

EVA TAYLOR

b. Jan. 22, 1895, St. Louis, MO, d. Oct. 31, 1977, Mineola, NY

Eva Taylor (who was born Irene Gibbons) recorded frequently in the 1920s and '30s, usually with groups organized by her husband, Clarence Williams. A fine singer with a likable and easy-to-understand voice, Taylor performed as a child, touring Australia and New Zealand (1900 and 1914) and Europe (1906). In 1922 she became a pioneer radio performer and also began her recording career. During the next 15 years, Taylor appeared on countless records, including 72 issued under her own name, many with Clarence Williams' groups, and memorable dates with the Charleston Chasers. She was usually backed by a hot jazz combo but occasionally just by her husband's piano. In addition, Taylor appeared in stage shows and revues and in the late 1920s had her own radio show on NBC.

Eva Taylor, who recorded two final numbers with Williams in 1941, largely stopped singing in the early 1940s except for special appearances. After her husband's death in 1965, Taylor came out of retirement to perform and record in Europe (albums in 1967, 1974, and 1976), still sounding quite cheerful and musical.

7 Vol. 1/Sept. 1922-Sept. 5, 1923/Document 5408
9 Vol. 2/Sept. 5, 1923–Nov. 4, 1927/Document 5409
8 Vol. 3/Feb. 17, 1928–Sept. 23, 1932/Document 5410
8 Edison Laterals 4/July 31, 1929–Mar. 30, 1977/Diamond Cut 303

Eva Taylor never made any pretense at being a blues singer. Although often used as a vehicle to promote her husband's songs, she was a fine jazz vocalist, one of the first nonblues jazz singers on records. The 72 selections that she recorded as a leader during 1922–32 have been reissued in full on the three Document CDs. Taylor's easy-going style is recognizable from her debut 1922 recording, and she was quite consistent throughout her career. *Vol. 1* has her joined by Williams' piano and in some cases his Blue Five of 1922–23, with such players as Johnny Dunn, Thomas Morris, Charlie Irvis, and (on "Oh Daddy Blues" and the humorous "I've Got the Yes! We Have No Banana Blues") clarinetist Sidney Bechet. Among the other selections are "Baby Won't You Please Come Home," "That Da-Da Strain," "12th Street Rag," "Farewell Blues," and "Original Charleston Strut."

Vol. 2 finds the recording quality improving and the accompaniment as well, including Williams, Morris, Irvis, Bechet, Jabbo Smith, and Ed Allen. There are quite a few memorable selections on this set, including "Jazzin' Babies Blues," "Old-Fashioned Love," "Ghost of the Blues," "Señorita Mine," a definitive version of "When the Red, Red Robin Comes Bob, Bob Bobbin' Along," "Nobody but My Baby Is Getting My Love," "Candy Lips," and "If I Could Be with You." *Vol. 3* covers the 1928–29 period and has appearances from Williams, flutist Albert Socarras, King Oliver, Omer Simeon, and a white group called the Knickerbockers. Among the better numbers are "Back in Your Own Back Yard," "Have You Ever Felt That Way," "Moanin' Low," and "When I'm Housekeeping for You." Eva Taylor stopped recording as a leader after 1929 (although she continued under Clarence Williams' name) except for two cuts from 1932, vocal trios with Williams and Lil Armstrong that wrap up the Document series.

Edison Laterals 4 is an intriguing CD that partly duplicates Classics' *Vol. 3*. Its first eight selections (from July–October 1929) include six duplicates plus previously unreleased versions of "In Our Cottage of Love" and "Oh Baby, What Makes Me Love You So?" In addition, there are three "new" alternate takes from these dates, all originally cut from the Edison label. On October 5, 1976, there was an event honoring some of Edison's former recording artists, and Eva Taylor is heard saying a few words and singing "Baby Won't You Please Come Home" a cappella! In addition, *Edison Laterals 4* has Taylor at a March 30, 1977, concert performing five standards from the 1920s (backed by an unidentified pianist), still sounding in prime voice. So 11 of the 17 selections on the Diamond Cut CD are unavailable elsewhere, making this a disc that should be of strong interest to Eva Taylor collectors.

JASPER TAYLOR

b. Jan. 1, 1894, Texarkana, TX, d. Nov. 7, 1964, Chicago, IL

Jasper Taylor (who also played drums) was a pioneering washboard player who may very well have been the very first to make the household appliance into a musical instrument. He began his career performing locally in Texas, hitting the road in 1912 to travel with Young Buffalo Bill's Wild West Show.

Taylor toured Mexico with the Dandy Dixie Minstrels, studied xylophone, and worked in Memphis theaters, including with both W.C. Handy and Jelly Roll Morton. After moving to New York in 1917, he made his recording debut with Handy. Taylor served in France during World War I and, after his discharge, performed in New York with Will Marion Cook and W.C. Handy.

Moving to Chicago, Taylor worked with the Chicago Novelty Orchestra (1922), Joe Jordan's Sharps and Flats, Dave Payton, Fess Williams, and Tiny Parham. For recordings, Taylor played washboard on sessions with Jimmy O'Bryant (1924–25), Ruth Coleman (1925), the Dixie Washboard Band (1926), and the Blue Grass Foot Warmers (1926), stuck to woodblocks on dates with Jelly Roll Morton (1923) and Freddie Keppard (1926), and played a drum set with Joe Jordan (1926), Fess Williams' Joy Boys (1928), and Reuben Reeves (1929). Taylor also led two sessions of his own during 1927–28, including one date ("Stomp Time Blues" and "It Must Be the Blues") that features Freddie Keppard and Johnny Dodds.

In the 1930s Taylor played drums in theaters and ballrooms, eventually becoming a part-time musician while working by day as a shoe repairman. In later years, Jasper Taylor worked with pianist Freddy Shayne (1944), Punch Miller, Natty Dominique (1952), Lil Armstrong (1959–60), and his own Creole Jazz Band in 1962.

JACK TEAGARDEN

b. Aug. 29, 1905, Vernon, TX, d. Jan. 15, 1964, New Orleans, LA

One of the greatest jazz trombonists of all time, Jack Teagarden amazed New Yorkers when he arrived in town in 1928, immediately overshadowing the trombone styles of Miff Mole and Kid Ory. His younger brother was trumpeter Charlie Teagarden, a fine Dixieland player who early on had stints with Ben Pollack (1929–30) and Red Nichols, while his younger sister was pianist Norma Teagarden. Jack (known later on as Mr. T.) started on piano when he was five, baritone horn at seven, and trombone at ten. He moved to Chappell, Nebraska, with his family in 1918. Teagarden first worked professionally in local theaters with his mother, a ragtime pianist. He gigged in Texas with Peck Kelley's Bad Boys (1921–23) and worked in a variety of territory bands, including Doc Ross' Jazz Bandits (1925–27), making his recording debut in late 1927 with Johnny Johnson's Statler Pennsylvanians (two very obscure titles). Teagarden worked with Wingy Manone for a week and played with a variety tour before joining Billy Lustig's Scranton Sirens at the Roseland Ballroom in New York in February 1928.

Teagarden's appearance in New York immediately caused a major stir, for here was a trombonist who played his instrument with the fluidity of a trumpeter, creating warm legato lines full of the blues. Although Jimmy Harrison with Fletcher Henderson had paved the way, Teagarden immediately became the pacesetter on his instrument, an extremely influential trombonist who made both Kid Ory and Miff Mole sound wooden and dated in comparison. Teagarden also became an important singer, helping to make "Basin Street Blues" and "Beale Street Blues" into standards and influencing Bing Crosby's style with his lazy relaxed approach and his ability to infuse pop tunes with the blues.

After playing with Tommy Gott for two months, Teagarden became a longtime member of Ben Pollack's orchestra, staying nearly five years (June 1928–May 1933). He was in great demand for record dates and a partial list of his work during 1928–33 includes Roger Wolfe Kahn (Mr. T.'s outstanding solo on "She's a Great, Great Girl" really launched his recording career), Eddie Condon (1928–29, including "I'm Gonna Stomp, Mr. Henry Lee" and "That's a Serious Thing"), Louis Armstrong ("Knockin' a Jug"), the Big Aces, Hoagy Carmichael (a 1930 date with Bix Beiderbecke), the Charleston Chasers (1931), the Dorsey Brothers Orchestra, Benny Goodman, Ted Lewis, the Louisiana Rhythm Kings, Jimmy McHugh's Bostonians, Irving Mills' Hotsy-Totsy Gang, Mills' Merry Makers, the Mound City Blue Blowers (1929), the New Orleans Ramblers, Red Nichols (1929–31), Jack Pettis, Willard Robison, Gil Rodin, Cornell Smelser, Bessie Smith (her final recording from 1933), Joe Venuti, Fats Waller (1929), and Virginia Willrich's Texas Rangers (1929). In addition, Teagarden led eight sessions of his own during 1930–34.

After leaving Pollack, Teagarden freelanced for a few months and then signed a five-year contract with Paul Whiteman (December 1933–December 1938). At first it looked like a good deal, locking up secure work during the Depression, but it was a mistake. When the Ben Pollack Orchestra collapsed a year later, the musicians were hoping to regroup under Mr. T's leadership, but he was tied up. Bob Crosby took over the band instead. Teagarden was underutilized by Whiteman, and, with the rise of the swing era, he became impatient to be free. By the time his contract ended and Teagarden finally formed his own big band in January 1939, there was so much competition that he did not stand a chance. The Jack Teagarden Orchestra lasted eight years, into 1947, but the leader had to declare bankruptcy when it broke up. Fortunately, he still had his talents and his name; a stint with the Louis Armstrong's All-Stars (1947–51) got him back on his feet again. Jack Teagarden, who never declined or altered his style, led a Dixieland combo during his final 13 years before his unexpected death from a heart attack.

8 1930–1934/Oct. 1, 1930–Mar. 2, 1934/Classics 698

7 That's a Serious Thing/Mar. 14, 1928–July 8, 1957/Bluebird 9986

10 The Indispensable Jack Teagarden/Mar. 14, 1928–July 8, 1957/RCA 961 327

1930–1934 has all of Jack Teagarden's early recordings as a leader, some of which were formerly

Trombonist Jack Teagarden, pictured with Earl Hines and Louis Armstrong in the late 1940s when he was a member of Armstrong's All-Stars.

rare. The seven sessions range from dance band music to Dixielandish, although in each case Teagarden is joined by 10- to 13-piece bands, sometimes drawn from the Ben Pollack (soon to be Bob Crosby) Orchestra. Key sidemen include tenor saxophonist Eddie Miller, Benny Goodman, Charlie Teagarden, Pee Wee Russell, Fats Waller (who shares vocals with Teagarden on "You Rascal You" and the silly "That's What I Like About You"), and Bud Freeman. Highlights include Waller's appearances (two of the songs were formerly put out only by a collector's LP), "Somebody Stole Gabriel's Horn," "I Just Couldn't Take It Baby," and Tea-

garden's initial recording of "A Hundred Years from Today."

However, during his first decade on records, Teagarden's most significant sessions were as a sideman. *That's a Serious Thing* has 21 selections, mostly from 1928–47 (including "I'm Gonna Stomp, Mr. Henry Lee," "That's a Serious Thing," and "She's a Great Great Girl") plus three later numbers with Louis Armstrong and two from 1957 with Bud Freeman. But get the two-CD *The Indispensable Jack Teagarden* (from French RCA) instead, for it has a better selection of songs (31 gems in all) and alternate takes of the three mentioned songs, plus strong samplings of Teagarden's work with Ben Pollack, Paul Whiteman, and the Mound City Blue Blowers.

LPS TO SEARCH FOR

The Great Soloists—Featuring Jack Teagarden (Biograph 2) has Teagarden as a sideman with Jimmy McHugh's Bostonians, Mills' Merry Makers, Cornell Smelser, Ben Pollack, Wingy Manone, and Frankie Trumbauer, dating from 1929–36. *King of the Blues Trombone* (Epic 6044) is a superb three-LP boxed set with 48 of Teagarden's best recordings owned by the Columbia family of labels, dating from 1928–40. Teagarden is featured with Jimmy McHugh's Bostonians, Mills' Merry Makers, the Whoopee Makers, Jack Pettis, Goody and his Good Timers, Joe Venuti's New Yorkers, Ben Pollack, Benny Goodman (1933–34), Frankie Trumbauer (1934–36), and Bud Freeman, plus his own combos and his big band of 1939.

THELMA TERRY

One of the great mysteries of the 1920s was Thelma Terry—who was she? Very few female instrumentalists led records in the 1920s (Lovie Austin is one of the only ones that come to mind), extremely few females recorded during the decade on any instrument but piano or violin, and female bassists were virtually unknown on records. And yet Thelma Terry recorded six numbers in 1928 with her Playboys, playing string bass at the level of a Steve Brown (her main influence) and Wellman Braud. When it is considered that Bill Johnson was one of the very few bassists (of any sex) to lead a record date in the decade (and not till 1929), the fact that Terry was also an attractive young female almost becomes irrelevant in discussing how unique she was.

And yet nothing is known about her beyond a few pictures and her playing on her two sessions in Chicago. Her nine- to ten-piece band includes trombonist Floyd O'Brien and Gene Krupa on the first four songs and pianist Bob Zurke on the last two numbers. All of Thelma Terry's recordings were reissued as part of the *Chicago Hot Bands 1924–1928* (Timeless 1–041) and also on *The Obscure and Neglected Chicagoans* (IAJRC 1007). But where she gained her talent and inspiration from, and what happened to her after 1928 is not known.

FRANK TESCHEMACHER

b. Mar. 14, 1906, Kansas City, MO, d. Feb. 29, 1932, Chicago, IL

An enthusiastic if sometimes erratic clarinetist and altoist, Frank Teschemacher certainly had the spirit of the 1920s in his playing. He grew up in Chicago, started on violin when he was ten, and played mandolin and banjo before learning alto sax when he was 14. Teschemacher played violin in the Austin High School Orchestra and made friends with other, like-minded jazz-loving students, including Jimmy McPartland and Bud Freeman. Inspired by the New Orleans Rhythm Kings, Tesch played with his friends in the Blue Friars (1924) the same year that he began studying clarinet. The band gradually evolved into the Red Dragons and Husk O'Hare's Wolverines. During 1926–28 Teschemacher worked with Muggsy Spanier, Floyd Town, Sig Meyers, and Art Kassel. On December 9 and 16, 1927, he made his recording debut, cutting four sides with the McKenzie-Condon Chicagoans. The first half of 1928 brought sessions with Charles Pierce, the Chicago Rhythm Kings, and the Jungle Kings plus one title ("Jazz Me Blues") under his own name.

In June 1928 Teschemacher followed the other Chicagoans to New York, subbing with Ben Pollack's band, spending a month with Red Nichols, and recording with Miff Mole, Eddie Condon, the Dorsey Brothers Orchestra, and the Big Aces. But Teschemacher became homesick for Chicago and returned in September. He freelanced during the next couple of years, including playing with Charlie Straight, Floyd Town, Benny Meroff, and Jess

Stacy. He made recordings with Wingy Manone, Ted Lewis (a couple of humorous items), Elmer Schoebel, and finally the Cellar Boys (1930); there were 34 recordings in all. Although his playing was not flawless, Teschemacher was gradually improving technically without losing his enthusiasm. His contemporaries always said that he was a much better player live than in the studios, where he sometimes became nervous. At times Tesch's playing is a little reminiscent of early Pee Wee Russell's.

Teschemacher toured with Jan Garber's orchestra in the fall of 1931 and then became part of cornetist Wild Bill Davison's new big band. After just a couple of gigs, and a week before the band was to have an important opening, Frank Teschemacher was killed in an accident when Davison's car was blindsided by a taxi cab; he was two weeks short of his 26th birthday.

LPS TO SEARCH FOR

In the late 1970s/early '80s, the Time Life label came out with a series of three-LP box sets that summed up the recorded legacy of an early jazz giant. *Frank Teschemacher* (Time-Life 123), the last in the series, was quite unusual because of both Tesch's lack of name value (particularly compared to Louis Armstrong and Duke Ellington) and the fact that this set has every recording he ever made. The extensive 48-page booklet is a real plus, and each of the 34 recordings is discussed thoroughly, along with the ill-fated clarinetist's life. In addition, six other recordings are included that Frank Teschemacher might have been on (though that is doubtful): dates by Lennie Hayton, the ironically titled Original Wolverines (in 1928, four years after the real Wolverines!), and Howard Thomas.

LORENZO TIO JR.

b. Apr. 18, 1884, New Orleans, LA, d. Dec. 24, 1933, New York, NY

Lorenzo Tio Jr. was a notable clarinet teacher who was also a pioneering jazz musician. His father Lorenzo Tio Sr. (1866–1920) was a well-respected clarinetist, as was his uncle Papa Luis Tio (1863–1927). In 1897, Lorenzo Tio Jr. began playing with the Lyre Club Symphony Orchestra. In the early 1900s he played jazz around the New Orleans area, becoming one of the first musicians to alternate between jazz and classical music. In 1910, Tio started associations with the Onward and Excelsior Brass Bands. It was at that time that he became a very important clarinet teacher. His students would include Johnny Dodds, Jimmie Noone, Albert Nicholas, and Barney Bigard, among others.

Tio played with Oscar Celestin (1913–15) and was in Chicago with Manuel Perez and Charles Elgar in 1916 but returned to New Orleans, where he worked again with Celestin (1917). His most important musical association was with Armand J. Piron (1918–28), visiting New York with Piron in late 1923 and making 13 recordings (including one song backing singer Esther Bigeou). Tio's sophisticated and melodic clarinet fit in perfectly with Piron's jazz-oriented society music.

After leaving Piron in 1928, Lorenzo Tio Jr. played in New Orleans with the Tuxedo Brass Band, and during his last three years (1930–33) he freelanced in New York.

DAVE TOUGH

b. Apr. 26, 1908, Oak Park, IL, d. Dec. 6, 1948, Newark, NJ

Dave Tough was an important part of several jazz styles in his career, including classic jazz, swing, bebop, and Dixieland. Tough began playing drums quite young, and, although he attended Oak Park High School, he was good friends with the aspiring musicians in the Austin High Gang. Tough was a professional musician by 1923 and became full time two years later. He worked in Chicago with Sig Meyers, Husk O'Hare's Wolverines, Art Kassel, Jack Gardner, Eddie Condon, and other short-term groups.

On a lark, he sailed to Europe with clarinetist

Danny Polo in the summer of 1927; otherwise he would have been on the McKenzie-Condon Chicagoans recording dates instead of Gene Krupa. Tough worked in Belgium, France, and Germany (making his recording debut in Berlin with New Yorkers Tanzorchester and also recording in Paris with Lud Gluskin), came back to New York briefly, and played in Paris with Mezz Mezzrow (1929). Back in the United States, Tough worked with Benny Goodman and Red Nichols and in 1929 recorded with the Charleston Chasers, the Louisiana Rhythm Kings, the New Yorkers, and Nichols. A serious illness forced him to stay out of music during most of 1930–34.

An intellectual who was also an alcoholic who weighed so little that it seemed he could be knocked over by a breeze, Tough was a very subtle and creative drummer who hated to take solos. He stayed busy during the swing era, playing with the big bands of Tommy Dorsey (1935–38 and 1938–39), Benny Goodman (1938), and Jack Teagarden, in addition to playing Dixieland with Eddie Condon and Bud Freeman. In the military, he toured with Artie Shaw's Naval Band (1942–44) and, upon his discharge, was a member of Woody Herman's First Herd (1944–45), debating the merits of bebop (which he supported) in print with Eddie Condon. After various illnesses, Dave Tough died at the age of 40 when he bumped his head falling down in a Newark street.

ALPHONSO TRENT

b. Aug. 24, 1905, Fort Smith, AK, d. Oct. 14, 1959, Fort Smith, AK

Alphonso Trent was the leader of one of the top territory bands of the late 1920s. He learned piano as a child, played locally in Arkansas, and in 1923 led a band based in Oklahoma. After studying at Shorter College in Little Rock, Trent worked with Eugene Crook's Synco Six, a group that he took over in 1924, when he was 19. The Alphonso Trent Orchestra played regularly at the Adolphus Hotel

in Dallas, Texas, for several years. Although always based in the Southwest, Trent's band had four record dates in Richmond, Indiana (two in 1928 and one apiece in 1930 and 1933), that resulted in eight titles that are included on *Richmond Rarities* (Jazz Oracle 8008). The orchestra visited New York in 1929 and occasionally played on riverboats. Among Trent's more notable sidemen were trumpeters Irving Randolph, Peanuts Holland, and Harry "Sweets" Edison, trombonist Snub Mosley, and violinist Stuff Smith.

Alphonso Trent retired from music in 1934 but came back in 1938 (when he had a sextet that included electric guitar pioneer Charlie Christian), leading small bands into the 1950s.

FRANKIE TRUMBAUER

b. May 30, 1901, Carbondale, IL, d. June 11, 1956, Kansas City, MO

The master of the now largely extinct C-melody sax and one of the top saxophonists of the 1920s, Frankie Trumbauer was an important force during the era. Tram was raised in St. Louis, where he played piano, trombone, flute, and violin before switching to C-melody sax; he also learned alto and bassoon (both of which he would record on during rare occasions). Trumbauer led his first band in St. Louis when he was 17. After serving in the Navy, he played in St. Louis and the Midwest with Max Goldman's orchestra, Ted Jansen, Earl Fuller, Gene Rodemich (with whom he made his recording debut), the Benson Orchestra of Chicago (1922–23), Joe Kayser, and Ray Miller (1923–24). Guesting on the second recording date by the Mound City Blue Blowers ("San" and "Red Hot"), Trumbauer displayed an original style that was already quite mature. He can also be heard on records with the Benson Orchestra of Chicago, Ray Miller, and the Cotton Pickers. Trumbauer became a major influence on the styles of both Lester Young and Benny Carter.

Trumbauer first met Bix Beiderbecke in late

**Frankie Trumbauer, a masterful saxophonist who became
an early inspiration for both Lester Young and Benny Carter.**

1924, and they initially recorded together as the Sioux City Six. The lives of Tram and Bix overlapped often during the next six years. Trumbauer became the musical director of Jean Goldkette's orchestra (1925–27); Bix joined in 1926. Tram had short spots on some of Goldkette's records but was not overly featured. However, as with Bix, 1927 was a breakthrough year. In addition to the Goldkette recordings, he began leading his own series of record dates for Okeh, which continued until 1930, switching later to Brunswick, Columbia, and Victor. Beiderbecke was on all of the sessions from 1927–28, and the first three dates yielded such classics as "Trumbology" (a feature for the C-melody saxophonist), "Singin' the Blues" (Tram's opening solo is almost as famous as Bix's), "Clarinet Marma-

lade," "Ostrich Walk," "Riverboat Shuffle," "I'm Coming, Virginia," and "'Way Down Yonder in New Orleans." After the Goldkette Orchestra broke up, Trumbauer and Beiderbecke were members of Adrian Rollini's short-lived big band (September–October 1927) before joining Paul Whiteman. Trumbauer also recorded in 1927 with the Broadway Bellhops, the Chicago Loopers, Joe Herlihy, and Red Nichols.

Unlike Beiderbecke, who was a happy-go-lucky alcoholic with a serious playing style, Trumbauer was a sober and reliable musician whose solos could often be whimsical, although his occasional attempts at vocalizing (such as on "Futuristic Rhythm") are good-humored but amateurish. Tram was with Paul Whiteman until 1936, having short solos on many of Whiteman's records although being heard at his best on his own sessions. By 1929 Bix was largely replaced (at his own request) by Andy Secrest on the Trumbauer dates. Most of the later Tram sessions (from 1934 on) featured Jack Teagarden. Because Trumbauer remained in Whiteman's band for so long, his chances of having a successful solo career became slim despite his talents. He co-led the Three T's with Jack and Charlie Teagarden in late 1936, moved to the West Coast, worked with George Stoll, and organized his own big band (1938–40), which recorded 17 titles in two sessions in 1940 but did not catch on.

Always greatly interested in flying, Trumbauer worked as a test pilot throughout World War II. In late 1945 Tram returned to music for a year, working a bit in the studios and appearing on a few obscure recordings, but he permanently retired from music in 1947 to work for the Civil Aeronautical Authority in Kansas City. Frankie Trumbauer made his final appearance as a musician at the Dixieland Jubilee's Bix tribute in October 1952, playing "Singin' the Blues" one last time.

9 Tram 1/June 14, 1923–May 22, 1929/The Old Masters 107
8 Tram 2/Sept. 18, 1929–Sept. 8, 1930/The Old Masters 108
8 Tram 3/Apr. 10, 1931–Feb. 23, 1934/The Old Masters 109
Frankie Trumbauer's dates as a leader from 1929 to early 1934 are reissued in full on these three well-conceived CDs. *Tram 1* is particularly interesting because it has Tram's most significant solos as a sideman, featuring him with the Benson Orchestra of Chicago (1923), the Mound City Blue Blowers ("San" and "Red Hot"), the Cotton Pickers, Ray Miller, Red Nichols, Paul Whiteman (1928–29), and the Mason-Dixon Orchestra (including a classic version of "What a Day"). Also included are two previously unreleased numbers featuring Bee Palmer. She was not much of a singer, but on 1929's "Singin' the Blues" she pioneered vocalese (putting words to recorded solos), 20 years before Eddie Jefferson and Jon Hendricks! *Tram 1*, which wisely bypasses Trumbauer's 1927–29 sessions with Bix Beiderbecke (which are continually reissued under the cornetist's name), also has the saxophonist's first dates as a leader (May 21–22, 1929), with Andy Secrest in Bix's place.

Tram 2 continues the Frankie Trumbauer Story with his somewhat obscure post-Bix dates as a leader, his key solos with Paul Whiteman's orchestra, and two songs with Joe Venuti's Blue Four (doubling on bassoon with the last). Highlights include "Nobody's Sweetheart," "Manhattan Rag," "Runnin' Ragged," "Happy Feet," and "New Tiger Rag." *Tram 3* has 23 additional selections from Trumbauer's recording groups, ranging from commercial sides where the ensembles are joined by a vocal group (The King's Jesters) to a couple of Bing Crosby vocals (including an exciting "Some of These Days") and the first session with Jack Teagarden. My fingers are crossed that The Old Masters label will eventually have a *Tram 4*, covering the remainder of Trumbauer's 1934 sessions plus his work in 1936 and possibly 1940.

RAY VENTURA
b. Apr. 16, 1908, Paris, France, d. Mar. 29, 1979, Majorca, France

Pianist Ray Ventura began leading his Collegians in 1928, when he was 20. Although the average age of his band members was 21, the ensemble quickly became France's top jazz group, recording some intriguing music during 1928–29 a bit reminiscent of Ben Pollack and the Dorsey Brothers Orchestra. Ventura was largely responsible for the arrangements while having Bob Vaz play piano. By 1930, the band became much more commercial, emphasizing French tunes although occasionally playing swing in the late 1930s; Django Reinhardt was a guest on one session.

LPS TO SEARCH FOR
Ray Ventura and His Collegians (Wolverine 4) has 15 selections from 1928–29, virtually the entire jazz

output from Ventura's band. The singers (Americans) are not so hot, but the ensembles have their exciting moments and the guest soloists include clarinetist Danny Polo and cornetist Philippe Brun.

JOE VENUTI

b. Sept. 16, 1894, Leeco, Italy, d. Aug. 14, 1978, Seattle, WA

A brilliant violinist who had a long and episodic career, Giuseppe "Joe" Venuti was at the top of his field throughout the 1920s and ranks as the first major jazz violinist, a player who largely introduced the violin to jazz as a solo instrument. Venuti grew up in Philadelphia and was a childhood friend of future guitarist Eddie Lang. The violinist worked in Atlantic City with Lang as early as 1919 and played with Bert Estlow's quintet (1921), the Hotel Knickerbocker Orchestra, and Red Nichols. Venuti directed the Book-Cadillac Hotel Orchestra for Jean Goldkette in 1924, making his recording debut.

After moving to New York in 1925, Venuti was very busy, appearing on countless recording sessions, including with Goldkette, Roger Wolfe Kahn, Frankie Trumbauer, the Dorsey Brothers, and Hoagy Carmichael. Venuti teamed up with Eddie Lang in many settings, ranging from commercial dates behind singers and dance bands to hot jazz sessions. As a leader on records, Venuti recorded exciting violin-guitar duets with Lang (including "Stringing the Blues"), freewheeling jazz dates (often with his Blue Four) and also with a jazz-oriented dance band filled with top musicians.

Venuti gained a well-deserved reputation for being an inventive practical joker during this period. His best-known escapade took place when he telephoned a couple of dozen bass players with an alleged gig, asking them to show up with their instruments at a busy corner. He drove around the block in his car and enjoyed watching the chaos that resulted!

Venuti worked with the Adrian Rollini Big Band during its short run in 1927, co-led a group with

Lang, and was a member of Paul Whiteman's orchestra for a year (May 1929–May 1930), appearing in a wonderful 90-second clip with Lang in the 1930 movie *The King of Jazz*. He kept busy during the early years of the Depression, mostly playing in the studios but also appearing on occasional jazz dates. On February 29, 1933, he unwittingly recorded with Eddie Lang for the last time, just shortly before Lang died from a botched tonsillectomy.

The guitarist's death shocked Venuti, who at first used Dick McDonough in Lang's place. He led a few more record dates during 1933–34 (including a memorable outing with Benny Goodman) and visited London in 1934. However, 1935 started a 33-year period in which the violinist slipped into obscurity. Venuti led a largely unsuccessful big band during 1935–43. He became an alcoholic, and, although he continued working (including a regular spot on Bing Crosby's radio show in the early 1950s), he was often difficult to locate and rarely recorded. However, the Joe Venuti story ended happily, because he made a major comeback starting in 1968 that found him in prime form and quite busy during his final decade.

10 The 1920s and 1930s Sides/Sept. 29, 1926–Sept. 10, 1931/ JSP 3402

9 Fiddlesticks/Oct. 22, 1931–Jan. 25, 1939/Conifer 172

8 Stringing the Blues/Nov. 8, 1926–May 8, 1933/Koch 7888

5 Venuti and Lang/Nov. 8, 1926–May 8, 1933/ABC 836 200

The JSP double CD contains 42 selections by Joe Venuti's small groups, all of his combo dates as a leader during 1926–31. The great majority of these performances are classics, for they find Venuti and Eddie Lang constantly inspiring each other and their guests, who include Arthur Schutt, Adrian Rollini, Don Murray, Frank Signorelli, Rube Bloom, Jimmy Dorsey, and Frankie Trumbauer. Among the gems are "Stringing the Blues," "Wild Cat," "The Wild Dog," "Kickin' the Cat," "Beatin' the Dog," "Sensation," "Runnin' Ragged," "Raggin' the Scale," and "Little Girl" (with a vocal from composer Harold Arlen). *Fiddlesticks* perfectly complements the JSP release, for this single CD has 20 additional performances from a slightly later period. The recording date of October 22, 1931, by the Venuti-Lang All-Star Orchestra (with a frontline of Benny Goodman and Jack and Charlie Teagarden), resulted in very exciting versions of "Beale Street Blues," "After You've Gone," "Farewell Blues," and "Someday Sweetheart." Also on this CD is Venuti's final recording with Lang, two orchestra features for the violinist, the last Venuti Blue Five date (from 1935, with both Adrian and Arthur Rollini), and the only four recordings by the Joe Venuti Big Band, whose titles are "Flip," "Flop," "Something," and "Nothing!"

Stringing the Blues is a double-CD straight reissue of a former double LP. The 32 selections are a bit of a grab bag, with 17 of the numbers that are duplicated on the JSP set, eight features for Eddie Lang (including several guitar duets with Lonnie Johnson), and seven other selections (including three featuring Tommy Dorsey's trumpet). Overall it is a fine sampler of the Venuti-Lang legacy, but the JSP set is preferred. The ABC *Venuti and Lang* CD is of lesser interest, since nearly all of the 16 selections (eight led by Venuti, three by Lang, two apiece by Frankie Trumbauer and Red Nichols, and the only rarity, Red McKenzie's "My Baby Came Home") are easily available elsewhere. Produced by Robert Parker, this CD is most notable for the recording quality, which often makes it sound like it is in stereo. (Due to the release of the JSP CD, the ratings for the ABC and Conifer Venuti sets have been readjusted from what they received in my *Swing* book.)

LPS TO SEARCH FOR

Overlooked in CD reissues thus far are Joe Venuti's dates leading a larger dance band during 1928–33. All of the music is available on *Big Bands of Joe Venuti, Vol. 1* (JSP 1111) and *Big Bands of Joe Venuti, Vol. 2* (JSP 1112). With the many vocals from

Scrappy Lambert, Smith Ballew, Don Elton, and Frank Luther, these recordings may not be as significant as the Blue Five performances, but there are some solid solos along the way from Venuti, trumpeters Leo McConville and Manny Klein, Tommy Dorsey, Jimmy Dorsey, and Jack Teagarden.

SIPPIE WALLACE

b. Nov. 1, 1898, Houston, TX, d. Nov. 1, 1986, Detroit, MI

In the 1980s, Sippie Wallace (who was born Beulah Thomas and was sometimes billed as "The Texas Nightingale") was the last of the surviving classic blues singers. She had been part of a very musical family that included two brothers who played piano (Hersal Thomas, who died of food poisoning in 1926, and the boogie-woogie pioneer George W. Thomas who recorded as Clay Custer). In addition, her niece was singer Hociel Thomas. Wallace began singing and playing organ in church. In the late 1910s, her family moved to New Orleans. Sippie gained experience working locally and throughout the South. After moving to Chicago in 1923, she began recording for the Okeh label. Wallace made 45 recordings during 1923–29 with such sidemen as Clarence Williams, Thomas Morris, Charles Irvis, Louis Armstrong, Sidney Bechet, King Oliver, Hersal Thomas, and Johnny Dodds.

Wallace worked throughout the 1920s, retired to Detroit after the Depression hit, and spent decades confining her singing to church (other than making recordings in 1945, 1958, and 1962). Sippie Wallace, after being persuaded by Victoria Spivey to resume singing, made a comeback starting in 1966 and worked fairly often during her final 20 years, being encouraged and to an extent sponsored by blues/pop performer Bonnie Raitt (a longtime admirer) near the end.

8 Vol. 1/Oct. 26 1923–Aug. 20, 1925/Document 5399
8 Vol. 2/Aug. 20, 1925–Sept. 25, 1945/Document 5400

All of Sippie Wallace's pre-1958 recordings are on these two CDs. *Vol. 1* has backing by Eddie Heywood Sr., Hersal Thomas, Perry Bradford's Jazz Phools, King Oliver, Clarence Williams, and two of Williams' groups, including a quintet with Louis Armstrong and Sidney Bechet ("Baby, I Can't Use You No More" and "Trouble Everywhere I Roam"). Primarily sticking to blues, Wallace certainly gets her message across on such songs as "Up the Country Blues," "Mama's Gone, Goodbye," "Let My Man Alone Blues," and "Devil Dance Blues." *Vol. 2* has two additional dates with Armstrong along with such tunes as "Murder's Gonna Be My Crime," "Suitcase Blues," "Special Delivery Blues," "A Man for Every Day in the Week," and two versions of Wallace's most famous song, "I'm a Mighty Tight Woman." After the May 6, 1927, date, Sippie recorded only two songs in 1929 and then two in a quintet with Lonnie Johnson and pianist Albert Ammons in 1945, otherwise unfortunately staying off records completely until 1958.

FATS WALLER

b. May 21, 1904, New York, NY, d. Dec. 14, 1943, Kansas City, MO

Although Thomas "Fats" Waller's greatest commercial successes were during the swing era, he was a major part of the New York jazz scene in the 1920s, as a pianist, organist, and songwriter if not yet a vocalist. Waller began playing harmonium at five and piano at six, performing in his school orchestra (which was led by altoist-arranger Edgar Sampson). His father was a church minister who was quite strict and wanted the youth to stick to religious music, but Waller was more attracted to popular music and the leaders of the new stride piano style, particularly James P. Johnson. After his mother died, Waller befriended James P. and his wife, moving in with the Johnsons and becoming the pianist's protégé. In 1919, when he was 15, Fats was hired as the Lincoln Theatre's house organist, stomping off improvisations for silent movies and developing the first jazz style on organ. During some of the shows, he gave the young Count Basie organ lessons. Waller began making piano rolls in the early 1920s (making 20 in all); he composed "Squeeze Me" (his earliest song), cut his first solo records in 1922, and often played at nightly rent parties with Johnson and Willie "the Lion" Smith.

Waller was quite busy on several fronts in the 1920s. He accompanied many singers on records during 1923–29, including Gene Austin, Alta Browne, Juanita Chappelle, W.C. Elkins, Porter Grainger, Rosa Henderson, Bert Howell, Alberta Hunter, the Jamaica Jazzers, Caroline Johnson, Anna Jones, Sara Martin, Hazel Meyers, Maude Mills, Andy Razaf, Carroll Tate, and Clarence Williams. He made guest appearances on hot jazz dates with the Fletcher Henderson Orchestra ("Henderson Stomp" and "The Chant" in 1926 and "Whiteman Stomp" and "I'm Coming Virginia" the following year), Johnny Dunn (1928), the Louisiana Sugar Babes, Nat Shilkret, James P. Johnson, McKinney's Cotton Pickers (1929), the Little Chocolate Dandies (1929), and the Mound City Blue Blowers (1930). Fats worked with lyricist Andy Razaf for the shows *Keep Shufflin'* (1928), *Hot Chocolates* (1929), and *Load of Coal*, writing such songs as "Ain't Misbehavin'," "Honeysuckle Rose," and "Black and Blue." He appeared at Carnegie Hall in James P. Johnson's *Yamecraw*. Waller also led an impressive and diverse series of recording dates for Victor during 1924–30 that included groundbreaking jazz organ solos, heated band jams (including "The Minor Drag" and "Harlem Fuss"), and such classic piano solos as "Handful of Keys," "Ain't Misbehavin'," "I've Got a Feeling I'm Falling," and "Smashing Thirds." And he did all of this while drinking, eating, partying, and carousing excessively!

Outside of a possible vocal on "Red Hot Dan" on one of his sessions from 1927, Waller did not sing at all on records until 1931. He began to emerge that year as a vocalist on solo versions of

Imagine spending a night trying to keep up with the constantly partying Fats Waller!

"I'm Crazy 'Bout My Baby" and "Draggin' My Heart Around" and on sessions with Ted Lewis and Jack Teagarden. Waller was with the bands of Otto Hardwicke and Elmer Snowden during 1931–32 and visited France and England in 1932. Although off records altogether during 1932–33 (other than a date with Billy Banks), he began to make a name for himself by appearing regularly on the radio, hosting *Fats Waller's Rhythm Club*. The Victor label took notice and in 1934 signed him up to record what would be a very extensive series of recordings with his Rhythm, a two-horn sextet. Fats Waller's jovial personality, ability to satirize songs in hilarious fashion, and brilliant stride piano playing soon made him a household name, and he became one of the most beloved of all jazz musicians, staying very active up until his death in 1943.

8 Piano Masterworks, Vol. 1/Oct. 21, 1922-Sept. 24, 1929/Hot 'n' Sweet 5106

9 Turn On the Heat: The Fats Waller Piano Solos/Feb. 16, 1927–May, 13, 1941/Bluebird 2482

10 Fats Waller and His Buddies/May 20, 1927–Dec. 18, 1929/ Bluebird 61005

Piano Masterworks, Vol. 1 has all of Fats Waller's piano solos from the 1920s (including all the alternate takes) except for the two from December 4, 1929. Although many of the selections are purposely melodic (such as the original version of "Ain't Misbehavin' ") rather than overly adventurous, there are some exceptions, including the virtuosic "Handful of Keys" and "Valentine Stomp." *Turn On the Heat* is a two-CD set that duplicates all of the music on the Hot 'n' Sweet CD except for Waller's two solos from 1922 ("Muscle Shoals

Blues" and "Birmingham Blues") and a third take of "I've Got a Feeling I'm Falling." However, the twofer easily compensates by also having Waller's 17 additional piano solos from his later years, including "African Ripples," "Clothes Line Ballet," "Tea for Two," and "Honeysuckle Rose," along with a pair of piano duets ("St. Louis Blues" and "After You've Gone") with Bennie Payne (Cab Calloway's regular pianist) in 1930.

With the exception of a few alternate takes, all of the pianist's small-group sessions as a leader from the 1920s are on *Fats Waller and His Buddies*, including such exciting numbers as "The Minor Drag," "Harlem Fuss," "Ridin' but Walkin'," "Fats Waller Stomp," and "Red Hot Dan." The sidemen include Charlie Irvis, Eddie Condon, Red Allen, Jack Teagarden, and Thomas Morris. The CD also includes six of the seven performances by the Louisiana Sugar Babes (all but the alternate for "Willow Tree"), which have restrained playing from Jabbo Smith, Garvin Bushell (clarinet, alto, and bassoon), James P. Johnson, and Waller on organ.

LPS TO SEARCH FOR

Fats Waller recorded 24 unaccompanied organ solos (counting alternate takes) during 1926–29, most of which are quite scarce on CD. Sixteen are on *Young Fats at the Organ, Volume 1* (French RCA 741.052), which will certainly be a difficult LP to get hold of. Also of strong interest is *Fats Plays, Sings, Alone and with Various Groups* (French CBS 63366), a gap filler that has Waller's two 1922 piano solos, his colorful guest appearances with Ted Lewis, Jack Teagarden, Billy Banks' Rhythmakers, the Little Chocolate Dandies, and the Mound City Blue Blowers, and his two solo piano-vocal numbers of 1931 ("I'm Crazy 'Bout My Baby" and "Draggin' My Heart Around") that foreshadow the success he would start having three years later.

FRED WARING

b. June 9, 1900, Tyrone, PA d. July 29, 1984, State College, PA

Fred Waring's fame was gained as the head of a glee club and vocal ensemble that engaged in chorale singing. However, early in his career, his big band occasionally played jazz. He led Waring's Banjo Orchestra (a quartet with two banjos, including himself) while attending college at Penn State. By 1922, when he left college to work full time as a bandleader-vocalist, the group was known as Fred Waring's Collegians and was up to ten pieces. Turning down an offer to join Paul Whiteman, Waring began recording with his orchestra in 1923 (one of their first songs, "Sleep," became their permanent theme song), and his ensemble worked steadily throughout the 1920s, using Paul Mertz as one of their main arrangers starting in 1927. Waring's principal goal (just as Stan Kenton's was 20 years later) was to play for concerts rather than dances, and to a large extent he was successful, even early in his career.

Fred Waring's Collegians appeared in the 1929 film *Syncopation* and on stage in 1930 in *The New Yorkers*. After 1932, what little jazz they played was dropped in favor of dance music and vocal features.

6 **Vol. 1: The Collegiate Years/Apr. 4, 1925-Dec. 14, 1928/The Old Masters 126**
6 **Vol. 2: The Broadway Years/Jan. 23, 1929–Nov. 16, 1932/ The Old Masters 129**

Jazz was only a flavor in Fred Waring's music of the 1920s, and his band lacked any major soloists. But the ensembles were clean, the musicianship was high, and quite frequently his band swung. Each of these CDs from The Old Masters label has 24 selections, and together they reissue the bulk of Waring's most interesting recordings of the 1920s. The music ranges from jazz and humorous novelties to ballads and period pieces, with Poley McClintock occasionally taking a short surprise vocal chorus, sounding just like Popeye!

WASHBOARD RHYTHM KINGS

During the early 1930s, it seemed as if a large portion of jazz was disappearing (particularly from records), with sweet bands, commercial dance orchestras, and soothing vocalists dominating. However, there were a few spirited ensembles that defied the trend. Seventeen overlapping groups recorded as the Alabama Washboard Stompers, the Washboard Rhythm Kings (the most popular name), the Five Rhythm Kings, the Washboard Rhythm Band, the Washboard Rhythm Boys, and the Georgia Washboard Stompers during 1930–35. What these bands offered were good-time music, usually featuring a washboard player, two or three horns, and spirited group vocals, falling stylistically between Dixieland and swing. Among the musicians who recorded with these enthusiastic and often-spontaneous ensembles (some of whose members are unidentified) were Teddy Bunn, trumpeters Taft Jordan and Valaida Snow, singers Jake Fenderson and Leo Watson, pianist Clarence Profit, banjoist-vocalist Steve Washington, and Ben Smith on clarinet and alto. But although they managed to survive the early years of the Depression, the Washboard Rhythm Kings and the other similar bands were considered obsolete once the big bands of the swing era began to dominate pop music.

8 Vol. 1/Apr. 2, 1931-Mar. 1, 1932/Collector's Classics 17
8 Vol. 2/Mar. 1, 1932–Nov. 23, 1932/Collector's Classics 18
8 Vol. 3/Oct. 5, 1932–Aug. 19, 1933/Collector's Classics 25
8 Vol. 4/Mar. 8, 1933–Sept. 12, 1933/Collector's Classics 26
8 Vol. 5/Mar. 24, 1930–July 19, 1935/Collector's Classics 30

These five CDs (115 selections) bring back most but not all of the numerous performances by the Washboard Rhythm Kings and its related groups of 1930–35. Each set is full of good-time music, and the sets are somewhat interchangeable despite the constant shifting of personnel. *Vol. 1* has Teddy Bunn on ten of the numbers and quite a few examples of this spontaneous jam band covering other groups' hits, including "Minnie the Moocher," "You Rascal You," "I'm Crazy 'Bout My Baby," "Star Dust," and "Georgia on My Mind." *Vol. 2* consists of four complete sessions from 1932 and is highlighted by "You Can Depend on Me," "Was

That the Human Thing to Do," "Tiger Rag," and "Sloppy Drunk Blues."

Vol. 3 has some fine trumpet work from Valaida Snow, spirited vocals from George "Ghost" Howell, and an early vocal version of "I'm Getting Sentimental Over You." The hotter numbers include "Sentimental Gentleman from Georgia," "I Would Do Anything for You," "Blue Drag," and "Old Man Blues." *Vol. 4* features three complete sessions from 1933, with spots for trumpeter Taft Jordan (closely emulating Louis Armstrong) and pianist Clarence Profit. Highlights include "Hustlin' and Bustlin' for Baby," "Dinah," "Happy as the Day Is Long," and "Hot Nuts." *Vol. 5* gathers together music from various sources (including performances by the Washboard Serenaders, the Scorpion Washboard Band, the Tramp Band, and the Five Rhythm Kings), with selections from 1930–31 (including "Kazoo Moan," "Washboards Get Together," "Please Don't Talk About Me When I'm Gone," and "Call of the Freaks") plus a London session from 1935.

All five CDs are easily recommended to fans of this brand of good-time music, which is very different from what listeners would normally expect from the music of the early Depression years! Hopefully there will be further Washboard Rhythm Kings releases from the Danish Collector's Classics label in the future.

BENNY WATERS

b. Jan. 23, 1902, Brighton, MD, d. Aug. 11, 1998, Columbia, MD

Benny Waters had a remarkably long career, being quite active as an alto saxophonist when he was in his mid-90s, recording on his 95th birthday, in 1997. Waters began playing music on the organ when he was three, in 1905. He also played a little bit of piano and trumpet before learning clarinet and tenor sax at seven. As a teenager, Waters performed with Charlie Miller's band in Philadelphia (1918–21). He studied at the Boston Conservatory and worked around Boston for a few years, including as

Ethel Waters proved during the 1920s and '30s that she could sing anything with class, swing, and emotion.

a music teacher; one of his students was Harry Carney. In 1925 Waters moved to New York, where he was a member of Charlie Johnson's orchestra for seven years, playing tenor and clarinet in addition to contributing many arrangements. During this era he also recorded with Clarence Williams (1928) and King Oliver.

However, it would take many years for Waters to achieve much fame. He worked with the Hot Lips Page big band (1938), Claude Hopkins (1940–41), Jimmie Lunceford (1942), and Jimmy Archey's Dixieland band (1950–52). Waters spent 40 years (1952–92) playing steadily all over Europe in swing and Dixieland settings. After he returned to the United States, Benny Waters surprised Americans in the 1990s with his forceful, fairly modern, and

still very viable playing, touring with the Statesmen of Jazz and working in New York clubs up until the end of his life. He was one of the final living links to mid-1920s jazz.

ETHEL WATERS

b. Oct. 31, 1896, Chester, PA, d. Sept. 1, 1977, Los Angeles, CA

Ethel Waters was one of the first black singers to "graduate" from the blues into popular music. In fact, in the 1920s and '30s, it was often obvious that she could sing practically anything. Waters sang in church choirs as a child and, while working as a maid as a teenager, she won local talent contests. She performed early on in Philadelphia and Baltimore and was nicknamed "Sweet Mama String-bean" due to her being tall and thin. That would be an ironic title (quickly dropped) after she gained a lot of weight during the 1930s.

Moving to New York in 1917, Waters was a major attraction almost from the start. Her flexibility and very clear enunciation helped her stand out from many of her contemporaries. Following in the wake of Mamie Smith's "Crazy Blues," Waters was one of the first black singers signed up for records. During 1921–24 she recorded blues and some popular songs (including "There'll Be Some Changes Made" and "That Da Da Strain") for the Black Swan label. Waters appeared in shows (including *Blackbirds* and the *Black Bottom Revue*) and by the mid-1920s was competing favorably with Bessie Smith (to whom she effectively paid tribute on her recording of "Maybe Not at All"). In 1925, Waters began recording for Columbia, cutting such winning jazz numbers as "Sweet Georgia Brown," "Go Back Where You Stayed Last Night," "I've Found a New Baby," and "Sugar." She introduced "Dinah," enjoyed having Joe Smith in her backup group, and cut a few classics (including "Guess Who's in Town" and "Do What You Did Last Night") while accompanied by James P. Johnson.

Unlike the careers of most classic blues singers, Ethel Waters' career did not slow down during the Depression. In 1929 she introduced "Am I Blue" in the underrated movie *On with the Show* (one of the few times from the era when a black performer was treated with some dignity on film). Waters' recordings became more orchestral and commercial in general yet retained a jazz feeling and consisted mostly of superior songs. Although she could not avoid all of the racial stereotypes, Waters was one of the very few blacks to become a stage and movie star in the 1930s and '40s while remaining in the United States. She appeared in the shows *As Thousands Cheer* and *Heat Wave*, recorded with Duke Ellington (1932) and Benny Goodman (1933), and introduced "Stormy Weather." As the swing era began, she was the best-known black female singer in

jazz and a major influence on Mildred Bailey and Lee Wiley.

Ethel Waters became more involved in acting by the end of the decade (starring in the 1942 movie *Cabin in the Sky*), continued singing into the early 1950s, and spent her last years heavily involved in religion.

7 1921–1923/Mar. 21, 1921–Mar. 1923/Classics 796
8 1923–1925/Mar. 1923–July 28, 1925/Classics 775
9 1925–1926/Aug. 25, 1925–July 29, 1926/Classics 672
10 1926–1929/Sept. 14, 1926–May 14, 1929/Classics 688
9 1929–1931/June 6, 1929–June 16, 1931/Classics 721
9 1931–1934/Aug. 10, 1931–Sept. 5, 1934/Classics 735

Fortunately all of Ethel Waters' vintage recordings are currently available on CD. The performances on *1921–1923* (which include five instrumentals by her backup group) are mostly obscure, and the technical quality is sometimes primitive. But even in 1921, Waters was a major and highly individual singer. Among her 22 numbers are "Oh Daddy," "There'll Be Some Changes Made," "Oh Joe, Play That Trombone," and "Memphis Man." The singer grew in power and depth as the 1920s progressed. With assistance from Joe Smith, Lovie Austin's Blues Serenaders, and Fats Waller on various selections of *1923–1925*, Waters is heard in her prime on "You Can't Do What My Last Man Did," "Craving Blues," "Sweet Georgia Brown," and "Go Back Where You Stayed Last Night."

Joe Smith also pops up on four songs on *1925–1926*, including a joyful "I've Found a New Baby." Other highlights include the original version of "Dinah," "Maybe Not at All" (which has Waters' imitations of Bessie and Clara Smith), "Shake That Thing," "Sugar," and "Heebie Jeebies." *1926–1929* is even better, with memorable renditions of "I'm Coming Virginia," "Home," "Take Your Black Bottom Outside," "Someday Sweetheart," "Some of These Days," "Guess Who's in Town," "My Handy Man," "Do What You Did Last Night," and the first classic version of "Am I Blue." James P. Johnson is a major asset on four songs.

On *1929–1931* Waters is backed not by black jazz players but by white studio musicians who fortunately could play jazz (including Tommy Dorsey, Jimmy Dorsey, Benny Goodman, Muggsy Spanier, and Joe Venuti). The emphasis is more on straightforward versions of current pop songs. But even though "Three Little Words'" is overly sentimental, there are fine versions of "True Blue Lou," "Waiting at the End of the World," "Memories of You," "You're Lucky to Me," and "Please Don't Talk About Me When I'm Gone." *1931–1934* wraps up Ethel Waters' preswing-era output, with her being joined on various selections by the Duke Ellington Orchestra ("I Can't Give You Anything but Love" and "Porgy"), white studio players (the initial version of "Stormy Weather"), Bunny Berigan ("Heat Wave), a Benny Goodman-led pickup group ("A Hundred Years from Today"), and musicians from the Chick Webb Orchestra. *1935–1940* (Classics 755), which completes the series, will also be of strong interest to Ethel Waters fans.

CHICK WEBB

b. Feb. 10, 1909, Baltimore, MD, d. June 16, 1939, Baltimore, MD

One of the top drummers to emerge in the late 1920s, the short-lived William "Chick" Webb led a very popular swing band which was at its prime during 1934–39. Cursed with tuberculosis of the spine and hunchbacked, Webb overcame his affliction to become an influential drummer and bandleader, the king of the Savoy Ballroom. He began playing drums as a teenager. After moving to New York in 1925, Webb led bands in various clubs. He recorded two numbers with his Jungle Band in 1929. The year 1931 was a turning point, for that is when Webb and his ten-piece band began playing at the Savoy. He led a three-song session that year (with a band that included Jimmy Harrison and Benny Carter) but did not start recording in earnest (other than two numbers in 1933) until 1934.

During his final five years, Webb introduced several Edgar Sampson songs (including "Stompin' at the Savoy" and "If Dreams Come True"), won battle of the band contests against Benny Goodman and Count Basie, and featured the young Ella Fitzgerald. Tragically he lived to be only 30, but he packed a lot of living into that short time.

10 1929–1934/June 14, 1929-Nov. 19, 1934/Classics 502

The first half of Chick Webb's recording career is covered in full on this CD, including Webb's two cuts with his 1929 Jungle Band ("Dog Bottom" and "Jungle Mama") and his 1931 session. Otherwise the music dates from 1933–34 and is early swing, highlighted by Taft Jordan's Louis Armstrong imitation on "On the Sunny Side of the Street," "When Dreams Come True," "Stompin' at the Savoy," and "Don't Be That Way." Except for a few titles, all the rest of Chick Webb's recordings (not counting his performances with Ella Fitzgerald) are available on the equally rewarding *1935–1938* (Classics 517).

SPEED WEBB

b. July 18, 1906, Peru, IN, d. 1980s?

Lawrence "Speed" Webb led a top territory band in the 1920s and '30s. But unlike the bands of Alphonse Trent and Zach Whyte, Webb's orchestra never recorded and is unfortunately totally lost to history. Webb played violin and mellophone as a child, switching to drums. He gained his nickname (Speed) for his skills as a baseball pitcher but chose music as his career. Webb played locally in Indiana (1923), studied embalming at the University of Illinois, and, back in Indiana, was a founding member of the Hoosier Melody Lads in 1925, becoming the band's leader. Webb's only record date, four songs for Gennett in 1926, was never released. During 1927–29, the drummer relocated the band to California, where the group provided the music for several films. Back in the Midwest, during 1929–38 Webb led his orchestra, sometimes under the names of the Hollywood Blue Devils, the Dixie Rhythm

Kings, Jack Jackson's Pullman Porters, and the Brown Buddies. Among his sidemen at various times were trumpeter Roy Eldridge, trombonist Vic Dickenson, and pianists Art Tatum and Teddy Wilson.

In 1938 Speed Webb permanently left music. He earned a master's degree in embalming in 1942 and ran a mortician business in Indiana for many years.

TED WEEMS

b. Sept. 26, 1901, Pitcairn, PA, d. May 6, 1963, Tulsa, OK

Ted Weems led a popular orchestra during the swing era that became best known for its hit "Heartaches." A decade earlier, in the 1920s, he had a superior jazz-inspired dance band. Weems, who played violin and trombone, worked earlier with Paul Specht and led his first band in 1922. In 1923 his orchestra had a best-selling record of "Somebody Stole My Gal." With Parker Gibbs taking vocals (later succeeded by Art Jarrett, Wes Vaughan, Elmo Tanner, and Perry Como) and such fine soloists in the late 1920s as clarinetist Don Watt, trumpeter Art Weems (Ted's brother), and Dudley Fosdick (on mellophone), Weems performed a variety of danceable jazz, novelties, and college songs. In 1929, "Piccolo Pete" (followed by "Harmonica Harry") was a big hit. That year Weems relocated from New York to Chicago, where he worked and broadcast regularly (when not touring) during the next 12 years. He broke up the band in 1941 in order to join the Merchant Marines but regrouped after World War II. In 1947, Weems' 1933 recording of "Heartaches" unexpectedly became a big seller. Ted Weems kept his orchestra together into the 1950s, and in later years he worked as a disc jockey in Memphis.

8 Marvelous/July 19, 1926-Sept. 15, 1929/Memphis Archives 7013

Eighteen of Ted Weems' better recordings from the 1926-29 period are on this CD, which unfortunately does not list the personnel. These renditions of "That's My Girl," "Miss Annabelle Lee," "From Saturday Night Till Monday Morning," "What a Day," and "Piccolo Pete" are gems, showing that Ted Weems had one of the finest jazz-oriented dance bands of the period.

LPS TO SEARCH FOR

Most of Ted Weems' valuable late-1920s recordings have not yet been put out on CD. *1928–1930* (The Old Masters 23) repeats only four numbers (including "Piccolo Pete" and "What a Day") from the *Marvelous* CD and has a strong sampling of slightly later material, including "Harmonica Harry," "The Man from the South" "Slappin' the Bass," "One-Man Band," and "Egyptian Ella."

DICKIE WELLS

b. June 10, 1909, Centerville, TN, d. Nov. 12, 1985, New York, NY

Dickie Wells was a very significant trombonist with Count Basie's orchestra during the swing era but his pre-Basie years were interesting too. Wells grew up in Louisville, Kentucky, studying music starting when he was ten, playing baritone horn at 13, and switching to trombone at 16. He became a professional soon after beginning on trombone, where his speechlike and humorous style made him popular. Wells moved to New York, joining Lloyd Scott's group (with whom he made his recording debut in 1927), and he stayed with the band after it was taken over by Cecil Scott (1927–30). Wells is quite colorful on his 1929 recordings with Scott's Bright Boys, being memorable (and sometimes hilarious) on "In a Corner" and "Lawd, Lawd."

After leaving Scott, Wells worked with Elmer Snowden (1930–32, including appearing in the 1933 short film *Smash Your Baggage*), Russell Wooding (1932), Benny Carter (1932–33), Fletcher Henderson (1933), and Teddy Hill (1934–37), also recording with Henry "Red" Allen, Spike Hughes, and Horace Henderson. But all of this was just a warm-up to Dickie Wells' becoming a longtime member of Count Basie's band in July 1938.

ARTHUR WHETSOL

b. 1905, Punta Gorda, FL, d. Jan. 5, 1940, New York, NY

Arthur Whetsol's lyrical style and haunting tone on trumpet worked perfectly as one of the voices in Duke Ellington's orchestra. He was born Arthur Schiefe, eventually taking his mother's maiden name of Whetsol. He grew up in Washington, D.C., and was a childhood friend of Duke Ellington, first performing with the pianist in 1920. Whetsol also worked with Claude Hopkins and the White Brothers Orchestra. He traveled with Elmer Snowden to New York in late 1923 to join the Washingtonians; soon afterwards Ellington became the band's pianist. Whetsol's sweet-toned trumpet worked very well with the alto of Otto Hardwicke, but after a few months he returned to Washington, D.C., to study medicine at Howard University.

His studies completed, in March 1928 Arthur Whetsol rejoined Ellington, who had taken over the Washingtonians from Snowden and made the band into a major success, performing nightly at the Cotton Club. Whetsol's lyrical sound was a perfect contrast to the extroverted plunger work of Bubber Miley (and his successor, Cootie Williams). His playing as first trumpeter on slower numbers such as "Mood Indigo" and "Black Beauty," although sounding simple, would in later years trouble those other trumpeters who tried to duplicate his effortless style. Whetsol is quite prominent in the 1929 Ellington short film *Black and Tan*, playing "Black and Tan Fantasy" as a duet with Duke.

Arthur Whetsol was a key member of Duke Ellington's orchestra until the summer of 1936, when a brain disease forced him to retire. He made a few brief attempts to come back but died in 1940, at the age of 34.

PAUL WHITEMAN

b. Mar. 28, 1890, Denver, CO, d. Dec. 29, 1967, Doylestown, PA

Paul Whiteman was billed as "The King of Jazz" in the 1920s and, although the title was inaccurate, he did lead an impressive and technically skilled band, the best known and most popular orchestra of the decade. His father, Wilberforce J. Whiteman, was a highly respected music teacher in Denver whose students included Jimmie Lunceford. The younger Whiteman began playing violin when he was seven and performed with the Denver Symphony Orchestra during 1907–14. He worked in San Francisco (including with the San Francisco Symphony Orchestra), was briefly in the Navy (leading a 40-piece band), and in 1918 began leading his own dance band at San Francisco's Fairmont Hotel.

Whiteman's background was in classical music, but his main goal became to "uplift" dance music and jazz to a high level of respectability, to "make a lady out of jazz," taming and civilizing the wild music and making it accessible to a large audience. Whiteman, who largely gave up playing violin by the early 1920s, took his orchestra to Los Angeles later in 1918, spent time in Atlantic City, and in 1920 moved his home base to New York. With Henry Busse as his star soloist, Whiteman had major hit records in "Whispering" and "Japanese Sandman," also introducing "Wang Wang Blues" in 1920 and "Hot Lips" (which was composed for Busse) in 1922. His favorite personal recording was "When Day Is Done."

A household name throughout the United States by 1922, Whiteman toured Europe in 1923 and 1926. On February 24, 1924, his concert at Aeolian Hall, which was billed as "An Experiment in Modern Music," introduced George Gershwin's *Rhapsody in Blue*, with the composer heard on piano. In subsequent years Whiteman also introduced Gershwin's Concerto in F and his main arranger Ferde Grofé's *Grand Canyon Suite*. Although his orchestra played dance music and some jazz, Whiteman

The best-known bandleader of the 1920s, Paul Whiteman sought to tame and "civilize" jazz.

was always interested in presenting a wide-ranging program that included semiclassical works too. His band almost always included strings along with the usual instruments and an expanded rhythm section. In fact, as his orchestra grew, it sometimes resembled an elephant, weighed down by technically skilled but unswinging players.

By 1926, Whiteman was widely known as "The King of Jazz," yet his orchestra was quite weak in the jazz department. He recognized that fault and so went about fixing the problem. A couple of promising jazz singers, Bing Crosby and Al Rinker, were teamed by Whiteman with Harry Barris and featured as the Rhythm Boys. Red Nichols, Tommy Dorsey, and Jimmy Dorsey all spent some time in the orchestra. And in the fall of 1927, after both the Jean Goldkette Orchestra and the short-lived Adrian Rollini big band failed, Whiteman hired most of their best players, including Bix Beiderbecke, Frankie Trumbauer, Bill Rank, Min Leibrook, and arranger Bill Challis. Hoagy Carmichael debuted his "Washboard Blues" with Whiteman, and in 1929 Joe Venuti and Eddie Lang were hired. All of these acquisitions did not mean that Whiteman was letting his orchestra become freewheeling, but he liked to use the jazz voices for color and their short solos for variety in his shows. Particularly during 1928–29, Whiteman's orchestra recorded quite a few rewarding jazz performances.

Meanwhile Paul Whiteman's Concert Orchestra grew and grew. By 1929 he had four trumpeters, four trombonists, six reed players, a full string section, two pianos, banjo, guitar, bass sax, tuba, bass, drums, and up to six vocalists to choose from. When Bix Beiderbecke became ill and had to depart, Whiteman hired the soundalike Andy Secrest (repeating his feat of 1928, when he quickly got Harry Goldfield to take over for Henry Busse, who had quit after an argument). When Bix unexpectedly returned, Whiteman kept both cornetists for a time until Bix permanently left later in 1929. In early 1930, at the height of his fame, Whiteman was in Hollywood with his 27-piece (not counting singers) orchestra, filming *The King of Jazz*. Unfortunately the movie is as overblown as much of Whiteman's music, but it does have a few great moments, including 90 seconds of Venuti and Long, the Rhythm Boys singing "Mississippi Mud," a version of "Happy Feet," and a humorous comedy routine by the virtuosic trombonist Wilbur Hall.

Returning to New York and finding the Depression in full swing, Whiteman decided it was time to cut back. He streamlined his group to a mere 20 pieces (Venuti and Lang departed, as did the Rhythm Boys) and emphasized dance music for a time. In the 1930s, Mildred Bailey (the first female singer to be featured regularly with an orchestra), Miff Mole, Bunny Berigan, Jack Teagarden, and Charlie Teagarden were among the more notable new musicians in the orchestra (Frankie Trumbauer and Bill Rank remained for many years). However, Whiteman was overshadowed during the swing era and seemed a bit directionless, holding onto his classical roots and original goals (which were now outdated) while allowing his big band to swing only now and then. He kept the orchestra together until the mid-1940s (recording "Traveling Light" with Billie Holiday in 1942), had a few short-term reunions, and in later years worked at ABC. Paul Whiteman spent his last decade running a farm in New Jersey.

7 Greatest Hits/Aug. 19, 1920–1928/Collector's Choice 61
6 King of Jazz/Aug. 23, 1920–1936/ASV/Living Era 5170
5 Music for Moderns/Apr. 1927–Oct. 5, 1928/Naxos 120505

8 Original 1927 Recordings/July 13, 1927–Nov. 23, 1927/Nostalgia Arts 3006

Considering how much Paul Whiteman recorded in the 1920s, it is surprising that there are not more CDs available of his music, although his 1927–29 recordings that include Bix Beiderbecke contributions are continually reissued under the cornetist's name. *Greatest Hits* mostly lives up to its title, featuring some of Whiteman's best-selling records of 1920–28, including "Japanese Sandman," "Whispering" (a million-seller in 1920), "Hot Lips," "Three O'Clock in the Morning," and the second version of *Rhapsody in Blue*. The jazz content is light but the music is enjoyable. The same can be said for *King of Jazz,* which covers a wider period of time (less successfully) with only a few duplications; highlights include a few Bix numbers, "Whiteman Stomp," and "Happy Feet." *Music for Moderns* has some of Whiteman's more "experimental" and classical-oriented pieces of 1927–28, including the four-part "Suite of Serenades" (by Victor Herbert), "A Study in Blue," "Sea Burial," "Caprice Futuristic," the original version of Gershwin's Concerto in F, and the second *Rhapsody in Blue*. Interesting music but very little jazz other than Henry Busse's trumpet chorus on "When Day Is Done."

Original 1927 Recordings features all of the Whiteman sessions from July 13 to November 23, 1927, concluding with "Washboard Blues," which was the first appearance of Bix Beiderbecke with the band. The diverse material finds Whiteman changing his focus from dance music to jazz while still featuring some semiclassical works. Highlights include "Whiteman Stomp," "Sensation," "Shaking the Blues Away," and the remake of "Wang Wang Blues" (released for the first time in 70 years). Jimmy Dorsey, Tommy Dorsey, Joe Venuti, and Bing Crosby all make notable appearances. Recommended.

A reappraisal of Paul Whiteman's pre- and post-Bix recordings is long overdue.

LPS TO SEARCH FOR

The double-LP *Jazz à La King* (French RCA 42413) has 33 selections that do an excellent job of tracing Paul Whiteman's musical evolution from 1920 to 1936, from "Wang Wang Blues," "Hot Lips," and an intriguing 1926 exploration of "St. Louis Blues" to "Mississippi Mud," Mildred Bailey on "Rockin' Chair," and 1936's "Saddle Your Blues to a Wild Mustang." *An Experiment in Modern Music* (Smithsonian Collection 2-0518) is a two-LP set that recreates the program of Whiteman's 1924 Aeolian Hall concert. The vintage recordings are by Whiteman, the Original Dixieland Jazz Band, the Great White Way Orchestra, Art Hickman, Zez Confrey, the Broadway Dance Orchestra, Jean Goldkette, and others, giving an idea of what the concert must have sounded like. A bonus is the original (and superior) version of *Rhapsody in Blue* from 1924.

Featuring Bing Crosby (Columbia 2830) has 16 selections from 1928–29, with Crosby singing (often as part of a group) on all but one number. Only four tunes feature Bix Beiderbecke, so there are some rarities here, including "Coquette," "At Twilight," and "I'm a Dreamer, Aren't We All."

ZACK WHYTE

b. 1898, Richmond, KY, d. Mar. 10, 1967, KY

Zack Whyte led one of the top territory bands of the late 1920s/early '30s. A banjoist, Whyte studied at Wilberforce, Ohio, and played in a group led by Horace Henderson (1922). In 1923 he put together the Chocolate Beau Brummels, which he led for the next 15 years. Unlike Speed Webb, Whyte was fortunate enough to record six selections, all in 1929 and available on *Richmond Rarities* (Jazz Oracle 8008). Trumpeter Sy Oliver, tenor saxophonist Al Sears, and pianist Herman Chittison were in the recorded band, while sidemen from later editions included Roy Eldridge and trombonists Quentin Jackson and Vic Dickenson. Zack Whyte retired from music in 1938.

CLARENCE WILLIAMS

b. Oct. 8, 1893, Plaquemine Delta, LA, d. Nov. 6, 1965, New York, NY

An adequate pianist, a cheerful singer, and an enthusiastic jug blower, Clarence Williams is most important as a songwriter, an organizer of scores of recording sessions (nearly all of which are quite rewarding and exciting), and a hustler for the music he loved. Williams grew up in New Orleans, played piano in Storyville, and was an emcee, dancer, and singer with Billy Kersan's Minstrel Show. He was writing songs by 1913. When he received a $1,600 check for a song he had forgotten about ("Brownskin, Who You For") that had been recorded by a band in New York, he began paying close attention to music publishing. Williams worked in vaudeville as a dancer, played duos with violinist Armand J. Piron, and toured with W.C. Handy (1917). He also co-ran a publishing company with Piron.

Around 1920, Williams moved to Chicago, where he at first had a music store before putting together a very successful publishing company. In 1921 he married singer Eva Taylor (their marriage lasted until his death, 44 years later) and recorded six songs as a vocalist. Williams also began writing a series of notable songs (some of which were co-composed with Spencer Williams, who was no relation); among the ones that became standards are "Baby Won't You Please Come Home," "Royal Garden Blues," "Sugar Blues," "Everybody Loves My Baby," "'Tain't Nobody's Business If I Do," and "I Ain't Gonna Give Nobody None of My Jelly Roll."

Things really picked up in 1923, and soon Williams had a very profitable system working for him. He wrote songs, published them himself, sold the sheet music, had his wife sing the tunes on the radio, and arranged to have them recorded by some of the finest small-group players of the 1920s. It helped that he was a talent scout for Okeh during 1923–28 and was constantly setting up record dates. Williams recorded 162 selections (not count-

A masterful businessman and talent scout, Clarence Williams organized scores of rewarding record dates.

ing alternate takes) under his own name during 1923–31, everything from piano solos to performances with fairly large bands. His sidemen included Sidney Bechet, Thomas Morris, Charlie Irvis, Louis Armstrong, Buster Bailey, Bubber Miley, Tommy Ladnier, Jimmy Harrison, Coleman Hawkins, Floyd Casey, Albert Socarras, Louis Metcalf, Cecil Scott, King Oliver, and James P. Johnson, plus such standbys as Ed Allen, saxophonist-clarinetist Arville Harris, banjoist Leroy Harris, Cyrus St. Clair, and Eva Taylor. In addition, Taylor recorded frequently during this period under her own name (with her husband on piano), and Williams recorded using such pseudonyms as the Barrelhouse Five Orchestra, the Bluegrass Footwarmers, the Dixie Washboard Band, the Four Spades, the Jamaica Jazzers, the Lazy Levee Loungers, and the Seven Gallon Jug Band, in addition to making guest appearances on records by James P. Johnson, King Oliver, and George McClennon's Jazz Devils.

Williams also worked very often with blues singers. He helped Bessie Smith get signed in 1923 and, in addition to appearing on some of her dates, he backed Texas Alexander, Lil Harden Armstrong, Anna Bell, Ester Bigeou, Bessie Brown, Laura Bryant, Butterbeans and Susie, Dora Carr, E.L. Coleman, Rosetta Crawford, Cora Garner, Horace George, Fannie Mae Goosby, Annette Hanshaw, Lucille Hegamin, Katherine Henderson, Alberta Hunter, Bertha Idaho, Edith Johnson, Elizabeth Johnson, Margaret Johnson, Maggie Jones, Virginia Liston, Billy and Mary Mack, Daisy Martin, Sara

Martin, Lizzie Miles, Monette Moore, Andy Pendleton, Sam Robinson, Irene Scruggs, Clara Smith, Hazel Smith, Laura Smith, Mamie Smith, Victoria Spivey, Charlie and Effie Tyus, Sippie Wallace, Ethel Waters, and Margaret Webster. Considering that he was no great shakes as a pianist, it is remarkable that he recorded with nearly every important classic blues singer of the 1920s.

Williams' importance waned gradually during the 1930s. After recording nothing as a leader in 1932, he cut 71 titles during 1933–35 (not counting dates with the Alabama Jug Band and the Birmingham Serenaders), 21 in 1937, three in 1938, and a final pair in 1941. After the late 1930s, Williams concentrated mostly on composing. In 1943 he sold his publishing catalogue to Decca for $50,000 and, other than for a few very rare appearances, retired from music. Clarence Williams, who lost his sight in 1956 after being knocked down by a taxi, spent his last years running a bargain store in New York, still happily married to Eva Taylor. His legacy to 1920s jazz is enormous.

8 1921–1924/Oct. 11, 1921–Nov. 6, 1924/Classics 679
9 1924–1926/Dec. 17, 1924–Feb. 1926/Classics 695
9 1926–1927/Mar. 7, 1926–Jan. 29, 1927/Classics 718
9 1927/Mar. 8, 1927–Sept. 23, 1927/Classics 736
9 1927–1928/Oct. 1927–Aug. 1, 1928/Classics 752
8 1928–1929/Aug. 1928–Jan. 1929/Classics 771

The long string of Clarence Williams recordings represents a huge treasure. Williams never "went commercial" by utilizing a dance orchestra, strings, or overly complex arrangements. His band performances perfectly balanced the strong melodies with space left for hot solos by his talented sidemen. It is very fortunate that the Classics label, on 14 CDs, has reissued the "complete" Clarence Williams (even if it does not include alternate takes).

1921–1924 has Williams' six very rare vocals from 1921, four piano solos, and dates with his Blue Five. Sidney Bechet is heard on his recording debut (outstanding versions of "Wild Cat Blues" and "Kansas City Man Blues"), and Louis Armstrong pops up on three numbers in 1924 (including "Everybody Loves My Baby"). *1924–1926* has Louis Armstrong on the first 13 selections, six of which also include Bechet. "Mandy, Make Up Your Mind" features Bechet taking a unique solo on the bass sarrusophone (the only time he used that instrument), while "Cake Walking Babies from Home" finds the two masters challenging each other, with Armstrong winning. The post-Armstrong selections (which sometimes feature Joe Smith, Bubber Miley, Ed Allen, Charlie Irvis, Buster Bailey, and Coleman Hawkins) are not exactly throwaways either; check out Hawkins (on baritone!) during "Dinah." *1926–1927*, which has notable contributions from Miley, Tricky Sam Nanton, Ed Allen, Louis Metcalf, Tommy Ladnier, Jimmy Harrison, Buster Bailey, and Coleman Hawkins, is full of gems. Highlights include "Jackass Blues," "Morocco Blues," "Senegalese Stomp," and especially a two-clarinet jam on "Candy Lips."

1927 consists of 22 selections recorded in less than a seven-month period. With Ed Allen, Buster Bailey, Charlie Irvis, Red Allen (in his recording debut), and Louis Metcalf taking key solos, the music is top-notch, particularly "Cushion Foot Stomp" (heard in three different versions), "Old Folks Shuffle," Williams' vocal on the charming "When I March in April with May," and "Shooting the Pistol," which has from Albert Socarras what is probably the first jazz flute solo on record. *1927–1928* has two Williams piano solos, two numbers in which his singing is backed by James P. Johnson (including the eccentric "Farm Hand Papa"), and band sides with Ed Allen, Buster Bailey, Coleman Hawkins, King Oliver, and Benny Waters; highlights include "Jingles," "Church Street Sobbin' Blues," "Sweet Emalina," and "Mountain City Blues." King Oliver makes some notable appearances on *1928–1929*, including on "Bozo" and "Bimbo." The usual players (plus Eddie Lang) uplift such tunes as "New Down Home Blues," "Organ Grinder Blues," "Have You Ever Felt That Way," and "Pane in the Glass."

8 1929/Jan. 1929–May 28, 1929/Classics 791
8 1929–1930/June 21, 1929–Apr. 23, 1930/Classics 810
8 1930–1931/May 22, 1930–Feb. 19, 1931/Classics 832
7 1933/May 15, 1933–Sept. 1, 1933/Classics 845
6 1933–1934/Dec. 6, 1933–June 28, 1934/Classics 871
6 1934/July 6, 1934–Oct. 3, 1934/Classics 891
6 1934–1937/Sept. 11, 1934–Apr. 8, 1937/Classics 918
4 1937–1941/1937–1941/Classics 953

There is less variety in personnel on *1929* (Ed Allen and Arville Harris are constants) and a fair number of remakes, but there are a lot of excellent performances, including "Steamboat Days," "Baby Won't You Please Come Home," "In Our Cottage of Love," and "Breeze." *1929–1930* benefits greatly from James P. Johnson's being on eight of the selections, including "You've Got to Be Modernistic," and two piano duets with Williams (the humorous "How Could I Be Blue" and "I've Found a New Baby"). Other hot numbers include "High Society," "Railroad Rhythm," and "Whip Me with Plenty of Love." The rise of the Depression did nothing to change Clarence Williams' music, as can be heard on *1930–1931*, which includes "You're Bound to Look Like a Monkey When You Get Old," "He Wouldn't Stop Doin' It," "Papa De-Da-Da," and four versions of "Shout, Sister, Shout" (each with different personnel). Among the musicians are Cecil Scott, pianist Herman Chittison, Ikey Robinson, Ed Allen, Red Allen, and Lonnie Johnson.

After so much activity, Clarence Williams was mostly absent from records for over two years. In 1933 he returned, but, despite plenty of spirit, many of the performances by his core quartet (with Ed Allen, Cecil Scott, and Floyd Casey) are somewhat predictable. Best are a couple of numbers with Albert Nicholas and jams with a jug band that includes both Herman Chittison and Willie "the Lion" Smith on pianos. Things slipped a bit at the time of *1933–1934* due to an excess of vocals, including seven by the insipid (if enthusiastic) Chick Bullock; only three of the 23 songs are instrumentals. Still, there are moments, thanks to James P. Johnson's help on many of the songs. But for the first time it sounds as if Williams was running out of fresh ideas and strong material. *1934* features (in addition to Williams' dates) the Alabama Jug Band numbers, with Willie "the Lion" Smith and Ikey Robinson making strong contributions. Highlights include "Sugar Blues," "Jerry the Junker," and "The Stuff Is Here and It's Mellow." Ed Allen, Cecil Scott, and Buster Bailey (on the 1937 session) are the main soloists on *1934–1937*, which finds Williams entering the swing era with his approach unchanged. Chick Bullock's three vocals do not help, but there are plenty of spirited moments from the combos. But obviously, since there were no recordings at all in 1936, things were greatly slowing down.

1937–1941 is the 14th and final CD in Classics' comprehensive Williams series. It is the weakest disc overall, although it should be of interest to historians. The first 15 selections are listed as being by "Clarence Williams' Swing Band"), but that septet (with Allen, Bailey, Scott, and Russell Procope on alto and clarinet) has little to do on most of the tunes (all spirituals) other than back William Cooley's dozen somewhat-pompous vocals. Also on this CD are three songs from a 1938 organ-piano-drums trio that does not include Williams (Babe Matthews has two vocals) and two final numbers from 1941, with Clarence Williams and Eva Taylor getting together one final time with old friend James P. Johnson.

5 The Complete Sessions, Vol. 1/July 30, 1923-Nov. 12, 1923/ Hot 'n' Sweet 5107
5 The Complete Sessions, Vol. 2/Nov. 14, 1923–Mar. 4, 1925/ Hot 'n' Sweet 5109
6 1927 to 1934/Jan. 25, 1927–July 6, 1934/ABC 836 829

The two CDs from the Hot 'n' Sweet label differ from the Classics CDs in that they include not only some numbers from Williams' Blue Five but his accompaniment to a variety of blues singers. *Vol. 1* (which starts with Bechet on "Wild Cat Blues") finds the pianist backing Sara Martin, Mamie Smith, Rosetta Crawford, Sara Martin, Margaret Johnson, and Eva Taylor, while *Vol. 2* also has selections with Virginia Liston, Maureen Englin, and Sippie Wallace. The blues dates are available in more complete form elsewhere through the Document label. The ABC release has producer Robert Parker cherry-picking through Clarence Williams' output to come up with 16 selections (including "Candy Lips," "Walk That Broad," and "Organ Grinder Blues"), which he magically turns into stereo. Excellent music, but get the best Classics releases instead.

CLAUDE WILLIAMS

b. Feb. 22, 1908, Muskogee, OK

One of the last survivors of the 1920s, Claude "Fiddler" Williams almost found fame twice but is actually better known today than he was during his early days. Doubling on violin and guitar, Williams first worked professionally with Terrence Holder's Dark Clouds of Joy in 1927, staying with the band after Andy Kirk became its leader in 1929. He recorded on violin with Kirk during 1929–30 (being its top soloist, other than Mary Lou Williams) but departed five years before the band hit it big in 1936. Williams worked with Alphonso Trent (1932) and in Kansas City with George E. Lee (1933) and Chick Stevens (1934–35). Williams joined Count Basie in 1936, playing rhythm guitar and violin. He was with Basie when the band went to New York, made its initial recordings, and had its first early successes. However, Williams was replaced by guitarist Freddie Green in early 1937 because producer Johnny Hammond did not care for violin soloists. While Green worked with Basie for 50 years, Williams returned to the Midwest, where he was in obscurity for decades.

Happily, Claude Williams gained some recognition when he began playing and recording with pianist Jay McShann in the late 1960s. He has been quite active ever since, touring with the Statesmen of Jazz and recording as a leader, still playing in fine form at this writing, at the age of 93.

COOTIE WILLIAMS

b. July 24, 1910, Mobile, AL, d. Sept. 15, 1985, New York, NY

Charles Melvin "Cootie" Williams gained fame in the 1930s with Duke Ellington's orchestra, recognition that might have gone to Bubber Miley if Miley had not drunk himself out of Ellington's band. Williams started off playing trombone, tuba, and drums in school. He was largely self-taught on trumpet and gained experience gigging in his native Alabama, touring with the Young Family Band (which included the young Lester and Lee Young), and working in Florida with clarinetist Eagle Eye Shields and Alonzo Ross' De Luxe Syncopators (1926–28).

Moving to New York in 1928, Cootie Williams recorded with James P. Johnson ("Chicago Blues" and "Mournful Tho'ts"), worked with Chick Webb, and spent a couple of months in Fletcher Henderson's orchestra (recording "Come On, Baby" and "Easy Money"), where he played opposite Rex Stewart, another future Ellington band member. After the alcoholic Bubber Miley was fired from Ellington's orchestra, in February 1929 Cootie Williams took his place. Miley was famed for his wizardry with mutes and for the unusual tonal distortions that he created. Williams played open horn for his first couple of weeks with Duke, until he realized that he had been hired in Miley's spot. With the assistance of Tricky Sam Nanton, Cootie soon mastered the plunger mute, and in time he surpassed his predecessor.

Cootie Williams is heard on most of Ellington's recordings of 1929–40 (finding his own niche opposite Arthur Whetsol, Freddy Jenkins, and later

Rex Stewart) and developing into one of the top trumpeters of the decade. After leaving Ellington, he worked with Benny Goodman for a year (1940–41), led a big band of his own (1941–48), had an R&Bish combo that was based at the Savoy, and (following a 22-year "vacation") ended his career back where he belonged, with Duke Ellington (1962–74).

FESS WILLIAMS

b. Apr. 10, 1894, Danville, KY, d. Dec. 17, 1975, New York, NY

A gaspipe clarinetist-altoist who was also a good-humored singer, Stanley "Fess" Williams (the uncle of bassist-composer Charles Mingus) led a popular jazz ensemble during the second half of the 1920s. He started on violin but by the time he was 15 was playing mostly clarinet in addition to learning saxophones. Williams worked in Cincinnati during 1914–23, leading local bands starting in 1919. After playing with Ollie Powers in Chicago, he moved to New York in 1924. The following year Fess formed his Royal Flush Orchestra, a septet that eventually grew to be 11 pieces. The band's home base was the Savoy Ballroom during 1926–27, and it recorded 23 numbers during this time. None of the sidemen (which included trumpeter George Temple and trombonist Jelly James) became famous, and the leader's solos could be overly exuberant and corny, but the band had plenty of spirit.

Williams spent most of 1928 in Chicago, fronting Dave Peyton's band (recording two numbers as Fess Williams' Joy Boys that are available on *Hot Stuff*—Frog 28) while his own orchestra continued playing in New York. Fess returned to the Big Apple in the spring of 1929, led his band again, and recorded an additional 28 selections during 1929–30. The basic style was unchanged, with heated ensembles, a happy feel, and the leader's over-the-top clarinet and alto usually in the lead.

Fess Williams led his orchestra until the beginning of the swing era (unrecorded sidemen included Bob Shoffner, Rex Stewart, Albert Nicholas, and Garvin Bushell), leaving music by the mid-1930s, except on a part-time basis, to work in real estate.

LPS TO SEARCH FOR

Fess Williams recordings are not too common on CD but, except for eight selections from 1926–27, all of his dates were reissued on LP. *Fess Williams and His Royal Flush Orchestra* (Fountain 116) has 16 early titles, including two that were previously unreleased and a pair of numbers by the band without Williams (released as by Jelly James' Fewsicians). *Volume One* (Harlequin 2039) and *Volume Two* (Harlequin 2040) have all of Williams' 1929–30 recordings, including some alternate takes and such heated performances as "Here 'Tis," "Hot Town," "Buttons," "Musical Camp Meeting," "'Leven-Thirty Saturday Night," "I'm Feelin' Devilish," and the hilarious "Playing My Saxophone." And for those listeners who cannot get enough Fess, there is *Volume Three—The Rare Masters* (Harlequin 2052), which has additional alternate takes and rare performances from 1926–30.

MARY LOU WILLIAMS

b. May 8, 1910, Atlanta, GA, d. May 28, 1981, Durham, NC

Sometimes called jazz's greatest female musician but in reality one of jazz's finest pianists, period, Mary Lou Williams had a lengthy and productive career. Like Coleman Hawkins and Duke Ellington, she was always modern, constantly evolving with the times. Born Mary Elfrieda Scruggs, she moved to Pittsburgh with her family when she was four. Growing up poor, she attracted a lot of attention with her brilliant piano playing (which was largely self-taught), gigging as a child from the age of six. The youth worked as Mary Lou Burley (using her stepfather's surname) in shows before she was a teenager. She was always working, touring throughout the Midwest and marrying alto and baritone-saxophonist John Williams when she was 16. Mary Lou Williams' first recordings were made in 1927: eight titles with the Synco Jazzers that were released four apiece under the names of singer Jeanette James and John Williams (reissued on the CD *Alexander, Where's That Band*—Frog 13). When her husband joined Terence Holder's Dark Clouds of Joy later in the year, the pianist took over the Synco Jazzers for a time.

By 1929, Andy Kirk was the leader of the renamed Twelve Clouds of Joy and Mary Lou Williams was often present at the band's performances. She contributed arrangements to the group and subbed on piano for their first recording sessions, in November. Because she fit in so well, the record label's producers insisted that she be on piano for all of Kirk's other recordings from 1929–30. A brilliant stride player, Williams made her first two solo piano records ("Night Life" and "Drag 'Em") on April 24, 1930. Finally, in 1931 she became Kirk's regular pianist.

During the next 11 years, Mary Lou Williams was Kirk's star soloist and main arranger. She modernized her style in the mid-1940s (embracing bebop) and had a very productive career, sounding quite contemporary as late as the 1970s but without ever losing sight of her roots in classic jazz.

🔟 1927–1940/Jan. 1927–Nov. 18, 1940/Classics 630

This CD has two of Mary Lou Williams' four recordings with Jeanette's Synco Jazzers and all four of her numbers with John Williams' Synco Jazzers (the same group) in 1927. In addition, Williams is heard on her two piano solos from 1930 ("Night Life" and "Drag 'Em"), one from 1939 ("Little Joe from Chicago"), ten trio numbers (1936–38), and six combo numbers (1940) that feature tenor saxophonist Dick Wilson. These are virtually all of Mary Lou Williams' recordings outside of the confines of Andy Kirk's orchestra during her early days, and they show the distinctive stride pianist adjusting her style quite well to swing music.

SANDY WILLIAMS

b. Oct. 24, 1906, Somerville, SC, d. Mar. 25, 1991, New York, NY

An excellent big band trombone soloist, Sandy Williams worked steadily for 20 years. He grew up in Washington, D.C., and started on tuba before switching to trombone. Williams performed locally with Claude Hopkins (1927–29) and was a member of the pit orchestra at the Lincoln Theatre. Moving to New York, the trombonist worked with Horace Henderson's big band (1929–31), graduating to become a soloist with Fletcher Henderson (1931–33), with whom he recorded and made a strong impression.

After leaving Henderson, Williams was a fixture with the Chick Webb Orchestra during the swing era (1933–40). His later jobs included associations with Benny Carter (1940), the Coleman Hawkins big band (1940–41), Sidney Bechet, Fletcher Henderson again (1941–42), the big bands of Cootie Williams (1942–43) and Roy Eldridge (1944), Art Hodes, Rex Stewart (including a tour of Europe in 1947), and various Dixieland combos. Unfortunately Sandy Williams' alcoholism took its toll by the late 1940s, and, after a breakdown in 1950, he dropped out of music. He made a brief comeback in the late 1950s before dental problems permanently forced him out of music again.

SPENCER WILLIAMS

b. Oct. 14, 1889, New Orleans, LA, d. July 14, 1965, Flushing, NY

Spencer Williams was a top songwriter and lyricist. He was raised in Birmingham, Alabama, studied at St. Charles University in New Orleans, and worked as a pianist and vocalist in Chicago during 1907–16, having a regular day job as a Pullman porter. With the dawning of the Jazz Age, Williams became quite active as a writer, collaborating with Fats Waller on "Squeeze Me" (1918) and with the unrelated Clarence Williams on "Royal Garden Blues." Other future standards that he wrote or cowrote during the next decade include "I Ain't Got Nobody," "Basin Street Blues," "Mahogany Hall Stomp," "I Found a New Baby," "Everybody Loves My Baby," "Shim-Me-Sha-Wobble," and "I Ain't Gonna Give Nobody None of My Jelly Roll."

Williams, who made his recording debut playing behind Lizzie Miles on one song in 1923, worked in Europe during 1925–28, including with Josephine Baker. In 1930 he sang and played on records with Lonnie Johnson and Teddy Bunn. In 1932 he moved to France, and, other than singing on a few numbers with Freddie Johnson's orchestra in 1933, he was not heard on records again. Spencer Williams, who left music other than for occasionally writing song lyrics, lived in England (1936–51) and Sweden (1951–57) before spending his last years in New York. The jazz repertoire would have been much poorer without his contributions.

GARLAND WILSON

> b. June 13, 1909, Martinsburg, WV, d. May 31, 1954, Paris, France

A flashy stride pianist, Garland Wilson has been largely forgotten but he was a fine player in his prime. He started playing piano at 13, studied at Howard University, moved to New York in 1929, and was a fixture in Harlem clubs for three years, including accompanying singer Monette Moore. In 1932 Wilson moved to France, at first working as actress-singer Nina Mae McKinney's accompanist. Wilson played regularly in England and France throughout the remainder of the 1930s. Because of World War II, Garland Wilson was back in the United States by 1939. In 1951 he moved back overseas, spending his final years in France.

8 1931–1938/May 18, 1931–Mar. 9, 1938/Classics 808
All of Garland Wilson's recordings as a leader are on this single CD, piano solos from 1931 (two lengthy test pressings made for producer John Hammond and not released for decades), 1932–33,

1936, and 1938 plus a pair of duets with violinist Michel Warlop and two vocals by Nina Mae McKinney. Other than a few numbers backing others, this disc has Garland Wilson's entire recorded legacy, and it finds him to be an excellent pianist, particularly on slower numbers.

SAM WOODING

> b. June 17, 1895, Philadelphia, PA, d. Aug. 1, 1985, New York, NY

Sam Wooding and his orchestra introduced jazz in the 1920s to many areas of the world that had never heard it before. As a pianist, Wooding worked in Atlantic City during 1912–14. He moved to New York in 1914, served in the Army during World War I, and in 1919 began leading his Society Syncopators. In 1922 he recorded two songs apiece with Johnny Dunn, Lucille Hegamin, and Alberta Hunter. In May 1925, Wooding and his orchestra sailed for Europe as the band accompanying *The Chocolate Kiddies* revue. Jazz was very new to Europe and much of the world at the time, so Wooding's concerts in Berlin, Scandinavia, Russia, Turkey, Romania, Hungary, Italy, and other spots throughout the continent were quite historic. Among his sidemen during this period were Tommy Ladnier, trombonist Herb Flemming, Garvin Bushell, altoist Willie Lewis, and clarinetist Gene Sedric. Wooding's band recorded 18 selections in Berlin during two record dates in 1925–26.

In 1927 Sam Wooding's orchestra played in South America before returning to the United States in the summer. After performing on the East Coast, Wooding and his band went back to Europe in June 1928. During the next three years they played in Germany, Scandinavia, France, Italy, and Spain. In addition to Ladnier, Lewis, and Sedric, other major musicians included trumpeter Doc Cheatham, Albert Wynn, and pianist Freddy Johnson; Wooding was mostly conducting and arranging at that point.

His ensemble recorded 31 additional selections during sessions in Barcelona and Paris.

As was true earlier, Wooding's music alternated between hot jazz, dance music, and mildly humorous (if often exuberant) novelties. By the time of its 1929 sessions and especially by 1931, the playing of the Sam Wooding Orchestra (which had lost touch with newer developments in the United States) had fallen behind the times and was sounding dated. The orchestra broke up in Belgium in November 1931.

Wooding returned to the United States and led bands around New York until 1935, not making much of an impression or making any further recordings. He dropped out of full-time performing, gained a masters degree in music, and during 1937–41 led the Southland Spiritual Choir. In later years Sam Wooding was a music teacher (trumpeter Clifford Brown was one of his students). He also toured the world in a duo with vocalist Rae Harrison in the 1960s and made a surprisingly modern (but not particularly successful) big band record in the 1970s that had no real connection to his earlier, trailblazing work.

LPS TO SEARCH FOR

Sam Wooding's orchestra recorded 49 selections (counting alternate takes) during 1925–26, 1929, and 1931, which will make two interesting CDs someday. In the meantime, most of the music has not been reissued in recent times. Sam *Wooding's Chocolate Kiddies* (Jazz Panorama 20) has 15 of the numbers from 1925 and 1929, displaying the sometimes uncomfortable alternation between jazz and dated novelty effects.

LAMMAR WRIGHT

b. June 20, 1907, Texarkana, TX, d. Apr. 13, 1973, New York, NY

Lammar Wright was significant for his association with two important groups. When he was 16, in 1923, the young trumpeter joined Bennie Moten's orchestra, staying for five years and taking many of the solos. When he left in 1928 to become a member of the Missourians, his timing was perfect, joining the band in time for its three recording sessions of 1929–30, sharing the trumpet solos with R.Q. Dickerson. After the Missourians were taken over by Cab Calloway, Wright stayed on, playing with Calloway until 1942, although getting relatively few solos.

After the Calloway years, Lammar Wright played lead trumpet with the big bands of Don Redman (1943), Cootie Williams (1944), Claude Hopkins (1944–46), and Lucky Millinder (a few times during 1946–52), eventually becoming a studio musician and a music teacher.

ALBERT WYNN

b. July 29, 1907, New Orleans, LA, d. May 1973, Chicago, IL

Albert Wynn was a talented trombonist who never achieved much fame but worked for decades. Born in New Orleans, he grew up in Chicago, playing in the Bluebirds' Kids band in the early 1920s. Wynn toured with Ma Rainey (with whom he made his recording debut during 1926–27) and worked and recorded in St. Louis with Charlie Creath's Jazz-o-Maniacs (1927). He made his most significant recordings in 1926 (two selections with his Gut Bucket Five) and 1928 (four numbers at the head of a sextet that have been reissued on *Get Easy Blues*—Frog 9, highlighted by "She's Crying for Me"). Wynn sailed to Europe, played in France and Germany, and was a member of the Sam Wooding Orchestra (1929–31). After the breakup of the Wooding band, the fluent trombonist stayed in Europe until returning home in September 1932.

Back in Chicago, Wynn worked with Carroll Dickerson, Jesse Stone, Reuben Reeves (1934), Richard M. Jones (with whom he recorded in 1935), Jesse Stone's Cyclones, and Jimmie Noone. After stints with the big bands of Fletcher Henderson (1937–39) and Earl Hines, Wynn primarily freelanced with trad bands in Chicago for decades, including groups led by Baby Dodds and Lil Armstrong. Albert Wynn owned a record store, was part owner of the Ebony Lounge, performed as a member of Franz Jackson's Original Jazz All Stars (1956–60), led a record date in 1961, and recorded and played with Little Brother Montgomery as late as 1964.

VARIOUS ARTISTS

"**V**arious artists" CDs are often extremely valuable for 1920s collectors, and the reason is logical: Many artists and bands recorded less than a full CD's (or even LP's) worth of material during their careers, sometimes just two or four selections. Fortunately there are many worthwhile "various artists" collections to choose from, with the best ones containing the complete output of several groups/musicians or at least the jazz high points.

7 Alexander, Where's That Band?/June 1926–Dec. 1928/Frog 13

The Paramount label made its mark with its blues recordings (and its notoriously loud surface noise), but the company also recorded some worthwhile jazz in the 1920s. The 26 selections on this CD feature several intriguing groups: Kline Tindull's Paramount Serenaders, Preston Jackson's Uptown Band (which is also heard backing Elzadie Robinson), Wilson's T.O.B.A. Band, the two selections by the Parham-Pickett Apollo Syncopators, the Synco Jazzers (under the direction of either Jeanette James or John Williams), two sessions from 1927 led by Dave Nelson, and Clarence Jones' Sock Four. Overall the music is not essential (most historic are the Synco Jazzers selections, because of the six numbers that were Mary Lou Williams' debut on records), but it will fill some gaps in 1920s collections.

7 Art Deco: The Crooners/Sept. 1926–Oct. 6, 1941/Columbia/Legacy 52942

When one thinks of "crooners," Bing Crosby comes immediately to mind. This two-CD set has Bing singing two songs ("How Long Will It Last" and "Cabin in the Cotton") along with mostly rare performances from a variety of male singers, including Willard Robison, Gene Austin, Seger Ellis, Smith Ballew, Lew Bray, Harlan Lattimore, Russ Columbo, Red McKenzie, Cliff Edwards (eight songs from 1932–34), Pinky Tomlin, Chick Bullock, Jack Teagarden, Harold Arlen, Buddy Clark, Eddy Howard, Frank Sinatra (with Harry James), and Dick Haymes. The majority of the 49 performances fit into the classic jazz and early swing era, and, although not all of the music is jazz, most of it should be of strong interest to vintage collectors.

8 Art Deco: Sophisticated Ladies/Apr. 5, 1929–Dec. 17, 1940/Columbia/Legacy 52943

A two-CD set that is a companion to *Art Deco: The Crooners*, this reissue has 50 selections from Ruth Etting, Helen Morgan, Greta Keller, Annette Hanshaw, Ethel Waters, Connie Boswell, the Boswell Sisters, Francis Langford, Alice Faye, Lee Wiley, Helen Ward, Ella Logan, Maxine Sullivan, Mildred Bailey, Nan Wynn, and Ginny Simms. Not every top female jazz-oriented singer from 1930–40 is here (Billie Holiday and Ella Fitzgerald are obvious omissions), but this set can introduce listeners to a wide variety of often-overlooked female singers. The song choices are particularly excellent.

7 Big Charlie Thomas/Nov. 23, 1925–Jan. 1927/Timeless 1–030

This CD has an odd concept. There may or may not have been a cornetist named Big Charlie Thomas (Margaret Johnson called him that on one song) and nothing at all is known about him; even if he really existed! However, the 25 songs on this CD (plus four songs not included, three of which are similar, alternate takes) seem to have the cornetist in common, even though individual selections have been misidentified in the past as being by

Jabbo Smith, Louis Metcalf, or even Louis Armstrong. Whoever Charlie Thomas might have been, he had only a brief recording career, but in his 11 months on record (plus two songs from January 1927 with singers Joe Sims and Clarence Williams), he appeared on many important sessions. Included on this unusual reissue are mostly high-quality dates with Sara Martin, Clarence Williams, Margaret Carter, Buddy Christian's Jazz Rippers, Thomas Morris' Seven Hot Babies ("Georgia Grind" and two takes of "Ham Gravy"), the Okeh Melody Stars, Bessie Brown, Rosa Henderson, and the Dixie Washboard Band. But was there really a Big Charlie Thomas, and what ever happened to him?

6 **Blue Ladies/Mar. 7, 1921–Oct. 1, 1925/Memphis Archives 7017**

There are 18 performances on this CD, a cross section of the many classic blues singers who were recorded in the early 1920s in the wake of Mamie Smith's "Crazy Blues." Most of the performances (and some of the performers) are obscure, making this disc a good introduction to the style. Heard from for one song apiece are Edith Wilson, Mamie Smith, Clara Smith, Bessie Smith, Clementine Smith, Sara Martin, Maggie Jones, Margaret Johnson, Rosa Henderson, Lucille Hegamin, Ida Cox, Dora Carr, Mary Stafford, Viola McCoy, Ethel Ridley, Trixie Smith, Ma Rainey, and Ethel Waters.

7 **Blue Yodelers 1928–1936/June 18, 1928–Sept. 1, 1936/Retrieval 79020**

The crossover between jazz and country music was at its peak in the late 1930s with the rise of western swing, which was essentially swinging jazz with the instruments (and sometimes the melodies) of rural white America. However, a decade earlier, a few vocalists who helped pioneer country music sometimes sang blues and used jazz musicians. This CD has eight numbers by Jimmie Rodgers (including "Blue Yodel No. 9" with Louis Armstrong), nine songs from Roy Evans (assisted along the way by James P. Johnson, the Dorsey Brothers, and even

Benny Goodman), and the final rare session by minstrel singer Emmett Miller from 1936. Although it can be a bit disconcerting to hear occasional yodels in these settings, the performances generally work quite well.

5 **Boogie Woogie Blues/Sept. 1922–Dec. 1928/Biograph 115**

The 16 performances on this CD are piano rolls. The emphasis is on blues (although there are some nonblues included too), with many of these piano rolls being a bit rare. Featured are Cow Cow Davenport, James P. Johnson, Clarence Williams, Clarence Johnson, Jimmy Blythe, Everett Robbins, Hersal Thomas, and Lemuel Fowler. As usual with piano rolls, the rhythms are a bit metronomic and the overall ambiance is less connected to the 1920s than that of actual piano solo recordings, but this set has its moments of interest.

8 **The Chicago Hot Bands 1924–1928/Sept. 8, 1924–Oct. 22, 1928/Timeless 1–041**

A variety of mostly lesser-known Chicago bands are represented on this CD, with the 26 selections being in chronological order. Featured are two cuts apiece from the Benson Orchestra of Chicago and Lloyd Turner's Villa Venice Orchestra, the one title from Al Katz's Kittens ("Ace in the Hole"), two songs from Al Handler's Alamo Café Orchestra and Sol Wagner, four numbers by Ray Miller, five from the Louisiana Rhythm Kings (the 1928 version, which was really the Coon-Sanders Orchestra), two from altoist Danny Altier's band (featuring Muggsy Spanier), and all six performances by Thelma Terry's Playboys (along with a rare photo of the leader). There is lots of hot jazz on this disc.

7 **Chicago Rhythm 1912–1926/Nov. 1912–June 26, 1926/Jazz Oracle 8010**

Cornetist Al Turk led record dates featuring his nine-piece band in October 1924 and June 1926, resulting in the 13 songs that lead off this CD. The music is a bit derivative but swinging in its fashion, fine examples of jazz's modern mainstream of the period. Highlights include Isham Jones' "Spain," "Shine," "King Porter Stomp," and "Snag It." The second half of the program starts with two songs from 1912–13 featuring the vocals of Gene Greene (billed as "The Rag-Time King"), with backing from pianist Charley Straight. Concluding the disc are seven selections from Straight's Rendezvous Orchestra of 1923 and four from his band of 1926. Straight's performances are the most jazz-oriented recordings of his career, including "Buddy's Habits," "Forgetful Blues," a classic rendition of "Deep Henderson," and two versions of "Hobo's Prayer."

6 College Rhythm/Aug. 18, 1927–Oct. 15, 1934/Memphis Archives 7021

During the second half of the 1920s, a large number of songs were recorded celebrating the party side of college life. Eighteen tunes (including "Collegiate Fanny," "Campus Capers," "Collegiate Love," "She's the Sweetheart of Six Other Guys," and "Freddy the Freshman") are heard on this set, performed by such ensembles as George Olsen ("Varsity Drag"), Kay Kyser, Ted Weems, Harry Reser, Gene Kardos, and a few other white orchestras. The cheerful music is quite fun and spirited, if not necessarily essential.

6 Crazy Clarinets—Raucous Reeds/Apr. 17, 1929–July 10, 1930/Jazz Crusade 3019

Included on this CD is music available elsewhere but well worth owning in one form or another. Wilton Crawley's three band dates of 1929–30 (with Red Allen, Jelly Roll Morton, and Charlie Holmes) are here, along with 12 of Fess Williams' better performances from the same period. The gaspipe clarinet playing of the two leaders is an acquired taste but can easily be enjoyed by listeners who are not too straight-laced!

6 The Crown House Bands, Vol. 1/Mar. 15, 1931–Mar. 3, 1933/The Old Masters 115

Very little is known about pianist Russ Carlson, who led the High Steppers on record dates during 1931–33 for the budget Crown label. Twenty-four of their titles (some of which were issued under other names) are on this CD. The personnel is unknown, other than Carlson and the singers (Elmer Feldkamp, Charlie Palloy, Dick Robertson, Harold Van Emburgh, John Amendt, and the team of Les Reis and Artie Dunn), but the performances are quite musical, being excellent examples of high-quality early-Depression dance band music.

6 Dallas Rhythm/Sept. 1924–Nov. 1, 1929/Jazz Oracle 8021

By the mid-1920s, jazz existed all across the United States, even if most of the pacesetters were in Chicago and New York. Although Dallas was never thought of as a hot spot, it had its own local scene. Pianist Jack Gardner (who was not the same Jack Gardner who played piano with Wingy Manone) led one of the city's top bands and had extensive record dates in 1924–25, resulting in 16 titles plus two songs backing blues singer Irene Taylor. Although none of the sidemen became famous, Gardner's orchestra played excellent jazz-oriented dance music. Also on this CD are two songs from Randolph McCurtain's College Ramblers in 1925, three songs from a St. Louis band led by pianist Phil Baxter in 1925, and one of two songs ("Marbles") from a 1929 Dallas band led by violinist Herman Waldman.

7 Don't You Leave Me Here/Aug. 9, 1926–May 20, 1931/Frog 12

At first glance, this CD appears to be a close rerun of Frog 8 (*Hot Notes*), but in reality nearly all of the music is alternate takes; it is strange that nothing is said about that on the outside of the disc! There are four alternate takes and three previously unissued performances by the Savoy Bearcats (a great band), alternates of two of Lloyd Scott's three numbers, one by Leroy Smith, two from Bubber Miley, two by Joe Steele, and ten from Charlie Johnson's orchestra. In addition, the master take of Russell Wooding's "That's My Desire" (with Alberto Socarras on flute) wraps up this excellent collector's disc. But get *Hot Notes* first.

5 Douglas Williams 1928–1930/Jan. 31, 1928–June 5, 1930/ Jazz Oracle 8012

Virtually nothing is known of clarinetist Douglas Williams other than that he lived in Memphis at the time he made the 24 Victor recordings (his entire output, other than two unissued sides) that are on this CD. Williams was a decent player who sometimes used gaspipe effects, although he seemed capable of playing fairly straight too. Included on this collection are two numbers in which he backs the vocal team of Alfoncy and Bethenea Harris, trios with pianist Edgar Brown and drummer Sam Sims, three duets with Brown, and three quintet dates with Brown, Sims, and sometimes cornetist Nathaniel Williams and guitarist Melvin Parker. Decent but not essential music.

6 Edison Diamond Disc—Fox Trots/Jan. 9, 1920–Oct. 18, 1923/Diamond Cut 307

The 20 selections on this CD are fine examples of early 1920s dance music, put out originally by the Edison label. The recording quality is quite good for the period, although there is relatively little jazz to be heard, since nearly all of the music was written out. Among the bands heard from are Kaplan's Melodists, the Green Brothers Novelty Bands (with Charles Hamilton Green on xylophone), Harry Raderman ("Make That Trombone Laugh"), and the Broadway Dance Orchestra.

3 Florida Rhythm/Aug. 22, 1927–Aug. 14, 1931/Jazz Oracle 8011

This is a rather esoteric CD centering around the activities of Robert Cloud, an alto and tenor saxophonist who had ambitions to be a top composer and was involved in writing gospel pieces by the early 1930s. In reality, he was a rather minor figure, and it is not even known if he is on all of the 25 selections included on this disc. Of greatest interest are eight numbers by Ross De Luxe Syncopators from Savannah, Georgia. The recording quality is quite echoey, with the band and the occasional vocalists being decent but not outstanding. The Jack-

sonville Harmony Trio (two vocalists and pianist Sugar Underwood) is heard performing four of Cloud's songs (none of which caught on), and Cloud is featured jamming with the Q.R.S. Boys and the Georgia Jumpers (groups that feature Benny Nawahi on steel guitar), backing the pompous singer Rollin' Smith, leading two songs, and accompanying three singers on a pair of his gospel tunes on piano. Overall, nothing all that significant or memorable occurs.

7 Gennett Rarities/July 7, 1927–Oct. 2, 1929/Jazz Oracle 8009

The first half of *Gennett Rarities* features selected performances from bands recorded in Birmingham, Alabama. There are tunes from the Triangle Harmony Boys, Eddie Miles' Florentine Orchestra, pianist George Tremer ("Spirit of '49 Rag"), Dunk Rendleman's Alabamians, and Frank Bunch's Fuzzy Wuzzies. Most intriguing are four songs (their complete output) by the Black Birds of Paradise. "Bugahoma Blues" is excellent, but on "Tishomingo Blues" trumpeter Shorty Hall makes quite a few clams! Also on this disc are the four enjoyable numbers recorded by Syd Valentine's Patent Leather Kids (a trio with trumpeter Valentine, pianist Slick Helms, and banjoist Paul George recorded in Richmond, Indiana) and four songs in which the Patent Leather Kids accompany singer Horace Smith.

8 Get Easy Blues/Jan. 21, 1928–Nov. 2, 1930/Frog 9

A variety of Chicago sessions from 1928–30 are on this superior reissue. Included are the dates by the Levee Serenaders (a Jelly Roll Morton group with Frances Hereford singing "Midnight Mama" and "Mr. Jelly Lord"), Jasper Taylor's Original Washboard band (with Johnny Dodds), pianist Lil Hardaway's sextet, Sammy Stewart's orchestra, Albert Wynn (his four selections), Jimmy Wade's Dixielanders, Jimmy Bertrand's Washboard Wizards (a 1929 quartet with Punch Miller, Darnell Howard, and Jimmy Blythe), the Beale Street Washboard Band (Johnny Dodds, trumpeter Herb Morand, Frank Melrose, and Baby Dodds on washboard), and

Frankie Franko's Louisianians. These 26 selections, which often elude reissue series, are consistently enjoyable and a superior example of late 1920s hot Chicago jazz.

8 Go Harlem—New York Columbia Recordings, Volume 2/ May 25, 1927–June 25, 1931/Frog 38

Eight different groups are featured on this survey of New York recordings from 1927–31. Trombonist Te Roy Williams has two hot numbers ("Oh Malinda" and "Lindbergh Hop") with an eight-piece group featuring Rex Stewart, James P. Johnson leads three combo dates (including Cootie Williams, Charlie Holmes, Fats Waller, Louis Metcalf, and Ward Pinkett), there are two songs apiece from Jasper Davis' orchestra, Marlow Hardy's Alabamians (recorded the day of the Wall Street crash!), and Trombone Red's Blue Six, plus there are four tunes from Vance Dixon's Pencils and six by King Carter's Royal Orchestra (which is really Mills' Blue Rhythm Band). There are no slow moments throughout this highly enjoyable and valuable disc.

5 The Golden Years in Digital Stereo: The Blues/Jan. 31, 1923– July 7, 1933/ABC 836 046
6 The Golden Years in Digital Stereo: British Dance Bands/ Feb. 12, 1926–Dec. 13, 1935/ABC 836 045
6 The Golden Years in Digital Stereo: Hot Violins/Dec. 10, 1926–Dec. 21, 1937/ABC 836 049

Australian sound engineer Robert Parker devised a method in which he makes 1920s classic jazz sound as if it were recorded in stereo. He has produced a series of samplers for a few labels, including the BBC (found under Jazz Classics in Digital Stereo) and ABC (the Australian Broadcasting Corporation). Since these are samplings of Parker's favorite recordings, none of these discs pretend to be "complete." Each one mixes common selections with rarities. *The Blues* has one song apiece from 14 blues singers (including Ida Cox, Rosa Henderson, Ma Rainey, Bessie Smith, and Ethel Waters) plus Jimmie Rodgers' "Blue Yodel, No. 9" and a number by the Memphis Jug Band. *British Dance Bands*

effectively demonstrates that there was excellent jazz being played overseas (by the likes of Jack Hylton, Fred Elizalde, Ambrose, Billy Cotton, and lesser-known groups). And while the pacesetters of the jazz fiddle (Joe Venuti, Eddie South, Stephane Grappelli, and Stuff Smith) are all represented on *Hot Violins*, there are also selections from the lesser-known Laurie Bookin, Hugo Rignold, Emilio Caceres, Michel Warlop, and the team of Eric Siday and Reg Leopold.

9 Happy Rhythm—New York Columbia Recordings, Vol. 1/ Jan. 6, 1925–Sept. 5, 1930/Frog 32

A cross section of excellent New York recording groups is featured on this CD. The Cotton Club always had top bands, so it is not surprising that the six selections from the 1925 Cotton Club Orchestra (which three years later would re-emerge as the Missourians) are excellent. Also featured on this highly recommended disc are the Get Happy Band, the Gulf Coast Seven, the Blue Ribbon Syncopators, Fowler's Favorites (led by pianist Lemuel Fowler), Leroy Tibbs' Connie's Inn Orchestra, the Musical Stevedores, and Bennett's Swamplanders. Among the many top musicians heard from are R.Q. Dickerson, Louis Metcalf, Sidney Bechet (with the Get Happy Band), Tricky Sam Nanton, Thomas Morris, Jimmy Harrison, Buster Bailey, Charlie Holmes, and Albert Socarras.

7 Harps, Jugs, Washboards and Kazoos/June 1926–Oct. 10, 1940/RST 1505

A variety of good-time jazz/blues bands are featured on this set. The first 14 selections have all of the recordings by the Five Harmaniacs, a group consisting of harmonica, kazoo, a second kazoo player who doubles on jug and washboard, banjo, and guitar. Among the tunes performed are exuberant versions of "Sadie Green, Vamp of New Orleans," "Coney Island Washboard," and "What Did Romie-O-Julie When He Climbed Her Balcony." Also featured on this collection are recordings by similar groups called the Salty Dog Four, the

Scorpion Washboard Band, and Rhythm Willie. Fun pre-skiffle jive music.

6 Hot and Rare/Oct. 15, 1926–Jan. 28, 1935/Diamond Cut 203

The 24 selections on this disc feature mostly white bands (other than Charlie Johnson), generally from 1926–30, with an emphasis on obscure performances. The groups heard from include a couple of Harry Reser units, Blue Steele, the Wanderers, Ted Weems ("What a Day"), Roane's Pennsylvanians, Mal Hallett, Adrian Schubert's Salon Orchestra, Phil Baxter, and Earl Gresh's Gang Plank Orchestra. Included are fine performances of hot dance music, although the programming is somewhat random.

9 Hot British Dance Bands/Oct. 7, 1925–July 8, 1937/Timeless 1–005

Although jazz was not rampant in England during the 12 years covered by this collection (it was very much underground music), even the top society bands occasionally performed jazz. The 22 selections on this CD, programmed in chronological order, feature 22 different British bands at their hottest, with the quality being quite high. Highlights include the Kit-Cat Band (in 1925) playing "Riverboat Shuffle," the Devonshire Restaurant Dance Band's "Sugar Foot Stomp," Jack Hylton's "Tiger Rag," the Arcadians Dance Orchestra on "'Leven-Thirty Saturday Night," Madame Tussaud's Dance Orchestra's "Rockin' in Rhythm," Harry Roy's "Milenberg Joys," and Ambrose's remarkable "Cotton Pickers' Congregation."

5 Hot Dance of the Roaring '20s/Sept. 15, 1928–July 16, 1929/ Diamond Cut 202

The Edison label recorded a lot of high-quality dance music during its final few years before it ceased operations in the fall of 1929; little has ever been reissued. The emphasis on the 21 numbers put out on this CD is on the melodies, danceable tempos, and smooth ensembles. There is some jazz content here and there (often in the arranged passages of some of the performances' last chorus), but this is primarily dance music rather than spontaneous jazz. Heard from are such anonymous orchestras as the Piccadilly Players, B.A. Rolfe's Lucky Strike Orchestra, and the Golden Gate Orchestra, along with other, similar ensembles.

8 Hot Notes/Aug. 23, 1926–June 4, 1929/Frog 8

The Savoy Bearcats (an exciting ten-piece band) recorded six songs during 1926, and all of them are on *Hot Notes*, highlighted by a version of "Stampede" that is faster than Fletcher Henderson's, "Senegalese Stomp," and "Nightmare." Also on this intriguing CD is Everly Preer singing "If You Can't Hold the Man You Love" (backed by a contingent from Duke Ellington's band in early 1927), the three recordings by Lloyd Scott's band, two songs from Joe Steele (1929), three by Leroy Smith (1928), and the master takes from all of Charlie Johnson's recordings of 1927–29 (leaving out his first session). Easily recommended, particularly for the Savoy Bearcats numbers, except perhaps to listeners already owning the Charlie Johnson recordings.

8 Hot Stuff—Black Chicago Big Bands 1922–29/1922– Aug. 16, 1929/Frog 28

Chicago was the home for quite a few black big bands in the 1920s, orchestras that played theaters and dance halls throughout the city. On *Hot Stuff*, the first two selections ("Wolverine Stomp" and "Ivy") are test pressings from the completely unknown Sunset Band in late 1922, an ensemble that might have been led by Carroll Dickerson and included Buster Bailey. The bulk of this CD features the one session by Elgar's Creole Orchestra (including a particularly eerie version of "Nightmare" and exciting work by the two cornetists on "Brotherly Love") and all ten performances by Walter Barnes' Royal Creolians during 1928–29; Barnes and nine of his musicians would tragically perish in a fire in 1939. Also on *Hot Stuff* are the two songs that Fess Williams recorded with his Joy Boys while spending a year in Chicago, the earlier of two dates by Carroll Dickerson's Savoy Orchestra (featuring trumpeter Willie Hightower and the nucleus of Louis Armstrong's Savoy Ballroom Five on "Missouri Squabble" and "Black Maria"), and the two band sides by cornetist Oliver Cobb's Rhythm Kings.

5 The Jazz Age/New York in the Twenties/Feb. 11, 1927– Oct. 7, 1930/Bluebird 3136

Although not a bad sampler when it was first released in 1991, this 22-song CD's value has dropped a bit since then due to more complete reissue programs. It features Red Nichols on six numbers (three are alternates) with a 1928 octet and Red and Miff's Stompers, seven tunes by Ben Pollack's orchestra (including "Waitin' for Katie" and "Buy Buy for Baby"), five solid performances from 1929 by Phil Napoleon's Emperors, and four cuts by Venuti and Lang.

6 Jazz Classics in Digital Stereo: Vol. 1: New Orleans/July 17, 1918–Sept. 15, 1932/BBC 588

5 Jazz Classics in Digital Stereo: Vol. 2: Chicago/Sept. 17, 1926–Sept. 12, 1934/BBC 589

5 Jazz Classics in Digital Stereo: Vol. 3: New York/May. 29, 1925–Aug. 26, 1935/BBC 590

6 Jazz Classics in Digital Stereo: Vol. 4: Hot Town/Dec. 14, 1926–Dec. 4, 1933/BBC 591

On these four CDs, producer Robert Parker (who can magically make 1920s performances sound like they were originally recorded in stereo) reissues 20 selections apiece (16 on *Hot Town*), dividing the music into overlapping areas of the country where particular styles originated (even if the music was sometimes recorded elsewhere). *New Orleans* has selections from Jelly Roll Morton, King Oliver, Johnny Dodds, Louis Armstrong, Freddie Keppard, Oscar Celestin, the New Orleans Owls, Louis Dumaine's Jazzola Eight, the NORK, the ODJB, Red Allen, the Jones-Collins Astoria Hot 8, Monk Hazel, and Sidney Bechet. As usual, the music is not programmed in chronological order (the ODJB actually closes this set), the sessions do not pretend

to be complete, and the song choices seem almost random at times.

Chicago has more Morton and Oliver, Carroll Dickerson, Richard M. Jones, Frankie Trumbauer, McKenzie-Condon's Chicagoans, Hoagy Carmichael, the Mound City Blue Blowers, and a dozen other groups of the era represented on one number apiece; nothing that is not easily available elsewhere. *New York* has Morton and Oliver again, along with Fletcher Henderson, Bessie Smith, Paul Whiteman, Duke Ellington, Cab Calloway, and many others.

Hot Town mostly features bands based in other cities (including Dave Taylor, Alonzo Ross, Eddie Johnson, Charley Williamson's Beale Street Frolic Orchestra, Blue Steele, Troy Floyd, and Paul Howard's Quality Serenaders). Slatz Randall's "Skirts" is a classic, although the inclusion of Fess Williams ("Hot Town") and Duke Ellington ("Daybreak Express") had more to do with the songs' titles than with their location (which was New York). But as is always true with these type of sets, they are recommended to beginners if found at a low price, but serious collectors will consider them a frivolity.

7 Jazz from Atlanta 1923–1929/Timeless 1–038

Recorded during field trips by the Okeh and Columbia labels, two Atlanta bands (Charles Fulcher's orchestra and Warner's Seven Aces) were well documented in their hometown. Fulcher, who played clarinet, violin, and trombone in addition to taking vocals, was also a talented songwriter whose best-known song, "My Pretty Girl," was recorded by Jean Goldkette. Fulcher recorded a dozen songs in all (during sessions in 1923, 1925–26, and in New York in 1929); the nine most jazz oriented are on this CD, including two selections by Fulcher's Dance Trio that has him showcased in a group with piano and banjo. In general the leader is better than his sidemen. Warner's Seven Aces, which recorded 30 selections during 1923–27 (16 of which are included) are on a higher level. The versatile band is heard in top form on "Bessie Couldn't Help It," "When My Sugar Walks Down the Street," "Who'd Be Blue," and "Don't Take That Black Bottom Away."

9 Jazz in California 1923–1930/Aug. 21, 1923–June 25, 1930/ Timeless 1–034

High-quality jazz existed in the Los Angeles area as early as 1921 when Jelly Roll Morton and King Oliver independently visited. Other than one song recorded in Oakland, all of the music on this collection was recorded in Los Angeles or nearby Culver City. Heard from are Sonny Clay's Plantation Orchestra, Vic Meyers, Henry Halstead, Reb Spike's Majors and Minors, Tom Gerunovich's Roof Garden Orchestra, and most importantly the complete output (13 performances) of Paul Howard's Quality Serenaders, one of the hottest bands of 1929–30. The Quality Serenaders, which boasts trombonist Lawrence Brown and Lionel Hampton (on drums) in its lineup, was an exciting octet that played arrangements by its altoist Charlie Lawrence and was filled with excellent (if now little-known) soloists. Even if the other bands were not excellent, this CD would be recommended for the Paul Howard sides alone.

9 Jazz in Saint Louis 1924–1927/Dec. 2, 1924–May 2, 1927/ Timeless 1–036

Although simplified jazz-history books make it sound like New Orleans musicians of the early 1920s took steamboats up the Mississippi River to Chicago, the Mississippi does not go that far North! However, some musicians did go up North via St. Louis, while the top St. Louis jazz musicians often played on riverboats. Best known among the hometowners were Charles Creath and Dewey Jackson. This CD has all of the recordings by both, with Creath's Jazz-o-Maniacs having its dozen recordings (from 1924–25 and 1927) reissued and showing that it ranked with Bennie Moten's orchestra as the best jazz band of the time located outside of New York, Chicago, and New Orleans. Dewey Jackson's

Peacock Orchestra's three numbers are highlighted by a classic version of "She's Cryin' for Me." Also on this disc are numbers by Phil Baxter's Texas Tomies, the Palledo Orchestra of St. Louis, Benny Washington's Six Aces, Jesse Stone's Blue Serenaders, and "Soap Suds" from a Jelly Roll Morton-led group called the St. Louis Levee Band.

7 Jazz in Texas 1924–1930/Oct. 1924–June 9, 1930/Timeless 1–033

Dallas, Houston, and San Antonio bands are represented on this collection, including Jimmy Joy's St. Anthony's Hotel Orchestra, Lloyd Finlay's, Fatty Martin, Randolph McCurtain's College Ramblers, Leroy's Dallas Band, and Fred Gardner's Texas University Troubadours. While those groups are generally excellent, the main reason to acquire this disc is for the pair of two-sided selections ("Shadowland Blues" and "Dreamland Blues") and "Wabash Blues," as played by Troy Floyd's Plaza Hotel Orchestra. The future Count Basie tenor saxophonist Herschel Evans is heard on "Dreamland Blues," while trumpeter Don Albert has a few impressive solos.

7 Jazz Is Where You Find It 1924–1930/Mar. 25, 1924–Apr. 7, 1930/Timeless 1–048

This is a particularly intriguing collection, featuring obscure but worthy bands from cities where listeners might not have expected jazz to have flourished in the 1920s. Best known is the Blue Ribbon Syncopators (their first date from Buffalo). Buffalo is also represented by George Warmack, and there are bands that recorded in Richmond, Virginia (Roy Johnson's Happy Pals and the Bubbling Over Five), Asheville, North Carolina (Foor-Robinson's Carolina Club Orchestra), Indianapolis (Charlie Davis' Orchestra), Annapolis (the U.S. Naval Academy Ten playing "Navy Girl" and "My Dream Ship"), Framingham, Massachusetts (Frank Ward), Cleveland (Emerson Gill and Harold Ortli's Ohio State Collegians), Knoxville, Tennessee (Maynard Baird playing "Postage Stomp"), Butte, Montana (Ernest

Loomis), St. Paul, Minnesota (George Osborne), Seattle (Jackie Souders), and Minneapolis (Arnold Frank and his Roger's Café Orchestra). Lots of collector's items!

7 Jazz the World Forgot, Vol. 1/Oct. 26, 1923–May 23, 1931/ Yazoo 2024

7 Jazz the World Forgot, Vol. 2/July 30, 1923–Sept. 5, 1930/ Yazoo 2025

There are two ways to look at this pair of reissues. Both CDs contain 23 selections from the classic jazz era, and there are dozens of gems, with quite a few of the performances being a bit obscure. But unfortunately, the programming is quite random, personnel and exact dates are not listed, and there is no "plot" or purpose to these releases, other than that the music is quite good. So what should have received ratings of 9 or even 10 gets only a 7 due to the packaging. Still, there is a great deal of fine music to be enjoyed here. Among the artists heard on *Vol. 1* are Sam Morgan, Paul Tremaine (the classic dance band chart "Four-Four Rhythm"), Bennie Moten, Frenchy's String Band, Ben Tobier's California Cyclones, George McClennon's Jazz Devils, King Oliver, and the Hottentots. *Vol. 2* has the Whoopee Makers, Dixon's Jazz Maniacs, Thomas Morris' Seven Hot Babies, Johnny DeDroit, and the Five Hot Chocolates, among many others.

7 Lost Chords/Jan. 10, 1920–Sept. 23, 1944/Retrieval 79018
Richard Sudhalter's large book *Lost Chords* covers white musicians' contributions to jazz during 1915–45, not by dismissing the black artist's significance but by focusing on a variety of underrated and often overlooked players. This double CD was released in conjunction with the book, and it has 49 performances, mostly from the 1920s and '30s along with a few later Dixieland numbers, ranging from the ODJB to Bobby Hackett. Most of the selections are available elsewhere, but there are a few rarer numbers, including cuts by the Original Memphis Melody Boys, the California Ramblers, Paul Mares (1935), and guitarist George Barnes.

7 Memphis Stomp/Feb. 24, 1927–June 6, 1930/Frog 24
Memphis, famous as a blues center, has spawned some worthwhile jazz through the years. On this CD (in which all but one session was recorded by Victor during its field trips to Memphis), singers Saide McKinney and Baby Moore are backed by a duet consisting of cornetist Charley Williamson and pianist James Alston, Jimmie Lunceford's Chickasaw Syncopators perform two numbers ("In Dat Mornin' " and "Sweet Rhythm") from 1930, and the complete output of Williamson's Beale Street Frolic Orchestra (four songs and four alternates by a sextet that includes cornetist Williamson and Alston) and the Memphis Stompers (eight numbers and three alternates, directed by drummer Snooks Friedman) is included. Excellent music that does not sound as if it were being played by territory bands.

6 The Music of Prohibition/Dec. 1, 1919–Feb. 2, 1942/Columbia/Legacy 65326
This CD has 22 selections that were used in the soundtrack of an Arts & Entertainment TV network special on Prohibition. Oddly enough, four of the numbers were recorded after Prohibition was repealed. A few songs (the State Street Swingers' "You Drink Too Much," the Mississippi Sheiks' "Bootlegger Blues," and Bert Williams' "The Moon Shines on the Moonshine") have to do with liquor, but most of the selections are just high-quality (if generally familiar) jazz performances by Harlem big bands, including those of Cab Calloway, Duke Ellington, Fletcher Henderson, Don Redman, Chick Webb, and (from Kansas City) Bennie Moten. Excellent music but nothing particularly rare or unusual.

8 New Orleans in the '20s/Mar. 15, 1924–Jan. 23, 1925/Timeless 1–014
During two field trips (March 15–17, 1924, and January 22–23, 1925), the Okeh label recorded many bands that were based in New Orleans. Nine of the bands are heard on this CD, although unfor-

tunately not the two hot numbers by Brownlee's orchestra (a heated octet that included cornetist Sharkey Bonano). The generous set does features Johnny DeDroit's New Orleans Orchestra, the only recordings by Fate Marable (two disappointing songs), two songs apiece by the Original Crescent City Jazzers (with cornetist Sterling Bose), Johnny Bayersdorffer's Jazzola Novelty Orchestra (an appealing if otherwise unrecorded band), and the Halfway House Orchestra (the session with Leon Roppolo). Also on this CD are the first sessions by Tony Parenti's Famous Melody Boys and Oscar Celestin's Original Tuxedo Jazz Orchestra, the one number recorded by John Tobin's Midnight Serenaders, and the reunion session by the NORK from January 23, 1925. The NORK date (Roppolo's last recordings) features classic versions of "I Never Knew" and "She's Crying for Me Blues."

7 New York Horns/Feb. 12, 1924 – Oct. 19, 1928/Hot 'n' Sweet 5102

This European CD starts off with 11 selections featuring Bubber Miley from 1924, before the cornetist had his sound completely together; he is heard with the Kansas City Five and the Six Black Diamonds and on four duets (two versions of two songs) with organist Arthur Ray that are quite atmospheric. Also on this CD are the Kansas City Five, with Louis Metcalf in Miley's place, and sessions from the Blue Rhythm Orchestra, the Gulf Coast Seven, the Five Musical Blackbirds, and Te Roy Williams. These hot jazz performances feature such players as trombonist Jake Frazier, Jimmy Harrison, Buster Bailey, Thomas Morris, James P. Johnson, and Rex Stewart.

6 New York Jazz in the Roaring Twenties/Apr. 16, 1926 – Jan. 27, 1928/Biograph 129

Although Tommy Dorsey, Red Nichols, and Jimmy Dorsey get top billing on this CD, the Dorsey Brothers are only sidemen on a few selections. There are four cuts from Red and Miff's Stompers, seven by the California Ramblers, two songs from Joe Herlihy's orchestra, and one by Phil Napoleon. All of the music was originally put out by the Edison label in the late 1920s, so the playing time is longer than usual, sometimes exceeding four minutes. The Red and Miff's Stompers performances (which include "Black Bottom Stomp" and "Stampede") are readily available elsewhere, but some of the other performances (particularly by the California Ramblers) are scarcer.

9 The Obscure and Neglected Chicagoans/1925 – Dec. 21, 1929/ IAJRC 1007

This very interesting CD can be divided into three segments. First there are three sessions that answer the question "What happened to the Wolverines after Bix Beiderbecke left?" After recording two titles with Jimmy McPartland, the band continued changing personnel. This disc begins with two titles that they recorded as Dud Mecum's Wolverines (a mid-1925 sextet with cornetist Frank Cotterel, clarinetist Jimmy Lord, and tenor saxophonist George Johnson) and also has six songs from 1927 – 28 by The Original Wolverines, which, under the leadership of pianist Dick Voynow, welcomed back McPartland and played in a similar style as the original band. Although the music is excellent, the Wolverines would finally fade into history after 1928. Also on this CD are 11 of the most jazz-oriented performances by Ray Miller's orchestra (five feature Muggsy Spanier) and all six songs by Thelma Terry's Boyfriends, the total output by this completely overlooked bassist-bandleader.

7 Odds and Bits 1926 – 1930/Mar. 10, 1926 – Nov. 1929/Timeless 1 – 055

A few of the selections on this hodgepodge collection are available elsewhere (including some of the Charley Straight selections), but there are also quite a few rarities. Featured are Straight's orchestra of 1926 and 1928, Husk O'Hare's Footwarmers, Cline's Collegians from Dallas, Harris Brother's Texans, the Marigold Entertainers, Slatz Randall (a

Minneapolis band heard playing a memorable rendition of "Skirts"), Moe Baer's Wardman Park Orchestra, George Belshaw's KFAB Orchestra, Herman Waldman, and Henry Lange. These gems (in some cases the absolute best of these groups, in other cases their complete output) are drawn from the Brunswick/Vocalion catalog.

4 Oriental Illusions/Aug. 10, 1922 – Oct. 14, 1938/Memphis Archives 7018

This is a rather frivolous reissue, made up of 16 songs that have something to do with Asians and Orientals in their titles. Included are such tunes as "Singapore Sorrows," "China Boy," "China Girl," "Hong Kong Blues," "Oriental Man," "Nighttime in Old Shanghai," "Limehouse Blues," and "Shanghai Shuffle." Some of the performances are rare ("Chinatown, My Chinatown" by Roane's Pennsylvanians and "Sing Song Girl" by Sleepy Hall's Collegians) but, since no Asian groups are represented, this collection is just silly.

8 The Original Memphis Five/Napoleon's Emperors/The Cotton Pickers 1928 – 1929/June 13, 1928 – July 9, 1929/Timeless 1 – 049

This CD has the last sessions (other than a date in 1931) of the Original Memphis Five, Napoleon's Emperors, and the Cotton Pickers. The first two groups have similar personnel, with Phil Napoleon, Tommy Dorsey, Jimmy Dorsey, and sometimes Joe Venuti, Frank Signorelli, Eddie Lang, Joe Tarto, and Stan King or Vic Berton. Half of the Cotton Pickers dates have a similar lineup, but its first two sessions actually feature Tommy Dorsey (on trumpet) and Glenn Miller, along with Jimmy Dorsey. No matter, the music throughout (which includes a version of Libby Holman singing "Moanin' Low") is high-quality and fairly freewheeling 1929 jazz.

5 Piano Wizards/Feb. 16, 1927 – June 30, 1939/Memphis Archives 7015

As is true of many of the Memphis Archives releases, this collection is based on a theme, with the songs being almost randomly picked and programmed. Fifteen pianists are heard on 18 tunes, including Fats Waller, Jelly Roll Morton, Earl Hines, Art Tatum (his remarkable 1933 version of "Tiger Rag"), Duke Ellington, and Bix Beiderbecke ("In a Mist"), plus obscurities by Reginald Forsythe ("St. Louis Blues" from 1934) and Jabo Williams. Fine music, but nearly all of it is available more coherently elsewhere.

9 Ragtime to Jazz 1 — 1912 – 1919/1912 – Nov. 1919/Timeless 1 – 035

8 Ragtime to Jazz 2 — 1916 – 1922/Dec. 20, 1916 – Dec. 1922/Timeless 1 – 045

These two CDs both contain a lot of rare early material. *Ragtime to Jazz 1* has very early piano solos by Roy Spangler and Mike Bernard, two of James Europe's first four recordings (1913's "Too Much Mustard" and "Down Home Rag"), performances by the Versatile Four and Wilbur Sweatman, four numbers from the Original Dixieland Jazz Band (including the first jazz recordings: "Darktown Strutters Ball," and "Indiana"), and songs from the Frisco Jass Band (including "Night-Time in Little Italy"), Earl Fuller's Famous Jazz Band (with Ted Lewis), Eubie Blake's Jazztone Orchestra, Dabney's Band, and the Louisiana Five. This is mostly very intriguing music, although a definitive series of pre-1917 ragtime has yet to be compiled on CD.

Other than Fred Van Eps' "Teasing the Cat," from 1916, *Ragtime to Jazz 2* focuses on early jazz rather than the prejazz period. Heard from are the ODJB, Earl Fuller, Paul Biese's Novelty Orchestra, the Louisiana Five, Yerke's Novelty Five, a Vincent Lopez group, the Whiteway Jazz Band, Eubie Blake, Brown and Terry Jazzola Boys, Lanin's Southern Serenaders, Mamie Smith's Jazz Hounds, Ladd's Black Aces, Husk O'Hare, Bobby Lee's Music Landers, the Syncopating Skeeters, and a couple of completely unidentified bands. Even the most veteran of all collectors will not already own all of this valuable material.

6 Rags to Rhythm/Jan. 24, 1906–July 15, 1926/Memphis Archives 7011

This CD has some pretty rare material along with an excellent concept, but its execution is a bit flawed. The idea is to trace music from early ragtime performances into the beginnings of the Jazz Age. However, the programming is not in strict chronological order, and the music chosen from the 1920s is mostly fairly common. Most valuable are the prejazz performances by James Europe (1913's "Down Home Rag"), pianist Mike Bernard, Arthur Pryor, the United States Marine Band, Collins and Harlan, the glass xylophonist Chris Chapman (a 1908 version of "Dill Pickles Rag"), and banjoist Vess Ossman. The eight numbers from 1923–26 (by Jelly Roll Morton, Oscar Celestin, King Oliver, the NORK, pianist Willy White, and a duo called Hot and Heavy) all have "Rag" in their titles but do not necessarily have much to do with ragtime. Still, collectors of early ragtime performances may want this CD.

8 RCA Victor 80th Anniversary, Vol. 1: 1917–1929/Feb. 26, 1917–Nov. 14, 1929/RCA 68777

In 1997, RCA came out with eight single CDs (also available as an eight-CD set), each of which documents a decade. The 1920s CD (which actually starts in 1917 with the ODJB's "Livery Stable Blues") is excellent and well conceived. Represented are the ODJB, the Original Memphis Five, the NORK, Jelly Roll Morton (three songs), Bennie Moten, Jean Goldkette ("My Pretty Girl" and "Clementine"), Red and Miff's Stompers, Fletcher Henderson, Duke Ellington, Paul Whiteman, Joe Venuti, McKinney's Cotton Pickers, Charlie Johnson, Eddie Condon, Earl Hines, the Missourians, Red Allen, Fats Waller, King Oliver ("Too Late"), and the Mound City Blue Blowers. The quality of the music attests to the importance of the Victor label in the 1920s.

★ Rhapsodies in Black—Music and Words from the Harlem Renaissance/Aug. 1921–Oct. 3, 1935/Rhino 79874

The Harlem Renaissance of the 1920s is celebrated on this four-CD set with poetry readings of 20 vintage pieces (read by black celebrities of today), 65 early recordings, and a very good booklet. Of course, jazz was not a direct part of the Harlem Renaissance; in fact much of the middle-class black culture of the period rejected jazz as barbaric, so it is a bit ironic that the recordings often sound fresher than the well-intentioned poetry. The music is of a consistently high quality and includes a lot of less obvious choices, such as Wilbur Sweatman's "Indianola," Cleo Brown's "Lookie, Lookie, Lookie, Here Comes Cookie," Paul Whiteman's "Charleston," pianist Fred Longshaw's "Chili Pepper," Fess Williams' "Do Shuffle," and Buck and Bubbles' "Lady Be Good." The poetry readings are brief, so get this set for the interesting variety of music.

9 Richmond Rarities/Sept. 16, 1927–Mar. 24, 1933/Jazz Oracle 8008

Despite its generic title (all of the dates on the CD were recorded in Richmond, Indiana), the contents of this disc are actually the complete output of four colorful territory bands. Alex Jackson's Plantation Orchestra's four numbers are highlighted by a memorable version of "Jackass Blues," and Red Perkins' Dixie Ramblers was a fine band captured in 1931. Better known are the orchestras of Alphonso Trent and Zack Whyte. Trent's four sessions feature such players as trumpeter Mouse Randolph, trombonist Snub Mosley, and particularly violinist Stuff Smith; their versions of "After You've Gone" and "St. James Infirmary" are classics. Zack Whyte's Chocolate Brummels recorded on four occasions, with trumpeter-arranger Sy White, tenorman Al Sears, and pianist Herman Chittison all making strong contributions.

5 Riverboat Shuffle/Feb. 1, 1926–Oct. 1, 1936/Memphis Archives 7004

Eighteen songs having something to do with riverboats and/or the Mississippi River are gathered together in this odd collection, which does not give either exact recording dates or complete personnel listings. There are some classics on the program, including the Boswell Sisters' "Roll On, Mississippi, Roll On," Frankie Trumbauer's "Riverboat Shuffle," and Paul Robeson singing "Ol' Man River" plus some memorable obscurities, but overall this is a rather lightweight and insignificant set.

9 Riverside History of Classic Jazz/1920–Oct. 7, 1954/Riverside 005

Put out originally as a five-LP set by Riverside in 1956, this three-CD box (which is a straight reissue) still holds up very well. It consists of six songs apiece under the categories of Backgrounds (including early blues, gospel, and ragtime), Ragtime, The Blues, New Orleans Style, Boogie Woogie, South Side Chicago, Chicago Style, Harlem, New York Style, and finally New Orleans Revival. A perfect introduction to 1920s jazz and the music that immediately followed.

9 Sizzling the Blues/Mar. 5, 1927–Dec. 15, 1929/Frog 5

It was thanks to the occasional field trips conducted by Okeh, Columbia, Victor, and Brunswick that some of the bands in New Orleans were documented in the 1920s; if only there had been much more recorded! On this CD, Louis Dumaine's Jazzola Eight (an octet with cornetist Dumaine and trombonist Earl Humphrey) is heard on all of its recordings: four instrumentals plus dates backing singers Genevieve Davis and Ann Cook. Also included are two bands featuring trumpeter Sharkey Bonano and clarinetist Sidney Arodin (pianist Johnnie Miller's New Orleans Frolickers and drummer Monk Hazel's Bienville Roof Orchestra) and one of the great ensembles of 1929: the Jones-Collins Astoria Hot Eight. Co-led by trumpeter Lee Collins and tenor saxophonist David Jones, the Hot Eight (which includes Arodin and Joseph Robechaux) recorded four hot titles plus two alternate takes, all of which are on the highly recommended *Sizzling the Blues*.

7 Texas and Tennessee Territory Bands/Aug. 26, 1927–July 1, 1931/Retrieval 79006

Five of the best southern territory bands of the 1920s are represented on this intriguing CD: Blue Steele, Slim Lamar, Mart Britt, Sunny Clapp, and Phil Baxter. The only sidemen who became known a little bit later on were cornetist Tony Almerico, clarinetist Sidney Arodin, and pianist Terry Shand, but the musicianship is pretty decent and the music generally swings well. Serious 1920s jazz collectors will want this one!

7 That's My Stuff/Aug. 21, 1929–Nov. 20, 1930/Frog 7

Although the golden age of Chicago jazz began to end in 1927 when many of the top players began to emigrate to New York, there were still many top players that stayed in the Windy City for the next decade. The music on this CD includes Omer Simeon's two recordings as a leader (accompanied by Earl Hines), the clarinetist leading a contingent from the Earl Hines Orchestra behind singer Helen Savage, the four selections by the Dixie Rhythm Kings, and sessions by the overlapping bands of Alex Hill, Harry Dial, and Lloyd Smith. This was still a fertile music scene, but one that the rise of the Depression would soon curtail on records.

4 This Is Art Deco/Jan. 7, 1913–Jan. 1982/Columbia/Legacy 57111

This 20-song CD was meant to help introduce listeners to Columbia's new "Art Deco" reissue series. However, that program did not last very long! The performances (mostly vocals) on this disc (which are programmed in chronological order) have relatively little in common, but there are some classics, including Bert Williams' "Nobody" (1913), Al Jolson's "Swanee," Cliff Edwards' "Fascinatin' Rhythm," and Sophie Tucker singing "Some of These Days," concluding with Alberta Hunter in 1982 performing "You Can't Tell the Difference After Dark." But overall, this is a confusing batch of music.

VARIOUS ARTISTS

8 Those Fabulous Gennetts, Vol. 1 1923–1925/May 25, 1923–Aug. 31, 1925/Timeless 1–062

Although the Gennett label is best remembered for its famous recordings with the NORK, King Oliver, the Wolverines, and Jelly Roll Morton, it also documented many lesser-known but talented players who were based in the Midwest. Featured on this CD are dates by Howard Lanin's Arcadia Orchestra, Guy Lombardo's Royal Canadians (four jazz-oriented numbers from its debut session of March 10, 1924), the Romance of Harmony Orchestra, the Lange-McKay Orchestra, Ross Reyndols' Palais Garden Orchestra, Perley Breed's Shepard Colonial Orchestra, Richard Hitter's Blue Knights, Marion McKay ("Doo Wacka Doo," which at one time was believed to have had a cornet solo by Bix Beiderbecke), the Chubb-Steinberg Orchestra (their three numbers that include cornetist Wild Bill Davison), Wally Erickson's Coliseum Orchestra, and Henry Thies' Castle Farm Orchestra. Despite its obscurity, in general the music is quite rewarding, giving listeners many early examples of jazz-oriented dance bands.

8 Thumpin' and Bumpin'/Nov. 18, 1929–June 9, 1931/Frog 11

A variety of intriguing New York sessions are on this disc. James P. Johnson leads a band (that includes King Oliver, Fats Waller, and an odd vocal group) on "You Don't Understand" and "You've Got to Be Modernistic." Dave Nelson's two 1931 sessions with the King Oliver Orchestra are included, as are a Eubie Blake dance band session from 1931 and the three titles from Russell Wooding's Grand Central Red Caps. Of greatest importance are the four numbers from Cecil Scott's Bright Boys (including very colorful and humorous versions of "Lawd Lawd" and "In a Corner") and the six titles from Bubber Miley's Mileage Makers. Of the latter, "I Lost My Gal from Memphis" and "Black Maria" compensate for the final, somewhat sappy session (which has Edith Wilson's vocals), although overall Miley is not as well featured as one would hope.

6 Tin Pan Alley Blues/May 4, 1916–Mar. 1925/Memphis Archives 7003

After W.C. Handy had a hit with "Memphis Blues" in 1912, and especially after Mamie Smith's recording of "Crazy Blues" in 1920 caused a sensation, the word "blues" was attached to all kinds of songs, many of which were not even blues. This potentially intriguing set emphasizes vaudeville-type blues but waters down the message by including some real blues (such as Bessie Smith's "St. Louis Blues" and Trixie Smith's "Railroad Blues") and less relevant material. Most interesting are the rare early examples of vaudevillians, including Nora Bayes' "Homesickness Blues" (1916) and Marie Cahill's "Dallas Blues" (1917). Also heard from are Belle Baker, Al Bernard, Eddie Cantor, Irving Kaufman, Viola McCoy, Ethel Ridley, Mary Stafford, and Edith Wilson.

6 Unreleased Edison Laterals/Feb. 10, 1928–Apr. 6, 1929/Diamond Cut Productions 201

Although Thomas Edison was not a fan of jazz (even he could not be a genius at everything!), his Edison label was technically advanced, and some jazz-oriented dance bands were documented. On this 1992 CD of previously unreleased material, the most interesting selections are three songs apiece by a later version of the California Ramblers and singer Vaughn de Leath. Otherwise there are performances by Al Friedman's orchestra, Bob Pierce, Tom Timothy's Frivolity Club Orchestra, Parker and Donaldson, the New York Military Band, B.A. Rolfe, the Piccadilly Players, the Golden Gate Orchestra, the Seven Blue Babies, Winegar's Penn. Boys, and Steel Jamison; all very obscure names not only today but in the late 1920s too!

8 What Kind of Rhythm Is That?/1927–May 6, 1931/Frog 31

Although the programming jumps around geographically on this CD, the music is happily in chronological order. Most valuable is the release of all six numbers by George E. Lee's orchestra, Julia Lee's two songs, and the only two numbers ("Blue

Devil Blues" and "Squabblin' ") recorded by Walter Page's Blue Devils. In addition, there are all the performances by Bill Brown's Brownies, the Chickasaw Syncopators (Jimmie Lunceford's debut recordings from 1927), Maynard Baird's Southern Serenaders, Hunter's Serenaders (which has a guest vocal by Victoria Spivey), and Grant Moore's New Orleans Black Devils. There are a lot of gems on this recommended CD.

LPS TO SEARCH FOR

Although the majority of the most important recordings of the 1920s have now been reissued on CD, there is still a lot of valuable material that is not yet available. The Arcadia label in the 1970s came out with a lengthy series of superior releases. *A Bag of Sleepers Volume 1* (Arcadia 2003) has selections featuring Hoagy Carmichael, Johnny Burris' orchestra (which in 1929 had some of the future members of the Casa Loma Orchestra), and a fine Midwest band led by singer Howard Thomas. *A Bag of Sleepers Volume 2* (Arcadia 2004) has very obscure material from 1925–30 (including titles from the Original Atlanta Footwarmers, Ducky Yountz, and Dexter's Pennsylvanians), while *A Bag of Sleepers Volume 3* (Arcadia 2005) consists of numbers from Bernie Schultz, the Cotton Pickers, Berlyn Baylor, Dick Kent, Joe Ward's Swanee Club Orchestra, Roy Wilson's Georgia Crackers, Jack Davies' Kentuckians, and Lawrence Welk. Welk's band in 1928 does a credible job on "Spiked Beer" and "Doin' the New Low Down," although obviously this was not the eventual direction of the bubble-meister's career!

While *Chicago in the Twenties Volume 1* (Arcadia 2011) has music by Elgar's Creole Orchestra, Caroll Dickerson, and Sammy Stewart that has been reissued on CD, *Chicago in the Twenties Volume 2* (Arcadia 2012) includes worthy obscurities from Elmer Kaiser, the Super Syncopators, Charley Straight, Husk O'Hare, the Midnight Serenaders, Bill Haid's Cubs, and the Manhattan Entertainers. *Twin Cities Shuffle* (Arcadia 2016) is an interesting survey of jazz bands from Minneapolis and St. Paul (including Eddie Carlew's Baby Aristocrats Orchestra, Walter Anderson's Golden Pheasant Hoodlums, and Slatz Randall). *West Coast Jazz Volume 1* (Arcadia 2001) has music from Los Angeles by Kid Ory (1922), Sonny Clay, Reb Spikes, the Dixie Serenaders, and Curtis Mosby (including the soundtrack to Mosby band's appearance in *Hallelujah*). *West Coast Jazz Volume 2* (Arcadia 2002) focuses more on obscurities, including the Wilshire Dance Orchestra, Tom Gerunovitch, the Mezzanine Melodies, and two numbers made by Fred Elizalde before he returned to England.

Black and White Ragtime (Biograph 12047) consists mostly of rare piano solos that are ragtime oriented, including titles by Eubie Blake, Fletcher Henderson, Jesse Crump ("Mr. Crump's Rag), Zez Confrey ("Kitten on the Keys"), and Vera Guilaroff (a 1926 version of "Maple Leaf Rag"). One of the odder 1920s LPs is *It Sounds Like Bix* (Broadway 104), consisting of 16 recordings that have cornetists or trumpeters who sound close to Beiderbecke. All have long been disproved (several are actually Andy Secrest), although the Biltmore Hotel Orchestra's "So Long Blues" is awful close. *The Princeton Triangle Jazz Band* (Biograph 12014) has 13 of the 17 recordings made by college bands from Princeton, dating from 1923–24 and 1926–28. The last edition of the group, which includes cornetist Bill Priestley, three reeds, and Squirrel Ashcraft on accordion, is particularly interesting, with its four numbers ("You Know Who," "Everybody and You," "China Boy," and "That's a-Plenty") showing the strong influence of Bix Beiderbecke and Frankie Trumbauer.

White Hot Jazz (Broadway Intermission 115) includes five hot early numbers by the Casa Loma Orchestra, a few rarities, and more familiar material from Jack Pettis and the Cotton Pickers. *White Hot Jazz Volume II* (Broadway Intermission 117) has common pieces by Boyd Senter and Phil Napoleon but rarer sides from Jackie Sounder, the Garden Dancing Palace Orchestra, Carson Robison's Kansas City Jack-Rabbits, and even Kay Kyser (two surprisingly hot numbers from 1929).

In the 1960s Columbia came up with quite a few very impressive box sets (usually three or four LPs), including boxes dedicated to Fletcher Henderson (*A Study in Frustration*), Duke Ellington, and Mildred Bailey. *The Sound of New Orleans* (Columbia C3L 30), *The Sound of Chicago* (Columbia C3L 32), and *The Sound of Harlem* (Columbia C3L 33) each contain 48 selections of consistent high quality, along with impressive and informative booklets. They each succeed magnificently at capturing the wide variety of vintage jazz heard in each of the cities during the 1920s and early '30s. *The Original Sound of the Twenties* (Columbia C3L 35), another three-LP set, sticks mostly to 1926–29 and sometimes wanders a bit further afield, with numbers from Rudy Vallee, Kate Smith, and other nonjazz singers, but also has valuable recordings from Paul Whiteman, Duke Ellington, Louis Armstrong, and others. The four-LP *Thesaurus of Classic Jazz* (Columbia C4L 18), although largely duplicated on CD by now, is a must for Red Nichols fans, since it has many titles by Miff Mole's Molers, the Charleston Chasers, the Redheads, and the Arkansas Travelers.

The Folkways label put out quite a few "various artists" jazz albums, some of which were more valuable than others. *Jazz—Some Beginnings* (Folkways 31) includes Bert Williams' classic "You Can't Get Away from It" (from 1913), early sides by James Europe and Fred Van Eps, and tunes from the likes of Gene Fosdick's Hoosiers, Vic Meyers, and C.A. Matson's Creole Serenaders. *They All Played the Tiger Rag* (Folkways 48) has no fewer than 15 versions of "Tiger Rag", including renditions by the ODJB, the NORK, Paul Howard's Quality Serenaders, Duke Ellington, and even Charles Dornberger. *They All Played the Maple Leaf Rag* (Herwin 401) has the same concept, versions of the ragtime hit by the likes of Jelly Roll Morton, James P. John-

son, W.C. Handy, Sidney Bechet, and ten others.

While most of the music put out by the Historical Records label in the 1970s has since been duplicated on CD, the releases from Harrison (one of the great 1920s labels of the 1970s/'80s) have such obscure (but usually very worthy) music that the performances are still quite scarce. *Blue Notes and Hot Rhythm* (Harrison I) features numbers from Fred Hall, the Ambassadors, Bert Stock, the Ipana Troubadours, Milt Shaw's Detroiters, and Julie Wintz. *Candullo-Creager-Finley and James* (Harrison Q) lives up to its title, with hot dance band music from Joe Candullo, Willie Creager, Bob Finley, and Billy James.

Dance Bands Play Hot (Harrison U) features titles from Joe Herlihy, Arthur Schutt (two songs from 1930), Roy Ingraham, Del Delbridge, Chic Scoggin, Gerald Marks, Eddie Droesch, and George Posnak; talk about obscure! *Four Four Rhythm* (Harrison P) has Ina Ray Hutton's Melodears, Paul Tremaine, Everett Hoagland, Roane's Pennsylvanians, Cline's Collegians, and Tal Henry. *14 Great Hot Dance Sides* (Harrison A) ranges from Glen Gray and Jack Pettis to the Dixie Dance Demons and the Ten Freshmen. *From Collectors' Shelves* (Harrison F) includes performances by Pat Dollohan, Harris Brothers' Texans, and the High Steppers, plus seven numbers from Henny Hendrickson's Louisville Serenaders.

Gennett-Champion Collection (Harrison B) is highlighted by Paul Cornelius' "Sentimental Gentleman from Georgia," Bud Ritchie's "Slappin' the Bass," and Carl Fenton's "Steppin' Along." *Jazzin' Around* (Harrison K) has a few bigger names than usual (Blanche Calloway from 1934–35, Sam Wooding, and Billy Banks) along with Nick Nichols and Eddie Deas' Boston Brownies. *Let's Start with Jack Teagarden* (Harrison C) consists of obscurities from ten bands, including Ina Ray Hutton, Alex Bartha, Mills' Merry Makers, and Teagarden ("You're Simply Delish").

Record Session Specials (Harrison D) includes titles from the Whoopee Makers, Hal Kemp, Ben Bernie, and Bert Lown, among others. *Shake It Down* (Harrison H) consists of 14 selections from eight bands, including Ellis Stratakos' Hotel Jung Orchestra, Doc Daugherty, and Smith Ballew. *Shuffle Your Feet* (Harrison R) has numbers from the Georgia Cotton Pickers, King Carter's Royal Orchestra, Lew Leslie's Blackbirds Orchestra, and Eubie Blake's 1931 orchestra, while *Syncopated Jamboree* (Harrison M) includes music from such bands as Adrian Schubert's Salon Orchestra, Jack Linx's Society Serenaders, Johnny Clesi's Areoleans, and Oreste's Queensland Orchestra. So overall, the Harrison label came out with many LPs that are well worth placing bids for on auction lists by 1920s collectors.

The Legendary Earl Baker Cylinders/Red Nichols Transcriptions (Jazz Archives 43) is for the true 1920s jazz fanatic. In the fall of 1926, cornetist Earl Baker invited some of the members of the Ben Pollack Orchestra to his home for jam sessions. He recorded some of the music on his cylinder machine, and they went unissued and forgotten for 53 years, until released on this 1979 album. The music is often quite noisy and features just incomplete bands, with up to four horns but only a banjo or guitar as the rhythm section. But the reason these performances are notable is that they include the earliest recordings of both Benny Goodman and Glenn Miller, slightly predating their studio sides with Ben Pollack. Also on this LP are performances by Red Nichols from 1929–30 that were made specifically for radio shows, including fine versions of "They Didn't Believe Me," "I May Be Wrong," and "That's a-Plenty," plus a medley featuring three trumpets, piano, and harp.

During 1929–32, the *Hit of the Week* series featured one-sided cardboard records by a variety of top dance bands. *The Cardboard Dance Hall* (Sunbeam 9) has 16 of these performances by such bands as Fred Rich (a classic version of "Little Girl"), Sam Lanin, Harry Reser, Harlem Hot Chocolates (which was really Duke Ellington), Don Voorhees, and Ben Pollack. *Columbia Gems of the Twenties* (Sunbeam 3) has more conventionally released dance band music from 1925–26 by the likes of Francis Craig ("Steady Roll Blues"), Art Kahn, Paul Specht, Fred Rich, and Earl Gresh's Gangplank Orchestra. The double-LP *Dime Store Dance Bands 1927–1933* (Sunbeam 17) consists of 32 performances from the late 1920s and early Depression years, dance band selections put out by budget labels. Although Jack Teagarden, Annette Hanshaw, and the Georgia Cotton Pickers make appearances, most of these selections are by fairly anonymous if enjoyable ensembles, including the White Way Serenaders, the Benjamin Franklin Hotel Orchestra, and Teddy Joyce's Penn Stage Recorders, casting light on some jazz-influenced music that has little chance of being reissued on CD anytime soon.

Black and White Jazz in Europe, 1929 (Wolverine 5) features music recorded in Paris and Berlin by Sam Wooding, Gregor's Gregorians, and Lud Gluskin's Ambassadonians. *With a Bow to Bix* (Wolverine 3) shows the Bix Beiderbecke influence on such 1920s trumpeters as Leroy Morris (with Marion McKay's orchestra), Bob Mayhew (with Hal Kemp), Philippe Brun, and Norman Payne, plus, from later years, Esten Spurrier and Tom Pletcher.

Hopefully more of these recordings will eventually surface on CD.

RECOMMENDED BOOKS

Fortunately there is no shortage of books available that cover early New Orleans jazz, ragtime, and jazz of the 1920s. Here are 69 of the best, all of them recommended.

BIOGRAPHIES

Louis Armstrong

Louis Armstrong by Hugues Panassie (Charles Scribner's Sons, 1971)

Louis Armstrong—An Extravagant Life by Laureen Bergreen (Broadway Books, 1997)

The Louis Armstrong Companion edited by Joshua Berrett (Schirmer Books, 1999)

The Louis Armstrong Story 1900–1971 by Max Jones and John Chilton (Da Capo Press 1988)

Satchmo by Gary Giddins (Doubleday, 1988)

Sidney Bechet

Sidney Bechet—The Wizard of Jazz by John Chilton (Oxford University Press, 1987)

Bix Beiderbecke

Bix—Man and Legend by Richard Sudhalter and Philip Evans with William Dean Myatt (Schirmer Books, 1974)

The Leon Bix Beiderbecke Story by Philip and Linda Evans (Prelike Press, 1998)

Buddy Bolden

In Search of Buddy Bolden—First Man of Jazz by Donald Marquis (Louisiana State University Press, 1978)

Baby Dodds

The Baby Dodds Story by Baby Dodds and Larry Gara (Louisiana State University Press, 1992)

Duke Ellington

Ellington: The Early Years by Mark Tucker (University of Illinois Press, 1991)

The World of Duke Ellington by Stanley Dance (Charles Scribner's Sons, 1970)

James Reese Europe

A Life in Ragtime by Reid Badger (Oxford University Press, 1995)

Earl Hines

The World of Earl Hines by Stanley Dance (Da Capo Press, 1977)

Claude Hopkins

Crazy Fingers by Warren Vache Sr. (Smithsonian Institution Press, 1992)

Alberta Hunter

Alberta Hunter by Frank Taylor with Gerald Cook (McGraw-Hill, 1987)

James P. Johnson

James P. Johnson by Scott Brown and Robert Hilbert (Scarecrow Press, 1986)

Scott Joplin

King of Ragtime by Edward A. Berlin (Oxford University Press, 1994)
Scott Joplin by James Haskins and Kathleen Benson (Doubleday & Co. 1978)

Jelly Roll Morton

Mister Jelly Roll by Alan Lomax (Pantheon Books, 1993)
Oh, Mister Jelly by William Russell (Jazz Media APS, 1999)

Red Nichols

Red Head by Stephen Straff (Scarecrow Press, 1996)

Original Dixieland Jazz Band

The Story of the Original Dixieland Jazz Band by H.O. Brunn (Louisiana State University Press, 1960)

Andy Razaf

Black and Blue by Barry Singer (Schirmer Books, 1992)

Bessie Smith

Bessie by Chris Albertson (Stein and Day, 1982)

Jack Teagarden

Jack Teagarden by Jay D. Smith and Len Guttridge (Da Capo Press, 1988)

Frankie Trumbauer

Tram by Phillip Evans and Larry Kiner (Scarecrow Press, 1994)

Fats Waller

Ain't Misbehavin' by Ed Kirkeby (Dodd, Mead & Company, 1966)
Ain't Misbehavin' by Joel Vance (Berkley Medallion Books, 1977)

Mary Lou Williams

Morning Glory by Linda Dahl (Pantheon Books, 1999)

AUTOBIOGRAPHIES

Louis Armstrong

In His Own Words by Louis Armstrong, edited by Thomas Brothey (Oxford University Press, 1999)
My Life in New Orleans by Louis Armstrong (Da Capo Press, 1954)

Sidney Bechet

Treat It Gentle by Sidney Bechet (Da Capo Press, 1978)

Clyde Bernhardt

I Remember by Clyde Bernhardt (University of Pennsylvania Press, 1986)

Barney Bigard

With Louis and the Duke by Barney Bigard and Barry Martyn (Oxford University Press, 1988)

Garvin Bushell

Jazz from the Beginning by Garvin Bushell with Mark Tucker (University of Michigan Press, 1988)

Lee Collins

Oh Didn't He Ramble by Lee Collins with Mary Collins, Frank Gillis, and John Miner (University of Illinois Press, 1989)

Eddie Condon

We Called It Music by Eddie Condon with Thomas Sugrue (Da Capo Press, 1992)

Bud Freeman

Crazeology by Bud Freeman with Robert Wolf (University Of Illinois Press, 1989)

Ethel Waters

His Eye Is on the Sparrow by Ethel Waters with Charley Samuels (Da Capo Press, 1992)

COLLECTIONS OF VALUABLE INTERVIEWS

American Musicians II by Whitney Balliett (Oxford University Press, 1996)
From Satchmo to Miles by Leonard Feather (Da Capo Press, 1984)
Hear Me Talkin' to Ya edited by Nat Hentoff and Nat Shapiro (Rinehart and Co., 1955)
Hot Jazz—From Harlem to Storyville by David Griffiths (Scarecrow Press, 1998)
The Poets of Tin Pan Alley by Philip Furia (Oxford University Press, 1990)
Selections from the Gutter edited by Art Hodes and Chadwick Hansen (University of California Press, 1977)
Voices of the Jazz Age by Chip Deffaa (University of Illinois Press, 1990)

ESSENTIAL PHOTO BOOKS

Black Beauty, White Heat by Frank Driggs and Harris Lewine (William Morrow and Co., 1982)
A Pictorial History of Jazz by Orrin Keepnews and Bill Grauer Jr. (Bonanza Books, 1981)

RAGTIME BOOKS

They All Played Ragtime by Rudi Blesh and Harriet Janis (Oak Publications, 1971)
This Is Ragtime by Terry Waldo (Da Capo Press, 1991)

OTHER IMPORTANT BOOKS ON THE CLASSIC JAZZ ERA

The Best of Jazz by Humphrey Lyttelton (Taplinger, 1982)
The Best of Jazz II by Humphrey Lyttelton (Taplinger, 1982)
Chicago Jazz by William Howland Kenney (Oxford University Press, 1993)
Early Jazz by Gunther Schuller (Oxford University Press, 1968)
Goin' to Kansas City by Nathan Pearson Jr. (University of Illinois Press, 1994)

A History of Jazz in Britain, 1919–50 by Jim Godbolt (Quartet Books, 1984)

Jazz—A History of the New York Scene by Samuel Charters and Leonard Kunstadt (Da Capo Press, 1981)

Jazz Masters of New Orleans by Martin Williams (Macmillan, 1967)

Jazz Masters of the Twenties by Richard Hadlock (Macmillan, 1965)

Jazz Masters of the 1930s by Rex Stewart (Da Capo Press, 1972)

Jazzmen edited by Frederic Ramsey Jr. and Charles Edward Smith (Harcourt Brace Jovanovich, 1967)

Jazz Styles in Kansas City and the Southwest by Ross Russell (Da Capo Press, 1997)

Lost Chords by Richard M. Sudhalter (Oxford University Press, 1999)

Spreadin' Rhythm Around—Black Popular Songwriters 1880–1930 by David Jasen and Gordon Gene Jones (Schirmer Books, 1998)

Swing Out—Great Negro Dance Bands by Gene Ferrett (Da Capo Press, 1993)

REFERENCE BOOKS

All Music Guide to Jazz, 3rd edition, edited by Michael Erlewine, Vladimir Bogdanov, Chris Woodstra, and Scott Yanow (Miller Freeman Books, 1998)

The Biographical Encyclopedia of Jazz by Leonard Feather and Ira Gitler (Oxford University Press, 1999)

Who's Who of Jazz by John Chilton (Chilton, 1978)

JAZZ ON FILM

Jazz and Hollywood have never had a comfortable relationship, with the movie industry often seeming incapable (with just a few exceptions) of producing a halfway realistic film on the exciting jazz life without resorting to clichés. It is remarkable that such early figures as Jelly Roll Morton, Bix Beiderbecke (the very flawed and confusing 1990 Italian film *An Interpretation of a Legend* does not really count), Fats Waller, King Oliver, the Original Dixieland Jazz Band, and Sidney Bechet have not been the subjects of movies, for their stories are particularly fascinating.

As far as early jazz musicians actually appearing in films, the fact that sound films did not become common until late in the 1920s meant that many of the pioneers went completely undocumented. The Original Dixieland Jazz Band did appear in the 1917 silent film *The Good for Nothing*, while the team of Sissle and Blake were in a couple of experimental sound shorts in the early 1920s. The first example of a jazz band appearing on film seems to be a rather notable clip of the 1925 Ben Bernie Orchestra playing "Sweet Georgia Brown" (with Jack Pettis taking a strong solo). With the coming of sound, the possibilities were endless but unfortunately mostly not taken, and King Oliver, Jelly Roll Morton, the Fletcher Henderson Orchestra (even in its later years), and Freddie Keppard never made it to film. Ted Lewis' *Is Everybody Happy* (filmed with Muggsy Spanier and Don Murray) and a Ben Pollack short with Benny Goodman and Jimmy McPartland have yet to be found.

Fortunately some early greats had better luck. Bessie Smith appeared in the ten-minute film *St. Louis Blues*, Louis Armstrong (who would later appear on film regularly) was captured as early as 1933 playing three songs, Duke Ellington's short *Black and Tan* (1929) has some prominent Arthur Whetsol, and, most remarkably, a few years ago a newsreel was discovered of Paul Whiteman's orchestra in 1928 playing "My Ohio Home"; Bix Beiderbecke can be seen if not really heard. Ethel Waters appears in 1929's *On with the Show* (singing "Am I Blue"), Curtis Mosby's Dixieland Blue Blowers are prominent in a nightclub scene in 1929's *Hallelujah*, and Paul Whiteman is saluted in the intriguing if flawed *King of Jazz* (1930), which gives listeners valuable glimpses of Joe Venuti, Eddie Lang, and the Rhythm Boys, although Frankie Trumbauer and Andy Secrest are barely seen at all. Also well worth looking for is *The Big Broadcast* (1932), which features valuable performances by Bing Crosby (singing "Dinah" while accompanied by Eddie Lang), the Boswell Sisters, Cab Calloway, and the Mills Brothers.

By far the best video collection of classic jazz film performances currently available is *At the Jazz Band Ball* (Yazoo 514). Included are performances by the Dorsey Brothers (a brief "Get Out and Get Under the Moon" in 1929), Duke Ellington (a medley from 1929's *Black and Tan* and a great version of "Old Man Blues" from the Amos 'n Andy movie *Check and Double Check*), the Boswell Sisters ("Crazy People"), Louis Armstrong (a 1931 newsreel appearance and the 1933 concert that consists of "I Cover the Waterfront," "Dinah," and "Tiger Rag"), the long-lost Bix clip, dancer Bill "Bojangles" Robinson, the bulk of Bessie Smith's film *St. Louis Blues*, Ben Bernie's 1925 performance of "Sweet Georgia Brown," two numbers from Tommy Christian's hot 1928 dance band, and a few other items.

The 1987 video *Duke Ellington* (Jazz Classics 101) has the two Ellington shorts *Black and Tan* (1929) and *Symphony in Black* (1935), and a Soundies version of "Cotton Tail"; these performances have also shown up unannounced now and then on cable television channels. *Jazz Women* (Rosetta 1320) consists of nine performances from 1932–50, including Nina Mae McKinney's "Everything I've Got Belongs to You" (with Eubie Blake's orchestra in 1932) and the only film footage of Ida Cox (from 1939).

Two other valuable CDs feature classic jazz greats in later years. *The Sound of Jazz* (Rhapsody 2001) is a justly famous television special from 1957 that is full of memorable moments. Most relevant to this book are two performances from the Red Allen All-Stars ("Wild Man Blues" and "Rosetta") featuring Allen, Rex Stewart, Pee Wee Russell, and Coleman Hawkins. *Chicago and All That Jazz* (Vintage Jazz Classics 2002), a 1961 special hosted by Garry Moore, stuffs far too much in too short a period of time, celebrating Chicago jazz of the 1920s. There are brief moments that are historic, including a recreation of the ODJB with Tony Sbarbaro; a version of "Jelly Roll Blues" with Red Allen, Kid Ory, and Buster Bailey; silent home movie footage of Bix and some Jean Goldkette sidemen; and "China Boy" by a reunion of the Chicagoans.

There should have been so much more on film by the classic jazz greats, but at least we have the records!

JAZZ IN 1933

In many ways, the jazz scene looked quite bleak as the year 1933 began. The record industry had collapsed, dropping from 100 million records sold in 1927 to just 6 million in 1932. The annual sales of phonographs had shrunk from 1 million to just 40,000. The first to be dropped by the record industry were the black jazz artists, such as Jelly Roll Morton, King Oliver, and Bessie Smith, while the white jazz musicians were generally heard during the early 1930s anonymously in large commercial orchestras. The premature deaths of Bix Beiderbecke, Don Murray, Frank Teschemacher, Jimmy Blythe, Jimmy Harrison, Carleton Coon, and Bubber Miley left major holes in jazz that would be very difficult to fill. Even the election of Franklin D. Roosevelt could be considered at that moment to be a bad sign for jazz, since his vow to end Prohibition would mean the closing of speakeasies that had formerly featured jazz.

But as it turned out, there were also many hopeful signs for jazz's future. Louis Armstrong had had a successful tour of Europe in 1932, Duke Ellington was roundly hailed as a genius, Cab Calloway had become a national name, and the film called *The Big Broadcast* displayed the very promising talents of Bing Crosby, the Boswell Sisters, and the Mills Brothers in addition to Calloway. Jazz might have been pushed underground to an extent, but there were many promising newcomers on the scene, including the amazing pianist Art Tatum, trumpeter Bunny Berigan, and tenor saxophonist Chu Berry. Although jazz big bands were not yet common, the Casa Loma Orchestra and the outfits led by Ellington, Fletcher Henderson, Earl Hines, Bennie Moten (in Kansas City), Chick Webb, and Jimmy Lunceford were all performing rewarding music. And radio, which had helped make Ellington and Calloway household names, had unlimited potential for exposing new talents.

Unknown to virtually everyone at that point in time (certainly no one predicted it in print) was that in 2½ years, the big band era, which was spearheaded by such studio musicians as Benny Goodman, Tommy Dorsey, Jimmy Dorsey, Artie Shaw, and Glenn Miller, would be launched and jazz would make a major commercial comeback under the new name of swing. And even the various styles of classic jazz would gradually reappear, starting in the late 1930s with the New Orleans revival movement. Many of the survivors of the 1920s who were fortunate enough to still be active in the 1940s would have opportunities to work regularly again.

Seventy years after it ended, the classic jazz era is today recognized not only as the soundtrack of the 1920s and an important chapter in the history of jazz, but as one of the most fun and rewarding periods of music ever.

Photo Credits

Ray Avery Jazz Archives: 23, 26, 28, 37, 47, 50, 57, 63, 69, 78, 81, 96, 103, 109, 120, 129, 133, 152, 160, 171, 180, 211, 230, 234, 239, 242, 247, 250

Photos by Duncan Schiedt: 59, 177

About the Author

Scott Yanow has been a self-described jazz fanatic since 1970 and a jazz journalist since 1975. Jazz editor of *Record Review* (1976–84), he has written for *Downbeat, JazzTimes, Jazziz, Jazz Forum, Coda, Jazz News, Jazz Now,* and *Strictly Jazz* magazines. Yanow currently is a regular contributor to *Cadence, the L.A. Jazz Scene, Mississippi Rag, Jazz Improv, Jazz Report,* and *Planet Jazz.* He has penned over 250 album liner notes and is estimated to have written more jazz record reviews than anyone in history. Editor of the *All Music Guide to Jazz* and author of *Duke Ellington* and *Trumpet Kings,* Yanow also wrote *Swing, Bebop,* and *Afro-Cuban Jazz* for the *Third Ear—The Essential Listening Companion* series, and is proud of having written five full-length reference books in 22 months. It is his goal to collect every good jazz record ever made, and to have time to listen to them!

INDEX

A

A. G. Allen's Minstrels, 155
Abbey, Leon, 223
Abbott, Larry, 60, 197
Adrian Rollini's Orchestra, 29, 158, 165, 208, 235
Adrian Schubert's Salon Orchestra, 264, 275
Ahl, Fred Arthur. *See* Hall, Fred "Sugar"
Ahola, Sylvester, 12–13, 15, 86, 113
Alabama Jug Band, 13, 53, 203, 218
Alabama Washboard Stompers, 241
Alabamians, 154, 200, 221
Alamac label, 163
Albert, Don, 71, 266
Albert, Tom, 35
Albert Ammons' Rhythm Kings, 199
Albert Wynn's Gut Bucket Five, 108
Albin, Jack, 130, 172
Alexander, Charlie, 70
Alexander, Texas, 123, 178
Alex Calamese's Virginia Ramblers, 56
Alexis, Ricard, 53
Alex Jackson's Plantation Orchestra, 270
Algiers Brass Band, 53
Al Goering's Collegians, 156, 189
Al Handler's Alamo Café Orchestra, 260
Al Katz's Kittens, 260
Allen, Ed, 13, 53, 62, 66, 227
Allen, Henry, Sr., 14, 53
Allen, Henry "Red," 8, 13–15, 113, 114, 146, 170, 195, 201, 203, 223, 245
Allen, Jap, 222
Allen, Ken, 128
Allen, Moses, 139
Allen, Red, 16, 17, 23, 25, 42, 52, 56, 62, 92, 99, 102, 105, 107, 111, 141, 151, 160, 161, 162, 163, 178, 196, 201, 218, 223, 240, 261, 265, 270, 281
Allen's Brass Band, 176
All-Star Orchestra, 138, 145, 165
Almerico, Tony, 271
Alphonso Trent Orchestra, The, 233
Al Simeon's Hot Six, 71, 208
Alston, James, 267
Alston, Ovie, 112
Altier, Danny, 221, 260
Alvin, Danny, 135
Alvis, Hayes, 118, 214
Ambassadors, 166, 188, 189, 274
Ambrose, 12, 15, 263, 264
Ambrose, Bert, 12
Amendt, John, 261
Anderson, Gene, 67
Anderson, Ivie, 79
Anderson, Kenneth, 214
Anderson, Missouri, 117
Anderson, Walter, 273
Andrade, Vernon, 39, 44, 147, 209
Andrew Preer's Cotton Club Orchestra, 66
Andrew Preer's Cotton Club Syncopators, 146

Andy Kirk Orchestra, 45, 46
Andy Kirk's Twelve Clouds of Joy, 130
Anton Lada's Louisiana Five, 175
Apex Club Orchestra, 173, 174
Arbello, Fernando, 112
Arcadian's Dance Orchestra, 264
Arcadian Serenaders, 35, 140
Archey, Jimmy, 15–16, 31, 113, 242
Arkansas Travelers, 155, 170, 171, 193, 204, 274
Arlen, Harold, 259
Armand J. Piron's New Orleans Orchestra, 35
Armstrong, Lil Hardin, 16–17, 18, 67, 70, 115, 155, 177, 204, 228
Armstrong, Louis, 4, 6, 7, 8, 9, 11, 12, 13, 14, 16, 17–21, 22, 23, 25, 26, 28, 32, 33, 39, 40, 44, 45, 46, 48, 56, 57, 63, 66, 67, 69, 70, 71, 74, 75, 76, 84, 92, 94, 99, 102, 104, 107, 108, 109, 110, 111, 114, 115, 116, 117, 125, 132, 137, 141, 151, 153, 157, 165, 167, 170, 173, 176, 177, 178, 184, 186, 189, 193, 195, 201, 202, 203, 204, 205, 207, 212, 213, 215, 217, 218, 221, 222, 223, 224, 227, 229, 230, 237, 238, 260, 265, 274, 276, 277, 280, 282
Armstrong's Stompers, 20
Arndt, Felix, 3
Arnheim, Gus, 63, 64, 198
Arnold Dupas' Orchestra, 169
Arodin, Sidney, 41, 271
Arthur Fields and His Assassinators, 93
Artie Shaw's Gramercy Five, 86
Ash, Paul, 150, 174
Ashcraft, Squirrel, 273
Austin, Gene, 191, 238, 259
Austin, Lovie, 22, 61, 68, 71, 176, 184
Austin High Gang, 7, 56, 145, 147, 168, 177
Austin High School Gang, 134, 225
Autrey, Herman, 39

B

B. A. Rolfe's Lucky Strike Orchestra, 264
Baer, Moe, 269
Bailey, Buster, 9, 15, 22–23, 39, 67, 89, 102, 105, 115, 151, 193, 210, 212, 216, 217, 227, 263, 264, 268, 281
Bailey, Mildred, 11, 23–24, 63, 73, 74, 90, 91, 95, 134, 140, 174, 175, 197, 243, 259, 274
Bailey, Pearl, 195
Bailey's Dixie Dudes, 156
Bailey's Lucky Seven, 76, 166, 183, 208
Baird, Maynard, 266, 273
Baker, Belle, 272
Baker, Earl, 275
Baker, Josephine, 27, 112
Ballew, Smith, 11, 73, 131, 139, 145, 150, 191, 192, 198, 204, 237, 259, 275
Bang-Up Six, 101
Bank, Paul, 135
Banks, Billy, 14, 57, 151, 203, 225, 274

Baptiste, Jules, 203
Baquet, George, 25
Barbarin, Isadore, 24
Barbarin, Paul, 24–25, 201, 204
Barbecue Joe and His Hot Dogs, 140, 141
Bard, Lola, 182
Barefield, Eddie, 113
Bargy, Roy, 25
Barker, Danny, 24
Barnes, Faye. *See* Jones, Maggie
Barnes, George, 131, 267
Barnes, Paul, 53
Barnes, Walter, 33, 56, 150, 264
Barnet, Charlie, 106, 175, 192
Barrelhouse Five, 13, 53
Barris, Harry, 63, 198
Bartha, Alex, 274
Bartlette, Viola, 22, 34, 35, 68, 176, 184
Basie, Count, 135, 136, 160, 164, 165, 185, 238, 244, 245, 266
Bastin, Harry, 190
Battle, Edgar "Puddinghead," 130
Bauduc, Ray, 156, 183, 191
Baxter, Phil, 261, 264, 266, 271
Bayersdorffer, Johnny, 268
Bayes, Nora, 272
Baylor, Berlyn, 273
Bayou Boys, 34
The Beale Street Washboard Band, 68, 70, 262
Beaman, Lottie, 199
Beasley, Irene, 90, 166
Beatty, Josephine. *See* Hunter, Alberta
Bechet, Sidney, 4, 5, 6, 9, 17, 18, 20, 25–27, 35, 39, 42, 65, 66, 68, 78, 84, 111, 114, 115, 116, 123, 132, 133, 137, 141, 142, 147, 157, 158, 161, 162, 173, 184, 187, 188, 209, 210, 216, 218, 227, 237, 238, 263, 265, 274, 276, 277
Beiderbecke, Bix, 7, 8, 12, 27–31, 34, 43, 49, 50, 54, 56, 72, 88, 89, 90, 98, 131, 132, 134, 135, 143, 145, 146, 149, 151, 154, 158, 165, 167, 168, 170, 191, 194, 200, 202, 204, 205, 206, 208, 226, 233–234, 268, 269, 273, 275, 276, 280, 281, 282
Beise, Paul, 32
Bell, Alfred, 224
Bell, Anna, 13, 203
Belshaw, George, 269
Ben Bernie Orchestra, 280
Benbow, William, 157
Benedetti's Six Crackerjacks, 169
Benford, Bill, 15, 31, 83
Benford, Tommy, 31, 162
Benjamin Franklin Hotel Orchestra, 275
Bennett, Cuban, 51
Bennett, Hip, 219
Bennett's Swamplanders, 220, 263
Bennie Moten Orchestra, 164, 185
Benny Goodman Orchestra, 130
Benny Goodman Trio, Quartet, and Sextet, 86, 89–90, 103, 225

Coon, Carleton, 58, 282
Coon-Sanders Nighthawks, 58–60
Coon-Sanders Novelty Orchestra, 58
Coon-Sanders Orchestra, 260
Cooper, Jerry, 74
Cooper, Jimmie, 146
Copeland, Andrew, 215
Copeland, Martha, 146, 149
Cordella, Charlie, 41
Cordilla, Charles, 168, 169
Cornelius, Paul, 274
Costello, Johnny, 182, 183
Cotton, Billy, 263
Cotton Club Orchestra, 67, 146, 154, 263
Cotton Pickers, 60, 166, 173, 183, 204, 208, 235, 269, 273
Cottrel, Frank, 268
Count Basie Orchestra, 164
Cox, Ida, 4, 22, 61–62, 92, 102, 132, 176, 186, 207, 211, 215, 216, 222, 260, 263, 281
Craig, Francis, 275
Crawford, Jimmy, 139
Crawford, Joseph. See Petit, Buddy
Crawford, Rosetta, 26
Crawley, Wilbur, 261
Crawley, Wilton, 9, 62
Crazy Kats, 116
Creager, Willie, 274
Creath, Charlie, 13, 62, 65, 84, 117, 122, 132, 141, 146, 157, 203, 207, 209, 266
Creath's Jazz-o-Maniacs, 266
Creole Jazz Band, 6, 16, 176, 177, 178, 203, 205, 207, 228
Creole Orchestra, 4
Creole Serenaders, 35
Crescent City Jazzers, 35, 140
Crippen, Katie, 102
Crosby, Bing, 11, 23, 38, 63–65, 73, 74, 101, 127, 134, 153, 197, 198, 225, 229, 235, 236, 259, 280, 282
Crosby, Bob, 35, 36, 63, 73, 127, 167, 190, 191, 221, 229, 230
Crosby, Israel, 102
Crump, Jesse "Tiny," 61, 273
Cuffee, Ed, 144
Cummins, Bernie, 65
Curl, Langston, 144
Curti, Guido, 169
Curtis Mosby's Blue Blowers, 40, 94, 205, 280
Cush, Frank, 139
Custer, Clay, 237
Czars of Harmony, 141

D

Dabney, Ford, 219
Dabney's Band, 269
Dahlgren, Gene, 128
Daily, Frank, 226
Daily, Pete, 146
Dale, Flora. See Henderson, Rosa
Dandridge, Putney, 122
Dandy Dixie Minstrels, 228
Dane, Barbara, 39
Daniels, Douglas, 221, 222

Daniels, Wilbur, 221, 222
d'Arcy, Phillip, 94
Darensbourg, Joe, 39
Dat Dere. See Hanshaw, Annette
Daugherty, Doc, 275
Davenport, Cow Cow, 217, 260
Dave's Harlem Highlights, 167
Davies, Jack, 273
Davis, Benny, 183
Davis, Bobby, 44, 45, 77, 91, 113, 131, 138
Davis, Charlie, 266
Davis, Genevieve, 271
Davis, Jasper, 146, 148, 220, 263
Davis, Julia, 132, 176
Davis, Leonard, 62, 65, 119
Davis, Meyer, 90, 219
Davis, Milton, 85
Davis, Wilmer, 169, 203
Davison, Wild Bill, 23, 41, 141, 160, 182, 232, 272
Deas, Eddie, 274
Deauville Dozen, 204
DeDroit, Johnny, 186, 267, 268
Deep River Boys, 131
DeFaut, Volly, 31, 42, 65–66, 89, 151
De Forrest, Maud, 102
Delbridge, Del, 274
Delk, Lillie, 48
DeParis, Sidney, 66, 119, 133, 162, 195
DeParis, Wilbur, 23, 43, 66, 157, 203
Deppe, Lois, 51, 108
Deppe, Russell, 86
Deschamps, Rosa. See Henderson, Rosa
Devine's Wisconsin Roof Orchestra, 49
Devonshire Restaurant Dance Band, 264
Dewey Jackson's Peacock Orchestra, 266
Dexter, Fred, 49
Dexter's Pennsylvanians, 273
Dial, Harry, 56, 66, 271
Dickerson, Carroll, 16, 18, 19, 20, 39, 48, 56, 66–67, 71, 75, 107, 109, 112, 117, 137, 199, 214, 225, 264, 265, 273
Dickerson, R. Q., 46, 67, 263
Dickerson Orchestra, 67
"Dippermouth." See Oliver, King
D'Ipplito, Vic, 134
Disney, 76
Dixie Daisies, 90, 101
Dixie Dance Demons, 274
Dixie Duo, 33
Dixie Four, 42, 119
Dixie Jazzers Washboard Band, 158
Dixieland Jug Blowers, 68, 70, 71, 99, 100
Dixieland Thumpers, 35, 71
Dixie Rhythm Kings, 155, 196, 209, 271
Dixie Serenaders, 273
Dixie Stompers, 105
Dixie Syncopators, 169, 178, 179, 184, 205
Dixie Washboard, 13
Dixie Washboard Band, 53, 228, 260
Dixon, Lawrence, 176
Dixon, Mary, 13, 146
Dixon, Vance, 176, 263
Dixon's Jazz Maniacs, 267

Doc Cook's 14 Doctors of Syncopation, 58
Doc Cook's Dreamland Orchestra, 107, 191, 203
Doc Cook's Gingersnaps, 128, 129, 173
Doc Holly's Band, 155
Doc Hyder's Southerners, 101
Doc Ross' Jazz Bandits, 229
Dodds, Baby, 4, 11, 16, 18, 67–68, 70, 71, 126, 141, 162, 176, 177, 178, 223, 262, 276
Dodds, Jimmy, 34
Dodds, Johnny, 6, 8, 9, 16, 17, 18, 20, 22, 32, 35, 42, 48, 55, 56, 67, 68–71, 71, 75, 99–100, 109, 119, 122, 130, 137, 141, 145, 155, 162, 173, 175, 176, 177, 178, 184, 185, 187, 199, 204, 205, 218, 223, 228, 232, 237, 262, 265
Dodds, Warren. See Dodds, Baby
Dodds' Black Bottom Stompers, 70
Dollohan, Pat, 274
Dominique, Anatie. See Dominique, Natty
Dominique, Natty, 22, 32, 33, 68, 69, 70, 71, 174, 223, 228
Don Nelson's Paramount Serenaders, 126
Don Redman Orchestra, 195
Dornberger, Charles, 274
Dorsey, Georgia Tom, 12, 193, 194
Dorsey, Jimmy, 9, 10, 44, 49, 50, 54, 60, 71–72, 76, 81, 88, 89, 95, 96, 97, 99, 113, 114, 127, 136, 138, 154, 156, 170, 171, 172, 175, 184, 195, 198, 207, 237, 244, 268, 269, 282
Dorsey, Johnny, 73
Dorsey, Tommy, 9, 34, 35, 44, 49, 50, 54, 60, 71, 72, 73, 81, 85, 86, 88, 89, 95, 96, 97, 106, 108, 127, 138, 143, 154, 159, 184, 188, 198, 207, 217, 220, 226, 233, 237, 244, 268, 269, 282
Dorsey Brothers, 34, 36, 37, 45, 54, 131, 134, 143, 150, 156, 158, 166, 167, 192, 198, 206, 226, 235, 260, 280
Dorsey Brothers Orchestra, 24, 64, 72–74, 130, 204, 208, 229, 231
Dorsey Brothers' Wild Canaries, 72, 146
Dorsey Concert Orchestra, 73
Dorsey's Novelty Six, 71, 72
Dot Dare, 90
Dougherty, Eddie, 122
Douglas, Louis, 132
Douglas, Russell, 131
Dowell, Edgar, 223
Downey, Morton, 188
Droesch, Eddie, 274
Duchin, Eddie, 135
Dudley, Roberta, 48, 85, 184, 185
Dud Mecum's Wolverines, 268
Duhe, Lawrence, 25, 48, 85, 176
Duke Ellington and the Washingtonians, 78
Duke Ellington Orchestra, 92, 93, 111, 117, 153
Dumaine, Louis, 265, 271
Dunham, Sonny, 52
Dunk Rendleman's Alabamians, 262
Dunn, Artie, 261
Dunn, Johnny, 8, 55, 67, 74–75, 121, 148, 162, 163, 216, 227, 238

Herlihy, Joe, 194, 234, 268, 274
Herman, Woody, 124
Herman Kenin's Multnomah Hotel Orchestra, 128
Herriford, Leon, 40, 205
Herring, Clara, 132
Heywood, Eddie, Jr., 115, 238
Heywood, Eddie, Sr., 62, 142
Hickman, Art, 92
Hicks, Edna, 102, 132, 148, 176
Higginbotham, J. C., 9, 15, 42, 51, 99, 102, 107, 111, 116, 151, 162, 192, 201, 202
Higgins, Billy, 220
High Hatters, 197
High Steppers, 261, 274
Hightower, Lottie, 48
Hightower, Willie, 67, 125, 137, 205, 265
Hilaire, Andrew, 107, 162
Hill, Alex, 55, 107–108, 112, 147, 170, 208, 214, 271
Hill, Bertha "Chippie," 18, 20, 56, 108, 126, 150, 203
Hill, Teddy, 189, 201, 205, 245
Hines, Earl, 10, 12, 13, 16, 18, 19, 20, 48, 51, 67, 70, 84, 86, 100, 106, 108–111, 113, 119, 155, 173, 174, 176, 196, 199, 209, 214, 221, 225, 227, 269, 270, 271, 276, 282
Hinton, Milt, 186, 187, 221, 227
Hitch's Happy Harmonists, 49, 50
Hite, Les, 19, 40, 94
Hite, Mattie, 102
Hitter, Richard, 272
Hoagland, Everett, 274
Hobson, Ray, 187
Hodes, Art, 33, 41, 66, 68, 84, 108, 141, 157, 170, 205, 209
Hodges, Johnny, 10, 26, 40, 72, 79, 92, 98, 111
Hokum Trio, 108, 200
Holiday, Billie, v, 90, 91, 211, 259
Holiday, Clarence, 159
Holland, Peanuts, 233
Hollis Peavey's Jazz Bandits, 56
Holloway, Mike, 186
Hollywood Blue Devils, 244
Holman, Libby, 60, 127, 269
Holmes, Charlie, 62, 107, 111, 148, 151, 201, 202, 261, 263
Holt, Ted, 139
Hometowners, 93
Hooper, Lou, 219
Hooper, Louis, 106
Hopkins, Claude, 12, 16, 27, 107, 111–112, 123, 194, 214, 219, 242, 276
Horace Henderson Orchestra, 105
Horace Henderson's Collegians, 51, 118, 224
Horne, Lena, 100, 210
Hot Air Men, 166
Hot and Heavy, 270
Hot Eight, 271
Hotel Roosevelt Orchestra, 31
Hot Lips Page Orchestra, 208
Hot Shots, 20
Hottentots, the, 267
Howard, Bob, 56

Howard, Darnell, 32, 35, 95, 110, 111, 112–113, 126, 150, 187, 196, 201, 220–221, 223, 224, 262
Howard, Earle, 13, 83
Howard, Eddy, 259
Howard, Jane, 158
Howard, Lionel, 15
Howard, Paul, 40, 94, 113, 265, 266, 274
Howard Lanin's Arcadia Orchestra, 272
Howe, George, 111, 201
Hudson, Bob, 42, 224
Hudson, Ed, 43, 223
Hug, Armand, 168
Hughes, Phil, 91
Hughes, Spike, 14, 51, 72, 113–114, 245
Humes, Helen, 223
Humphrey, Earl, 271
Humphrey, Jim, 127
Hunt, Pee Wee, 52, 89
Hunter, Alberta, 6, 11, 18, 20, 22, 26, 79, 102, 114–115, 116, 132, 149, 166, 176, 210, 215, 216, 238, 271, 276
Hunter's Serenaders, 273
Hurley, Clyde, 190
Husk O'Hare's Footwarmers, 268
Hutchenrider, Clarence, 52
Hutchinson, Jimmy, 187
Hutton, Ina Ray, 274
Hylton, Jack, 99, 113, 115–116, 263, 264
Hyman, Johnny, 168, 186

I

Idaho, Bertha, 13
Imperial Band, 71
Imperial Orchestra, 4, 85, 187
Ina Ray Hutton's Melodears, 274
Indiana Brass Band, 53
Indiana Syncopators, 183
Inge, Edward, 195
Ingraham, Roy, 274
Invincibles String Band, 167
Ipana Troubadours, 90, 274
Ira Coffey's Walkathons, 66
Irving Aaronson's Commanders, 132, 146
Irving Miller's Brown Skin Models, 155
Irving Mills' Blue Babies, 22
Irving Mills' Hotsy Totsy Gang, 30, 90, 145, 154, 156, 166, 188, 189, 202, 208, 229
Irving Mills' Modernists, 189
Irvis, Charlie, 9, 78, 116, 119, 137, 142, 159, 165, 216, 219, 227, 237, 240
Isham Jones Orchestra, 124

J

J. C. Cobb and his Grains of Corn, 35
J. C. Higginbotham's Six Hicks, 202
Jack Carey's Crescent Brass Band, 48
Jack Davies' Kentuckians, 273
Jack Hylton Orchestra, 115
Jack Linx's Society Serenaders, 275
Jack Pettis' Pets, 188
Jackson, Alex, 224, 270
Jackson, Cliff, 13, 44, 106, 116, 148, 165
Jackson, Dewey, 53, 62, 66, 84, 116–117, 137, 266

Jackson, Franz, 208
Jackson, John, 114
Jackson, Mary, 102
Jackson, Mike, 115, 158
Jackson, Papa Charlie, 61, 130, 187, 194
Jackson, Preston, 117, 126, 201, 259
Jackson, Rudy, 33, 79, 117–118, 210
Jackson, Tony, 4, 101, 118, 155
Jacksonville Harmony, The, 262
Jack Teagarden Orchestra, The, 229
James, Billy, 274
James, George, 65, 199, 214
James, Harry, 190, 259
James, Jeanette, 259
James Reese Europe's Society Orchestra, 209
Jamison, Steel, 272
Jan Garber Orchestra, 85
Janis, Conrad, 204
Janis, Harriet, 3
Jarrett, Art, 245
Jasper Taylor's Creole Jazz Band, 55
Jasper Taylor's Original Washboard band, 262
Jass, 38
Jaxon, Frankie "Half Pint," 35, 117, 150, 155, 200, 208
Jazzbo's Carolina Serenaders, 166, 183, 184, 208
Jazz Cardinals, 130
Jazz-O-Maniacs, 62
Jazz Pilots, 197
Jazz Wizards, 125–126
Jean Goldkette Orchestra, 35, 40, 88, 89
Jefferson, Blind Lemon, 12, 222
Jefferson, Eddie, 235
Jefferson, Hilton, 102, 105
Jeffersonians, 48
Jeffries, Herb, 111
Jenkins, Freddie, 79, 118, 146, 170, 212, 213
Jenkins' Orphanage Band, 159
Jenney, Jack, 175
Jesse Stone's Blue Serenaders, 266
Jim Jam Jazzers, 39
Jimmie Lunceford Orchestra, 139
Jimmie Lunceford's Chickasaw Syncopators, 267
Jimmie Noone's Apex Club Orchestra, 55, 191, 205
Jimmy Bertrand's Washboard Wizards, 68, 112, 150, 262
Jimmy Blythe's Ragamuffins, 130
Jimmy Joy Orchestra, 126
Jimmy Joy's St. Anthony's Hotel Orchestra, 266
Jimmy McHugh's Bostonians, 145, 188, 191, 229, 231
Jimmy Powell's Jazz Monarchs, 53, 66
Jimmy Wade's Dixielanders, 108, 112, 150, 262
Jimmy Wade's Syncopators, 221
Joe Haymes Orchestra, 72
Joe Jordan's Sharps and Flats, 13, 228
Joe Mooney Quartet, The, 226
Joe Robichaux's New Orleans Rhythm Boys, 25
Joe Venuti-Eddie Lang All-Star Orchestra, 90
Joe Venuti's Blue Four, 235
Joe Ward's Swanee Club Orchestra, 273
John Hammond's Spirituals to Swing, 121, 133, 217

Meyers, Sig, 65, 221, 231, 232
Meyers, Vic, 266, 274
Mezzanine Melodies, 273
Mezzrow, Mezz, 16, 27, 42, 56, 68, 107, 132, 133, 141–142, 147, 157, 193, 209, 218, 233
Midnight Airedales, 138, 143, 144
Midnight Rounders, 32, 35
Midnight Serenaders, 273
Midway Dance Orchestra, 40
Midway Garden Orchestra, 65, 204
Miff Mole's Molers, 83, 155, 156, 166, 170, 172, 274
Miles, Eddie, 262
Miles, Josie, 102, 146, 215, 220
Miles, Lizzie, 146, 147–148, 178, 199
Miley, Bubber, 8, 14, 39, 49, 50, 78, 79, 106, 116, 118, 142, 146, 148–149, 157, 162, 165, 176, 178, 209, 214, 216, 219, 261, 268, 272, 282
Miller, Charlie, 241
Miller, Clarence, 155
Miller, Eddie, 168, 191, 230
Miller, Emmett, 260
Miller, Glenn, v, 35, 54, 60, 72, 73, 99, 140, 143, 145, 149–150, 170, 172, 190, 191, 269, 275, 282
Miller, Johnnie, 271
Miller, Luella, 117
Miller, Punch, 32, 35, 150, 178, 179, 186, 187, 188, 228, 262
Miller, Ray, 66, 72, 140, 151, 155, 205, 221, 233, 235, 260, 268
Miller, Sodarisa, 176
Millinder, Lucky, 123, 151, 216
Mills, Donald, 152–153
Mills, Harry, 152–153
Mills, Herbert, 152–153
Mills, Irving, 22, 30, 79, 80, 90, 107, 149, 151, 153–154
Mills, John, 152–153
Mills Blue Rhythm Band, 14, 22, 67, 93, 107, 111, 151–152, 154, 263
Mills Brothers, 11, 36, 47, 64, 152–153, 195, 280, 282
Mills' Merry Makers, 90, 154, 229, 231, 274
Mills' Modernists, 154
Mills' Musical Clowns, 90, 189
Milo Rega's Dance Orchestra, 196
Milt Shaw's Detroiters, 274
Mississippi Maulers, 138, 156
Mississippi Sheiks, 267
Missourians, The, 46, 48, 67, 154–155, 270
Mitchell, George, 58, 69, 155, 162, 174, 196, 201
Moe Baer's Wardman Park Orchestra, 269
Moeller, Whitey, 124
Mole, Miff, 9, 34, 44, 45, 54, 60, 68, 76, 83, 91, 95, 97, 127, 131, 138, 139, 143, 151, 154, 155–156, 158, 166, 170, 171, 172, 173, 183, 202, 204, 208, 225, 226, 228, 229, 231, 274
Mollick, Jack, 94
Monk, Thelonious, 121
Monk Hazel's Bienville Roof Orchestra, 271
Montgomery, J. Neal, 107

Moody, Julia, 102, 149, 215
Mooney, Dan, 225–226
Mooney, Joe, 225–226
Moore, Baby, 267
Moore, Big Chief Russell, 23
Moore, Bill, 32, 44, 91, 138, 156–157, 188
Moore, Clarence, 200
Moore, Freddie, 157
Moore, Grant, 273
Moore, Monette, 119, 132, 149, 157, 176, 220, 224
Moore, Vic, 32
Morand, Herb, 188, 262
Morehouse, Chauncey, 73, 86, 88, 89, 130, 157–158
Morgan, Helen, 259
Morgan, Russ, 86
Morgan, Sam, 5, 53–54, 158, 267
Morris, Leroy, 275
Morris, Thomas, 44, 83, 106, 116, 119, 142, 149, 158–159, 165, 215, 217, 224, 227, 237, 240, 263, 267, 268
Morrison, George, 130, 139
Morrison, Henry "Chick," 205
Morse, Al, 94
Morse, Lee, 159, 166, 173
Morton, Baby, 69
Morton, Benny, 102, 105, 159–160, 195, 223
Morton, George, 151
Morton, Jelly Roll, 4, 5, 6, 7, 8, 12, 14, 17, 24, 27, 31, 33, 39, 42, 43, 44, 56, 62, 66, 67–68, 69, 70, 71, 75, 83, 86, 95, 101, 107, 112, 113, 116, 118, 123, 132, 137, 141, 146, 148, 149, 150, 155, 163, 167, 168, 169, 170, 175, 177, 178, 179, 184, 185, 186, 188, 189, 200, 201, 203, 205, 207, 208, 209, 217, 218, 225, 228, 261, 265, 266, 269, 270, 272, 274, 277, 282
Morton, Tom, 182, 183
Mosby, Curtis, 40, 94, 163–164, 273, 280
Mosby's Blue Blowers, 163
Mosely, Snub, 270
Mosiello, Mike, 94
Mosley, Snub, 31, 233
Moten, Bennie, 135, 136, 164–165, 185, 215, 266, 267, 270, 282
Moten, Buster, 164
Mound City Blue Blowers, 99, 134, 143, 144, 150, 202, 229, 231, 233, 235, 238, 240, 265, 270
Muggsy Spanier's Ragtimers, 41
Murphy, Turk, 86
Murray, Don, 88, 136, 165, 168, 188, 236, 280, 282
Musical Stevedores, 118, 146, 220, 263
Mutt, King, 150
Mutt Carey's Jeffersonians, 107, 185, 205
Myers, Wilson, 221
Myers' Sax Band, 207

N

Nance, Ray, 165
Nanton, Tricky Sam, 9, 40, 79, 116, 149, 159, 165, 263

Napoleon, Phil, 5, 8, 45, 54, 60, 95, 96, 156, 165–167, 182, 183, 184, 207, 208, 226, 265, 268, 269, 273
Napoleon, Ted, 184
Napoleon's Emperors, 269
Napoli, Filippo. See Napoleon, Phil
Nash, Joey, 201
Nashville Jazzers, 158, 159
Natoli, Nat, 89
Nawahi, Benny, 262
Nelson, Arnett, 224
Nelson, Big Eye Louis, 25, 209
Nelson, Dave, 22, 61, 167, 178, 259, 272
Nelson, Lucille. See Hegamin, Lucille
Nelson, Ozzie, 225
Nesbitt, John, 144
New Georgians, 86
New Jersey Dixieland Brass Quintet, 226
New Orleanians, 186
New Orleans Blackbirds, 156, 166, 188
New Orleans Blue Five, 158, 159
New Orleans Bootblacks, 16, 69, 70, 71, 155, 184, 204
New Orleans Feetwarmers, 27, 132, 133
New Orleans Owls, 167–168, 169, 265
New Orleans Ramblers, 229
New Orleans Rhythm Boys, 198–199
New Orleans Rhythm Kings, 6, 8, 9, 28, 29, 35, 40, 41, 65, 84, 98, 136, 143, 161, 165, 168–169, 188, 189, 190, 204, 224, 231, 265, 268, 270, 272, 274
New Orleans Wanderers, 16, 69, 70, 71, 155, 184, 204
Newton, Frankie, 147, 205
New York Military Band, 272
Nicholas, Albert, 15, 33, 107, 111, 126, 162, 163, 169–170, 178, 189, 201, 232
Nichols, Earl, 275
Nichols, Ed, 147
Nichols, Nick, 274
Nichols, Red, 9, 12, 28, 32, 34, 37, 44, 45, 57, 60, 72, 76, 83, 84, 86, 90, 95, 97, 100, 131, 132, 135, 138, 140, 143, 146, 150, 155, 156, 158, 170–173, 183, 184, 186, 200, 202, 204, 225, 226, 228, 229, 231, 233, 234, 235, 265, 268, 274, 277
Noble, Ray, 13, 35, 85, 150
Noble Sissle's Sizzling Syncopators, 132
Noone, Jimmie, 4, 9, 24, 25, 39, 42, 55, 56, 58, 68, 71, 75, 89, 92, 107, 108, 109, 110, 117, 122, 128, 137, 155, 167, 173–174, 184, 185, 188, 191, 203, 205, 209, 225, 232
Noone, Jimmie, Jr., 174
Norville, Kenneth. See Norvo, Red
Norvo, Red, 24, 32, 50, 143, 174–175
Nunez, Alcide "Yellow," 4, 5, 175, 179, 180, 202

O

O'Brien, Floyd, 147, 231
O'Bryant, Jimmy, 22, 61, 132, 157, 175–176, 193, 207, 228
O'Donnell, Johnny, 86
O'Hara, Ted, 128

Scott, Cecil, 15, 205, 245, 272
Scott, George, 154
Scott, Howard, 102
Scott, James, 2
Scott, Lloyd, 205, 261, 264
Scott's Bright Boys, 245
Scott's Symphonic Syncopators, 205
Scoville, Glenn, 168
Scroggins, Virgil, 221–222
Scruggs, Irene, 169, 179, 184
Seaberg, Artie, 181
Sears, Al, 39, 270
Sears, Jerry, 144
Secrest, Andy, 30, 49, 89, 190, 205–206, 235, 280
Sedric, Gene, 141
Seger, Ellis, 259
Seidel, Ed, 50
Selby, Arlene, 56
Selby, Norman, 56
Selvin, Ben, 90, 91, 196, 206–207
Senior, Milton, 144
Senter, Boyd, 9, 149, 166, 207, 208, 273
Sepia Serenaders, 220
Seven Blue Babies, 272
Seven Gallon Jug Band, 218
Seven Hot Babies, 159
Seven Little Polar Bears, 197
Seven Missing Links, 173
Seven Rag Pickers, 197
Seven Wildmen, 197
Shand, Terry, 271
Sharp, Gus, 155
Shavers, Charlie, 69, 115, 151, 174, 218
Shaw, Artie, 54, 86, 127, 141, 175, 194, 233, 282
Shaw, Milt, 166, 274
Shayne, Freddy, 228
Sherwood, Bobby, 35
Shields, Larry, 9, 139, 175, 180, 181, 182
Shilkret, Nat, 90, 138, 194, 226, 238
Shoffner, Bob, 22, 126, 176, 177, 201, 207–208
Shukin, Leo, 132
Siday, Eric, 263
Siegal, Al, 169
Sigler, Maurice, 137
Sigler, Vincent, 220
Signorelli, Frank, 60, 73, 81, 134, 140, 166, 171, 173, 181, 182, 183, 184, 207, 208, 236, 269
Silver Bells Band, 25
Silver Leaf Orchestra, 24, 75
Simeon, Al, 71
Simeon, Omer, 43, 66, 110, 111, 126, 150, 162, 196, 200, 208–209, 214, 222, 227, 228, 271
Simms, Art, 24, 117
Simms, Ginny, 259
Simpson, Cassino, 214, 225
Simpson, James, 185
Sims, Arthur, 5, 155, 187
Sims, Joe, 260
Sims, Sam, 262
Sinatra, Frank, 259
Singing Syncopators, 112

Singleton, Zutty, 11, 17, 18, 56, 62, 92, 109, 123, 141, 149, 162, 209
Sioux City Six, 30, 31, 34, 135, 234
Sissle, Noble, 5, 22, 27, 33, 34, 82, 83, 97, 117, 132, 149, 199, 200, 209–210, 215
Sissle and Blake, 280
Six Black Diamonds, 149, 219, 268
Six Hayseeds, 197
Six Hottentots, 171, 204
Six Jumping Jacks, 197
Sizzling Syncopators, 209
Skeete, Charlie, 15, 31, 65, 83, 98, 189
Slack, Freddie, 33
Sleepy Hall's Collegians, 269
Slevin, Dick, 143
Slocum, Charlie, 200
Small, Paul, 54, 198
Smelser, Cornell, 229, 231
Smith, Bessie, v, 4, 6, 11, 13, 18, 20, 23, 53, 61, 92, 95, 98, 102, 114, 120, 132, 193, 195, 196, 203, 210–212, 213, 216, 220, 229, 243, 260, 263, 265, 272, 277, 280, 282
Smith, Cal, 99, 100
Smith, Cladys. See Smith, Jabbo
Smith, Clara, 13, 18, 92, 102, 118, 122, 123, 205, 212–213, 215, 260
Smith, Clarence. See Smith, Pinetop
Smith, Clementine, 217, 220, 260
Smith, Elizabeth, 158, 217
Smith, Hazel, 178, 217
Smith, Horace, 262
Smith, Howling, 223
Smith, Ivy, 217
Smith, Jabbo, 8, 14, 43, 112, 119, 159, 196, 200, 209, 213–214, 227, 240, 260
Smith, Joe, 8, 102, 105, 115, 125, 144, 193, 212, 213, 214–215, 216, 217, 243
Smith, John C., 15
Smith, Joseph C., 92
Smith, Kate, 55
Smith, Laura, 158, 215
Smith, Leroy, 123, 261, 264
Smith, Lloyd, 271
Smith, Mamie, 4, 6, 16, 26, 39, 43, 44, 74, 75, 99, 101, 142, 146, 158, 163, 189, 215–217, 218, 220, 243, 260, 269, 272
Smith, Pinetop, 217
Smith, Rollin', 262
Smith, Ruby, 212
Smith, Russell, 214
Smith, Stuff, 23, 233, 263, 270
Smith, Sugar Johnny, 185
Smith, Tab, 123, 151
Smith, Trixie, 18, 42, 92, 102, 130, 215, 217–218, 260, 272
Smith, Willie "the Lion," 10, 13, 66, 111, 116, 120, 139, 146, 147, 167, 205, 216, 218, 238
Smitzer Trio, 119
Snooks and His Memphis Stompers, 219
Snow, Valaida, 241
Snowden, Elmer, 31, 44, 53, 65, 78, 92, 93, 97, 98, 116, 122, 123, 139, 146, 149, 165, 219–220, 223, 224, 239, 245
Snyder, Frank, 168
Socarras, Alberto, 10, 65, 148, 205, 220, 228, 261, 263

Society Orchestra, 82
Sonny Clay's Plantation Orchestra, 266
Soul Killers, 126
Sounder, Jackie, 267, 274
Soundies, 280
Sousa, John Phillip, 1, 2, 3, 5
South, Eddie, 10, 31, 33, 56, 107, 220–221, 227, 263
Southland Six, 166, 183, 184
Spangler, Roy, 269
Spanier, Muggsy, 31, 41, 66, 95, 99, 113, 114, 136, 147, 151, 156, 176, 190, 221, 231, 244, 260, 268, 280
Spargo, Tony, 11, 180
Specht, Paul, 12, 86, 204, 226, 245, 275
Speed, Samuel, 75
Spike, Reb, 266
Spike Hughes' Three Blind Mice, 72, 113
Spikes, Red, 273
Spikes Brothers, 94, 225
Spikes' Seven Pods of Pepper Orchestra, 6, 48, 184, 185, 200
Spirits of Rhythm, 39, 42, 143, 144, 221–222
Spivak, Charlie, 86
Spivey, Christian, 48
Spivey, Sweet Pease, 15, 201
Spivey, Victoria, 14–15, 20, 21, 48, 56, 122, 123, 147, 178, 201, 202, 209, 222–223, 225, 237, 273
Spriccio, John, 175
Spurrier, Esten, 275
Stabile, Dick, 32
Stacks, Tom, 197
Stacy, Jess, 30, 110
Stafford, Mary, 119, 260, 272
Stark, Bobby, 51, 102, 105, 215, 223
Stark, John, 2
Starr, Henry, 164
State Street Ramblers, 34, 35, 68, 70, 71, 112–113, 119, 186, 223–224
State Street Stompers, 55
State Street Swingers, 267
Steeden, Peter Van, 12, 13
Steele, Joe, 15, 16, 111, 189, 261, 264
Stein, Johnny, 4, 5, 175, 179, 186
Steinberg, Murphy, 40
Stein's Dixie Jass Band, 179
Stevens, Gababy, 168
Stevens, Joe "Ragababy," 41
Stewart, Priscilla, 176, 187
Stewart, Rex, 31, 51, 102, 105, 106, 118, 144, 157, 159, 189, 202, 208, 215, 219, 223, 224, 263, 268, 281
Stewart, Sammy, 105, 107, 109, 200, 214, 262, 273
Stilwell, Ray, 86
Stitzel, Mel, 65, 89, 168, 224–225
Stock, Bert, 274
Stoll, George, 235
Stomp Six, 66, 221, 225
Stone, Eddie, 124
Stone, Jesse, 135, 266
Straight, Charlie, 29, 140, 221, 231, 261, 268, 273
Straine, Mary, 102, 215
Strange, Jimmy, 100